MANCHESTER
A FOOTBALL HISTORY

BY THE SAME AUTHOR

HISTORICAL/FACTUAL

From Maine Men To Banana Citizens (1989), Temple Press

The Pride of Manchester (with Steve Cawley, 1991), ACL & Polar

Manchester: The Greatest City (1997 & 2002), Polar Publishing

Farewell To Maine Road (2003), Polar Publishing

Manchester City Hall Of Fame (2005), Hamlyn

Manchester City The Complete Record (2006), Breedon Books

Manchester City: 125 Years Of Football (2006), At Heart Publications

TELEVISION

The History Of Football (2007), Channel M

FICTION

Atkinson For England (with Mark Brown, 2001), Empire

BIOGRAPHY

Football With A Smile: The Authorised Biography of Joe Mercer, OBE
(1993 & 1994), ACL & Polar

MANCHESTER
A FOOTBALL HISTORY

GARY JAMES

PUBLISHED BY

First published in Great Britain in 2008 by
James Ward
PO BOX 822, HALIFAX, HX1 9FX

www.manchesterfootball.org

info@manchesterfootball.org

A catalogue record for this book is available from the British Library.

Designed by Trevor Hartley

ISBN 978-0-9558127-0-5

James Ward 705

Printed and bound in Great Britain by CPI
Antony Rowe, Chippenham, Wiltshire.

CONTENTS

PART TWO – MANCHESTER MATTERS

INTRODUCTION

PRODUCED to coincide with the 400th anniversary of football being banned in Manchester, the aim of this book is to detail the importance of football to Manchester and its neighbouring boroughs. A book focusing on Manchester football clearly has two main sporting organisations at its core, however this publication simply does not focus on City and United, instead it attempts to consider the relationship between the other League and former League sides of the conurbation.

It's always difficult to identify what constitutes Manchester itself – Old Trafford is outside of the City's boundaries but very much a part of Manchester as far as United fans and most neutrals are concerned – and so I've decided to focus on the boroughs within the M60 and those the motorway enters. This includes the boroughs of Manchester, Bury, Oldham, Rochdale, Salford, Stockport, Tameside and Trafford, however I have excluded Wigan and Bolton. I believe the stories of the sides from those two boroughs are more appropriate in another volume I intend writing, although you will find the occasional reference to sides from those boroughs within this volume.

The eight boroughs featured in this book have, over the last century been fortunate to have seven League sides, with Salford being the only borough not to have possessed a League side (though United is on its doorstep). In addition each borough has known great periods of success, failure and to varying degrees tragedy.

No one living within the region can fail to be aware of the importance of the game of football and even if residents do not attend games they must surely be aware of the positives the game brings. Today, Manchester is known around the world more for its sport than for any other aspect of Mancunian life, while the towns of Oldham, Bury, Rochdale, and Stockport remain in the public consciousness partly because of their football sides. Interestingly, Tameside is not so well known around Britain as those boroughs, could this be because Tameside has never had one dominant club. The borough does have several great non-league sides – had Tameside possessed one significant club utilising the name Tameside would the borough be known nationally in the same manner as, say, Rochdale?

Possibly because of the rivalry between the sides in the region few books have considered how football developed across the area. For at least three decades there have been plenty of books on United and in the last decade or so City has seen a plethora of material produced on its existence. Similarly, the last few years have seen books on all the region's League sides. But each book has been aimed at the supporters of individual teams and not the region as a whole. This means that some stories such as the formation of the PFA, the role of Manchester Central FC, and even the contribution to the game of Ernest Mangnall have either been missing, or have been considered only from the perspective of one club. This book aims to improve that situation and put into perspective the history of the game within the region.

It has to be stressed that this is not supposed to be a comprehensive story of every game in the region, or of every side, or indeed of every player. Club histories, player biographies, and other club specific works already provide that. Instead this book utilises the stories of the region's clubs to develop particular themes or ideas through the decades.

One of the main aims is to help the reader, via an entertaining narrative and statistical records, understand why football is such an important part of Mancunian life. From the beginning the game has been a significant – but often overlooked – part of the region's social history and even economy. This book covers some of the well-known stories but also takes a look at aspects of the game that many readers will be unfamiliar with. In addition, some of the more famous or popular stories concerning specific players or games have not been included as these have been well documented elsewhere and do not necessarily develop the Mancunian story. I would have loved to have covered the stories of every player, every final, League Championship, and significant match played by each of our clubs but it was simply not possible. Instead I have tried to identify stories that typify a period, or link with the main thrust of the chapter, and I have where possible tried to provide information that has not previously been published, or material that has been miss-reported over the years.

Within the pages of this book stories can be read highlighting:

- the banning of football in the city four hundred years ago
- why rugby and football share a few Manchester firsts
- Manchester's role in the national formalisation of the game
- which Manchester side was the first English team to play competitive football in Scotland
- why a street in Wolverhampton contains a memorial to an old Mancunian ground
- Which present day League side wanted to change its name to Manchester Football Club during the early 1890s but was blocked by the FA
- how Bury found major success before any of the region's other sides
- for the first time the true date when Newton Heath became Manchester United
- how City benefited by having one of the biggest newspaper barons of the 20th Century as chairman
- the scandal that led to the formation of the PFA
- how a City director led United's 1909 FA Cup homecoming
- how the region's most successful manager of the period walked out on United for life at City
- the story of how Tameside's only League representatives resigned because of lack of support despite getting crowds higher (on average) than Rochdale's all time average (and FC United's average during 2005-6)
- how City and United combined to stop a third Manchester side from threatening their existence
- what Rochdale achieved 8 years before City, 20 years before United, and 27 years before Oldham
- how supporters are beginning to regain control of the game within the region

There have been many great moments in the region's footballing history but what has rarely been considered is how the region's sporting successes have influenced the development of the region and its prestige. In 1904, following City's first FA Cup win, manager Tom Maley was amazed at the size of the city centre's first homecoming parade. He told City's officials and Manchester's journalists at the end of the parade:

"Perhaps love of sport had something to do with the bringing together of so great a gathering, but love of Manchester, had much more to do with it."

Maley's views were significant and within two days of the comments being made the Manchester Evening Chronicle claimed that Manchester was now the second city of the Empire. It was a bold statement, but it was also totally understandable. The celebrations and attention paid to the game had brought the people together (the rivalry of later years was not evident as all Mancunians wanted all Mancunian sides to bring honour to the city at this point), and such a show of solidarity in a celebratory manner gave a very positive demonstration of what made Manchester special.

Moving to today, football is just as significant – if not more so – than it was a century ago. Today tourists flock to Manchester because of the game, while supporters around the world tend to know at least the name Manchester United. Whenever Old Trafford stages a European game, hundreds of rival fans visit City's stadium – In March 2007 over 400 Lille supporters booked hospitality, toured the stadium and visited City's museum ahead of their meeting with the Reds. The staging of events such as World Cup games, England internationals, European Cup finals, UEFA Cup finals, European Championships etc. provide a direct focus on the region, while players from the region have found great success on both the national and international stage. For example, 1966 World Cup final hero Geoff Hurst was born in Ashton, as was 2006 Italian World Cup winner Simone Perrotta.

Manchester and its neighbouring boroughs has a lot to be proud of, and this book celebrates the entire region's history and heritage.

Throughout the pages of this book I have tried to ensure I correct inaccuracies and challenge myths developed over the years, and so some of the material included is at odds to that perceived as fact by supporters of the region's clubs. Where this occurs I have tried to explain the conclusions I have reached and the differences between the text here and the 'established facts'. Every effort has been made to ensure that the facts and figures in this book are correct, but it has to be stressed that research is still ongoing in many areas and readers may have information which helps. Past experience shows that new information emerges following publication – it always seems to happen!

Should new information come to light, or indeed errors be spotted within this volume, then I would be delighted to receive such information in writing, addressed to me care of the publishers.

Inevitably, mistakes will creep into this volume, but please understand that extensive work has been performed to try and ensure the information recorded is as factually correct as possible. I am particularly pleased that the early years of the sport within the region are recorded here, but I accept that I have had to focus more on the city of Manchester than the neighbouring towns. Clearly, the development of each club is covered but whenever talking about the region as a whole Manchester itself has had to dominate. Nevertheless, I'm sure every fan – no matter which team you support – and every neutral will find enough in this volume to entertain, inform, and enjoy.

To all those who feel strongly that a book on Manchester football should only cover those sides playing within the City of Manchester I apologise. However, had I taken that as my own boundary I would have had to exclude many aspects of footballing life that nationally everyone associates within the city. For example, the history of United after their move to Old Trafford would have been excluded. Similarly, there may be some who believe that 'M' postcodes should have been the main focus of the book, but the allocation of 'M' postcodes seems to bear little relation to civic boundaries or for that matter football interests.

There may also be supporters of Bury, Oldham, Rochdale, Stockport and the non-League sides who feel appalled that their club has been described as a 'Manchester club' within this book. I know this is technically wrong however, in my defence, I'd like to stress that I have done this because I believe every club has contributed significantly to the region's footballing success and deserves to take centre stage. I intend producing similar volumes on Lancashire, and other neighbouring areas over the coming years but feel the stories of sides such as Bury are much more relevant to the Mancunian story than other areas of Lancashire. You may disagree, but personally if I supported Bury I'd use this book to show that my side had achieved significant success before either City or United, and that if the entire history of the region is taken as a whole the Shakers natural position would be as third most significant side in the region.

I have enjoyed writing this book – even if it has taken at least three years longer to write than initially anticipated – and I hope this comes through the text. In total I have been researching specifically for this book for over a decade, and still I believe there's much more to uncover about the game in our region. Nevertheless, I am pleased with the material included here and the story this book tells. Hopefully, you'll be equally pleased with the result.

I hope this volume encourages you to find out more about your local club whether it be a Premier League side or one playing in North West Counties Division Two, or one of many surviving from week to week on park pitches across the region. Not all of our sides can attract crowds of 75,000 plus, but they do all carry hope, ambition, and at kick off in every game in the region no individual can predict exactly how the game will unfold. That's the beauty of football and in the Manchester region we are blessed with an incredible number of football clubs.

ACKNOWLEDGEMENTS

As with every book I write there are many, many people who have helped during the production of this book. Some, such as the employees of all the clubs in the region have provided significant help, others have helped with occasional comments, but I am grateful to them all for their assistance. One of the joys of writing this book is that, like ***Football With A Smile*** (the authorised biography of Joe Mercer written in 1993), I have been privileged to meet so many interested people from a wide variety of clubs.

I have enjoyed my discussions, visits, and email contact with present day personnel at professional clubs Bury, City, United, Oldham, Rochdale, and Stockport, and am very grateful for the support and interest shown at each club. Of course, support has also come from a variety of non-League sides and other sports organisations. Significant support has come from: Altrincham, Ashton United, Droylsden, FC United of Manchester, Hyde United, the Lancashire FA, the Manchester FA, Manchester (rugby) FC, the PFA, the RFU, Stalybridge Celtic and so on.

In addition I have received great support, assistance and inspiration from (listed in alphabetical order): Eric Alexander, Ron Atkinson, Len Balaam, Peter Barnes, Mike Barnett, Earl Barrett, Julian Baskcomb, David Bernstein, Lawrence Bernstein, Chris Bird, Susan Bookbinder, Mike Bradley, Phil Brennan, Adam Brown, Tony Bugby, Andy Burton, Mark Bushell, Peter Carlisle, Steve Caron, Phillip Carter, Doug Cheeseman, Ian Cheeseman, Pat Crerand, Jack Crompton, Kevin Cummins, Paul Davies, Andy Dickman, Tommy Docherty, Willie Donachie, Garth Dykes, Sir Tom Finney, Geoff Fisher, Steve Fleet, Mike Flynn, Jimmy Frizzell, Ray Goble, Peter Godkin, Bob Greaves, Bernard Halford, Steven Hall, Ross Hamilton, Alan Hardy, Trevor Hartley, Henry Hochland, Mark Hodkinson, Paul Hodkinson, Brian Houghton, David Johnson, Alan Jubb, Stephen Kelly, Mark Kennedy, Tony Lees, Andy Lyons, Jean-Francois Maille, David Meek, David Mercer, David Moor, John Motson, Tommy Muir, Jane Muskett, Ian Niven jnr, Paul Parker, Mark Parlett, Mike Pavasovic, Ken Ramsden, Roger Reade, James H Reeve, Stuart Renshaw, Andy Ritchie, Joe Royle, Ken Smallwood, Jed Smith, Gordon Sorfleet, Jules Spencer, Mike Summerbee, Gordon Taylor, Richard Tucker, Tom Tyrell, Dave & Sue Wallace, Andy Walsh, Andy Ward, Richard Whitehead, Mark Wilbraham, Chris Williams, and Mark Wylie.

During the writing of this book I was saddened to hear of the death of Dennis Chapman and of David Mercer. Dennis was a fan of Manchester City and had helped me enormously over the years with a variety of books and other activities. His statistical records and programme collection were second to none, while his positive approach was always appreciated. David, the son of former City manager Joe Mercer, has also helped me significantly over the years. I was particularly grateful for his support during my research for ***Football With A Smile***, the life story of David's father.

The following museums, libraries and media organisations have provided support and assistance: the BFI, Channel M, Manchester Central Library, Manchester City Museum, Manchester Evening News, Manchester United Museum, National Football Museum, the newspaper archive of the British Library at Colindale, the People's History Museum, the Reporter Group, Tameside Libraries, and the World of Rugby. It is worth stating that the museums of City and United are staffed by people who truly care about the history of their sides. Often these museums, and others like them, are perceived as being focused solely on the past, however it has to be stressed that both City and United's museums care passionately about the future of their clubs. If used correctly by their parent organisations they can help strengthen marketing, publicity and a whole host of modern day activities for their clubs

Inevitably, thousands of individual newspaper editions have been consulted during the production of this book, particularly those national and local editions produced in Manchester. These include:

The Bury Times
Manchester Courier
Manchester Evening Chronicle
Manchester Evening News
Manchester Weekly Times
Oldham Evening Chronicle
The Reporter (various locally branded versions)
Rochdale Observer
Salford Chronicle
Stockport Express & Advertiser
Daily Dispatch
Athletic News
Sporting Chronicle

Plus of course all modern day national newspapers, football magazines, and club-based material.

Club historians and fellow members of the Association of Football Statisticians have assisted and, as always, I am grateful to them all. We are fortunate in the Manchester area that we have so many dedicated football historians. Similarly, I would like to thank all the journalists, photographers, and officials who have helped chronicle the game throughout the history of the region. The majority of photographs come from the archives of the football clubs featured, the *Manchester Evening News*, Edward Garvey, and the author.

I have also received help and support from Keith Barraclough. Keith has, together with his wife, proof read sections of this book and has helped to ensure the book remained on track.

Of course the staff at my publishers James Ward need thanking for their efforts in making this a great publication. As does Trevor Hartley who has, once again, performed miracles with the design of this book and its cover.

As always, I would like to say 'thanks' to my family for their continuing support. This book has taken a lot longer than I had planned, but at last we can see the result of all this work.

Finally, one of the most positive elements of my research has been the support I have received from across the region's footballing fraternity. No matter which sides people came from, or personal preferences, everyone has been keen to see this work produced. I know Manchester is a special city and its neighbouring boroughs make this a great region, and the research for this book has proved there are a great deal of people across the region who play a significant part in the development of football. There are many unsung heroes at every club and on every park in the region. Please spare a moment to ensure you recognise those who ensure the game continues to be the region's number one sporting activity next time you attend a game, or play for your Sunday league side.

NOTES ON THE TEXT

The book has been divided into two parts with the first section covering a chronological story of football within the region and the second focusing on aspects such as ground developments, the media, and statistical information.

Within the first section the chronological story is not followed completely as I have often diverted away from a strict timeline to focus on the development of a club or a theme, such as bribery and scandal in chapter eight. I hope this is not too confusing, and that the overall flow of the book still works.

Within the chronological story of the game I have included tables showing seasonal average attendances, and league positions of each of our Football League/Premier League sides. This has been included to help provide appropriate comparisons between the clubs.

For each side's League position, a final place per season has been allocated to each side based on the total number of teams in the League at that time. This has been calculated by taking the total number of sides in each division and calculating a final place. So, for example, in 1892-3 Newton Heath were placed 16th in Division One while Ardwick were 5th in Division Two. As there were only 16 clubs in Division One, Ardwick's position has been calculated as being 21st in the entire League. Similarly, in 2006 Rochdale were 82nd in the League based on 20 sides in the Premier, 24 in the Championship, 24 in League One, and Dale finishing 14th in League Two.

For seasons when Division Three North & South existed, the final position of sides in Division Three North has been calculated as if the southern division did not exist. This has led to a significant fall down the table for Oldham Athletic in 1958 when the Fourth Division was created out of the bottom sides in each regional Division Three.

In addition it should be remembered that the size of the Football League has varied over the years so, in 1902 Stockport actually finished second bottom (35th place) in the entire two division League, and Newton Heath finished fourth bottom.

Occasionally, due to the nature of football within Manchester some stories are touched on in more than one section of the book. To ensure each chapter can be read in isolation, I have occasionally repeated key information to aid the reader.

Finally, as this book is such a significant volume, it is recognised that some detail, for example each side's trophy record may be out of date within a short timescale. It should be stressed however that this book is intended as a history of the Mancunian game rather than a review of the modern era.

CHAPTER ONE

SETTING THE SCENE

Manchester, on the south side of the Irwel river, stondeth in Salfordshiret, and is the fairest, best builded, quickest and most populous tonne of all Lancastreshire. John Leland, 1538

To understand the role football plays in Mancunian life it is first important to appreciate how the city and its surrounding area evolved, and how sport took a hold of the region. Today Manchester is known throughout the world primarily for its football – even in the American cartoon series *The Simpsons* Ryan Giggs (although it was misspelt) has been mentioned in an episode in which the family come to England, while another episode talks of a fictitious British TV programme following the lives of a family of soccer hooligans who support a team called Manchester who play in red – but clearly the region developed substantially before the game ever took a hold of the people.

The Manchester conurbation consists of several towns and two cities (some would argue that Stockport should be the region's third city) each with its own identity, and at various points in history different areas within that conurbation have taken prominence. The first proper reference to what is now Manchester comes with the Romans. The outpost Mamucium was established in AD70, close to the junction of the rivers Medlock and Irwell, and over the course of the following three hundred years a small town became established around the original Roman fort. It is worth noting from a footballing point of view that the eagle which forms part of Manchester City's modern day emblem (and also used by Manchester United in 1958) highlights the Roman influence.

In AD 410 the Romans withdrew from the Castlefield area and the Saxons renamed it Manigceastre, however in 870 the Danes seized the town and within 50 years, under the new version of the name Manceastre, it became a frontier town between Mercia and Northumberland. During the tenth century the church of St. Mary was established at the top end of present day Deansgate, close to the modern day cathedral, and the town started to develop in that area.

After the 1066 invasion by William the Conqueror the manor of Manchester was valued at £1,000 and was given to a Norman Knight, Nigellus. It passed to his son-in-law, Albert de Gresley, in 1129, and remained in his family for several generations. In 1230 Salford was granted a charter and became a free borough while Manchester followed in 1301. At the time lord of the manor, Thomas de Gresley, surveyed his land and noted several important areas, including Manchester itself and one hamlet which would ultimately be known for having a Football League side (Ardwick):

"There is a mill at Manchester, running by the water of the Irk, value ten pounds, at which the burgesses and all the tenants of Manchester, with the hamlets, and Ardwick, Pensham, Crummeshall, Moston, Notchurst, Getheswych, and Ancotes ought to grind."

By the 1500s the town had grown and the collegiate church of St. Mary, the present day cathedral, had been established, and within a century a Free Grammar School became established, followed by Humphrey Chetham's hospital and library (arguably the first free public library in Europe) in 1635 close by.

In between these dates football was perceived as a significant problem within Manchester. It seems amazing to think that the main activity the world of the 21st century would identify Manchester with, was in actual fact perceived as one of the region's biggest problems four hundred years earlier. In 1608 the sport was banned by the Manchester Court Leet:

"Whereas there hath been heretofore great disorder in our town of Manchester, and the inhabitants thereof greatly wronged... by a company of lewd and disordered persons using that unlawful exercise of playing with the footeball in ye streets of the said town, breaking many men's glass windows at their pleasures, and other great enormities.

"Therefore, we of this jury do order that no manner of persons hereafter shall play or use the footeball

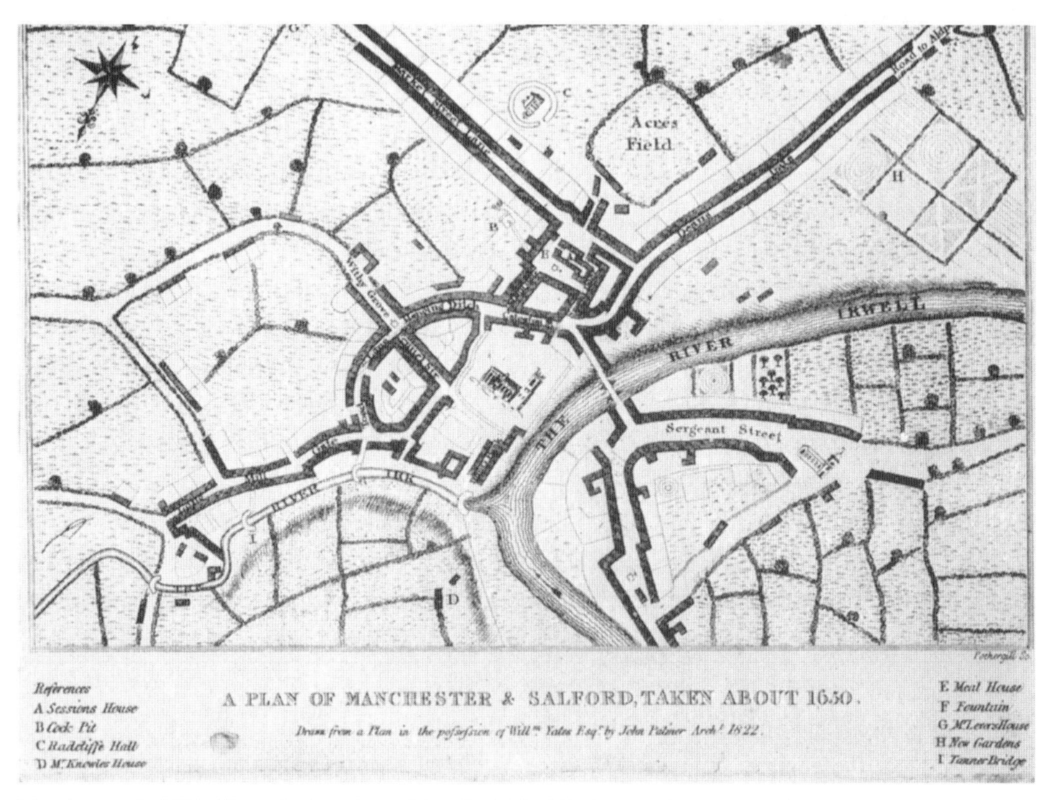

Manchester in 1650. Note the location of the Cock Pit (B) close to the present day entrance to the Arndale Centre on Market Street.

in the said town of Manchester, sub pena to every one that shall so use the same, for every time, twelve pence."

At this time football was played in the streets with players rampaging through without a care for what damage was caused. This was of course a significant enough reason to object, however another aspect was that the game did not develop skills that would prove useful from a military perspective. Activities such as archery clearly helped develop military skills but football had little to offer. In fact various leaders had objected to the game for at least three centuries as it was seen as a foolish activity and a complete waste of time. Edward II had banned the game on 13th April 1314, and then Edward III issued a royal proclamation in 1349 deploring the fall in popularity of archery and he commanded that all able bodied men should pass their leisure time with bows and arrows to ensure an adequate supply of archers in the event of war. He announced that anyone found *"attending to throwing stones, skittles, quoits, fives, football or hockey, or wrestling, or cock-fighting or other foolish games like these which are of no use"* would be imprisoned.

Similar bans had been introduced in 1389 by Richard III, and in various regions such as the City of London (1572) over the years.

In 1618 two 'offic'rs for ye footeball' were employed in Manchester – George Richardson and Robarte Boardman. Exactly what their duties were and the hours they worked is not clear, but it is known that they were expected to keep the streets safe from the distractions of the game.

As the 1600s also saw the English Civil War, It is clear there was great concern that young men could be distracted by an activity that had little to offer but pleasure. On 5th July 1642 the first activity in the Civil War took place in the Manchester area between Charles I's troops and the Manchester Parliamentarians, and this was reported in London as the beginning of a civil war.

From a football perspective the 1608 ban was followed by further bans in 1656 and 1657 as the popularity of the game increased again. Interestingly, one of the main acceptable sports of the period was one which today the majority would find totally abhorrent – cock-fighting. The sport, if that is an appropriate term, was encouraged during the 1700s as an orderly activity and there were even inter-county tournaments. Simon Inglis, in his **Played In Manchester** book, talks of a Lancashire-Cheshire 'match' being staged at the Royal Exchange in Manchester in 1786. There were also cockpits set up across the city with Market Street housing one in 1650, and others appearing at Cross Street (1730), the top of Deansgate (1760), Kersal Moor (also the site of Manchester's racecourse from 1681 to 1847); and at Chorlton. The 'sport' was eventually banned in 1849, although reports of its activity continued into fairly modern times.

Another activity popular in Manchester which would later be condemned was bear-baiting. Images survive of bear-baiting being performed during the 1700s at a site close to the modern day Printworks and Triangle (Corn Exchange) shopping centres. Baiting of bulls and bears was common across the region, while other bloodsports such as hunting were also popular. Inglis reports that:

"For the privileged few, hunting in the Manchester region can be traced back to at least the early 14th Century. Two hunting parks have been identified; at Bradford on the River Medlock, and Alport, in the Castlefield area. There was an enclosed deer park at Blackley, and one at Dunham Park, Trafford, where examples of deer-leaps survive; that is, platforms built on the outer side of walls, allowing deer to enter but not exit from the park. The deer park at Bramall Hall was certainly in use in 1577."

The site Inglis mentioned at Bradford is close to the present day City of Manchester Stadium.

The eighteenth century saw Manchester grow at a phenomenal rate with developments such as the creation of St. Ann's Square and the areas around King Street, visible signs of a lively region. Manchester's wealth was growing as a result of its involvement with the cotton trade.

By 1788 the combined population of Manchester and Salford was 50,000 and in 1847 St. Mary's collegiate church was designated a cathedral. Six years later Manchester was granted its city charter, but earlier, in 1819, one of the most important moments in Manchester's history occurred when the Manchester reform meeting held in St. Peter's fields, close to present day St. Peter's Square, ended with the infamous Peterloo Massacre. The meeting was planned to be a visible but peaceful demonstration against the Corn Laws and part of a campaign for parliamentary reform, but it became much more than that. The authorities tried to put an end to the meeting shortly after it started and as a result conflict arose. John Tyas, writing in **The Times** editorial on 19th August gave his opinion of the day:

"It appears by every account that has yet reached London, that in the midst of the Chairman's speech, within less than twenty minutes from the commencement of the meeting, the Yeomanry Cavalry of the town of Manchester charged the populace sword in hand, cut their way to the platform, and with the police at their head, made prisoners of Hunt and several of those who surrounded him - seized the flags of the Reformers - trampled down and cut down a number of the people, who, after throwing some stones and brickbats at the cavalry in its advance towards the hustings, fled on all sides in the utmost confusion and dismay.

"Of the crowd ... a large portion consisted of women. About 8 or 10 persons were killed, and, besides those whom their own friends carried off, above 50 wounded were taken to the hospitals; but the gross number is not supposed to have fallen short of 80 or 100, more or less, grievously wounded."

The report included some important questions:

"Was that [meeting] at Manchester an 'unlawful assembly'? Was the notice of it unlawful? We believe not. Was the subject proposed for discussion an unlawful object? Assuredly not. Was anything done at this meeting before the cavalry rode in upon it, either contrary to law or in breach of the peace? No such circumstance is recorded in any of the statements which have yet reached our hands."

The injustice of Peterloo helped to shape Mancunian life and gave the residents of the city their strong belief in fairness, equality, and justice. It is no coincidence that movements like the co-operative movement became established in the region. Perhaps Peterloo also helped define the typical Mancunian as someone who would not simply accept life as it is.

Manchester developed quickly during the nineteenth century due to its location and the opportunities it presented. The close proximity of the Pennines, together with a damp climate – surprisingly some tourist officials in modern day Manchester have tried to discourage their staff from talking about the city's reputation for rain, even though this helped create the modern city - helped industry grow as the many rivers and streams encouraged the construction of water-powered cotton mills.

Cotton, which had been imported since the eighteenth century, brought the textile industry to Manchester and ultimately became the city's number one industry. The raw material was

A contemporary representation of the Peterloo Massacre

transported to the region via the Mersey and Irwell rivers – both had been navigable to some extent from the early 1700s with full development coming in 1740 – while the development of canals such as the Bridgewater made the region even more accessible. The Bridgewater Canal opened between Worsley and Manchester in 1763 and over the following decades the canal was extended to Runcorn and linked to other canals such as the Trent & Mersey and the Leeds & Liverpool. This opened up the region and allowed barges to travel right into the heart of industrial Manchester.

Manchester's accessibility was further improved in 1830 with the opening of the Liverpool and Manchester Railway, the world's first steam passenger railway. Interestingly, at its opening the people of Manchester demonstrated their free spirit when they pelted the passenger carriages with stones. The reason is that they wanted the Duke of Wellington, one of the main guests, to suffer for his part in the Peterloo Massacre – many Mancunians blamed him for the heavy-handed military presence. Mancunians have never been afraid of venting their feelings.

Within eleven years Manchester was connected by rail to Hull, Birmingham and London, as well as Liverpool, and therefore little could stop the industrialisation of the region. The rest of the 1800s saw thousands of people settle in the area as they searched for work and a future for their families. It is hard to accept that families willingly travelled from relatively pleasant villages all over the British Isles, and in some cases much further afield, to settle in an area that was becoming heavily polluted and industrial. The main reason they settled in the Manchester area was financial. Although working conditions were often difficult, the region on the face of it could at least guarantee employment. Farming was always at the mercy of the weather, but in Manchester the new mills seemed able to guarantee employment.

The region welcomed new residents from Ireland - particularly after the suffering they endured as a result of the Potato Famine – and also Germans, Italians, Polish, and members of the Jewish community. This great mix helped the Manchester psyche develop further.

Manchester, or Cottonopolis as it was nicknamed, became the most important industrial centre in the world. The pace of change was fast and the region prided itself on being at the cutting edge of industry, thinking, and achievement. The saying *"What Manchester does today, the rest of the world does tomorrow"* became known around the world, and Mancunians loved everything that saying embodied.

The region's growth continued, although there were significant problems and hardships along the way, throughout the nineteenth century. Sport and recreation itself became more important as the century progressed and, according to Simon Inglis, cricket made its mark with the first recorded Manchester game occurring around 1823 at the Adelphi ground in Salford (Lancashire CCC had originally formed as Aurora CC between 1818 and 1823). Then in 1846 three public parks opened in the region – Queen's Park (Harpurhey), Peel Park (Salford), and Philips Park (Bradford).

Philips Park, widely acknowledged as the first municipal park in the world, was named after Mark Philips, a reforming politician who was one of two MPs elected to represent Manchester after the Great Reform Act of 1832 had restored representation to the area. The site guaranteed an area of green amongst a rapidly developing industrial landscape and this area became crucial to the development of sport in the city. Ultimately, the park became recognised for a variety of leisure activities – it even had an outside swimming pool that was used by water polo teams training for the Olympics – but Manchester United's second ground (Bank Street) and Manchester City's modern day venue (City of Manchester Stadium) would later become its neighbours.

After the development of Philips Park, the sporting life of Manchester grew rapidly. The Factory Act of 1847 reduced the working week for women and children, and over the decade that followed further improvements meant that the working week for men was to exclude Saturday afternoons from the normal hours of employment. This gave time for sport to develop.

A variety of sports including cricket, cycling, lacrosse, water polo, tennis, and bowls flourished by the end of the nineteenth century but there was one team sport above all others that became the region's predominant sporting activity - football.

The game became much more formal during the 1800s when public schools incorporated team games into their timetables as a means of teaching pupils a more ordered way of life. Rules were developed and followed thereby teaching participants about structure and discipline, and it was believed the benefits of team-spirit, co-operation and so on would help educate. It has to be remembered as well, that education at a public school was something only the wealthy (and a few residents living close by) could afford and that it bore no relation to the intelligence of those attending the schools. It has therefore been suggested by some, notably Percy M Young in his

Ancoats in the late 19th Century

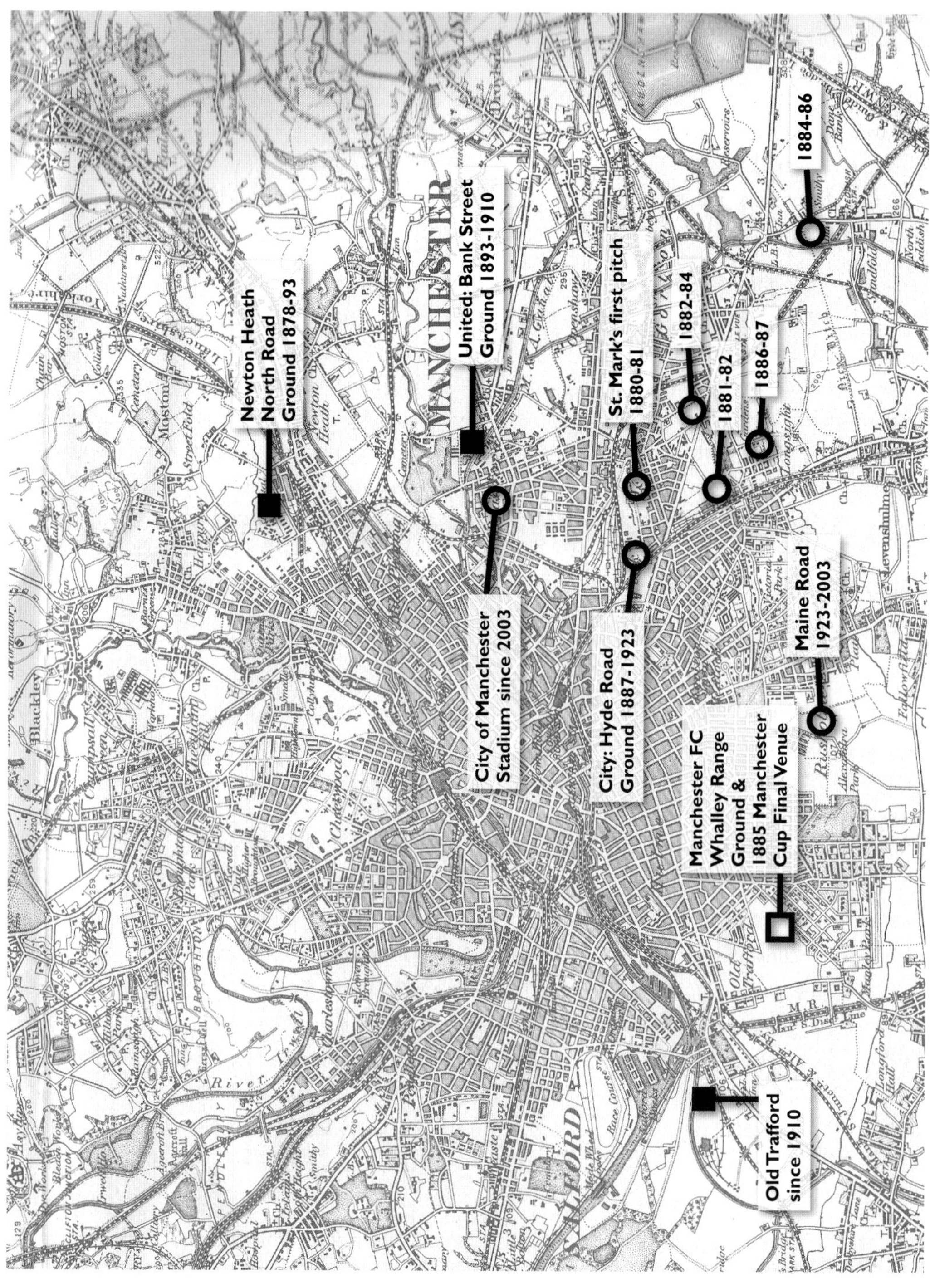

An 1896 map of Manchester marked with the locations of each of City and United's grounds since formation

○ = City's grounds

■ = United's grounds

History of British Football, that sport offered schools an outlet to teach their *"less intelligent charges"* a *"basic moral philosophy."*

According to Young, the formal development of football came in 1846 with the publication of *The Laws of Football As Played At Rugby School*. These laws established the game of rugby football, however it is generally accepted that the game of rugby was first created two decades earlier. In December of 1880, in a letter to *The Meteor* (the Rugby School magazine), former pupil Matthew Bloxam talked of the defining moment in 1823 when the game of Rugby was born:

"A boy of the name Ellis – William Webb Ellis – a town boy and a foundationer... whilst playing Bigside at football in that half-year [1823], caught the ball in his arms. This being so, according to the then rules, he ought to have retired back as far as he pleased, without parting with the ball, for the combatants on the opposite side could only advance to the spot where he had caught the ball, and were unable to rush forward till he had either punted it or had placed it for some one else to kick, for it was by means of these placed kicks that most of the goals were in those days kicked, but the moment the ball touched the ground the opposite side might rush on. Ellis, for the first time, disregarded this rule, and on catching the ball, instead of retiring backwards, rushed forwards with the ball in his hands towards the opposite goal, with what result as to the game I know not, neither do I know how this infringement of a well-known rule was followed up, or when it became, as it is now, a standing rule."

The importance of Webb Ellis' actions have over the years been dismissed by some. In fact, the view that he had invented the game did not surface until four years after his death and doubts have been raised about the story ever since 1895 when it was first investigated by the Old Rugbeian Society. There are many who still dispute the story, however the Rugby World Cup is now named after Webb Ellis, and he is widely acknowledged as creating the game, even if he himself did not make that claim.

The Webb Ellis story is important for a couple of reasons. The formation of Rugby was the first recognised adoption of rules for football as a team game (ultimately leading on to the development of association football), and secondly William Webb Ellis himself was often recorded as being a Mancunian by birth. This means that a Manchester man was in at the start of the formal creation of the game. Modern day historians accept that Webb Ellis' father's roots were in the Manchester region, and most tend to claim Webb Ellis himself was born in Salford, however the man himself stated on the 1851 census that he was born in Manchester. The family moved to Rugby after William's father was killed in action during 1812 as William's mother was determined that her children would receive a good education. They lived within ten miles of the Rugby school clock tower and as a result were entitled to free education as a 'foundationer' (hence the use of the word in Bloxam's comments).

Webb Ellis' actions precipitated one version of the sport, but almost every school tended to have its own rules, and therefore a different form of football. It is widely acknowledged that the first school to tackle the formalisation of association football was Cambridge University. One of the key figures, H.C. Malden, documented his view of the steps taken in 1848 to create the Cambridge rules in a note from 8th October 1897:

"I went up to Trinity College Cambridge. In the following year an attempt was made to get up some football in preference to the hockey that was then in vogue. But the result was dire confusion, as every man

played the rules he had been accustomed to at his public school. I remember how the Eton men howled at the Rugby men for handling the ball.

"So it was agreed that two men should be chosen to represent each of the public schools, and two who were not public school men, for the 'Varsity. G. Salt and myself were chosen for the 'Varsity. I wish I could remember the others."

Malden remembered that there were fourteen people present and that Harrow, Eton, Rugby, Winchester, Shrewsbury were amongst those represented. He then gave his account of the meeting:

"We met in my rooms after Hall, which in those days was at 4.pm.; anticipating a long meeting, I cleared the tables and provided pens, ink and paper. Several asked me on coming in whether an exam was on!

"Every man brought a copy of his school rules, or knew them by heart, and our progress in framing new rules was slow. On several occasions Salt and I, being unprejudiced, carried or struck out a rule when the voting was equal. We broke up five minutes before midnight. The new rules were printed as the Cambridge Rules, copies were distributed and pasted up on Parker's Piece, and very satisfactorily they worked, for it is right to add that they were loyally kept, and I never heard of any public school man who gave up playing from not liking the rules."

These rules became the first formulated rules of association football and were influential in the creation of the Football Association rules of 1863, but Cambridge was not the only educational establishment whose rules were influential. From a local perspective the rules of Harrow school were adopted by Bolton side Turton in 1872, which is regularly recorded as the first 'soccer' team in Lancashire. However, much more significantly than that, there is evidence (as can be seen in the following chapter) that a team from Manchester competed in an association game played to Harrow rules during the 1860s.

Once the Football Association was formed in 1863, and the FA Cup created in 1872, the game developed to the FA's rules. Any club wanting to develop had to adopt those rules, otherwise they would struggle to find appropriate competition. Public schools continued – and still continue – their own variety of the game, but from a national perspective only one set of association rules could develop.

Within Manchester, rugby remained the dominant version of football for several years, but the transformation to the association game began during the 1870s.

CHAPTER TWO

MANCHESTER FOOTBALL CLUB

Pluck frequently made up for inexperience. Most of us were learners and representatives of public schools where the Rugby game was unknown. Richard Sykes, 1907

BY 1870 the population of central Manchester was estimated to have grown to approximately 350,000 from only 235,000 in 1840 and 75,000 in 1800. This growth was as a result of the development of industry within the city, which also caused the population of Manchester's neighbouring towns to grow. The hatting trade in Stockport and the cotton trade throughout the region caused many to move to the area for employment.

Streets were developed at an incredibly fast rate and the conurbation of Manchester quickly subsumed smaller villages such as Ardwick Green and Clayton to create a vast conurbation which, by the early twentieth century, stretched from Reddish in the east to Trafford in the west.

This influx of people led to a variety of social issues. Inevitably, poor housing, large families and low incomes caused deprivation, but there were also distractions with alcohol proving to be one of Manchester's biggest issues. Many of the region's leading figures were concerned about these conditions and, over time, efforts were made to improve the social wellbeing of the local population. They tried to encourage the locals to focus on sporting activities and they used sports to raise funds for the needy.

On 29 December 1862 football was used, perhaps for the first time, to aid the people of the Greater Manchester region when a charity match was staged between Sheffield and Hallam to raise funds for the Central Relief Committee, an organisation set up in Manchester to help those suffering as a result of the Cotton Famine that was seriously affecting the well-being of the area. This game is also noteworthy as it saw Sheffield's Major Nathaniel Creswick punch a man called Waterfall, one of his opponents, after some rough play. A general fracas followed which only ended when a group of supporters tried to stop the players from fighting. Once calm was restored Hallam's Waterfall was the only man punished – he was sent to keep goal for the rest of the game! An act more in keeping with modern day playground football.

Considering the actions at that game, it is clear that football was still developing as a sport. In the north-west it is widely recognised that the first Lancastrian association football club was Turton, which was created in 1872 and published its first rules in 1873. However some sources

The Cotton Famine – operatives waiting for their breakfast in Mr. Chapman's courtyard at Mottram.

talk of Manchester's first club being Hulme Athenaeum formed a decade earlier in 1863. This was documented in Percy M Young's *A History of British Football*, published in 1968, and is the first mention specifically of an association side within Manchester.

Sport of all descriptions was developing rapidly in the region, and so events took place with little publicity. It is therefore difficult to pinpoint specific landmark moments, and so the identity of the first association football side in Manchester is not entirely obvious. Respected football historian Percy M Young claimed Hulme Athenaeum played at a ground in Moss Side, but it is unclear who their opponents were or what form of football they actually played. The FA was formed in 1863 and clearly their rules eventually dominated the game, but it took several years for that to occur, and so it is very difficult identifying whether Hulme Athenaeum played a form of association football, or whether the game was more akin to rugby. Young suggests they played a form of association football.

In 1866 another team is recorded as playing a version of association football in the area, the Manchester Football Club. This side played at Whalley Range, and it appears that this was an offshoot of the rugby playing Manchester Football Club which still exists today.

Rugby was the dominant local sport at the time and so it does make sense that the leading association football sides of the period would evolve from rugby playing roots. Rochdale AFC can trace its roots back through rugby union side Rochdale St. Clements, although this had more to do with the availability of the ground rather than a desire by a committee to play the association game.

Manchester Football Club was founded by Richard Sykes, a former captain of football at Rugby School. This was, and still is, a rugby playing side and, from an association football perspective, the growth of rugby in Manchester is significant. Research for this book suggests that Manchester FC were not only the first rugby side, but they were also the first significant local association football side.

The first rugby game played in Lancashire took place on 19th December 1857 when a team of Mancunian 'Gentlemen' faced a Liverpool side at Edge Hill with a ball supplied by Sykes. Few games occurred during the early 1860s but Sykes managed to set up his side at a ground near Alexandra Park, Moss Side, and then in 1862 in Whalley Range, and rugby developed.

In 1907 Sykes wrote a letter to Manchester FC's president, Roger Walker, from his home in California (Sykes had moved to the States and helped to introduce the game into California) giving his memories of the formation of the club. He also gave the first clue as to when Manchester FC first played association football:

"It was sometime in 1860 that I was invited to play in a trial game on a field adjoining the Western Cricket Ground [Pendleton]. Howard Aston, late of Cheltenham College and captain, Tom White of the 84th Regiment [garrisoned at Ashton under Lyne], an old Rugbean were prominent on this occasion. This game led to the formation of the Manchester Football Club, our games usually being played at Whalley Range. I believe I was the first captain and held the position until about 1869. Our games were amongst ourselves and our matches against Liverpool and the Academicals of Glasgow or Edinburgh. I recollect a Sheffield match, but I believe the Harrow Association game was attempted on that occasion.

"The recollections of the game at Whalley Range are most pleasant as they were played always with good humour and were unattended by serious accident. Pluck frequently made up for inexperience. Most of us were learners and representatives of public schools where the Rugby game was unknown."

The reference to the Harrow Association game does mean that Manchester FC, although known throughout the Country as a rugby side, did play association football on occasion. The reasons for their interest in the game probably ties in with Sykes' final comment where he mentioned that most of the players were learners. Although he was referring to rugby it is possible Manchester FC contained a group of young men who simply wanted to compete in a team environment. The boundaries between rugby football and the association game at this stage were not so clear. The FA was only formed in 1863 and in areas such as Manchester the intricacies of either sport were not generally known.

Manchester

The Manchester FC coat of arms.

Many association football sides, including Rochdale and the Yorkshire side Bradford Park Avenue, evolved to some extent out of rugby roots, and the problems of professionalism, which would later cause the split within rugby itself, were not an issue during the 1860s. Football did become professional as the century progressed and ultimately the two sports did not mix, however for Manchester FC it appears the two activities co-existed for some time. It has to be stressed though that rugby was by far the more dominant activity.

Little hard evidence exists of association games played by Manchester FC, however the reference to the Harrow game against Sheffield must have meant that game was played prior to 1867 as Sykes became injured and did not play again for the side. Interestingly, when Sykes settled in the States he owned considerable areas of land and created a number of towns. One was named Edgeley, after the place of his birth Edgeley Park. **The Edgeley Centennial Book** recorded:

"The father of our city was Richard Sykes, an English gentleman, who was born on May 11, 1839 in Edgeley Park, Stockport, Cheshire, England. He was educated in England and became a partner in a syndicate of investors. In August, 1881, he came to America to check on his land holdings and to buy more."

In terms of association football little is known until 1876-77. The club's own records state that they played three association games against 'the Sheffield club' by the end of 1876-77. Sheffield is recognised as the oldest association football club in the world and these meetings suggest Manchester FC showed sufficient interest to compete on three occasions against one of the most famous sides of the period.

Interestingly, of those three association games, it was reported there were two serious accidents affecting players, whereas the same club had played over 100 rugby games by the end of 1876-77 and suffered only two serious injuries. Perhaps the view existed that the association game was more dangerous than rugby.

In November 1877 Manchester FC faced Darwen in the first FA Cup tie ever played in Manchester. Further games in the competition occurred in 1883 starting with a first round tie against Stoke. The team for that game was: AR Andrews (captain & goalkeeper), JM 'Junior', Walker, Hay, Sumner, Cornall, Sinclair, C Coulthurst, J Acton, Bassett & Newby. It is unclear if any of these were also rugby players, but the Walker family had strong links with the rugby side. It is also known that rugby fixtures were played at the same time as some of the association games. A 15-0 defeat against Queen's Park, Glasgow, followed the Stoke tie and it seems association football soon disappeared as an activity for Manchester FC.

By the early 1890s association football was not an activity Manchester FC seemed interested in, although they would occasionally be referred to in association circles. The greatest mention and impact the side was to have on the game during the decade came in 1893-94 when Newton Heath (latter day Manchester United) attempted to change their name. For several years both Ardwick and Newton Heath wanted to attract larger support and, perhaps, be the first to truly represent the entire city. Ardwick were trying to relaunch themselves as Manchester City FC in April 1894 while Newton Heath were keen to adopt the title of Manchester FC. Which came first is open to debate, however it is known that Ardwick directors had applied to have Manchester City FC affiliated to the Lancashire FA on 4th April, while on 9th April Manchester FC announced they would be writing to the Rugby Football Union to complain about Newton Heath's intention to adopt their name.

It seems both Ardwick and Newton Heath were in a race to select and use Manchester in their title, but whereas Ardwick's directors had been discussing the restructure of the club for at least a couple of months, there is no evidence to suggest how early Newton Heath chose to adopt the name of Manchester FC.

Regardless of which came first, it is clear that Ardwick's transformation to Manchester City FC went ahead with relative ease, although some members of the old club were against the idea, while Newton Heath's transformation did not occur. The official complaint from Manchester (rugby) FC went to the Rugby Union officials and the following was minuted in April:

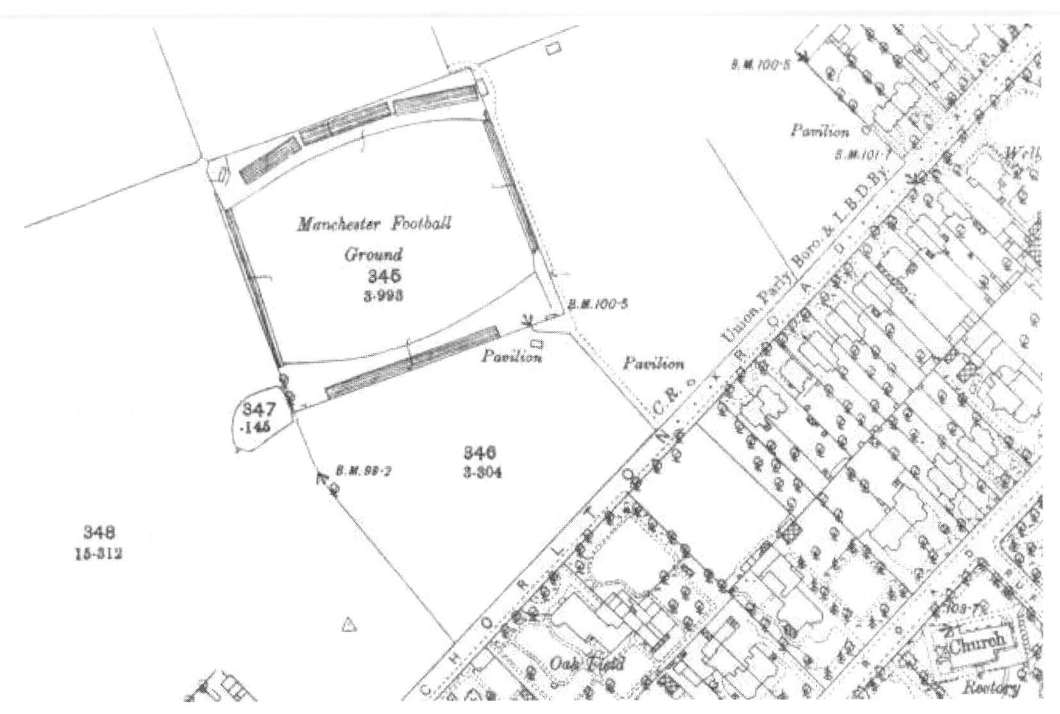

A plan from 1899 showing the Manchester FC ground in Whalley Range.

"Newton Heath FC - It was decided that the Honorary Secretary be instructed to inform the Newton Heath Football Club and the Football Association that the Rugby Union object to the club taking the name of Manchester FC. That the sub-committee previously elected to deal with the question of the naming of clubs be asked to meet a committee of the FA to deal with the above and professional laws."

The reference to professionalism was crucial in this comment as the Rugby Union was seriously concerned with all aspects of professionalism and a year after this comment the great split between Rugby Union and the northern clubs (Rugby League) occurred. Clearly it was hoped that a meeting with the FA would result in some form of agreement between Union and association football, and potentially the re-naming of Newton Heath may have been some sort of bargaining tool, although this is highly unlikely.

Ultimately, Newton Heath did not take on the name of Manchester FC but whether this was because of Manchester FC's complaints or pressure applied by the FA is not known, but it is significant that Newton Heath did not make a name change until 1902. Perhaps there was only one name they wanted – Manchester – and any other form of the name did not appeal. The selection of Manchester City's new name was not contested by any other body, and that name was used by the club to claim that they were a side representing the entire 'City of Manchester'.

Today Manchester FC remains the oldest rugby side in the region and, thanks to their record in the FA Cup and their friendlies with Sheffield, they are also Manchester's oldest surviving soccer club, even if they do not play the game today. Interestingly, the distinctions between the two main forms of football – rugby and association – during the 1880s led to the coining of the term 'soccer'. Many assume the word is an American creation, however it's roots lie in the development of the game in England. According to anecdotal evidence the phrase became common following its first use by Charles Wreford Brown. An Oxford student, who would later play international football for England and become vice-president of the FA, Brown is alleged to have been asked if he wanted to play 'rugger', a common term for rugby football. He replied that he wanted to play 'Soccer' (his abbreviation for 'association').

From that point on the new term was often used by serious followers of the game, and it was not until the split within the rugby game that the more recognised terms of Rugby Union, Rugby League and Football came to differentiate the three sports in England.

CHAPTER THREE

THE GROWTH OF FOOTBALL

The result on that fateful day is of course etched in every record book. Hyde lost 26-0, an FA Cup record. But Hyde were only a small team and very young. Proud Preston were the best in the world and soon to be the first ever Football League champions.

"Mottram Road to Maine Road – A History of Football in Hyde", Mike Pavasovic 1985

AS time moved on local sides started to develop around the city and the neighbouring towns, but the confusion about whether they played a form of soccer or a form of rugby continues to this day. Bolton Wanderers were the first of the Greater Manchester sides to be formed when in 1874 a teacher at Christ Church called a meeting of teachers and other young men. From that meeting Christ Church Football Club was formed and in 1877 the name was changed to Bolton Wanderers. However in 1894 the Bolton newspaper ***The Football Field*** claimed that Christ Church had played rugby for its first two years of existence, while other sources claim the club alternated codes depending on the wishes of their opponents. Whatever the truth, it is clear that Bolton was the first of the region's leading sides to be formed.

In 1878 the Lancashire FA was formed and this helped to formalise local rules and provide competition with the formation of the Lancashire Cup in 1879-80. Darwen were the first winners after beating Blackburn Rovers 3-0 in the final, but there was only minor representation from the Manchester region. A significant number of teams from Bolton took part but, apart from those sides, the only other one from the Manchester region was Manchester Wanderers.

Wanderers remained a significant local side for several years, but ultimately they were unable to develop and eventually disappeared as the other Mancunian sides came to prominence.

Within Manchester itself the game was developing and Newton Heath Lancashire & Yorkshire Railway, which eventually became Manchester United, is believed to have been formed in 1878, then two years later Manchester City's predecessor was formed as St. Mark's (West Gorton). The reasons for the creation of these two sides are significantly different, however the fact that both organisations were to develop in the east of the city is significant.

East Manchester was a densely populated, heavily industrialised area with significant social issues. Football provided a great release from the worries of the region. The areas of Ardwick,

Made 16th August, 1879, at the Coffee Tavern, Darwen Street, Blackburn.

North End (Bolton)	v	Turton.
Padiham	v.	Haslingden.
Astley Bridge	v.	Rising Sun (Blackburn).
Accrington	v.	Halliwell.
St. Paul's (Bolton)	v.	St. Mark's (Blackburn).
Lower Darwen	v.	Darwen Rangers.
Bolton Olympic	v.	Lynwood (Darwen).
Darwen St. James	v.	Haslingden Grane.
Middleton	v.	Edgeworth.
Cloughfold	v.	Great Lever.
Darwen Grasshoppers	v.	Darwen.
Cob Wall	v.	Manchester Wanderers.
Livesey United (Blackburn)	v.	Halliwell Jubilee.
Bolton Hornets	v.	Blackburn Christ Church
Enfield	v.	Blackburn Rovers.
Bolton Wanderers	v.	All Saints (Bolton).
Blackburn St. George's	v.	Lower Chapel (Darwen)
Bolton Rovers.	v.	Eagley
Church	v.	Blackburn St. Andrews
Blackburn Park Road	v.	Emmanuel (Bolton).

Manchester's representatives were few in the inaugural Lancashire Cup.

Longsight, Gorton, Beswick, Clayton, Newton Heath, and Failsworth still retained their individual identities, but were very similar in terms of type of residents, industry, and housing. They were mainly working class areas and sport was used to help provide leisure activities.

Saturday afternoons were the ideal time for sporting activities as workers would often finish their toil at lunch time on a Saturday and the afternoon provided a great time to let off steam. Perhaps, because of the individual identities of each of the districts or towns, football clubs developed to represent the various localities. Even towns such as Gorton were split into different communities and so sides such as Gorton Villa grew at a similar rate to Manchester City's predecessors in the same area.

A little further east from the city centre, the neighbouring towns of Tameside were equally as passionate and determined to create sides to represent their communities. Ashton and Stalybridge in particular seemed to have many teams by the mid 1880s. A review of the **Gorton Reporter** – the leading newspaper for the whole of east Manchester and Tameside (it produced separate issues for many of the local towns) - for January 1885 shows several sides from Ashton-under-Lyne, including: Hurst Ramblers, Darnton Road, Hurst Brook Rovers, Hurst Knowl Light Foots, Hurst Star, Hurst, and Hurst Brook Olympic. Another side, Bardsley, was mentioned from the border of Oldham and Ashton, while the newspaper also talked of other Ashton based sides over the weeks that followed. Mike Pavasovic, an expert of football in the Tameside area, believes this area was particularly strong during football's formative years:

"The oldest club in Tameside is Hurst, present day Ashton United, formed in 1878, but there were

many other teams around during the 1880s. Some were just regulars at local pubs or churches. These clubs came and went throughout the early years. Ashton and Stalybridge had a variety of clubs, but areas such as Audenshaw and Denton also had their own sides.

"In 1887 Hyde played Denton on land near the Bankfield Hotel and some records say there were about 10,000 people there. It was a real grudge match and in the **North Cheshire Herald** *the week after a poem appeared which basically told the story of how 'Hyde people' do not like 'Denton people' and never will. After another game – a victory over Hurst – someone controversially produced 'sympathy cards'. The secretary of Hyde had to offer a formal apology afterwards. The rivalry was pretty intense."*

Inevitably with so many sides in the east Manchester area football fixtures were relatively easy to arrange, but competition was still too flexible for most people's liking. A prime example – and also a fairly typical one – came in the 3rd January 1885 meeting between Levenshulme and West Gorton. The away team, West Gorton, were recorded as winning the match but the game was never actually finished. Levenshulme disputed the only goal and walked off the field, refusing to accept either the goal or the result. It was a situation repeated around the region.

In an attempt to formalise competition for local sides the Manchester FA was formed in 1884 and a cup competition – the Manchester Cup – was created. At the time this was a major landmark and gave all sides something to aim for. It is difficult appreciating the scale and importance of this act now, but in 1884 football was still developing. None of the leading sides had any real chance of success, but the Manchester Cup allowed all member sides to enter the competition and to play ties against other progressive sides from the region.

Manchester FC and Hurst had both competed in the FA Cup by this stage and understood the importance of real competition. In fact, Hurst was actually Manchester's only undefeated entrant in the FA Cup at this point. They entered the competition in 1883-84 and defeated Turton 3-0, then defeated Irwell Springs from Bacup 3-2. However Irwell protested about the result and the FA ordered a replay. Sadly, the match report from the ***Manchester Courier*** of December 1883 fails to mention any protest and simply describes the tie as a 'very fast game'. Hurst decided they would rather pull out of the competition than face a re-match, and Irwell progressed. Interestingly, Irwell who played near the Roebuck Inn, at a ground called the Broad Clough, had also lost their first round match to Rossendale 6-2 on 17 November 1883 but the FA disqualified Rossendale for professionalism. Irwell faced Bolton Wanderers in the third round and inevitably were defeated, this time 8-1.

So Hurst and Manchester recognised the excitement that could be generated by competition and they inevitably became founder members of the Manchester FA, as did Newton Heath LY & R and Gorton AFC (the renamed St. Mark's/MCFC side). It should be recognised that Hurst had also joined the Lancashire FA in July 1881.

The idea of local pride fitted perfectly with the concept of local competition and so the Manchester Cup and other similar local cup competitions, for much of the decade that followed, became more important than the FA Cup. This may seem strange, but the FA Cup would often involve a lot of travel and some of the region's clubs simply could not afford to travel. Newton Heath chose only to enter the competition once pre-1889 and even then they had endured a bad experience when a tie at Fleetwood Rangers in October 1886 ended 2-2 and the referee tried to persuade the Heathens to play extra-time. The Heathens, perhaps thinking about rail travel back to Manchester, refused and the tie was awarded to Fleetwood.

HURST v. ST. MARK'S, WEST GORTON (ASSOCIATION RULES).

This match was played on Saturday last on the ground of the former, at Hurst, in very stormy weather. The visitors won the toss, and elected to play with the wind in their favour. The home team kicked off, taking the ball close to the visitors' goal, when Lawton, dashing in, shot the ball between the posts. The visitors kicked off from the centre, and after a little give-and-take play in midfield, the home forwards again came away, and, not to be denied, Lawton scored goal No. 2. Shortly after this half time was called. Ends having been changed, they [illegible] with two goals to the bad and a strong wind against them, kicked off. During the second half the visitors' team were hard pressed, and many shots were made at the visitors' goal, but the wind carried them wide of the mark. Ultimately the visitors' forwards getting possession made a good run, and Lomas, the Hurst custodian, had to run out to save his charge, kicking the ball, which bounded from one of the visitors close to the Hurst goal, but [illegible] neck of time came to the rescue, and visitors took the corner, but nothing [illegible] the visitors had to act on the defen- [illegible] of time Axon scored the third goal, saying the ball had been over the goal [illegible] saw this, and the visitors kicked [illegible] Time was now called, having the [illegible] goals, one disputed, to nil.

[illegible] (ASSOCIATION RULES)

[illegible]day, on the ground of the [illegible] return match. The ground [illegible]quently the falls were very [illegible] the toss, and elected to play [illegible] Lawton kicked off with a [illegible] goal was soon in danger. [illegible] the ball well in front [illegible] the spot scored goal No. 1. [illegible] visitors' backs were equal to [illegible] the ball into mid field, and [illegible], but its keeper [illegible]

The first recorded meeting between Hurst and St Mark's (City) from December 1880

Interestingly, local football remained more important than the FA Cup for many years. In April 1885 the FA Cup final between Blackburn Rovers and Queen's Park was hardly covered locally. It had only one paragraph in one local newspaper while a friendly between Hurst V Rawtenstall had over three times the space, although the fact that the local match had been controversial may have played a part. With the score at 3-0 to Hurst the referee walked off following a dispute about a goal, and while he was off the field Hurst scored their fourth.

The first season of the Manchester Cup proved to be very exciting with games involving Hurst and Newton Heath grabbing much attention in the local newspapers. In fact the two sides competed in the first Manchester Cup final. This was played at Manchester FC's Whalley Range ground and had an attendance of approximately 3,500. The Ashton club won 3-0 and, at the end of the match, all the Hurst players were lifted shoulder high by their fans, and there was tremendous excitement on the pitch. It was perhaps the first time a Manchester side had experienced success that actually meant something.

HURST CLARENCE v. ST. MARK'S, WEST GORTON.

The above clubs met for the first time this season to play a game of football (association rules) on Saturday last, on the ground of the latter. The weather was very fine, which brought a good number of spectators to witness the game, which proved to be a friendly one. The home team chose the way to play, which was a little down hill, but not much. The visitors put the ball in motion, which was kept in play for some time when the visitors got a corner kick which proved successful for them, as they scored from it. The home team then put the leather about, both teams showing some good play, nothing more being done until half-time was called. Half-[illegible] the home team put the ball in motion, the visi[tors] of it now put two more goals to the list, tha[t] team three goals to the bad. Time being ca[lled] pleasant games ended in favour of Clarence [illegible] nil. Teams: Hurst Clarence—J. Hindle, [illegible] J. Barton, backs; J. Dickin (captain), [illegible] backs; E. A. Lees, H. Bickerton, J. P[illegible] Turton, and A. R. Adams, forwards. St. [Mark's] goal; W. Sumner (captain) and E. Greve[illegible] and A. Macdonald, half backs; W. C[illegible] Downing, R. Millard, R. Hopkinson, and [illegible] Umpire, J. E. Bickerton.

NEWTON H[EATH]

This match, unde[illegible] Heath on Saturday [illegible] a victory for the ho[me] were scored for New[ton] the other being put [illegible] their own backs [illegible] Thomas. E. Thoma[s] following were the te[ams] [illegible]ner and Hopkinson, Beastowe and Pickin[g] centre [illegible]

[illegible] v. BENTFIELD, GREENFIELD.

[illegible] at Longsight on [illegible] West Gor[ton]

Hurst Clarence faced St Mark's (City) in November 1881.

The Manchester Cup, seen in 2008 at Manchester City's museum.

Hurst could rightly claim to be the best in the area, and after the game finished the President of the Manchester FA, Mr. Colbert, presented the cup to J. Ingham, Hurst's captain. *The Reporter* then described the fantastic parade that took place all the way back to Ashton:

"All the way from Whalley Range the victors kept cheering and the band playing, the cup being held up in front of one of the carriages in which the journey to Ashton was made. On arriving in town their cheers were redoubled and they received a great ovation in the streets.

"The victors crowded into the Pitt & Nelson, and Mr. Joseph Fletcher, holding in his hand the cup which was filled with liquor, and addressing the captain of the club, said he had great pleasure in presenting to Mr. Ingham the cup on behalf of the Hurst Cricket & football Club."

Joseph Fetcher was the landlord of the Pitt & Nelson and according to *The Reporter* he made a speech saying that he:

"had lately been in Blackburn and he could assure them that the fame of the Hurst club was well known in that district and he was certain that the next season they would be called upon to play with teams from that district, the Mother of the Game."

This was undoubtedly the finest moment for any of the Manchester clubs at this stage in history, and Hurst were worthy recipients of the praise. Hurst had done more than most to encourage the game to develop and, as well as entering the FA Cup, they also tried to arrange fixtures with teams beyond the Manchester boundaries. In March 1885 they had welcomed Welsh side Rhyl to Hurst with the Ashton side winning 8-1 before 3,000 fans. On Good Friday they

NEWTON HEATH (L. Y. R.) v. WEST GORTON.

This match, under Association rules, was played at Newton Heath on Saturday last, and, after a pleasant game, resulted in a victory for the home team by three goals to nil. Two goals were scored for Newton Heath in the first half, one by J. Jones, the other being put through the West Gorton goal by one of their own backs whilst attempting to stop a shot from E. Thomas. E. Thomas also kicked a goal in the second half. The following were the teams: West Gorton – Kitchen, goal; Sumner and Hopkinson, backs; Greves and [illegible], half backs; Beastowe and Pilkington, right wings; McDonald and [illegible], centre; [illegible]d and Pervor, left wings. Newton Heath – Shaw and Morris, backs; [illegible] and Fulton, [illegible]rs and Latham, right wings; Thomas and J. [illegible]opwood and Edwards, left wings.

A match report from Newton Heath (United) V West Gorton (City) in November 1881.

played their return match and, in one report from the period, it was suggested that over 750 fans had travelled from Ashton for the game which Hurst won 4-0. Considering the nature of travel, working conditions, and the state of the game at the time, this was a major achievement, although the club's own records suggest the total crowd was around 750.

With the Manchester Cup now providing a focus Manchester's sides had something to push for. Newton Heath (Manchester United) won the trophy in 1886 by defeating Manchester FC, and then in 1887 West Manchester won the trophy for the first time. The following three seasons saw sides from Denton, Hooley Hill, and Royton reach the final but Newton Heath managed to lift the trophy on each occasion. Then in 1891 Ardwick, the team that had evolved from St. Mark's and would ultimately become Manchester City, defeated the Heathens in the final.

For the following twenty years or so the competition would be dominated by sides that are today known as well-established Football League sides – Bury (first success 1894), Bolton Wanderers (1895), Stockport County (1898), and Oldham Athletic (1914).

Local success in the Manchester Cup helped to establish the sides, however football was developing throughout the country with sides from the north-west, predominantly northern Lancashire, and the Midlands becoming recognised as the powers of the game. It should be recorded that by 1890 the FA Cup had already seen winners from Blackburn (Rovers & Olympic), and Preston. The best any of the sides from the Greater Manchester area had managed was when Bolton Wanderers reached the semi-finals in 1889-90, but other than that Manchester struggled. Ignoring the sides from Bolton, Manchester's first competitors in the FA Cup were:

1877-78	Manchester FC
1878-79	Birch
1883-84	Hurst, Manchester FC
1884-85	Hurst
1885-86	Hurst
1886-87	Newton Heath
1887-88	Hurst, Hyde, Denton, Heywood Central, West Manchester & Bury
1889-90	Newton Heath
1890-91	Ardwick AFC, Newton Heath

The first actual FA Cup tie played by a club from the present day M60 boroughs of Manchester was Manchester's 3-0 defeat at Darwen on 7 November 1877. Sadly, none of the leading local or national papers of the day covered this game as coverage of association football remained poor in Manchester. By 1880 however, some – but by no means all - newspapers included match reports and general footballing gossip. The coverage at a local level in the Manchester branded newspapers, i.e. the *Evening News*, *Evening Chronicle*, *Courier*, and *Mail* was patchy.

From 1880 the *Manchester Courier* tended to focus on big games, such as the Lancashire Cup or those played against recognised non-local opposition, while the *Evening News* barely covered football at all. Newspapers tended to rely on the clubs themselves sending in reports and the *Courier* often fielded complaints from sides who felt their match reports were a little biased. On a fairly regular basis in the early 1880s the *Courier* asked clubs to be fair and balanced in their reports, although it is clear from their own reporters that the *Courier*'s journalists were keen to stress the qualities of the local sides above non-Mancunian sides.

On 8th November 1880 the only association football match covered in the *Courier* was Sheffield's 2-1 victory over Manchester Wanderers at Brook's Bar. Every other report was of rugby games involving teams with seemingly bizarre names such as Newton Heath Orleans. Whether this was because of a lack of fixtures, or simply because the sides failed to send in detailed reports is not clear, but it does seem as if the *Courier* would have printed every report it received no matter how big or small the side. On 22nd November every Lancashire Cup game was reported on, so perhaps there simply were not that many matches in early November 1880, although later that month would see both St. Mark's (City) and Newton Heath (United) have games reported.

By October 1883, when the second FA Cup game featuring a side from the area occurred association football was starting to receive a good level of coverage, or at least FA Cup games were being documented extensively in the leading newspapers of the day. The *Manchester Courier* even had a regular journalist called 'Dribbler' focusing on the association game. Match reports appeared for this second FA Cup tie, incidentally the first to be played by a local side at home in the competition, and the competitors were Hurst who defeated Turton 3-0.

The following November saw Manchester FC manage a 2-1 victory at Stoke. Manchester's tie with Stoke was viewed by Dribbler as a significant point in the development of the game in the city, particularly as prior to the tie only Nottingham Forest had managed to defeat Stoke that season. Even the attendance – estimated as 700 – was viewed as significant for this fixture:

"In the English Cup tie at Stoke a most disappointing blow was given to the home team by Manchester, who defeated the noted Staffordshire club by two goals to one. Judging from what I saw on Saturday, I should say that each team had its weak points. The visitors were not nearly so strong in the forwards as the home team, while the latter were lamentably weak in the back division as compared with that of Manchester.

"I feel quite confident that the Manchester team have more about them than past form would imply, all they want is more thorough combination in forward play. Walker and 'Junior' as backs, and Sumner and Hay half backs, are players deserving of the trust placed in them, as their play on Saturday was the chief feature of the match. Stoke have been defeated only once this season previous to their engagement with Manchester on Saturday."

Interest in association football increased as a result of this victory and this interest intensified when it became clear Manchester would face the great Scottish side Queens Park in the next round. This was to be a British first for Manchester as the tie, played at Queens Park's temporary home of Titwood, the home of Clydesdale Cricket Club, was the first FA Cup tie played in Scotland. Therefore Manchester was the first English side to play a competitive club fixture north of the border. Queens Park had entered the FA Cup in its inaugural season, but this was the first time they had competed in a home fixture. They were Scotland's dominant club and were in the process of building Hampden Park, hence the temporary use of the cricket ground.

Sadly, the game was one step too far for Manchester and they were defeated 15-0. It has to be stressed though that the Scottish side were formidable opponents and that they went on to reach the final itself. On route to their final appearance they defeated two of the leading English sides of the period, Aston Villa (6-1) and Blackburn Olympic (4-1).

Earlier, it was mentioned that the Hurst-Turton match of October 1882 was the first home game involving a Manchester side in the FA Cup. This is true, but it was not the first FA Cup tie in the city as two FA Cup semi-finals had been played at Manchester's Whalley Range ground in the early 1880s.

On 15 March 1882 Blackburn Rovers defeated Sheffield Wednesday 5-1 in a replay, played in front of a crowd reported as 10,000, while the following year Blackburn Olympic defeated Old Carthusians 4-0 on their way to becoming the North's first FA Cup winners. These games were important as they demonstrated the attention football could generate in the area. For any neutral fixture to attract a crowd of around 10,000 must have been a phenomenal achievement at the time and possibly inspired others and, maybe, this was part of the reason for the creation of the Manchester Cup in 1884.

It should be highlighted that on 6 December 1882 a grand footballing conference was held in Manchester whereby representatives from each of the four home nations' football associations came together. The idea was that this group would produce a uniform code of laws and would become the new guardians of the game. The Manchester Conference led to the creation of the "International Football Association Board" which became established in the summer of 1885.

The IFA Board became the only body able to change the laws of the game until, of course, the formation of FIFA in 1904. It has to be stressed however that the British football associations did not support FIFA's authority for many years, and even as recently as 1960 a major four volume work entitled ***Association Football*** by AH Fabian & Geoffrey Green claimed that the IFA Board was still the only body which could change football's laws. Clearly this is no longer true, as FIFA controls football on an international level.

One surprising aspect of the development of football within Manchester was the role of the university. In general universities played a leading role in the development of football however this does not appear to be the case in Manchester. Sources from the early 1880s suggest the university was not too active with association football and in 1883 Dribbler, writing in the ***Manchester Courier,*** went as far as suggesting the university was lagging behind clubs such as Manchester FC and the other developing sides.

An Owens College side was in existence, but after one particular game against Cheadle in Fallowfield the Dribbler suggested that simply using the name Owens College meant that the university was not supportive of the game in the way it should be. He called for the side to be named the Victoria University (the university had originally been Owens College but had improved its name and status in 1880 when it was renamed the Victoria University). He argued that such a change would help the university become a leading player in the development of the association game.

Whether the university was more interested in other sports or not is immaterial today, however it is clear that most of Manchester's earliest sides came from the working classes rather than the education elite. The earliest entrants in the major competitions tended to come from the industrial towns and districts of the area.

It is worth pausing to mention more of Manchester's early FA Cup entrants. Hurst were clearly the most interested in the competition but they did not enter until 1883. By that time Birch had become Manchester's second entrants, entering in 1878, but they never actually played in the competition as they were drawn away to Darwen and pulled out before the game took place.

The same thing occurred on 15 October 1887 with several local sides, but this date is important because it was also the first to see widespread Mancunian interest in the competition. On that day

Denton, who played at a field dubbed Chapel Green, were drawn away to South Shore (Blackpool) but for an unknown reason pulled out. Presumably the cost of travelling, or the time taken to travel caused too many problems for the Dentonians. Bury also pulled out of their tie at Blackburn Rovers (although we do know their game was declared void as a result of player ineligibility) and had to wait until 1891 before they finally managed to play a proper game in the competition when they defeated Witton 3-1 in the first qualifying round.

Another local side, Heywood Central, who played at the Phoenix Pleasure Ground near the Britannia Hotel in Heywood, were defeated 8-1 at Higher Walton. They entered the competition every year between 1887 and 1894-95 but 1887 was the only time they played in the competition proper. Hurst defeated Astley Bridge 5-3 but were subsequently disqualified after a protest from Astley. At Fleetwood Rangers West Manchester were defeated 4-1 at the same time, while the biggest FA Cup story of them all as far as the Manchester area is concerned occurred at Preston and featured Hyde FC.

Hyde FC were formed in 1885 at a meeting attended by about 40 men in the White Lion public house in the middle of the town centre, and it is clear from the start that the side was quite ambitious for the period. At the start of the 1886-87 season one of the giants of the period, Blackburn Rovers, were invited to Hyde for a friendly. Hyde lost 8-0 but afterwards members of Blackburn's side stressed that they believed Hyde had potential to go far. It may have been these comments that encouraged Hyde to enter the FA Cup the following season and ultimately make history.

They did enter the competition for 1887-88 and, as with the previous year, they opened the season with a friendly against significant opposition. This time Bolton defeated Hyde 8-1. When the FA Cup draw was made Hyde were drawn away at Preston North End. Mike Pavasovic, author of **Mottram Road to Maine Road – A history of football in Hyde**, believes Hyde saw themselves on a par with some of these sides:

"When Hyde were founded they became a successful club locally quite quickly. They spent a lot of money on attracting some of the biggest clubs to come to Hyde for games and they felt their place was at a higher level than perhaps some of the other local sides. This caused the others to think that Hyde were getting too big for their boots.

"When they were drawn against Preston – arguably the world's greatest team at the time - everyone knew it was an impossible task for Hyde to win. There was an odd comment in the **North Cheshire Herald** *by a reporter called Rover who said:'a man is a man, but if a pig could fly, Hyde would beat Preston and I will eat my hat. He meant they stood no chance."*

ARDWICK v. HYDE.—(Ardwick District Charity Cup, second round).—At Ardwick. Hyde kicked off. Ardwick scored first from the toe of Drinkwater, and from the kick off they took it down and scored again. Then Parker scored for Ardwick, and all the first half Ardwick pressed. On change of ends, with wind in their favour, it was thought that Hyde would press, but it was not so. Parker, Hodgetts, and Callagan scored, and from Manning, at half back, Callagan scored. Then Hyde scored one. McKenzie afterwards scored the eighth for Ardwick, the result being :—

ARDWICK .... 8 goals.
HYDE .... 1 "

This victory by Ardwick over Hyde was eventually scrubbed from the records as Hyde complained about the state of the pitch. The replay ended 3-1 to Ardwick at Hyde.

Walkden—Cooke 2, Boone, 2, Hurst 2, Gardrer 1, and Price 1.

BELL'S TEMPERANCE v. BURNLEY UNION STAR.—Played at Burnley. A very fast and even game ensued, the Stars winning by 2 goals to Bell's 1 goal.

HURST v. OSWALDTWISTLE ROVERS.—At Hurst, before 2000 spectators. Garnett started the ball at 4·35, the visitors arriving late. The play ruled fast, and ten minutes from start the visitors rushed one through. Soon after Gabbust centred finely to Garnett, who equalised, and in another minute Mulholland put on a second. In the second half both sides played up determinedly, each goal being visited in succession, Hurst pressing a good deal, but no more goals were scored, Hurst winning by 2 goals to 1.

LONDON v. STAFFORDSHIRE.—Played at Kennington Oval, before 400 spectators. London eleven without Old Carthusians or Westminsters. London pressed at first; Roberts fisted out, then Bambridge nearly scored for London; Sayer and Shutt took the ball down, and Roberts saved a fine shot. Davies kicked grandly for London, who had first three corners. Mills and Roberts saved five grand shots; Ingram twice shot outside Stafford's goal. No score at half time, but London was hard pressed in the second half. Playford passed to Bambridge, who gave it to Ingram, and the latter scored first goal amidst great applause; Playford narrowly missed another amid great excitement. Then Bambridge almost scored again. The Southern combination was perfect. Staffordshire got three corners, but could not score. At length the ball was heaved through in a scrimmage. Five minors were added before time, and Staffordshire getting the best of it, got 3 more goals. Result:—

STAFFORDSHIRE .... 4 goals.
LONDON 1

STAFFORDSHIRE.—W Rowley, Stoke, goal. C Mason, Wolverhampton Wanderers, and T Hawkins, Mitchell St. George's, backs. A Bailey, Mitchell St. George's; G Shutt, Stoke: and A Lowder, Wolverhampton Wanderers, half-backs. J Sayer, Stoke; C Shaw, Walsall Town; J Brodie, Wolverhampton Wanderers; W Vickerstaffe, Leek; and W Harrison, Mitchell St. George's, forwards.

A match report from the Umpire newspaper of Hurst V Oswaldtwistle in February 1887

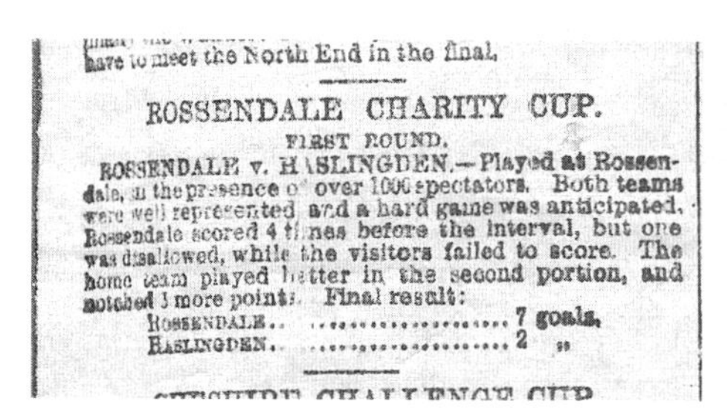

have to meet the North End in the final.

ROSSENDALE CHARITY CUP.

FIRST ROUND.

ROSSENDALE v. HASLINGDEN.—Played at Rossendale, in the presence of over 1000 spectators. Both teams were well represented and a hard game was anticipated. Rossendale scored 4 times before the interval, but one was disallowed, while the visitors failed to score. The home team played better in the second portion, and notched 3 more points. Final result:

ROSSENDALE.. .... 7 goals.
HASLINGDEN.. .... 2 "

The Rossendale Charity Cup (February 1887) - competitions like these sprung up all over the region prior to the formation of the Football League

Preston had reached the semi-finals the previous season and were recognised as a leading side. For Hyde the game was expected to be exceptionally tough, and the Hyde players must have been both excited and apprehensive about the game. However there was some controversy pre-match. According to Mike Pavasovic, Preston had already arranged a fixture with West Bromwich Albion and wanted to play the FA Cup tie midweek. Hyde, perhaps because of the complications a midweek game would have caused at the time, refused. As a result Preston made it clear that they would do all they could to win the match.

The game commenced at 3.30 and within five minutes Fred Dewhurst had headed Preston's first goal. A relentless attack on the Hyde goal followed and after 12 minutes Drummond netted the second. Jimmy Ross scored the third five minutes later, then Dewhurst headed a fourth almost immediately.

According to the **Lancashire Evening Post** the Preston goalkeeper did not touch the ball until the 25th minute when he took a goal kick, but by this point Hyde were already a struggling side. Almost immediately after the goal kick Preston challenged Hyde's goal again:

> *"Drummond was responsible for the fifth goal and a minute later Graham with a grand shot put on the sixth and Thompson added the seventh with a fairly long swift shot making the third goal inside of five minutes. Three minutes from half time Jack [Nick] Ross placed himself in the proud position of having a goal to his credit. Thompson notched the eleventh and Gordon the twelfth, at which score the game stood at half time."*

Hyde came out for the second half determined to demonstrate an attacking spirit and they briefly put Preston under some pressure, but Preston soon regained the initiative and the goals flooded in. The match reports for this game simply list the scorers from this point on as, presumably, the pace was so frenetic that it was impossible for the reporters to record the general action.

The final score was 26-0 but there was a little more controversy and confusion according to Pavasovic. After the third goal, scored in the 17th minute, Hyde's centre-back Bowers left the pitch with a sprained arm and Preston allowed the Hydonians to bring on another player for the second half even though substitutions were not allowed at this point in football history. Presumably they had felt a half time 12 goal lead was enough of a cushion.

The referee, R.G. Barlow of Manchester, also played his part in the large victory by playing an additional five minutes during which time Preston's last goal was scored. The reason this additional time was played remains unclear, although some at the time suggested the referee was simply too involved with the action to check his watch, while others over the years that followed claimed his watch had stopped and that an additional ten or fifteen minutes had actually been played. Whatever the truth it is clear that this was a remarkable victory for Preston, and it was also clear that sides from the Manchester area were still some way off competing with the best.

Despite the scoreline, Hyde's goalkeeper Bunyan was actually one of the heroes of the day. According to the **Preston Guardian**:

"It is only fair to the Hyde custodian to say that had he been a less able man there is no telling what the score would have been. Times innumerable he stopped shots which brought forth cries of 'through' and was repeatedly cheered right lustily."

Interestingly, in the match preview the **North Cheshire Herald** had predicted a fine performance:

"I wish them every success and especially Bunyan who in goal will I hope prove a clinking opponent of the North Enders."

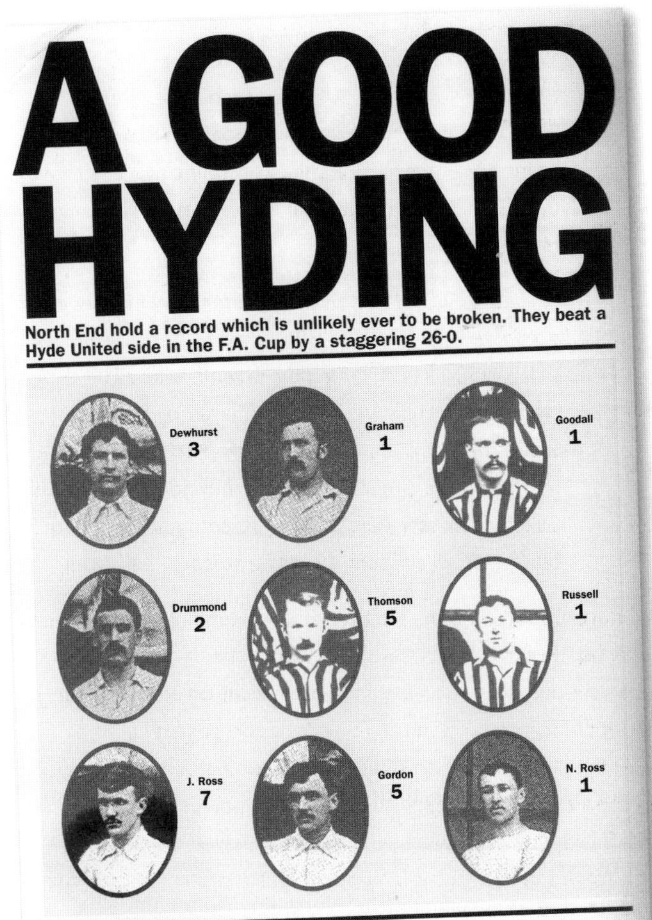
A GOOD HYDING

North End hold a record which is unlikely ever to be broken. They beat a Hyde United side in the F.A. Cup by a staggering 26-0.

Dewhurst 3
Graham 1
Goodall 1
Drummond 2
Thomson 5
Russell 1
J. Ross 7
Gordon 5
N. Ross 1

The journalist Tityrus, real name J.A.H. Catton, wrote of the quality of Preston some forty years later and ended his feature with:

"Of course, the 'cup-tie' with Hyde remains a historical feat, a record. Charles Bunyan, who was the goalkeeper for Hyde, assured me one day at Brussels that it was a wonder Preston did not get forty goals. That may be, but there came a time when the whole eleven of Hyde were backs. Such are some of the great deeds of Preston."

Mike Pavasovic also believes the Hyde goalkeeper was the star man:

"Bunyan played for a number of clubs, including Newcastle, and he was an absolute star. In fact there's a story that the Hyde team bought him a suit as a gift following his great performance. I don't know if it's true, but it does look like he was Hyde's best man."

On the 15th October 1887 a game took place at Deepdale which was to be written into soccer history books and remain there for years to come. It was that 26-0 game most schoolboys hear about from their fathers and grandfathers. It was no exception. Did all the team score and who got the most goals? These were just two questions I wanted answering as a schoolboy.

Only a "fair muster" of spectators assembled at Deepdale for this English Cup First Round tie against the Hyde club from the Manchester area. Sam Thomson turned out for his first game of the season and took his place at the front. Fred Dewhurst got the ball rolling, scoring the game's first goal with less than five minutes gone.

It was twenty five minutes before Addison, North End's goalkeeper, got his first touch of the ball, by which time Drummond, J.Ross and Dewhurst had added to the scoreline.

Within five minutes another three goals were in the bag from the likes of Drummond, Graham and Thomson. North End's right wing then got into the act with Gordon and J.Ross grabbing goals eight and nine.

Double figures were reached when Nick Ross came up from full-back to blast one past Bunyan, Hyde's goalkeeper. Before the bemused crowd had stopped applauding Thomson and Gordon had made it 12-0. All before half time. Talk about one way traffic!

By this time the match reporter's pencil must have been blunt and all he could do to keep pace was to record the goalscorers as the total totted up to that now famous 26-0 scoreline.

A hundred years on, to commemorate the famous win, North End played an exhibition match at Hyde. Despite a replica kit and a few centre partings, the score was a more respectable 4-1 win.

For the budding statisticians the second half goalscorers were: Thomson, Thomson, J. Ross, Thomson, J.Ross, J.Ross, Gordon, Russell, J.Ross, Gordon, Gordon, Dewhurst, J.Ross and finally, Goodall.

Just for the record Bob Howarth, North End's right back, did not manage to score. And the goalkeeper, Addison, was said to have had a quiet game.

Above and previous page: **Memories of Hyde's 26-0 defeat as documented in "North End: A Pictorial History of Preston North End"**

From a Manchester perspective it should be noted that Preston's leading scorer Jimmy Ross, who is usually credited as scoring eight of the goals, went on to become a major star during Preston's first Football League season of 1888-89 and also became a hero at Manchester City when he teamed up with Billy Meredith between 1899 and his shock death in 1902. He also had a great sense of humour. Tityrus:

"Ross was as cunning as a monkey and as accurate with a ball as a professional billiards player. Moreover, he was one of the very best story tellers I ever heard. On one occasion when he played with a scratch team at Stonyhurst College he kept a room full of reverend fathers convulsed with laughter by his anecdotes and experiences."

After the game Hyde and Preston regularly played each other in friendlies, and the two sides also met to raise money for the victims of the Hyde coal mining disaster of 1889 – that same year Newton Heath LY&R and Ardwick met under floodlights at Belle Vue to raise money for the families. This is believed to be the first floodlit match played in the area, although there is anecdotal evidence to suggest that Preston played Ardwick at Hyde Road around the same time under artificial light.

In 1987 Preston and Hyde United met to remember the 1887 game. This time Preston defeated Hyde 4-1 on the old plastic pitch at Ewen Fields. Another re-match was staged in 2007.

There are records of this period in many different locations, including Manchester United's museum. In fact at Old Trafford details of the Manchester Cup entrants for the 1887-88 are held. These show basic information on each entrant, including their headquarters and, where known, the colours of their shirts. The teams listed were:

TEAM	**HEADQUARTERS**	**COLOURS**	**DATE FORMED** (AS RECORDED IN UNITED'S MUSEUM)
Ardwick	Hyde Road Hotel	Royal Blue & White vertical stripes	1887
Denton	Ashton Road, 1/2 mile from Denton Station	Red & White	
Eccles	Ellesmere Park	Light & Dark Blue	
Farnworth Parish Church	Lord Street, Kearsley	Blue & White	1884
Greenheys	Alexandra Park	Navy Blue & White	1882
Gorton Villa	Bulls Head Hotel, Reddish Lane	Red & Blue	1883
Hurst	Church Inn	Red & White	1878
Hooley Hill	Canning Street, 1/2 mile from the Pack Horse Inn, Guide Bridge	Red, White & Blue	1884
Hyde	Opposite the Bankfield Hotel	Oxford/Cambridge Blue halves	1884
Heaton Park		Blue shirts, White shorts	1886
Lower Hurst	Park Road, near infirmary	Blue & White	1884
Manchester FC	Hullard Hall Lane	Blue & White quarters, White shorts	

TEAM	HEADQUARTERS	COLOURS	DATE FORMED (AS RECORDED IN UNITED'S MUSEUM)
Manchester Clifford	Trafford Hotel, Old Trafford, 1/2 mile from Old Trafford Station	Maroon & Blue	1884
Miles Platting			
Newton Heath LY&R	North Road, 1/2 mile from Newton Heath Station	Green & Yellow	1878
Oldham Olympic	Copster Hill & Noggin Inn, Hollins	Chocolate, Blue & White	1885
Royton	Dog & Partridge, Royton	Blue & White	1886
Stalybridge St. Georges	Bulls Head Inn & Crookbottom	Blue & White	1883
Stretford	New Angel Hotel	Chocolate & White	1885
Ten Acres	Three Crowns Hotel & Ten Acres Lane		1884
West Manchester	Brooks Bar & Northumberland Hotel	White	1884
West Gorton Athletic	Church Lane, Gorton & New Inn Hotel, Gorton Lane	Red & White quarters	1885

Inevitably, the specific details of some of these clubs, most notably the years of formation, may have varied slightly, however the list provides a general view of the game as it was from a local perspective.

These records provide the first documentary evidence of Ardwick (City's) use of blue and white. For many years it has been assumed the club did not wear blue until the 1890s and the adoption of the title Manchester City, however the author of this book has always held the belief that blue had been the club's preferred colour since the formation of Ardwick. These details suggest this to be true, although it is intriguing to note that the side wore a form of royal blue and that the shirts were striped in 1887. This is out of character with the club's later style. Incidentally, it is often recorded that City wore white at times in the 1890s. This is not now accepted as fact as City typically wore their shirts for several years and it is believed the pale blue shirts faded after extensive washing.

By the end of the 1880s sides within the Manchester area were trying to compete with some of Lancashire's biggest names, however none of the region's sides were competing on a level footing. Elsewhere football was developing rapidly and the experience of Preston and West Bromwich Albion, and potentially others, when they had to cancel lucrative friendlies to play much less attractive opposition in the FA Cup, caused some to consider a way of guaranteeing the best quality opposition every week. Aston Villa's William McGregor considered what could be done and on 2nd March 1888 he sent a letter to Blackburn Rovers (FA Cup winners 1884-1886), Bolton Wanderers (Lancashire Cup winners 1886 after defeating Blackburn Rovers in final), Preston North End (FA Cup semi-finalists in 1887 and by the time the letter was sent they were scheduled to play West Bromwich Albion in the 1888 final), West Bromwich Albion (FA Cup finalists in 1886 & 1887 and scheduled to face Preston in 1888 final), plus his own club Aston Villa.

McGregor opened his letter with:

"Every year it is becoming more and more difficult for football clubs of any standing to meet their friendly engagements, and even arrange friendly matches. The consequence is that at the last moment, through cup-tie interferences, clubs are compelled to take on teams who will not attract the public.

"I beg to tender the following suggestion as a means of getting over the difficulty. That ten or twelve of the most prominent clubs in England combine to arrange home-and-home [sic] fixtures each season, the said fixtures to be arranged at a friendly conference about the same time as the International conference. This combination might be known as the Association Football Union, and could be managed by a representative from each club."

McGregor went on to suggest they meet on the eve of the FA Cup final in London, and also asked for suggestions for names of other clubs which might be worth contacting. Other Lancastrian and Midland clubs were added to the list, and a meeting was held in London with ten clubs, including the two FA Cup finalists, attending. The Association Football Union was dropped as a title and replaced with The Football League, although McGregor personally did not like the use of the word League as at the time it was often used for political organisations.

Although Manchester's clubs were not ready to compete in the League, the city itself did play a key role in the formation of the world's first football league. On 17 April 1888 the first true meeting of the League was held at the Royal Hotel, Manchester. This formally agreed the creation of a twelve club League and the associated rules of the competition. None of the 12 clubs were from the south, as there were no professional sides south of Birmingham.

The original twelve included Bolton Wanderers, Accrington and Burnley, and McGregor made it clear from the outset that he believed the League should be as widespread as possible. Clearly, the lack of southern clubs was an issue, but McGregor wanted to ensure that a maximum of one team from each town could be included. This caused some controversy – McGregor's Aston Villa seemed to block another Birmingham side, Mitchell St. George, from taking part (West Bromwich Albion was not regarded as part of Birmingham at the time) – but would have worked in Manchester's favour as Liverpool (Everton), Birmingham (Aston Villa), Wolverhampton, Derby, and Stoke were already represented and a representative from a city the size of Manchester would have proved beneficial. As many footballing meetings, conferences, and other football related matters occurred in the city, it seems likely a Manchester side would have been included had one been ready.

Much has been made in recent years of Newton Heath's standing in the game at this point and it is fair to say that the Heathens were one of Manchester's more successful sides after winning the Manchester Cup in 1886 and appearing as finalists in 1885 and 1887. They would ultimately win the trophy in 1888 for a second time, but at the time McGregor and Co. were planning their League Newton Heath, like the other Mancunian sides, were actually one of the teams they wanted to avoid playing. Newton Heath had only played in one FA Cup tie – and that ended controversially when they refused to play extra time – and were not recognised by the larger Lancastrian sides as a serious contender at this point. Many United histories claim the Heathens applied and were rejected by the new League committee after receiving one vote, but that simply is not true.

The League was created by invitation with no sides applying during 1888, and the League itself evolved as time moved on. It was not seen as something every aspiring team had to be in during 1888, and even some of the teams competing were not totally convinced from the outset. In fact

GORTON VILLA FOOTBALL CLUB.

The Gorton Villa Football Club opened the season on Monday. The continued popularity of the game was fully demonstrated by the venture; for, although the weather was quite summer-like, and appeared much more suitable for cricket than football, there was an attendance of interested spectators of over 1,500. The Church-lane ground appeared in excellent condition. No doubt before the close of the allotted time during which football may be legitimately engaged, it will be the arena on which many a hard-fought game will be fought. The Villa open the season with excellent prospects. They have secured as patrons Mr. William Mather, M.P., and Ernest F. G. Hatch, Esq. Mr. George Pilkington Dawson has been chosen the president, and there are quite a host of vice-presidents. The hon. corresponding secretary is Mr. W. G. Struthers, of Oldham-street, Gorton, the hon. financial secretary Mr. C. J. Walker, whilst Mr. S. Sibberin, of the Chapel House Hotel, which is the dressing-room, is the hon. treasurer. The list of fixtures for the season are better than those of last year, and the patrons of the club may justly expect a good return for their money. This year will see a number of new men in the Villa ranks. Amongst them will be found Nussey, the famous full back from the Hurst team, and who will this year lead the Villa "lambs." A companion of his, Broughton, of the Hurst team, has also engaged with the home club. Besides these, the committee have secured the services of Pickford and Craythorn, late of the Look combination; Duncan, formerly of Halliwell and Glasgow Thistle teams; and Roach, from the Oswestry Club. The games of Monday and Tuesday last terminated unfavourably to the local club. This should not be looked upon with too despondent feelings. Both matches ought to be regarded as trial matches more than anything else. Then also it should not be forgotten that Witton is acknowledged to be a superior combination to that of the Villa; and the defeat of the local men at their hands was by no means unexpected. Newton Heath, too, have been regarded in past years as a superior team to Gorton, and the latter were by no means disgraced on Tuesday when they were defeated by two goals to nothing. Gorton Villa had never played together before Monday; both Witton and Newton Heath have been practising together for weeks. When the Villa men have settled down and become acquainted with each other's play they will be able to give a good account of themselves. It has already been made abundantly clear that the back division is all that could be desired, but the forwards need strengthening. The matter may be safely left in the hands of the committee to do what is necessary. The following are the engagements for the season:—

First Team.		Second Team.	
Sep. 7—Halliwell	H		
14—Hyde	A	Hyde	H
21—Chester	H		
28—L C J T (1st round)		Stalybridge	A
Oct. 5—Denton (English Cup Tie	A		
12—Denton	H		
19—L J C T (2nd round)	"		
26—English Cup Qualifying Com. (2nd round)		Hatherlow	A
Nov. 2—Oswestry	H		
9—Newton Heath Central	H		
16—Welsh Druids	H		
23—Chester, and M and D C C (1st round)	A	Denton	A
30—Blackburn Park Road	H		
Dec. 7—Manchester Welsh	A	Manchester Welsh	H
14—Hyde	H	Hyde	A
21—Hurst	H		
25—			
28—Haydock	H		
1890			
Jan. 4—			
11—Northwich Victoria	H		
18—			
25—Denton	A	Stalybridge	H
Feb. 1—Haydock	A	Hatherlow	H
8—Manchester Welsh	H		
15—Hurst	A	Denton	H
22—M and D C tie (3rd round)			
Mar. 1—			
8—Newton Heath Central	A		
15—1st round 2nd stage, M and D C tie			
22—Ramsbottom	H		
29—			
Apl. 5—Ramsbottom	A		

GORTON VILLA v. WITTON.

The above clubs opened their season on Monday at Gorton, before 2,000 spectators. The Villans had hardly their full team, although they were fairly represented. Turner scored twice for Witton and Halston once in the first half, whilst Peach was instrumental in getting one through for the homesters. The second half was all in favour of Witton, who pressed continually, Turner scoring the fourth goal, and a fifth was the result of a scrimmage. The Villa put in a rush towards the close, but failed to effect any material advantage, and at the finish Witton were credited with the victory by five goals to one. Teams:—Witton: Torries, goal; Shorrocks and Tattersall, backs; Halston, Franklin, and Pickup, half-backs; Turner, Brown, Smith, Fletcher, and Isherwood, forwards. Gorton Villa: Greenhalgh, goal; Ferguson and Murray, backs; Jukes, Myatt, and Claythorne, half-backs; Peach, Duncan, Pickford, Struthers, and Roach,

Gorton Villa, the main rivals to City's predecessors, received significant local support. This article outlines their fixtures for 1889-90

even the method of awarding points was not decided until several games in the competition had been played.

Newton Heath did not apply as J.J. Bentley, Bolton's secretary and ultimately a key figure at United, suggested most of the northern names to McGregor and he chose the sides he knew were the best from his involvement with the Lancashire FA. The Heathens, like the other Manchester sides, were simply not ready.

Of all the other local sides it is possible that Hurst was the only credible challenger for a place. They had competed in the FA Cup on a regular basis, played fixtures across the north-west and Wales, and were recognised as a progressive outfit. Another contender, had the League been created a few years earlier, would undoubtedly have been Manchester FC. Manchester FC had shown interest in serious competition from the earliest days and their ground had clearly impressed the FA with two semi-finals played there. There was also an international between England and Ireland there on 28 February 1885 watched by a crowd of 6,000.

It appears that the original Manchester FC had given up on soccer by 1888, certainly at a major level, and so the opportunity of joining the League never really came. Perhaps this had more to do with the conflict between professionals and amateurs during the decade. In 1884 thirty-one clubs met in Manchester – where else - determined to break away from the FA unless professionalism was adopted, and in July 1885 professionalism was legalised.

It seems Manchester FC had no intention of becoming a professional outfit. Indeed, if this association football club really was an offshoot of the rugby club, it is clear that professionalism was indeed something the club did not support as Manchester FC remained very much an amateur side, preferring to follow the Rugby Union code when most significant northern sides chose to become professional sides (ultimately following the Rugby League code). It is unclear whether the club known as Manchester FC whose headquarters are recorded by Manchester United's museum as Hullard Hall Lane, is actually the same club that entered the FA Cup in the 1870s.

In 1888 Newton Heath, despite not forming part of the new Football League, did take steps to formalise their fixtures for 1888-89. Working with several other ambitious clubs spread across the north and midlands they created an alternative competition called the Football Combination, however the Combination was much less formal than the League.

Created on 27th April 1888, the Combination allowed each of its twenty member clubs to arrange its own fixtures and they could play as many games as they wished. The only stipulation was that they had to take part in at least 8 games. Newton Heath were excited by the prospect of organised, regular competition and published their own fixture list as a result. For perhaps the first time, they felt confident of a successful season. Their first Combination game saw them win 4-3 against Darwen on 22nd September 1888 and, in total they played 11 matches, winning 7, drawing 2 and losing 2.

Newton Heath were the only Manchester representatives in the Combination, but they found the competition frustrating. Although many of the sides, including former FA Cup winners Blackburn Olympic, were of a significant standard, few of the sides could fulfil all their fixtures. In fact Olympic themselves had to pull out. Games were cancelled at short notice and the free and easy way of arranging fixtures was no better than what had gone before. On 5 April 1889 eleven clubs, including the Heathens, pulled out and the Combination effectively collapsed.

The Heathens' ambitions were now much higher and they applied to join the Football League. The League had determined that the bottom four clubs in 1888-89 would stand for re-election and, again, Manchester played its part in the League's first re-election contest. The meeting was held at the Douglas Hotel in Manchester and nine sides applied to join the League while four sides sought re-election. Those seeking election were allowed a maximum of five minutes to explain why their side was ready to compete in the League. Afterwards the vote was taken with Newton Heath collecting one vote out of the 48 cast - each existing League side had to vote for the four out of the 13 that they wanted to see in the League – and finished ninth in the election. As the meeting was held in Manchester the Heathens had been hopeful, but sadly they left disappointed,

Despite the frustration felt, the Heathens worked with some of the other sides rejected and other members of the old Combination to set up a new competition – The Football Alliance. This really was a move forward and one that Newton Heath were right to play a significant part in. As with the Football League, the Alliance was made up of 12 northern and midlands sides with Darwen, Bootle, and Newton Heath being the only sides from the Lancashire area taking part. The Heathens finished eighth while Sheffield Wednesday were champions.

THE ALLIANCE.

Results up to date :—

	Plyd	Won	Lost	Drn	Goals For	Goals Agst	Pts
Stoke	20	11	2	7	49	37	29
Sunderland Albion	16	9	1	6	53	19	24
*Notts Forest	19	9	3	7	61	27	23
Birm'hm St. George's	16	9	5	2	47	40	20
Grimsby Town	18	8	6	4	25	25	20
Walsall Town Swifts	17	7	6	4	26	41	18
Newton Heath	20	7	10	3	35	51	17
Darwen	18	7	8	3	49	44	17
Small Heath	19	7	10	2	55	52	16
Crewe Alexandra	19	6	10	3	47	54	15
Bootle	18	2	9	7	31	40	11
Sheffield Wednesd'y	18	2	11	5	30	24	9

* Two points deducted for playing an unregistered player.

22nd March 1891 - Newton Heath lie in seventh place after a 3-1 defeat by Birmingham St George. The Heathens ended their second Alliance League season in ninth place.

THE UMPIRE, SUNDAY, SEPTEMBE

Grimsby Town v. Newton Heath. — At Grimsby, before 3000 spectators. Walker started for Grimsby, and the visitors took the ball to the home goal, but nothing resulted. By some neat work the ball was worked to the other end, where Ross had a chance, but he headed over. Some smart play ensued on both sides, each team obtaining a fruitless corner. A good run by the Grimsby forwards resulted in Cosgrove scoring from a slow shot. Newton Heath rushed the ball to the other end, but nothing but a corner was obtained, which proved abortive. The visitors was now having the best of matters and Stewart equalised with a good shot. Keeping up the pressure the visitors had one or two chances, Ramsay having particularly hard lines in not scoring. Just before half-time Cosgrove added the second for the fishermen, the game at half-time standing 2 goals to 1 in favour of Grimsby Town. The second half was keenly contested, each side playing their best. After about half-an-hour's play Cosgrove added the third for the home team, and the game ended:—

GRIMSBY TOWN .... 3 goals.
NEWTON HEATH .... 1 „

Small Heath v. Sunderland Albion.—At Birmingham. In the first half the Heathens pressed

ASHTON DISTRICT LEAGUE.—Ashton North End v. Hurst Nook Rovers. —On the North End ground, before about 1500 spectators. After about fifteen minutes' play, the North End scored the first goal, followed shortly after by another. At half-time the home team led by 2 goals to nil. In the second half the game became very rough, the visitors being penalised on two or three occasions, and the final result was—North End, 3 goals; Nook Rovers, 2.

Manchester v. Hurst.—At Alexandra Park, before a moderate assembly. At the commencement of the game the homesters went off with a rush, but Roby, for Hurst, was the first to score, followed by a second by Morris. Powell and Spencer then scored for Manchester, which made the score equal. Morris again put one through and Powell did likewise, so that at half-time the score was 3 goals each. After change of ends Morris scored after five minutes' play. Eventually Haughton and Maddocks each scored for Manchester, and at the close the score was:—

MANCHESTER .... 5 goals
HURST .... 4 „

A section of the Umpire newspaper from September 1890 showing games involving sides from Hurst, Ashton and Newton Heath (present day United).

Manchester v. Buxton.—At Alexandra Park. Powell started for Manchester, who assumed the offensive, but the Buxton team were in good form and repulsed the home team in good style. Eventually Goswell, from play in front of goal, sent in a good shot, which Cliff failed to save. Half-time: Manchester, 1 goal; Buxton, nil. On change of ends, the play became very fast; but it was soon evident that the good passing of the home forwards would non plus their opponents. Goswell scored 3 goals and Spencer 1. Just before time Kitchen scored for Buxton, and the game ended with the result—

MANCHESTER .... 5 goals.
BUXTON .... 1 „

Ardwick v. Bury.—At Ardwick. This being the first meeting of the club, great interest was manifested, and there were 6000 present when Campbell started for the home team. The visitors took the lead, and Fielding scored twice. The home team then attacked, but Shorrocks played a grand defence, and the visitors again scored before half-time by Conway. The second half opened fast, and Bury gained two fruitless corners. Holt had to save several difficult shots at the other end. The home team at length scored, Whittle sending the ball through. Hodgetts and Campbell both missed splendid chances of scoring. Result:—

BURY .... 3 goals.
ARDWICK .... 1 „

Gorton Villa v. Shrewsbury Town.—At Gorton, before 1000 spectators. The visitors were fairly outclassed by the grand display of the home team, who scored 9 goals in the first half to Shrewsbury 1. The second half was more even, each side scoring 2 goals. Result:—Gorton, 11 goals; Shrewsbury Town, 2.

A typical programme of games for October 1890 - note that around 6,000 watched Ardwick V Bury.

LANCASHIRE LEAGUE.

Results up to date.

	Pld	Won	Lst	Drn	Goals For	Goals Agt	Pts
Heywood	2	2	0	0	9	5	4
Bury	1	1	0	0	7	1	2
Heywood Central	1	1	0	0	5	1	2
Rossendale	1	1	0	0	4	1	2
Union Star	2	1	1	0	3	5	2
Blackpool	2	1	1	0	5	8	2
Fleetwood Rangers	1	0	0	1	2	2	1
Southport Central	1	0	0	1	1	1	1
West Manchester	2	0	1	1	5	6	1
Nelson	2	0	1	1	2	8	1
Oswaldtwistle Rov'rs	1	0	1	0	3	4	0
Higher Walton	2	0	2	0	1	5	0

Bury v. Nelson.—At Bury, before 4000 spectators, in splendid weather. Bury faced the sun, and the game commenced hard and fast, Garner scoring for Nelson. After twenty minutes play, Bury had again a near squeak, but quickly recovering, commenced a grand attack, Conway scoring the first goal. The visitors fell off, and Bury continuing the pressure, Cooper scored three times in succession, the home team leading at half time with 4 goals to 1. The second half opened disastrously for Nelson, Bourn scoring in two minutes. The visitors played a disheartened game, and missed many excellent chances. Fielding made a sensational run, and finished by scoring, and Conway scored nicely. Noble was severely taxed in goal, but played a fine game, Bury showing up with all-round excellence. Result:—

BURY .... 7 goals
NELSON .... 1 „

A match report from September 1890 showing Bury's 7-1 victory over Lancashire League rivals Nelson.

The Alliance was not the only means by which local sides were able to play football on a more organised basis as Bury, in particular, took a lead role in creating healthy competition for itself and neighbouring clubs. On 26th March 1889 the Bury committee discussed the possibility of creating a Lancashire League. This led to a meeting with other clubs at the Saddle Hotel, Bolton and eventually the Lancashire League came into force for the start of the 1889-90 season. The founder members were Blackpool, Bury, Earlstown, Fleetwood Rangers, Heywood, Heywood Central, Higher Walton, Hyde, Nelson, Oswaldtwistle Rovers, Blackburn Park Road, Rossendale, Southport Central and West Manchester.

The Lancashire League kicked off on 14th September 1889 with instigators Bury facing the Preston side Higher Walton at Gigg Lane before a crowd of around 2,000. The game ended in a draw with the first champions of the new league being Higher Walton with runners up Bury missing the title by a point. The following season however Bury won the Lancashire League.

The problems of impartiality seemed to dog the non-formal, or so called 'friendly', fixtures played within the region and this may have influenced Bury's decision to formalise fixtures. On 16th March 1889 Bury travelled to Denton and were leading after thirty minutes. Four minutes into injury time at the end of the first half the Dentonians equalised. In the second half the neutrality of the referee was called into question by the **Bury Times**:

"The whistle sounded to recommence and Conway appealed to the referee for fair play. This was met with a challenge from the official to step into the next field and fight it out. Steele [Bury's captain] most commendably declined to continue the game until the referee was displaced. After ten minutes for consideration and no response, Steele led his men from the ground. The referee was Edwards, a registered professional with West Manchester, who is only waiting for his liberation from that club to join Denton. He was totally unfit to act as referee and the audacity of Denton putting up such a man is almost incredible. Denton will certainly not figure on Bury's list of fixtures again!"

Football continued to develop across the area and in 1892 both Newton Heath and Ardwick joined the Football League. At that point the League increased to two divisions with Newton Heath applying and being accepted into Division One. Ardwick chose simply to apply to join the Second Division even though twelve months earlier they had only missed out on being accepted into Division One by two votes and they received a total of four votes. Newton Heath had received none that year. Had Ardwick applied to join Division One

MANCHESTER CUP.—Semi-Final.

Newton Heath v. Stockport County.—On the Ardwick club ground, before 5000 spectators, Stockport kicked off and after 10 minutes' play Milarvie scored for the holders. The game was even for a time in which Upton had hard lines in striking the upright with a capital shot. Just before the interval Milarvie scored the second shot for Newton Heath. The second half was hotly contested and Smith scored for the county. Stewart added the third for Newton, and a good game ended.

NEWTON HEATH .... 3 goals
STOCKPORT .... 1 "

LANCASHIRE JUNIOR CUP.—Final.

Ardwick v. Blackpool.—Played at Preston, before 6000 spectators. Ardwick kicked off with the wind, and had the best of the opening exchanges, but Blackpool scored in three minutes. The Mancestrians, by dint of good forward work, equalised from the foot of Lambie, this goal being most cleverly obtained. Davidson showed up with some fine kicking. The game was very fast, and each goal in turn was rapidly visited. Blackpool scored twice, and led at half-time by 3 goals to 1. On resuming the game was most evenly and hotly contested, though the Blackpudlians were most persistent in their endeavours to score. Robson and Milarvie defended gallantly, and were undoubtedly the means of saving a more severe defeat. The Fylde men were much quicker and smarter on the ball, though each side strove their utmost. There was no further score, and Blackpool again won the Cup by 3 goals to 1.

The Heathens defeat County 3-1 in the 1891 Manchester Cup semi final at Hyde Road. Ardwick defeated Newton Heath in the final.

A season ticket for Ardwick from the 1892-93 season.

in 1892 it is possible both Manchester sides would have been accepted, but the Manchester vote may also have been split which would have caused neither side to make it.

Surprisingly, considering their development of the Lancashire League, Bury chose not to apply. It is possible they may have found their way among football's elite had they applied.

The fortunes of the region's first two League sides were not great. Newton Heath ended their first couple of seasons as bottom side in the First Division and were relegated in 1894 (they had survived in 1893 as they had been successful in the promotion deciding Test Matches, but they failed in these the year after). There had even been controversy with the club taking the *Birmingham Daily Gazette* to court. The reason? The newspaper had dared to say that the style of play employed by Newton Heath in their 14th October 1893 4-1 victory over West Bromwich Albion was:

"Not football but simply brutality. Perrins kicked Geddes in the spine of the back, raising a lump as big as a duck egg" and that another player was maliciously kicked on the ankle and another on the back of the head. The alleged libel concluded with the remark that the Heathens style would *"perhaps create an extra run of business for undertakers."*

On 10th March 1894 the **Gorton Reporter** detailed the court's verdict. The judge reported that there had been libel but that no substantial damage had been caused. The judge ordered the newspaper to pay one farthing damages, but that both sides pay their own legal costs (considerably more than a farthing). In effect the Heathens were ridiculed for taking the matter to court.

For Ardwick, 1892-93 saw the side finish fifth in Division Two, but in 1894 they finished 13th out of 15 sides and collapsed financially with the 14th April 1894 **Gorton Reporter** announcing:

"On Monday evening Newton Heath played Ardwick 'for the last time', as the posters pathetically put it. In the future the Manchester City club, which will shortly be affiliated with the Lancashire Association, will occupy the old Ardwick venue, arrangements having been made with the MS & L Railway Company."

The Newton Heath-Ardwick match had been a friendly, ending 2-1 to the Heathens, but the real story was clearly the transformation of the Ardwick side into Manchester City. Many people over the years, including City's own personnel, have focussed solely on the development of Manchester City in 1894, but research in recent years clearly demonstrates that Ardwick evolved into City. More or less the entire playing staff and committee of Ardwick became City's. Manchester City was launched in April 1894.

While Ardwick were struggling during 1893-94 some members of the committee, most notably secretary Joshua Parlby, saw how important Manchester itself was becoming. Parlby had a burning desire to see the Blues successful after becoming involved with the side shortly after arriving in Manchester from Stoke.

At one point Ardwick had almost lost their Hyde Road ground when the landlords, the Manchester, Sheffield, and Lincolnshire Railway Company, gave notice that they wished to close the entrance adjacent to the Hyde Road Hotel. It seems that the railway company had plans to recover the ground from the club for breaching the agreement - presumably Ardwick were behind in their rent. By this time Chesters brewery were significant benefactors of the club and they had spent over £2,500 repairing the ground, and investing in the bars. They were not prepared to lose that investment, nor the potential beer sales a popular football club would create. The brewery persuaded the railway company to keep the entrance open for the rest of the season, and at the same time lease the ground to them instead of Ardwick. Chesters would pay the rates and bear the expense of keeping the ground in a fit state for football. On 25th March 1894 they also agreed and signed a document to underlet the ground to the football club.

A couple of weeks later, on the 8th April, with one game remaining, and Ardwick trapped in the re-election zone, the **Umpire News** reported on confusion surrounding the future of the club. The article outlined plans by some season ticket holders to form a new club called Manchester City Football Club. It also claimed that on Wednesday 4th April 1894 Manchester City F.C. applied for affiliation to the Lancashire F.A. The Lancashire F.A. stated that it would accept City's

FOOTBALL
CLUB.

application providing that the club could produce an agreement proving that it had a ground to play on. City immediately stated that they would be using the Ardwick ground. However, influential committeeman John Allison felt that the club should continue as Ardwick. The club appeared to be split in two with Allison finding support to play on from the bulk of the Ardwick committee, while Joshua Parlby charmed the fans to back his bold plan for a new 'Manchester' club.

Parlby's enthusiasm persuaded many ordinary supporters the time was right to lay the name Ardwick to rest, and move forward with a more ambitious title. He recognised the need to build a strong identity and, possibly because of his own arrival in the city, he wanted to establish a Mancunian identity. Most of the committee, including the influential Lawrence Furniss (born in Matlock), had arrived in Manchester at some point over the previous thirty years or so, as had many of the club's fans and the vast number of Manchester residents.

The selection of the Manchester City name was directly aimed at creating a side to represent all of Manchester and so, Parlby hoped, there was to be an organisation to represent all Mancunians no matter what their social status, background, or place of birth. Clearly Manchester FC, the rugby club, was still in existence but by 1894 rugby was no longer the region's number one sporting activity, and therefore the side was not as popular as either Ardwick or Newton Heath. Had rugby remained the dominant game, then Manchester FC would probably have assumed the lead role, but as football was now the lead sport both Ardwick and Newton Heath needed to establish themselves as the number one. Adopting the name Manchester City gave the Blues the edge, but interestingly the lead almost went to Newton Heath.

During 1893-94 it is known that the Heathens tried to adopt the name Manchester FC, but this was blocked by both the FA and the Rugby Union. Had the Heathens selected any other form of the Manchester name it is possible they would have gained the initiative.

As it is, Manchester City can claim quite rightly that its name was selected because the organisers wanted to establish a team for all citizens of Manchester, and that the club has always existed to represent Manchester. The combination of the name, the year, and the opening of the Ship Canal gave City the edge from a representative point of view and it is a fact that City has always prided itself on being 'Manchester's club'.

This was a very important moment in the city's history. Manchester was the world's first industrial city and was still growing at an incredible rate with many ambitious developments taking place. In fact on New Year's Day 1894 Queen Victoria opened the Manchester Ship Canal - a sign that the city's growth would continue for some time as the canal offered Manchester terrific development possibilities as an inland seaport. There was still great suffering and discomfort in the area - any city developing at the speed Manchester had in the latter half of the nineteenth century would have experienced this - however this was compensated for by the terrific pride the population felt in the city's many achievements. Now Parlby and his supporters wanted a football team to represent the whole of Manchester, a team that everybody could feel equally proud of.

The *Umpire News* reported that many Mancunians who had not previously supported Ardwick, were rushing to back the new venture. Applications poured in to purchase shares in the new club and Parlby appeared to be achieving the first stage of his plan. His next steps saw him secure the ground and use his skills of persuasion to bring John Allison and the others round to his way of thinking.

On Thursday 12th April at a rather crowded meeting of 'Manchester City' supporters, it was

A map showing most of the Tameside area as recorded in 1896.

announced that opposition to the new club had been abandoned, and that everyone was pulling behind the new 'City' club. A couple of days later Ardwick played their last game - a 5-2 defeat away to Walsall Town Swifts - finishing the season thirteenth out of fifteen.

On Monday, 16th April, Manchester City Football Club Limited became a registered company and Parlby's next task was to somehow get the club accepted into the Football League. The restructuring of the club meant that Manchester City had to apply to join the League as if they had never previously existed. There had been a question of Ardwick's debts but by 12th May the *Gorton Reporter* noted that they no longer hung over Manchester City – although it was not common knowledge at the time, director Lawrence Furniss paid Ardwick's debts out of his own pocket and as a result had to put back his own wedding for three years!

At the League AGM Parlby spoke in a confident manner of the strengths of the side, and made a point of saying that Ardwick's two major strengths – support and the Hyde Road ground – would be utilised to make Manchester City an even stronger club. Somewhere in his logic it appears he stressed that with Newton Heath failing in Division One, the new Manchester City side would add something neither Manchester club had previously. His persuasive powers worked and City gained enough votes to force their way into the Second Division, while Parlby himself headed the poll for a place on the League Management Committee – this was a rather cunning way to ensure that Manchester would receive appropriate support throughout the season from the men in control of the League. This was the start of City's first golden age which lasted until 1905.

In an article published some fifty years after Parlby's stirring speech, the moment was remembered as one of the most important in the history of the game in the region. Apparently, Parlby impressed the League leaders and every year his speech was referred to in one way or another. Whether stories of the speech were handed down and developed by each storyteller is

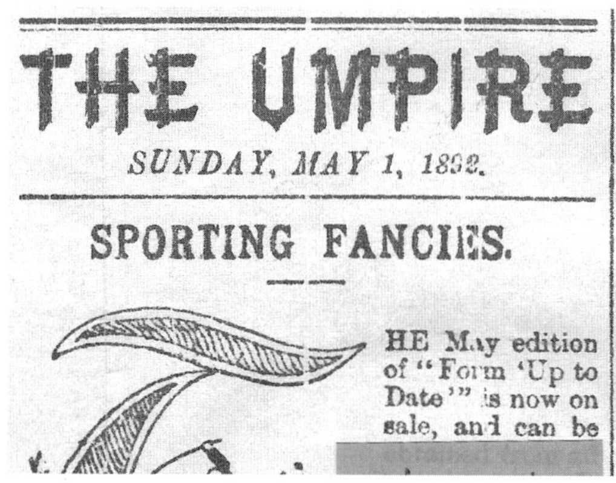

THE UMPIRE

SUNDAY, MAY 1, 1892.

SPORTING FANCIES.

HE May edition of "Form 'Up to Date'" is now on sale, and can be

show among Lancashire Rugby clubs next season.

Bury's victory over the famous cupfighters, the Blackburn Rovers, was highly meritorious, and they fully deserve the honour of holding the handsome Lancashire Cup for the next twelve months. To win the Cup the first time of entering the competition, beating such clubs as Newton Heath, Accrington, Everton, and the Rovers (the last three clubs without losing a goal), is an achievement of which any team might be proud, and we heartily congratulate the Lancashire League champions on making such a brilliant wind-up to a very successful season.

General comment on Bury's remarkable success in the 1891-92 Lancashire Cup final over Blackburn Rovers.

not known, but without Parlby's persuasion, and some would say behind the scenes connivance, the club would probably have never arisen from the ashes of Ardwick.

Manchester City's first season saw the Blues finish ninth in Division Two, but the following season (1895-6) they managed to finish second and enter the promotion-deciding test matches. Sadly, a loss of form and a rather amazing organisational own-goal – the management put admission prices significantly higher for the first test match and fans boycotted the game as a protest (typical City!) – caused City to lose out. However, it did remind club officials that the very existence of the club owed everything to the people of Manchester, and that the fans would always be keen to ensure the club remained theirs no matter who the actual owners would be.

Sixth place in 1896-97 was followed by a third place finish, then the final year of the 19th century brought real delight for the Blues when they took the Second Division title for the first time in their history. Six points behind the Blues were another relatively local side, Glossop North End, and the two sides became the first to gain automatic promotion to Division One. The test matches had been scrapped.

Despite this great transformation of the Blues, City were not the first of the region's sides to enjoy promotion as Bury, who only joined the League in 1894 (and faced City in their first League game), were promoted via the Test matches at the end of their first season. Bury also became the first of the region's sides to win a major national tournament when they finished that first season as champions of Division Two.

By the end of the decade City and Bury were competing in Division One, Newton Heath in Division Two. Stockport were seeking admittance to the League, Pine Villa had been reformed as Oldham Athletic and were members of the Manchester & District Alliance, while Rochdale had yet to be created.

ATTENDANCE DETAIL
SEASON BY SEASON - 1892-1894

Season	Ardwick	Newton Heath
1892-93	3000	7000
1893-94	4000	7000

LEAGUE POSITION
SEASON BY SEASON - 1892-1894

Season	Ardwick	Newton Heath
1892-93	21	16
1893-94	29	16

CHAPTER FOUR

THE RECTOR'S DAUGHTER

In 1879 Miss Connell set about the idea of the Working Men's club, unfortunately the men were a little reticent with only a handful turning up at the first few Tuesday night sessions. She persevered and gradually, after several attempts, the working men's meetings became popular, especially when the committee decided to form a cricket team and a lending library. *Manchester The Greatest City*, Gary James, 1997

WITH Ardwick re-forming as Manchester City in April 1894 the sporting importance of the city moved to a higher level. Every week the Manchester name would appear on fixture lists throughout the country, and any success for the club would now bring the Manchester name to the fore, rather than a district of the city. Similarly failure or scandal would also reflect on the city.

The selection of the Manchester name was very important for the club, but when considering the roots of the organisation, it is clear that the club had always striven to be representative of the local community. To understand this fully it is essential the early history of the Blues is considered.

For many decades City's roots have been inaccurately recorded, with some claiming Manchester City FC, as we know it today, has little if anything to do with the clubs that preceded it. Even the club itself has often ignored its early history and focussed on its formation as City in 1894 as the most important date. By doing this the Blues have regularly played down the importance of the club's early history, and of the side's first successes. Even those who have documented the club's birth as a church team in 1880 have regularly incorrectly quoted the names of the founders.

The book that has come closest to accurately recording the facts of City's birth was the 2006 version of ***Manchester City The Complete Record***. That book documented that the initial formation owes a great deal to a young woman called Anna Connell. Anna, the daughter of Arthur Connell the rector of St. Mark's Church, was determined to ensure some of the ills of 19th century Manchester were eradicated. West Gorton, like so many districts of the world's first industrial city, had developed at an alarming rate. Factories and terraced housing, in many cases of a poor quality, were swallowing up almost every area of greenery surrounding the city, and areas such as Ardwick, Beswick, Bradford, Clayton, and Gorton, grew from relatively small villages to become densely populated districts of the city within twenty years.

A blue plaque marking City's birth on the former Aces public house in West Gorton.

The church opened in 1865 with Arthur Connell as the first rector. It is now believed that his daughter Anna was born on 24th December 1851 in Clones, present day County Monaghan in Eire, and as she grew she, together with her younger sister Georgina, spent considerable time and effort working with the local community. In 1871 she worked as a Governess for a while at Coppull, near Preston, but by the late 1870s she was back in West Gorton. Around that time Georgina helped to create an organisation for the women of the parish, but Anna worried about the male population of West Gorton. Gang warfare, known as 'scuttling' by locals, regularly seemed to break out between the different communities of east Manchester with windows broken, people injured and many residents afraid of going out. Those were exceptionally harsh times and although gang warfare and the like have since become much more prevalent, many of the issues of today were significant in the 1870s. Anna's view was that she could change that and to some extent she did.

St. Mark's Church West Gorton.
Right: **The much-loved Rector of St Mark's Arthur Connell. His daughter Anna worked hard to establish activities for the young men of the West Gorton area.**

Poverty, domestic violence, alcoholism, racial tension and gang warfare affected most Gortonians and, to be frank, most residents of the working class districts of the city. By 1877 the population of the Gorton area was reported as being in excess of 30,000 and conditions were extremely poor. Scuttling was reported in the local newspaper often and in May 1879 the **Gorton Reporter** revealed that over 500 had taken part in one battle alone. The districts of Gorton, Openshaw, and Bradford were exposed to regular outbreaks. One report from this period appeared in the **Reporter** as if it were a match report under the title 'Openshaw V. Gorton'. The following extract describes the scenes close to Clowes St:

"According to one of the witnesses the bother commenced soon after breakfast and was on more or less all day. When Constable Wilson arrived on the scene, a little before seven o'clock in the evening, he found gathered on one side of Gorton Brook some lads and lasses from Openshaw and on the opposite side of the brook a similar gang of lads and lasses belonging to Gorton. They were engaged in the delightful occupation of storming each other.

"Some of them, said the officer, had their belts off, but they were not sufficiently close to be able to use them. This is bad, but the state of terrorism excited by the scuttlers' conduct is worse. In explanation of the fact that rowdyism was allowed to go on for so long a time, it was stated that the people living in the vicinity were afraid to inform the police, as they know that the result would be that their windows would be broken.

"This will give to those people who happily live in districts where scuttling is unknown some idea of what it means."

Perhaps Anna wanted to provide activities to release aggression in a more productive manner than the scuttles, or maybe she simply felt that organised male activities would help develop the community identity. The scuttles encouraged the wrong kind of community identity.

It was not only the violence but also poverty that worried locals. In January 1879 Arthur Connell set up a soup kitchen and a relief fund for the local poor. On its first day of operation 300 people queued for soup, bread and other food, and within a week over 1500 gallons of soup, 1000 loaves of bread and ten tons of coal had been distributed from the church.

Anna was convinced other activities could discourage the men of the parish from taking part in the drinking and violent activities, while some form of organisation could be set up to improve the racial tension. The local population of east Manchester was made up of several nationalities including Italians, Irish, German, and Polish. There was a significant Jewish population in the city and, although it is not often considered, most English Mancunians were themselves immigrants to the city from other parts of the Country. These had arrived from all over the nation looking for work on the railways – as the history of Newton Heath demonstrates - and in the engineering works and cotton mills of the city. There was a real mix of accents, backgrounds, and interests. The two significant figures of authority were usually the local church, or the local employer. Anna Connell recognised this and decided to work with figures from the local ironworks to help improve the lives of Gortonians.

Alongside William Beastow and Thomas Goodbehere, two highly respected figures from Brooks' Union Ironworks (later known as Brooks & Doxey's), she set about creating a series of men's meetings. Beastow had previously tried – and failed – with a similar venture, but Anna was convinced that the concept could work. Her aim was to encourage the local men to meet regularly and discuss the major issues, both spiritual and social, of the day. Unfortunately the men were a little reticent with only a handful turning up at the first few Tuesday night sessions. She persevered – walking from house to house trying to persuade the men to attend - and gradually after several attempts the working men's meetings became popular, especially when the committee decided to form a cricket team and a lending library.

It was William Beastow's idea to form the cricket side and it is believed it was also his idea to create a football team. Beastow, for this reason, should be regarded as the true founding father of the club. Ongoing research suggests that the cricket team was formed as early as 1875, possibly earlier.

Due to his position at the local ironworks and at the church, Beastow was able to encourage young men to participate in the new venture. During the development of the football team he managed to recruit respectable, hardworking players, including his two sons, Charles and John, but it is significant that many of the other young men involved were exactly the type of people Anna had tried to engage with.

The football team became known as St. Mark's (West Gorton) and the first known game took place on 13th November 1880 against the Baptist Church from Macclesfield. However this may not be the very first game played by the club – it seems highly likely that there would have been an earlier game but so far extensive research has failed to identify a specific match. It does seem likely that Beastow, Connell, Goodbehere, and the other key figures would have sought as many fixtures as possible. It is also worth noting that research has failed to identify an earlier Newton Heath (Manchester United) game – the first known Heathens match was against a Bolton Wanderers XI seven days later.

The first known St. Mark's game was staged between sides containing twelve players each. This may have been to accommodate all those who arrived with the Macclesfield side, or it may have simply been agreed some time in advance. It hardly matters as it was the game itself that was important, although it proves that football as we know it today was still developing.

The first match report appeared in the **Gorton Reporter**, and a review of that newspaper's sports coverage makes it clear that the attempts by William Beastow and the others to stage the first game must have been great as none of the other match reports detailed under the heading 'Football' refer to Association Football. All the other 'football' matches reported are rugby football games featuring local sides – Reddish, Failsworth Rangers, Newton Heath Rovers, Newton Heath, Blackley, Sandfield Hornets, and St. Mary's (Failsworth). The Association game was very much the minor sport with rugby remaining the area's key winter sport.

It is worth noting that research in recent years has identified that every member of that historic first known St. Mark's side was aged 20 or younger with the youngest being 15. Again, this proves beyond doubt that Anna's aim to give the young men of the area something positive to focus on was succeeding.

In November 1885 the **Gorton Reporter** referred back to the early 1880s while commenting on a Gorton (St. Mark's evolved into Gorton) game against Gorton Villa:

"There was a pretty fair attendance of spectators, notwithstanding the unpropitious weather. The way in which Association games draw the Manchester public is wonderful, considering that it is not much more than three years since the dribbling code of football was introduced into this district."

Clearly that report was incorrect as Beastow had encouraged competition during 1880.

Two weeks after the first reported game in 1880, it was recorded that St. Mark's had achieved a draw in Harpurhey against a side called Arcadians, and then on 19th March 1881 St. Mark's achieved their first known victory as they defeated Stalybridge Clarence 3-1. Clarence, however only had eight fit players and three men from the crowd made up their eleven man side.

The St. Mark's Church side developed rapidly that season. Captain Anstruther, the Archdeacon of Manchester, told the men of Anna Connell's Men's Meetings. His words were paraphrased in the **Gorton Reporter**:

"It must be a great source of encouragement to see how the movement had been taken up, and the highest credit was due to Miss Connell for the way in which it had been carried out. No man could have done it – it required a woman's tact and skill to make it so successful."

The following season, 1881-2, saw the side face Newton Heath (present day Manchester United) for the first time, and play their home matches at the Kirkmanshulme Cricket Ground south of Hyde Road.

Newspaper reports from the period seemed uncertain as to what the team name was. Sometimes the side were known as St. Mark's (West Gorton) sometimes as West Gorton (St. Mark's). This has led to some suggesting that the church removed its patronage, or that there were concerns over the number of non-parishioners in the side. This seems unlikely as all the key figures within the club remained significant figures at St. Mark's Church itself. It seems more likely that the person submitting the reports to the local newspaper was simply inconsistent. Certainly

Gorton AFC photographed in October 1884. It is believed the suited man on the left with a stick is key committee man Lawrence Furniss, while the man on the far right is understood to be William Beastow - the man who presented the new black shirts to the club.

indications are that the church was delighted with the direction of the club during its first couple of seasons.

In April 1882 a report on the opening of the cricket season highlighted that St. Mark's had a good series of fixtures and it is clear that many of the cricketers were also the people playing football. Both sports co-existed for some time at St. Mark's though it is not clear where the cricket team played, or how long it survived.

Later that year the side was asked to move on by the Kirkmanshulme cricket team and the footballers took up residence at a park off Queen's Road further east along Hyde Road. Often described as 'Donkey Common' this was more of a football pitch than any of the club's previous grounds, however moving there did cause a number of issues for the club. The words 'St. Mark's' were finally dropped completely from the side's name. Also, reports suggest there was a merger with another Gorton side which, ultimately, led to friction.

By 1884 the old St. Mark's men decided to break away from the merged side and reform under the name of Gorton Association Football Club. Edward Kitchen, Walter Chew, Lawrence Furniss, and William Beastow – all influential figures at St. Mark's Church – seemed to be the key players. Beastow was Chairman while Furniss found the club's new ground – at Pink Bank Lane (south of the Belle Vue Pleasure Gardens). Another St. Mark's churchwarden James Moores became Club President. It seems the experience at 'Donkey Common' had forced the men to challenge what they wanted from the club. Did they want a side simply to provide an outlet for physical activity each week, or did they want to create an ambitious club run on professional lines? It seems the answer was the latter.

The East Manchester area continued to be plagued by many of the problems Anna Connell had wanted to tackle in the 1870s, and so there was still a great deal of activity both within the St. Mark's community and the football team. 1884-85 was an important season as one of the more headline grabbing scuttling cases was reported in the Manchester press. It was recorded that on 7th December 1884 gangs from Gorton and Openshaw fought with sticks, broken bottles and stones in Gorton itself. In January 1885 five of the young men were charged with rioting – three were aged 16, one 17 and one 18 - but from a football perspective it is significant that two of the ringleaders were sixteen year olds from the site of City's initial birth (Clowes Street and Thomas Street). The area desperately needed the club to continue its development and provide a positive distraction for the youths. Clearly, they could not all play for the side, but they could support the club or help in other ways.

With the desire to develop strengthened, Gorton took on a more professional approach and they applied to join the newly formed Manchester County FA. In addition, one of the original founders, William Beastow, presented Gorton with its first known formal kit. Various shirts had been worn prior to 1884 – some reports talk of scarlet and black stripes although this does not appear to have been West Gorton's formal colours – but 1884 was the year when a proper kit was identified for the first time. The new colours were black with a white 'Maltese style' cross.

The development of Gorton continued throughout the mid 1880s, however 1887 was to prove perhaps the most important year of the period. They had spent the previous couple of seasons playing at the Bull's Head in Reddish Lane, on the very edge of Gorton. This was really as far away from Clowes Street as the side could go while remaining in Gorton and so the club's identity was in danger of disappearing. Likewise association football was becoming more popular in the area and sides, such as Newton Heath, were beginning to move upwards winning trophies such as the Manchester Cup.

They also vowed to return to their Clowes Street roots, although they recognised that this was not entirely possible – Clowes Street remained one of Manchester's most densely populated areas – but captain Kenneth McKenzie did manage to find an area of wasteland not too far away at Bennett Street, Ardwick, close to Hyde Road.

After a great deal of effort the pitch was ready by the end of August 1887, while the club was also relaunched as Ardwick AFC (the new ground was just within the boundaries of Ardwick and not Gorton, although it has to be stressed that this ground was closer to Clowes Street than any other Gorton venue used by the club after its first season). In addition, this area was actually part of the St. Mark's parish until the erection of St. Benedict's, Ardwick in 1880. So this could truly be said to be within the boundaries of St. Mark's at the time the club was initially created.

Despite the closeness of St. Mark's the Hyde Road Hotel became Ardwick's headquarters. Stones from this building, demolished in 2002, now form part of the City of Manchester Stadium's Memorial Garden. According to the records at Manchester Central Library, St. Mark's itself was demolished in 1974 with a replacement church dedicated to Emmanuel opening in June 1975 close to another former home for the club, Gorton Park.

With the club full of ambition, a grand opening fixture was arranged for 10th September 1887. Ardwick's first opponents were to be Salford A.F.C. yet for some unknown reason they failed to arrive at the new Hyde Road ground. A band had been hired and a crowd of over five hundred had turned up, only to discover that Ardwick's birth was to be a farce. Over eighty years later, Francis Lee made a famous quote about the possibility of the club winning 'cups for cock-ups'. He was talking about the club's 1970s ability to make the easy difficult, but he could have been referring to almost any period in the club's history. It seems that this 'grand opening' was the first but by no means the last 'own-goal' in the club's professional history.

The following week the ground was used for a match - this time Hooley Hill from Denton defeated Ardwick 4-2 in a game played in 'delightful weather' according to one newspaper report. Even so, the quality of the Hyde Road playing surface was quite poor - one of Ardwick's goals was scored from the midst of a puddle, despite the fact that it had not rained at all. Later in the season Ardwick's 8-1 demolition of Hyde in the Ashton & District Cup had to be replayed due to complaints from the Hydonians that the ground was unfit for football. The replay took place at Hyde with Ardwick dominating the game so much that the home side continually sent the ball as far away as possible. The match report commented on the amount of times the ball had to be retrieved from the field next to the Hyde ground. Not surprisingly Ardwick easily beat the home side 3-1.

Ardwick v. Heywood Central.—At Ardwick, before 5000 spectators. Weir started for the home team, and they were not long before they began to take the upper hand. One of the visitors' backs deliberately fisted the ball, and from the free kick McWhinnie scored; the visitors then gained two fruitless corners; the central forwards continued to press, but Douglas and Robson defended well. The home forwards then broke away, McColl being prominent: Rushton shooting through. The home team were now having most of the play, and Weir added 2 goals before half-time. The home forwards went away from the start and Weir shot over. The game then became very even, the home half-backs showing up well. McWhinnie then got one through and Weir followed with a sixth after the goalkeeper had twice saved. McColl soon after put in a long shot which McWhinnie headed through. McColl had then to leave the ground through receiving a nasty knock in the face. The home team, however, continued to press, Jarrett putting in some good work, Ardwick eventually winning by 7 goals to nil.

Everton v. Nantwich.—At Nantwich. Each team distinguished itself in turn, the home half-backs doing good service. At half-time the game was—Everton, 5 goals; Nantwich, 1. Final result: Everton (i.e., the reserve team), 6 goals; Nantwich, 1.

Match report from Ardwick's meeting with Heywood in September 1890.

Gradually Ardwick became a strong side and they also increased their support. In 1889 a grandstand capable of holding 1,000 spectators was built. From that point on the club grew at a rapid rate.

Ardwick's desire to become one of the region's elite clubs grew. The Manchester Cup had been established in 1884-5 and this soon became the most prestigious competition available to local sides. In April 1891 Ardwick reached the final for the first time and defeated Newton Heath 1-0 in the first final played between these two sides. The influential Ardwick captain Davie Weir scored the only goal in the seventh minute. According to match reports the game was rather even, although Ardwick did actually have another goal disallowed. Nevertheless, the victory finally made the footballing fraternity sit up and notice the Blues (the new colours being adopted in 1887). Newton Heath had featured in every Manchester Cup final since inception, and so by winning the trophy Ardwick were suddenly thrust into the local spotlight.

Success in the trophy perhaps went a little to their heads when at the 1891 Football League AGM Ardwick - along with Darwen, Newton Heath, Nottingham Forest, Stoke, and Sunderland Albion - applied for the first time to join the 'big boys' when the League was expanding from 12 to 14 clubs. All the applicants, with the exception of Ardwick, were members of the Football Alliance - a league originally set up to rival the Football League. Considering this was their first experience of the voting system, the Blues performed exceptionally well gaining four votes – the most of all the non-elected clubs – and four more than near rivals Newton Heath could muster. The two new places were filled by Stoke, who had won the Alliance, and Darwen.

Ardwick were however asked to join the Alliance League for the 1891-2 season instead.

The defeat of Bolton Wanderers by Ardwick in the Manchester Cup competition probably surprised no one more than Ardwick people themselves. Certainly the eleven have done one or two fine performances during the season, but nothing to lead their most sanguine supporter to believe them capable of defeating such a team as the Wanderers. However, they did so, and, what is more, did it by playing better football than their opponents. This is the second time David Weir's men have won the cup, and the victory will do much to enhance the reputation of the team.

The Manchester Cup was retained in 1892 when Football League side Bolton Wanderers were defeated 4-1, but earlier in the year there was real concern that the side might not survive. On 16th January 1892 the **Gorton Reporter** was highly critical of the state of the Blues. It highlighted financial problems and then asked:

"Will the finances at Ardwick allow them to exist another season?"

Joining the Football League was Ardwick's ultimate aim and when a decision was taken in April 1892 to form a second division of twelve clubs and expand the First Division to sixteen Ardwick's chance came. The Blues joined Division Two, finishing fifth in 1892-3 but they struggled in 1893-4, finishing 13th out of 15. Early into 1894 however steps were already underway to dramatically change their fortunes and as April progressed it became clear that Ardwick were to become re-established as Manchester City FC. The new club became a registered company on Monday, 16th April, with its registered address being given as 31 Halsbury Street, Stockport Road, Manchester.

Above: **City's Billy Gillespie attacks in a game believed to be the Boxing Day 1898 derby with Newton Heath at Hyde Road. City won the game 4-0 with goals from Meredith, Gillespie, Dougal and Williams.**

Right: **City defend a corner from Newton Heath with Welsh international Di Jones the player closest to the camera.**

City, Division Two champions in 1899. The great Billy Meredith can be seen on the far left of the front row.

Making reference to the end of Ardwick A.F.C., the club's new motto was *'Even in our own ashes live our wonted fires'*.

By the time of City's 1899 Second Division title, Anna Connell was no longer in the Gorton area. However she must have gained a great deal of satisfaction from knowing that her club had developed into one of the game's elite within twenty years of its birth. Her idea had been to use activities such as football to build community spirit and to provide young men with an outlet, and by 1900 her side had already achieved much more than her original aims.

ATTENDANCE DETAIL
SEASON BY SEASON - 1894-1898

Season	City	Newton Heath	Bury
1894-95	6000	6000	3900
1895-96	10000	5500	6000
1896-97	8000	6200	6150
1897-98	8000	6125	5200

LEAGUE POSITION
SEASON BY SEASON - 1894-1898

Season	City	Newton Heath	Bury
1894-95	25	19	17
1895-96	18	22	11
1896-97	22	18	9
1897-98	19	20	14

Manchester City Fixtures.

Date.	Club.	For	Agt	Date.	Club.	For	Agt
Sept. 1--				Jan. 2--*h*	Glossop North End..		
" 3--*h*	Grimsby Town	7	2	" 7--*h*	Newton Heath		
" 10--*a*	Newton Heath	0	3	" 14--*a*	New Brighton		
" 17--*h*	New Brighton......	1	1	" 21--*h*	Lincoln City		
" 24--*a*	Lincoln City	1	3	" 28--	E.C. 1st r'nd proper.		
Oct. 1--*h*	Woolwich..........	3	1	Feb. 4--*h*	Luton Town		
" 8--*a*	Luton Town	3	0	" 11--*a*	Leicester (L.C.)		
" 15--*h*	Leicester Fosse	3	1	" 14.-	Shrove Tuesday		
" 22--*a*	Darwen..........	2	0	" 18--*h*	Darwen		
" 29--*a*		2	1	" 25--*a*	Gainsborough		
Nov. 5--*a*	Barnsley	1	1	Mar. 4--*h*	Barnsley (L.C.)		
" 12--*a*	Glossop North End..	2	1	" 11--	Manchester Cup ..		
" 19--*h*	Walsall	2	0	" 18--*a*	Walsall		
" 26--*a*	Burton Swifts	3	3	" 25--*h*	Burton Swifts		
Dec. 3--*h*	Burslem Port Vale..	3	1	" 31--*h*	Gainsborough		
" 10--	Loughborough	3	1	April 1--*a*	Burslem Port Vale..		
" 17--*h*	Loughborough	5	0	" 3--*a*	Woolwich..........		
" 19--*h*	Fleetwood Rangers	6	1	" 8--*h*	Small Heath		
" 24--*a*	Blackpool..........	4	2	" 15--			
" 26--*h*	Newton Heath	4	0	" 22--*h*	Blackpool..........		
" 27--*a*	Small Heath	1	4	" 29--			
" 31--*a*	Grimsby Town						

Manchester City Notes.

THE XMAS EVE and Boxing Day of 1898, will be green spots in the memory of the thousands who interest themselves in the well-being of the City Club, because the Xmastide was in all respects a merry one in the most respectable interpretation of the word. It brought four points and 8 goals to 2, and considerable joy, which would have carried it almost to the point of frenzy if success had attended the efforts at Small Heath, on Tuesday. But let that pass. The Blackpool match on Saturday was a foregone conclusion, and it may be dismissed with the observation that the City players did not find so very much difficulty in finishing on the right side, their shooting being as deadly as it has so frequently been recently.

Monday was the great day, and the "Citizens" can congratulate themselves upon a magnificent display, and a thoroughly merited victory. Although it is to the interests of both Clubs that they should do as much as possible to assist each other to the first division, sentiment was not permitted to intervene, as the City directorate recognised that the Club had to make their bow to opponents on foreign ground, which has already been trodden by the "Heathens," therefore, it was not advisable to lose the chance of any points. It was borne in mind that Newton Heath had been to Woolwich, Leicester, New Brighton, and Small Heath, places which were strange to City up to that point of the season.

It is not putting a too formidable construction upon the facts to say that Newton Heath were almost completely overwhelmed, and while there was much to praise with the combination, fineness of attack, and dash of the City, it must be conceded that their opponents helped them more than a little. "Di" Jones practice of going close to his half-backs came off for once in a way, but that was through the other half-backs not tumbling to his presence. Meredith played a grand game up to the time he was hurt, but it says a great deal for the other forwards, that two goals were scored after he was rendered nearly helpless. Every man did himself credit, and the play of the City was worthy of such a great occasion. Four to none was a great blow to the "Heathens," but they courted it, and have themselves greatly to blame for it.

Above: **General comment on City from the official Manchester programme from the end of 1898 - that season City won the Division Two title for the first time.**

Left: **Billy Meredith takes a corner shortly before half time in City's Boxing Day 1898 derby with Newton Heath at Hyde Road. Notice the boys' band are ready to play.**

CHAPTER FIVE

THE HEATHENS

These were hardy lads who toiled hard for their daily bread and played football like demons on Saturdays. They were not pampered in seaside hotels, fed on special diet or trained to the ounce, but they could play a trifle nevertheless. *Association Football & the Men Who Made It*, 1905

ALTHOUGH Manchester City's exact roots have only been accurately documented in recent years, the beginnings of Manchester United as Newton Heath at first glance appear to have been extensively documented. It is fairly common knowledge that United began life as a club formed by workers from the Newton Heath base of the Lancashire & Yorkshire Railway in 1878. However, it is also clear looking at all previous publications on the Reds that there are still many unknowns and myths surrounding the club's birth.

One mystery concerns the lack of match reports from Newton Heath's first couple of seasons. Unlike St. Mark's (City) there are no match reports for the club's first season, let alone the details of any game the club could accept as its first. In fact it is not until 20th November 1880, according to the *Manchester United Pictorial History And Club Record* (published by Temple Press in 1986), that specific details of a completed game do appear. Interestingly, this is exactly one week after the St. Mark's first reported game and, if this truly was the Heathens first competitive game, then it means City's competitive roots go back further than United's. This seems unlikely as St. Mark's had only considered playing football since the summer of 1880, while the Heathens are understood to have been tinkering with the game since 1878.

The Three Crowns in Newton Heath was used as Newton Heath's base during the early years of the club.

On 20th November 1880 Newton Heath were defeated 6-0 at Bolton where they faced the Wanderers' second team. According to the **Bolton Evening News**, the Heathens wore green and gold, while Bolton wore scarlet and white quarters. The Heathens colours were important as these are widely acknowledged to have been worn to reflect the livery of the Lancashire and Yorkshire Railway Company.

Although November 1880 seems to be the date accepted by some United publications as that of their first known game, it is clear that the organisation had existed for some time by that point. ***The History of the Lancashire Football Association***, published during the 1920s, claims the club was founded in 1878, as does the 1905 ***Book of Football***, but hard evidence is difficult to come by of the specific moment or action that caused the creation of the club. In terms of United's own records, the museum contains a fixture list from 1882 which states: "Established 1878", while a brochure for the 1901 fund raising bazaar at St. James's Hall in the city centre seems to be the first officially produced acknowledgement of 1878:

"Very ancient people will refer you to the existence of a Newton Heath Football Club some time during 1878, and they will tell you that the lads who kicked a ball often got into trouble with others who preferred the summer game, because the former often spoilt the ground for the 'wielders of the willow'. Side games were mostly played, and football proper was in its infancy, few then having any idea it would grow into such a fine healthy man. Side games were not exciting enough, and local clubs were invited to do battle, among them such teams as Manchester Arcadians, Dalton Hall, Naughton Dale, Hurst Brook Rovers, Outringham Park, and Blackburn Olympic 2nd, the latter being a big standing dish for a long time..."

Looking at these comments it is clear that the writer managed to condense several seasons of activity into one simple paragraph, as the opponents mentioned did not play Newton Heath until the 1880s. Nevertheless, it does give some information on the structure of the organisation in the 1870s. The comments about playing 'side games' is important as this shows that the whole concept of the organisation in its earliest days was to create competition for sides/teams from different sections of the railway company to compete against each other. This concept, similar to the ideas of the world's oldest club Sheffield FC, meant that the game was being played competitively but between sides within the same organisation.

In Manchester during 1878 there were very few clubs playing association football, certainly there were too few to enable regular competition to occur, and so the concept of playing games amongst themselves was something the Newton Heath organisers could control. They could certainly guarantee fixtures and, although no evidence exists, it is possible to think of games being played on a regular basis between the different areas of work, or the different nationalities employed, the different ages and so on.

The local newspapers, most notably **The Reporter**, covered sport exceptionally well during the 1870s and 1880s and almost every activity connected with the game from a local perspective is documented, although it tended to require one of the club's committee to send in match reports and other news. Despite extensive research of **The Reporter** no evidence of a Newton Heath game has been identified during the 1870s, even though much detail of other sporting activity from the Newton Heath area appears. For example on 12th October 1878 there is extensive coverage of rugby in the area including a report of Newton Heath beating Fairfield by two touchdowns to one. Similarly, the reports of rugby side Newton Heath Orleans were featured in the **Manchester**

Courier during 1880. As there is no mention of association football being played by Newton Heath in these publications, it seems highly unlikely the Heathens played competitive games prior to 1880.

According to the 1882 fixture list the club was known as 'Newton Heath (LYR) Cricket and Football Club' and so the question of which was the more dominant sport also raises its head. Cricket was certainly the more popular sport for Mancunians in the 1870s, and its possible cricket was the only game played in 1878 & 1879 by the Heathens. Interestingly, research in 2008 by City fan Paul Toovey has identified that City's predecessor St Mark's was playing cricket in 1875, but the Blues tend to focus on their first competitive football game as being their formation date.

Whatever the truth about the Heathens' first competitive game, it is clear that these early days were a period of trial and error. The club had been created by the Dining Room committee of the railway works with the aim of developing team spirit, social skills, and generally to improve the quality of their workforce and to improve their employees' lives. This was a time when employment was beginning to change and many employers were looking at ways to make life better for their workers. Manchester, and in particular East Manchester, was a heavily industrial area, with very little going for it except, of course, work. The area gave employment to an enormous population and the railways, together with heavy industry, and the region's canals, meant an influx of people during the nineteenth century. The Newton Heath Lancashire and Yorkshire Railway depot had itself grown at a rapid rate and the workforce had arrived from many different parts of the British Isles, many from Ireland.

The 1978 publication *There's Only One United* by Geoffrey Green, included a few snippets of a letter from the secretary of another railway side, Newton Heath Loco. This provides a few clues as to the roots of Manchester United, and gives details of when the Dining Room committee first tried to improve matters for workers. It stated that a series of Improvement Classes were instigated in 1859 and that this ultimately led to the formation of various sports clubs. The Carriage and Wagon Department formed Newton Heath LYR and played at North Road, while the Motive Power section became known as Newton Heath Loco and played at Ceylon Street. It also suggested that games were played on an inter-department basis in the beginning and that the Carriage and Wagon department ultimately pulled out of internal competition to compete against other sides in the region – it is the belief of this author that the change of direction occurred in 1880 and that the game against Bolton Wanderers' second team was one of the side's first (possibly the actual first) competitive matches.

In his book Green makes a point of saying that he believes the roots trace back to 1878 and he even took time to dispel a belief that the club's formation had occurred some time later:

"The precise date of the birth is buried in the mists of time. As well search for a footstep on a sandy beach, long since washed away by the sea. A variety of reference books over the years have invariably pointed to 1885 as the start of it all, due probably to the fact that it was in that year that Newton Heath LYR first came to some attention by reaching the final of the Manchester Senior Cup where they lost to another local side called Hurst."

The date of 1885 was occasionally recorded as the side's birth in earlier publications – the authoritive *Encyclopaedia of Sport* published in 1959 recorded the birth as that date – but as Green pointed out that date does not bear any relation to the truth and, as with so many myths in the history of our local sides, it probably appeared as a mistake in one publication and then was repeated over and over again.

Assuming Newton Heath LYR was created as a sports club in 1878 it is clear that the earliest years were very much small scale in comparison with the later achievements of the Reds. The club's first ground was at North Road (present day Northampton Road) and was a very basic venue. According to the **Book of Football**:

"The Newton Heath Club did not have very inviting playing headquarters, for even in the early eighties the field was little better than a clay pit, and all round the ground was a perfect quagmire. There was no dressing tent on the ground. Bless you, the arrangements were far too primitive for that! The team changed at the Three Crowns public house, Oldham Road, and then had a sharp run to the playing field. After you had played in a hard match you had a sharp run back, a wash and a rub down and you felt as fit as a fiddle."

By 1882 the Heathens are known to have played several friendly matches against teams such as Hurst, Manchester Arcadians, Blackburn Olympic's second team, Bootle reserves, and the forerunners of City - St. Mark's. The first meeting with St. Mark's in November 1881 ended in a 3-0 win at North Road, with the return resulting in a 2-1 defeat at Kirkmanshulme CC. The club was developing and when they produced their fixture card for the 1882-83 season they announced 26 fixtures including games against fellow railway team Southport LYR, and the reserve side of 1883 FA Cup winners Blackburn Olympic.

The club president was recorded as Mr. F. Attock. Research for this book has identified, for the first time in a publication connected with Manchester football, that his full name was Fredrick Attock, and that his age in 1882 was 36, and that he was employed as the Carriage and Wagon works superintendent.

A quick analysis of his own life shows the state of Manchester, and in particular east Manchester, at the time of the publication of the fixture list. Fredrick Attock shared a house with his two young sons – Fredrick William, aged 6, and George Henry, aged 8. Both were born in Essex, suggesting that the Attocks had only arrived in Newton Heath at some point between 1876 and 1881 (they are Newton Heath residents at the time of the 1881 census). In addition to Fredrick and his sons, Fredrick's mother, Hephzibah Attock, aged 70 in 1882, and servants Mary Forturn (52) and Jane Smith (36) lived in the family home, Sommerseat House.

Not one of the residents had been born in Manchester. Jane was from Chester, Mary from Ireland, Hephzibah from Lincoln, and Fredrick himself was born in Liverpool – so the first president of Newton Heath was born on Merseyside!

Both Hephzibah and Fredrick were widowed, and so the children had already known hardship in their young lives and a move from Essex to Manchester was significant. Attock was clearly wealthier than many of the side's first players, but like so many Manchester residents of this period he had moved to the city through work and not directly through choice. This is the very reason both City and United's roots owe a great deal to the large influx of people into the region during the 1800s.

How long Attock remained in Manchester is not clear, but by the time of the 1901 census he was recorded as being a retired engineer and lived in Westmoreland, while his sons were both living in Lancashire with Fredrick junior in Horwich and George close to Lancaster. It is hard to establish whether any of the family knew or understood the sporting implications of their time in Manchester.

As well as Attock, the 1882 fixture card talks of vice presidents, committeemen, the club captain, secretary and vice captain. The full names of some of these have now been identified and these include vice president Thomas Gorst, born in 1830 in Liverpool! (another Liverpudlian), who lived at 5 Church Terrace and was employed as a railway clerk; and vice captain John Cramphorn who was 23 in 1882 and lodged at 31 Ten Acres Lane. He was born in Shalford, Essex. At both Cramphorn's and Gorst's addresses lodged other railway workers from other parts of the British Isles – again demonstrating how cosmopolitan, for the period, the area was.

Under Attock's presidency the club developed and in 1883-84 they entered the Lancashire Cup for the first time but were defeated 7-2 in the first round by the team of the period Blackburn Olympic. The following season with the creation of the Manchester Cup the Heathens' chances of success improved considerably, and the side performed exceptionally well. They went on to defeat Dalton Hall in an extraordinary game for the time. The Collegians – the side were university students based at Dalton Hall (recognised as the first purpose built hall of residence in the country when it opened in 1882) – were leading 2-0, in a match that was described as "fast, furious, and exciting", after only 15 minutes at the Hurst ground on the outskirts of Ashton-under-Lyne. A fightback from the Heathens followed, and by half time the score stood at 2-1.

In the second half Newton Heath maintained their fightback and after equalising they took the lead. Dalton Hall made it 3-3, and when the whistle was blown the two sides decided to play two periods of extra time, each lasting 15 minutes. This is believed to be the first occasion the Heathens ever played extra time, and it has to be stressed that this was not necessarily the norm at that time. In the first period of extra time Newton Heath made it 4-3 and despite frenetic play afterwards that is how the game ended.

The Heathens faced Hurst in the first final of the competition, but the Ashton side managed a 3-0 win. Despite the defeat it is clear that the Heathens were at long last starting to develop a good reputation.

In 1886 they reached the final of the Manchester Cup again and this time they defeated the region's most famous club of that era, Manchester FC, to win the trophy for the first time. However there was some controversy, as Manchester believed the Heathens' winning goal was both handball and offside. Nevertheless a victory was a victory and the Manchester Cup was the first trophy ever won by the side.

By the end of the 1890-91 season the Heathens had played in the first seven finals of the Manchester Cup. They had won the trophy on four occasions (beating Manchester, Denton, Hooley Hill, and Royton) and been beaten by Hurst, West Manchester, and Ardwick (City). This incredible record ensured the Heathens' name grew and on 20th October 1886 they competed in their first FA Cup tie – a 2-2 draw at Fleetwood Rangers (the Heathens refused to play extra time and the tie was forfeited). This meant the Heathens were the fourth local side, after Manchester, Birch, and Hurst to compete in the competition, however the experience at Fleetwood set the tone for the following couple of years and the side did not enter the competition again until 1889-90.

One of the great advantages the Heathens had over other sides in the region during this period was their ability to guarantee work for star players. While most of the local sides were independent of local industry the whole concept of Newton Heath was that it was a works team, therefore only workers from the railway works were supposed to play for the side. Rather than limiting team selection this allowed the Heathens to attract players by also guaranteeing them employment.

One famous story from the club's early history focuses on Pat O'Donnell (some sources call him Pat McDonnell) who, according to legend walked all the way from Glasgow to Newton Heath looking for work. The Lancashire & Yorkshire Railway Company gave him a job and ultimately he became part of the Newton Heath team. Other quality players were given work simply to help them strengthen the club, so much so that the **Manchester Evening News** focused on the ethnic make-up of the side in an article from October 1887:

"Burke, Davies, Powell, Owen and Doughty are all Welshmen, while Tait is a Scotchman and O'Donnell, Irish. In fact with the exception of Wright we do not recognise a local man in the team."

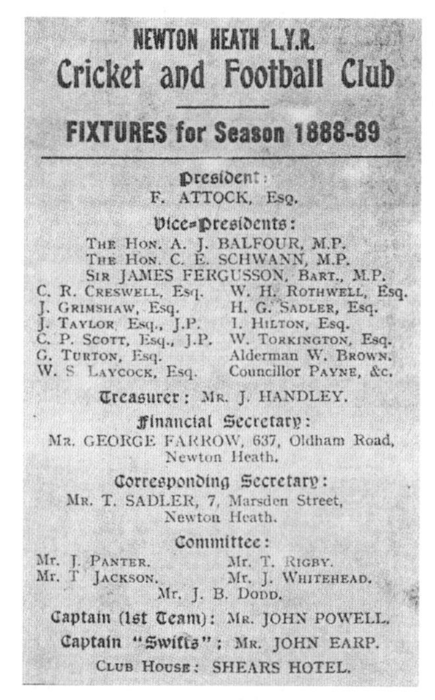
NEWTON HEATH L.Y.R.
Cricket and Football Club

FIXTURES for Season 1888-89

President:
F. ATTOCK, Esq.

Vice-Presidents:
THE HON. A. J. BALFOUR, M.P.
THE HON. C. E. SCHWANN, M.P.
SIR JAMES FERGUSSON, BART., M.P.
C. R. CRESWELL, Esq. — W. H. ROTHWELL, Esq.
J. GRIMSHAW, Esq. — H. G. SADLER, Esq.
J. TAYLOR Esq., J.P. — I. HILTON, Esq.
C. P. SCOTT, Esq., J.P. — W. TORKINGTON, Esq.
G. TURTON, Esq. — Alderman W. BROWN.
W. S. LAYCOCK, Esq. — Councillor PAYNE, &c.

Treasurer: MR. J. HANDLEY.

Financial Secretary:
MR. GEORGE FARROW, 637, Oldham Road, Newton Heath.

Corresponding Secretary:
MR. T. SADLER, 7, Marsden Street, Newton Heath.

Committee:
Mr. J. PANTER. — Mr. T. RIGBY.
Mr. T JACKSON. — Mr. J. WHITEHEAD.
Mr. J. B. DODD.

Captain (1st Team): MR. JOHN POWELL.
Captain "Swifts": MR. JOHN EARP.
CLUB HOUSE: SHEARS HOTEL.

Fixture list for Newton Heath showing Fredrick Attock as President. Note the mention of MP AJ Balfour - ever the politician he held a similar role at Ardwick/Manchester City.

By the late 1880s discussions were taking place on the formation of a national league, and ultimately in 1888 the Football League was formed without any Manchester clubs as members. Over the years another myth, often recorded in official United publications, has developed that the Heathens attempted to join the League from its inception and that they were rejected at the League's formation meetings. Those same publications claim the Heathens were by far the most successful of the region's clubs at this stage. Neither of these claims is true. The Heathens did not apply to join the League at formation and they had won the Manchester Cup the same number of times as Hurst and West Manchester. They had competed in the FA Cup fewer times than Hurst and Manchester FC, and they had hardly gained any form of reputation outside of the region. They were no different from the other sides, but they were certainly not the most likely of the region's sides to enter the League. In fact Hurst or West Manchester would have stood more of a chance.

Those that suggest the Heathens applied in 1888 actually downplay the achievements of the club over the years that followed as a rejection suggests there were issues with the club. In truth the Heathens themselves had a more pragmatic approach. It appears the Heathens did want stronger competition but did not feel the rigidity of a League competition would be appropriate. Instead they helped to create an alternative and more informal competition called the Football Combination.

The Combination allowed each competing club to select its own fixtures, and so a fixture list could contain anything from eight games (minimum allowed). This was a major step forward for Newton Heath and it is fair to say that forming this league did more to develop the club's name than anything the side had previously been involved with. They were the only Manchester representatives.

Unfortunately, the Combination was not a success and on 5 April 1889 eleven clubs, including the Heathens, pulled out, causing the Combination to collapse. It was at this point that the side realised it had to compete within a more rigid format, and so they applied to join the Football League at the end of the League's first season. Unfortunately, Newton Heath collected only one vote out of the 48 cast and they finished ninth in the election. This failure could have killed the side's spirit, but instead the Heathens joined with other rejected teams and some of their former Combination colleagues to create The Football Alliance – a 12 team league competition.

Newton Heath ended the first Alliance season eighth, but at least they were now competing on a much larger stage than before. Again they applied to join the more high-profile Football League, and again they were rejected – Sunderland became the first new side to be admitted that season. Unfortunately no record exists of the number of votes the Heathens received.

Another Alliance season followed with the side finishing ninth out of 12 clubs, but the Heathens had also won their first FA Cup tie when they defeated Higher Walton 2-0 in the first qualifying round, sadly they lost the second qualifying round tie at Bootle 1-0. Inevitably, as members of the Alliance Newton Heath decided to apply for election to the Football League again in 1891. This time they were hopeful of success as the League was to be extended to 14 clubs from 12. Also included amongst the aspiring clubs were another Manchester side, Ardwick.

The League still wanted to spread its influence, and therefore towns or cities without a League side seemed to be at an advantage, however with both Newton Heath and Ardwick up for election

A Heathens team group from 1892.

there was a real possibility that the vote for a Manchester club would be split – this may have had a bearing on later events.

The other aspiring sides were Darwen, Nottingham Forest, Stoke, and Sunderland Albion. Of these only Ardwick were not members of the Alliance. Incredibly though, the election saw Newton Heath finish bottom without gaining a single vote. Darwen and Stoke both received seven votes and were accepted into the League, while surprisingly Ardwick managed to secure four votes and ended up receiving more votes than any of the other non-elected sides. Interestingly, the prospect of the two Manchester sides causing the vote to be split clearly did not materialise.

In 1891-92 a determined Newton Heath, under the leadership of secretary Alf Albut, finished second in the Alliance and immediately they applied to join the League. There had been some difficulties along the way, with the **Gorton Reporter** focusing on disharmony within the ranks during January 1892:

"The Newton Heath (LYR) Committee had before them several members of the team on Monday night who all complained of the selfish actions of Donaldson in not passing the ball during the last four matches. It is said that this has been the cause of the inability of the team to win several Alliance matches."

At the time of the comment Newton Heath had drawn four consecutive games but in the next match – at home to Crewe on 30th January – no one had cause to complain about Donaldson as the player netted a hat-trick in a 5-3 victory.

Other media coverage tended to focus on the quality of the side and on 16th January 1892, a week after a 1-1 draw at Bootle in the Alliance, **The Reporter** talked of how well the side had been viewed at Bootle:

"Newton Heath have earned such a great reputation for themselves of late. The visitors are a fine body of men and the dashing game they played throughout would have made them easily victorious but for the stubbornness of the Bootle defence."

By the time of the Heathens application to join the League, it had been decided the League would be increased into two divisions and rather than accept a place in the Second Division the side became determined to gain a First Division spot. Ardwick, who had competed in the Alliance for only one season, did not make an application to join the top division and settled instead for a place in the Second Division. Whether the two sides discussed the possibility of splitting the vote is not clear, but had Ardwick applied to join Division One it does seem highly likely the Manchester vote would have been divided with, potentially, both sides missing out.

When the vote was performed the Heathens gained six votes – only one vote more than rejected side Sheffield United – and alongside The Wednesday and Nottingham Forest they managed to become a First Division side. In June that year they became a Limited Company and, according to records at United's museum they finally dropped the references to the railway from their name, although some sources claim this had been done a few years earlier.

The first League game the Heathens competed in was an away game at Blackburn Rovers on 3rd September 1892. That match ended in a 4-3 defeat but a week later the side picked up its first point with a 1-1 draw at home to Burnley. A couple of defeats followed before another point was gained at West Bromwich Albion, then on 15th October the first victory of the season was an incredible 10-1 win over Wolves at North Road.

Despite this victory the Heathens ended their first League season as the bottom club out of 16. With a Second Division in place Newton Heath avoided the ignominy of re-election – something which could easily have gone against the side as League sides during this period would often base their voting on non-footballing ability and the quality of the North Road venue, the finances of the club, and a whole host of other reasons would play a part. Likewise the Heathens were safe from automatic relegation – this was not introduced until 1898-99 – but they did have to compete in the promotion deciding Test Matches (similar to modern day play-offs). In 1893 each of the bottom three sides competed against one of the top three sides in Division Two at a neutral venue to determine which teams would compete in the higher division. The Heathens managed a 1-1 draw at Stoke against Division Two Champions Small Heath (present day Birmingham City) and then in the replay they won 5-2 at Bramall Lane to retain their place in the top division.

By the start of the following season the Heathens had moved to their second ground, Bank Street in Clayton (often referred to as Bank Lane during the 1890s). Problems with the rental and charging of admission at North Road had forced the club to move on. The move to Bank Street could not have been ideal, as the new ground was a good two to three miles from North Road and it was certainly not within the Newton Heath district. In addition it was close to chemical works, a coal mine and lots of heavy industry. It was not a perfect place by any stretch of the imagination, but at least it offered the side the potential to develop. The site found allowed a larger paying public to watch the side, and over the years the venue would improve.

The one surprising aspect of the move at the time was why the club did not change its name. A move so far from the club's roots would normally have brought about a change. Across at Ardwick,

A team group of Newton Heath from 1895-96 - *Back (L to R)* **AH Albut (secretary-manager), F Paley (Trainer), John Dow, William Douglas, FW Palmer (director), Fred Erentz, Will Davidson, G Faulkner (director).** *Middle:* **W Crompton (director), George Perrins, James McNaught, Willie Stewart, H Jones (Vice President).** *Front:* **John Clarkin, Bob Donaldson, Joe Cassidy, Dick Smith, James Peters.**

the Blues had changed their name from Gorton AFC to Ardwick AFC when they moved a few yards over the border into Ardwick, so why the Heathens did not change at first appears to be a mystery, however research for this book has identified that the side did consider a change within a year of the move.

In 1894 they applied to alter their name to Manchester FC. Potentially, the move to Clayton caused the club to consider its name and, as they were competing against sides named Sunderland, Nottingham (Forest), Derby (County), Sheffield (United) and so on they may have felt it was time to adopt the name of the city rather than a district.

The name change was ultimately blocked by the Rugby Union and the Football Association as detailed in Chapter Two.

One of the biggest problems facing the side around this time was its League form. The 1893-94 season followed a similar vein to the previous campaign with the side finishing bottom of the First Division again. This time they struggled in the Test Matches and were defeated 2-0 by Second Division champions Liverpool at Blackburn. They became the first of the Manchester region sides to be relegated, but twelve month later they had a chance to return to the First Division when they ended the season third, behind champions Bury - more of that later- and Notts County. Again, this meant Newton Heath were in the Test Matches but their game against the First Division's 14th club (3rd from bottom) Stoke at 'neutral' Port Vale ended in a 3-0 defeat.

Newton Heath Notes.

ACT 1.

IF they had so arranged it the Newton Heath officials could not have found a better team than Chorley to test the abilities of their eleven. It was plain to be seen that the Juniors, if we may call them such, intended to obtain a victory, and in failing to do so they experienced exceedingly hard lines. They were much the better team, and showed the weak points of the Heathens to a nicety. The latter team played the usual friendly game, but some of them found it out to their cost, and were probably surprised when they found themselves left off the team. "Curly" Jones was the only one of the new comers that did anything like, and he really played a "class" game. The forwards put no devil into their play, and the way some of them shaped would have disgraced a school-boy. Cairns did well at times, but both Brooks and "Chorley" Jones did little of any good. Being the opening game was an excuse, and we have hopes of their turning out good men. Cartwright rambled about a good deal, but it was probably with a view to help Morgan. You are dis-discharged, Walter, this time, but don't do it again.

ACT 2.

When they came to serious business, however, the Heathens played a very different kind of game. Of course alterations had been made in the forwards, and the ever-popular Fred was standing by the side of the very happy Harry. It was evident from the start that they meant business, and although Old Sol was looking straight into their faces, and a powerful wind tried to smash up their combination, they stuck to their guns, and Private Cassidy hit the target before the interval. The second half saw the Heathens in good trim, attack and defence both being good. Goal number two was not long in coming, and although the Gainsborough men tried hard they failed to get a solitary point. Thus the Heathens booked their first League points. It was a brilliant win, and proves that the locals are a very good lot. If the team is kept together success is assured.

A "GRATE FITE."

The game at Clayton last Saturday proved a battle royal. Right from the start both teams went at it hammer and tongs, with the result that play was fast and furious. There was very little in the teams, but the winners were entitled to their honours. In the closing stages much feeling was imparted into the game and the referee had a warm time of it. If Saturday's form is kept up the attendance at Combination fixtures will improve considerably.

General comment on Newton Heath from the official Manchester programme following the 2-0 defeat of Gainsborough Town on the opening day of the 1898-99 season.

In 1896 the Heathens missed out even on the Test Matches as they ended the season sixth, but the following year they competed again as runners up to Notts County. By this time the format of the games had been changed with matches being played on a mini-league basis. The two First Division sides would face the two Second Division teams on a home and away basis, and each victory would be awarded two points and each draw one. The Heathens managed to beat Division One's bottom club Burnley 2-0 at Bank Street but they had already lost the home fixture by the same score. They then drew with Sunderland in Clayton, putting them on three points.

Away at Sunderland the final match would ultimately determine which of the two sides would earn a place in Division One as the north-east club had only managed two draws at this point. In the end the Heathens were defeated 2-0 and promotion was missed again with Sunderland retaining their place in Division One and Division Two champions Notts County taking the other place at the expense of Burnley.

December 1898 - The editor of the official Manchester programme sings the praises of a pub close to the site of the present day City of Manchester Stadium.

ON RETURNING from the match, at Newton Heath, last Saturday, our representative called at the "Holt Town Tavern," in Mitchell Street, to have a chat with mine host (Alec. Peak), and was pleased to sample some of his fine Ales and Cigars, which proved to be of excellent quality. Patrons are also treated to a first-rate concert on Monday, Friday and Saturday nights.

The team sheet for the 10th September 1898 Manchester derby. Newton Heath won 3-0 with goals from Boyd, future Blue Cassidy and Collinson.

NEWTON HEATH v. MANCHESTER CITY.

NEWTON HEATH.

Goal.
Barrett
1

Right Back. Stafford *Capt.* 2
Left Back. Erentz 3

Half-Backs.
Draycott 4 — Morgan 5 — Cartwright 6

Right Wing. Bryant 7 — Collinson 8
Centre. Boyd 9
Left Wing. Cassidy 10 — Gilliespie 11

Left Wing. Williams 12 — Whitehead 13
Centre. Gilliespie 14
Right Wing. Smith 15 — Meredith 16

Half-Backs.
Holmes 17 — Smith 18 — Munn 19

Left Back. Read 20
Right Back. Moffat 21

Goal.
Williams
22

MANCHESTER CITY.

Kick-off 3-15 — Referee, Mr. John Lewis.

NOTE.—In case of any Final Alteration in the Teams as given above, a notice will be sent round the Enclosure giving the name of the substituted player, and the number of the position in which he will play.

The Heathens never again competed in the Test Matches and with automatic promotion introduced in 1898-99 it was hoped the side would automatically prove capable of competing at the highest level, but the side never again challenged for promotion as Newton Heath. They did finish fourth in consecutive seasons (1898 and 1899) but their last season as the Heathens (1901-02) saw them finish in their lowest League position at the time – fifteenth out of 18 clubs. With serious financial problems the club was in a desperate position throughout 1901-02.

ATTENDANCE DETAIL
SEASON BY SEASON - 1898-1902

Season	City	Newton Heath	Bury	Stockport
1898-99	10000	7775	4525	
1899-1900	16000	6225	5775	
1900-1	18300	5475	6950	3725
1901-2	17000	4650	6200	3050

LEAGUE POSITION
SEASON BY SEASON - 1898-1902

Season	City	Newton Heath	Bury	Stockport
1898-99	19	22	10	
1899-1900	7	22	12	
1900-1	11	28	5	35
1901-2	18	33	7	35

CHAPTER SIX

THE BIRTH OF BURY

Few clubs can boast of a more interesting career than the Bury Football Club. Right from the inception of the organisation in the early months of 1885 their career has been marked by a series of triumphs which has won the club distinction even among the high class company in which they now figure. Starting from the humblest level, the highest sphere has been attained only by the exercise of much self-denial by real enthusiasts and unremitting attention to the well being of the organisation and directors. In the course of their career Bury have won every cup and trophy for which they have entered, with the sole exception of the League Championship and the Sheriff of London Shield.

The Book Of Football, 1905

AS the new century commenced football within the region was increasing in stature and importance and true success for three of the region's sides was to occur within the first decade of the century. In fact by the outbreak of war in 1914 the clubs in this area had won between them two League titles, five FA Cups and the Second Division title on four occasions.

In 1900 the First Division already contained two of our featured sides – City and Bury – and by 1910 two of the other local League sides of the period - Newton Heath (reformed as Manchester United), and Oldham Athletic - would also compete at the highest level possible. In addition three of those sides would find major trophy success with the first truly successful side from the region being Bury.

The 1905 ***Book Of Football***, the first serious work covering any of our local clubs, highlighted Bury as one of the game's greatest sides. Certainly their comments on the Shakers were significantly more positive than either of the other Manchester region sides featured (City & United).

The specifics of Bury's formation in 1885 are no longer entirely clear however a brochure from 1925 included a potted history of the club:

"At the time of the club's birth few people in the district gave much thought to the association code. The majority preferring Rugby and sharing their affections and spare cash between Bury and Tottington. But those who had witnessed Soccer in towns such as Sheffield, Bolton – ardent and enthusiastic –

conceived the idea of introducing the Association game, put their heads together, and held several informal meetings."

Although this account is perhaps the one that is closest to the truth, there are still some errors in the explanation, particularly the section referring to rugby dominating activity in the town. Modern day historian Gordon Sorfleet, and others connected with Bury, recognise that Bury FC were not the first association football club in the town. Sorfleet:

"The Bury Times carried match reports at this time from a variety of local teams, but basically a meeting was held between two church teams. They combined and that was that. Off they went."

The dominance of rugby is often referred to when considering the club's early history, even the **Book Of Football** talked of it, and the reason for this seems to be that Bury Football Club was actually the local rugby side, similar to Manchester FC, and so the new soccer club was usually reported as Bury Association Football Club to differentiate between the two sides.

The first informal meeting of the club was held early in 1885 at the Waggon and Horses public house on Walmersley Road, and then on Friday, April 24th 1885 at 8pm a public meeting was staged at the White Horse Hotel – a site occupied in 2007 by the Royal Bank of Scotland on The Rock. At this meeting the club formed a 12 man committee and appointed all the key positions. They also set out to find a venue.

The committee soon opened negotiations for a plot of land known as "Mr. Barlow's field, Gigg Lane." Thomas Barlow was an agent for the Earl of Derby and lived at Bankfield Farm (present day Bankfield Nursing Home), and the football club began negotiation with Barlow to become sub-tenants of a field at the south-west corner of the farm – this became the Gigg Lane ground, and today it is the oldest ground of a League side in the region.

There is really nothing very heinous about the transfer system. If one League club takes a famous player from the ranks of another League club, thereby strengthening its playing resources, it is only fair that it should pay for the privilege. It is generally supposed that Everton paid Bury £400 for the services of Settle, their famous forward.

In April 1899 Jimmy Settle was transferred from Bury to Everton for an astounding fee of £400. His career blossomed at Goodison before he returned to the Manchester region in 1908 where he played for Stockport. By that time he'd appeared in 6 England internationals.

A series of friendly games and minor competition, such as the Lancashire Junior Cup, followed, with the first known match taking place on 5th September 1885 against Little Lever. Seven days later Wigan Borough was defeated 4-3 at Gigg Lane. Incidentally, Gigg Lane's reputation for a quality playing surface was noted from the beginning. The **Book of Football** highlighted that Bury's pitch was from the earliest days:

"regarded as one of the best playing surfaces in England, being well drained and covered with a thin carpet of grass even at the end of the season."

At the end of the first season the report and accounts made poor reading with the club struggling financially. Fortunately, despite a loss of around £8 the committee agreed the club should continue and several local businessmen were persuaded to get involved but the position hardly improved. By the start of 1887-88 the club were reportedly £100 in debt.

The previous season saw Bury attempt to improve their status with a formal application to enter the FA Cup, however the FA claimed they received Bury's application too late and so the side had to wait until 15th October 1887 for their first taste of significant competition.

Bury faced Blackburn Rovers away but, surprisingly, they pulled out of the fixture shortly before the game was due to start as the committee suddenly realised they would be fielding a number of ineligible players. Ironically a situation that also affected Bury in 2006-07. Incredibly though they kept this news from the two sets of players and presumably the crowd, and so the two sides faced each other believing the game was the most important competition Bury had played in at that point, but in truth it was only a friendly. The game ended in a 10-0 victory for Rovers, but the tie was classed as a Blackburn 'walkover' by the FA with the game marked as 'scratched' in official documentation.

The journalists reporting on the Blackburn match believed the game to be a genuine tie and so, even to this day, some sources claim the 10-0 defeat is Bury's record FA Cup loss, but in truth the game was irrelevant.

The following season, perhaps understandably, Bury did not enter the FA Cup. In fact they did not play in the competition at all until 1891. Instead Bury decided to take matters into their own hands and organise a much more formal and regular competition. With the Football League nearing the end of its first season Bury's committee decided to work with other sides to create a local league. Ultimately the Lancashire League was created and in 1891 Bury were Lancashire League champions for the first time. They received the trophy at the League's annual meeting in Southport on 16th May 1891 but amazingly the trophy was not stored at Gigg Lane afterwards, instead it was taken to club President Sir Henry James' house in London.

Bury was developing at a rapid rate and, after further local successes and a visit from the Canadian touring XI, the Gigg Lane committee contemplated on applying to join the Football League. Surprisingly a vote was taken and the committee decided by three votes to two, with four abstentions, not to make an application. It is a pity they did not as 1892 was the year the Second Division was created with both Ardwick and Newton Heath managing to join the League that season. Had Bury applied, then their proud record, which was certainly on a par with both clubs at this stage, would probably have seen them elected.

Incidentally, the nickname 'The Shakers' came about during the 1891-92 season. According to Peter Cullen, writing in **Bury's Official History**:

"It was at the 1892 Lancashire Cup Final on 23rd April that the club's nickname of 'The Shakers' first came into being. Mr J.T. Ingham was Chairman-cum-Team Manager at the time and it is this gentleman who is alleged to have been questioned about his team's ability to beat the supposedly stronger opponents that day. It has been recorded down the years since that Mr Ingham retorted 'We shall shake 'em. In fact we are the Shakers' and that the press and supporters alike seized on the phrase which has led to its general recognition as the club's nickname ever since. Some reports suggest that Mr Ingham may have actually uttered the phrase at the semi-final game against Everton but what is certain is that Bury Football Club's nickname came into existence during the famous Lancashire Senior Cup success of 1892."

By the end of 1893-94 Bury were clearly one of the north-west's strongest non-League sides and with both Ardwick and Newton Heath competing in the Second Division, Bury must have been aware that at this time they possessed as much ability to live amongst the Country's leading clubs as Manchester's two sides. The **Bury Times** recognised that the town's team were at a critical point in their history. The newspaper concluded one article at the start of May with:

"Bury will have to cease to act as the mainstay of the Lancashire League and turn to a league in which something will be found that reawakens the interest of its members."

Gordon Sorfleet shares the view that Bury were treading water:

"They got fed up of winning the Lancashire League year in year out. They needed stronger competition."

On 11th May the Bury committee agreed to submit an application to join Division Two. Ten days later the Football League held its Annual General Meeting at the Boars Head Hotel, Withy Grove, Manchester. Prior to this meeting it was already known that the Division would be increasing from 15 teams to 16, and so as result of this and other factors it was agreed that four of the nine sides up for election would be accepted. Bury received 17 votes and was accepted into the division after only nine years of existence. This in itself was a major success.

From a regional perspective Bury's opening game was newsworthy not simply because it was their first League fixture, but also because it was the first game Ardwick played under their new name of Manchester City. The match, played on Saturday 1st September 1894 started with City scoring after only three minutes, but Bury managed to equalise five minutes before half time – their first League goal was netted by captain Billy Barbour. The Shakers then went on to control much of the match and this first Bury-City fixture ended 4-2 to Bury. They went on to win a further 14 consecutive home fixtures in what was to become a truly great season. Sorfleet:

"It was a great first season of League football. Unbeaten at home. Unbelievable for such a new team. Compared with today's game it's totally unthinkable, especially for a town the size of Bury."

Bury ended their first season in the League as Second Division champions and became the first of the region's sides to win a major national trophy. Not only did they win the title, but they did it in style with a nine point lead over nearest rivals Notts County – this margin remained a record until 1974 when Middlesbrough had a 15 point lead but crucially they had played an additional 12 games.

In 1895 however promotion was not guaranteed and Bury had to compete in the end of season Test Matches, similar to modern day play-offs, against Liverpool, the bottom club in Division

APRIL 26, 1900.] *SPORTING SKETCHES.* 13

Football Association Cup: Final Tie.

(Illustrated with Instantaneous Photographs by the Standard Photo Co.)

FOR the first time since 1883 a Southern club this season reached the final stage of the above competition, but Southampton failed to outplay the survivors of the North—Bury—and were well beaten by 4 goals to nil, at the Crystal Palace on Saturday. Few finals have created more widespread interest than this year's, and many of the enormous crowd present on the ground were there in the hope of seeing the coveted Cup once more return to the South. These hopes were dashed to the ground, however, and, as the Mayor of Southampton said afterwards, his men were beaten by a superior side on the day's play. The terrible heat wave which has seemingly transported London from mid-winter into a very fair imitation of the dog days, made even watching football a trial. A blazing hot sun poured down upon the greensward, and incidentally also upon the perspiring tens of thousands of excited partisans of the rival organisations who sat, stood, and sweltered long before the match was advertised to commence. An hour before the match there were fully 30,000 spectators present, and when the game started the attendance was quite up to that of the last few years—in fact, officials even declared greater than ever before.

Bury won the toss, and Southampton kicked off shortly before time. Southampton had the

A STOPPAGE OWING TO SLIGHT INJURY TO PRAY.

their faces, doubtless had a lot to do with it, but even allowing for this their play was feeble.

The second half was expected to be more in Southampton's favour, but the lead established by Bury seemed too big to wipe off. The opening stages certainly favoured them more, but they never seemed able to play the same sprightly football that Bury had done in the first half. Chadwick had several attempts with long shots, but the direction was almost invariably bad. Wood and Milward continued to peg away most pluckily, Milward making several attempts to score, but they were all futile. In saving a long shot from Pray, Robinson tipped the ball over the bar. Richards took the corner beautifully, and Plant, with a lightning shot, scored again for Bury. This was the climax of Southampton's misfortunes, and from that time forth the game fizzled out tamely, the final score being 4—0 in favour of the Northerners.

There can be no doubt at all that Bury deserved their victory, their work being better all round than that of the Sotonians, who seemed tired and stale. It was a great disappointment to the South and the Southern League's supporters, but Southampton never deserved to win, and another year must elapse at any rate before the South of England secures its ambition and "lifts the cup."

The 1900 FA Cup final saw Bury defeat Southampton to become the first of the Manchester region sides to win the trophy.

Southampton's 'keeper Robinson is left stranded as Bury score.

A Bury throw in against Southampton in the FA Cup final.

One, at neutral Blackburn. Bury took a 32nd minute lead, but after 76 minutes a Liverpool forward, Bradshaw, fouled Bury's 'keeper Archie Montgomery. Montgomery retaliated and was sent off (the first Bury player dismissed in the League). Fortunately, Bury managed to hang on, and their first season ended with promotion to Division One.

Not only were Bury the first local side to achieve promotion they were also the first to win the FA Cup. When they defeated Southampton 4-0 in the 1900 final it was the first truly significant success by any of the region's clubs and for the Shakers to achieve that success was remarkable. Today the majority of residents in the Manchester region have no idea of Bury's proud early history and most South East Lancashire residents would probably suggest that either City or United were the first significant trophy winners, but clearly they would be wrong.

Bury's 1899-1900 FA Cup run became a major story but it also ran alongside the story of the Boer War in Africa. The Boer War inevitably was the biggest national story of the period, but the involvement of the Manchester Regiment and others from the region made every conflict seem more personal than perhaps previous wars had been. The **Athletic News**' famous journalist JAH Catton had been following Bury's exploits in the Cup and was also a very proud Englishman. In 1926 he looked back on his own career and claimed that Bury's 1899-1900 quarter-final replay was the most significant day in football history he had personally experienced.

The game was played on 1st March 1900 and news of the relief of Ladysmith was filtering through. Although much of what he wrote has long since escaped the consciousness of Lancashire's population, it is worth documenting in full his article to give a flavour for the period and of how football provided an outlet for national rejoicing. Catton wrote:

"This was to be a day of general rejoicing and thanksgiving – a prelude to the Mafeking celebrations in May. As it happened, on that day Bury were to meet Sheffield United in a replayed Association Cup tie at Gigg Lane.

"By common consent every football enthusiast who could, set out for the little town celebrated for blankets, black-puddings, and the barracks of the First Manchester's, a regiment which had taken a momentous part in the South African War. So I bent my steps towards the Bury football ground, about eight miles from my home. The factories had closed. Business was at a standstill. This was Ladysmith Day, and there was a pulse quickening Cup-tie against a team which were the holders of the Cup - a team which included William Foulke, the mighty; Needham, the tiny Titan; "Cocky" Bennet, the surefoot, who could shoot a ball with wonderful velocity; and many another fine player, including Beer, who is now connected with Birmingham after some years in the Colonies. No doubt Beer will recall the events of that day.

"When I got into the thoroughfare leading to the gates of the Bury ground it was thronged with thousands of folk struggling to gain entrance. The position looked hopeless. As the folks say in Lancashire, 'There's always most thrutchin' where there's least room' - and thrutchin' means pushing, shoving, squeezing, and crushing. It was all very good tempered, as, of course, everybody wanted to go one way. Still, when thousands of folks are eager to pass through one gate, one bottle-neck, the situation is tense with all the good humour in the world. I was behind a heap of struggling and grunting humanity, and I wondered how I should get on to that old farm land which Bury have converted into a football arena. My motto was: 'Wayte awhyle - wayte awhyle'.

"When I was getting anxious a group of soldiers from Bury barracks marched up. The crowd ceased to jostle and began to cheer. As if by order they voluntarily opened out to let the men in khaki through

to the ground. The platoon virtually marched in, and espying my opportunity I dashed to their rear and practically walked in under cover of a military escort. The little trick amused me - almost as much as the tie itself - for had not this contingent arrived the match would have been half over before I should have reached the gates.

"As the Bury ground was at that time, a gathering of over 20,000 excited and joyous folks was a splendid frame to the moving picture of earnest teams. Eight or nine of the players have joined the ever-increasing majority, but they all acquitted themselves like true athletes. I always considered that Bury won the Cup on Ladysmith Day, although they had afterwards to meet Nottingham Forest in the semi-final tie and Southampton in the last scene of all. In that era Bury had a Cup team to be proud of-in my opinion, a side superior to that which carried off the trophy a second time in 1903. With such back divisions as Darroch and Davidson, and Prey, Leeming, and George Ross, it is not astonishing that Sheffield United and Nottingham Forest were the only opponents who could score against them.

"Think of the vanguard with such sturdy Lancashire lads as Richards and Wood, both from Middleton, on the right, the late James M'Luckie, of Jordanhill, the tall and menacing Scottish centre, the late Charles Sagar, of Turton, nearly six feet of willowy wizardry, and J. Plant, the Bollington boy, who always played in such tattered and supple shoes, held together with yards of tape, that he called to mind Tom Bury, of Darwen, who preferred such fragile footgear that it was always said he played in his wife's elastic–side boots.

"Tom Bury was a gradely Lancashire lad, and there were three of them in this forward line of Bury on Ladysmith Day, while Jack Plant, as harmless as a dove, but such a fine player, came from the next county - the plains of Cheshire. And that is how I escaped a bit of rib-cracking at Bury, and enjoyed a match that will never fade from memory."

From a Bury point of view the quarter final was inevitably eclipsed by the semi-final, and then by the region's first national final. Surprisingly, Bury were actually favourites for the trophy on cup final day with many journalists expressing the view that opponents Southampton had no hope of defeating the Lancastrian side.

Southampton were accurately recorded as a non-League side, however they were significantly members of the Southern League and although this was not part of the Football League, many of its teams were as strong, if not stronger, than some Division One sides. It should be remembered that the Football League still predominantly consisted of northern and midlands sides and that the majority of southern clubs continued to compete in the Southern League. Southampton were one of the league's more successful clubs, winning the title on several occasions, and so when they faced Bury they were still one of the south's most advanced sides.

GEORGE ROSS.
George Ross, the veteran captain of the Bury F. C., first played with the Bury Wesleyans, and joined the Bury Club in 1887. He is a Scot by birth, but came to Bury when only a few months old. He has risen with the club from its infancy to the giddy heights of fame, and probably no player in the country possesses a more varied or valuable collection of gold medals which he has won during the nineteen years he has played for the club

The **Daily Telegraph** reported on the final, but tended to focus on Southampton rather than Bury:

"Southampton came to Crystal Palace with high hopes of becoming the first 'outsiders' to win the FA Cup since the inception of the Football League. But Bury proved too much

for them and ran out easy 4-0 winners. Perhaps it was the occasion that got to the non-Leaguers, although they had played on the ground in the semi-finals. They had also disposed of three First Division sides on their way to the final - Everton 5-0, Newcastle 4-1 and West Bromwich 2-1 – all at the Dell. Only fellow Southern Leaguers Millwall gave them any trouble, drawing their semi-final 0-0 before going down 5-0 in the replay at Reading.

"Nearly 69,000 turned out on a blazing hot April day to watch the final. Southampton kicked off with the sun in their eyes, and found themselves three goals down within 25 minutes, two of them from centre-forward McLuckie. They came back into the game for spells in the second half, but never seriously challenged Bury's lead, and a fourth goal for the northerners 10 minutes from time was the final nail in their coffin."

The **Sporting Sketches** newspaper was a little more balanced and described the game as being dominated by Bury once the first goal was scored:

"From the goal kick Wood got down and forced a corner for Bury, from which McLuckie scored the first goal after ten minutes' play. Bury, having established a lead, pressed hotly, tricky work by Sagar and Plant leading up to a regular bombardment of the Southampton goal, and Plant sent in a hot shot, which Robinson saved grandly, but could not clear, and Wood dashed up and scored a second goal just twenty minutes from the start. This had a thoroughly demoralising effect on the Hampshire men, who were being outplayed."

The report continued to stress Bury's domination and then ended:

"There can be no doubt at all that Bury deserved their victory, their work being better all round than that of the Sotonians, who seemed tired and stale."

This great 4-0 victory was followed in 1903 with an even more incredible 6-0 victory over Derby County in Bury's next FA Cup final. Not only was the final score remarkable but Bury also became the first side since Preston in 1889 to win the trophy without conceding a goal in the competition. According to the **Book Of Football** published in 1905 Bury's success was: *"a finer record than that established by Preston North End in the early days of the game"* as Bury had played more ties than Preston.

In the seasons that followed the Shakers established themselves as a respectable mid to lower end of the table side finishing 11th, 9th, 14th, 10th, and 12th before ending 1900-01 in fifth place. Of course, by that time Bury had already become the region's first FA Cup winners, but they were also crucially the region's most successful side in the League.

Bury's success is often overlooked when residents of Greater Manchester talk about football but without Bury's achievements during these formative years for the game in the region it is possible that the other sides may not have developed.

City joined Bury in Division One in 1899 while United gained promotion for the first time in 1906. Both sides would ultimately eclipse Bury's achievements, but for a few years at least Bury was the region's best and most successful side. Bury led the way while both City and Newton Heath were struggling to make a name for themselves.

A PEEP INTO FUTURITY.

Some day, perhaps, in the far, far distant future, when most of us are dead and gone, Manchester City and Bury may be able to decide as to which of them is most entitled to the possession of the Manchester Senior Cup. The "Daily Dispatch" published a cartoon on their series of drawn games, and we have taken the liberty of reproducing it.

City and Bury seemed to be perfectly matched when they competed in the Manchester Cup final. After a goalless game in April 1904 the competition was eventually decided on 5th December 1904 when Bury won 4-0.

The Bury team of 1905-06.

Future Prime Minister Arthur Balfour attends Hyde Road for City's 2-0 victory over Stoke in September 1900. Balfour, photographed here shaking hands with City Captain Billy Meredith, was a patron of the club and attended City's 1904 FA Cup final win.

CHAPTER SEVEN

MANCHESTER'S RISE

Perhaps love of sport had something to do with the bringing together of so great a gathering, but love of Manchester, had much more to do with it. Tom Maley, 1904

THE first Manchester challenge for the League title itself came in 1904 when City came close to achieving the double, however before that can be detailed it is important to consider the fate of both Newton Heath and Stockport County.

During the early years of the twentieth century both the Heathens and County were struggling in Division Two. County had joined the League in 1900, so in a sense, any struggles they endured during the early years of the century have to be put into perspective. Their first three seasons of League football ended with County finishing 17th out of 18 clubs in Division Two, and the general feeling was that the side were really competing at a level higher than they realistically should have expected to play at.

Stockport County photographed in April 1900 - shortly before being accepted into the Football League.

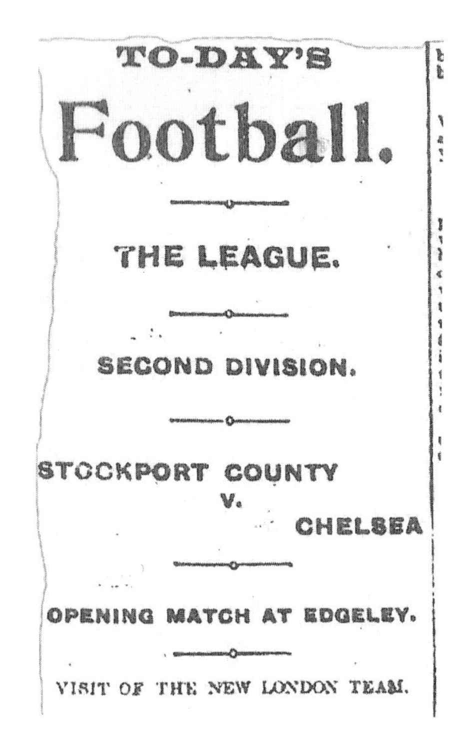
TO-DAY'S

Football.

THE LEAGUE.

SECOND DIVISION.

STOCKPORT COUNTY
v.
CHELSEA

OPENING MATCH AT EDGELEY.

VISIT OF THE NEW LONDON TEAM.

STOCKPORT COUNTY v. CHELSEA.

There was a large gate at Edgeley Park, Stockport. Foulke won the toss, and in the presence of a crowd of 5,000 strong Manson kicked off against the wind. Heywood pulled the Chelsea left up in grand style, and Hall was applauded for tricky work. Pemble was first tested with a long shot from Miller, but there was nothing behind it. Schofield forced a corner, and to clear Foulkes ran out and sent away. Cresser met the rebound and grazed the bar with a terrific drive. Stockport were now having the best of the game, and pressed. Half-time:—No score. Chelsea restarted with a rush, Pemble having to clear a long shot from Moran. Chelsea attacked, and Cresser proving a failure at half-back. Moran and Copeland had much their own way on the Chelsea right. Dodd beat Foulke after the latter had saved a penalty. Result:—

STOCKPORT COUNTY 1
CHELSEA 0

On the opening day of the 1905-06 season Stockport defeated new club Chelsea in both sides' first game since joining the League. County had been rejected in 1904 but managed to gain election in 1905.

In May 1902 – after their second League season came to an end – County's annual meeting was a difficult one. The Chairman of the club made a statement describing how much the club was struggling. He told the attendees that County had liabilities of £900 and that he felt only the working men of Stockport were supporting the club. The Gentlemen, he felt, were the ones who had let Stockport down. He then made a somewhat strange statement about the playing squad, saying that those players who had been used to playing in the Lancashire League were good men, and were easily motivated, however since joining the League he felt that the majority of players had been 'pampered'. He claimed that Stockport were unable to do anything with the 'higher class men of the second league'. He added that they *"wanted carting about wherever they went, and they almost wanted carrying!"* Who knows what he would have thought about Premier League players in the 21st century.

As a result of the problems at Stockport, the committee decided to hold a bazaar to raise funds. The saddest part of this period for County however came in 1904. They finished 16th, their highest position at the time, but unfortunately they found themselves in the re-election zone. Sadly, County received fewer votes than existing League sides Leicester Fosse and Glossop, and Doncaster Rovers who went on to replace County. It was a bitter blow, but County were not to be beaten and twelve months later they applied to return to the League and were successful. It helped that the two divisions were to be increased from 18 to 20 clubs each, thereby meaning an additional four clubs would be needed. A two-stage vote occurred with all those clubs applying to join the League joining the three bottom sides in Division Two in the first part. The three clubs receiving most votes, which included Chelsea, were awarded places in Division Two, then another vote was taken for the remaining four places. Stockport scraped through and there was some justice as County beat Doncaster Rovers for the final place. From that point on County appeared to have a new lease of life and the 1905-6 season ended with them in 10th place in the division.

Newton Heath's struggles were more far-reaching in terms of their consequences. The Heathens had been elected into Division One in 1892 when the League was expanded but looking at the hard facts of their results and performances it is clear they were some way short of the quality required. They were relegated in 1894 after finishing bottom of Division One for successive seasons and these struggles may well have set the tone for the following decade. Had the Heathens been elected into Division Two instead of the top flight in 1892 it is highly probable their development would have matched – maybe eclipsed – that of Manchester City and Bury.

By 1900 Newton Heath appeared to make fourth place of Division Two their own as they continually fell short of sustaining a credible promotion challenge. Then an appalling tenth place finish was followed in 1902 by fifteenth spot and, although the Heathens were one place above the re-election zone, they were on level points with the 17th placed side Chesterfield.

This appalling finish – the club's worst until 1934 when they finished twentieth – came at the end of an immensely difficult season. During the previous season a bazaar was held at St. James' Hall in the city centre with the aim of raising £1,000 to solve the Heathens financial worries, but it was not a major success despite strong support from leading Manchester MPs and rivals Manchester City. In fact it is known that several of the official patrons who had donated money and were recorded as key contributors were connected with the Blues. These included directors John Allison, John Chapman (City Chairman), Edward Hulton and the famous kit manufacturer of the period Alec Watson (Watson went on to supply cup final shirts to City). Of these it is recorded that City gave £10 and Chapman £1 1s.

V. HAYES
Manchester United.

Vic Hayes, born in Miles Platting, played for Newton Heath/United from 1901-07 and again from 1908-10. he later moved into coaching and had spells in a variety of European locations including Madrid, Vienna, and Norway. In 1913 he became the Rochdale player-manager but left them in 1919 after they failed to join the Football League.

Naturally, the Blues felt Manchester needed two major sides in the city and wanted to see the Heathens develop. Financially, however, the side remained in an appalling state and close to extinction. Around this time the Newton Heath secretary, Alf Albut, wrote to JAH Catton, a leading journalist with the **Athletic News**, of the predicament the Heathens were in:

"The last three weeks I have been living on the ground – buck-navvying until there is not a 'buck' left in me. I am quite a 'doe'. Previous to that time I always had the front door locked to keep out the bum-bailiffs, and you would have to knock at the front door 'til the devil fetched you before I should have shown myself. We have had the honour of having the gas cut off. To see half a pound of candles – eight pound to the weight – stuck in four ginger beer bottles, all alight and aglow, at a directors' meeting is immense. It knocks the electric lights to Hades. At the ground we have, I think, done some hard work."

According to Catton, writing in the mid-twenties after United's first golden period, Albut was one of the most influential men in the development of United, for if he had not carried out the desperate activities of 1901-02, the club would have died before it had had chance of salvation.

On the 11th January 1902 it was revealed in the **Gorton Reporter** that a winding up order had been granted for the club:

"At the Ashton Under Lyne County Court on Thursday afternoon Dr. Bradley, barrister, instructed by Messrs Brett, Hamilton and Tarbolton, solicitors of Manchester, applied to the judge on behalf of Mr. W.J. Healey of Salford for a compulsory winding up order against the Newton Heath Football Club Co. Ltd. There was no appearance to the petition."

The article went on to describe the position of the club. It seems that William Healey, a former director of the club, was owed £242 17s 10d and that he had brought the petition with great reluctance as he still felt part of the club. According to the article Newton Heath had become a limited company on 2nd June 1892 and issued 2000 £1 shares.

It is interesting to note that Newton Heath must have been in serious disarray at this point as not one member of their board or committee was able to oppose the petition. However, the most amazing aspect from a modern perspective is that the judge seemed to be unaware of what football was all about. **The Reporter** quoted verbatim his findings and questions:

"His Honour: 'What is a Football Club Limited?' 'How do they carry on business?' 'Do they make money?' Dr. Bradley said the club engaged professional players to play matches and took gate receipts. He didn't suppose that a company of this kind was formed with the object of gain. It was formed with the object of ascertaining the liabilities and seeing that they did not exceed a certain amount. According to what the receipts were they paid the players.

"His Honour: 'Was it a success?' Dr. Bradley: 'At first it was, but lately it has not been.' His Honour: 'Has it paid any dividends?' Dr. Bradley: 'I don't think so. I think I may safely say it never has paid any. The object being not to pay dividends, but to play football. The club is in the Second Division of the League'."

According to **The Reporter** it was revealed in court that Newton Heath had previously offered to pay William Healey 10s per £1 owed but they failed to achieve this and so Healey felt he had no choice but to pursue the winding up. The judge granted the winding up and it was noted that there was no opposition at all.

Two days later the **Athletic News** recorded further problems for the Heathens:

"experiencing the qualms of such a severe financial shock that they were on Saturday unable to fulfil their engagement with Middlesbrough."

The game was actually scheduled as a home fixture and was ultimately played in April, but this was another serious indication of the club's plight.

Inevitably, as with so many situations like this, many attempts were made to keep the Heathens going further and the affair dragged on for some time, although the official receiver seemed very keen to resolve the matter as soon as possible. On 25th January however it was reported that the official receiver wanted the court to grant a cattle dealer from Salford called William Walker to re-possess the plot of land used by Newton Heath at 'Bank Lane, Clayton'. Apparently, this land, which was in effect the Bank Street Ground, had been leased from Walker since 13th May 1898. The order was granted by judge Reginald Brown and the receiver also announced that an offer had come in for £110 by someone wanting to purchase the stands and the fixtures and fittings. The receiver stated that this could be settled within two days of the order being carried out.

On Wednesday 5th February a meeting of all the creditors was held at the official receiver's office on Byrom Street where it was agreed the Heathens' total liabilities stood at £2,670. One shareholder, recorded as Mr. Robinson, claimed the Heathens' liabilities were this high because of the poor weather affecting games and attendances and it seems the official receiver supported this claim as he concluded that he did not want the club wound up yet.

There may be some truth in the comments regarding the weather as the Heathens fixture against Blackpool on 25th February was played in heavy snow with only around 2,500 fans attending – Newton Heath's average in 1900-01 had been 5,475. Reports of that match also note that the Heathens were under new management, so it does appear as if the receiver was doing all he could to keep the club going, although by the end of February the Football Association announced they had held a meeting with representatives of Newton Heath (L&Y) FC saying they had formed a new club called Newton Heath Football Club and that the new club would be able to fulfil all the existing fixtures and satisfy the terms of the players contracts. Whether this was simply part of the receiver's strategy or a move by others is not clear, but it does show that there were many people in the Newton Heath area who were keen to keep the Heathens operational.

On 1st March details of the Heathens financial affairs were made public. These showed that Newton Heath had 171 shareholders and that they had taken up 787 of the 2000 shares created in 1892. There was then a breakdown of everything the club had received in terms of gate money and its expenditure covering the period 1892 to 30th April 1901:

INCOME	
Gate Receipts:	£27,373
Tickets (presumably bought in advance):	£1,483
Donations:	£335
EXPENDITURE	
Salaries & Wages:	£20,408
Gatemen:	£530
Referees:	£539
Training:	£828
Football Utensils:	£417
Legal:	£271
Rents & Tax:	£1,137
Hotels & Travel:	£2,814
Printing & Stationery:	£1,359
Police:	£318
Total Assets =	£127

Throughout March 1902 the receiver worked to establish a way forward for the business but was ever mindful of the non-footballing offers that had come his way for the land and stands. A series of meetings were held, but to the outside world in general it appeared as if the club would disappear completely at the season's end. Then on 12th April 1902 matters were brought to a head when the club captain Harry Stafford wrote a letter to various newspapers outlining his dissatisfaction with the progress – or lack of it – being made. Stafford attended a meeting aimed at saving the club but wrote:

"It's surprising and disheartening that no real tangible effort has been made."

Stafford claimed that he and four other men – he did not name them at this stage – had offered to find £1,000 but that when he spoke with two of the Newton Heath directors he was surprised at their attitude. He claimed that they believed they should be recompensed for their shareholding while Stafford felt they were the men responsible for the financial mess. He urged supporters and businessmen to apply pressure on the existing directors to force a change in the set up.

As Stafford was the club captain this was an amazing act. Could you imagine Roy Keane taking on a similar role when the furore surrounding the Glazer takeover was announced? Stafford's role was unprecedented in football but it did prove successful. As a result of his pleas pressure was applied and a public meeting was held on Thursday 24th April 1902 at the New Islington public hall in Ancoats. This meeting is the most important and significant in the early history of the club and it is fair to say without it Manchester United would not exist today. Amazingly however every publication and official word on the formation of Manchester United produced over the last fifty years or so has incorrectly recorded the date and some of the details of this meeting.

Like so many other footballing clubs, myths have developed and inaccuracies overlooked as writers and researchers have simply been happy at accepting the story as previously recorded without researching the original material. Every Manchester newspaper of the period has been reviewed for this book and it is clear the meeting was definitely held on 24th April. So, for the first time, it can clearly be stated that Manchester United Football Club was created on 24th April 1902 and not on 28th April as United's own official histories claim, nor the 26th as the enormous *United Opus* records.

The *Manchester Evening Chronicle* was the first to report the story with their 25th April edition, while the *Manchester Evening News* followed on 26th April. They each carried reports of the name change. Inevitably, as the name change is one of the most fundamental moments in the club's history there have always been plenty of stories about how the name Manchester United came about and what other alternatives were considered. Sadly, for such a famous club, even these stories appear to be untrue. To try and understand the truth it is worth detailing here the most comprehensive article that appeared in a local newspaper at the time. The *Gorton Reporter*, which via various locally named editions covered east Manchester, reported on 26th April 1902 – two days after the meeting was held but crucially two days before United claim the meeting was held – that the meeting's chairman, James Brown, brought up the subject of the name Newton Heath:

"It had been mentioned to him that during the season one or two visiting clubs had been deluded by the name of the club in taking the wrong car through being mistaken as to the situation of the ground. In consequence delay in commencement of the matches has been entailed. On this ground, and others of even a stranger character, he would suggest that the club's name should be changed, on approval of the League and the FA, to that of Manchester United.

"The question was asked would the new club be likely to be re-admitted to the Second Division under the name of Manchester United? In reply, Mr. West (the secretary) said they would have to apply but did not expect a difficulty. But he did say that as the bulk of supporters were from Newton Heath that he would like to some how retain that name "

So based on this report it is clear that James Brown was the man who officially brought up the subject of the name and it does appear that he himself was the man who came up with the

Manchester United tag, while existing secretary James West was keen to see the Newton Heath name retained. He suggested using a combination of the name Manchester with Newton Heath but the overwhelming choice on the night was to go with Manchester United. In the years that have followed, particularly since the publication of *There's Only One United* by Geoffrey Green in 1978 it has been claimed that Louis Rocca – a major force behind the development of United – was actually the man who came up with the name Manchester United. Green:

"According to the redoubtable Louis Rocca it was he who hit on the title now made famous through the land. 'I got up and suggested Manchester United. The name was taken'."

Contemporary reports of the meeting make no such comment, and clearly state that it was Dentonian James Brown who made the suggestion, though it is unclear as to whether he actually came up with the name.

Sadly, Brown's name has been largely overlooked by United historians over the years. Even the *Official Manchester United Illustrated History*, published in 2001 (and reprinted on several occasions since), and the *Manchester United Pictorial History & Club Record*, published in 1986, misspelt his name as James Bown.

Another rumour that seems to have become fact over the years is the actual debate surrounding the name. According to most modern day historians there were three main choices of name – United, Manchester Celtic and Manchester Central. Again, contemporary reports suggest this is untrue. Brown was quoted as suggesting the United name but at no point is there a suggestion that other names were discussed. In fact, the name Manchester Central could not have been suggested as that name had already been utilised by another club. Match reports for Manchester Central appeared in local 'papers as early as 1892, and their ground was recorded as Birch Park. In fact in January 1892, as the Heathens were planning to apply to join the Football League, Manchester Central faced East Manchester side Gorton Villa twice. The first of these games took place on New Year's Day and resulted in an 8-0 defeat. The second occurred three weeks later in Gorton – the Heathens must have been aware of their existence. Central, nicknamed at the time as the Mancunians, were not a great side but they did exist and therefore it is highly unlikely members of the Heathens ever contemplated selecting that name, particularly after the experience of 1894 when they were stopped from utilising the name of Manchester F.C. Central ultimately failed but another Manchester Central became prominent during the 1920s and is documented later in this book. It is also worth noting that a side from Newton Heath – Ten Acres – had changed their name to Newton Heath Central in August 1888 and although there's no evidence to suggest they featured in any shape or form in 1902, it is unlikely the Heathens committee would have selected a name that could have brought comparisons with another Newton Heath side of the past.

The idea of calling United Manchester Celtic also seems untrue, although many people connected with Manchester football pre-war openly claim that United were known as a catholic club and therefore the Celtic connection does seem a possibility. However, there is still no actual proof that this was discussed in the April meeting. The only other suggested name appears to be West's suggestion of a name along the lines of 'Manchester Newton Heath F.C.'.

The closest any local newspaper came to documenting the actual discussion on the name other than he *Reporter* was the *Manchester Evening News*. Of all the Manchester 'papers, the *Evening News* was the one closest to the club. It had an office at the Bank Street ground and worked closely with the team to create publicity for the Heathens. In their 26th April 1902 edition the Evening News explained the main reason for the change:

"The proposal to change the name of the Newton Heath club to Manchester United will not be received with favour in certain quarters, but there is no doubt that it is a step in the right direction. Visiting teams and their supporters have many times been led astray by the name of the club, and have journeyed either by car or train to Newton Heath only to find that they were miles away from the home of the club.

"A mistake of this kind not very long ago put a team in a very awkward position. They reached the old ground in North Road, and then found it a difficult matter to procure conveyances to take them across to Clayton. The result was that the players reached the ground within five minutes of the fixed time for starting the game. We should imagine that the League clubs will support the change."

Why the name 'United' was chosen is not clear. Naturally, the name suggested togetherness, but it is also worth remembering that the name United was very much in vogue during this period. Often sides are named after another successful club, for example names such as North End proved popular following Preston's successes in the 1880s and led to sides such as Glossop North End and Manchester North End, so it is possible the use of United by other significant sides may have had a bearing. In 1902 Sheffield United were FA Cup winners (and finalists in 1901 when the replay was played at Bolton). In fact the FA Cup final actually took place on 19th April 1902 with a replay on 26th April, and so the Yorkshire side were definitely in the headlines at this point.

Regardless of where it came from, the moment the name was chosen and the four main backers found, Manchester United propelled forward in a positive manner. By the start of May major changes were under way both within the running of the club and at the Bank Street ground. Due to its close relationship with the side at the time, the Evening News was keen to stress the changes. On 2nd May they reported:

"Dr. Bishop will now act as Chairman. The two open stands adjoining the present covered one are to be roofed, and the large open stand behind the Clayton goal is also to be covered. At the opposite end of

Three players well known in our region. George Ross made 366 League appearances for Bury before joining non-League Rochdale in 1906. Billy Meredith had a highly successful career with City and United but also played for Stalybridge Celtic during the First World War. David 'Di' Jones played for Newton Heath before they joined the League, then Bolton, then City from 1898 until his shock death in 1902 - he was injured in a public practice match and died a week later.

the ground the work of erecting a new stand has already commenced. It has been decided to reserve the existing covered stand for donors and moderately high priced season ticket holders, and amongst the new arrangement on this particular stand will be a number of plush seated chairs. These, when the game is not in progress, will be stored in a room which is to be provided for the purpose. The dressing rooms and the referee's room are also to be considerably improved."

Some supporters today may compare the treatment of the donors and wealthier supporters as being typical of Manchester United's modern day image, however this is a little unfair. Back in 1902 these people saved the club from extinction and were far from the 'prawn sandwich' brigade Roy Keane spoke of. They deserved to be looked after and the United of 1902 certainly tried to do all it could to look after those men. One of these investors was brewer John Henry Davies. Davies was a director of Walker & Homfrays and of the Manchester Brewery Company, while his wife was the daughter of Henry Tate from the Tate & Lyle sugar company. According to United's own publications, he was not particularly interested in football until he met up with Harry Stafford in 1901.

Legend has it that Stafford had taken his St. Bernard Dog, Major, to the 1901 St. James's Hall bazaar to raise funds, and that the dog had a collection box fastened around its neck. The dog was allowed to roam around the stalls collecting money, but somehow it went missing. Eventually, It seems the dog was found by Davies and, recognising that this dog must have had an owner and was not a stray, he set about trying to find the owner. Ultimately Davies located Stafford and the brewer started to ask Newton Heath's captain about the collection tin. Stafford explained about the Heathens' financial worries and Davies became one of the wealthy backers in Stafford's plan to save the club in 1902. In addition, Stafford gave Davies the dog for his daughter to look after. Both Davies and Major the dog were regarded as the real saviours of the club, and Davies did go on to first save then transform the club, however once he passed away during the 1920s, United struggled financially.

It is possible Davies already knew of the benefits Chesters brewery had gained by their close relationship with City. The Blues used a public house owned by Chesters as their HQ and the brewery had exclusive rights to sell beer at the ground. Clearly, in the days before sponsorship and shirt advertising linking up with a football club would not have brought the kind of attention to a company present day support would, but simply the opportunity of selling beer at the ground, advertising in the club programme, and so on would prove of financial benefit.

By August 1902 a new Manchester United was ready to compete in the League and there was much optimism. On 22nd August 1902 the **Manchester Evening News** commented on a topic that was still causing some discussion amongst fans – the name change. Surprisingly, many supporters were voicing concern about the new name and so the **Evening News** tried to explain the advantages. The 'paper tried to be positive:

"Changing the name of the club was not at all palatable to many of the old supporters, but a change of name worked wonders in the neighbourhood of Hyde Road, and there is every likelihood of the same happening at Clayton."

On 6th September the first League game under the new title ended in a 1-0 victory at Gainsborough Trinity, and the following week a crowd of around 20,000 watched another 1-0 victory (over Burton United) for the new United in a much improved Bank Street. The size of

MANCHESTER'S GREAT FOOTBALL DAY: SCENES AT HYDE-ROAD.

Above: **The first Division One Manchester derby was eagerly anticipated. A crowd recorded as 40,000 packed into City's Hyde Road ground as City defeated United 3-0 on 1st December 1906.**

Left: **The first Division One derby match to be staged in Clayton saw a 1-1 draw between United and City in 1907. Note the supporters sat on the roof.**

the crowd was viewed as being remarkable for the side with the *Manchester Evening Chronicle* believing it was a record:

"The gate the club drew on Saturday was such as to fill the hearts of the officials with glee. I have no means of knowing but I doubt if Newton Heath ever had a 20,000 gate except for a special match."

United were on the march.

Elsewhere around Manchester the various clubs were having mixed fortunes. Bury, despite being Cup winners in 1900, were apparently having a dreadful season in terms of attendance. The *Manchester Evening News* of 19th April 1902 reported:

"If gates can be taken as any criterion, interest in the doings of Bury seems to be on the wane. Recently the gate receipts at Gigg Lane have been remarkably low, and Saturday's engagement with the Wolves was no exception. There were only about 2,500 spectators and the receipts amounted to £35."

Despite the poor attendance the report went on to talk about the generous nature of Bury folk and, with reference to the Ibrox disaster, detailed:

"A collection was taken for the fund which's being raised on behalf of the sufferers from the terrible catastrophe at Glasgow. Despite the poor attendance, the sum of £8 odd was raised, and this was increased by another £1 at the reserves match on Monday evening."

For non-League Stalybridge the financial situation was reported as *"not at all favourable"*, while Stockport County were suddenly displaying good form on the pitch:

"Now that Stockport County are doomed to apply again for re-election to the Second Division, the players have displayed form which, if shown earlier in the season would have placed the club in a respectable position in the table."

Over at Manchester City's Hyde Road ground success on the pitch was poor, while the financial situation was incredible. The Blues were relegated at the end of the 1901-02 season but the Manchester Evening News highlighted a situation for perhaps the first time that still rings true:

"It is of course generally known that Manchester City Football Club have done remarkably well in the matter of 'gates' but few people will be prepared for the astonishing statement that the receipts for the First Division matches at Hyde Road amount to nearly £7,000. There are not two clubs in the League that have done better from this point of view, and the publication of the figures will only intensify the regret that a club which can command such support will have to spend next season in the Second Division."

Modern day supporters would probably see this as 'typical City'.

The following seasons saw football develop on a much more professional scale with City determined to return to the top division; Manchester United keen to make their mark; Bury enjoying their dominance of the local scene; and in Stockport it was clear County needed to overcome a number of problems if they too were to become an established side. For each of those sides the following decade or so was to bring some significant success. Stockport was perhaps the side that struggled most, but by 1914 they had established themselves as a Second Division side – something no one seriously anticipated back in 1902.

In 1903 Manchester City won the Second Division title for the second time while United's first season ended in a highly respectable fifth place finish. The real stars of the season though were once again Bury.

Monday, April 27, 1903

CITY FOOTBALL GROUND BROKEN INTO: Depredations By Boys.

Yesterday evening the secretary's office on the Manchester City Football Club's ground, Hyde Road, was broken into and ransacked.

Three boys suspected to be connected with the affair were brought up at the City Police Court this morning.

Their names were Joseph Harrison, Harry Davenport and Leonard Foulds; each gave an address in Ardwick.

It is alleged they first broke into the premises of a stonemason and afterwards got on the football ground. A bundle of season tickets, some stamps, a pocket knife, keys and other small articles were afterwards missed from the club. Many windows were broken.

Each boy was ordered to receive six strokes of the birch rod.

In 1903 young offenders breaking into City's ground were punished with the birch.

Billy Gillespie scores twice as City defeat Bury 3-1 in the Division One derby between the 1903 Cup winners and the eventual 1904 FA Cup holders.

From the start of the season Bury impressed and on 18th October 1902, after a six match unbeaten run, they headed the Division One table. The lead was only held briefly as form dipped a little, and sadly they ended the season in eighth place – their worst position since 1900 – but in the FA Cup they shone, just as they had three years earlier.

Victories over Wolves, Sheffield United, and Notts County brought them a semi-final appearance against Aston Villa. Before a Goodison Park crowd of around 50,000 Bury took a thirteenth minute lead. This was increased to 2-0 three minutes after the interval, then in the 60th minute Billy Richards made it 3-0. Prior to the final there was a little controversy as Bury and their opponents Derby County both traditionally wore white shirts and blue shorts. According to Bury officials, the Lancashire side were adamant that they should wear white as they had worn white longer than the Rams, but Derby countered 'We are the older organisation'. With no solution in sight the sides tried to get the Football Association to make a decision and, as perhaps everybody in Bury expected, the FA chose to pass the decision back to the two sides. Ultimately, commonsense prevailed and both decided to wear an alternative strip. Derby chose red shirts and black shorts, while Bury chose the extremely light shade of blue traditionally worn by Manchester City for their shirts.

Cambridge Blue, as both Bury and City described it at the time, was an unusual colour for football sides and, as far as can be identified, Bury were the first side to find success wearing that colour. Bury's shorts were navy blue. Potentially the selection of Cambridge Blue may have had something to do with the Cambridge roots of the game.

Bury's experience in 1900 seemed to work in their favour as they took the opportunity to methodically plan their excursion for the final. They chose to stay from Thursday through to Saturday at the White Swan Hotel, Upper Norwood – a short distance from the Crystal Palace ground. The aim was to guarantee the players a good sound sleep in the days leading up to the final. Derby County, meanwhile, did not leave their Derbyshire headquarters until Friday afternoon, having trained in the morning.

For supporters the excitement was high and on the Friday afternoon and the Saturday morning seven special trains left the stations at Knowsley Street and Bolton Street for the journey to London. Some have estimated that around 2,000 Bury fans made the journey. It has to be stressed that this in itself was a major achievement. Money was tight and most working men in Bury would have had enormous problems trying to get time off work. Inevitably, some factories closed for the Saturday – remember most industry continued to operate on Saturday mornings – but the whole concept of holidays was yet to be properly established. Because of this travel to London was extremely rare and most of the travellers would have been travelling for either their first time or, if they had been one of the lucky ones in 1900, for the second time in their life.

The London media made much of their arrival in the city and boasted about the amount of beer and whisky stored at each mainline London station awaiting the arrival of the Lancastrians. St. Pancras alone had laid aside three rooms for Bury fans with 40 barrels of beer, 200 cases of bottled beer and a plentiful supply of whisky.

While some Bury fans would have enjoyed this aspect of the trip, it is also true that many others would have wanted to see London's sights. According to the **Bury Guardian**:

"Whichever way one turned, one met Bury people sporting their colours. It was impossible to get away from residents of one's own town."

BURY F.C.
WINNERS OF THE F.A. CUP, 1902-03.

J. Johnson, J. Lindsay, F. Thorpe, H. Montieth, G. W. Ross (Captain), J. McEwan. W. Richards, W. Wood, C. Sagar, J. Leeming, J. Plant.

Inside the ground the *Bury Times* seemed delighted with the turnout from the media:

"Quite a number of photographers were in evidence, while a cinematograph was taken to the top of one of the stands. The Derby men were the first to take the field and were greeted with a roar that was very easily outclassed when the Red Rose representatives were led on by captain George Ross."

The comment about the cinematograph is interesting as it is clear this match was filmed, however no surviving footage has yet been traced. The same situation exists for 1904 when City's cup final against Bolton was filmed. According to the *Manchester Evening Chronicle* of 25th April 1904, two days after the final, footage was on show:

"Cinematograph pictures of the match are on view at the St. James' Hall. The pictures are excellent and Meredith is shown scoring the winning goal."

The 1903 game itself has often been claimed to be a totally one-sided affair with Bury easily outclassing Derby, although it is fair to say it did not start that way. Although the Shakers took the lead in the twentieth minute via George Ross, the score remained 1-0 until three minutes into the second half. The Derby 'keeper Jack Fryer was suffering from a groin strain leading some to suggest post-match that he should not have played, however pre-match every one connected with Derby wanted to see him take to the field.

Fryer struggled, especially after receiving a knock while trying to stop Bury's second goal. He was forced to receive treatment, and Bury scored a third while Charlie Morris deputised. Fryer, limping badly, valiantly returned to the nets believing he could keep his side in the match, but a fourth goal followed then, after 68 minutes the Derby 'keeper felt he could no longer play on and, as he trudged off towards the dressing rooms, Bury netted number five. A sixth goal came after 75 minutes, and the match ended 6-0. This remains the largest winning margin in the FA Cup Final.

The newspapers were inevitably full of stories connected with the final, but sadly the general comments of the day tended to focus on Derby's failure rather than Bury's success. The **Morning Leader** was typical of the coverage:

"As a Southampton [Bury's opponents in 1900] director remarked after the game, 'our display was bad enough, but at least the four goals against us were good ones. This was more like opera bouffe'."

The **Daily Chronicle**: *"Briefly and candidly the cup final was a fiasco. Nothing like it had ever been seen before. Bury defeated Derby County by six goals to none, and it might have been twenty. That it was not is testimony to the mercy exercised by the victors rather than to the defence of the losers."*

Celebrations followed for Bury at the Trocadero in Piccadilly Circus, then the Tavistock Hotel where the club stayed until Monday. A League game at West Bromwich Albion followed before the Shakers made it back to Bury on Monday night. Bury's modern day press officer Gordon Sorfleet believes this was a highly significant moment in the history of the region:

"To win the FA Cup twice in only four seasons and by a 10-0 margin over the two games says a lot about the strength of Bury at the time. Unfortunately not that many fans could make it to either final, remember Bury was a working class team and we didn't have the money then – and we certainly don't have it now – to really build on that win. The success was real achievement and there were thousands upon thousands at the train station when the team came home. Can you imagine how great that felt for the town? The two finals were the first proper successes the town had ever known."

Inevitably the whole town celebrated and the **Bury Guardian** printed a small story its reporter claimed to have overheard on the Monday morning after the final, but before the homecoming, concerning a man who had been celebrating:

"A Bury Employer (to employee who has arrived late): Hullo, Jack, you are late this morning how is it? Employee: I had a dream, and overslept myself. Employer: What has that to do with it? Employee: Well, I dreamt I was at the Cup tie final. The game ended in a draw, and the referee ordered extra time. If it hadn't been for that extra time I should have been at work early."

Bury were the dominant force locally and later that month, on April 27th Bury collected the Lancashire Senior Cup after beating Everton 1-0 at Gigg Lane. Two days later the Shakers then drew 2-2 with Manchester City in the Manchester Senior Cup Final and jointly held the trophy for twelve months with the Blues. The Shakers therefore won all three major cup competitions available to Manchester's clubs within the space of ten days. It was a phenomenal achievement. Gordon Sorfleet:

Above: **The 1903 FA Cup final ball.**

Right: **The FA Cup won by Bury in 1900 & 1903, City in 1904 and United in 1909.**

HOME-COMING OF THE BURY TEAM.

(From the "Daily Dispatch.")

"You have to put it all into context. Bury only joined the League in 1894 while the two Manchester clubs had been members since 1892, and so promotion in the first season and two FA Cup wins within those first nine years is an achievement I can't think of any other team matching, and it can certainly never happen again. Sadly, I do think this was the turning point for football though. I believe that the money men started to take over – even then – and when you look at the sides who won the trophy in the years that followed they were mainly big city teams."

Sorfleet's views appear correct, as it was not until 1912 that a 'town' won the trophy again when Barnsley defeated West Bromwich Albion. From a pure Manchester viewpoint the transformation between relatively small town success to big city success is easily demonstrated with the two year period starting with Bury's 1903 victory. In 1904 Manchester City won the FA Cup for the first time in their history and narrowly missed out on the title in the same season. According to the **Manchester Evening Chronicle** over 30,000 travelled from Lancashire to London, while in the days leading up to the final the same newspaper treated the final as a significant moment in the development of the region. Their coverage contained many aspects on the periphery of the game, as perhaps a modern day tabloid would, with the most entertaining story seeing the newspaper employ a 'phrenologist' to determine whether City or their opponents Bolton would win based on

At the time they called it the Lancashire Invasion - these City fans took time out to visit St Paul's Cathedral while in London for the 1904 final.

Manchester City's players and officials when the team won the F.A. Cup in 1904. Left to right, front row: Hendren, Billy Meredith, Booth. Centre Ashworth, A. Turnbull, Gillespie, Threlfall, Frost, J. Broad (trainer). Back: Burgess, Livingstone, Dr. Holmes, Hillman, T. Maley (secy.), Hynds, and Dearden

their intellect. The phrenologist determined that City were the brainier side based on the shape and size of their heads!

"The Lancastrian Invasion", as the 1904 final became known as in London, saw Manchester sport dominate newspaper coverage for the first time. The ***Manchester Evening Chronicle*** found the Londoners reaction to City and opponents Bolton's arrival humorous:

"The true character of the London invasion could not be gleaned until midnight and during the early hours of Saturday morning. At Euston, St. Pancras, King's Cross and Marylebone, the trains, heavy laden, steamed in continuously. 'What a cheer!' I heard a jovial porter say, shortly after midnight. 'This is great, ain't it? Blimey! Did you ever see so many pubs in bottles? What, oh! Don't they grub?' And truly, the trippers upheld the tradition of the North. Each little party seemed to have brought their own stack of provisions for the weekend. Nine gallon barrels of beer, stone jars of whisky and big baskets filled with 'baggins' were almost as plentiful as blackberries in Autumn, while there could never have been as many toastmasters on Euston station before, 'Good Health!' rang perpetually in one's ears. 'Hooray!', 'Play up, City!'

The excited Mancunians would have re-enforced their stereotypical view of the North with their flatcaps, beer, and odd-looking food. Many Mancunians decided to shelter at the train stations as the London weather was particularly poor early on. St. Pancras station was reported to have had more people packed onto its platforms that morning than at any other earlier time, while at least sixteen thousand people arrived at Euston during the night with nowhere else to go.

In 2008 this image was discovered in the collection of Billy Meredith's grandson with a comment on the back saying that this was City's train for the 1904 FA Cup final.

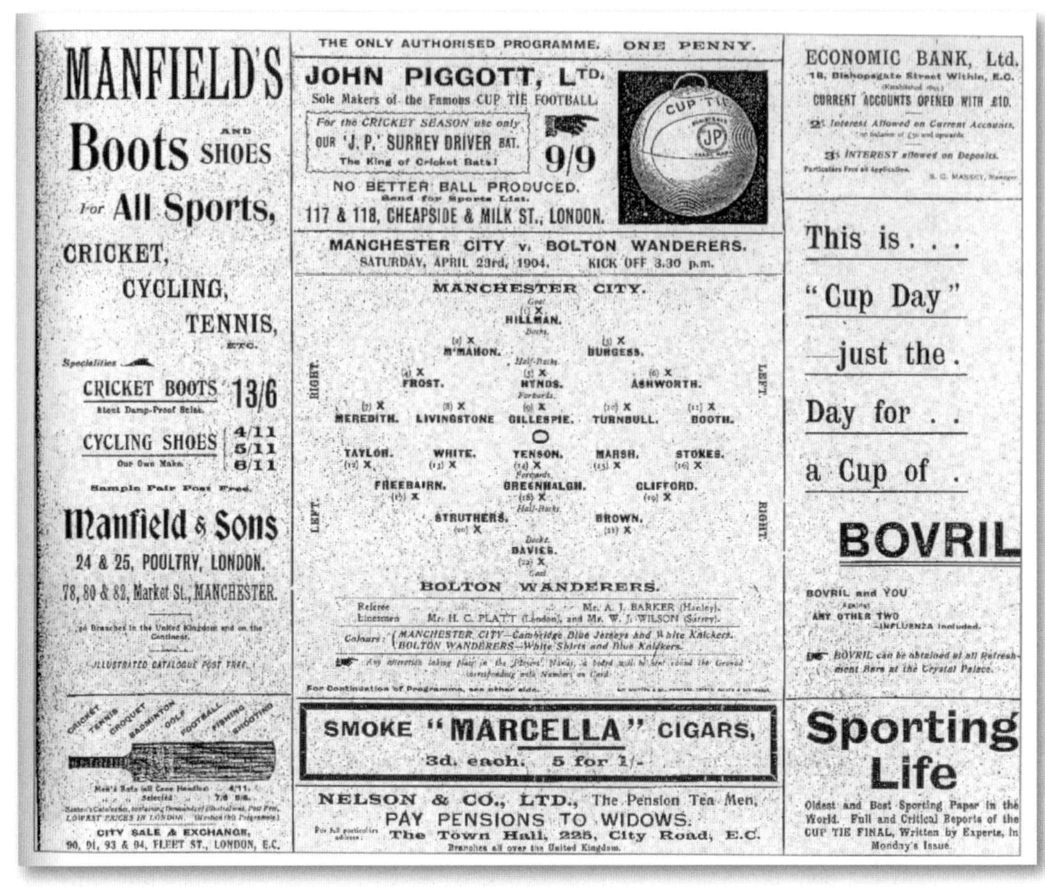

MANFIELD'S Boots AND SHOES For All Sports, CRICKET, CYCLING, TENNIS, ETC.

Specialities

CRICKET BOOTS 13/6

CYCLING SHOES 4/11 5/11 6/11

Our Own Make.

Sample Pair Post Free.

Manfield & Sons

24 & 25, POULTRY, LONDON.

78, 80 & 82, Market St., MANCHESTER.

ILLUSTRATED CATALOGUE POST FREE.

THE ONLY AUTHORISED PROGRAMME. ONE PENNY.

JOHN PIGGOTT, LTD.

Sole Makers of the Famous CUP TIE FOOTBALL.

For the CRICKET SEASON use only OUR 'J. P.' SURREY DRIVER BAT. The King of Cricket Bats!

9/9

NO BETTER BALL PRODUCED.

117 & 118, CHEAPSIDE & MILK ST., LONDON.

MANCHESTER CITY v. BOLTON WANDERERS.

SATURDAY, APRIL 23rd, 1904. KICK OFF 3.30 p.m.

MANCHESTER CITY.

Goal (1) X HILLMAN.

Backs (2) X M'MAHON. (3) X BURGESS.

Half-Backs (4) X FROST. (5) X HYNDS. (6) X ASHWORTH.

Forwards (7) X MEREDITH. (8) X LIVINGSTONE (9) X GILLESPIE. (10) X TURNBULL. (11) X BOOTH.

TAYLOR. (12) X WHITE. (13) X TENSON. (14) X MARSH. (15) X STOKES. (16) X

Forwards FREEBAIRN. (17) X GREENHALGH. (18) X CLIFFORD. (19) X

Half-Backs STRUTHERS. (20) X BROWN. (21) X

Backs DAVIES. (22) X Goal

BOLTON WANDERERS.

Referee Mr. A. J. BARKER (Hanley).

Linesmen Mr. H. C. PLATT (London), and Mr. W. J. WILSON (Surrey).

Colours: MANCHESTER CITY—Cambridge Blue Jerseys and White Knickers. BOLTON WANDERERS—White Shirts and Blue Knickers.

For Continuation of Programme, see other side.

ECONOMIC BANK, Ltd.

18, Bishopsgate Street Within, E.C.

CURRENT ACCOUNTS OPENED WITH £10.

2% Interest Allowed on Current Accounts.

3% INTEREST allowed on Deposits.

This is . . . "Cup Day" —just the . Day for . . a Cup of . BOVRIL

BOVRIL and YOU Against ANY OTHER TWO —INFLUENZA included.

BOVRIL can be obtained at all Refreshment Bars at the Crystal Palace.

CRICKET TENNIS CROQUET BADMINTON GOLF FOOTBALL FISHING SHOOTING

CITY SALE & EXCHANGE, 90, 91, 93 & 94, FLEET ST., LONDON, E.C.

SMOKE "MARCELLA" CIGARS, 3d. each. 5 for 1/-

NELSON & CO., LTD., The Pension Tea Men, PAY PENSIONS TO WIDOWS. The Town Hall, 225, City Road, E.C.

Branches all over the United Kingdom.

Sporting Life

Oldest and Best Sporting Paper in the World. Full and Critical Reports of the CUP TIE FINAL, Written by Experts, in Monday's Issue.

The team sheet taken from the 1904 FA Cup final programme.

Reports suggested though that those Mancunians who left the safety of the stations took flight in a similar manner to a young bird leaving its nest for the first time as the Blues fans were eager to leave, but uncertain what they would find. Gradually, as more left their nest others plucked up courage to discover what London was really like. By ten o'clock the sun was shining and most Blues had taken flight.

The journey to London was also a great adventure for City's officials. They obtained a horse-drawn carriage and, with eleven or twelve on the roof, and around six inside, they travelled south. Interestingly, the journey was not only made by City's directors, but they were joined by many other leading figures from the region. Former City secretary-manager Sam Ormerod travelled – even though he was now County's manager – and JJ Bentley, the former Bolton secretary-manager and future United manager, was also on board the City carriage.

The Cup Final itself was fairly tight with the Blues beating Bolton 1-0 thanks to a disputed goal from captain Billy Meredith. Incidentally one of the most newsworthy incidents of the game came straight after the goal when a City fan invaded the pitch as part of his celebration. The police raced on to the field after him and once caught he was seen being led away, however the *Sporting Chronicle* revealed that the supporter had so impressed the police with his support and devotion to City that they released him and allowed him to find a spot on the terraces – it is doubtful they would have been so supportive in later City finals.

A scene from the 1904 FA Cup final between City and Bolton.

Once the Blues won the Cup, the most significant aspect was the homecoming itself. Within the city most Mancunians were keen to stage some form of celebration, however the city council and senior figures within the constabulary were not interested. They argued that too much time had already been spent on football and that Manchester was an industrial city and simply had to get back to work. Fortunately the people thought differently.

The story behind this perhaps helps to explain why the game eventually got hold of Mancunians in a way that today makes it perhaps the one industry that Manchester is known for more than any other. Although Bury had already been twice successful in the FA Cup, City's success in 1904 was the first time the main conurbation had had reason to celebrate. Prior to 1904 Lancashire CCC had found success but cricket did not appeal to the greater part of Manchester's population, plus Lancashire was not seen as a pure Manchester institution. Other major activities occurring around the city had focused on one-off events such as major races at the Manchester Racecourse, or festivals lasting several days – a Manchester Wheelers cycling festival attracted around 50,000 to Alexandra Park in 1883 according to some sources. The FA Cup success was different because it was the first time a major sporting organisation appealing to all areas of society from the city had achieved national acclaim.

Although most Mancunians were keen to see the conquering City side bring home the Cup, the civic leaders and police rather surprisingly refused to support any plans for celebration. When a civic reception was suggested Manchester's leaders gave a response along the lines of 'Manchester is an industrial city and has no time for merriment'. When asked about a special home-coming, the Chief Constable retorted, *"I am not interested!"* It was all quite sad but, perhaps they simply did not understand what positive impact football could have on the lives of Mancunians. Maybe they were concerned that too much time had already been spent organising the trips to London and so on.

Unfortunately for the Police Chief, the people of Manchester were interested in welcoming back their heroes and huge crowds took to the streets of Britain's first industrial city to see its trophy winners.

The homecoming took place two days after the final as City had been forced to play their crucial final match of the season on the Monday night following the final. They travelled to Liverpool for their game over the weekend, were defeated 1-0 by Everton, then travelled back to Manchester for a Monday night homecoming. The Blues missed their scheduled train, and so the Cheshire Lines Railway Company put on an extra train from Liverpool. As the news travelled that the Blues were travelling people turned out at some of the stations on the route to cheer the side on. At Warrington Station a large crowd gathered and Billy Meredith leaned out of a carriage window holding out the Cup to let everyone catch a sight of the trophy.

In Manchester, the parade started at 9.30 in the evening. Sadly, the defeat at Everton caused City to finish the season as runners-up to Sheffield Wednesday. Nevertheless, this was still Manchester's highest League position at the time.

When the Blues arrived back at Manchester a horse drawn carriage, driven by Albert Alexander senior – a man who would later be vice-chairman of the Blues and would also lead United's homecoming in 1909 – took the players on the first homecoming parade the city had known. According to the newspaper coverage the parade saw a large force of mounted police take the lead; followed by the St. Joseph's Industrial School Band; then came a stage coach dressed in Cambridge Blue and White carrying the players, led by Meredith lifting the Cup at regular intervals; this was followed by a four-in-hand carrying the directors and press. Then came the ground committee – an important group of enthusiasts who basically managed City's Hyde Road ground and performed a variety of duties from stewarding to the upkeep of the pitch – then came mounted police. The procession travelled from Central Station, to Peter Street, Deansgate, Market Street, Dale Street, London Road, Ardwick Green, and ended at the Ardwick Conservative Club (not, surprisingly, the Hyde Road ground).

The **Athletic News** followed the triumphal procession:

"As soon as they caught sight of the trophy trimmed with blue and white ribbons which Meredith now and then raised above his head, they gave vent to prodigious cheering. Most of the windows of the upper stories were packed with people whose plaudits, added to by the blowing of a bugle here and there, and the music of the band, made a deafening sound.

"To the accompaniment of incessant cheering, the procession made its way at walking pace down Dale Street where what might be called the welcome of the middle-classes was exchanged for that of the proletariat. It came from rough working men and larrikins and beshawled women and children in arms and hand, and was hearty if not heartier than had gone before."

As can be seen from that comment, City's homecoming united Mancunians in a way no other success had managed. That day Manchester recognised the benefits of footballing success, and that day Manchester found its sporting identity. Thousands of ordinary people mixed with wealthier citizens on the streets and there was nothing the police or the city council could do to stop them. The St. Joseph's Band played "See the Conquering Hero Come" but reports told of how they almost lost their instruments as the police struggled to clear a path. According to the **Manchester Evening Chronicle** every building was packed with onlookers. Special mention was made of the packed windows at the Midland Hotel and then later the article talked about the latter stages of the journey:

"In Piccadilly, the scene was one which beggars description. The windows of the hotels were packed, electric standards and the statues on the Infirmary Esplanade [those occupying modern day Piccadilly] were invaded, flags were waved, and bugles were sounded. All vehicular traffic was at a standstill. The tops of the tramcars were utilised as stands for viewing the procession, and all along London Road, Downing Street, and Ardwick Green the same spectacle of indescribable enthusiasm prevailed.

"Some alarm was occasioned in Downing Street by some well-meaning enthusiast discharging a squib, which shot across the road alighting amongst the people."

Reports describe a wide range of people from different social classes taking to the streets while the **Manchester Evening Chronicle** claimed:

"There is nothing in the annals of football that will compare with the magnificent reception which was accorded the Manchester City football team on the occasion of their return to Manchester last night in the proud position of holders of the English Cup for the first time in Manchester's career. Notwithstanding the lateness of their arrival, the whole population of the city seemed to have turned out to do them honour. The enthusiasm recalled 'Mafficking (sic) Night'."

City manager Tom Maley summed up the importance of the moment accurately when he told officials and the press that he was deeply moved by the reception and *"the appreciation of the people of Manchester of what [City} had been able to achieve."* He added: *"Perhaps love of sport had something to do with the bringing together of so great a gathering, but love of Manchester, had much more to do with it."*

A pre-League team group from 1911-12 of Rochdale. Jack Reynolds *(front row, far left)* **later became famous as manager of Dutch side Ajax (1915-25 & 1928-47).**

Two days after football had dominated all Mancunian activity, the *Manchester Evening Chronicle* claimed that Manchester was now the second city of the Empire. It was a bold statement, but it was directly connected with what had occurred earlier that week. Football really had changed the atmosphere for all in the world's first industrial city and the following January the people of Manchester ensured the players were thanked for their boost to the region's image. At a special commemorative dinner held at the Grand Hotel on Aytoun Street on 9th January 1905, the players, trainer Jimmy Broad, and Secretary/Manager Tom Maley were presented with commemorative gold watches paid for by collections amongst Mancunians.

Mancunians were suffering great hardship at the time, both financially and health wise, and so the fact that fans performed collections and helped raise funds to recognise City's achievement is very significant. This act alone proves how important the game had become to the people of the region.

The winter of 1904/5 was particularly harsh with many locals dying of cold and malnutrition, and unemployment was high. It was not a good time to look after your family in the city. A relief fund was set up and popular music hall entertainer and supporter of City at the final (he would also support United and is claimed to be the man responsible for United's 1909 Cup Final shirt design) George Robey, brought a 'Team of Internationals' to Hyde Road on 23rd January to raise money. At that game, and others at Hyde Road, blankets were carried around the pitch for people to throw coins into. Although City was by this stage a wealthy and successful club, many Mancunians had little else to cheer. Football gave Mancunians a successful escape from the grim reality of life in Edwardian Manchester.

ATTENDANCE DETAIL
SEASON BY SEASON - 1902-1904

Season	City	United	Bury	Stockport
1902-3	16000	11875	7850	4100
1903-4	20000	18775	6675	3800

LEAGUE POSITION
SEASON BY SEASON - 1902-1904

Season	City	United	Bury	Stockport
1902-3	19	23	8	35
1903-4	2	21	12	34

Haddon]

J. W. SUTCLIFFE.

A Yorkshireman with the distinction of having played for England under both the Rugby and Association codes. Standing 6ft., and weighing 13½st., he has to be reckoned with as a defending force. Has played in the ranks of the Bolton Wanderers, Millwall, and Manchester United. Joined Argyle at the end of last season. His judgment and resource are as good as ever. Obtained his Rugby cap for England against the Maoris in 1888-9.

During the early years of the Twentieth Century rugby and football continued to co-exist. United goalkeeper John Sutcliffe was also an accomplished rugby player.

CHAPTER EIGHT

SCANDAL & UNION

Why wasn't evidence allowed to be heard from Meredith? Why wasn't the public allowed to see the evidence? Why was Leake not suspended for the assault (with others) on Turnbull in the passage after the Aston Villa game? And why hadn't Leake brought his charges of bribery immediately, instead of waiting until a charge was hanging over himself? The Athletic News, 1906

WHEN Bury won the FA Cup in 1900 and 1903 their success seemed appropriate. It seemed fair. Bury were viewed as the type of football team the FA encouraged. They represented their local community, their ground was in a pleasant location, and they seemed to follow tradition. There was some talk of Bury being fortunate, but in the main the focus was all on events on the field rather than off it.

By Summer 1904 however the FA felt the game was changing in a way they did not like, and it seems there was a fear that the balance of power was to move towards big city, wealthy clubs, with Manchester City's 1904 FA Cup success proving too much for some to bear.

Prior to City's win the FA Cup had been won by some big city sides – Aston Villa, West Bromwich Albion, both Sheffield clubs, Wolves, both Nottingham clubs, and Spurs – but most of these were viewed as the game's aristocracy while others were still relatively minor in stature. City was different. The Blues were perceived as being more professional in their outlook, and their rapid rise – from their reformation as Manchester City in 1894 to Cup winners in ten seasons – was viewed suspiciously by some.

In 1903-04 City not only won the FA Cup but they also finished runners up in the League Championship race (Manchester's highest League position at the time). The previous season they had been a Second Division side.

This transformation caused some to see the Blues as a nouveau riche club determined to buy success. It was well known across the game that City had a number of high profile supporters including the newspaper baron Edward Hulton, who had been on the Board for a while and whose newspapers tended to promote the northern, professional clubs' views. The Football Association, 'a southern body dominated by amateurs' according to northerners at the time, were unhappy with Manchester's success. According to John Harding's biography of Billy Meredith, ***Football Wizard***, the FA believed that clubs such as City were too professional and that there was a real danger of football's amateur, sporting, nature being lost forever. In truth it had already gone, but many FA Councillors liked to keep up the pretence.

As far as the FA were concerned, City's rapid development had to have come via illegitimate means. They decided to investigate and within two weeks of the FA Cup final the FA secretary, F.J. Wall, and a member of the FA General Council, John Lewis, arrived at Hyde Road demanding to see the club's books. They spent the whole close season examining City's accounts determined to find proof of illegal wages and bonuses, yet found nothing tangible.

The FA did eventually find discrepancies in the transfers of Frank Norgrove and Irvine Thornley from Glossop - there were forged receipts for unusual payments coinciding with the players' transfers. The FA decided these were actually signing on fees paid to the players in excess of the £10 maximum then allowed.

Previously, the FA had insisted on maximum signing on fees and, of course, there was the £4 maximum wage rule. Most First Division clubs regularly broke the rules but some were adept at balancing the books and not bringing due attention to themselves, as Meredith once said: *"Of course clubs are not punished for breaking laws. They are punished for being found out."*

In October 1904 City were fined £250 and Hyde Road was ordered to be closed for two games. In addition, three directors were banned for three years, while the Finance Director was suspended for life. This was a major blow for the club and for the men involved, especially as three of the men – Joshua Parlby, John Chapman, and Lawrence Furniss – had been instrumental in City's development. Furniss was perhaps the most important man in the club's development, and had been with the side since the early 1880s.

The player Irvine Thornley was suspended for the rest of the season. He had been with the club since April and was already popular with the supporters, however his transfer had already brought him great hardship. His move from Glossop to City had caused him to give up his involvement with his family's butchery business. Perhaps that is the reason he is believed to have received an illegal payment – maybe City recognised that the player was sacrificing a share in a lucrative business for the uncertainties of professional football in a heavily industrialised city.

Despite the off the pitch problems, City had a good 1904-05. In fact the Blues challenged for the League title again and, with three games to go, they were three points behind leaders Everton. It was an intriguing situation, especially as on 21st April City and Everton would meet at Hyde Road.

Sadly, the game was ill tempered and, although City won 2-0 with goals from Tom Hynds and George Livingstone, an off the ball incident turned the game into a major news story. Everton's Tom Booth brutally 'flattened' City's Frank Booth. The Manchester man retaliated and both players were cautioned, but Mancunians felt this was totally unfair. The police had to escort the players from the pitch and it was perhaps only the fact that City had defeated the League leaders that stopped the situation from deteriorating further.

City were now only one point behind Everton with two games remaining, but Newcastle were also a threat. Any of those sides could win the title, and on the final day Newcastle were away at Middlesbrough while the Blues travelled to FA Cup winners Aston Villa. Everton were League leaders by a point but their season had finished.

At Villa Park, the home side had no time for any of Manchester's sides and they tended to share the FA's view of City - young upstarts with no tradition. As an analogy with the modern era it is safe to say that Villa were the aristocracy of football, whereas City were perceived in a similar manner to Abramovich's Chelsea, where money was no object and tradition was irrelevant. In the eyes of many, they had appeared from nowhere to challenge the establishment and at this point in football history, the establishment would always win.

Villa were determined to put City in their place and unfortunately the Blues made it easy for them. City conceded three goals and struggled, but two second half goals brought the Blues back into contention. During the final thirty minutes the game became progressively more violent with City star Sandy Turnbull seemingly involved in every incident. The **Bolton Football Field** reporter outlined his view:

"Turnbull was in his dourest dribbling mood, dashing about the ball with his whole heart set on victory. Leake found him a real hard opponent and, becoming annoyed at the rough impact, gathered up a handful of dirt and hurled it at the City man. Turnbull was not hurt and responded with an acknowledgement favoured by the bourgeoisie - thrusting two fingers in a figurative manner at the Villa man. He then says that Leake appeared to look towards the referee as though appealing, and not catching his eye, 'gave Turnbull a backhander'. The latter immediately responded with his fists and Leake was restrained by his fellow players from retaliating further."

Although Turnbull had developed a reputation for a rough style of play it appears that he was not the guilty one this time. Unfortunately, Leake was viewed as a gentleman and many were convinced that he would only react, not provoke. The Villa biased **Sports Argus** tried to convince its readership that Leake was entirely innocent and that he had merely enquired what Turnbull was doing rather than throw dirt at him and give him a 'backhander'. It also stated that the City man had hit Leake at least twice. No one else saw this of course.

The game continued but frequent fights broke out, spoiling any chance of City equalising and ultimately the realisation dawned that the Blues had lost out in the title race. However, the controversy did not end with the final whistle. The **Bolton Football Field** reported:

"Turnbull was coming off the ground (I think he was almost the first of the City players) and was going down the covered passage to the visitors' dressing room when someone, not a player, sprang out from the urinal and grabbed Turnbull, pulled him inside the Villa dressing room and the door was shut behind him. I thought the whole thing was in fun until, within a few seconds, the door was opened and Turnbull was pitched out heavily, by whom I could not see. He was yelling with pain and fright, and he had obviously been badly handled for his right cheek was grazed with a black mark or dirt (something like a cyclist describes as a cinder rash) and he had a mark on his ribs where he had been kicked."

Turnbull had been the victim of a deliberate attack by Villa men but incredibly the **Birmingham Sports Argus** tried to justify it. Significantly, it was not merely the Villa players and employees who were attacking the City men as police had to be called into the ground to protect the Blues. Leaving Villa Park was also a nightmare as an angry mob stoned the City party. A season that had promised so much ended in disgraceful scenes at a ground that was supposed to be one of the best in the Country, against a team that was supposedly one to respect.

The FA had to act and they set up a special committee to investigate, but it quickly became apparent that the investigations were out to identify problems with City, not focus on the Villa violence. Meeting behind closed doors, the committee interviewed player after player in their quest for the full facts. This seemed rather suspicious, especially to the northern newspapers who were now convinced that the committee were fishing for a bigger catch than merely a disrepute charge against one or two players. With the FA meeting in secret rumour spread throughout football, with most northerners convinced the 'southern' FA would make City the scapegoats.

Eventually on 4th August 1905, a month before the new season started, the FA committee produced their surprising findings. Firstly, they suspended the referees of the games against Everton and Villa for a month each for failing to control the games. They then announced that Tom Booth of Everton would have a suspended sentence of one month, and that City's Sandy Turnbull would be suspended for one month. Amazingly, there was no mention of Villa's main protagonist Alec Leake, and then came the most shocking news of the whole affair:

"The Commissioners also reported on statements brought to their notice with regard to W. Meredith of Manchester having offered a sum of money to a player of Aston Villa to let Manchester City win the match. W. Meredith is suspended from football from 4th August until April 1906."

Mancunians were outraged that football's greatest player could be found guilty of bribery. Meredith told the press:

"I am entirely innocent and am suffering for others. Such an allegation as that of bribery is preposterous! I could never risk my reputation and future by such an action and I repeat that I never made such an offer. It is totally unjustifiable and grossly unfair. This sort of thing will demoralise Association Football. Manchester has not many friends among the Association officials and I doubt if the decision will be reversed or the suspension lessened if the whole case is reopened and enquired into."

He added that Aston Villa had too much influence within the FA and that: *"Manchester City is becoming too popular to suit some other clubs."*

The general feeling was that City had suffered because football in Manchester was simply too popular. Aston Villa supporter Simon Inglis covered the story in his 1980s review of football's major scandals, **Soccer in The Dock**, and he stated:

"Alec Leake was not even mentioned, even though it had been plainly stated that Turnbull had been assaulted by Villa players after the game. Small wonder therefore that in the eyes of many neutrals the FA appeared to bear a grudge against Manchester City, a nouveau riche club with no traditions. Villa, in contrast, were solidly reliable, brimming with honours and very much part of the football establishment. Some commentators noted caustically that Leake was an England international while the other players were not. Meredith meanwhile complained, 'Had I been anyone but a Welshman I should have been better dealt with.' But Harricus of **Athletic News** *said the FA's methods had seemed 'un-English, most autocratic and arbitrary."*

The Blues had suffered merely because of who they were and not through the actual actions, nevertheless the FA must have had some evidence to suggest that Meredith was guilty. Over time further details emerged that Leake had actually laughed off Meredith's alleged bribery attempt at the time, thinking it to be very much a joke. The FA commission heard a rumour of bribery and they started to investigate further. They found a 'responsible gentleman from Birmingham' who claimed he had overheard the conversation – it was never revealed who this man was. Leake was interrogated further and was apparently forced to admit that Meredith had attempted to bribe him. Meredith claimed that he had not but did admit to having a conversation with Leake. Instead of offering him £10, he claimed to have offered his congratulations to the Villa man for winning the FA Cup.

The matter did not end there, however. City were far from happy and the northern sporting press tended to support the view that their punishment had been unjust. They published many negative comments about the FA and its councillors became angry. They felt that their actions were right and, if anything, became more interested in the affairs of City because of the proclamation of innocence. They appointed an auditor, Tom Hindle, to keep a close watch on the club and report anything out of the ordinary. Because of the state of most leading clubs at the time, not only City, it was not long before Hindle became suspicious.

Meredith, while banned from all football activity, still appeared at Hyde Road asking for his wages and generally expecting the Blues to look after him:

"Though the FA suspended me, I felt strongly that my club would see that I was not the loser financially. At the beginning of the trouble it looked as if the club was going to recognise this, but later I found them shilly-shallying and putting me off until I got tired."

Understandably, for a man who had dedicated over ten years to the club he expected that club to care for him, especially when on the first day of the ban (4th August 1905) manager Tom Maley sent him a letter suggesting that he would always be a member of the City, but would have to 'lie low' until Hindle had gone away. The fact was that the Blues were not allowed to support him - the FA had made it quite clear that the player and the club were not to support each other. Because of this, every visit or demand by Meredith caused the club tremendous embarrassment. There is no doubt that the club wanted to look after him, after all they needed him to return once his suspension ended, however they were forbidden from doing so. Meredith, without any other form of income at this stage, needed the money. He often turned up and Hindle, the FA auditor, saw him arguing with officials on several occasions. Hindle persuaded City to report Meredith to avoid further FA investigations.

The letter presented an unpleasant picture of City's relationship with Manchester's first truly great captain:

"I am instructed by my directors to bring to the notice of your Association the conduct of William Meredith, a player of this club at present under suspension. This player has been in attendance at almost all the principal matches at our ground and invariably frequented the dressing room and offices despite requests not to do so."

The letter sent on 14th February 1906 went on to say that Meredith had periodically approached the board for his wages, and that when his requests were turned down that the player made threats. This was something City did not want to say, however it seemed the only way to avoid further investigation. Unfortunately, it backfired.

Meredith was so appalled that he started to speak out about the alleged bribery. The FA immediately set up a new commission and started to investigate the bribe further, but they also now chose to question players about illegal payments. Meredith claimed that he had offered Leake £10, but told the commission that this was at Tom Maley's suggestion with full approval from the rest of the City team.

Maley was adamant that he did not have anything to do with the alleged bribery attempt, but he did say he was aware that three players had talked about the idea. Apparently, one of them had stated that he would not stoop so low.

The other issue being pursued by the commission was the question of illegal payments. Maley did not deny that payments had been made to players more than the maximum, but claimed that this was common business practice in England and that he only continued to follow the club's standard practices. He stated that if all First Division clubs were investigated, not four would come out 'scatheless'. It is a fact that had the FA carried out a similar investigation at most of the leading clubs they would have found the same situation. Unfortunately, City were the team under the spotlight and, as they and their friends in the media, had already criticised the FA they were to be the ones taught a lesson. The **Athletic News** (owned by City's wealthy backer Edward Hulton) not only blamed the FA it also pointed the finger at Meredith:

"The famous footballer determined not only to admit that he had made an offer to Alec Leake - an offence which ought to have ended his football career - not only that he had been most lavishly and generously paid by the club which ran dreadful risks to give him all they had except the goalposts, but dragged everyone else he could into the same mess. No sense of gratitude for all the managers who, over the years, remunerated him so that he became comparatively rich, no ideals of friendship for the men who, admitting his enviable playing skills, had done everything they could for him, and no feeling of loyalty for the comrades who had fought side by side with him in many a scrap of hard games restrained this man from divulging the secrets of his masters and colleagues. It would have been honourable to confess his own deeds, to express his sorrow and promise an amendment that he promised to fulfil but he took a course that amounted to revenge after he had been simply killed by kindness by the club whose colours he wore."

On Thursday 31st May 1906 the FA commissioners reported their findings. They were of the opinion that City had been overpaying for years and that the club was actually suffering from too much player-power. With the maximum wage at £4, it was revealed that Meredith had been earning £6 and that Livingstone had demanded and received £6 10s. Even the amateur Sam Ashworth had received £50 on top of £25 expenses, and was subsequently declared a professional by the commission.

Then came the most devastating blow - a total of seventeen current and former players were to be suspended until 1st January 1907. Maley and the former Chairman Forrest were to be suspended from English football sine die, while two other directors were to be suspended for seven months. City were fined £250 and the suspended players had to pay a total of £900 in fines. It is a fact that no club in the history of football has ever suffered to such an extent, regardless of tragedy or bans.

The club was virtually dead, although around this time the **Athletic News** journalist James Catton, who used the pen name Tityrus, warned that City were *"like the poor. We always have them with us. It seems we cannot escape from them."*

City's first golden period ended in shame. The 1905-6 season, which had seen the Meredith-less club challenge for the title once again, ended with the Blues in fifth place. Not surprisingly, a loss of form had coincided with the FA investigation.

Three players appealed as they had been reserve players during 1904-5 and, even after bonuses were included, had not received the maximum £208. Their appeal failed, as did a petition signed by 4,128 Mancunians against all the suspensions. Billy Meredith was highly critical of the hypocrisy of the whole affair:

"The League met and representatives of each club voted in favour of the punishment meted out to us being enforced. And while their representatives were passing this pious resolution most of them had other representatives busy trying to persuade the 'villains whose punishment had been so well deserved' to sign for them under conditions very much better in most cases than the ones we had been ruled by at Hyde Road."

Regardless of the approaches going on in the background, City still held the banned players' registrations and would do so until the end of December. On 1st December 1906 City defeated United 3-0 in the first Division One derby of all time (United had been promoted the previous season), but the most noteworthy event of the day actually took place in the Hyde Road offices after the game, when bargaining for the banned players commenced in earnest. The players bans were due to be lifted on 1st January, but as there were so many involved, and the purchasing clubs were keen to see the players take the field immediately into the New Year, the transfer deals had to be completed quickly. In reality the bargaining had been going on for some time, especially for the international players, but the FA agreed that deals could be struck in December. For the City management the sooner the event was over the better. It was already twenty months since the infamous game with Villa and the Blues were simply unable to move forward, especially as much needed capital would be gained by the Hyde Road sales. It is worth noting that the main business was carried out at the ground, although some activity did take place subsequently at the Queen's Hotel in the city centre. Some footballing historians have mistakenly located the whole sale at the Queen's Hotel – this is not true.

According to reports there were representatives from at least eight clubs with the majority interested in the tough England left-back Herbert Burgess, known by City fans as the Mighty Atom. Rumours circulated that Burgess had signed for Celtic for a sum of around £1,000 and also claimed he was going to Everton as part of a player exchange. Eventually, he signed for United for the sum of £750, much to the disgust of both Celtic and Everton. Everton were so incensed that City had transferred Burgess to their friends at United they complained to the League, causing City further heartache. The *Daily Dispatch* reported the sale under the heading ***'More rumours and a few facts'*** on 6th December:

"The inexorable laws of the Football Association have decreed that he shall not play again for City, and therefore it is only fitting that he should go to Clayton. I think the supporters of the City club will be pleased that the matter is definitely settled, for I am sure they would prefer that Burgess remained in Manchester."

In addition to Burgess, United's first truly great manager, Ernest Mangnall, signed Sandy Turnbull, Jimmy Bannister, and the man who was such a hero to the Mancunian masses Billy Meredith. Each of these signings is officially recorded as 5th December, although there is no doubt that Meredith had signed for the Reds some months earlier on a free transfer. The fact that City received nothing for their brilliant captain angered many, and for a time the Blues had tried to sell him but Meredith, totally bemused by the whole affair, produced an agreement between him and City stating that he would be entitled to a benefit match and a minimum sum of £600. This was the main reason he had pursued the club throughout his suspension.

The FA again became involved and declared that they could force the Blues to honour the agreement. Meredith was adamant that the club should not receive a penny for his transfer:

"The City club put a transfer of £600 on my head. And United were prepared to pay it. But I refused to let them pay a halfpenny. I had cost no fee and I was determined that I would have no fee placed on my head.........I was prepared to fight the matter. The City club were not. I was given a free transfer and, as a result, I got £500 from a gentleman to sign for Manchester United and he also paid the £100 fine to the F.A."

In addition to the transfers to United, it is worth detailing what occurred to a few of the other Hyde Road favourites. Johnny McMahon and Frank Booth signed for the 1903 FA Cup winners Bury for a total of around £750. Tom Hynds moved to Arsenal. Former Celtic man George Livingstone returned to Glasgow with Rangers, although two years later he would travel back to Manchester to join Meredith and Co. at United. Sammy Frost and goalkeeper Jack Hillman signed for Southern League Millwall, although it was not a particularly good move for the 35 year old 'keeper as, a short while later, an elbow injury ended his career and left one arm permanently crooked. For Frost the move was at first a perfect one as it enabled him to return to his successful chain of sweet shops he had been forced to leave behind when he signed for City in 1901. However, in March 1926 he committed suicide after problems with his business life.

Another player worth mentioning is the bustling cult hero Billy Gillespie. The controversial player was so disgusted with how he and his colleagues had been treated that he emigrated and refused to pay his FA fine. It was the kind of act that helped develop Gillespie's relationship with the fans, and one which all Mancunians wished the other players and officials would have been able to perform. Interestingly, Gillespie eventually settled in the mining town of Butte, Montana (USA), later made famous as the hometown of daredevil motorcyclist Evil Kneivel.

As Gillespie believed, the investigation had seemed unfair, and it had a major impact on Manchester football. It led to the near destruction of City, while it also indirectly helped United establish themselves as a major side and was a key factor in their first success. The men who transferred to United immediately had a major impact on the fortunes of the Reds.

The four players – Bannister, Burgess, Turnbull and Meredith - all made their United debuts on New Year's day 1907 against, ironically, Aston Villa. It was with some satisfaction that Sandy Turnbull, the man who had been a central figure on the day of the infamous Villa-City match of 1905, netted the only goal of the match. Meredith had set the goal up of course with a terrific cross. Interestingly, the crowd that day was recorded as 40,000 by the United management. This crowd matched the attendance for the visits of City and Bolton but was significantly higher than United's average. In 1905-6 the Reds averaged 13,950 as they were promoted from Division Two, then in 1906-07 the average attendance increased to 20,725.

The impact on the Reds was huge. As well as a substantial increase in support United found the players helped transform the side from one that had finished second in Division Two, to one that finished eighth in Division One. Prior to Meredith & Co. arriving the Reds record was not a great one as they struggled to establish themselves in the top division. They were on 18 points after winning 6 games, drawing 6 and losing 9, while with Meredith & Co. they achieved 11 victories,

2 draws, and only 4 defeats. No mater what anyone may say today it is absolutely clear that the arrival of the former City men created United's first glory period.

In 1907-08 the Reds won the title for the first time, becoming the first Manchester side to win the League, and Meredith & Co. were clearly key players in that achievement. Sandy Turnbull was the leading goalscorer with 25 goals from 30 games – this made him United's record goalscorer with a figure not bettered until Rowley netted 26 in 37 games during the 1946-47 season.

The Reds had a phenomenal season and were more or less certainties for the title by the time of the Manchester derby of 18th April 1908 at City's Hyde Road ground. That game ended goalless and United went on to win the title nine points clear of City, who finished third on equal points with second placed Aston Villa. Although United's success brought much pride and satisfaction to the region, it is fair to say that one of the major talking points for all football enthusiasts was the role of the former City men. City's third placed finish was a remarkable achievement considering the problems that had ripped apart the Club, but it was clear that Meredith & Co. were the difference between the Blues and the Reds. The fact that they helped City to glory in 1904 and then United in 1908 is hugely significant.

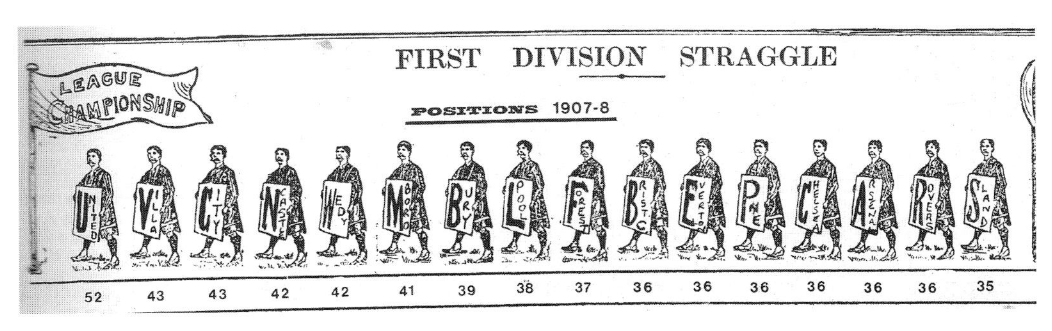

United in 1908 photographed at Bank Street with the Charity Shield, the League Championship trophy and the Manchester Cup. Manager Ernest Mangnall is pictured on the far right with the bowler hat.

As well as helping to transfer the balance of power from City to United there was also one other significant development on the game locally (and nationally) – the formation of the players union, the PFA. Although the PFA was not formed until 1907, it was clearly the illegal payments scandal that was a catalyst. Billy Meredith believed in justice and, although the game was itself a cynical and ruthless one, the player always tried to do the right thing. The stories of bribery are difficult to accept and even if it was true the view that Meredith was simply carrying out a plan hatched by several people perhaps has some credence. As far as illegal payments were concerned Meredith would have felt these were only fair and just, after all these were only illegal in the eyes of the FA, not the fans, not the players, not the directors. Why could not football clubs pay players a rate applicable to their value to the club?

Throughout industrial Manchester at this time there was much debate concerning working conditions and wages, and whereas some of the region's industries could more or less guarantee a job for life, or at least gave that perception, footballers only had a very small working career. After the game they would be left to find new jobs. The 1904 FA Cup winning team would prove to be a great example to Meredith. Despite bringing the city great honour, many of the players struggled to make new lives once their careers ended.

Throughout his suspension Meredith is believed to have considered the injustices he and his team mates suffered, and it is possible he also thought back to the problems encountered in 1902 when two of the City team, Di Jones and Jimmy Ross, passed away. Jones had cut his leg in the annual public practice match and within a week had died. On 27th August the *Manchester Evening News* reported that he had died at Bolton from blood poisoning and lock-jaw, while Ross had also died suddenly earlier that year. According to the *Evening News* Jones' death in particular was tragic:

"Jones fell upon a piece of glass, lacerating his left knew severely. Despite every attention he died as

stated. He was 35 years of age. As a mark of regret the Manchester City directors have agreed to cancel all trial matches arranged for this week."

Neither player had enough savings or investments to look after their families after their deaths and so the precarious nature of a footballers life was obvious to Meredith and his colleagues.

John Harding stated in his history of the PFA, **For The Good Of The Game**, that City *"denied all liability for Jones, claiming he had not been 'working' at the time of the injury"*, but this is not accurate. The Blues did stage a benefit match against Bolton at Hyde Road for 'the widow and children of the late 'Di' Jones' on 9th September 1902 and held various collections. As can be seen by the additional payments they made to players around this time it seems highly likely the club would have done more than most to ensure their players and families were looked after. Harding's comments are out of character with the City of the period and of the rich legacy it possessed – remember the Blues had grown out of a desire to make conditions better for all Mancunians and many of the original leaders such as Lawrence Furniss were still involved at the time of Jones' death. His comments are typical of football in general and of the life of most workers during the early years of the Twentieth Century. It is worth remembering that one of City's wealthiest backers at this time was the newspaper magnate Edward Hulton whose newspapers, in particular the **Athletic News**, tended to write positively about players' rights.

It is known that Jimmy Ross was one of the founders of the original players' union, founded in 1897. In February 1898 that union had drawn up its rules and made them public at a meeting held at the Spread Eagle Hotel in Manchester. It was also revealed that 250 League players had signed up. Unfortunately the union collapsed at the end of the 1900-01 season.

Meredith may well have been thinking about the injustices of his own career and the impact the deaths of Jones and Ross had on their families during his suspension. What is known is that during 1907 Meredith was openly talking about resurrecting the union in some way. The **Athletic News** supported the idea:

"We cannot conceive of any player with a grain of sense refusing to support the establishment of a body for the protection of his own interests."

On 2nd December 1907 the first meeting of the new union was held at the Imperial Hotel, London Road, Manchester. This building, one of Manchester's most important landmarks, was allowed to be demolished in the 1990s and much of the site is now covered by part of the Malmaison Hotel.

Attending the first meeting were four members of the 1904 Cup winning side (three of whom were then with United) – Burgess, Meredith, McMahon, and Turnbull; another City man - Thornley; four further Reds – Broomfield, Downie, Roberts, and Sagar; plus a few individual players from other, mainly northern clubs (although a Tottenham player did attend).

From that point on the new union became more formal. John Davies, the wealthy brewer and United chairman became a vice-president, as did Jimmy Catton, the editor of the **Athletic News**. A solicitor was appointed who was also a director of City, and basically the local clubs tended to support the new movement. It seems, though hard evidence is hard to come by, that the larger clubs like City and United were keen to challenge the wage controls that limited their potential. As City had proved in 1904 the game was changing and the larger city clubs knew they could attract more significant crowds than the smaller town teams and, from a regional perspective, the two FA Cup finals of 1903 and 1904 demonstrate how the game was developing. Bury were a successful and popular side but they could never hope to challenge their more wealthy neighbours on a regular basis. Their 1903 success was a major triumph and demonstrated how any side could find success, but City's 1904 success was not perceived by the FA in the same light. Sure it was a major success, but was this the start of a period when wealth would dominate the game?

Much has been made over the years of the fact that many of the founding fathers of the union in 1907-08 were United players. Harding claimed:

"Manchester United were unquestionably the team of the moment. Massive crowds were turning out to watch this classic eleven as they swept all before them. They were a glamorous side at a time when the popular media – newspapers, particularly, but also music halls – were successfully establishing and exploiting footballers as attractive entertainment figures."

Although these comments do make some sense, they are not quite accurate. It is very easy, particularly with the history of clubs such as United, Liverpool, Arsenal, or even Chelsea to paint a picture of popularity and strength from the start. To portray the clubs as an early version of what a modern day audience might expect, but United in December 1907 had not yet won a major trophy. In 1906 the Reds had been promoted after 12 seasons in Division Two as runners up to Bristol City, and they did not really make much progress until the arrival of Meredith & Co. from City at the start of 1907.

After Meredith's arrival United went from potential relegation candidates to only losing 4 of their remaining 17 games. The 1907-08 season started with an even better run, and so the Reds were certainly challenging for the title, but they were not yet recognised as the side Harding claimed. In addition, United were not the dominant club in terms of support. In the 1906 promotion season they averaged 13,950 (8th best in the League), 1906-07 this increased to 20,725 (4th best behind Newcastle – who averaged 33,650, Villa, and City), and then in 1907-08 they went on to average 20,050 (4th behind Chelsea – who averaged 30,850, Newcastle and City).

City director Albert Alexander provided the horse and carriages for both City's homecoming in 1904 and United's in 1909. Alexander is seen here in between United manager Ernest Mangnall and captain Charlie Roberts.

Billy Meredith - a proud Welshman.

What is true however is that United wanted success and that they wanted to become one of football's elite. As with City in 1904 they saw opportunities to establish themselves but they knew they needed the best players available and they also knew, again like City, that they could raise more funds than the smaller teams and therefore could pay those players more – if they were allowed. This is the crucial point in the support of the union by both United and City. As Manchester's leading side City recognised the opportunities a strong, successful, popular team could bring, while United had the ambition and drive to become a significant power. Teams like Bury could not hope to compete, even at this point in football. Once football gave better conditions, money, and opportunities to players, then the smaller sides would struggle and the game would become more professional.

United's chairman Davies helped to fund transport for the union's benefit games. He recognised that supporting the union would benefit his club, however by 1909 the mood changed somewhat. The union decided to take Reading to court on behalf of one of its players who was seeking compensation under the Workman's Compensation Act of 1906. The view was that the club was taking too much time settling the claim and that the only way to resolve the issue was by taking legal action. Union secretary Herbert Broomfield, who by this time had been a player with United and City, carried out most of the union's action – in fact without Broomfield it is believed the union would have crumbled.

The situation worsened with the FA insisting that they alone decided disputes between football clubs and players and that: *"All such disputes must be adjudicated by it and not taken to a court of law."*

Broomfield countered this and all other claims with strong argument, but it was not long before it became clear that this issue would become a make-or-break moment for Meredith's union, as the press liked to dub it. Leading figures started to criticise the union, and then the FA removed its official recognition for the organisation. This was a major blow and before long rumours of a potential players' strike were circulating with newspapers full of comment and rumour. Both sides appeared confrontational at times. The union chairman, Harry Mainman, said in April 1909: *"We look upon the clubs as enemies of the players."*

The union solicitor, City director Wilkinson, resigned as he recognised a conflict of interests, and United's management were becoming less supportive. The FA also made an announcement which was aimed at killing off the union:

"It will be necessary for players to withdraw from membership of the Union if they desire to continue their connection with the FA."

This statement had a significant impact with the entire management committee of the union, except for secretary Broomfield and chairman Mainman, resigning. The summer of 1909 saw Broomfield, who had made four appearances as goalkeeper for City in 1908-09, consider both his playing future and the options for the union. His career had been plagued with injury and with the demands of the union taking up much of his time it was clear where he felt he had to focus. His hard work on behalf of the union that summer helped to determine the strength of the union in the decades that followed.

As the new 1909-10 season approached the situation came to a head at United. Their players had refused to resign from the union and so were suspended by the Reds. According to most

Charlie Roberts leads United out for the 1909 FA Cup final wearing the new white kit with a red V and red rose - some sources claim music hall artist George Robey supplied the kit.

sources, United did not tell the players of their suspensions at first, and that the first Charlie Roberts knew of it was when the newspapers were delivered to his newsagent's shop. The following Friday Roberts and the other players arrived at United demanding their wages, but there was nothing for them. In effect they were banned from the ground, so Roberts and the others talked with Broomfield and he arranged for them to train at the Manchester Athletic Club ground in Fallowfield - site of the 1893 FA Cup final.

A number of journalists and photographers were contacted and Roberts created a famous story when:

"After training a day or two a photographer came along to take a photo of us and we willingly obliged him. Whilst the boys were being arranged I obtained a piece of wood and wrote on it, 'Outcasts Football Club 1909' and sat down with it in front of me to be photographed. The next day the photograph had a front page of a newspaper, much to our enjoyment, and the disgust of several of our enemies."

On 11th August it was announced that Newcastle United's players would support United's men, and pretty soon other significant clubs would follow, including Oldham, Everton, Liverpool, and Sunderland. Ultimately the growth in support made the threat of a players' strike likely, and inevitably this forced the parties together. After various meeting suspensions were lifted, wages were to be paid, the union recognised, and the strike avoided but there were plenty of complications along the way. Inevitably both the union and the FA claimed victory, but one of the key men, Billy Meredith, felt Broomfield deserved most praise:

"Herbert Broomfield is the first player who has pointed out to the players that they can protect themselves by unity and that if their cause was right they had no reason to fear saying so. He faced the power of the FA fearlessly, endured insult and abuse from his critics, worked night and day, travelled thousands of miles and spent at least £200 of his money because he would not touch Union funds until he had the consent of members to do so... How many men would have dropped into the background as Broomfield has done, allowing others more popular with the FA than he is to voice his views in order that his presence should not hinder a settlement? Very few, I think. A grander, pluckier fight was never made than Broomfield has made!"

The formation of the Professional Footballers' Association, as it became known, owes much to the men of the region who made a stand. The creation of the union clearly came about as a result of a desire by those punished as part of City's illegal payments scandal to improve conditions for

A famous moment in the early history of the PFA - these players were stopped from training at United and this image of their rival training session helped convince other players of the importance of the players' union.

their fellow professionals, and its success and continued growth came from the stand made by the Outcasts in 1909. Manchester gave birth to the union and, in 2008, the PFA is still based within the city centre, close to St. Peter's Square where the union's office was first set up above Billy Meredith's shop. During December 2007 a 100th anniversary game was staged at, appropriately, the City of Manchester Stadium.

In the years that followed the City scandal the importance of the players' union grew, but there were still serious financial hardships for players. Even the most successful of players found life outside of the game tough. It is perhaps for these reasons that another significant scandal was to affect Mancunian football within a decade.

ATTENDANCE DETAIL
SEASON BY SEASON - 1904-1907

Season	City	United	Bury	Stockport
1904-5	20000	15400	9125	Non League
1905-6	18000	13950	8900	4900
1906-7	22150	20725	10350	4875

LEAGUE POSITION
SEASON BY SEASON - 1904-1907

Season	City	United	Bury	Stockport
1904-5	3	21	17	Non League
1905-6	5	22	17	30
1906-7	17	8	16	32

CHAPTER NINE

PINE VILLA BECOMES OLDHAM ATHLETIC

The Pine Villa AFC has secured the Oldham Athletic Grounds, and the club will be known in future as the Oldham Athletic Club. Oldham Standard, 1899

OLDHAM ATHLETIC joined the League in 1907 and, as with Bury when they first joined the League, the Latics developed at a rapid rate and for a time eclipsed the region's other sides.

Oldham first saw light of day as Pine Villa AFC. The first time the club appears to have been mentioned was when Pine Villa defeated Booth Hill Albion 4-0 on 16th November 1895. According to Stewart Beckett, author of a variety of excellent publications on the Latics, the team was first formed when Fred Goddard, the son of the landlord of the Featherstall & Junction Inn, decided to create a side. His father, John, was a keen association football enthusiast and he was on good terms with the key figures behind another side Oldham County. County had been formed only the previous March but they had staged a number of fundraising activities at John Goddard's pub and it must have been obvious to the Goddards that the association game was one that appealed to pub regulars, especially as County were quickly accepted into the Lancashire League.

In September 1895 County faced Everton Reserves and, despite indifferent form, by November the sky-blue shirted side would have been recognised by the Goddards as something to emulate.

John Goddard arranged with County for the two sides to share County's Hudson Fold ground, positioned between the Union Work House and Pine Mill, and Pine Villa became established. Almost immediately the fledgling club hit a problem when County created a reserve side, leaving no free Saturdays for Pine Villa to use Hudson Fold, and so the younger side moved to Berry's Field, off Garforth Street, Chadderton.

For the first couple of seasons Villa competed in friendly matches and it was not until 1897-98 that truly competitive football was played by the side. They joined the Oldham Junior Association Second Division and they ended their first season as champions of the division, and the following year they finished as runners-up in the First Division,

Pine Villa were growing quickly and, despite problems over a venue (the side had moved to the Shiloh ground in 1898 but it was only a basic venue), they clearly needed to move up at least another level. A committee meeting at the Black Cow Inn, the club's headquarters on Burnley Brow, on 18th July 1899 brought a significant leap forward for the club when George Elliott, a liquidator for the Oldham County club, suggested Villa take over the County's ground.

The previous year or so had been difficult for County. As the town's most senior club they had great vision and in 1896 had developed a new ground on Sheepfoot Lane which they called the 'Athletic Grounds', however the move signalled a decline in County's fortunes and finances, and in November 1897 a winding up order was served. The club went into voluntary liquidation and Pine Villa's chance to establish themselves as the town's premier club presented itself.

FOOTBALL.

The Pine Villa A. F. C. has secured the Oldham Athletic Grounds, and the club will be known in future as the Oldham Athletic Club.

How the Oldham Standard reported the name change in July 1899.

Pine Villa moved to the 'Athletic Grounds' and as a result decided to change their name. Presumably the 'Athletic' came from the venue, but the side clearly saw this moment as the chance to become the town's most significant club with the adoption of the name Oldham. It is worth remembering that sides such as Newton Heath had not quite grasped the importance of adopting their wider conurbation's name at this point, and so the adoption of Oldham in their title did suggest they wanted to set themselves apart from the other local soccer sides.

At the new location the side joined the Manchester Alliance and seemed much more positive in its outlook, however the club did decide to retain a link with the past when it chose to wear Pine Villa's colours of red & white shirts and dark blue shorts.

The 1899-1900 season saw Athletic finish third in the Manchester Alliance and also reach the final of the Alliance's cup competition and, partly because of the success and partly because of the support the club was receiving, the side joined the semi-professional Manchester League (alongside Northwich Victoria and Hyde). Sadly, the move was not the success Oldham anticipated and poor performance on the pitch, together with rent problems, caused the club to struggle. A ground move became essential, though that hardly improved matters as the side had to spend money on improving the venue – the old Hudson Fold ground.

Despite the negativeness of 1901, Athletic did progress and in June 1902 the side was invited to join the Lancashire League, however the committee decided to decline the offer – they recognised that County had moved forward too quickly and perhaps wisely felt another season or so of consolidation was needed before they made the big leap forward.

The following season Athletic won the Manchester Junior Cup – goalkeeper Robert Newton saved a penalty in the last minute – and in 1903-04 they finished third, but the club had been in trouble with the FA following crowd trouble at the end of a 3-0 defeat by Tonge FC. The Hudson Fold ground was closed for six weeks after fans had attacked the referee.

On 5th May 1904 a meeting of the committee discussed a number of changes for the club including the desire to apply to join the Football League, and create a reserve team to play

Manchester League Match.

FAILSWORTH

VERSUS

Oldham Athletic

At Hudson Fold, Werneth

SATURDAY NEXT, Octr 11th 1902

Goal	J. Heys
Right Full Back	G. E. Kirkman
Left "	J. Shenton
Right Half Back	A. Brember (Captain)
Centre "	J. Schofield
Left "	J. B. Prosser
Right Wing Outside	C. Barratt
" Inside	G. Rothwell
Centre	W. H. Midwood
Left Wing Inside	W. C. Charnock
" Outside	C. Dawson
Reserve	

Kick-off at 3-15 p.m.

Players meet at Train Leaves Failsworth Station

not later than at 2-15 (Headquarters "Westhulme Hotel" Featherstall Rd Werneth

J. LEECH, Hon. Secretary.

J. B. Fielding, Printer and Bookbinder, Canal Bridge, Failsworth.

Oldham lost this Manchester League game at Failsworth 2-1 on 11th October 1902.

The Featherstall Junction public house.

in the 'B' Division of the Lancashire Combination. It was also proposed that the club should negotiate with brewers JW Lees for a return to their Athletic Ground.

This positive air did not last however as in the AGM held on 10th May 1904 only one of the existing committee, Arthur Barlow, managed to keep his place. Working with nine new committee men must have been difficult for Barlow, especially when the optimism of the previous week was replaced with a decision to remain at Hudson Fold and to apply to join the Lancashire Combination 'B' Division, instead of the Football League.

In the Combination Oldham proved successful and ended the 1904-05 season in third place and were promoted to the 'A' Division. A mediocre league season followed but Oldham entered the FA Cup for the first time, reaching the fourth qualifying round after defeating Ashton Town, Fairfield, Stalybridge Rovers. League side Hull defeated them 2-1, but simply reaching that stage was a significant step and again encouraged the committee that League football was something the club could seriously push for. In April 1906 the club decided it was time to act.

At the meeting the club decided to become a limited company and to apply to join the Football League. In addition, the meeting vowed to appoint a manager and start negotiations to return to the Athletic Ground – present day Boundary Park. By the end of the month Rossendale United's assistant secretary David Ashworth was appointed as Oldham's new secretary-manager, and then in May an agreement was reached with JW Lees for Oldham to return to their old ground.

Everything looked positive and when the Football League election meeting was held there was a strong feeling that Oldham would make it. In the end Athletic missed election by a solitary vote – existing League sides Chesterfield, Burton United, and Clapton Orient were all re-elected but Latics were only one point behind Orient.

The following month solicitor Charles Sutcliffe was elected to the board of directors. This was an interesting move as Sutcliffe, who often acted as a solicitor to Manchester United, was also a significant figure in both the Lancashire FA and the Football League. He was on the League Management Committee and was certainly a very influential man. Inevitably, at the end of 1906-07 Oldham applied to join the League again, but this time the committee went further than any side had previously gone to seek election. They produced a detailed document explaining their strengths which was distributed to all voting clubs, while window stickers appeared across the town and were left at every town the club visited during the 1906-07 season. It was an audacious move.

Oldham are on the ball in this third round FA Cup tie with United at Boundary Park in February 1913. The game ended goalless with Latics winning the replay 2-1 at Old Trafford before 33,500 fans.

The 1913 FA Cup semi final at Ewood Park saw Oldham lose 1-0 to Aston Villa. Goalkeeper Matthews watches as Villa miss a great opportunity..

Whether Oldham's lobbying was a step too far is not clear, but the Latics failed in their bid. Understandably, everyone connected with Oldham was disappointed by the vote. The board then immediately decided to try and join the Southern League in place of Fulham (who had been accepted into the Football League). The move would give Latics a greater level of competition but inevitably there would be significant cost and travel implications, but more importantly they would face competition from another northern team for the vacant place. Bradford Park Avenue made the same approach to the Southern League and it was the Yorkshire club who were accepted. It is believed they made a better offer than Oldham to compensate teams travelling north.

The double blow of rejection from both leagues occurred within consecutive days and Oldham pondered what action to take. Some reports suggested they tried to join the Midlands League but ultimately Oldham announced they would be staying in the Lancashire Combination. Then the whole situation turned again as Burslem Port Vale announced that they would be resigning from the Football League because of financial trouble. Latics, Burton United, and Rotherham Town immediately applied to replace the side, and a special meeting of the League was held at Blackpool. At that meeting, on 15th June 1907, Oldham were finally admitted into the Second Division.

On 7th September Oldham travelled to Stoke for their opening League fixture and the Latics upset the form book with a 3-1 victory. Another victory – 2-1 at home to West Bromwich Albion – followed and Latics went on to enjoy a good first half of the season. Only three of the opening 16 games ended in defeat, but the second half saw the side falter a little. They ended their first League season third in Division Two, and missed promotion by two points. It was a major achievement and the previous November the side had also won the Lancashire Cup.

There had been at least one black moment during the season however. In February Boundary Park witnessed a controversial game against Fulham where the referee made a series of decisions which the home fans objected to. At the end of the match the referee was escorted from the field by a policeman and afterwards the London side's coach was stoned as it left Boundary Park by angry supporters who had waited behind. There was even a story that Latics' 'keeper Bob Hewitson had thrown a missile at the referee during the match.

The FA inquiry found Oldham guilty of misconduct and fined them £10 while Hewitson was found guilty of throwing mud at the referee and of inciting a riot! He was banned for fourteen days, but once his suspension was lifted he only played two further games before being suspended by Oldham for insubordination. He was transferred to Tottenham in the close season.

Despite the problems with the Fulham game, Oldham had every reason to be proud of their record. Two seasons later true success arrived with Latics' promotion as runners-up to City to Division One, but it had been a very tight race. In fact only one point separated champions City and fourth placed Derby County. Oldham achieved promotion with a 3-0 victory in their last game – at home to Hull – before 29,083.

In 1910-11 Oldham ended the season as the region's second highest club. United were champions, Oldham were seventh, and for the first time both City (17th) and Bury (18th) were lower than Latics, but this was soon to be eclipsed in both the League and the FA Cup. In 1913 Oldham defeated Bolton, Nottingham Forest, United, and Everton to reach the FA Cup semi-final. Sadly Aston Villa won the semi at Blackburn Rovers 1-0 before 41,956, but at least Oldham had proved during the run that they could defeat sides which had previously seen themselves as of a significantly higher status. The following season, buoyed by the arrival of former United Cup winning captain Charlie Roberts, Oldham finished fourth and were the highest placed side in the region for the first time, and then in 1914-15 the Latics finished second, but manager David Ashworth had left the club before the season had started to take over at Stockport County. He said at the time:

"I was asked to renew my contract, but I considered a proposition made to me when I secured promotion had not been fulfilled, so I refused."

Ashworth's replacement was Herbert Bamlett and under his guidance Oldham missed the title by a single point, with Everton taking the last Championship before the League programme was suspended. The title could have been Oldham's but the last two games (against Burnley and Liverpool) ended in defeat while Everton beat City and drew with Chelsea. Incidentally, had City defeated the Merseyside club then Oldham and City would both have ended the season on 45 points, while Everton would have had 44. The title would have been decided on goal average and Latics would have been the successful side. Oldham journalist Tony Bugby believes the title should have been Latics':

"There's no question that they should have won it, but they blew it at the end of the season. They had a really good side at that point and the success should have really developed but the outbreak of war ended that opportunity. Oldham had been on a real high, but after the war it took them a very long time to get got going again."

The outbreak of war and ultimate suspension of the League programme came at a bad moment for Oldham. Clearly, there is never a good time for conflict but from a pure footballing point of view the side's development was halted. Instead of 1914-15 being seen as a progression – and all evidence suggests Latics could have achieved more - it was to become the club's high point.

The war caused Oldham to lose the initiative, and in 1923 Oldham dropped to Division Two. They would not return to the highest domestic level until 1992.

ATTENDANCE DETAIL
SEASON BY SEASON - 1907-1908

Season	City	United	Oldham	Bury	Stockport
1907-8	23000	20050	10350	11825	5200

LEAGUE POSITIONS
SEASON BY SEASON - 1907-1908

Season	City	United	Oldham	Bury	Stockport
1907-8	3	1	23	7	33

CHAPTER TEN

MORE SCANDAL

A plot to cheat the public, to sell to the faithful followers of football a sham instead of the genuine article, to rob bookmakers by criminal fraud, and to conspire for the suppression of the truth has been revealed. For the moment the game of Association Football, as played by professionals, staggers under the grave scandal that the League match between Manchester United and Liverpool last spring was a complete and deliberate fake Athletic News, 1915

FOLLOWING Manchester's first League title success in 1908 United went from strength to strength. They won the FA Cup in 1909, moved to Old Trafford in 1910, and managed another League title in 1911. Ernest Mangnall, United's secretary-manager, was perceived by many as the major influence in each of those achievements and it is clear that he had established a highly successful side and had created, in Old Trafford, the most modern stadium in the Country, although the ground building programme was not completed entirely to Mangnall's satisfaction. The plans for Old Trafford were scaled down with only one roofed stand erected, where Mangnall had planned for two, but nevertheless this was still a remarkable venue.

It is worth also considering Mangnall's impact on reserve football at this stage. In 1911 the reserve sides of the significant local League clubs competed in the Lancashire Combination, however other clubs competing in that competition were turning against the League sides believing they were blocking their own development. As a result officials connected with the Combination were finding themselves cold-shouldered and in some cases voted off committees. Mangnall felt the situation needed resolving:

"The League clubs were indignant and determined not to tolerate these caucus meetings any longer. As secretary of the club I knew that Manchester United had not only made up its mind to withdraw from the Lancashire Combination, but that its intention was to make application for admission to one of the Manchester leagues. I then submitted a scheme to Mr. JH Davies, President, and he gave me authority to proceed carte blanche as best I thought. Of the clubs interviewed I got promises of support from Bolton Wanderers, Bury, Crewe Alexandra, Glossop, Manchester City, Manchester United, Oldham Athletic, Preston North End, Stockport County, and Southport Central. The idea at that time was to fill in the vacant Saturdays by means of a subsidiary competition. After an Annual General Meeting of the LFA at the Winter Gardens, Blackpool on 24th May 1911, I called a private meeting."

City director WA Wilkinson acted as chairman, with Everton's Will Cuff as secretary, while Mangnall outlined his plan. The aim was for the Lancashire based League sides to withdraw from the Combination and create a new competition. Four days later the group met again. This time every League side in Lancashire plus Stockport County and Glossop attended. In addition, chairman Wilkinson allowed representatives from non-League sides Darwen, Chester, and Rochdale to address the meeting. Each non-League representative made an impassioned speech urging the League sides not to withdraw but their pleas were in vain.

At another meeting, on 29th May at Manchester's Imperial Hotel (site of the meetings to create the players' union a few years earlier) the name "The Central League" was adopted, and then in June the founding 13 members held another meeting to select a further five clubs. As with the Football League an election was carried out with Southport Central, Huddersfield Town, Rochdale, Barnsley and Crewe Alexandra all admitted. Clearly, Rochdale's speech at the Blackpool meeting had actually worked in their favour with the representatives from the other sides keen to see them included in the new competition. However, Rochdale had to withdraw before the competition started after the Combination objected and the FA blocked their move. Sadly, Rochdale made a loss of £600 on the season due to the decrease in receipts caused by the loss of League sides to the Central League. The Dale applied to join the new league again and this time everything was above board and the side moved into the competition for the 1912-13 season.

This had been a good period for Dale with 1912 seeing the side defeat City 2-0 in the semi-final of the Manchester Cup, then they faced United in the final. The game ended goalless 'after a grand struggle' then the replay saw the two sides draw again (1-1). It was decided the two sides would share the trophy and although the cup was not won outright by the Dale, this was a remarkable success especially as this was the first season Rochdale had entered the competition.

United of course were still managed by Mangnall at this point, but the following September he stunned the Reds when he chose to leave the club and join rivals City.

From that point City and United's fortunes went in opposite directions, and by the time the Football League was suspended due to the outbreak of the First World War the Blues were once again the higher placed side, while the Reds were struggling.

It seems appropriate to consider at this point the development of Oldham Athletic. The Latics joined the League in 1907 with their first match being a 3-1 victory at Stoke on 9th September 1907. Further success followed in the following match when 14,397 saw West Bromwich Albion defeated at Boundary Park. That season the Latics finished third in Division Two. It was a significant achievement and two years later, Oldham gained promotion as runners up to City. They finished seventh, eighteenth, ninth and fourth in the following four seasons, and had reached the FA Cup semi final (1913) after defeating Bolton, Nottm Forest, United, and Everton along the way. Their development also enabled them to attract well known players from the other Manchester sides such as Jimmy Broad jnr from City and Charlie Roberts, United's Cup winning captain.

The Latics were improving year after year, then shortly after the 1914-15 season commenced war broke out. For the first time ever it was suggested the League should be suspended until the war was over, however as most people seemed convinced the war would be over by Christmas the Football League decided the League programme should continue.

For Oldham the 1914-15 season became one of the Club's greatest of all time. Of the opening 20 fixtures only two ended in defeat, but a few poor results in January and February caused the side to slip a little. Nevertheless they remained serious challengers for the title and in mid March they defeated one of the challengers Everton 4-3 at Goodison. By the time of their game with Middlesbrough on 3rd April they were fourth, just two points behind League leaders City. With a fixture coming against City on 5th April it was clear the Latics could put matters into their own hands.

Sadly, the Middlesbrough match was a disaster with major implications for the club. Within twenty minutes of the start of the match Oldham had conceded three goals, but the Latics were convinced that one of those goals should not have been allowed, then their anger intensified when a penalty appeal was turned down for no obvious reason. Despite their anger the players remained relatively calm and pulled a goal back. Unfortunately, shortly into the second half there was a clash between rival players which first resulted in a penalty (converted by Middlesbrough) then the sending off of Oldham's full back Billy Cook. The other players felt this was totally unjustified and swarmed around the referee. The crowd became agitated and according to the ***Oldham Standard***:

"Eventually the referee was seen to take out his watch and, after looking at it a little while, walked off the ground. The players of both sides following."

The game was abandoned with 31 minutes remaining and the referee later admitted that he'd given Cook a minute to leave the field. The Oldham man was reported as saying:

"You can give me an hour if you want but I'm not going."

It was later claimed by the media that this was the first time a game had been abandoned as a result of the actions of one player. The general consensus was that Cook should not play again for some considerable time with the controversy and media interest reaching similar levels to that which would later greet Eric Cantona's exploits in 1995 when he lunged at members of the Crystal Palace-United crowd.

Whether Oldham ignored the media, or were simply being stubborn is not known, but amazingly Cook played against City two days after the Middlesbrough game. Ultimately he was banned for a year, but the Latics continued to play him until the sanction was imposed. With Cook still in the side Oldham could only manage a draw against leaders City. They seemingly lost the opportunity on that day but that draw was enough to cause City a few jitters. Another draw for the Blues at Bradford City opened up the title again and the Latics, Blackburn, and Everton were now able to challenge City's ambition. In fact the Manchester Blues were now in freefall and their final three matches, including a crucial home game with contenders Everton, all ended in defeat. Had they defeated both Oldham and Everton then they would have won the title.

For Oldham victories over United and Sheffield United made it look as if the title could be theirs but a draw at Aston Villa was followed by successive defeats to Burnley and Liverpool. The side to benefit from the failure of City and Oldham was Everton. The Merseysiders ended up winning the title with 46 points, Oldham were second with 45, and City ended in fifth place with 43 points. Both Blackburn and Burnley had leapfrogged over them. Oldham's chance of major glory was over.

The First World War was not over by Christmas and by the 1914-15 season's end it was clear the war would continue for some time. For much of that season United were struggling to avoid relegation and on Good Friday a highly significant game with Liverpool was alleged to have been fixed. It is worth mentioning that former Blues – and victims of the FA's investigations into City less than a decade earlier - Sandy Turnbull and Billy Meredith took part in what became a highly controversial match.

On Good Friday 1915 United faced mid table Liverpool as part of their desperate fight against relegation to Division Two. The Reds managed to achieve a 2-0 victory before 18,000 – United's second highest crowd of the season. The victory helped lift United and, when the season ended, they avoided relegation by a point.

The United victory ultimately helped the Reds survive, but at this time the *Manchester Football Chronicle* was not too positive about United's future:

"If the club does go down the present team would not be at all likely to regain the senior division. My own opinion is that of recent seasons there had been far too much talk about money at Old Trafford and too little about football. It is prosperity which has caused the decline. The Manchester United players have been treated magnificently by the club. They have been given benefits of handsome guarantees when the club was really not in a position to wisely do anything of the kind. From all I can gather the golden time of the player has gone."

Almost immediately after the match rumours of match-fixing started to appear. The newspapers commented on Liverpool's laid-back approach, while fans and even the referee felt they had witnessed a peculiar game. In fact during the match sections of the Old Trafford crowd jeered, despite United's win. The Reds even missed a penalty which some observers believed was a step too far and caused others to think it was the scoreline, rather than the result, that was important to the players on the pitch.

The *Daily Dispatch* hinted at a few problems. Under the headline ***"Liverpool beaten – lifeless football in second half"*** it made comments such as:

"It was a game which would scarcely send the most enthusiastic United supporter mad with delight. The second half was crammed with lifeless football. United were two up with 22 minutes to play and they seemed so content with their lead that they apparently never tried to increase it. Liverpool scarcely ever gave the impression that they would be likely to score."

The *Manchester Football Chronicle* was a little more positive in its report on 3rd April, but it still pointed to some form of match-fixing. Under the headline ***"A Surprising Display"*** it read:

"Yesterday's match at Old Trafford provided a fairly good first half, but proceedings after the interval were dull, tame, unenthusiastic and generally most disappointing. Neither team showed any real energy after the United had gained a lead of two goals and the football in the concluding stages was the poorest seen on the ground this season.

"Some of the comments I heard were very strong but quite justifiable. One famous old player said, 'You don't need the War to stop the game, football of this sort will do it soon enough'. Personally, I was surprised and disgusted at the spectacle the second half presented. Hodge, Spratt, Anderson and Montgomery were the best men on the United side. Anderson scored both goals and his first was a beautiful shot. The opening was cleverly made for him by Montgomery who in the first half was the cleverest middle-man on the field. Spratt gave a splendid display and was the strongest back on view. He often beat Sheldon in

masterly style. O'Connell missed a penalty but did a lot of good work and Norton was a big improvement on Wall at outside left."

As the weeks progressed rumours increased that there had been something 'fishy' going on. A £50 reward was offered by a betting organisation if someone could come forward to substantiate an allegation that the match had been fixed. They believed an unusual quantity of bets had been placed on the scoreline of 2-0 to United. The **Sporting Chronicle** published a notice from a bookmaker called: "The Football King":

"We have solid grounds for believing that a certain First League match played in Manchester during the Easter weekend was 'squared', the home club being permitted to win by a certain score. Further, we have information that several of the players of both teams invested substantial sums on naming the correct score of this match with our firm and others. Such being the case, we wish to inform all our clients and the football public generally that we are withholding payment on those correct score transactions, also that we are causing searching investigations to be made with the object of punishing the instigators of this reprehensible conspiracy. With this object in view, we are anxious to receive reliable information bearing on the subject and we will willingly pay the substantial reward named above [£50] to anyone giving information which will lead to punishment of the offenders."

The Football League set up a commission to investigate the match which included, bizarrely, Charles Sutcliffe who also worked as a solicitor for United. Presumably there would have been a conflict of interests. In addition, the commission seemed to bundle along at one point much to the disgust of the **Manchester Evening Chronicle**. On 30th October it revealed the surprising news that the commission had only just asked for the names of the players taking part in the game:

"If the controlling body of the game have not this most necessary information after all the hubbub and inquiry that has been going on for seven months past, the followers of the pastime who have waited the result of the investigation with such interest are hardly likely to have more than a hazy idea for the central figures in this momentous matter, at all events not when the decision is given, whenever that may be."

On 23rd December 1915 the commission finally gave its verdict, with most Mancunians reading the news in the Christmas Eve issues of the local newspapers. The findings were that several players had hatched a plot to fix the result and scoreline of the match for financial gain. Eight players were to be permanently suspended from taking part in football or football management and were banned from entering any football ground in the future. The eight players included four from Liverpool and Turnbull, Whalley, and West from United. Another player, Lol Cook (ex-Stockport County) from Chester was also banned but no one quite understood his involvement. **The Liverpool Echo** reported:

"Confusion arose in our minds when the name Cook was included. William Cook is the long-time Oldham back, but Lol Cook played for Stockport County and never for Oldham."

At no time in the years that have followed has Cook's role been accurately revealed.

Another player was also named. City's Fred Howard was to be suspended for 12 months once football was resumed after the war, while the report also suggested that other members of United were involved, although it admitted it could only punish those it could prove had done wrong.

The findings were a major shock but as December neared its end more information and stories surrounding the game emerged. The implications were felt immediately as well. The morale boosting 1915 Christmas Day derby match between City and United at Hyde Road was affected as both Enoch West (United) and Fred Howard (City) were dropped. Similarly Turnbull and Whalley were stopped from playing for the Footballers' Battalion against Birmingham.

So what were the reasons for the match-fixing? Some have suggested United's potential relegation had something to do with it, but that is a bit of a red herring. It is fair to say that had United been enjoying a good season the prospect for a 'fix' would have reduced – odds of 7-1 would not have been offered had United been mid-table – but the game was still several weeks off the end of the season and so it is unlikely an attempt could have been made to avoid relegation in this manner that early. However the result did cause Chelsea to be relegated instead of the Reds. The **Athletic News**, despite its Manchester-leanings, was not impressed:

"Manchester United have been extremely fortunate in escaping from the consequences of the acts of men for whom they are technically responsible. The United players have for years caused much trouble. The forbearance of the FA some years ago and the beneficent neutrality of the League has saved the club. Manchester United enjoy a place they have not honestly won and Chelsea are called upon to suffer an indignity they do not honestly deserve."

The real motivation was money, although the **Athletic News** was quick to point out exactly how much United's first team had earned:

"The wages of the players in 1913-14 were £5,573 15s and in 1914-15 £5,810 1s 11d. There does not appear such a reduction here as should tempt any man to scheme for money in an illegitimate manner. The football which the United team showed last winter was not worth £112 per week. The players had bonuses of £60, and the travelling expenses cost £909. The receipts of the first team matches declined from £13,397 to £6,081, and the total revenue fell from £16,022 to £11,708. The debit balance is not surprising when the players take £5,810 out of £6,081 taken at the more important matches."

Enoch West in his pre-war United kit.

Even in the 1980s when Simon Inglis wrote **Soccer in the Dock**, a review of football's biggest scandals, the view was that the players were simply on the make. He stated:

"All this, added to the fact that men like West would have been about to receive lucrative benefits, made the illegitimate attempt to make a few extra pounds on Good Friday appear even more loathsome."

In 2003 Graham Sharpe, a senior figure in the bookmakers William Hill, wrote an in-depth volume focusing on the implications from a players' perspective as well as the general view. In **Free the Manchester United One** Sharpe argues that the players were simply trying to secure their futures. With the First World War raging the future of football, as with most of society, was uncertain. The players did not know whether they would be employed the following season, or whether the clubs would be able to pay them sensible wages. This certainly gave them reason.

Of the players banned one, Enoch West, vehemently denied having anything to do with fixing the match and spent the rest of his life trying to clear his name. Sharpe's book examines the full story in detail and it paints a very interesting picture of how appallingly West was treated in comparison with some of his colleagues, and Manchester United themselves. According to Sharpe:

PLAYER'S SUSPENSION.

Claim for Damages and an Injunction.

PLAINTIFF'S DENIALS.

F.A. Allegations of "Squared" Match.

The hearing was begun in the King's Bench Division yesterday of an action in which Enoch James West, professional footballer, of Railway-road, Old Trafford, Manchester, claims damages for alleged libel against the Football Association, Limited, and Messrs. E. Hulton and Co., Ltd. Plaintiff also asks for an injunction restraining the Football Association from putting into force a resolution suspending him from taking part in football or football management.

Messrs. Hulton admitted publication of certain statements about plaintiff's conduct as a football player, but pleaded justification and fair comment.

Mr. Cyril Atkinson, K.C., and Mr. J. D. Crawford appeared for plaintiff, Mr. Rawlinson, K.C., M.P., and Mr. H. T. Waddy for the Football Association, and Mr. Rigby Swift, K.C., and Mr. B. Campion for Messrs. Hulton.

In opening the case, Mr. Atkinson said West, who was now engaged in the Ford Works, at Manchester, was playing for Manchester United until the end of 1915. He was engaged for three years, receiving £4 10s. a week for one year, and £5 a week for the last two years, the club undertaking also to give him a benefit which should amount to £500.

Enoch West's attempts to clear his name.

"United, who had condemned the match fixing, but had nonetheless benefited substantially as a result, do not seem to have offered to do the decent thing and sacrifice the two points they 'won' from the game and which ultimately kept them above the relegation positions."

The game had a further impact on the League. Once the First World War ended Chelsea made their formal appeal against being relegated, and the League Management Committee agreed that:

"it would be unjust that Chelsea should be relegated to the Second Division."

It also determined that United could not now be relegated and so came up with a rather unusual plan. It decided that either the League should be increased to 22 clubs in each division, or that Division One alone be extended, and that Chelsea and United would in effect fight to avoid relegation, with the lower club going down no matter where they actually finished. In the end both divisions were increased by 2 clubs and so United, and Chelsea remained in Division One. Tottenham were still relegated (they'd finished bottom), but perversely Arsenal (fifth in Division Two) were promoted. The reasons for this antagonise Spurs fans to this day, but are not worth exploring in a book on Manchester football. Suffice to say, that United and Arsenal both benefited from the match-fixing scandal, while the players of Liverpool and United, most notably West, were the real losers.

The suspension of the Football League during the war caused a restructure of first team competition. Regional leagues were created for 1915-16 with Stockport County, Bury, Oldham Athletic, Rochdale, City and United all forming part of the Lancashire section. That section was exceptionally strong, especially as the top five placed clubs in the Football League at the end of 1914-15 had all come from Lancashire, with two from the Manchester region itself.

Wartime football was far from perfect, but the regional competition ensured interest was high for all of Manchester's clubs. In terms of success City won the Lancashire Regional Tournament and the Lancashire Tournament (South) in 1915-16 & the Lancashire Subsidiary Tournament C in 1918-19; Rochdale won the 1916-17 Lancashire Subsidiary Tournament; and Oldham won the Lancashire Subsidiary Tournament B in 1918-19.

Once the war ended in 1918 thoughts turned towards the future of League football. The League was resurrected in 1919. For some sides, such as City, the return enabled them to re-establish themselves as a power but for others, most notably from a regional perspective Oldham, the war had ended their opportunity of major success.

The scandal that had affected United continued to make news for several years, but locally

Oldham secretary-manager David Ashworth watches as future Oldham player Charlie Roberts leads United out for the 1913 FA Cup tie. The match ended in a no score draw.

another team was to be caught out in the immediate post war period. In April and May 1920 Bury faced Coventry in successive end of season games. The first match ended 2-2 with the return finishing 2-1 to Coventry at Gigg Lane on 1st May. The results enabled Coventry to finish 20th in Division Two – crucially two points above the re-election zone. These results were viewed as suspicious but little of note was discussed in Bury until 15th January 1923 when director Richard Wood resigned.

Other resignations followed in February and gradually the news emerged that Wood had asked two directors - Read and Horrocks - to resign from the Board when he became aware of allegations of match fixing in those matches with Coventry City in 1920.

On 6th March 1920 the FA sent a letter to Bury saying that Read and Horrocks would face charges of match fixing. The letter said:

"Information has been received by us of alleged wrongful practices - the squaring of a match played between Bury and Coventry City in 1920. A commission has been appointed and will sit at the Grand Hotel, Manchester on Friday next, 9th inst. At 2 p.m."

"It is requested that your club be represented and that there should also attend, your Chairman Mr J. W. Horrocks, your vice-chairman Mr F. Read, your Secretary-Manager Mr W. S. Cameron and your player T. Cornthwaite.

"It is also desirable that the following officials and players should have an opportunity of attending before the commission and giving information upon the matters to be considered. As we do not know their address we should appreciate you informing them of the terms of this letter. Colonel Hall, Mr Unsworth, Mr Duckworth, Mr Helm, Mr Brown, Mr Allan, Mr Unsworth, Mr Hamer, Mr Hird, Mr Goldie, Mr Heap, Mr Perry, Mr Ritchie, Mr Aitken."

When directors Read and Horrocks refused to resign Wood felt he had no choice but to tender his own resignation, followed by other members of the board.

An extraordinary meeting was called with the proposal being ***"the removal of the whole of the members of the existing board of the directors of Bury Football Club and the election of new members to the board of directors."*** The meeting, held on 22nd March, led to Read and Horrocks being voted off the board.

The FA's investigations continued for some time and then at the start of June Bury received notification of the commission's findings. The Directors' minute book recorded:

"Read letter from the Football Association enclosing copy of the decision of the commission appointed to investigate matters affecting the Bury and Coventry clubs. The commission which has enquired into matters affecting these clubs, whilst not having been able to ascertain all the facts, is satisfied from the evidence that an arrangement was made that the match played at Bury in 1920 should be won by the Coventry City club.

"That the following officials and players of the clubs were parties to or had knowledge of the arrangement. Bury FC : Messrs J .W. Horrocks (Chairman), F. Read (Director), W..S. Cameron (Secretary-Manager), J. Allan, R. Perry, W. Ritchie, J. Goldie and T. Cornthwaite (players). Coventry City: Messrs J. Marshall (Chairman), D. Cooke (formerly a Director) and G.D. Chaplin (player).

"Messrs J. W. Horrocks, F. Read, W. S. Cameron, J. Allan, W. Ritchie, J. Goldie, J. Marshall, D. Cooke and G.D. Chaplin are suspended permanently and T. Cornthwaite for twelve months from the 29th May 1923 from taking part in football or football management."

In addition both Bury and Coventry were fined £100 each, and like the scandals affecting City in 1905 and United in 1915 the affair brought major suffering and disgrace to the players involved, and like the City scandal the club itself also suffered significantly.

ATTENDANCE DETAIL
SEASON BY SEASON - 1908-1911

Season	City	United	Oldham	Bury	Stockport
1908-09	20000	17375	11625	9900	6075
1909-10	18275	16950	11525	8125	6525
1910-11	26000	19950	13525	8550	4850

LEAGUE POSITIONS
SEASON BY SEASON - 1908-1911

Season	City	United	Oldham	Bury	Stockport
1908-09	19	13	26	17	38
1909-10	21	5	22	13	33
1910-11	17	1	7	18	37

CHAPTER ELEVEN

STOCKPORT COUNTY

The players from both sides were cheered loudly by the spectators as they left the field with one Leicester supporter exclaiming of County 'What go, what devilment they have'. And so it was generally agreed by all that Stockport had made a good start to their Football League campaign.

Cheshire Daily Echo, 1900

IN between the two world wars several significant stories highlighted and to some extent shaped the role of Stockport County within the Manchester region. The first of these came at the end of 1920-21 when it was clear the Football League was to be restructured. A Third Division, made up predominantly of southern clubs had been created at the start of that season, and a northern section of the Third Division was to be created for the start of the 1921-22 season. Sadly, Stockport was the first side to be automatically relegated to the new division.

The final game of that relegation season was for many years regarded as a record with only 13 spectators paying to attend County's 7th May meeting with Leicester. The game was played at Old Trafford as Edgeley Park was closed for disciplinary reasons after trouble broke out during a match with Sheffield Wednesday on 2nd April, and the only time the game could be played was straight after United's home game with Derby County. The match had a 6.30pm kick off and ended goalless but the attendance of 13 was for many years quoted as the lowest official crowd.

In truth the attendance that day was somewhat larger. United had attracted around 10,000 people to their Division One game and it is now understood that somewhere in the region of between 1,000 and 2,000 people remained to watch County's match. From a Stockport perspective the interesting part is that those 13 who did pay clearly had no interest in watching United, otherwise they would have joined the other 10,000 for the earlier kick off and made sure they got real value for money.

Twelve months after this game County ended the 1921-22 season as inaugural Third Division North champions – the first title ever won by the club. They remained in the Second Division until relegation in 1926. The following season the side had two points deducted for playing ex-Bolton player Joe Smith on 19th March 1927 while he was unregistered.

A decade later scandal hit Stockport again when County won the Third Division North title for the second time. County director George Worsley was found guilty of making illegal payments to Carlisle United players if they could beat Lincoln City – County's main title rival. Carlisle

managed the win, and the loss of points dented Lincoln's challenge. County went on to win the title but it was not until the following season that the Football League commission announced their findings. As County had won the title by three points, rather than two, the Carlisle game did not actually have a final bearing on County's promotion, but Worsley's guilt did put a dampener on the success.

Illegal payments and the like were a far cry from the humble beginnings of the club. County was initially founded as Heaton Norris Rovers in 1883, by members of the Wycliffe Congressional Church meeting at McLaughlin's Coffee House in the town centre. Like much of the region rugby still tended to dominate the local sporting scene but association football was gaining ground. Likewise, Stockport and its various smaller villages and districts were growing and becoming more industrialised. The hatting industry dominated of course.

Several ground moves followed, together with a merger with Heaton Norris. Some sources claim this occurred in 1886, others say it was 1888 (they definitely dropped the word Rovers from their title that year). Whichever year is correct, it is clear that the combined side grew in popularity and in their approach. A reserve side and an A team was fielded in 1888 and then the following year Stockport became a county borough of Cheshire and as a result in this improved status the football team decided to rename itself Stockport County.

The name change was formally adopted on 24th May 1890 and, although Stockport's status changed in 1974 as a result of the county boundary restructure that saw the town become part of Greater Manchester the name survived – incidentally there were calls for the side to be renamed with Manchester South FC being suggested. Fortunately both the team and the town managed to retain its true identity. The first game under County's name ended in a 5-3 defeat to Hurst FC from Ashton Under Lyne.

County's status improved rapidly and the side joined the Football Combination in 1891. Three years of steady improvement followed with County finishing 11th, 6th and 4th in consecutive seasons. During this time they also became the first Combination side to reach the last 32 of the FA Cup. In 1894 County left the Combination as there was a feeling that the side really needed to establish itself in the Lancashire League. A ninth place finish followed in their first season there and by the end of the decade County were determined to raise their profile further, especially as they had defeated Second Division City in the Manchester Cup final of 1898 and the following year retained the trophy after defeating Division One side Bury. As a result of these successes Stockport applied to join the Football League in 1899. In the annual vote County finished fifth in the election race with 11 votes – incidentally Ashton North End also applied but did not receive a single vote in their favour.

The following season Stockport won the Lancashire League, winning 21 of their 28 games, and as a result their second application to join the Football League proved successful with County finishing second with 28 votes to Barnsley in the ballot. Another club from the area Stalybridge Rovers received only one vote.

An away trip at Leicester Fosse on 1st September 1900 gave Stockport a tough opening day fixture but the newcomers acquitted themselves well with a 2-2 draw. There was some amusement right at the start of the match however when the two captains Martin John Earp (Stockport) and George Swift (Fosse), together with the referee, realised none of them had brought a coin on to the pitch for the toss. A laughing crowd greeted the Leicester captain when he ran across to the crowd asking spectators if any of them had a coin!

Another interesting snippet concerning County's captain Earp is that the Sheffield born player became known around the town because he objected to changing with the rest of the team at the Nursery Inn, instead he would change on his own at the George Hotel on Wellington Road North before travelling a good ten minutes to County's Green Lane ground by hansom cab.

County's first League season was not a success as they ended the campaign seventeenth out of eighteen clubs, two points behind 'safe' Barnsley in fifteenth place, in Division Two and was forced to apply for re-election. Surprisingly Stockport's re-election was not a formality and County tied in third place with Doncaster Rovers. Initially there were only three places available and so a second ballot was held between County and Doncaster with Stockport receiving eight votes more than the

					Goals		
	P.	W.	L.	D.	F.	A.	Pts.
Bradford .... (3)	35	23	3	9	87	37	55
Doncaster Rovers... (8)	35	21	9	5	71	36	47
Stockport County... (6)	35	20	9	6	75	44	46
Tranmere Rov. ... (9)	34	19	8	7	91	56	45
Lincoln City ....(11)	36	20	11	5	77	62	45
Bradford City .... (—)	36	15	10	11	78	55	41
Darlington .... (—)	34	18	12	4	78	57	40
Wrexham ....(13)	36	17	14	5	59	53	39
Southport ....(12)	36	17	15	4	66	57	38
Accrington Stan. (21)	36	15	13	8	67	59	38
Halifax Town ..... (4)	35	12	12	11	65	61	35
New Brighton .....(10)	34	11	12	11	54	48	33
Rochdale .... (2)	34	15	16	3	63	66	33
Rotherham United.(19)	35	11	15	9	58	59	31
Hartlepools Utd. (17)	36	13	18	5	60	72	31
Crewe Alexandra ...(15)	36	11	17	8	69	73	30
Chesterfield .... (7)	36	11	17	8	61	71	30
Ashington ....(16)	36	9	20	7	60	96	25
Barrow ....(22)	36	9	20	7	48	96	25
Wigan Boro' ....(18)	36	6	20	8	48	86	24
Durham City ....(20)	35	9	21	5	43	85	23
Nelson .... (5)	34	9	21	4	59	108	22

The figures in parentheses denote the club's position in the final table last season.

EVERY FORWARD SCORES.

Nelson Completely Outplayed by Stockport County.

Stockport County 8, Nelson 0.

Nelson were overwhelmed at Edgeley Park. Not for years have Stockport County scored as many goals in a League game, and the result was noteworthy from the fact that every forward found the net.

Scurr signalised his return to the side by scoring within five minutes, while Ramsden and Smith netted further goals before the interval. Nelson attempted to exploit the off-side game, but found it did not pay, and in the second half their defence was repeatedly in difficulties, goals being added by Smith, Ramsden, Boardman (two), and Burgess.

Wilson and Warhurst were the outstanding figures for Nelson, but Stockport County were clever all round, the attack, which included Boardman at inside left, giving a sparkling exhibition. Smith played finely, and both wings showed splendid tactics.

There was nothing amiss with the Stockport defence, which was not overtaxed.

Promotion chasing Stockport defeat bottom club Nelson 8-0 in Division Three (North) in April 1928. County missed out on promotion that season, finishing third. Only one side was promoted.

Yorkshire side and thereby securing their place in Division Two. In the end Doncaster also made it in to the League as New Brighton Tower resigned before the new season commenced.

Further struggles followed with County facing the ordeal of the re-election process every season until 1904 when finally County failed in the ballot. This failure was perhaps unfair as Stockport had actually started to turn the corner. Financially, a move to Edgeley Park in 1902 had helped and it certainly gave them great hope for the future, but the other League sides were clearly more concerned with the past than the future. A past which, according to the four volume **Caxton** publication of 1960, was riddled with problems of control:

"Things were so bad, the players got no wages, so they assumed management, picked their own teams and shared the gate money."

Not to be deterred by the problems, County applied to re-join the League in 1905 and were fortunate in that the decision had been taken to increase both Division One and Two to twenty clubs each. Finishing next to bottom in the vote, County scraped back into the League. The club's first game back in the League saw them face another new League side Chelsea. The London side had only been created that year and – a bit like the modern day Chelsea but interestingly not the position that has existed for most of the club's life – were perceived as a side ready to buy success. Despite Chelsea's determination to succeed, County managed a 1-0 victory thanks to a goal from Dodd (match reports suggest Dodd netted after Chelsea's enormous 'keeper 'fatty' Foulke had saved a penalty, but Stockport sources claim the scorer was Bob Manson).

From that point on the side seemed refreshed and they managed to not only survive but at times thrive, in the Second Division. Their best pre-war season coming immediately after their return to the League when they finished tenth in Division Two, while their worst season came in 1912-13 when they finished nineteenth out of twenty Second Division sides. Despite that disappointment however County were still in a fairly healthy position when war was declared. At the end of the 1914-15 season Stockport finished 14th but they also managed to win the Manchester Cup for the third time.

ATTENDANCE DETAIL SEASON BY SEASON - 1911-1915

Season	City	United	Oldham	Bury	Stockport
1911-12	24625	17200	11950	7875	6625
1912-13	24000	22675	10275	5050	5475
1913-14	27000	24825	12200	6975	7225
1914-15	21000	12325	9450	3750	5000

LEAGUE POSITIONS SEASON BY SEASON - 1911-1915

Season	City	United	Oldham	Bury	Stockport
1911-12	15	13	18	20	36
1912-13	6	4	9	31	39
1913-14	13	14	4	30	32
1914-15	5	18	2	31	34

CHAPTER TWELVE

FOR THE GOOD OF MANCHESTER?

In view of Manchester United's sorry position I think Manchester Central should have been admitted. But the League do not go over the heads of their members. Ivan Sharpe, 1931

THE period between the wars started with some of our clubs suffering more than others. Every club had been affected by the First World War of course, however it appears as if Oldham were the side to be most affected. Their chance to win major honours ended with war and post war they struggled, with the 1922-23 season culminating in relegation to Division Two. It would be almost another seventy years before the Latics returned to the top flight.

Oldham were not the first of the local sides to struggle post war, United were relegated in 1922, and their fall from grace was an indication of how the Reds were suffering off the pitch. The development of Old Trafford thirteen years earlier had severely stretched United's finances and with attendances not improving significantly after their ground move, income had not increased sufficiently to push the Reds on to further success.

Before the move United enjoyed average attendances of around 20,000, after the move the figure immediately dropped. By 1911 it stood at 17,000 despite United winning the title, but then it did rise for a couple of seasons before dropping to a little over 12,000 in 1914-15. It is worth stating that all attendances dropped during this period with the best in the League being City with an average of around 21,000.

Post war most sides experienced an increase in support and United did reach a new high of 35,000 in 1920-21, but that level did not last and financially United were crippled by the Old Trafford move.

There was better news at City, although their Hyde Road ground was beginning to prove too small post war. So great was the interest in the Blues that several games resulted in headlines focusing on the problems of crowd control. Gates were smashed down as fans poured into the ground and, despite significant investment pre-war, the Hyde Road ground was simply too small to accommodate the size of crowds they were attracting. A move was essential if the Blues were to capitalise on their popularity.

To emphasise the style of football for most spectators at this time, it is worth considering the views of City fan Harry Hughes. Hughes was born in August 1902 and during 1996 he talked of his first visit to a football ground. The ground was City's Hyde Road, but his comments could equally have applied to United's old Bank Street ground, or any of the other venues in the region, apart from possibly the modern Old Trafford:

"When I arrived I was mystified as to what to do, there were narrow holes for turnstiles and I didn't know what they were at all. Anyway I eventually paid my shilling and staggered into this vast multitude of people. There must have been 30,000 or more. I could hear the voices - a lovely rustling sound like wheat in the wind. The match was against Bolton Wanderers, I think, they were a real force in the land of course.

"The ground had metal stanchions - the lattice type - holding up the roofs and much of the ground looked similar. There were houses cutting into the Popular Side terracing, overlooking the ground and for years I used to ask my mother if we could flit and move into one of those so we could see the ground. During the games you could always see fellas hanging out of their windows, smoking and drinking pints of beer - a sort of executive box of the day.

"My mother used to say if you're going to the football make sure you don't come home injured and I used to reply 'I'm only watching, I'm not playing' because you didn't think you could get injured watching. Occasionally you'd get crushed a little, but there was never really any trouble.

"The funny part of all these games around this time was the Beswick Prize Band. It was nice to hear the crowd whistling the tunes - 'Oh, Comrades' and tunes like that. There was an old fella there - Patsy Hagan I believe his name was. He wore a great hat and carried a huge beagle stick, marching along, moving his stick, beating time. The band were all right - they played all the tunes and the crowd listened and whistled. Can you imagine the whole crowd whistling more or less all in tune? It was great, but this Patsy Hagan looked to be a staunch teetotaller, very serious. When he marched into the corners with his serious face, he'd wave his stick and turn around, and the crowd would point at him and laugh. It was very funny.

"Another funny thing used to occur with the lads selling 'Batty's Football Tablets'. That was a do in itself! The tablets were sold in little pokey bags - a penny a packet, and I remember that at my first game a fella right at the back threw a penny down and the Batty lad caught it. They used to do it all the time. Anyway, the Batty lad threw the packet back up, right to the man who wanted them! Occasionally, the packets would only go halfway up the terracing and the bag would be knocked to the buyer by the others in the crowd - each one knocking it on. Sometimes the bags would burst and we'd all get a tablet! That was part of the fun. Every home game you had to buy Batty's tablets.

"I remember that the Hyde Road crowd were always in good humour and, after that first game, I walked home - I don't think I touched the floor until I got home, I was full of it. I said 'that's for me, I'm going there again'. I loved it and couldn't wait for the next game. I dreamt about it all fortnight."

Sadly, fire in 1920 resulted in the destruction of the Hyde Road Main Stand and an urgent need for the club to bring forward their plans of moving home. Earlier in the season John Davies, United's Chairman, had suggested City could share Old Trafford, but at that time City did not feel the need, then after the fire the Blues went back to the Reds.

Within days the **Daily Dispatch** revealed that City had tried to negotiate for the use of Old Trafford but that United's terms had suddenly become prohibitive. Apparently the Reds now wanted a guaranteed income and to keep all receipts in excess of the corresponding fixtures from the previous season. They did state that they would pay City if the receipts did not match those of twelve months previous, but the chances of that actually happening were minimal. Many of City's games had been sell-outs and the Blues felt that, with a bigger venue, the crowds would have

Charlie Pringle (central figure, looking to his right) and other members of the City team messing around with the groundsman's wheelbarrow.

been higher. 'It was not the ground that attracted the supporters it was the team' was City's main argument. Considerable coverage of the period appears in the scrapbooks of City manager Ernest Mangnall, stored at United's football museum.

With the two sides failing to reach agreement, and the Blues determined not to cancel the Huddersfield fixture (to be staged exactly a week after the fire), City took the only option available to them and they patched up Hyde Road.

With the players changing at the neighbouring Galloways boilerworks, and a little discomfort in the press and officials section, the game against Huddersfield went ahead as planned. A crowd of 35,000, according to the *Daily Dispatch*, watched a 3-2 City victory but for Harry Hughes the most significant moment came on 27th November when United visited:

"United in their benign way offered the use of Old Trafford but City politely refused saying 'Don't worry we'll have a grandstand!' and y'know we did! We had one built by the time we played United. It was made of tongue and groove and varnished. In fact you could still smell the varnish all over the ground. It was pretty rough, but it served it is purpose, and as it was all new wood it must have been ten times stronger than the old stand.

"As usual the band came out, formed a circle on the pitch and played all the popular songs of the day. Then they started playing 'I wouldn't leave my little wooden hut for you' and the crowd wasn't slow to notice that, and we all started laughing. Then the referee came on, blew his whistle at the band and told

them to get off! So as they marched off they played 'Home Sweet Home' - very apt, very witty! Then we beat United 3-0!"

Clearly, the Blues could not afford to continue playing at a patched up venue, and the expense of building a modern main stand at the ground would not have proved value for money, so City had to move. The decisions that followed led to significant developments in the game across the region – City had planned on moving to the Belle Vue pleasure gardens, but instead moved to Maine Road thus causing Belle Vue to find new activities for its stadium including speedway and eventually a new football side Manchester Central FC. The development of the region's grounds is featured elsewhere in the book, but it has to be stressed that this was one of the most significant moments in the development of the game locally, as City's move meant the region had two venues capable of staging crowds of over 70,000.

For the smaller local sides the years that followed were mainly successful, although Bury were not quite ready to return to the top flight. They were an established Second Division side immediately after the war but retained an ambition to become one of the elite again. In 1924 they achieved promotion and remained there for most of the decade.

At Stockport finishing bottom of Division Two in 1921 could have caused significant problems for the side. That season a Third Division had been created of southern based sides, and in 1921-22 season a northern division was to be created. Stockport became the first side to experience relegation from Division Two to the Third Division. This could have brought a serious decline in County's fortunes but they won the first Division Three North title comfortably and returned to Division Two for the 1922-23 season. Simply winning a championship was a significant boost to the game locally and County's achievements in 1922 rank as highly as any of the region's earlier successes.

The creation of the northern division when announced on 7th March 1921 gave an enormous boost to the fortunes of other local clubs, and two of the region's sides made it into the new league – Rochdale and Stalybridge Celtic. Basically the development of the Third Division North resulted in the League accepting virtually all the prominent northern non-League sides of the period into the new division although it was not certain that Stalybridge would make it. They were still a relatively small side in comparison with the other Central League clubs and the Football League Management Committee decided that 14 clubs – Accrington, Ashington, Barrow, Chesterfield, Crewe, Darlington, Durham, Hartlepools United, Lincoln City, Nelson, Rochdale, Tranmere, Walsall and Wrexham – would be admitted automatically, while other contenders would have to go through a voting process. This process ultimately led to the election of Wigan Borough (34 votes), Halifax Town (25 votes), Southport (25 votes) and Stalybridge Celtic (25 votes). There were ten rejected sides, mostly from Merseyside and West Yorkshire including South Liverpool, Doncaster Rovers and Wakefield City (Wakefield remains the largest city without League representation today).

The fortunes of the two new sides were significantly different during the opening season of 1921-22. Rochdale found the new league difficult despite an opening day 6-3 victory over Accrington Stanley – five Rochdale goals were netted in the final 20 minutes. Victories became less commonplace with their first away win coming as late as 11th February at Lincoln but even then the side had relied on an own goal for the victory.

The season ended with Rochdale placed last (20th) in the division 3 points behind 19th placed

Halifax and the two sides became the first to face re-election from the division. They were both successful with Halifax receiving 42 votes and Rochdale gaining 31 – 22 more than their nearest rivals Doncaster Rovers. Over the course of the following seasons Rochdale improved and in 1923-24 they finished second to Wolverhampton Wanderers in the Northern table with 62 points, one point behind the leaders. This remains their highest points tally under the 2 points for a win system (it would also be the highest if 3 points were given for victories back then). Sadly, only one side was eligible for promotion as both the Northern and Southern sections of the Third Division shared the two promotion spots available.

For Stalybridge Celtic the opening years actually seemed more positive, however ultimately Celtic would be the first casualty of the new division. In the opening season Celtic finished 7th and had opened that campaign with a thrilling 6-0 demolition of Chesterfield – this remains Celtic's best result in the League.

There was a great deal of optimism around the town and when their second League season commenced it was anticipated Celtic would at least match the 1922 final position. Sadly an indifferent start, peppered with a few high scoring defeats meant the season could not be a successful one. Celtic were never a struggling side, but they did appear to be at best a mid-table side. Then from 7th October the side embarked on a fine run of results with only 2 defeats coming in 12 games (8 matches ended in victory). Those results lifted Celtic to fourth place and optimism took hold once more. Alongside this progress was made in the FA Cup and victories over Nelson (1-0) and Bristol Rovers (2-1 after a goalless game at Bower Fold in front of a crowd of 8,800) set up a meeting with one of football's leading sides of the period West Bromwich Albion.

At Albion on 13th January 1923 Celtic managed a goalless draw in front of a crowd recorded as 24,008 – the largest Celtic were to play in front of. That result suggested to Celtic's relatively small but loyal band of supporters that the club were destined for a bright future and an enormous crowd was anticipated at 12,000 capacity Bower Fold.

On the day supporters started queuing at 9.30 for a 2.15 kick off and by the time the game started an official crowd of 9,753 (paying £550) was recorded. It was a club record but still fell short of the 10,400 who had attended a Dick Kerr's Ladies match there in February 1921.

The game itself saw Celtic contain Albion for the first 81 minutes, but sadly Albion managed to net twice in that final period to knock Stalybridge out of the tournament. Sadly, the defeat hit Celtic extremely hard and they struggled to get that result out of their system. Only one point came in the following seven games and it was not until 17th March that their next victory came – 3-2 at home to Grimsby.

Despite the loss of form, Stalybridge managed to end the season in 11th place, however off the pitch the club's management team were seriously questioning whether the town could support a League side and, after much heartache, the decision was taken to withdraw from the League. It was an understandable decision as the club clearly struggled to pay its way, but considering the fortunes of many other clubs during this period it was perhaps the wrong decision. Stalybridge may not have been a well attended side on the face of it – their average in 1922-23 was the second worst in the League at 3,440 – but they were still attracting over 1,500 more than Durham City and they survived until 1928 without significantly increasing support.

In truth, Stalybridge's departure was a lesson to the other Manchester region sides. Their committee perhaps had more vision than any of the other sides in the region and with their resignation they knew they could guarantee a life for the club outside of the League. Sadly, a return to League football has never presented itself and it is interesting to note what could have been achieved had Celtic remained in the League. Would the club have followed a life similar to Rochdale, or would the side have established itself in a similar way to Bury?

At the time of Celtic's resignation, Stalybridge was part of Cheshire and the borough of Tameside was some fifty years off being created. As the Tameside area today consists of several individual towns, most with at least one strong football team of its own (Droylsden, Hyde, Mossley, the Ashton clubs etc.), it is difficult to understand how far any one of those sides could have developed. Often calls have been made for the borough's sides to merge to form one strong Tameside club, but it is highly debateable whether that would actually have benefited the game in general across the borough.

With Stalybridge's resignation came the end of a brief period when the immediate Manchester area could boast seven League clubs. Nine if Wigan Borough and Bolton Wanderers are included. At that same point the much densely populated Greater London area had ten, but no other region came close.

On the football field, apart from Stockport's Third Division North title in 1922 trophy success eluded the local sides through the immediate post war period, although Bury's second placed finish in Division Two in 1924 did bring a welcome return to the top flight for the region's first FA Cup winners.

The closest any side came to significant national success was when City finished runners-up to Burnley in 1920, but the Blues endured a relegation in 1926 – despite reaching the FA Cup final. In fact the story of City's 1925-26 season is one of the club's most famous. That season the Blues experienced an exceptionally poor spell during the opening months of the season. Only three of the opening 18 games ended in victory and manager David Ashworth, the man who guided Oldham into the League, moved on. It appears he was dismissed although records do not categorically state this. From that point until the latter stages of the season City did not appoint a new manager instead a committee, led by vice-chairman Albert Alexander snr, took charge.

Alexander guided City to the FA Cup final (defeating United in the semi-final at Bramall Lane), where they were defeated 1-0 by Bolton. The following Monday new manager Peter Hodge took charge of the side and his side won one of the two remaining fixtures. Had City drawn their final match, instead of losing it, they would have retained their top flight status, sadly a penalty save in that match cost the Blues dearly and they became the first FA Cup finalists to be relegated in the same season. The **Daily Telegraph** reported:

"Manchester City have become the first Football League club to reach the Cup final and be relegated in the same season. They went down in most unfortunate circumstances only eight days after los-ing 1-0 to Bolton at Wembley.

"What an extraordinary season it has been for City. They scored 89 goals, more than any relegated club in the history of the League. And they stormed into the Cup final after an orgy of goalscoring in earlier rounds. Then they couldn't score a single goal at Wembley. But it was a thrilling final. On the last day of the season, with Notts County already condemned to the drop, Leeds United and Burnley were a point behind Manchester. So City, with a superior goal average, needed only to draw their game at Newcastle even if the other two won. City lost 5-2 after missing a penalty, the other two both won 4-1... and City were down."

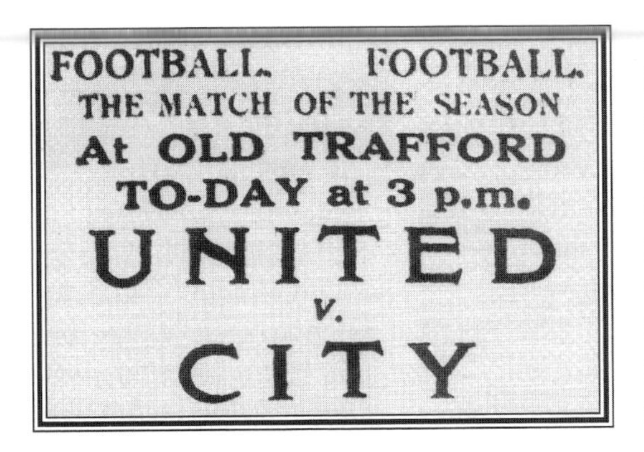

The big draw: City defeated newly promoted United 6-1 in this derby match at Old Trafford in 1926.

The phrase 'Typical City' seems to have been borne that season, especially as the season had also seen Alexander's Blues defeat United 6-1 in the largest derby victory at Old Trafford. United themselves had been promoted in 1925 as runners-up to Leicester, while Bury ended the 1925-26 season as our highest placed side. They finished the season in fourth place – at the time of going to press this remained their highest all-time finish.

Trophy success arrived in 1927-28 with City winning the Division Two title, but the highest placed local side that season was Bury who were fifth in Division One. Although there was much excitement across the region, particularly in Stockport where consecutive second placed finishes in Division Three North had suggested the side were close to success, the rest of the 1920s was not one of significant achievement. Relegation for Manchester United in 1931 was also an indication that the club had perhaps overstretched themselves with the move to Old Trafford two decades earlier.

It is true that the Old Trafford move did continue to have a bearing on United's development. At the time the move to the new site was seen as a chance to establish the Reds as a major side and in recent years, in fact since the 1950s, many have incorrectly talked of the move as propelling United forward, but this is far from the case. United's heartland was, like City, in the east of Manchester. The densely populated areas of Clayton, Newton Heath, Ardwick, Gorton, Openshaw and the rest were where the game grew.

United, in particular, owed their salvation in 1902 to a vast number of east Mancunians. They were the people who helped the club relaunch itself and they were the people who helped support the team. Sure the actual finances came from Stafford and the other investors in 1902, but without the ordinary workers of Clayton, Beswick, Newton Heath and surrounding districts the success would not have come. As United found trophy success in Clayton it seemed obvious that the side should have developed within the area, but no. For some reason the Reds chose to move across the city to the Trafford area. In fact the side was to move outside of the city of Manchester – a move which would forever give the supporters of City boasting rights.

The move to Old Trafford was the furthest move away from its roots any club had made including that made by Sheffield Wednesday to Hillsborough in 1899. It was a bold move and one which may not entirely have been done for the direct good of the supporters. It certainly gave the Reds an opportunity to develop a fantastic stadium, but it also alienated those supporters who worked in the Newton Heath and Clayton area and would not have time between finishing their shifts and making the journey across the city to Trafford. In addition, some of the locals may not have been able to afford the tram fare to United's new home. To get from Clayton to Old Trafford would have necessitated either two tram journeys or a significant walk into Manchester city centre, then a train or tram ride out again. It does not seem logical to put your most loyal supporters under this kind of pressure. With Manchester City remaining in East Manchester until 1923 workers in United's strongholds had the choice of a short walk (in some cases only a mile) or a quick tram ride to Hyde Road.

It is a fact that whereas United and City were close in terms of average attendance during the Reds final days at Clayton, the first season after the Reds' move to Old Trafford City's average rose by over 6,000. United's also increased initially, by about 3,000, but whereas City managed to first retain, then build on their new crowd despite a lack of success United in the main could not.

Of course success travelled with the Reds initially, but by the start of the 1930s with United in Division Two the loyalty of support was seriously tested. Any new fans the Reds had picked up from Trafford, Salford and the surrounding towns presumably continued to attend games, but the statistics suggest only the most dedicated of supporter would have travelled from Newton Heath and Clayton. At the end of the 1930-31 season United's average stood at 11,685 in a venue capable of holding at least a further 65,000.

This is extremely significant as within East Manchester there was a feeling that football was deserting the very people who had made it popular in the region. This problem was exacerbated when City moved to Maine Road in 1923. The new City venue could hold around 85,000, and with City's support tending to come from Gorton, Ardwick and some of the areas where United had also been strong, it was clear the local population had cause for complaint. The difference between City's move and United's was that Maine Road was not quite so far out of the city centre plus, for the majority of fans the 53 tram which cut through the eastern districts (passing the modern day City Of Manchester Stadium, and close to United's former home of Bank Street), travelled on to Moss Side. Later the 53 bus would follow this route and it would also stretch on to Old Trafford.

What City's move did do however was create a feeling that East Manchester needed its own side. As the two leading League sides in the region had both moved out of the eastern districts key local figures felt something had to be done, particularly as the area already possessed one magnificent sporting stadium and, in 1926, also possessed the new greyhound stadium – both sites had been considered by City as potential homes early in the 1920s.

So, a new football club was created called Manchester Central FC. Deliberately the initials MCFC were chosen and above the main entrance to the old athletics stadium on Hyde Road, less than a mile from City's old Hyde Road ground and about 500 yards from the St. Mark's Church Hall where City's predecessor was originally formed, those initials were placed in big bold overlapping letters. Anyone uncertain of how football had developed during the mid 1920s would have surmised that this MCFC was City not Central. In fact confusion on the identity of the club lasted into the 1970s and 1980s. Journalist Mike Pavasovic: *"I used to go to Belle Vue Speedway in the late seventies and eighties at the old Hyde Road stadium watching the likes of Peter Collins, and I*

The main entrance to Manchester Central's ground photographed in the 1950s. The old MCFC ironwork can still be seen in the semi-circle above the central entrance gate.

remember being stood and noticing in the old wrought-iron railings the initials MCFC. I thought it was City at first, but I later learned it was Central."

Central's match programme was printed by the same company that produced City's and its style, colouring and content was remarkably similar to the Blues. It should be said though that Central adopted a kit which could not be confused with either Manchester side. They chose to play in white shirts with black shorts.

There had been a Manchester Central at the turn of the century playing at Birch Park, but this new Central side had no connection. Similarly, comments that Central was a name that in 1902 Newton Heath almost chose instead of Manchester United seem wide of the mark. This Central side was formed in 1928 by local businessmen, including the key figure at this point behind Belle Vue Zoo and amusement park, John Henry Iles, although the man seen by most as the founder of Central was the former City director Mr. John Ayrton. Ayrton had been a City director between 1912 to 1927 (this included the period which saw the Blues move from Ardwick to Maine Road).

Apparently Ayrton had become disillusioned with life at Maine Road and felt the new ground was too far away from City's roots. At the time of Central's first game Ayrton was put forward as spokesman by the new club to explain their raison d'etre:

"Ever since the City club left the Hyde Road district I have thought of the desirability of having a club on this side of Manchester, and my numerous inquiries as to whether such an organisation would be welcomed in these parts were so well received that the idea quickly developed. This is a happy day for

those of us who have done the spade work, the first results of which you see today in the alterations and improvements effected on this famous old ground.

"Our whole object is to develop local talent, and gradually to build up the club so that one day it may take its place in the Third Division of the Football League. We believe there is no need for clubs to go to Scotland in search for young players. All our 21 reserves so far signed are local products, and our aim is to develop and, if possible, to make first class players of them. Manchester has the biggest sporting community in the provinces, and is well supplied with playing fields for youths; moreover, within a five mile radius of this ground there is a population of a million and a half to draw upon for support. Surely then we have every reason to hope that there is plenty of room for our club, especially as the two local League clubs are so far away from this district."

Ayrton and the other directors of the new club received substantial support from former City and United players, most notably Charlie Pringle (who left City at a stage in his career when he still had much to offer), ex-Blue Johnny McMahon and former United Captain Charlie Roberts (by this stage Roberts was running a successful tobacco and confectionary business, and his son played for Central). Another man involved from a coaching point of view was Charlie Pringle's father-in-law, Billy Meredith. Meredith remained the biggest name in Manchester soccer and had only finished playing in 1924 at the age of 49.

Eli Fletcher, the ex-Watford manager and another former City man, was also involved in coaching at Belle Vue. According to Ayrton:

"We have had the valuable help of those famous old players Messrs. W. Meredith, J. McMahon, and C. Roberts in selecting players from trials, and we are confident that we have begun our task along the right lines. Our first team is almost entirely composed of men of League experience. Jimmy Branston (goalkeeper) has played with Rotherham County and Preston North End; E. Gregory (right back) with Hurst; J. Mulligan (left back) with Manchester City and Southport; E. Regan (right half) with Wrexham; Charlie Pringle (centre half) with Scotland and Manchester City; J. Bain (left half) with Manchester United; J. Allen (outside right) hails from Paisley; W. Smith (inside right) has seen service with Huddersfield Town, Halifax Town, and Barrow; Frank McPherson (centre forward) with Barrow and Manchester United; R.S. Williams (inside left) was Chesterfield's leading marksman last season, and A.E. Trotter (outside left) was with Port Vale. In addition our trainer Eli Fletcher, the Manchester City back, will be available if wanted as a player."

Central's first game was in the Lancashire Combination on 25th August 1928 when they faced Lancaster Town. The side had been a late addition to the Combination and as a result Central's opening fixture list was a little uneven. Most of the Combination fixtures had been set up prior to Central's admission and therefore Manchester's newest club could only fit in where gaps existed. Despite their late addition Central made rapid progress. Ayrton:

"I want to take this opportunity of expressing my gratitude for the splendid manner in which my co-directors have co-operated to launch the club. The preparatory work has been arduous in view of the fact that the club's admission to the Lancashire Combination only dates from June, for only then could we start to put our plans into effect. The erection of the new covered and portable stands, with dressing rooms for players of both teams and match officials, offices and boardroom, and the building of a new entrance to the ground are all the work of a few weeks."

Billy Meredith, City trainer Jimmy Broad, and Charlie Pringle at Maine Road in the early 1920s. Meredith and Pringle would later help create Manchester Central FC.

Central's creation was viewed by the majority of East Mancunians as a positive move, and beyond Manchester there were also plenty of others who wanted to see the side successful. Blackburn Rovers, the FA Cup winners, agreed to play Central in their second home game. The match, played on 3rd September at Belle Vue, was probably the first to cause United and City to first look at Central as a threat. In the days leading up to the game Central made it clear that Blackburn were very supportive and that the Cup holders were to bring the FA Cup to Belle Vue. In addition, the former Blackburn player and one of England's greatest players of all time Bob Crompton was to start the game off.

Manchester Central September 1928.

Back (l to r): Gregory, Williams, Branston, Allan, Mulligan & Fletcher. Front (l to r): Regan, Smith, Pringle, McPherson, Bain & Trotter.

Inevitably, with the support of so many great players and of course the likes of Blackburn giving their good wishes, a promising start was made with Central ending their first season 7th out of 20 in the Lancashire Combination.

This wonderful first season convinced the management to apply to join the Football League at the end of that first season (1929). Central recognised that with strong businessmen and former players backing them, and with the vast population of East Manchester on their doorstep they had much to offer. That year nine sides entered the vote for election to the Third Division North and it was no surprise when Hartlepools United were re-elected with 33 of the votes, however two sides were up for re-election with Ashington failing to gain enough votes. They were replaced by York City, and Central received a mere two votes. Nevertheless, this was greater than four more established north-west sides.

The following season, Charlie Pringle was signed by Bradford City while Charlie Roberts junior was convinced by his father to concentrate on their business interests rather than play competitive football by the end of the campaign. Central's ambition remained high however and for the 1929-30 season they not only challenged for the Combination title, but they also fielded a reserve side in the Cheshire County League (a competition deemed by many on a par with the Lancashire Combination). This was significant as the only other second teams playing in this league were the reserves of Football League sides.

'Phone No.: OPENSHAW 698. Telegraphic Address: "MANCEN, MANCHESTER."
Club Colours: White shirts, black knickers.
Directors:
Mr. C. B. CLEGG, *Chairman*. Mr. G. HARDMAN, *Vice-Chairman*.
Mr. P. ELSON, Mr. J. AYRTON, Mr. A. M. BOOTH, Mr. C. O'BRIEN,
Capt. H. BAXTER.
Secretary: Mr. JAMES McMAHON.
Ground: BELLE VUE, HYDE ROAD, MANCHESTER.

MEMBERS OF THE LANCASHIRE COMBINATION

THE MANCHESTER CENTRAL FOOTBALL CLUB

FIRST SEASON 1928-29

OFFICIAL PROGRAMME

Vol. 1. No. 3. SEPTEMBER 8th, 1928. TWOPENCE.

MANCHESTER CENTRAL.

Back Row: Gregory, Williams, Branston, Allan, Mulligan, Fletcher.
Front Row: Regan, Smith, Pringle, McPherson, Bain, Trotter.

ALLIED NEWSPAPERS LIMITED, Printers, Withy Grove, Manchester

In the Combination Central finished second, one point behind Lancaster, and they also reached the second round proper of the FA Cup, defeating Mansfield Town (Roberts jnr netted one of Central's goals in the 2-0 victory). In the next round they faced Division Three North's Wrexham at Belle Vue before a crowd of approximately 8,500. Wrexham won the match 1-0 but the attendance proved Central could receive significant support. It is interesting to note that City had a crowd of 18,246 on the same day for the visit of Leicester while United were watched by a crowd of 18,182 the following day when they faced Everton. Both City and United's games had been Division One fixtures.

It is worth stating that, a bit like the modern day FC United, Central's players were still of quality and that the side did attract significantly better players than many of the other sides competing for a place in the Football League. One such star player who featured for Central around this time was goalkeeper Bert Gray. Gray was a Welsh international who had made 100 league appearances for Oldham, and 68 for City prior to joining Central in August 1929. Gray stayed at Central for about a year and played against Scotland whilst on Central's books. In total he made 24 caps, but it says much about the Belle Vue side that they could attract players of that quality.

4 Manchester Central Programme.

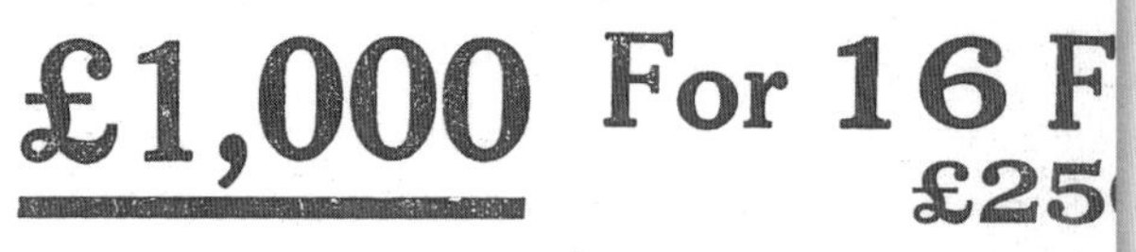
£1,000 For 16 F
£25
SEE TO-MORROW'S SUND

SATURDAY, DECEMBER 14th, 1929.

MANCHESTER CENTRAL

1 GRAY (A) Goal

2 HAMILTON Right Back — 3 ROBERTS (S) Left Back

4 BROWN Right Half-Back — 5 CLAYTON Centre Half-Back — 6 INCH Left Half-Back

7 ROBERTS (F) Outside Right — 8 PELAN Inside Right — 9 JONES Centre — 10 SMITH Inside Left — 11 PARTRIDGE Outside Left

Kick-off - 2-15 p.m.

Referee: P. G. BRUMMITT, Sheffield.

12 BELL Outside Left — 13 BAMFORD Inside Left — 14 MAYS Centre — 15 WOODHOUSE Inside Right — 16 LONGMUIR Outside Right

17 CROMPTON Left Half-Back — 18 READ Centre Half-Back — 19 DICKIE Right Half-Back

20 LUMBERG Left Back — 21 JONES Right Back

22 FINNIGAN Goal

WREXHAM

NEXT HOME MATCH.

LANCASHIRE COMBINATION

SATURDAY, December 21st. *Kick-off - 2-15 p.m.*

CENTRAL v. DARWEN

Welsh international 'keeper Gray was one of Central's stars.

With such a great season and with quality players, Central were encouraged again to apply to join the League in 1930. This time they received 13 votes but both Halifax and Barrow were re-elected. They applied again in 1931 but this time Rochdale were up for re-election and inevitably they received most votes, while the other side up for re-election Nelson were actually voted out and replaced by Chester. Central were fourth again in the voting system but only managed four votes. It soon became clear to Central's management that the election process would only succeed if the side leaving had very little to offer, as with Nelson.

For the 1931-32 season Central decided to concentrate on the Cheshire League instead of the Combination, and the side's reserves would move into the Manchester League. Then, just when hope of joining the League was disappearing, Wigan Borough announced they would be resigning from the League. Wigan Borough were a Third Division North side and their announcement on 26th October immediately threw Central a lifeline.

Wigan had been struggling for some time and with debts of £30,000 and dwindling attendances the decision was taken to pull out of the League. Central's forward thinking chairman, George Hardman, immediately leapt into action and prior to Wigan's decision he'd already put together a bid to replace the club. Hardman's offer was for Central to continue with the Wigan fixtures and for all existing results to stand. Their record was not great and stood at Played 12, Won 3, Drawn 1, Lost 8, Goals Scored 12, Goals Conceded 32, and Points 7.

On Monday 26th Hardman told reporters:

"Naturally we hope that Manchester Central will be able to take the place of Wigan Borough. We made our application to the secretary of the League last Friday. Of course the situation is full of difficulties, because if it is that we are fortunate enough to be elected in place of Wigan ten of Wigan's home fixtures would be at home when Manchester City, our nearest neighbours, are also at home. But a way out of the difficulties would no doubt be found if it is that we secure admission to the League.

"That we would do our best can be taken for granted. We have three times before made application for League status and if it is that the Management Committee look upon our application in a favourable light we shall do our best to strengthen the teams. All I hope is that our application is successful."

Central's acceptance into the League felt certain to succeed on that Monday, and the following day Nomad, writing in the **Manchester Evening Chronicle,** felt certain that the League would accept Central's bid. He was very much looking at the matter from a Central viewpoint, rather than City or United, and his only word of caution was that Central might find it difficult attracting enough support because of their potential fixture clash with City. He implied that it would be better for Central if they clashed with United as this would not really be an issue to Central and would not limit Central's support. The implications for United were not considered but they would have been disastrous.

Ultimately, it was the impact on the existing Manchester clubs that was to affect Central's chances. While City had been the fifth best supported side in the League with an average of 26,849 in 1930-21, United could only attract 11,685. The Reds had also been relegated and so opened 1931-32 in Division Two. Their home match on 24th October 1931 immediately prior to the announcement that Central wanted to join the League was attended by a miserable 6,694 but even that was almost double the opening match of the season when 3,507 witnessed a 3-2 defeat by Southampton on 2nd September. Old Trafford had not been developed for such a poorly supported and poorly performing side. If Central's League bid was deemed to damage any club it was clearly United who had most to lose.

It is fair to say that City's crowds had dropped during the period following the creation of Central. In 1927-28 the Blues were the best supported side in the entire League with an average of 37,468, so the club had lost around 11,000 fans during Central's growth, but commentators at the time seemed to imply that Central had not impacted on the Blues, nor did they feel the new club could damage City. The most respected journalist of the period, Ivan Sharpe from the Sunday Chronicle, knew Manchester football well and was well known by both Manchester League sides. He felt that Central should be admitted simply because he felt United were failing and that the new side would have no impact on City. Thinking about the Blues he stated:

"A third club in Manchester would not damage the City at all seriously. It would build up football interest. I don't like the way Manchester is slipping back in football. Where are those 30,000 football

followers who used to assemble at Old Trafford? The odd 25,000 are missing. Is football to lose them? It is time something was done about it."

In the **Daily Dispatch** another well-known journalist Adjutant commented:

"Manchester Central, potentially are not merely a Second Division, but a First Division club of the future. There should be room in Manchester for three League clubs and, after all, Belle Vue is a long way from Maine Road and longer still from Old Trafford."

Despite support and interest from all aspects of the media and the people of Manchester, ultimately it was the Football League clubs themselves that mattered. The Division Three North's Chairman Alderman Cropper of Chesterfield welcomed Central's bid and said that he had canvassed the views of other clubs and they were all keen to see Central join the League. Another of the region's sides Stockport County – perhaps the club after City and United with most to lose because of the close proximity of Belle Vue to the edges of Stockport – seemed extremely positive about Central. Although senior officials would not talk openly about the situation they did talk with Cropper and a former director, who refused to give his name because of concern for his own role within the game, told the **Evening Chronicle**:

"At Stockport we feel that Manchester Central have shown the right kind of spirit and enterprise. The Third Division wants clubs with enterprising people behind them, for there are too many members in the Division struggling."

United and City felt otherwise. The Blues and the Reds saw Central as a threat. The United Chairman GH Lawton refused to talk publicly but it was clear he had serious issue with Central's ambition. At City secretary Wilf Wild called a Board meeting to discuss the matter, and it is now understood that at that meeting the views of Manchester United were aired extensively. It seems that City, as the side in the strongest position, were able to exert more pressure on the League than United, and as the Blues and the Reds directors knew each other exceptionally well it was decided that City had to make the strongest complaint. United and City were rivals off the pitch but in so many other areas they were exceptionally close. City's vice-chairman Albert Alexander snr had a seat reserved for him in United's directors' box for every game – he was also the man who supplied the coach and horses for United's 1909 FA Cup homecoming - while Reds' officials attended City's home games. The two sides shared many ideals at this point and they also recognised the need to co-operate, although this did not always manifest itself.

So on 27th October City, on behalf of both sides, lodged a formal complaint. The reasons for the objection stated that gates were dwindling at both Manchester clubs – but by significant numbers at Old Trafford – as a result of the industrial depression and that was more or less it. The League Management Committee telephoned both the Blues and the Reds and, when questioned, the two sides aired the same objections. John McKenna, the Liverpool Chairman and President of the League, spoke directly with officials at both clubs, but particularly at United where he had been a guest at the opening of Old Trafford in 1910. Immediately on hearing United's concern Central's bid was rejected.

Central were hugely disappointed, as were a significant number of Mancunians. George Hardman spoke on behalf of his club:

"This is to be regretted, as we think there ought to be League football in the Belle Vue area, where there are 440,000 people within two miles, and a million people within four miles. This is surely enough for two Football League clubs in a place like Manchester. What about London? Their clubs have far more opposition than this and I don't believe even today London can compare with Manchester as a soccer hot-bed.

"All I have to add is that there seems to be a sad lack of enterprise all round in Manchester so far as League football is concerned. We shall carry on. Given reasonable support we shall continue making applications for admission to the Football League. We shall get there before long."

Whether Hardman deliberately ignored United when he made the comment 'two Football League clubs' or whether it was a simple slip of the tongue is not known, but it is clear that United's position was ultimately the deciding factor. Ivan Sharpe was of the opinion that the Reds were a dying club and he seemed to imply that Central would ultimately replace the Reds:

"In view of Manchester United's sorry position I certainly think Manchester Central should have been admitted. But the League do not go over the heads of their members."

Nomad, writing in the **Evening Chronicle**, held a similar view:

"Keen disappointment is expressed that Manchester is not to have a Third Football League club, especially as there is a splendid 45,000 ground available at Belle Vue, and that Manchester United are so signally failing to keep Manchester on the football map."

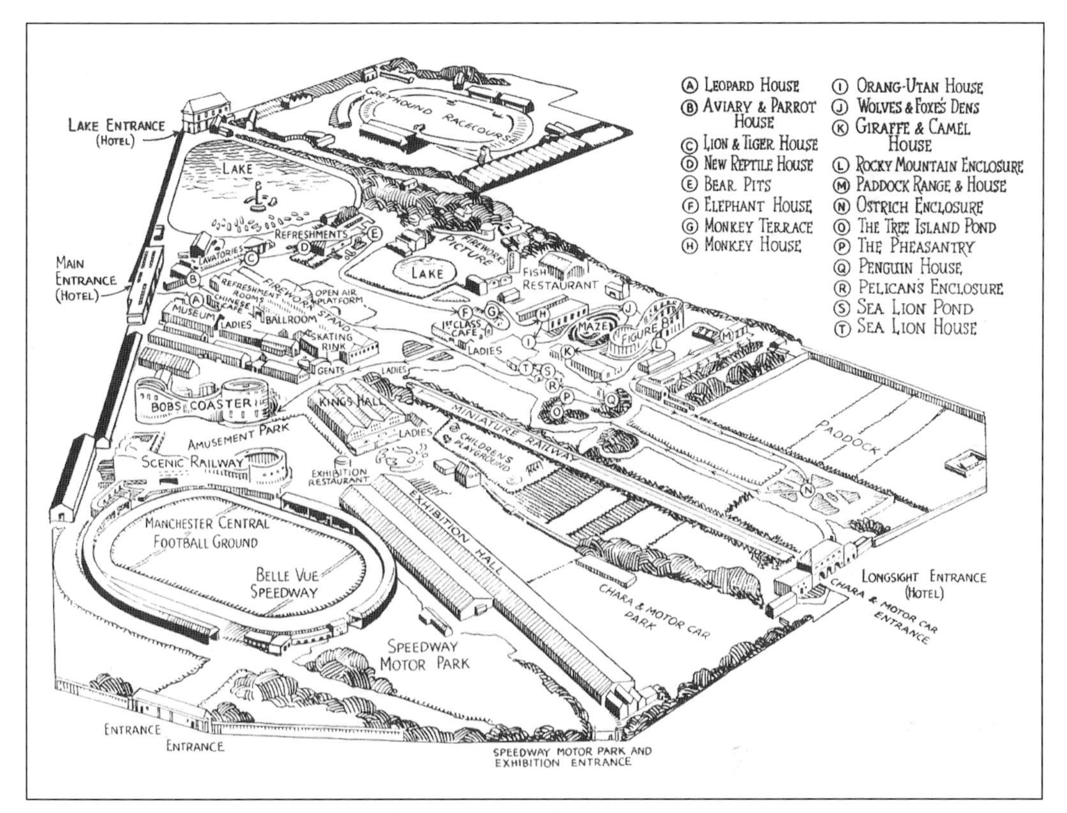

A 1931 plan of the Belle Vue site, showing Manchester Central's home.

Gorton Park (City's home 1882-84)
Present day
Greyhound
Stadium
Pink Bank Lane
(City's home
1884-85)
Belle Vue
(home of
Manchester
Central)
Kirkmanshulme Cricket Club
(City's home 1881-82)

Despite the League's decision the Third Division clubs did not give up hope. On 31st October Alderman Cropper decided to call a meeting of all Division Three North clubs in Manchester to be held on the first Thursday of November. He wanted all grievances out in the open and he invited both City and United to attend to explain their objections. This was a significant attempt by the Third Division sides to ensure they held the power to decide who is admitted to their division, however the Third Division clubs were still classed as minor clubs when it came to voting and so on. The clubs of Division One and Two held the real power.

The Football League's Management Committee were angry at the Third Division's plans and they forced Cropper to cancel the meeting. Whether this was because the other Manchester sides objected, or whether it was because the League saw it as an attack on their own power is not clear, but it is obvious that this was the final nail in Central's coffin. The League Management Committee protected its more powerful clubs at the expense of the smaller sides.

Wigan Borough's fixtures were expunged from the records and this caused serious issues for every Division Three North club, not least Lincoln who had defeated Wigan twice and were favourites for promotion, but ended up scraping into the top spot on the last day of the season on goal average. Financially, those teams that had not played both fixtures against Wigan lost income (in those days home and away income was split between the sides, so even away games affected the balance sheets), while the acceptance of Central would have brought significant crowds to at least the local sides of Stockport and Rochdale – a team that was in desperate need.

For Central all optimism was drained away. The club knew that it could be popular, it knew it had a lot to offer, and it also knew that the people of East Manchester in particular were on their side, however the realisation also dawned that so long as Manchester United remained in a perilous state in the League then the League Management Committee would always block their ambition. When the season ended – by which time they'd also faced Third Division North's champions Lincoln City in a FA Cup tie – Central decided not to apply for the League again. They had finished fifth in the Cheshire League which normally would not have deterred them, however the Football League was forced to restructure a little. Mansfield Town were moved from the Southern section (an additional vacancy was created in the South, filled by Aldershot) and so there was only one vacancy in the North. Rochdale, finishing 21st, were up for re-election and the only other applicants were Rhyl and Wigan Athletic. Wigan received no votes, Rhyl 2, and Rochdale 47.

By that time Central had decided to call it a day, and the club ceased to exist. Since that time the Central name has been used from time to time by small local sides, however during the 21st Century it became listed as one of the options for the new Manchester United side created by supporters disgruntled at the direction of the Reds. Ultimately the founders and supporters of the new club selected the name FC United of Manchester, however the option for Central was based on the incorrect assumption that Central had been one of the original options for Manchester United back in 1902. There is no evidence to suggest Central was an option in 1902, especially as there had already been a Manchester Central in existence during the decade prior to United's name change. It would have been ironic if Central's name had been chosen instead of FC United as it was Central that formed the biggest threat to United's existence back in 1931.

As far as 1930s Manchester is concerned the decision not to allow Central into the League did protect United, and once the club disappeared crowds at Old Trafford did increase – despite serious struggles on the pitch. So what would have happened if Central had become a Division

Three side? Inevitably Central would have capitalised on those United and City fans living in East Manchester, and potentially crowds for both sides would have dropped. Possibly by the time United were seriously in trouble financially and on the pitch – in 1933-34 they dropped to 20th in Division Two - Central may have overtaken them. Central could have achieved promotion to Division Two in 1933 and that would inevitably have created a real conflict between the two sides, especially as the Blues were enjoying great success in the FA Cup and challenging for the League title.

It is highly likely that Central, with significant financial backing from the Belle Vue complex, would have become a First Division side by the outbreak of war. Whether United would have survived is open to debate, but it does appear unlikely. Similarly, post war a financially strong Manchester Central would have had a significant advantage over City. Assuming United would have survived it is clear that a strong Central could have seriously affected City's post war development and by the mid-sixties when it is known that one of City's directors considered a merger with United, it is possible that a merger could have occurred with Central.

Moving to more recent times, Central's position in East Manchester would surely have stopped City's move to the City Of Manchester Stadium. Maybe it would have been Central inhabiting that venue instead, or maybe they would have taken over Old Trafford in the 1930s.

Clearly, all of this is irrelevant however it does demonstrate how the people of Manchester can impact the role of Mancunian sport. Central, created because the inhabitants of East Manchester felt deserted when first United then City moved away, went from nothing to serious League hopefuls with a 45,000 capacity venue in less than 3 years. In more recent times FC United of Manchester has been created as a result of supporter dissatisfaction in the direction of Manchester United and by 2007 the new club were already attracting significant crowds and gaining ground on the region's other clubs. They even had their own TV programme on Channel M. FC United are covered elsewhere in this book, but the parallels are clear. Will United and City ultimately combine to stop the new venture? Will FC United ever threaten the livelihood of City or United? It all seems unlikely, but the new side may affect the region's smaller clubs.

City and United's role in the Central affair clearly demonstrates the worst aspects of football in Manchester. Sure the Reds and Blues worked together and protected their own interests, but did they truly consider the positive impact Central could have had on the region? Clearly not.

ATTENDANCE DETAIL SEASON BY SEASON - 1919-1921

Season	City	United	Oldham	Bury	Stockport
1919-20	25240	27140	13725	5940	7300
1920-21	31020	35020	19200	11120	9100

LEAGUE POSITIONS SEASON BY SEASON - 1919-1921

Season	City	United	Oldham	Bury	Stockport
1919-20	7	12	17	27	38
1920-21	2	13	19	33	44

CHAPTER THIRTEEN

ROCHDALE

At a meeting convened by Mr. Harvey Rigg in the Central Council School, Fleece Street, last evening, with Mr Herbert Hopkinson in the chair, it was decided to form a club to be called Rochdale Association Football Club. Rochdale Observer, 1907

WHILE the role of Manchester Central brought question marks over the balance of power within the city, the twenties and thirties saw sides on the edges of the region bring pride to their communities.

In 1920 the first division of the Southern League in effect became the Third Division of the Football League and then in 1921 the League decided to create a northern version of the Third Division. Fourteen clubs were immediately accepted into the League without a vote, including a side from our region – Rochdale. Another Manchester region side, Stalybridge Celtic, was accepted after an election ballot. Stalybridge's League record was brief and is covered later in this book, while Rochdale have gone on to become known as one of football's stalwarts.

It took Dale only fourteen years from formation in 1907 through to League football, although it is worth noting that the roots of football in the town go back much further. Rugby was by far the predominant sport during nineteenth century Rochdale, and from a soccer point of view, near-neighbours Heywood Central were the first to make an impression.

Heywood were a member of the Lancashire Combination and, in 1887, they entered the FA Cup for the first time - only four sides from the Manchester area had entered before this date. Heywood continued to enter the competition until 1995, but as far as the town of Rochdale itself was concerned it was the following season when the first proper town club became established by members of the Rochdale Athletic Club and the Rochdale Athletic Ground Company. This Rochdale side joined the Lancashire Combination, with a reserve side in the Central Lancashire League.

Most of the sides competing in the Combination were the reserve sides of Football League clubs, and so the quality of the competition varied depending on the exploits of those clubs in the League. For Rochdale the opening season was however a good one, with the side finishing sixth – the highest of the non-reserve sides. Ahead of them were the reserves of Liverpool, Preston, Bury, City, and Blackburn Rovers. The club entered the FA Cup for the first time the following season and defeated Bay Moss Exchange 5-3 in the first qualifying round, and then drew 1-1 at home to Horwich. A 6-2 defeat followed in the replay, but Rochdale had also made the surprise decision to switch to the Lancashire League for that 1897-98 season instead of the Combination. The season was not a good one in the league and Rochdale finished third from bottom.

It is worth noting at this point that 1897 had also seen the formation of the Rochdale & District Amateur Association Football League, and so it is clear the game itself was developing in the town.

By the time of the start of the next season (1898-99) one of Rochdale's star players, forward Herbert Chapman, had moved to Grimsby Town. Chapman, formerly a Stalybridge Rovers player, would later find fame as the highly successful manager of Huddersfield and Arsenal. This perhaps heralded the start of the club's downfall as the new season saw Rochdale finish 12th out of 13 clubs, although the 1899-1900 season did see them finish a creditable ninth out of 15.

At the end of that season Rochdale moved out of their home, the Athletic Grounds, and moved into Spotland (the former home of rugby union side Rochdale St. Clements). Rochdale Hornets took over the Athletic Grounds as Rochdale's sporting clubs seemed to carry out their own version of musical chairs. The move more or less marked the end for Rochdale as severe financial problems caused a variety of issues. The side still managed to enter and compete in the FA Cup but it was proving difficult to plan. They defeated Rossendale United 1-0 in the first qualifying round, then won away at Freetown 3-0 but by the time of their third qualifying round game against Workington in November the side could not raise a full team. They withdrew from the competition, and on 1st January 1901 the cub officially folded.

Despite the death of Rochdale, football was still very much alive in the town and by the start of the new season another club, Rochdale Town, was created. Town, playing at Dane Street, joined the Lancashire League immediately, and they ended their first season in seventh place, and defeated Black Lane Temperance Club 7-2 in an FA Cup qualifying match. However, they were defeated by Barrow 4-0 in the third qualifying round. The following season they again finished seventh and enjoyed a brief run in the FA Cup, including a 1-0 victory at Second Division Blackpool.

In 1903-04 Rochdale Town became members of the Lancashire Combination's new second division and they also moved to Spotland. As with the earlier Rochdale club the move was not a success and by December 1903 financial problems killed the side. Atherton Church House took over Town's Combination fixtures, but senior football in the town now took a back seat. Rugby dominated with Harvey Rigg, the man who held the lease on the fields at St. Clements (Spotland), using his sports ground for local rugby competitions in the absence of soccer. Again this venture was doomed to failure. Rochdale Hornets created their own tournament at the Athletic Grounds and this limited Rigg's opportunities. The rugby enthusiast knew he needed to find new tenants for his land and following a great deal of effort on his part a meeting was held in May to discuss the creation of a new sports club. According to the **Rochdale Observer** of 15th May 1907:

"At a meeting convened by Mr. Harvey Rigg in the Central Council School, Fleece Street, last evening, with Mr. Herbert Hopkinson in the chair, it was decided to form a club to be called Rochdale Association Football Club."

Hopkinson was the secretary of the Rochdale & District Football League and was also a well known referee. He was clearly the sort of soccer enthusiast the town needed and between him and Rigg the town was blessed with a venue and a soccer visionary. Under his guidance Rochdale AFC were admitted into the Manchester League two weeks after formation.

A committee of other enthusiasts was created and from the start those men aimed for success. They immediately set themselves up as a professional outfit with captain Zach Holden being the first professional. Perhaps they had been inspired by the development of near-neighbours Oldham who would be accepted into the Football League that summer. Whether the wider committee had previously had any involvement with the other Rochdale sides is not entirely clear, however it is obvious they would have been keen to learn the lessons of the original Rochdale and the Town club. Inevitably though their first decision – to use Spotland – must have been a brave one, after all it was the transfer of the earlier clubs to Rigg's venue that started their demise.

A public practice match between the club's Manchester League side and the 'Rest' was held on 24th August 1907 with around 400 paying 1d to watch, and then on 3rd September the new side faced Oldham Athletic in a friendly. Inevitably, 'new' Second Division side Oldham won 4-1 but the interesting aspect from Rochdale's perspective was that the crowd was an encouraging 2,000. A similar number attended the club's first Manchester League fixture four days later when a 2-2 draw with Tonge marked the club's competitive debut.

The first season was not a particularly great one with Rochdale finishing tenth out of 16 clubs. They had also endured a few heavy defeats including a 9-1 away thrashing by League leaders Denton, but nevertheless the season had been an encouraging one from a supporter and committee perspective. On 30th April the club's management met to discuss the successes and failures of the season and as a result they decided that the club's development had been such that they should apply to join the Lancashire Combination. Ambition remained high and on 21st May Harvey Rigg gave a three minute speech to the Combination on why Rochdale deserved to join the league. In the subsequent vote Dale gained enough votes to place them second and they entered the league for the start of the 1908-09 season.

Rochdale's ambition during this period was encouraging and during the summer they signed several new players including Second Division Glossop's all-rounder Patrick Galvin and Salford United's goalkeeper John Taylor. It should be stressed that any player from Salford would have been highly regarded at this point as Salford were one of the region's most forward looking non-League sides. Remember that only twelve months earlier Salford had applied to join the League itself and that only the move of Manchester United to Old Trafford in 1910 would kill off Salford's own development.

The first Combination saw Rochdale finish tenth but again there had been many highs and several lows. From an attendance perspective the games with Heywood United both attracted crowds recorded as around 5,000 – the Dale's highest at the time – while only 150 watched Turton beat Rochdale 5-1 in January, although the game was played in deep snow! There were also a couple of controversial moments with the game against St. Helen's Town being the most newsworthy. In that match the referee had failed to turn up and so both sides agreed that a St. Helen's reserve could referee the game. Galvin, who had scored two goals for Dale and was clearly on top form, was sent off by the 'impartial' referee and the Spotland supporters became incensed. A spot of crowd disorder followed, but the game continued. It ended 4-1 to the home side, but Galvin became the first player to be sent off for the club.

The following season, 1909-10, Rochdale finished the season fourth and won promotion to the first division of the Lancashire Combination. Interestingly fate played its part as a November meeting with Haslingden was abandoned after 82 minutes with Haslingden winning 3-1, while the replay was played towards the end of the season and was won 2-0 by Rochdale. Had the earlier result stood, then Haslingden would have been promoted and not Rochdale.

During the summer the club became a limited company and applied to join the Football League. Sadly the application was perhaps a year or two early and the club only received one vote. It ended the election as the bottom of eight sides. Another application was made at the end of 1910-11, but the side once again received only one vote. This was a surprise as Rochdale had performed exceptionally well during the year with a remarkable run of results seeing the side win the Lancashire Combination. During the season they had defeated the reserve side of League Champions Manchester United, and had drawn 2-2 against Liverpool reserves in front of an Anfield crowd of 16,000. In the FA Cup a new Spotland record crowd of 9,933 was set for a tie with Luton Town of the Southern League.

After the disappointment of the League election vote Rochdale, along with representatives from Chesterfield, Darlington, Hartlepools United, and Lincoln, called for a Third Division to be created. They advertised in the leading sports paper of the day, ***The Athletic News***, and attracted 15 other applicants. Most of these sides were from the north and Midlands but Cardiff, Croydon Common, and Portsmouth also expressed an interest. The Southern League, which had wanted to become the Third Division a few years earlier, objected and, as a result of their strong relationship with the Football League, Rochdale's suggestion was defeated.

Around the same time Rochdale were also facing the prospect of another breakaway league damaging their livelihood. The Football League clubs whose reserve sides competed in the Lancashire Combination were considering pulling out of the Combination as they felt the other clubs were trying to limit the League side's influence. Rochdale, by this point the side with most to lose if the League clubs resigned, were determined to stop the move and Harvey Rigg made an impassioned speech at a breakaway meeting urging the sides not to resign. Sadly, the clubs still decided to create their own competition and the Central League was created. Rochdale, recognising that the Combination would now be much weaker, then decided to apply to join the Central League, and they were accepted. However, the Combination complained and the FA vetoed the move forcing Dale to remain in the Combination for another year.

The title was won again by Dale in 1911-12 with Rochdale's home form proving particularly impressive – they were unbeaten for three years at Spotland in league competition – and inevitably they applied to join the Central League during the summer. This time they were accepted and allowed to make the move.

The first season of Central League football for Dale saw the side finish a creditable seventh, and this was their best position until the restructure of the game during the war years. In 1915-16 they competed in the Football League Lancashire Section, alongside the first teams of all the significant Lancashire teams. As most of these teams had achieved success in the Football League or the FA Cup in previous years this was a particularly high standard of football – it is worth noting that four of Division One's top sides in 1914-15 would compete against Rochdale in this section. Inevitably this was the highest regular level of football the club had competed in since formation. Rochdale ended the season 13th with only Preston below them. The wartime leagues were restructured the following season with the Lancashire section holding two tournaments – the principal tournament of 30 games and a subsidiary tournament of six matches. Rochdale won the Subsidiary tournament after competing against Bolton, Bury and Oldham. They only dropped one

Rochdale photographed during the 1923-24 season. That season Dale finished second in Division Three (N) but only one side was promoted.

point – a 2-2 draw at Oldham – and they headed a table which saw the north-west's regular giants City, United, Everton and Liverpool below them. The following season they finished fourth after 30 games in the principal tournament – ahead of City and United! Sadly, once peacetime football was resumed Rochdale were unable to compete with Manchester's giants on an equal footing and the side returned to facing their reserve sides in the Central League.

In 1920 they finished 19th out of 22 Central sides, and then in 1921 they were tenth, but football was to be restructured and the Third Division North was created. As we saw in the previous chapter, Dale were founder members. So after only fourteen years Rochdale had gone from nothing in a town obsessed with Rugby to become a League side.

In 1924 Rochdale finished the season second by a point to Wolves in the Third Division (North), but with only one side from each of the regional Division Three's promoted Dale missed

October 1925 - a record crowd of 16,295 witness a 2-0 Rochdale victory over Bradford Park Avenue.

Rochdale in their stripes during the 1925-26 season.

out. Near misses followed in 1926 (third) and 1927 (second). Dale were struggling financially and by 11th November 1931 it was revealed that the club was about to go out of business. A special meeting was called where it was revealed that £400 was needed immediately to help put the club back on its feet.

On Christmas Day 1931 Rochdale suffered a 9-1 defeat at Tranmere – this remains their heaviest defeat (although there have been a couple of 8-0 results as well!). Later in the season with both finances and results poor the entertainer Gracie Fields offered support while former player – and by 1931 popular comedian – Harry Mallalieu organised a concert of 'Rochdale's finest talent'.

A season that had promised much – the opening day attendance of approximately 7,000 was almost twice the crowd of Manchester United's opening game – ended with the club in 21st place and with an average crowd of 3,070 (the third worst in the entire League).

Dale survived but they were rarely out of the bottom three for the rest of the decade. Nevertheless, they seemed to have grown stronger as an organisation and by the outbreak of war they were in their best position since the 1920s. They ended 1938-39 in 15th place and averaged 6,110.

ATTENDANCE DETAIL SEASON BY SEASON - 1921-1923

Season	City	United	Oldham	Bury	Stockport	Rochdale	Stalybridge
1921-22	25000	29100	16540	10040	10900	4530	5480
1922-23	24000	23550	13830	11840	12850	5125	3440

LEAGUE POSITIONS SEASON BY SEASON - 1921-1923

Season	City	United	Oldham	Bury	Stockport	Rochdale	Stalybridge
1921-22	10	22	19	33	45	64	51
1922-23	8	26	22	28	42	56	55

CHAPTER FOURTEEN

CELTIC AMBITION

A new record attendance of 7,475 was created with the visit of nearby Stockport County to Bower Fold on the last day of 1921, producing match receipts of £350. This first campaign in the Football League was seen as a success, and further progress was hoped for the forthcoming season. Rejected FC, Dave Twydell, 1988

ROCHDALE were not the only local side to join the League for the first time in 1921, Stalybridge Celtic also joined when the decision was taken to create a northern section of Division Three. Football had been strong in the town since the turn of the century but in those days the major side was Stalybridge Rovers, playing at Crookbottom Ground (between Wakefield Road and North End Road).

The Rovers were believed to have been formed during the early 1890s, competing in the Football Combination in 1894 and the Lancashire League in 1895. Rovers entered the FA Cup for the first time in 1894 and in 1899-00 they succeeded to pass the qualifying rounds – defeating South Liverpool, Stockport County, and Port Vale before facing Bristol City in the first round proper. The game ended in a 2-1 defeat before a 5,000 crowd in Bristol.

The FA Cup run immediately encouraged the club's leaders to apply to join the Football League in 1900, but Rovers only received one vote (Stockport County were elected). Nevertheless they persevered and the following season, as champions of the Lancashire League, they applied again. Sadly, despite a significant increase in support from the other sides, they failed again and over the years that followed their form suffered and the club entered a terminal decline. By the end of 1908 it seems the side had withdrawn from serious competition, and they certainly never entered the FA Cup again after a 7-1 defeat against St. Helen's Recreation during the 1907-8 season. Interestingly, another prominent non-league side Altrincham record details of an FA Cup meeting with Rovers from that same season. According to the Altrincham records, Rovers were draw away in the 1st qualifying round of the FA Cup but they refused to play the game at Altrincham's Pollitt's Field as the pitch was less than the FA stipulated minimum length of 110 yards – the actual length measuring 106.5 yards. So the game was switched to Rovers' Crookbottom ground and Altrincham lost 4-0.

It was around this time that Stalybridge Celtic entered the fray. Celtic was probably formed in 1906, although most sources state 1909 as the club's formation. Interestingly some Stalybridge

Celtic supporters claim the club was formed by the merger of Stalybridge Rovers and Stalybridge Town in 1906, but that does not seem consistent with Rovers own history. It is possible Rovers did merge with Celtic in 1909, but Celtic's own history does tend to go back to 1906.

Dave Twydell's **Rejected FC** claims a club was formed with the name Stalybridge Celtic in Harry Bayley's Billiards Room, and played its first game at Joe Walsh's meadow at Spring Hollows. Details of various friendlies appear in newspaper reports from this season but in truth very little substance appears until 1909. Some have suggested the original Celtic folded after one season, while others claim the club survived as a minor outfit before becoming forward thinking in 1909. What is known however is that two players – Storrs and Manwood played in the 1906 side and the 1909 team, and that one of the 1906 players, Herbert Rhodes, became the leading benefactor of Celtic in the years that followed. Rhodes was a keen sportsman and, as well as his football interests, he also captained Stalybridge Cricket Club.

In 1909 Rhodes paid for the development of Bower Fold into a properly enclosed ground, and it staged its first truly competitive game that September when Celtic faced Xaverian College in the Lancs & Cheshire League. The club developed relatively quickly from that point on and the following season they were losing finalists in the Ashton Junior Challenge Cup, and in the summer of 1911 they turned professional with Stalybridge Rovers' former player John Shand Johnston becoming player-manager. Johnston had also played in Bury's 1903 FA cup winning team and his leadership qualities were known throughout the region. He immediately guided the side to the championship of the Lancashire Combination Division Two in 1912, and runners-up spot (on goal average) in 1913.

The development of Celtic brought much attention and when the club applied to join the League in 1913 they managed to poll 6 votes – Blackpool and Stockport were relegated but Celtic were a creditable fourth out of 8 sides. The club recognised it needed stronger competition and so after missing out on the League, Celtic took the surprising decision to join the second division of the Southern League.

The Southern League was originally seen as a competitor to the Football League and the majority of its sides were significant southern-based clubs such as Southampton, Portsmouth and QPR. The Southern League's Second Division was mainly made up of teams from south Wales and also Stoke and Coventry. Celtic acquitted themselves well in their first season, ending the campaign as runners-up to Stoke. The success would normally have resulted in promotion – and another significant step towards establishing themselves as a potential Football League side – but the difficulties of travel and the outbreak of the First World War led to Celtic playing in the Lancashire Combination (southern section).

Celtic enjoyed some success during wartime competition, and post war the side returned to the Central League. With strong support – often reaching 4-5,000 – the club's ambition grew again. Then in 1921 the Third Division North was created and Celtic succeeded in winning enough votes to be elected (perhaps their experience in the old Southern League Division Two had helped establish their name).

Significantly, Celtic performed better than the region's other new League side Rochdale, but support was poor in comparison to the rest of the division. Tameside expert Mike Pavasovic believes this was significant:

"The people of Stalybridge supported Celtic, but they needed support from outside. It's back to the idea of the modern day Tameside area having several great non-League sides, with fierce rivalry. In some ways this makes it difficult for any one side to capitalise on all the football support in Tameside."

Herbert Rhodes had financed the club's development and clearly had invested a significant amount – some sources claim he had invested £25,000 in the period leading up to 1921 – but it was not possible for him to continue in this manner. In March 1923 a public meeting was held at the Town Hall, sadly demolished in the 1980s. Around 1,200 people heard Rhodes explain that the club needed an immediate injection of cash - £2,000 – plus support had to increase if the side was to continue in the League. It was suggested that Celtic should become a Limited Company and that a further £10,000 was needed to move the side to a new ground closer to the town centre. Bower Fold was very much on the edge of Stalybridge and it was felt that its location was seriously restricting pulling power. Pavasovic:

"The Bower Fold ground, which they still play at, was seen as a problem because it was too far out on a limb, particularly in the 1920s. At the time it was felt it would cost £10,000 to build a new ground, which was impossible to raise."

Despite the doom and gloom of the finances, it is clear that Celtic had achieved a significant amount during this period and it is also clear that support, as a proportion of the local population, was high. At this time records suggest the population of Stalybridge was around 24,000 while Football League records show that Celtic's average in 1921-2 was 5,480 and 3,440 in 1922-3, making a combined average of 4,460. This means approximately a fifth of the town's population watched home games. Other analysis, reported in **'Rejected FC'**, suggests that approximately half

CELTIC'S DEBUT IN FOOTBALL LEAGUE

the male adult population attended games at Bower Fold. Whatever the actual breakdown was, it is clear that the percentage of support was significant.

Much has been made over the years of Stalybridge's relatively near neighbours Glossop and the fact that Glossop was the smallest town to have a First Division side. At the time Glossop joined the League in 1898 its population was over 25,000 with an average attendance of just over 2,000. In the years that followed the town's population rose, however the highest average the Derbyshire side ever attained was only 4,000 in their promotion season of 1899-1900. Therefore Stalybridge's record is significant, particularly when other factors are taken into consideration such as the level Glossop were playing at, the proximity of good rail links (Stalybridge's station is a significant distance from the ground), and the competition around Stalybridge. It is fair to say that by 1921 when Celtic joined the League, many locals were already supporting established League sides Oldham and City (both within easy travelling distance for the period), and there were many, quality non-League sides within neighbouring Ashton, Mossley and the other towns of Tameside.

Once the debate over Celtic's finances was out in the open only a further £500 was raised, and the club resigned from the League. This now appears to have been somewhat premature and there is a feeling that had the side continued for another couple of seasons then the entire situation could have improved. The Third Division North was increased to 22 clubs the following season, and that would surely have helped finances improve, while Manchester City was to move to Moss Side in 1923 from the Ardwick area, thereby leaving the whole of East Manchester without a League side. Stalybridge lay on the very edge of the Manchester conurbation at the time, but this may well have been close enough to capture some support. In addition, the whole of present day Tameside was a densely populated area and as time moved on Celtic may have been able to develop along a similar path to Rochdale, Stockport or even Oldham as THE side for that part of the region.

As an area, present day Tameside is extremely strong in its involvement with football. With significant sides in each of the town's of the borough it is clear there is good support for the game, however once Stalybridge dropped out of the League this vast area had little opportunity to make an impression on the national stage. Celtic competed in the Conference, the unofficial fifth division of the League, during the 1990s, and for one season in the new century, but was unable to make the final leap back to the League. They also reached the second round of the FA Cup in 1994 and 2000 but were defeated by League sides Carlisle United and Chester City respectively.

Other Tameside clubs have gained national interest since 1923 - Ashton United attempted to join the League in 1947 while Droylsden, Hyde United, and Mossley have made FA Cup appearances – but none of them have ever had the opportunity or potential Stalybridge had in 1921. Having said that, for any team in Tameside to compete in the League was itself a significant achievement considering the volume of competition within the borough. Tameside residents should feel proud of Stalybridge's record and the fact that more sides from the borough have attempted to join the Football League than any other borough within the region. Salford has never had a League side, but Tameside has had one, plus five other sides bid to join the League.

Before leaving Stalybridge it is worth pausing to consider two significant footballing figures who played a part in the development of the game. Arthur Wharton – the first black goalkeeper in the Football League – was a Stalybridge Rovers player in 1896. Basically, after playing for Sheffield United and Rotherham, Wharton came to Stalybridge and played professional cricket for Stalybridge CC, and football for Stalybridge Rovers. He also coached Rovers.

In 1897 Ghana-born Wharton joined Ashton North End as captain, playing at centre-forward, and later kept goal for the side. In 1898 he returned to Stalybridge Rovers before moving to Stockport County in 1901.

The other leading figure in Stalybridge's early footballing life was Herbert Chapman. Chapman later became one of the game's most successful managers guiding both Huddersfield and Arsenal to phenomenal success in the 1920s and 1930s, but he did actually play for both Ashton North End and Stalybridge Rovers during the 1890s. In fact some sources claim Arthur Wharton coached him during 1896.

ATTENDANCE DETAIL SEASON BY SEASON - 1923-1930

Season	City	United	Oldham	Bury	Stockport	Rochdale
1923-24	27400	22360	10470	12820	11550	6360
1924-25	29000	30030	9350	19440	12670	5260
1925-26	32000	27647	11959	15728	8086	6030
1926-27	30848	26138	12555	15447	8998	6181
1927-28	37468	25555	13893	15608	8418	4222
1928-29	31715	23659	13206	14507	11947	5355
1929-30	33339	18599	17694	10435	9542	3440

LEAGUE POSITIONS SEASON BY SEASON - 1923-1930

Season	City	United	Oldham	Bury	Stockport	Rochdale
1923-24	11	36	29	24	35	46
1924-25	10	24	40	5	41	50
1925-26	21	9	29	4	44	47
1926-27	25	15	32	19	50	46
1927-28	23	18	29	5	47	57
1928-29	8	12	40	21	46	61
1929-30	3	17	25	27	46	54

Mr. James W. Gibson
Manchester United F.C.
Chairman 1931 - 1951
Manchester United Football Club acknowledge the debt owed to
Mr. James W. Gibson, who in December 1931 rescued the Club
from bankruptcy. Mr. Gibson rebuilt the Club and served
as Chairman until his death in 1951.
Also, in memory of the services of his son, J. Alan Gibson,
who served as a director from 1948 until 1984, when he
became a Vice-President of Manchester United F.C. He
continued to serve in this capacity until his death in 1995.

CHAPTER FIFTEEN

UNITED'S SALVATION & CITY'S SUCCESS

At one time, Manchester United and Wigan Pier had a close affinity as the butt of music hall comedians. One man more than any other changed all that – his name is James W Gibson. Mr Gibson, it can be said in complete truth, saved the club. That was in 1932. Manchester United Over The Years, 1947

THE 1930s were mixed for Manchester's clubs. We've already considered the development of Manchester Central and the impact that could – should – have had on the game and on Manchester City and United. It's now worth exploring in detail the state of the both the region's giants during that decade.

By 1930 Manchester United were in a desperate position. The glories of Ernest Mangnall's reign were long since forgotten as the Reds struggled to survive in the First Division. On 4th October 1930 the Reds were defeated 4-1 by City at Maine Road and then after a 5-1 defeat at West Ham seven days later – the club's 12th consecutive defeat (including two games of the previous season) – a group of supporters organised a meeting for the following Friday. That meeting was to discuss the possibility of boycotting home games and on 17th October 1930 around 3,000 supporters attended Hulme Town Hall to hear GH Greenhough, a shareholder, and secretary of the Supporters' Club, talk of the financial problems of the club. Apparently he had asked to see the United directors to ask where gate income had gone and why the club was so heavily in debt.

Greenhough's name was already familiar to supporters and the media, and his views were gaining a great deal of coverage, although the press tended to support United's leaders rather than Greenhough. In fact, after the Reds had lost to City, Ivan Sharpe, one of football's most respected journalists wrote of Greenhough in his commentary of United:

"Manchester United have become the football which the Fates are kicking. I wonder what Mr. Greenhough thought about it. Mr. Greenhough, you must know, is the Hitler of the Manchester United Supporters' Club. He is carrying the banner and using the megaphone at the Supporters demonstrations against the United directors for failing to get new players and stop the rot. Surely sorrow and sympathy must have crept into his hard heart on Saturday afternoon."

At the Friday night meeting a ballot was held to seek agreement that a boycott of the following

day's game with Arsenal should be staged, and it was decided by a large majority of attendees that the boycott should be performed. Former captain Charlie Roberts attended the meeting and Roberts, perhaps more than any other former United man including Meredith, was a man the fans could identify with.

Roberts was a local businessman at this point and had also helped establish Manchester Central FC. More importantly though, he was perceived as a true Red whereas Meredith was at this point more closely identified as part of City's history and heritage. It was only in the modern era when first a biography and then the creation of United's museum that Meredith's name has become more closely associated with the Reds. In 2004 his daughter Winifred recalled that City had always been his first love and that City supporters were always more appreciative of his skills than United (a point re-iterated in 2007 by Billy's grandson Ian Pringle).

Roberts was loved by supporters and his attendance at the meeting said a great deal about how he felt about the club. He wanted United to be successful and he cared, as supporters

James Gibson, regarded as United's saviour during the 1930s for his significant financial support of the club. Without him United would have died.

cared, for the club. He stood up and seconded a motion that the boycott be withdrawn, and added that the boycott would perhaps damage the players more than the management of the club. He felt the management were to blame and wanted them to be held accountable. He did not feel the boycott would be successful, nor did he feel it was the right way to approach the situation.

The meeting still vowed to boycott the game, but Roberts' views undoubtedly had an impact. They were reported in the media of the day and, in the main, the newspapers were not supportive of a boycott. On the day extra police were brought in fearing trouble, but the more militant members of the supporters organisations did nothing to actually prevent supporters from attending or cause any other form of trouble. Ultimately, the attendance for the game was 23,406 – the highest crowd of the season up to that point. However, this was some way short of the attendance many had predicted as Arsenal were FA Cup holders and their game at City two months later was to attract almost 57,000. Nevertheless, the attendance was regarded as not having been affected much by the boycott. In fact some sources during more recent times have claimed the attendance increased and an official book ***Manchester United – pictorial history and club record*** published in 1986 claimed:

"The plot failed and the game attracted the highest home gate that campaign."

In truth, that is inaccurate as the attendance was some 16,000 below the highest crowd (V. City, 7th February 1931).

Whether the boycott had any impact on the day or not is immaterial as United's struggles worsened during the season. Attendances dropped with even the Manchester derby attracting less than 40,000 – this remains the lowest Old Trafford derby crowd of all time – but more significantly this was one of only four United home fixtures to attract a crowd above 10,000 during 1931. The only crowds over 10,000 were: 39,876 (City), 33,123 (Wolves, 25/12/31), 11,745 (Bury, 21/11), and 10,834 (Chesterfield, 26/9).

On the final day of the 1930-31 season the Reds were relegated after a 4-4 draw with Middlesbrough, but they were a full nine points behind their nearest rivals and a total of ten points from safety. Under the headline: ***"At Lowest Ebb – Record Equalled At Manchester"*** the ***Athletic News*** journalist Wanderer reported:

"It is sad to relate that interest in the affairs of Manchester United is at the lowest ebb. Only 4,000 spectators saw the game with Middlesbrough, which rang down the curtain on a season that has been disastrous in more senses than one for the Old Trafford club. It even terminated with them having their name written down in records, for, relegated with 22 points, they now share with Middlesbrough the unenviable distinction of going into lower circles with the lowest number of points since the League was extended."

The actual crowd for the Middlesbrough match was 3,969 but even that was not the lowest of the season – that came on 25th March 1931 when only 3,679 attended the goalless match with Leicester City. Inevitably, the United manager Herbert Bamlett was dismissed and replaced by Walter Crickmer, with Louis Rocca acting as his assistant. Both men were United through and through and Rocca in particular had achieved a great deal over the years to make the Reds successful. He had worked tirelessly behind the scenes to increase support, and was a well known figure around the area. However, the two men had little chance to improve the situation, other than their own personal desire to save the Reds, and 1931-32 was another season of struggle.

The year also saw an enormous threat to United's existence with the continued development of Manchester Central. Central, who by summer of 1931 had mounted three unsuccessful bids to join the Football League, were growing in popularity. They were also based at Belle Vue, not too far from United's heartland of Clayton and Newton Heath.

Although Central had undoubtedly set themselves up as a result of dissatisfaction with City's move to Maine Road, their growth was not seriously impacting City but it was having a detrimental effect on the Reds. It is no coincidence that United's loss of support came at a time when Central were at their strongest. Sure, United were struggling, but football fans in the 1930s did not simply desert the game.

Another problem affecting football during the 1930s was of course the Depression, but City's crowds increased, so this perhaps shows that Mancunians were a little more selective over the type of football they wanted to watch.

The opening home game of the 1931-32 season saw a crowd of 3,507 attend as United were defeated 3-2 by Southampton and the Reds continued to struggle both on the pitch and financially. Then in October Wigan Borough resigned from the Football League Third Division North and Manchester Central offered to take their place. The Third Division accepted them at first, but ultimately the League blocked Central's bid and the danger of Central replacing United as Manchester's second team was over.

The following December, with United still in a desperate position, the **Manchester Evening News** reported a story that would ultimately change the direction of the club:

"Mr. JW Gibson, a Manchester businessman with no previous record in big football, has taken over Manchester United for a month, and he has paid the players' wages for this week. He has undertaken to be responsible for the Club's expenditure from December 16 [1931] until January 9. If during that time sufficient support is forthcoming at Old Trafford then he is prepared to consider securing a new manager, four first class players, and the construction of covered accommodation on the Popular Side of the ground."

Journalist Stacey Lintott, the **Daily Mirror** Sports Editor, is the man recognised as introducing Gibson to the Reds. During the 1950s Lintott wrote about the day he heard the news United were facing bankruptcy:

"The news was a terrific shock. Could nothing be done, I wondered. Suddenly I had a brainwave. For some time I had been lunching with a party that included Mr. James Gibson. I knew him to be a successful businessman with a weakness for taking over failing businesses and restoring them to solvency. Here was his big chance. He knew nothing of football, had no interest in the game, but that was not necessarily an obstacle. He also had a love of Manchester, and would deeply regret the collapse of such a famous institution as United."

Over the years it has been said that Louis Rocca had introduced Gibson to United, but Peter Harrington's book **The Gibson Guarantee** totally disputes this view and confirms that Lintott was the man.

One of the first steps taken by Gibson was to discuss United's predicament with Greenhough, the man described as the 'Hitler' of the United Supporters' Club by Ivan Sharpe. It was a shrewd move as Greenhough had many contacts amongst supporters and was clearly the type of man who would not be afraid to voice his opinions if Gibson's lack of footballing knowledge caused problems. Greenhough told the **Manchester Evening News** that he had met with Gibson and that he was impressed:

"I gave Mr Gibson the supporters' point of view and Mr Gibson said that he would be pleased to have the supporters with him if he took over the Club permanently."

Gibson knew how to gain full support and he clearly was a successful businessman with great knowledge of how to succeed. By bringing Greenhough on board Gibson had pacified one potential opponent. From a financial viewpoint he has also stood as guarantor to the club's bankers to the value of £40,000 – by doing this he saved United over £1,000 per month and accepted the full risk for the club. Although the situation is considerably different the 21st Century takeover of United by Malcolm Glazer could have learnt a great deal from looking at how the Gibson 'takeover' occurred. Neither Gibson nor Glazer were known as football fans, but they were both recognised as businessmen. Where they differ however is that one is viewed as 'saving the club' by fans, while the other is seen by some as using the club as a means of 'generating cash'. As Gibson recognised as early as 1931, the feelings and involvement of supporters is vital to the success of any of the region's clubs.

United's problems were not resolved immediately, but with the support of Greenhough the crowd for the Christmas day meeting with Wolves reached 33,123 – around eight times the size of the previous week's home game (4,697 V Bristol City)!

The Reds ended that season 12th in Division Two which, considering the negativity that surrounded the club prior to Gibson's involvement, was a significant success. A sixth placed finish came in 1932-33 but United were some way off promotion. The following year Gibson had negotiated with the Great Central and North Staffordshire Railway to open a station at the ground – a major boost to making the ground accessible – but on the pitch United needed to win their final game of the season to avoid relegation to the Third Division North. Ultimately they won the game 2-0 at Millwall, but Gibson's United seemed as far away from a return as they had at any point since relegation.

Fortunately the tide was about to turn and a fifth placed finish in 1935 was followed by promotion as Division Two Champions in 1936. Promotion was achieved with a 3-2 victory over Bury at Gigg Lane on 29th April, and on 2nd May a 1-1 draw at Hull City was enough to give the side the championship. The **Daily Mail** held Gibson as responsible for United's return:

"The public of Manchester owe it to Mr. JW Gibson that there will again be first class football at Old Trafford next season. Mr. Gibson shouldering all the burden of Manchester United, has been responsible for as much as £25,000."

Of course, the United fairytale was not quite at an end, and the 1936-37 season saw United

Arsenal 2 City 1, 21st January 1933. Goalscorer Fred Tilson watches as Jimmy McMullan tries to head the ball while Arsenal 'keeper Moss punches clear.

relegated in 21st place while neighbours City won the Championship. Clearly, the Reds still had much to do if they were to turn around the situation. One area where United were starting to have the lead though was in youth football. Under Gibson's guidance Walter Crickmer and trainer Tom Curry set up the Manchester United Junior Athletic Club with the aim of finding and developing young talent. The old Broughton Rangers Rugby Ground, The Cliff, was obtained (interestingly, Broughton Rangers had moved to Manchester Central's old Belle Vue ground in 1933 after Central had collapsed) and the move became instrumental in re-establishing the side as a credible force over the following decade.

Crucially, United's spell in Division Two was only brief and the Reds immediately returned to the top flight. Going in the other direction however were City who were relegated as reigning champions of the League!

From that point on United were to become an established trophy winning side, only facing relegation once during the following seventy years.

Across Manchester the story of City during the 1930s was predominantly one of success. In fact from the end of the First World War through to the late 1930s the Blues seemed to thrive.

Pre-war it had been difficult for the Blues to recover from the scandal that had ripped the club apart in 1906, although there were still some significant moments along the way. The immediate period after World War One however saw the Blues develop at a phenomenal rate and re-establish themselves at the level they had held prior to the scandal. They rediscovered their drive and determination and in 1920-21 they made a serious assault on the League, finishing second to Burnley – it was the closest any of the Manchester region clubs had been to title success since Oldham's second placed finish in 1915. In addition, City were one of the most popular sides in the Country, and by the end of the 1930s the Blues held – or held for a period – several major attendance records and had been the best supported side in the League for several seasons.

The Blues have always been proud of their local support and certainly, as the inter-war period progressed they continued to view themselves as Manchester's club. The struggles of 1906 may have turned national support away, but locally the scandal had strengthened the supporters' resolve. The club still mattered enormously to Mancunians, and in March 1920 King George V's advisors recognised this. They chose City as the ideal venue for the King to meet typical Mancunians as part of his visit to the region. It was the first visit to a provincial ground by a reigning monarch and ideal from a royal perspective as the Blues were facing Liverpool and so the King would be seen as being interested in the northwest's two major cities, and he would be featured in the leading northwest newspapers of the day.

In the days before television, and even widespread newsreel footage, an appearance by the reigning monarch was seen as a significant event. Few had ever seen the King, apart from in newspaper photographs, and so there was more mystique about royalty. For City it was an historic moment and the Blues are unique as they have now had three venues visited by consecutive monarchs – King George was the present Queen's grandfather; her father attended a game at Maine Road in 1934 (though he wasn't King at the time); her husband attended a Maine Road derby in the 1960s; and she attended the City of Manchester Stadium with her husband in 2002 for the Commonwealth Games.

Despite many positives, it was not until the Blues moved to Maine Road in 1923 that the club was able to prove itself a major power once more. Unlike United's move to Old Trafford, which seemed to affect the club's ability to compete for at least a couple of decades, City's move was successful from the start. Huge crowds were now able to attend with over 76,000 attending a cup match during Maine Road's first season. At the time this was the largest football crowd ever recorded in Manchester, including three FA Cup finals (1893, 1911, & 1915).

In terms of match action, 1923-4 saw the Blues reach the semi-final of the FA Cup. This was a significant moment and a major national news story as Billy Meredith, City's great captain from 1904, had returned and was playing well enough to be selected at the age of 49 for first team duty. His final match was the semi-final with Newcastle at Middlesbrough's Ayresome Park ground. Sadly, a 2-0 defeat prevented Meredith from appearing at Wembley in the FA Cup final, although the Blues did make it in 1926 (sadly without Meredith).

Despite finishing third in 1929-30 it was not until 1931-32 that the side seemed ready to seriously challenge for major honours. That season City reached the FA Cup semi-final losing out to a goal in the final minute by Arsenal's Cliff Bastin, then twelve months later new manager Wilf Wild guided the Blues to face Everton in the 1933 final. That match ended in defeat, but 12 months later City were back for their third final in 8 years. This time City defeated Portsmouth in a game made famous for the exploits of 20 year old 'keeper Frank Swift. Swift fainted at the final whistle and his transformation from the third team to FA Cup winner in only six months made the headlines.

The game itself saw the Blues become only the second team in history to recover from a goal deficit at Wembley with Fred Tilson netting both City goals.

Throughout this decade City were second to Arsenal in terms of glamour, excitement and interest, and were perceived by the media and neutrals as Arsenal's main rivals. In terms of success

A Wednesday afternoon crowd of 68,614 witness City's 2-0 victory over Sheffield Wednesday in the 1934 FA Cup fifth round replay. That season Maine Road also housed its record crowd of 84,569.

and support they were certainly the north's glamour side. City tended to get the larger crowds, while Arsenal found more success, but the Blues had their moments. They came close to winning the title on a few occasions – in 1930 they were third; 1934 fifth; and 1935 fourth – with the League Championship finally arriving in 1937. They had to beat Arsenal of course to stand a chance of success and by the time of their meeting with the Gunners in April 1937, the two sides occupied the top two positions. It was a crucial meeting, but City did not start well and were easily outplayed by the Gunners during the opening minutes. Fortunately, City's confidence increased and gradually they gained control.

In the 35th minute City seized control and took the lead via Peter Doherty. Ernie Toseland made it 2-0 later and City overtook Arsenal at the top of the table, and gained the upper hand. They ended the campaign five points clear of third placed Arsenal and three points above second placed Charlton.

The 1936-37 Championship success was the high point of City's second golden age. It was the first time Manchester had won the title since Ernest Mangnall had guided the Reds to it back in 1911, and the Manchester region's trophy count now stood at 5 FA Cups (City 2, Bury 2, United 1) and 3 League Championships (United 2 City 1). The Blues themselves had appeared in 4 FA Cup finals – one more than the rest of the region combined – and had been runners up in the League twice.

16 MONDAY. DAILY

WONDER SHOOTING—CHAMPION MANCHESTER

By HENRY ROSE

Manchester City 4, Sheffield Wednesday 1.

MANCHESTER staged a miniature Wembley all on its own on Saturday. Excited "fans" swarmed over the field—policemen lost their helmets.

Manchester City had won the championship for the first time in their history. Great stuff.

And how they won it!

This was no scrambling victory but a triumph gained by some superlative football and three goals that memory will treasure for a long time. Oh, boy, what goals! Three in twelve minutes. Each is worth framing. Cold print cannot do them justice.

Nearly Broke The Net

The first. Percival to Doherty then a master touch by the Irishman to Brook, and that left of the wingman's seven-league boots almost broke the net.

The second. A "dummy" by Doherty to the Sheffield defence, a pass to Tilson, who scored with an effort that reminded me of the two he scored when the City won the Cup against Portsmouth.

Then the third, the gem of the lot. I never want to see a better. Forgive me but truth must bring in Doherty's name again. He started it at the halfway line. A dribble for twenty yards, a cross pass to Tilson. Another dribble. A cross pass back to Doherty. Back again and again, and a crashing shot home by Doherty.

I intended to criticise Brook for some inaccurate centres and wild shooting, but how dare any one criticise a player who can come across with two such goals as he scored?

His second—the last of the game—was from the centre forward position from a pass by—you've guessed it—Doherty.

Just before, the Wednesday—who never gave up trying—had made it 3—1 when Rimmer scored after Swift had made a brilliant save from Luke's shot.

Referee: R. W. Blake (Middlesbrough).

DONCASTER'S FUTURE

Doncaster Rovers have received an unofficial intimation that they may be invited to join the Southern Section of the Third Division next season instead of the Northern Section, from which they were promoted. It is not certain they will accept.

ALBION SAVED WHEN JONES LET FLY

By STANLEY HALSEY

West Bromwich Albion 1, Manchester United 0.

THIS was a hard game—hard to sit through. I'd have gone home long before the end if it hadn't been my duty to stay. Lots of spectators melted away.

Both teams were supposed to be fighting for safety-first points. But I've seen more fight in a schoolboy's game on a village green.

Mind you, I'm not forgetting the magnificent defence work of Vose, centre half, Roughton, left back, and Breen, goalkeeper, of Manchester United. These boys played with the full realisation that they were there to save their side from the Second Division.

Roughton, particularly, with his fierce but fair tackling and his shrewd covering was a tremendous asset. If only the forwards had gone for the ball as he and Vose did, Manchester would be nursing greater hope.

It was Jones, Albion inside right, who works more overtime than an armament factory, who knocked out that grand defence early in the second half.

DEMPSEY WALLOP

Jones, running into the inside left position, carried the ball with him. A defender intercepting, clouted the ball on to Jones's chin—a real Dempsey wallop. I thought that would stop him.

But no, Jones drove on for goal, snapped up the rebound and sent in a high, spinning semi-lob which found the net wide of Green's finger tips.

Pint-sized Boyes was so delighted, he tried to lift quart-sized Jones. Result: Jones got another wallop. Boyes dropped him.

It was a shot that could have been saved. If Breen had got that, his show

April 1937 - City are League champions while United are relegated.

The Oldham players gather at the start of the 1934-5 season.

City's championship winning team of 1936-37.

The Blues celebrated their 1937 Championship by accepting an invitation to become the first English side to play in the Berlin Olympic Stadium. The Blues toured Nazi Germany as part of a propaganda stunt that backfired on the German leaders – the visit coincided with the British Coronation and the Hindenburg airship disaster – and the Blues actually beat a German XI in one of several high profile games. In the Olympic Stadium itself Peter Doherty and the other City stars refused to give the Nazi salute, while the club's comedian, Frank Swift, deliberately performed exaggerated salutes and Heil Hitler at every opportunity on the tour!

With typical City style the following season was a shocker! The Blues struggled to find any form and more or less the same side that had won the Championship was relegated only twelve months later. They still thrilled on occasion and managed to score more goals than any other side in the First Division, but they were relegated with two points fewer than Grimsby in 20th place. A final day victory would have been enough.

It was a bad time to be relegated, and City could only manage a fifth place finish in Division Two during 1938-39. As with Oldham's second placed finish in 1915, the Blues were unable to build as shortly after the 1939-40 campaign commenced the Second World War caused the abandonment of the season. City were to endure their longest period of time (though not seasons) outside of the top flight. The great successes and developments of the 1930s should have seen the Blues establish themselves as a giant in the same way as Arsenal managed, however relegation shortly before the war ended all hope of that.

A quick survey of all the Manchester region sides at the outbreak of the Second World War paints an interesting picture. The Reds were promoted in 1938 on goal average (leapfrogging the Blues), while Stockport ended that season bottom of Division Two. It had been County's only season in the division during the decade, however County fans were well known for enjoying the ups and downs of supporting the side. While other supporters saw relegation as a major disaster, County fans tended to be a little more pragmatic and accept the nature of the club's existence. Back on the 8th August 1933 the **Cheshire Daily Echo** accurately recorded:

"The existence of Stockport County is not one of notable triumphs, and of success followed by success. It is a story of a club always fighting against adversity, of heroic efforts to keep going despite discouragement and ill luck, and yet I doubt whether any of the stalwarts who all along have backed up the club would have the story any less different, for the real test of loyalty is steadfastness in the face of misfortune."

Sure County fans wanted success but, as with the decades that have followed, they appreciated that the strength of the game was the fact that it could throw up surprises, disappointments and every range of emotion possible. As the 1930s were nearing their end the change in fortunes of City and United gave a clear example to all of how close every side was to both success and failure. The actual positions at the end of 1938-39 for all local league sides were:

United (14th, Division One)
City (5th, Division Two)
Bury (16th, Division Two)
Oldham (5th, Division Three North)
Stockport (9th, Division Three North)
Rochdale (15th, Division Three North)

ATTENDANCE DETAIL SEASON BY SEASON - 1930-1939

Season	City	United	Oldham	Bury	Stockport	Rochdale
1930-31	26849	11685	11313	8813	6937	3162
1931-32	24173	13011	8389	8594	5147	3070
1932-33	24254	20149	8254	9406	5210	4669
1933-34	30058	18338	8824	9616	8944	3823
1934-35	34824	22871	7576	9499	7352	4593
1935-36	33577	26070	5869	9241	7165	4827
1936-37	35872	32332	6433	12903	11011	4669
1937-38	32670	26633	9214	10120	14399	5374
1938-39	31291	30365	6828	10175	8933	6110

LEAGUE POSITIONS SEASON BY SEASON - 1930-1939

Season	City	United	Oldham	Bury	Stockport	Rochdale
1930-31	8	22	34	35	51	65
1931-32	14	34	40	27	56	65
1932-33	16	28	38	26	47	62
1933-34	5	42	31	34	47	66
1934-35	4	27	43	32	51	64
1935-36	9	23	51	36	49	64
1936-37	1	21	48	25	45	62
1937-38	21	24	48	32	44	61
1938-39	27	14	49	38	53	59

CHAPTER SIXTEEN

BUSBY BABES & McDOWALL'S MEN

Fourth place talent money was well earned. So shall we say that all's well that ends well, and add to that, confidently, the statement that if Manchester City can play as well right through the coming season as they did in the Cup Final, they can win, with a side of mainly experienced men, everything for which they enter. Playfair Football Annual 1956-57

THE Second World War had a dramatic effect on football in the region. Inevitably, many players, officials, and supporters were involved in the conflict and also, for the first time Manchester itself came under attack. The blitz caused significant damage to the city centre and industrial areas, including Trafford Park. From a footballing perspective the biggest wartime impact on Manchester came with the bombing of Old Trafford on 11th March 1941.

United's home suffered significant bomb damage on the night with the Old Trafford Main Stand almost entirely destroyed – the lowest section of terracing survived - and an area of terracing damaged. The pitch was also badly scorched. The Reds were unable to stage first class football there and so City offered the use of Maine Road. In addition, once the Old Trafford pitch was restored both the City and United reserve sides used United's home, while the first teams remained at Maine Road.

The rubble of the Main Stand has been cleared away at a bombed Old Trafford.

It is often stated that United's use of City's ground during the post war years brought the Blues a great deal of money, but the truth is somewhat different. The major beneficiary of United's time at Maine Road was the Reds themselves. They were able to attract significant crowds – larger than any held at Old Trafford – and as

FOOTBALL EDITION

Always goes first.. BIRD'S CUSTARD

Evening Chronicle

FLAG SAUCE —of course!

No. 15,186 Threehalfpence SATURDAY, APRIL 6, 1946 A KEMSLEY NEWSPAPER

SMITH'S FOUR AGAINST UNITED

City's magnificent win in a game of thrills

MANCHESTER UNITED .... 1 MANCHESTER CITY 4

By ALF CLARKE

MANCHESTER'S "Derby" match at Maine-road this afternoon was a game of thrills and sensations, and if the result was surprising it was no more than the City deserved. Hero of the match was Smith, three of whose four goals were scored in seven minutes.

Aston got the only goal for United after 53 minutes, and so atoned to some extent for his previous failures.

For the greater part of the game the United attack was a disappointment. The forwards played much too closely. On the other hand, the City opened out the play. They were strong alike in attack and defence.

For once in a way the United left wing had no punch.

Both teams were as announced.

UNITED. — Tapken; Whalley, Walton; Carey, Chilton, Cockburn; Delaney, Aston, Hanlon, Pearson, Rowley.

CITY.—Swift; Williams, Barkas; Walsh, Cardwell, McDowall; Dunkley, Herd, Constantine, Smith, Emptage.

Whalley won the toss for United and they had the sun at their backs in attacking the city end goal.

Rowley made progress down the left, but he was forced to put behind when tackled by Williams.

In the next minute the City became very menacing. Herd pushed the ball down the middle to Constantine, who bore down on the United goal, only to see Chilton make a magnificent tackle and charge down his shot.

There was another thrill at the [illegible] end when Carey, trying a

THE CITY POINT OF VIEW

EVERYBODY thought this was going to be a walk-over for United. On the contrary, the City were much the better side in the first 20 minutes, and had their inside forwards finished better City might have been further in the lead.

City, forwards did everything except score, Smith and Constantine failing close in, but I can remember Swift making two great saves from Hanlon.

A game of thrills, and when Smith headed a goal from Constantine's centre after 35 minutes it was no more than City deserved. There would be no doubt that

the ball off his head. The goalkeeper next made a smashing save from Hanlon when all seemed lost. He was injured in the effort and had to receive attention.

SMITH TAKES A CHANCE

After 35 minutes City took the lead. The goal followed a throw-in. Constantine broke through, veered to the right and centred, and SMITH, running in, got his head to the ball to deflect it out of Tapken's reach.

It was a lead which, on the play, City had scarcely deserved, though their fast, open play had always looked menacing.

The surprising thing about United had been the lack of thrust on their left wing. Indeed, there had been little effective shooting by any of their forwards.

Just before the interval City nearly got a second goal when Chilton only just succeeded in blocking a shot from Constantine. Then Herd shot wide.

Half-time: Manchester United 0, Manchester City 1.

SECOND HALF

After an early attack by United had been beaten back, City made progress, but Chilton turned the ball back to Tapken to clear. United's weakness in attack was young Aston, who just lacked the experience necessary for this type of game and a weak pass on his part again

NEARLY A GOAL. Constantine of City, m[illegible] a great effort but fails (above). Tapken, U[illegible]'s goalkeeper, goes down to make a great save (left).

HAGAN STAR FOR ARMY XI

F.A. XI 3, A.P.T.C. XI 5

HAGAN, of Sheffield United, was the star of the International Trial match at Wembley to-day. Partnering Compton again, he gave the F.A. defenders a gruelling time and

Bury outclassed at Middlesbrough

MIDDLESBROUGH ...... 3 BURY 0

BURY were well beaten at Middlesbrough, where the home team playing fast, clever football soon established the mastery.

Taylor, in the Bury goal made several brilliant saves, but little was seen of the Bury attack. Middlesbrough's forwards, with Murphy and Mannion outstanding, kept the Bury defence on the run.

Bury improved for a time after the interval, but Nash in the Middlesbrough goal dealt confidently with several shots.

Mannion who returned from the Middle East after four years' service in the Army, captained Middlesbrough. The crowd numbered more than 20,000 at the start.

Bury made two late changes. Bradshaw was unable to travel owing to the illness of his mother

Aston; Howarth, Hart, Halton; Roberts, N. Berry, Livingstone, Quigley, Kilshaw.

Middlesbrough, with the slight breeze, were first to attack, but Dews' final pass was short. Mannion was prominent, but Aston cleared.

Spuhler after a tussle with Aston, worked an opening for Dews, but Taylor easily saved the inside left's shot. Middlesbrough were doing most of the attacking.

IN THE AIR

Mannion often troubled the Bury defence. Walker worked his way through, but his shot was wide.

The ball was too much in the

City's George Smith scored four against United in this fixture in April 1946.

a result they made large profits. In addition, there was an unseen cost on the Blues which would impact the side for at least the following two decades, possibly longer, and that was the loss of support to United.

When City offered Maine Road to United they were simply offering their neighbours a chance to continue. Many connected with the club, such as members of the Alexander family and secretary-manager Wilf Wild, would have remembered the problems the Blues faced in 1920 when their Hyde Road Main Stand was destroyed. City desperately looked for an alternative and wanted to move to Old Trafford but the move was not financially viable, and so a little over twenty years later the City management felt they had to do something to help their neighbours.

City were not looking at the financial impact, or the desire to capitalise on the Reds' misfortune. Nor were they considering the potential impact on City or on Maine Road. Clearly, United could have turned City down and moved to another venue – any of the other League grounds in the Greater Manchester area would have welcomed them. In addition, the memory of Manchester Central's bid to join the League was still part of Mancunian life and so the Belle Vue ground with a capacity reported pre-war as 45,000 could easily have accommodated United for a while. In fact it is a wonder the Reds did not move there as that ground would have allowed United to move closer to their birthplace, although elements of the Belle Vue complex were utilised at various times throughout the war for military purposes.

The sharing of Maine Road was simply to allow United to survive. Nothing more, nothing less, but the Blues did try to make United feel at home. They accommodated their guests as best they could at a managerial and public level. A point proved by the fact that the Blues always advertised United's fixtures in their match programme, and always tried to help when it came to fixture allocation. City could have been awkward and insisted on their fixtures always taking priority but they did not. The Blues would often negotiate with the Reds when fixtures clashed and often, though not always, City would let United have Maine Road first – a point best demonstrated at the start of the 1946-7 season.

United's first post-war Football League match at Maine Road was a 2-1 victory over Grimsby Town in Division One on Saturday 31st August 1946. The game was watched by a crowd of 41,025, while City's first home game of the period was played in the late afternoon on Wednesday 4th September – a far from ideal time. The Blues felt United's Division One game should take priority, but because of this City could only attract 33,814 for the derby match with Bury in Division Two (the game would probably have attracted over 50,000 had it been on a Saturday). A regular kick off on the following Saturday saw City attract 49,046 for a goalless game with Chesterfield.

From a Red perspective the move was a good one, although there's no doubting that they would have preferred to be at Old Trafford. From a Blue viewpoint the shared use did have a detrimental effect on City's long term direction. Albert Scanlon, who would later become an important member of Matt Busby's fifties team provided his view of the two sides during an interview with journalist Jeff Connor in 2006:

"As a kid I supported City and Hulme [where he lived] was City territory. Maine Road was the only ground we ever went to. Wednesdays and Saturdays we were at Maine Road. We laughed at United.

"I can recall their first trophy win after the war. They won the Lancashire Cup and there was Johnny Carey stood on the steps at Maine Road with this little trophy and no one was really bothered 'cos it was United. But I was. Carey had come to our school once and he went through the usual routine of asking us all what we wanted to do when we grew up. I piped up 'I want to play for United' and they all laughed, Carey included. But I did in the end. Within a few years I was laying out Carey's kit in the first team dressing room."

The immediate post-war period was a boom time for football and many clubs recorded huge gates. In Manchester however supporters' loyalties were tested. Few fans ever travelled to away games but Mancunians were desperate to watch good football. United's use of Maine Road brought a solution for many former soldiers. In the 1980s Fred Burden, a former soldier living in East Manchester during the 1930s and 1940s described his experience of football during this period:

"As a boy I'd been a City supporter. Whenever I could I'd go to Maine Road and watch Big Swifty, Busby, Brooky and Doherty. There was only one team for me, although I did watch Central a bit as well until they were killed off. Then after the war it seemed natural to keep going to Maine Road. It was like home. It had a familiar feel. Of course with United playing there I then started to watch City one week and United the next. It was a natural thing to do.

"United had been the poor relations throughout my boyhood and when they came to Maine Road they were managed by a City player - Matt Busby. It seemed right to support him and to see United reborn. My first United games were really just out of interest or perhaps even sympathy. We'd all suffered in the war and there wasn't really any rivalry between the clubs.

Cup Exit of a Tired Town

By HENRY JONES

STOCKPORT COUNTY 3 SHREWSBURY TOWN... 2
(After extra time—at Maine-road, Manchester.)

THREE fugitive patches of colour emerged from this Marathon Cup-tie with its rather sombre background of crude moves and "let's-get-it-over" tactics in which Stockport went forward to a home third round tie with Torquay, leaving Shrewsbury with the memory of 352 minutes of endeavour and hope.

I pin-pointed McCulloch, Stockport left half with the classic style, ruddy-complexioned young Shrewsbury centre-forward Phillips, and Glaister, former Blackburn Rover, who, with a goal in two minutes, stopped Shrewsbury almost before they had started.

Phillips was the mystery man of the match. His dashing and vigorous display (topped with a goal) captured the imagination of the host of scouts and managers present.

Identity of the man Manager Leslie Knighton (in extremis regarding the selection of his side) had pulled from his magic bag of players, dwarfed other after-match talking points.

Lilting voice of this young man with a future quickly told me he hailed from Wales. Swansea-born, he has recently been demobilised from the R.A.F. and was playing his first game in Shrewsbury's Midland League side.

"Mystery Man"

Only a week ago he signed professional forms. On this showing he is going places. "I think I'll have difficulty in keeping him," Manager Knighton told me. He's surely right.

In al. three ties I have seen McCulloch has shown ability well above the class of football in which he plays. Fitting climax for him was the winning goal after five minutes of extra time.

His long, lobbed free-kick from 25 yards was the despair of Shrewsbury amateur keeper Clifford Smith. With the ball apparently well covered, he appeared to take a nudge from an opponent as McCulloch's foot connected.

Stockport's FA Cup second round replay win over Shrewsbury at Maine Road made the headlines in December 1947.

"But when it came to proper League and Cup football after the war that's when it all started to change for me. Busby's United were a better side than City and, with a young family, money became tight. I had to make a choice. By the time the Reds moved back to Old Trafford, I moved back with them. I didn't have enough money to watch them both and, in my mind at the time, I was still supporting Manchester. Busby was a Blue and I'd grown up watching him. When United won the Cup in 1948 all of Manchester was happy."

That 1948 Cup success was United's first trophy for 37 years – the longest spell either of the two main Manchester sides have endured without a major success (although at the time of writing in April 2008 City have gone 32 years without significant success – their longest spell). The *Daily Telegraph's* report of the final demonstrated United's achievement and also gave an indication of why many Blues fans were beginning to adopt United as their side:

"If ever a team deserved to win the Cup it was Manchester United. Their epic 6-4 victory at Villa Park in the third round set the ball rolling. All five of their opponents on the way to Wembley were First Division sides, United scoring 18 goals to six. But Blackpool were no slouches, 18 goals and only one conceded, and that in their heart-stopping semi-final at Villa Park with Spurs, when Mortensen equalised with four minutes to go and completed his hat-trick in extra time.

"When two great attacking sides play to their form to a man, and some above it, you have a classic. The Manchester forward line - Delaney, Morris, Rowley, Pearson, Mitten - were brilliant. For Blackpool, Matthews, the first Footballer of the Year, was his scintillating self until United cut off his supply of passes in the second half. Mortensen was ever-dangerous with his electric speed, while right-half and captain Johnston worked furiously in defence. The first drama occurred with 12 minutes gone, when Mortensen went racing through on goal and was brought down from behind by Chilton. Was it a penalty? It looked outside the box. But if the referee's decision was not right, it was certainly just, and Shimwell scored from the

spot. It took United 16 minutes to equalise, when Rowley made the most of a mix-up in the Blackpool defence. But Mortensen restored their lead just before half-time with a typically opportunist goal.

"Manchester began to take charge after the interval, but there were only 21 minutes left when Rowley equalised again with a spectacular diving header. The turning point came 10 minutes later. Mortensen broke through again and smashed a shot at goal which Crompton brilliantly held. He cleared the ball to right-half Anderson, who transferred it to Pearson, and the inside-left ran on to crack a low 25-yarder in off a post. Three minutes later, Anderson hit a speculative shot from way out, which curled into the net off a Blackpool defender. That was the end of a great Cup final."

Goalkeeper Jack Crompton's save from Mortensen was inevitably the turning point. Crompton:

"It was great to be at Wembley. Every boy's dream and to have played a part in such an important win... well, it's indescribable. When the save happened everyone thought Blackpool would score, and for

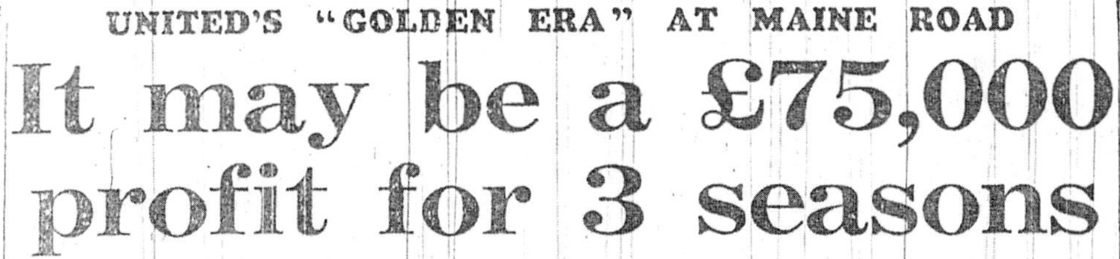

UNITED'S "GOLDEN ERA" AT MAINE ROAD

It may be a £75,000 profit for 3 seasons

BY TOM JACKSON

POST-WAR football has brought a financial boom to Manchester United. Final returns from their "golden era" at Maine Road, when they hired City's ground for senior matches, will probably reveal an aggregate profit of £75,000 on the last three seasons.

United's balance-sheet for 1948-49—their closing spell at Maine Road—will soon be issued to shareholders. It is believed to show all-time records in attendances, gate receipts, and profit on the season's working.

THE SCALE

THIS is how their profits have soared since normal League and Cup soccer was resumed after the war—season 1946-7 £13,393, 1947-8 £22,329, with last season's margin likely to be in the region of £40,000.

Attendances at remodelled Old Trafford are limited to below 60,000, and, therefore, United may not be able to show such handsome dividends at the end of the current season.

But already they have one source of satisfaction — bigger gates at Central League games. So far they have averaged 3,550 at Old Trafford and twice exceeded the 5,000 mark.

From a cash angle this means the difference between £44, which represented their takings at one reserve game last season, and £224, their highest so far.

When City used Old Trafford for Central League fixtures takings on one occasion were only £4 15s., barely enough to cover the transport of playing kit to the ground!

INSIDE BIG SOCCER with Eric Thornton

...es to town Arsenal?

...B MAY BE DECIDED UPON ...CESTER CITY 22-YEAR-OLD ...LUB DIRECTOR HAVE TAKEN

...date of the next meeting depends on how long these investigations take."

IN the office of Mr. Wilfred Wild, the City secretary, a bag of mail is gradually expanding and developing into a second and third bag—full of applications for tickets for next month's England-Ireland international at Maine Road.

But by the time the English and the Irish F.A.s and the League clubs and the season-...

MEETS THE BLUES

CUMMINGS
Burnley's centre half against City at Turf Moor on Saturday.

SOCCER

MANCHESTER CITY (v. Burnley), away, Saturday: Powell; Phillips, Westwood; Walsh, Fagan, Emptage; Oakes, Munro, Turnbull, Black, Clarke.

SOUTHPORT (v. Oldham), home, Saturday: Birkett; Beardshaw, Boyle; Hitchen, Bellas, Hacking; Rothwell, Dainty, Walsh, Wyles, Maddison.

RUGBY LEAGUE

ROCHDALE HORNETS (v. Swinton), away, Saturday: McGilvray; Nicholson, Winstanley, Butler, Williams; Jones, Wilde; Wagstaff, Croft, Gronow, Thorning, Fearnley, Tucker.

An article from October 1949 outlining the profit United made from their stay at Maine Road.

that to be turned into a goal so quickly, well it made the game. The commentators thought it was over and then it all changed with that save and goal.

"People told me afterwards that I must have played well because Matt [Busby] was not very demonstrative but afterwards he came up to me and I got a squeeze on the shoulder and a bit of a hug as well. So I must have done well!"

This victory had a significant effect on football support and there was no doubt that Busby's side were beginning to gain the upperhand in terms of support, and possibly success. In terms of overall trophy success at this point Bury, City and United had each won the FA Cup twice, but City had appeared in four finals, and had also won the League title. United had won two League titles but, apart from 1948, their successes had come during one three year spell, whereas City's had occurred during different periods. True United were a glamour side between 1907-1908 and 1910-11 but one spell of success was poor for a side that aimed to be one of football's biggest clubs. So when the Reds won the Cup in 1948 there was a feeling that the success was long overdue. The rivalry that would ultimately dominate Manchester football did not exist and so all Mancunians celebrated the success enjoyed by former Blue Busby and his side.

Friend of Busby, and former City Chief Scout, Harry Godwin talked of this time during the 1980s:

"United played at Maine Road just after the war, and because they were a better team

Former Blue Matt Busby became United's manager post-war.

than City they took over a lot of the support of the men whose loyalty had strayed while they were away in the services, and of their youngsters who were just getting interested. United were looking like a team, and they won the Cup in 1948."

In 2002 City supporter James Dowd gave his view of this period:

"There were about equal numbers of Blues and Reds at school. The banter and leg pulling was friendly and there was none of the nastiness which has sadly infected many rival supporters in a city like Manchester. We would often go together to Maine Road every week to see City and United alternatively. United shared City's ground because Old Trafford was a bombed wreck.

"We Blues grudgingly admired Red players like Johnny Carey, Stan Pearson, Bert Whalley, and above all Jack Rowley with his thunderous shot. But we staunchly insisted we liked the great Frank Swift better than all the United players put together! I am certain it was Frank who single-handedly retained the loyalties of many younger fans.

"When United moved back to Old Trafford several of my former school Blues moved with them. They preferred to watch the more successful team. Illogically I felt they were traitors. Go to Old Trafford? Never! It was a football lesson that a successful team will attract hangers-on. United have certainly gained a lot of hangers-on over the years from all over the country. In contrast nobody can accuse City of having fair weather fans for we have had to endure a lot of bad weather!"

James Dowd's views are clearly those of a loyal City fan, however he also recognised that the Blues did lose their way after the war:

"One of my most vivid memories is going to see Manchester Schoolboys, in their rugby style shirts, play in the late forties. One quick moving and clever forward stood out. He was called Dennis Viollet. Later, of course, he achieved fame with United. As he had showed his skills and promise on their ground why didn't the City management snap him up?"

The game James refers to may have been the Lancashire Schools Cup game between Manchester Boys and Salford Boys in April 1949. The match was covered extensively in the **Daily Dispatch** with respected journalist Archie Ledbrooke also commenting on Viollet's skills. As James pointed out Viollet should have been a Blue. Everything pointed to him joining City - his family were all Blues and he even played with Alex Herd's son David. City goalkeeper Frank Swift had noticed Viollet's skills and had mentioned him to the City management but for some unknown reason City ignored Viollet's obvious talents. Swift became angry with the club and insisted they meet with the Viollet family.

A meeting was organised, but the Viollets were left waiting in reception for over an hour. Dennis' father demanded to know what was happening and he was told the Scout had decided to go out instead. The Viollets, understandably stormed out of Maine Road and the following day when a cheery Frank Swift popped around to see how the meeting had gone the family told the City 'keeper what had happened. He was furious and marched to the ground to confront the scouting team. After an unproductive debate Swift decided to speak with his old friend Matt Busby and the following day the United manager personally visited the Viollet family. Inevitably Viollet signed for the Reds.

Former City director Ian Niven had known Viollet as a boy and was amazed with the whole affair:

"I was flabbergasted when I heard Dennis had signed forms with United. I thought it was a mere formality that he would be joining City. It shows how wrong you can be.

"One day I casually asked Dennis why he hadn't signed for City because I distinctly remember that all his family were 'dyed in the wool' Blues. He told me that he was waiting for someone from Maine Road to call and speak to him and his parents but nobody came."

The Viollet transfer clearly is not the most important post war story, however it does give a clear indication that it was this time that the Blues started to lose out locally to the Reds and suggests that for the first time in their history the club lost out to the Reds as a result of their own lack of a cohesive plan either on the pitch or off it. It has to be stressed that United seemed to be getting better organised at all levels and, perhaps because of the influence of former Blue Matt Busby, the Reds simply seemed to know how to progress. Of course United's new found direction may also have been impacted by the adversity of their ground problems. The bombing of Old Trafford perhaps brought home the realisation that United had to be focused and clear on what they wanted to achieve. With Busby in charge they had a recognised footballer, with great knowledge of the game and the way to succeed. This was somewhat different to how United had existed during the 1920s and 1930s.

Apart from the opening decade or so of both clubs' existence, the only time when United had held the upper hand over the Blues was the period 1907 to 1911 following City's illegal payments scandal. At that time the Reds were managed by Ernest Mangnall who, remains today the fourth most successful Manchester manager behind Alex Ferguson, Matt Busby, and Joe Mercer.

Of course United were a First Division side in the first post war season (promoted in 1938) while City, League Champions in 1937, were a Second Division side (relegated in 1938). Under Busby the Reds excited from the start and the opening post war season ended with the Reds missing the title by a point – Liverpool were the first post war Champions.

Busby was one of a new breed of managers who tried to work with the players rather than be hidden away in an office, seeing the team for a few seconds at the end of a training session. At City manager Wilf Wild had wanted the same approach since the 1920s when he first worked as assistant to Ernest Mangnall. At times Wild had managed to see a split between administrative duties and team matters, but for most of the period since 1932 he had performed both roles. Johnny Hart – a 1950s City star but also an office boy at Maine Road during the forties – was amazed at the dual role Wild, and others at clubs across the region, were expected to perform:

"I remember him in the dressing room giving his customary team talk – 'watch the first five minutes and the last five, and don't do anything silly' – then at about twenty to three there was a knock on the door. I followed him out, we walked down the tunnel and he picked up a loud hailer. He went on to the touchline, shouting instructions to the crowd on the Popular Side to move over, and make room for latecomers! Then he headed back to the dressing room to talk with the players a bit more. He had to share the role!

"On another occasion I remember the Chief Scout Albert Kavanagh coming in at about 11. Wild asked him where he was going. Albert said, 'I was thinking about going to watch some lads on Hough End.' Wild said 'No. I want you to go to Halifax.' Albert pointed out the time and how difficult it would be to get there on time, but it was no use. Then he said, 'I'll have no dinner', so Wild leans over. I thought he was going to get some money to give to him, but he opened up his own lunchbox, pulled out a scrappy sandwich and handed it to Albert: 'Here have this. Now get off to Halifax.' I couldn't believe it."

In November 1946 Wild managed to persuade the City directors to split the role. Maybe he had witnessed the way Busby was operating at United and wanted City to follow suit. Busby's former team mate Sam Cowan was given the manager's role and the Blues achieved promotion as Division Two Champions in his first season but, again proving the difference in direction between the Reds and the Blues, Cowan was dismissed at the end of that season as it was felt his domestic arrangements were too much of an issue – Cowan lived close to Brighton on the south coast and he could only be in Manchester for half the week. This did not seem to impact his control of the side, but it upset a few of the directors and his dismissal caused the Blues to stagnate for the following seasons, until ultimately they were relegated in 1950. The balance of power moved to United, particularly when they won the FA Cup in 1948, and the title in 1952.

The Blues still attracted large crowds for significant one-off matches but found it difficult to retain those figures every game. During the promotion season an official crowd of 69,463 (these figures tended not to include season ticket holders and this crowd was recorded at the time of having in excess of 70,000) watched a game with Burnley – this was around 3,000 more than title challenging United could attract for their highest attendance – and in the following season 67,782 watched the opening 4-3 victory over Wolves, but the biggest City home crowd of the season was the Manchester derby on 20th September 1947 and was watched by 78,000 fans.

By the time of the return match in April, watched by 71,690 also at Maine Road, it was clear that United's use of Maine Road was having an effect on City's support. Over the 19 League

Mid-1950s and fans board match buses in city centre Manchester.

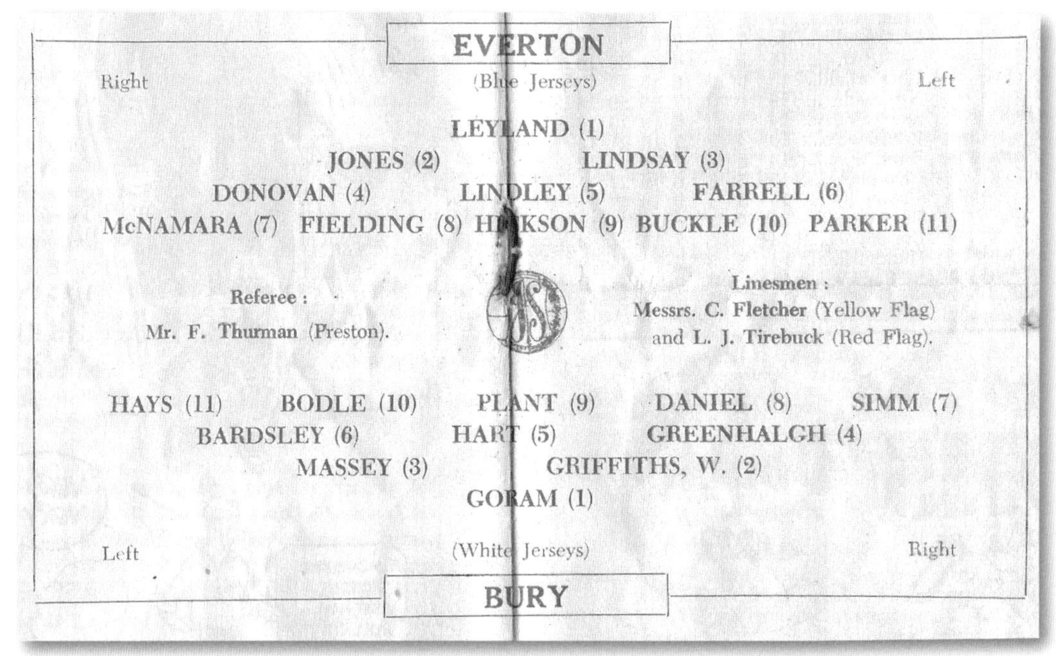

EVERTON
(Blue Jerseys)

Right — Left

LEYLAND (1)
JONES (2) LINDSAY (3)
DONOVAN (4) LINDLEY (5) FARRELL (6)
McNAMARA (7) FIELDING (8) HICKSON (9) BUCKLE (10) PARKER (11)

Referee :
Mr. F. Thurman (Preston).

Linesmen :
Messrs. C. Fletcher (Yellow Flag)
and L. J. Tirebuck (Red Flag).

HAYS (11) BODLE (10) PLANT (9) DANIEL (8) SIMM (7)
BARDSLEY (6) HART (5) GREENHALGH (4)
MASSEY (3) GRIFFITHS, W. (2)
GORAM (1)

Left — Right

(White Jerseys)
BURY

Bury draw 2-2 with Everton at Goodison Park on 3rd November 1951 in Division Two.

games United had played at home at Maine Road they had averaged approximately 54,000, while the Blues were watched by an average of around 43,400 over a similar number of games. Pre-war the disparity between the figures had worked in City's favour but the increased interest in sport following the war, and the fact that the two sides were playing at City's venue created this landmark change.

The attendance for the second derby is interesting. Why would around 7,000 fewer people attend the second derby at the ground that season? It seems highly unlikely, particularly as this occurred in April as United were challenging for the League title. It does not make sense, but it may say more about the way the game was perceived. The significance of this April derby match is that this was the first League game at Maine Road in which City were the visitors. They changed in the away dressing room; United's season ticket holders sat in their regular seats while City fans normally housed in those seats had to find alternative accommodation; the match programme was United's not City's; and even the flag raised proudly on the Popular Side, latter day Kippax, was United's not City's. For some fans this was a sign that Manchester was no longer predominantly Blue and that the Reds now held the upper hand. Maybe fewer City fans attended this game than a regular Maine Road game.

City played second fiddle to United in the immediate post war period, then in August 1949 United's spell at Maine Road ended. Regularly it has been stated that City gained a great deal of finance out of the arrangement but, when considering the impact in terms of loss of support and the finances raised by United during this period, it is clear that City were not significantly better off. According to ***There's Only One United*** by Geoffrey Green published in 1978, United were supposed to pay the Blues £5,000 in instalments for the 1947-48 season alone, although former directors of the Blues doubt this rental figure was actually paid - they claim the postwar spirit and City's relative wealth at the time gave them more of a charitable view of the situation.

For the purposes of this book we should assume it was paid in full, but it is worth noting that when compared with the profit made by the Reds the actual amount paid to City pales into insignificance.

An article in the *Manchester Evening News* (at the time perceived as Manchester's 'Red' paper as opposed to the *Evening Chronicle* which was perceived as 'Blue') of October 1949 highlighted the financial success of United's stay at Maine Road and suggested a return to Old Trafford may not be in United's interest. Under the heading ***"United's 'Golden Era' At Maine Road"*** it revealed that United were poised to announce an aggregate profit over the three Maine Road League seasons of £75,000 – easily an all time record. Also, this was a substantial turnaround from 1945 when the Reds were reported to be in debt for a figure in excess of £15,000. The report noted that the 1949-50 season might not be quite as profitable:

"Attendances at a remodelled Old Trafford are limited to 60,000 and, therefore, United may not be able to show such handsome dividends at the end of the current season."

Interestingly, the use of Maine Road contrasted substantially with City's use of Old Trafford for reserve fixtures. At one fixture the gate receipts were £4 15s with the *Evening News* pointing out that this was barely enough to cover the transport of the playing kit from Maine Road.

Once United moved back to Old Trafford the club continued to develop. Under Busby the Reds put a lot of emphasis on youth development. Together with assistant Jimmy Murphy, coach Bert Whalley, a former United and Stalybridge Celtic player, and former City scout Joe Armstrong, Busby placed his trust in the development of players. According to Busby, writing in 1980, Murphy, Whalley, and Armstrong were vital to his plans:

"Jimmy and I shared the club's secrets and worked together, checking out players, discussing possible signings, mulling over the progress made and the way we wanted things to go. Bert Whalley was another who did much to help the club. He had played for United at centre-half, without ever having established a regular first team place, but his heart was at old Trafford, and when an eye injury forced him to quit playing, he joined the staff.

Action from United's 3-0 victory over Athletic Bilbao at Maine Road on 6th February 1957. Exactly a year after this photo was taken many of the United players had been victims of the Munich Air Disaster.

Roger Byrne with the League Championship trophy won by United in 1957.

"When I was playing for City, Joe Armstrong was scouting for them. I didn't forget the shrewd job he had done at Maine Road, and he eventually landed at Old Trafford, to discover more potential star players than any of us. Joe worked for years, watched all manner of games in all kids of weather, and seldom made a mistake about a youngster."

Over time United's development of quality young players gained significant headlines, and by the mid 1950s after winning the League in 1952 and 1956 the press were dubbing the side the Busby Babes, although the term Busby Boys appears to have been utilised just as much at the time with the **Manchester Evening News** using the Boys tag during 1954 and the **Empire News** still using it in 1957 when the Reds won the title again. Of course the tag Busby Babes became known worldwide following the horrific Munich Air Disaster of 1958.

Across the City the 1950s saw City re-establish themselves as a force with former player Les McDowall instigating a number of significant tactical developments which helped to revolutionise the make up of the game. The most famous tactical plan was known as the Revie Plan, after City's famous centre-forward Don Revie. The plan saw Revie play a deep role which, although it sounds relatively simple today, totally bamboozled the opposition. A point best illustrated by the success McDowall's side enjoyed in the Manchester derby matches of 1954-55 – the first season the Revie Plan was adopted. That season the Blues defeated Busby's Babes in two League games and an FA Cup tie with an aggregate score of 10-2.

The Most Fateful Soccer Meeting?

WHEN Matt Busby and Jimmy Murphy danced their unashamed victory-jig on the Maine Road touch-line after that fabulous Manchester United — Bilbao European Cup match, it took me back 12 years and a 1,000 miles to one of the most fateful meetings in soccer.

BY FRANK SWIFT

The saga of the Busby Babes started when C.S.M. Busby, manager of a British Army side touring Italy just before V.E. Day, met the sports organiser of an Army rest-camp at Bari. The name was Murphy.

Like most of the tourists—of whom I was one—Matt Busby had formed a healthy respect for wing-half Jimmy Murphy during his West Bromwich and Wales playing days

But Busby admits he was doubly impressed by the Welshman's vigorous coaching and organising ability with the lads in Italy.

Says Matt: "I made a mental note there and then that Jimmy would be a useful asset to any football club."

To cut a long story short, a year after Busby had taken over at Old Trafford, he heard that "Murph" was out of the Army and looking for a job.

Before you could say "Bilbao" he was on Manchester United's staff.

So was launched the most successful partnership in post-war soccer management.

Jimmy, the junior partner, has done his job of grooming the youngsters so expertly that several League clubs have offered him a job as manager.

But Jimmy, who also looks after the Welsh national team, prefers to remain as Matt Busby's assistant. Busby certainly picked a winner in Italy.

* * *

THANKLESS JOB

THAT was just one example of Busby's now-legendary shrewdness, which I first recognised on the field as a Manchester City colleague of this former Scottish international half-back

If anyone was ever fitted for the thankless job of club management, it is Busby.

I am proud to think that I had a hand in launching his career in that direction.

That was when the soldier-footballers met in London before their Italian tour to pick the man in charge

From an exalted company of sergeant-majors and N.C.O.s that included Arthur Rowe, Cliff Britton, Joe Mercer, Tommy Lawton, Jimmy Mullen and Jack Rowley, Matt Busby was the unanimous choice.

And he did a perfect job.

* * *

WHAT A REFEREE

ANOTHER football fallacy exploded in my face at Maine Road—the one about British referees being the best in the world.

Herr Albert Dusch, of Germany, who packs 15st into a five-foot frame, looked a slightly comic figure when he came on to the pitch. But he soon made it clear that he would tolerate no funny business.

His was the best display of controlled, decisive refereeing I have seen this season. It earned him the respect and admiration of crowd and players alike.

So much so that, at the after-the-match banquet, several Spanish players asked for his autograph.

Herr Dusch, who told me he has refereed for 28 years, enjoyed the game immensely, and said that the sporting conduct of both sides had made his task easy.

The rotund German is too modest. His impartial strictness in penalising every infringement kept the sizzling game from boiling over.

And to rule out two Manchester United "goals" for offside within five minutes was a tremendous show of moral courage in that electric atmosphere, particularly as one involved a hairbreadth decision

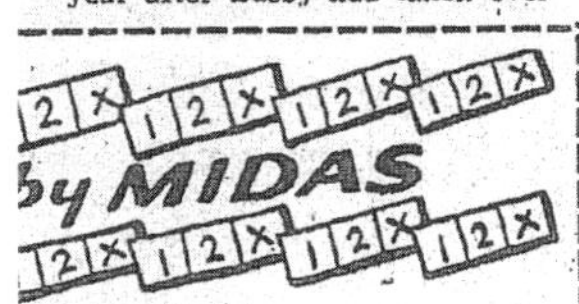

of two selections, and that the third block has two columns of three selections.

Match Ratings

HOMES

Aston Villa, Preston, Leeds, Wolves, Fulham, Swansea, West Ham, Plymouth, Barrow, Hull, Rochdale, Workington.

AWAYS

Everton, Sheffield, Wed., Doncaster, Middlesbrough, Stoke, Brighton, Chester, Stockport, Chesterfield, Rangers, Kilmarnock, Aberdeen.

DRAWS

Blackpool, Luton, Blackburn, Sheffield Utd., Colchester, Northampton, Q.P.R., Reading, Southend, Derby, Barnsley, Bournemouth, Huddersfield, Southampton.

POINTS POOLS

Littlewoods.—X X 2 2 2 2 1 2 1 2 X 2 2 2
Vernons.—X X X 1 2 2 2 1 2 1 2 2 2 1
Shermans.—X X X X 2 1 X 2 2 1 2 2 1
Copes.—X X 1 X 2 2 2 1 2 2 2
Murphys.—2 2 1 2 1 2 1 X X X 2 2
Zetters.—X X 2 1 X X 2 1 2 1 2 1
Soccer.—X X 2 2 2 2 1 1 1 2 1 X
Empire.—X X X 2 1 2 2 2 1 1 2 2

★ FIXED ODDS ★

A POPULAR guarantee table for Three Draws is that which covers eight matches in such a way that if four of them are right there will be a column of three draws correct. However, it is not necessary to write this 20-column table out in full, for it can be expressed in formula fashion.

Split your eight selections into two sets of three and a set of two, and put a bracket round each section. Label the sets of three A and B, and the set of two C. Then add these instructions:—

Perm:
3 from A = 1
3 from B = 1
2 from A with 1 from B = 0
2 from B with 1 from C = 6
2 from C with 1 from A = 3
= 20 lines @ 6d. = 10s.

It looks a lot, but this is easier than writing out the full 20

A Frank Swift article from February 1957 recalling the moment when Matt Busby and Jimmy Murphy first met.

The closest of these games was the September 1954 meeting at Maine Road which ended 3-2. Don Davies, the journalist who went under the pen name of An Old International and a victim of the air disaster in 1958, compared City's tactical qualities against United's youth:

"City were content to rely on smooth, ordered teamwork and a patient, logical build up as the best means to score goals, whereas United, though no less able to indulge in effective combination at will, seemed somehow drawn by youthful exuberance and perhaps the challenge of the occasion into heroic individual efforts that came so frequently to nought."

Despite City's dominance in those fixtures the Blues found it difficult to make a claim on the League title during the 1950s. In 1957-58 City scored more goals than any other side in the top two divisions when they netted 104 goals, however they conceded a remarkable 100 goals (becoming the first side to both score and concede 100 goals in a season) and ended the season fifth.

The closest they came to winning the title had been two years earlier, in 1955-56, when the Blues finished fourth (United were the Champions), but success did arrive in the FA Cup. In 1956 City defeated Birmingham City 3-1, but twelve months earlier the Blues had been unfortunate to be defeated by Newcastle after injury to Jimmy Meadows had caused City to be a man down for 71 minutes of the final.

Injury problems dominated the first three Manchester finals of the 1950s with the 1956 (City) and 1957 (United) finals both becoming remembered for the injuries sustained to the Manchester goalkeepers. In 1956 the story was all about City 'keeper Bert Trautmann, as the **Daily Telegraph** reported:

"Manchester City 'keeper Bert Trautmann played the last 15 minutes of the Cup final in great pain, not realising his neck was broken. With his side two up, this latest victim of the 'Wembley hoodoo' could have been excused for going off after a dive to save at the feet of Birmingham's Peter Murphy left him dazed and reeling. When the highly popular ex-German POW, newly elected Footballer of the Year, staggered to his feet, the fans burst out into a refrain of "For he's a jolly good fellow". He went up with his team-mates to collect his medal after their 3-1 victory, and it was only later that X-rays showed the fracture, which could easily have been fatal.

"This was a Cup final that had everything. Birmingham started as firm favourites after a dazzling Cup run that saw them reach Wembley without a single home tie, scoring 18 goals against two. Manchester City, by contrast, scraped through with single-goal victories in every round. And injuries forced a last -minute reshuffle of their team for the final. The out-of-favour Don Revie, dropped by both England and his club earlier in the season, was brought back from reserve-team football to play his deep-lying centre-forward role, and Bobby Johnstone was moved out to the right wing. These controversial moves by manager Les McDowall proved to be match-winners. If Trautmann's heroics stole some of the headlines, Revie was the man of the match. He set up the first goal with a long cross-field ball to Roy Clarke from near half-way, was in the box for the return pass, and back-heeled the ball for Joe Hayes to score - this after only three minutes.

"Birmingham equalised against the run of play after 15 minutes through Noel Kinsey. It was another 50 minutes before Jack Dyson restored Manchester's lead. And five minutes later the same player headed a long Trautmann clearance into the path of Johnstone, who beat the advancing Gil Merrick with ease to become the first man to score goals in successive Wembley finals."

Trautmann had in fact broken his neck and it was not until after the homecoming – in which he was clearly in agony – that the true extent of his injury became known.

The 'Wembley hoodoo' as it had been termed affected League Champions United the following year. Again, the *Telegraph* focussed on the goalkeeper's role:

"Yet again we have had to witness the sight of a team struggling through most of a Cup final with only 10 men. This time it was no accident, but a foul charge by Aston Villa's Peter McParland on Ray Wood that left the Manchester United keeper concussed and with a broken cheek bone. This, after only six minutes, completely disrupted a United side who were bidding to become the first club to bring off the League and Cup 'double' since Villa did it 60 years ago. But for Wood's injury, United would almost certainly have achieved it. Centre-half Jackie Blanchflower went in goal - and played a blinder! Edwards went to centre-half, where he is perfectly at home, and was another United hero. But Whelan's dropping back to left-half left the forward line unbalanced and lacking his goalscoring power (he was United's leading League scorer with 26 goals). A groggy Wood returned for 10 minutes half an hour later, but only as nuisance value on the wing.

"The reorganised Manchester side held out until midway through the second half, when two goals from outside-left McParland virtually killed their chances. With seven minutes to go, however, Taylor headed in an Edwards corner, and United brought Wood back into goal for a last desperate effort. But Villa's defence, admirably marshalled by Dugdale at centre-half, held out against all their opponents could do, and the Midlanders had won their record seventh FA Cup. Villa captain and inside-left Johnny Dixon had an outstanding match, but their star was Irish international McParland, always the danger man, although his second goal was arguably offside. His performance, however, should not be allowed to whitewash the unforgivable foul that laid out the United keeper. Wood had already caught the ball from McParland's header and was standing still, some four yards from his goal line, when the oncoming winger, who could easily have avoided him, crashed into him. At best, it was reckless and irresponsible. Yet the referee did not even caution McParland. Sadly, it left a nasty taste in the mouth."

Wood's injury was a devastating blow and did end with the Reds narrowly missing out on the double – the closest any of our sides had come since FA Cup winners City had missed the title by three points in 1904. These were great years for the Reds and consecutive League titles ensured everyone in football knew of Matt Busby's young side.

Across at City the Blues mid-fifties glory was not as great as the Reds, however the Blues seemed determined to build on their memorable FA Cup finals, particularly when exciting youngster Denis Law was signed from Huddersfield Town during the 1959-60 season. However, by that time the bulk of the 1956 FA Cup winning side had moved on and the Blues never really supplemented the Law transfer with other big arrivals. Without those transfers and with United dominant from a youth perspective in the region City missed their opportunity and, once Law was allowed to join Torino the year after arriving at Maine Road, the Blues embarked on a more small-time approach. Selling Law was a huge disappointment for fans and for the first time since 1930 – when goalscoring hero Tommy Johnson was sold against his wishes and the wishes of all supporters to Everton – the Blues had sacrificed their biggest star. The side would not compete for success again until the arrival of Joe Mercer and Malcolm Allison in 1965.

Of the other sides in the region the best placed side was undoubtedly Bury. Bury had been members of the Second Division since 1929 and when football resumed post war there was inevitably a great deal of excitement and interest in the club. Season tickets, selling at £1 10s for the terracing and £5 5s for the most expensive seats proved popular and the season ended with Bury boasting an average attendance of 14,764 – their highest since 1928 when they finished fifth in Division One. In addition, a profit of £1,591 was made on the season which enabled the directors to make a bold move. They reduced the price of season tickets. In 2007 much was made of Premier League sides cutting season ticket prices in a bid to make attending football more popular, but even the reduced prices were significantly larger in many cases than football should charge. In the late forties Bury's prices were already relatively low but the Bury directors were convinced their policy would pay dividends and when the total number of season ticket holders was revealed it stood at 1,749 – almost three times the figure in 1946-47!

Pleased with the response, Bury spent a record £4,000 on signing a City centre-forward Jimmy Constantine, and the 1947-48 season saw the average attendance increase to 16,037 despite a poor season on the pitch. It has to be stressed that during this period of increase Bury were the only Manchester region side in the Second Division – typically the supporters of City and United would help boost crowds for derby matches.

The increase in Gigg Lane attendance continued for the following couple of seasons but on the pitch little improved. On New Year's Eve 1949 everything looked positive with Bury beating Blackburn Rovers 3-0 to reach fourth place in the division but 1950 saw the side struggle and a dismal run saw only two wins in seventeen games. They ended the season in 18th place.

Twelve months later they avoided relegation with a 3-1 win in their penultimate game of the season but from a financial point of view the season had been a disaster. Excessive spending on transfers placed Bury in the red for the first time since 1939 and they recorded a record loss of £15,282. At the annual shareholders meeting on 26th July 1950 Acting Chairman Alex Lawson painted a particularly poor image of Bury's position:

"If we lose £15,282 again next season then we will go out of existence and it cannot happen. The average gate at Gigg Lane was 15,086 last season, as compared to the average in the Second Division of 23,386. It costs as much to operate a Second Division club as it does one in the First Division and yet our total gate receipts amount to little more than we are supposed to have paid for one player. Hence the importance of the players who have been transferred from the club. The population of Bury is by far the smallest of the towns in Division Two and by far smaller than many towns possessing Third Division clubs. Consequently our gates are not sufficient to run the club without being subsidised by transfer fees."

In terms of the wider context of football in the region, it was a fair assessment and suggested that Bury had been punching above their weight throughout their history. They were the first of the region's sides to find true success and at this stage in history they remained the Manchester region's third strongest club, with a record only City and United could match. Today few consider Bury to be one of the region's giants, but in truth their history and heritage makes them one of our biggest successes. It is a major shame the modern era has proved so difficult for the Shakers.

By the Fifties both Mancunian sides had eclipsed Bury in terms of attendances and success, but none of the other local sides had consistently been able to better Bury's achievements and records. Sadly, a loss of £4,859 followed and Bury ended 1951-52 in 17th place but only 3 points above relegated Coventry.

The financial position improved slightly in the following seasons, but the League position did

The Bury side from 1957-8 - this team finished fourth in Division Three (North).

not and each season seemed to end with the Shakers needing vital wins in their final games. Sadly 1956-57 was to see an end to Bury's proud record of never having been out of the top two divisions, and after a first half of the season had seen plenty of goals – both for and against – the second half tended to see the exact opposite.

Bury lost their final game of the season away at Stoke but there was still a faint hope of survival. Relegation rivals Notts County had three games remaining and there was hope of a fairytale ending for Bury, however County's rivals did not really have anything to play for and they defeated Blackburn in their first game of the three, thereby relegating Bury to Division Three North. *The Bury Times* was as stunned as most locals: ***"Shakers relegated after 63 years in senior football."***

It was a crucial period for Bury as the League structure was about to be reorganised with the regional Third Divisions being scrapped and replaced by a national Division Three and Four for the start of the 1958-59 season. This meant that Bury not only had to fight to gain promotion – only one place was available - but they also had to ensure they did not finish in the lower half of Division Three North – the bottom 12 clubs would be in the newly formed Division Four.

Fortunately Bury had nothing to worry about as far as relegation was concerned, but they did not manage to achieve promotion either, finishing fourth. There were a couple of significant moments from a local perspective however with Bury meeting Rochdale in their first ever League meeting. 10,000 fans travelled to Spotland in a crowd of 18,896 to see a 1-1 draw.

In 1959 Bury recorded their lowest finish at the time – ending the season tenth – and in 1960 they finished seventh in Division Three, but their overdraft had increased to £48,000 and the dawn of the sixties had to see the side return to the Second Division – a division still lower than the majority of fans wanted to see their side compete in.

The restructure of the League in 1958 was a desperate period for all the regional division's clubs. Locally, Rochdale, Stockport and Oldham, as well as Bury, were in danger of falling into the new Fourth Division and the 1957-58 season was at times a desperate race to ensure a top twelve finish. Rochdale, who had not finished higher than tenth since 1950, and Oldham, who had been 20th and 19th in the preceding seasons, were the two most vulnerable while Stockport had finished no lower than 11th since 1948.

In the end 1957-58 was perhaps the most dramatic season for the region's lower division sides as a whole and, apart from Bury, any of the other sides could have been relegated to the new Fourth Division. In the end only Oldham suffered the ignominy of becoming Division Four founder members – together with Crystal Palace and Coventry City Oldham hold the amazing record of being founder members of both Division Four and the Premier League. Oldham ended 1957-58 in fifteenth place on 45 points. Rochdale finished tenth on 46 points and Stockport finished ninth on 47 points.

How close each side came to relegation can be demonstrated by their results. Oldham and Rochdale faced each other in their penultimate game – a goalless draw. Had Oldham won then Rochdale would have been relegated instead, it was that close. At Stockport the situation had appeared equally as bad with only four games to go, but a run of 3 victories and a draw ensured just enough points to enter the new national Division Three.

The goalless derby game between Oldham and Rochdale at Boundary Park was watched by a crowd of 10,919 on 26th April 1958.

November 1950 - George Hardwick makes his Oldham debut.

For Oldham the opening Division Four season was a disaster. Latics should have challenged for one of the four promotion places but instead the club hovered around the re-election zone, and ended the season 21st out of 24 clubs. They were safe, but the future did not look bright. Similarly Rochdale and Stockport made history that season by becoming two of the first four sides to suffer automatic relegation to the Fourth. Rochdale ended the season bottom of Division Three while Stockport were 21st, in the last relegation spot, five points from safety.

With three sides competing at the lowest level the decade ended grimly. Oldham had to face the re-election ballot at the end of 1959-60 after finishing the season 23rd, five points from safety, while Stockport and Rochdale were tenth and 12th respectively. For Oldham this was an exceptionally difficult period, especially as the Latics had looked so strong earlier in the decade. Oldham Journalist Tony Bugby:

The Oldham Athletic badge during 1951 - apparently manager George Hardwick played his part if designing this badge.

"After the Second World War Oldham's position improved and it really coincided with the arrival of George Hardwick at Boundary Park in 1950 as player-manager. George was an interesting character and his arrival brought an upturn in the club's fortunes. They won the Division Three title in 1952-3. This was the first championship they had ever won in the club's history. That was quite remarkable considering they'd been in the League for so long. So that was a significant moment, but then the decade ended with more struggles and the creation of Division Four.

"Oldham suffered from bad timing again. There First Division development had ended with the suspension of football at the start of World War One, and then a downturn in form came just at the moment Division Four was born."

The future for all Division Four sides was expected to be a difficult one. Journalist Peter Morris, writing in **Football Monthly** in May 1958 was critical of the new league. He described Division Four as:

George Hardwick guided Oldham to the Division Three (North) title in 1952-53 and Manchester Cup success. Here he is with both the Division Three shield and the Manchester Cup.

"A league many think will kill off soccer's deadwood inside two years. The Football League set up, as we know it today, has for too long been cluttered with clubs who find it hard even to live from hand to mouth. Clearly, there can be no firm status for clubs in the new Fourth Division. As I see it, they will rank no higher than teams in the Southern and Midland Leagues, all of which can operate on a much looser shoestring season by season."

Morris painted a grim future for teams forced to travel from the north-west to places like Torquay, and he firmly believed the cost of travel and also the limited opportunity for progression – even though four sides would face promotion each year – meant that for the smaller sides Division Four would offer:

"A slow and painful death with the Football League exhibiting no more remorse than that expected from a solicitous family undertaker!"

So by the end of the 1950s the future looked bleak for Division Four sides Oldham, Rochdale and Stockport, while Bury lay in Division Three – a division their history suggested should have been beneath them. For City the post war period had not been particularly successful. The balance of power had shifted, giving United dominance, with City's mid fifties cup finals becoming the highlights of a period that brought much attention Old Trafford's way. For the Reds the successes under Busby had brought United into the general public eye for the first since 1911. Their pre-war financial problems and relegation struggles had been replaced with a new found wealth and exciting success on the pitch. Appearances in the European Cup, combined with three League titles and five finishes as runners-up during the fifties, meant they were the English team of the decade, although Wolves supporters would argue that point.

ATTENDANCE DETAIL SEASON BY SEASON - 1946-1954

Season	City	United	Oldham	Bury	Stockport	Rochdale
1946-47	39283	43945	10877	14764	8881	7577
1947-48	42725	54890	12950	16037	11024	8124
1948-49	38699	48808	15893	16360	10916	8616
1949-50	39381	43282	15185	16821	12013	8372
1950-51	35016	39008	13579	15101	10006	6519
1951-52	38302	42916	16153	14100	12030	4992
1952-53	34663	37571	17928	13420	8006	6182
1953-54	30155	35458	17859	13532	7678	6121

LEAGUE POSITIONS SEASON BY SEASON - 1946-1954

Season	City	United	Oldham	Bury	Stockport	Rochdale
1946-47	23	2	63	39	48	50
1947-48	10	2	55	42	61	56
1948-49	7	2	50	34	52	51
1949-50	21	4	55	40	54	47
1950-51	24	2	59	42	54	55
1951-52	15	1	48	39	47	65
1952-53	20	8	45	42	55	66
1953-54	17	4	44	39	54	63

LORD BURGHLEY

CHAPTER SEVENTEEN

THE MUNICH AIR DISASTER

To me personally, it has been a great shock. I had seen them, at Highbury the previous Saturday, give a wonderful exhibition of Soccer, one of the best for many years. I thought then, United, blossoming further with more experience, would become the finest Soccer machine of the century.

'Charles Buchan's Football Monthly', Charles Buchan, 1958

ONE event has been written about more than any other in the history of the game within the Manchester region and that event is also by far the most tragic and devastating moment in Mancunian sport. Ignoring stadium disasters such as Hillsborough, Bradford, and Bolton, the Munich Air Disaster was the worst tragedy to affect any English club. It brought the near destruction of an entire team of good quality, successful players.

The story of the disaster has been covered extensively over the years and has featured in many television documentaries and even in feature length dramatisations, however it is worth assessing the way the disaster took hold of the people of the region and how it was viewed by all Mancunians at the time.

The simple facts of the story are that 23 people, including eight Manchester United players, were killed in the disaster on 6th February 1958, but the circumstances surrounding it need explaining. United had progressed to the quarter-finals of the European Cup where they were to face Red Star Belgrade on a two-legged basis. The first leg, played at Old Trafford on 14th January was watched by a crowd of around 35,000 and ended in a 2-1 victory – Eddie Colman and Bobby Charlton the scorers. The following month, on 5th February, the Reds played the second leg and drew the game 3-3, thereby winning the tie 5-4 on aggregate. It was the second time United had reached the semi-final stage and there was a strong feeling this was to be United's year, although AC Milan and Real Madrid had also reached the semi-final stage. Madrid it has to be remembered had won the competition in its first two seasons, and would ultimately win the trophy for five consecutive seasons. Madrid were a phenomenal side.

As well as their progress in Europe the Reds were also challenging for the League title and had already reached the fifth round of the FA Cup, and many of their young players were national figures.

After the game in Belgrade the Reds stayed overnight in the city. There had been an official

Players, officials, and journalists make their way onto the plane out from Manchester together. United captain Roger Byrne can be seen wearing a light coat, with Duncan Edwards next to him. Former City and England goalkeeper Frank Swift is pictured slightly to the right of Duncan Edwards.

banquet after the match and manager Matt Busby spent much of the evening in the company of Frank Swift, his former City team mate who was by this time a leading journalist, and several other journalists and friends. The journey home began the next morning (Thursday) and for many years rumours that United were under pressure to return home to ensure they were back in plenty of time for their Saturday fixture with League leaders Wolves has been suggested. Clearly the Football League would not have wanted European football to jeopardise a game that was already viewed by many as the deciding factor in the Championship race (a Wolves victory would place United eight points behind the leaders with only 13 games to go), however it is highly debateable that the League or FA would have placed pressure on United at this moment. It is possible United felt the pressure of course, as they had gone against the English authorities the previous year by entering the European Cup.

At Belgrade there were a few delays caused by lost passports and the like, however the weather was also poor. The previous day's game had been played in wintry conditions and by the time the flight left Belgrade visibility was poor but still not bad enough to cause a cancellation. The journey back to Manchester was intended to get the players home by teatime, with a stop off at Munich for refuelling.

In Germany snow was falling and the conditions were deteriorating, however after a short refuel the plane was ready to take off again at 2pm. The pilot Captain James Thain and his co-pilot

Captain Kenneth Rayment prepared for take off with Rayment taking the controls. Thain later gave his version of what happened next:

"As Ken opened the throttles, which were between us on the central pedestal, with his right hand, I followed with my left hand. When they were fully open I tapped his hand and held the throttles in the fully open position. Ken moved his hand and I called 'full power' and, looking at the instruments in front of me, said 'Temperatures and pressures correct and warning lights out'. I then called out the speed in knots as the aircraft accelerated. The engines sounded an uneven note and the needle on the port pressure gauge started to fluctuate. I felt a pain in my left hand as Ken pulled the throttles back and said 'Abandon take-off'. I held the control column fully forward while Ken put on the brakes.

"What had happened was boost surging, which was not uncommon with Elizabethans at the time, particularly at airports like Munich, because of their height above sea level. Over-rich mixture caused the power surge, but though the engines sounded uneven there was not much danger that the take-off power of the aircraft would be affected. The Elizabethans were very powerful in their day and you could actually have taken off on one engine. Knowing that one cause of boost surging was opening the throttles too quickly, Ken said that at the start of our next run he would open the throttles a little before releasing the brakes and then continue to open them more slowly. Ken opened the throttles to twenty-eight inches, released the brakes; and off we went again."

The plane struggled further: *"I took the decision to abandon the take-off this time. We were halfway down the runway with the throttles fully open when I saw the starboard engine steady itself at fifty-seven-and-a-half inches but the port pressure run to sixty inches and beyond. I wanted to discuss this with the BEA station engineer.*

"The station engineer, William Black, came to the cockpit to check the trouble and we explained about the boost surging. He said it was fairly common at airports like Munich."

The engineer explained how Thain and Rayment could overcome the problem but also suggested he could retune the engines but explained that an overnight stop would then be required. This was not something the pilot felt was necessary, and so the decision was taken to make a third attempt at take off.

The United players, management and other passengers were in the airport building at this stage and so had to be recalled to the aircraft. In the airport building Duncan Edwards sent a telegram to his landlady saying: "All flights cancelled – stop – flying tomorrow – stop – Duncan." **Manchester Evening Chronicle** journalist Alf Clarke telephoned the newspaper with similar news.

For most of the players and some of the journalists the period in the airport was typical of the experience most feel when waiting for a delayed flight. Some of the players were buying drinks and snacks, others simply sitting around waiting. Journalists Franks Swift and Eric Thompson were lightening the mood. According to another journalist, Frank Taylor, in his eyewitness account of the disaster ***The Day A Team Died***:

"The comics, Frank Swift and Eric Thompson, had taken over. Eric, small and round, had picked up Big Swifty's overcoat and he was shuffling around the room like a lost grizzly bear, the coat almost trailing the floor, the arms hanging hugely by his sides. Big Swifty was trying to cram his massive torso into Eric's coat. 'Must have shrunk' he was saying with that gormless grin so famed in the sporting world. 'Or maybe I've growed on this trip'."

Earlier Swift had entertained some of the passengers with stories from his playing career.

Once the passengers returned to the plane Thain and Rayment attempted the third – and fatal – take off. Frank Taylor's book on the disaster has become the best eyewitness account of how the events unfolded, and he explores in detail the take off and events that followed. Suffice to say that at two minutes past three the pilots were given clearance to take off but were told that if they were not airborne by four minutes past three the clearance would become void. This suggests any take off later than four minutes past would not be allowed and a considerable wait would occur. Taylor:

"I wonder what went through their [the pilots] minds then? Did they feel under pressure? If they didn't get the aircraft airborne within the next two minutes, they might face a much longer delay on the ground. In the passengers' cabin, we didn't know the pilots had been warned they had two minutes to make up their minds whether or not to go."

The decision was taken to go and by this time the mood of many of the passengers was quite subdued. Some were extremely nervous about the flight, while others tried to focus on other things. Survivor Bill Foulkes later told journalists that the passengers had felt unsettled and that one of the players chose to move to the back of the aircraft where most of the journalists sat:

"David Pegg said 'I'm not sitting here. It's not safe', and went to the back of the plane. And I seem to remember Frank Swift standing up near the back and saying something like, 'that's right, lads, this is the place to be'. We set off and I remember looking out of the window. They had big windows, those Elizabethans. I remember seeing the snow coming down and the slush flying about and then there was a terrible noise, the kind you might expect to hear of a car suddenly left a smooth road and started running over rocks."

The plane's speed had been increasing until this point and despite the general air of anxiety all had seemed well. Captain Thain later told the German inquiry his view of what happened:

A section of the Manchester City museum in February 2008, remembering the Munich air disaster.

"When it reached 117 knots I called out 'V1' [velocity one, the speed at which it is no longer safe to abandon take off] and waited for a positive indication of more speed so that I could call 'V2' [119 knots – the speed required before taking off]. Suddenly the needle dropped back to 112, and then 105. Ken shouted 'Christ, we can't make it,' and I looked up from the instruments to see a lot of snow and a house and a tree, right in the path of the aircraft."

Later it was discovered that the engineer had incorrectly re-fitted the air speed indicator meaning it gave an incorrect reading. From that point on the plane careered off the runway and headed towards a house positioned beyond the airport. Thain:

"The aircraft went through a fence and crossed a road and the port wing hit the house. The wing and part of the tail were torn off and the house caught fire."

Little has been said over the years about the fate of the people living in the house at the time. The occupants were the Winkler family. The husband was out, presumably at work, and the eldest daughter was at a friend's at the time of the crash but the girl's mother, Anna, was at home sewing together with her three other children. According to German reports two of the children were having an afternoon nap and were thrown out of the burning house by Anna, who also escaped, while the other child – a four year old – managed to escape by crawling out through a window.

The left wing of the plane and part of the tail were ripped off the rest of the aircraft, while the cockpit smashed into a tree and the fuselage into a hut that contained a fuel-loaded truck. This exploded.

Hans Birnbaum, a Munich fuel merchant, was one of only a handful of witnesses and he said at the time:

"The visibility was poor so not many people saw what happened. I was only 200 metres away when the plane crashed and the force of the explosion of the petrol was so powerful that I was knocked down by it. When I got up I saw flames and smoke pouring out of two houses and debris flying through the air. I ran to the plane and saw the plane had broken in pieces."

What followed was a remarkable series of brave incidents by a number of the passengers, most notably goalkeeper Harry Gregg. Gregg actually returned to the plane to rescue a baby and its mother, and is recorded as dragging Bobby Charlton and Dennis Viollet clear, and of giving assistance to other members of the flight. He has regularly disputed the tag of 'hero' often used by the media when describing him. In truth though he was a hero.

Emergency vehicles ultimately arrived and the passengers – both those alive and those that had passed away – were rushed to the Rechts Der Isar hospital.

At the hospital it was not immediately obvious that the patients being brought in were connected with Manchester United. As far as the doctors were concerned these were victims of an air crash and who they were was irrelevant at first, then the head of the neuro-surgical department professor Frank Kessel started to treat the patients and he immediately recognised Frank Swift. Swift, at this point, remained a major international name and was hugely popular wherever he went. He was the first English goalkeeper to appear in the Berlin Olympic stadium – playing for English champions City in a highly publicised propaganda match against a German national XI in 1937 – and was well known to Kessel as the professor had actually lived in Manchester for a while and was known to attend football matches. He knew who Swift was, although he did not quite understand

A small housing estate in Newton Heath has streets named after the United victims of the air disaster.

why he was in Munich, and then he spotted Swift's old City teammate Matt Busby. *"Das ist ein Englische Fussball spiel"* he is reported to have exclaimed as he recognised that the combination of two former City players meant this was an English football team. Inevitably it became obvious the side was United.

Swift and Busby were both still alive at this point, although Swift was badly injured and died shortly afterwards as he was being carried into the hospital. Kessel had hoped to save the former 'keeper but sadly his main aorta artery had been severed apparently by his seat belt. Busby's life was also in the balance and he would have the last rites administered to him twice, but eventually after 71 days he returned to Manchester.

Two other men were also struggling – players Johnny Berry and Duncan Edwards. Berry also pulled through although his playing career came to an end due to the injuries he suffered, while Edwards fought on for 15 days before he died of kidney failure. It was the saddest moment for most Mancunians as Edwards' fight for survival had brought much hope, but the moment he passed away signalled the end of Busby's great side.

In total twenty-three people died as a result of the air disaster. They included eight members of United's playing staff:

GEOFFREY BENT (a reserve player for the Munich trip meaning his journey was ultimately unnecessary, 25 year old Bent had earlier made 12 League appearances for the Reds)

ROGER BYRNE (popular captain, Byrne made a total of 277 appearances in League, Cup and Europe, and had appeared in 33 internationals – he was two days short of his 29th birthday at the time of the crash)

EDDIE COLMAN (21 year old Colman made 107 League, Cup & European appearances)

DUNCAN EDWARDS (the most famous member of the team, 21 year old Edwards made 175 League, Cup and European appearances and had appeared in 18 internationals)

MARK JONES (24 year old Jones made 120 League, Cup and European appearances)

DAVID PEGG (22 year old Pegg made 148 League, Cup and European appearances and had made one international appearance)

TOMMY TAYLOR (26 year old Taylor made 189 League, Cup and European appearances and 19 internationals)

LIAM 'BILLY' WHELAN (Like Bent 22 year old Whelan was a reserve for the Belgrade game, in total he had appeared in 96 League, Cup and European games, netting 52 goals and made 5 Eire international appearances)

Three members of United staff:
WALTER CRICKMER (United secretary and manager in 1931-32 & 1937-45)
TOM CURRY (trainer and former Newcastle & Stockport player)
BERT WHALLEY (coach and former Stalybridge Celtic and United player)

Eight journalists:
ALF CLARKE (Manchester Evening Chronicle)
DON DAVIES (Manchester Guardian)
GEORGE FOLLOWS (Daily Herald)
TOM JACKSON (Manchester Evening News)
ARCHIE LEDBROOKE (Daily Mirror)
HENRY ROSE (Daily Express)
FRANK SWIFT (News of the World & former City goalkeeper and England captain)
ERIC THOMPSON (Daily Mail)

The other victims were:
TOM CABLE (steward)
Capt KENNETH RAYMENT (co-pilot)
WILLIE SATINOFF (Manchester businessman)
BELA MIKLOS (travel agent)

The following all survived the crash:

Johnny Berry – was in a coma for two months following the disaster and was never able to resume his playing career. He suffered brain damage and according to other survivors his hand-eye co-ordination had gone. Within 12 months of the disaster he and his family were ordered to leave their club house and his employment cards arrived in the post. Berry's problems continued throughout his life (he passed away in 1994) and understandably his wife never forgave United for their treatment of the family.

Jackie Blanchflower – suffered renal damage and various broken bones, including his pelvis, and despite his youth (he was only 25) he was unable to play again. He had been destined to play for Northern Ireland in the 1958 World Cup finals but struggled to make a decent non-footballing career instead. Like Berry, Blanchflower was told to leave his club house a few months after the disaster, even though his wife was pregnant and it was clear the family would struggle. New Chairman Louis Edwards gave him a job loading pies on to lorries at his meat factory and it was reported in ***The Lost Babes*** that he refused to go to Old Trafford after being turned away when he asked for match tickets for his doctor. He passed away in 1998.

Matt Busby – after a long fight to regain fitness Busby returned to his role as United's manager and ultimately created a new side which, in 1968, became the first English side to win the European Cup. He was awarded the CBE in 1958 and then was knighted in 1968. He remained a key presence at Old Trafford until his death in 1994.

Bobby Charlton – went on to become recognised as one of United and England's greatest players. He was part of Busby's new side during the Sixties and featured in the successes of that side. He was a member of the 1966 World Cup winning team.

Bill Foulkes – As with Charlton he managed to return to action and feature in the new United, winning the European Cup in 1968.

Harry Gregg – Appeared in the 1958 FA Cup final and remained with United until 1966. Had a spell as United goalkeeping coach from 1978 until 1981. He has remained keen to challenge perceptions of Munich throughout his life and has tried to fight to help the families of the victims and the survivors – the majority of whom found life extremely difficult after the disaster.

Ken Morgans – although he returned to action in April 1958 he was never able to establish himself in the side post-Munich. In March 1961 he was transferred to Swansea and also had a spell at Newport County.

Albert Scanlon – had been left for dead initially as rescue workers searched for those who looked more likely to survive. He suffered a fractured skull but managed to return to England within a month. Sadly he was transferred out of United in November 1960 and felt he had been betrayed by the club, in particular by new Chairman Louis Edwards and by Matt Busby. In later life Scanlon worked 12 hour shifts as a security guard.

Dennis Viollet – resurrected his career and played in the 1958 FA Cup final, however in January 1962 he was sold to Stoke City. According to friends his personality and approach to life changed significantly after Munich. In later life he suffered with a brain tumour – many believe this had been caused by the bang to his head he received at Munich – and he passed away in the States during 1999.

Ray Wood – By the time of Munich the 1957 FA Cup final 'keeper Wood had lost his place to Gregg and inevitably, post Munich, the 'keeper was unable to regain his position – he made one first team appearances (a 4-0 defeat at Wolves on 4/10/58). He was transferred to Huddersfield in December 1958 and played over 200 league games for them. He passed away in 2002.

The other survivors were:
Frank Taylor - the only journalist to survive and he went on to write the highly acclaimed *The Day A Team Died*. He was also awarded the OBE and passed away in 2002.
Peter Howard – Daily Mail Photographer
Ted Ellyard – Photographer
Mrs Vera Lukic and baby daughter **Venona** - Passengers (saved by Manchester United player Harry Gregg)
Eleanor Miklos - Wife of the travel agent that arranged the trip who died in the crash
George 'Bill' Rodgers - Radio officer
Belosja Tomasevic - Passenger
James Thain - Captain
Rosemary Cheverton – Stewardess
Margaret Bellis - Stewardess

Over the years Munich has come to mean different things. For some it is a strong reminder of the pioneering spirit of Fifties United and of the quality of those unfortunate young men who passed away in such devastating circumstances. Others have seen it as an important step towards the globalisation of the United name and brand. In fact there are some that see the disaster as a means of capitalising on tragedy and in Jeff Connor's publication *The Lost Babes* he explores in detail the way the disaster has been used to generate income for others – he talks of the 1998 benefit match which raised around £1m but over £90,000 was paid to Eric Cantona's agent for expenses in relation to the Frenchman's appearance in the game – and of the use of Munich in merchandise, museums, television and other areas of the media.

For most true Mancunian United-supporting families it is the players they think of first, rather than the specifics of the tragedy. Actor and Salford born United fan Christopher Eccleston talked of the players during an interview with Denis Campbell in 2002:

"Some of my earliest memories are of my dad talking about the Babes, specifically Duncan Edwards. 'He was a man at 16,' he always said. He was a great guy but kept his feelings to himself, but at any mention of that team he suddenly became filled with emotion.

"My mum was an Old Trafford trolley-dolly. She used to push a trolley round the side of the pitch selling Bovril. Just recently she said, very casually, 'When we finished work we used to see Duncan standing at the bus stop after the game eating fish and chips.' Can you imagine Ryan Giggs doing that? My dad would talk about them as players while my mum talked about their personalities, like 'Roger Byrne's very good looking but you can tell he's moody'."

Back in 1958 when the first news of the crash filtered back to Manchester, the city was in shock. No one could understand or accept what they were hearing. Former City Chairman Eric Alexander, who in 1958 was part of City's ground committee and was also working in the area, remembers the moment he heard the news:

"I heard people in the street on Deansgate shouting. I was struggling to make out what they were

saying but it sounded as if something had happened to United. The noise and emotion ran high and I had to find out. I rushed out on to the street and heard what had happened. It made me feel sick. It was one of those moments that you dread. It was awful.

"It affected everybody in Manchester. No question. We knew the players obviously, but we also knew the journalists. We all lost something very significant that day."

By 6pm a special edition of Alf Clarke's newspaper, the **Manchester Evening Chronicle**, was on sale:

"About 28 people, including members of the Manchester United football team, club officials, and journalists are feared to have been killed when a BEA Elizabethan airliner crashed soon after take-off in a snowstorm at Munich airport this afternoon. It is understood there may be about 16 survivors. Four of them are crew members."

It also included Clarke's match report and referred to his telephone conversation earlier in the afternoon.

Gradually accurate information started to emerge, but the strength of feeling was such that thousands of Mancunians walked the streets of the city dazed, shocked and confused. Clearly, the death of any of those players in tragic circumstances would have been greeted with a shared feeling of grief but the size of the disaster and the impact it had on football and on the city reached incredible levels. Supporters of all sides felt the grief and the relationship between the Manchester region clubs at this point was not a difficult one. There were rivalries of course, but with City and United both sets of supporters shared the pain of the tragedy. Matt Busby and Frank Swift were tremendous City heroes, while many of the players had grown up in the city and were known to Red and Blue alike. Viollet and Scanlon had been City fans as boys, while Byrne came from Gorton.

In the Busby household as the news filtered through members of his family and Swift's gathered on the day of the disaster. Little was known, but the news did come through that Busby was amongst the survivors. The **Manchester Evening Chronicle** reported the reaction:

"Said Mrs. Busby: 'Thanks God he's safe' but the family could not celebrate. They did not know whether he had been injured and also in the house was Mrs. Frank Swift, upset and ill with no news of her husband. Finally Mrs. Swift's son-in-law came to the house and said he would break the news to her that her husband was unaccounted for. He drove her home in his car."

Swift was of course a journalist by this point, and each of the journalists were major local figures. Don Davies, Henry Rose, Archie Ledbrooke and the others were well known and popular reporters who had covered the game in Manchester for many, many years. Davies, who went under the name of an Old International, had reported on almost every significant moment to affect Mancunian football for years.

Bert Trautmann, City's German goalkeeper, heard the news of the crash at home. He was listening to the radio and was immediately engulfed with sadness. One of the victims, Frank Swift, had been his predecessor at City, but most of the other victims were also known to him personally. Once he managed to gather his thoughts he started to consider how his understudy Steve Fleet was feeling. Steve's story is typical of the way the players felt:

EDDIE COLMAN
Manchester United

"It is one of those events that make you realise that life itself is a greater game than football. It matures you. It makes you realise what life is all about and though it's difficult at the time to understand, it did actually put football in its place. Football was not important in the weeks that followed the crash.

"I had lots of friends at United, but Eddie Colman was my best friend. Up to his death we were as close as anybody could be. He was going to be the best man at my wedding. When he died it was terrible. Eddie lived in Archie Street – the inspiration for Coronation Street – and I lived close by. On the night of the crash we all congregated at his house and we waited for news. None of us had a telephone in those days, so the only way we could find out what was happening was by going to the off-licence down the road and call United. I kept going off to do it. Les Olive was answering the 'phone at Old Trafford and he said to me 'Steve, I know you're very close to his family, can you tell them that Eddie's gone'. I then had to go back to Eddie's house and tell his mum and dad. Something you never think you have to do, especially at that age. His dad couldn't accept it. He said I must be wrong. He went down to the off-licence and made a call himself.

"It was awful, but that was the way it was for a lot of people."

The following day the City players met at Maine Road. Bert Trautmann rushed to see Steve Fleet: *"Bert understood more than anyone how I felt about losing Eddie. He taught me how to handle grief and come to terms with it. It was not easy but Bert had such humility and a caring attitude he helped me tremendously to overcome one of the worst periods of my life. He also offered to help United in any way he could. You see, we all knew the United players. We'd socialise with them, and they were just like us. Bobby Charlton, when he was living in digs, would sometimes come to our house for his tea. We were all close – Red or Blue didn't come into it."*

German-national Bert contacted United and offered to help with translation, contacts and with whatever the Reds felt they needed.

Despite their grief, the City players were told they had to carry on with their own preparations for Saturday's League game at Spurs. Cliff Lloyd, secretary of the Manchester-based PFA, had called for the suspension of the weekend's games – something City's players, and those of other clubs in the region desperately wanted – but within 24 hours of the crash the League insisted that only United's game would be called off.

Reluctantly, the Blues travelled to London on Friday 9th. It is known that later that day the City players went to a cinema in North London with the hope of watching the latest newsreel footage showing the tragic scenes however, according to **British Movietone**, newsreel footage did not arrive until four days after the disaster and so the players could only wonder what the devastating scenes were like. Although City players do hold a view that they saw some crash related footage that night in London. City were to play at Tottenham the following day, and were staying overnight in the capital. They felt isolated from the news and changed their routine in the hope that they could find out all they could.

Inevitably at Tottenham the players wore black armbands and, full of emotion, they lined up for a two-minute silence – impeccably observed by all fans. This silence was more personal than any the players had previously been involved with – only four days later Ken Branagan, Dave Ewing, Joe Hayes, Roy Little and others would attend the funeral of Gorton born United captain Roger Byrne. It wasn't the only funeral they attended, but it does indicate that the players' thoughts were hardly on a game that most players across the country had wanted called off.

Understandably the crash affected the City team that day and the Spurs game ended in a 5-1 defeat.

Similar scenes appeared at football matches across the country and locally Bury faced Oldham at Gigg Lane and the players and spectators stood in two minutes silence prior to kick-off as a mark of respect for the Munich victims. The Bury Silver Band played 'Abide with me'.

Many of the region's players mixed socially with United's.

The region was in a state of combined grief, and then the bodies started to be returned to Manchester. The Old Trafford gymnasium became a makeshift mortuary, while families made plans. Thousands of supporters, rival fans, and ordinary supporters gathered to pay their last respects and each funeral saw scenes of Mancunians lining roadsides as funeral processions passed by.

The story dominated every aspect of Manchester life and for those who had never quite grasped what the game was about and why it was so important to the region, this terrible disaster soon brought understanding, and it has to be stressed that this awful tragedy was not simply one affecting a single football team. It affected an entire city, region, and in many ways a nation. Many of the players were major international footballers, but more than that many of the other victims were highly respected, renowned journalists with a real passion for Manchester and its people. **Daily Express** journalist Geoffrey Mather provides his view of how the news filtered through the newspaper industry on his website **www.northtrek.plus.com**:

"As news spread, the city went silent. The grief settled like a fog: it was everywhere. Survivors were struggling for life, manager Matt Busby among them. I was features editor of the **Daily Express** *in Manchester. I was in the office being told by the then editor, Roger Wood, that I would be in charge of all inside pages apart from Sport. I could call on any sub-editor on the editorial floor whenever I liked.*

"The London editor, Sir Edward Pickering, was visiting at the time and decisions came quickly. William Hickey, normally on Page 3, was relegated to Page 13. Virtually the whole of the paper was United. I protested about my role. 'I know nothing about football' I argued. Roger Wood brushed that aside – 'I will put someone from Sport in a seat behind you'. And so the long night began and decisions made at that early stage paid off. There were not to be any edition times. The pages would roll as they were made ready. The paper churned out all night long. It was a superb operation on the part of staff. I lost count of the number of pages prepared, run, re-done. At some late stage - a landmark - I had a half page of thumbnail pictures of those involved. The **Daily Mail** *people were said to be reading our first edition to see whether their own man was alive.*

"Henry Rose, best-known of Northern sports writers, had gone down with the Busby Babes. Esther Rose, his niece, was the only one on the editorial floor who did not know this. When she was finally told, she was crying as she was led out of the office. Rose's executive chair was empty. His was a considerable presence whether in the building or Press box. The line-up as his funeral went by the office days later was almost Presidential."

Rose's funeral was the largest of the non-United players. *Express* journalist Desmond Hackett wrote a moving tribute to him and it is recorded that taxi drivers offered their services free to anyone who was going to the funeral. The funeral procession travelled by Rose's former office – his work place was actually every significant football ground in the country – the impressive glass fronted *Daily Express* building in Great Ancoats, and then travelled on to Southern Cemetery, close to Maine Road where some of the other victims, would be buried and where the great Billy Meredith would also be buried the following April.

Understandably, five decades later, the air crash still bears significance at Old Trafford. The Manchester United museum understandably pays tribute to the victims, but so does the Manchester City museum at the City of Manchester Stadium with a timeline recording the victims. This is significant because the disaster touched all Mancunians regardless of team supported, or played for.

Surprisingly, considering the strong feelings of the supporters of all of the region's clubs, the footballing authorities seemed to misjudge the mood. Not only had they refused to call off all games scheduled for the Saturday following the disaster, but they also made plans for the continuation of all competitions United were involved with. The decision was taken to progress with the League.

On 9th February it was reported that UEFA were considering what to do with the European Cup semi finals. Real Madrid had stated they felt the competition should be suspended and that the Reds should be awarded the European Cup – this was a generous move – but UEFA did not want to do that. Instead, UEFA said they would be speaking with the FA about the selection of a team to replace United in the competition. UEFA made it clear they wanted City to take United's place, while the Blues immediately made it known that they would not be interested in taking United's place, and that City would do all they could to help the Reds compete in the competition. Eric Alexander:

"Our thoughts were with United. They had to take part. Part of the recovery process had to be United's return to action – all Mancunians knew that - and we wanted to do all we could to help them go forward."

The FA's response was a surprising one and, when reported, it was said that the FA had stated that the decision would be theirs, not UEFA's. Fortunately, commonsense prevailed and the Reds were able to compete, however in the 1990s social commentators and writers talked of this period cynically and gave the impression that somehow City had tried to take some glory and had proactively pushed themselves forward as European replacements. This is totally unfair but the comment does show how much society changed in the decades after the disaster. Many football followers use the term 'Munich' as an insult, while others claim the Blues did not support United in their hour of need and tried to gain reflected glory via the European offer. The views of both groups are totally abhorrent.

Inevitably Manchester and football had to keep going although, understandably, United's game

Directors :
Messrs. A. DOUGLAS (*Chairman*) E. GILL D. F. HAMER F. R. JOLLY W. SMITH
Manager : Mr. LESLIE J. McDOWALL *Secretary :* Mr. WALTER GRIFFITHS
'Phone : MOSs Side 1191

Vol. 52 No. 16 (Entered at Stationers' Hall) SATURDAY, 15th FEB., 1958

By THE EDITOR

NEXT to Old Trafford, the impact of the Munich air disaster has been felt nowhere more severely nor with more regret than here at Maine Road. Players, officials and sports writers on that ill-fated plane were our friends and yours, and we feel it would be your wish that we suspend several of our usual programme features this week and pay our tribute to the memory of all who gave their lives in the line of duty.

Mr. ALAN DOUGLAS

(Manchester City Chairman)

I STILL cannot find words to express my deep regret and horror at the dreadful accident which hit our friends and neighbours at Old Trafford but on behalf of my directors, I should like to express sincere sympathy with the bereaved and injured. For many, many years there has existed a keen rivalry between the two clubs, but just as we at Maine Road have rejoiced in United's many triumphs, so now we share their sorrow. I would assure Mr. Harold Hardman, the chairman, his directors, and all associated with Manchester United, that while the blow they have received is a cruel one, it is not a knock-out, and we of Manchester City are convinced United will recover, and eventually return to their exalted place in the world of football. And if we can do anything to help them in any way, however small, to achieve that objective, we shall regard it as a privilege to do it.

Mr. LESLIE McDOWALL

(Manchester City Manager)

THE grievous blow delivered at local and international football is, from every point of view, as terrible in its individual context as it is to the relatives and friends of those who lost their lives. To all the bereaved I extend my sincere condolences. Yet even in this darkest hour of Manchester United's history, there is still hope for the future, and the superb courage and faith he showed in his fight for life will, I am sure, be repeated when my good friend Matt Busby resumes that other fight to keep United in the fore-front. Instead of the skill and devotion of surgeons and nurses who, under Divine guidance, brought him through his crisis, Matt will have the respect and affection of countless thousands to help him in his task. He will not let them down however long it may take, and I wish him a speedy and complete recovery followed by a quick and active return to the game to which he has given so very much.

Mr. WALTER GRIFFITHS

(Manchester City Secretary)

THE tragic death of Mr. Walter Crickmer has deprived United and football generally of one of its most talented officials. By virtue of United's performances at home and abroad, the success of their office management depended on a high degree of efficiency and patience, and these qualities Mr. Crickmer had in good measure. He was shrewd and he was kindly at all times, and he will be greatly missed at Old Trafford not only by players and officials, but by countless friends of whom I was privileged to be one.

LAURIE BARNETT

(Manchester City Trainer)

MEMBERS of the training, coaching and ground staffs have asked me to express their deep sympathy to all who have suffered as a result of the air disaster. In our particular duties, we had many opportunities of admiring the specialised work of Bert Whalley and Tom Curry, and of appreciating the tremendous part they played in the smooth and successful running of the United teams. They spared no effort in everything they did, and the glorious achievements of the club—and those yet to come—will be a lasting memorial to two loyal servants.

KEEP THIS COUPON and watch for ticket match announcements

MANCHESTER CITY F.C.
No. 12 15.2.58
TICKET COUPON

In Memoriam

Seven Manchester United players and three officials died in the air disaster at Munich. Here are their photographs.

ROGER BYRNE — GEOFF BENT

WALTER CRICKMER — EDDIE COLMAN — BERT WHALLEY — TOMMY TAYLOR

BILLY WHELAN — DAVID PEGG — TOM CURRY — MARK JONES

4

OTHER TRIBUTES

DAVE EWING

(Manchester City Captain)

IF I forget all else in my career, I shall always remember with gratitude the kindly, good-luck wishes extended to me by the United players when I made my League debut for City at Old Trafford just over five years ago. Since then I have played against United many times and have always felt privileged to do so. On and off the field they were a grand bunch of fellows, and it is impossible to realise we shall never see some of them again. On behalf of the City players, I should like to pay my tribute to the memory of all who died in the disaster, to offer sympathy with the bereaved, and to express the sincere hope that the injured will make a rapid and complete recovery.

Mr. W. H. MILES

(Chairman, Manchester City Supporters' Club)

ON behalf of officials and members of the City Supporters' Club, I should like to express deep sympathy with the relatives of all who lost their lives at Munich, and the hope that the injured may soon be restored to complete health. The loss of so many fine players and personal friends will leave an irreplaceable gap in the sporting lives of millions of football supporters all over the world and particularly in Manchester, but I am convinced that United's many followers will play their usual loyal part in helping this fine club recover from this terrible blow. And if we of the City Supporters' Club can help in any way towards that end, we shall be proud to do so.

ROY PAUL

(Worcester City and former Manchester City Captain)

I CANNOT express adequately my feelings at the loss of those great players against some of whom I played several times, nor of the sports writers whom I knew intimately and for whom I had such a high regard. They all had a part to play in this great game of ours, and right well they played it. We shall miss them all. To the United club in general and to their supporters, I would just say, "Carry on as they who are gone would have wished—and the best of luck to you all."

5

Above and facing page: **Some of the tributes featured in City's match programme for the game with Birmingham on 15th February 1958 - the first League match to be played in Manchester after the disaster.**

against Wolves was cancelled and their FA Cup tie against Sheffield Wednesday was delayed by four days. In between the fixtures of all other clubs continued as normal and the first senior match to be played within Manchester by either United or City was the Blues game against Birmingham City on 15th February 1958. This match has largely been forgotten by the media, but as the first game played after Munich the details of the day need to be remembered.

It was a deeply emotional affair, with few in the mood for football. It is clear there was no appetite amongst fans for the Birmingham game. It felt wrong to be playing an important match while people were still fighting for their lives, and others were being buried. Significantly, a lower crowd than usual – only 23,461 - attended Maine Road for this fixture. City's average for the six previous home matches had been 43,000, and the season's average would be 32,765.

The match programme was full of tributes with every editorial space, other than the Birmingham page and the teamsheet, being given over to the tragedy. There were photographs of all the victims. The programme editor accurately wrote:

"Next to Old Trafford, the impact of the Munich air disaster has been felt nowhere more severely nor with more regret than here at Maine Road. Players, officials and sports writers on that ill-fated plane were our friends and yours."

City Chairman Alan Douglas added:

"City are convinced United will recover and eventually return to their exalted place in the world of football. And if we can do anything to help them in any way, however small, to achieve that objective, we shall regard it as a privilege to do it."

Captain Dave Ewing talked of the United players:

"On and off the field they were a grand bunch of fellows, and it is impossible to realise we shall never see some of them again."

Former captain Roy Paul's comments included mention of the press:

"whom I knew intimately and for whom I had such a high regard. They all had a part to play in this great game of ours, and right well they played it. We shall miss them all."

This was still an emotional time for all Mancunians. The tragedy seemed to touch each and every Mancunian personally, and inevitably the game itself was played in an extremely mournful atmosphere. Abide with Me, with soloist Sylvia Farmer, was played by the Beswick Prize Band pre-match and every fan stood, head bowed to remember Manchester's victims. City fan Dave Wallace writing in Century City talks of the game:

"It was pouring down. I did not switch to the Kippax but watched it from the perimeter wall at the Scoreboard End. The band played Abide With Me and all in the Main Stand stood up removed their hats and sang it with their heads bowed. It made the hairs on the back of your neck stand up. The rain continued unabated and the game was called off in the fortieth minute, the pitch a quagmire. It was as though the heavens were sending a tearful message of sympathy to Manchester."

The heavy rain and miserable atmosphere proved to all that life was more important than a game of football.

United Chairman Harold Hardman and new secretary Les Olive were guests of honour, and they were encouraged by City to approach several City players to fill the gaps left by the crash. It was clearly something they did not want to do but it was absolutely vital, and attempts were made to sign City's Irish international Fionan 'Paddy' Fagan but for unknown reasons this failed. Many clubs, most memorably City, Liverpool, and Nottingham Forest, offered United whatever assistance they could.

The Munich disaster affected all Mancunians and all involved with sport in Manchester. In the years that have followed, the City-Birmingham game has largely been forgotten. As with all abandoned games it was wiped from the records, however perhaps there has also been a subconscious effort to forget the day as it was such a painful one. Manchester had not yet found the strength to carry on and look to the future – that would come with United's first home game.

On Wednesday 19th February an emotional night saw the Reds compete in their first post-Munich match. A highly emotional evening saw survivors Harry Gregg and Bill Foulkes take to the field with new signings Ernie Taylor and Stan Crowther (both given special dispensation to play in the FA Cup after competing for other clubs), and relatively inexperienced players Ian Greaves, Freddie Goodwin, Ron Cope, Colin Webster, Alex Dawson, Mark Pearson and Shay Brennan. Ian Greaves later admitted how he felt replacing Roger Byrne:

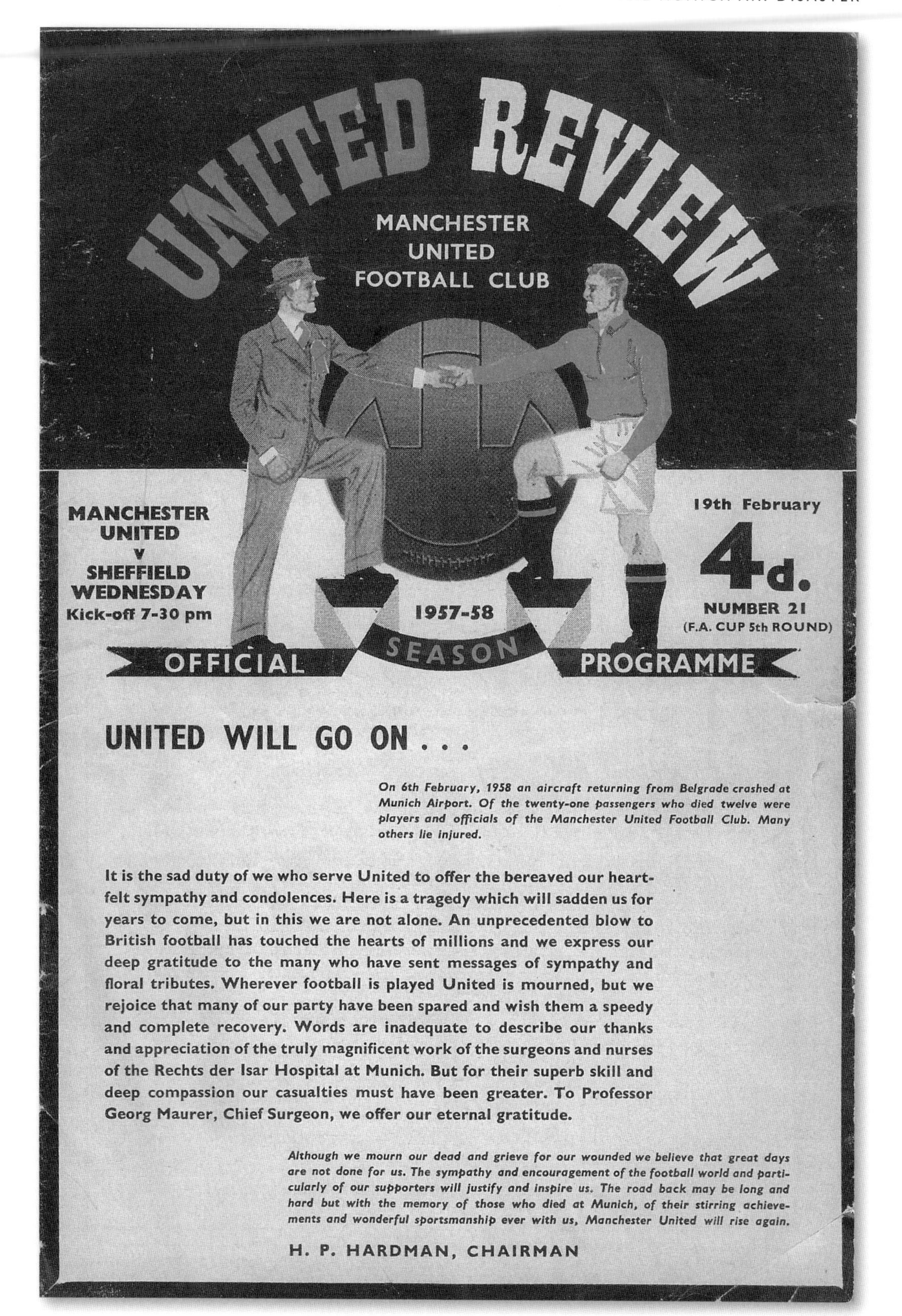

UNITED REVIEW

MANCHESTER UNITED FOOTBALL CLUB

MANCHESTER UNITED v SHEFFIELD WEDNESDAY Kick-off 7-30 pm

1957-58

19th February

4d.

NUMBER 21 (F.A. CUP 5th ROUND)

OFFICIAL SEASON PROGRAMME

UNITED WILL GO ON . . .

On 6th February, 1958 an aircraft returning from Belgrade crashed at Munich Airport. Of the twenty-one passengers who died twelve were players and officials of the Manchester United Football Club. Many others lie injured.

It is the sad duty of we who serve United to offer the bereaved our heartfelt sympathy and condolences. Here is a tragedy which will sadden us for years to come, but in this we are not alone. An unprecedented blow to British football has touched the hearts of millions and we express our deep gratitude to the many who have sent messages of sympathy and floral tributes. Wherever football is played United is mourned, but we rejoice that many of our party have been spared and wish them a speedy and complete recovery. Words are inadequate to describe our thanks and appreciation of the truly magnificent work of the surgeons and nurses of the Rechts der Isar Hospital at Munich. But for their superb skill and deep compassion our casualties must have been greater. To Professor Georg Maurer, Chief Surgeon, we offer our eternal gratitude.

Although we mourn our dead and grieve for our wounded we believe that great days are not done for us. The sympathy and encouragement of the football world and particularly of our supporters will justify and inspire us. The road back may be long and hard but with the memory of those who died at Munich, of their stirring achievements and wonderful sportsmanship ever with us, Manchester United will rise again.

H. P. HARDMAN, CHAIRMAN

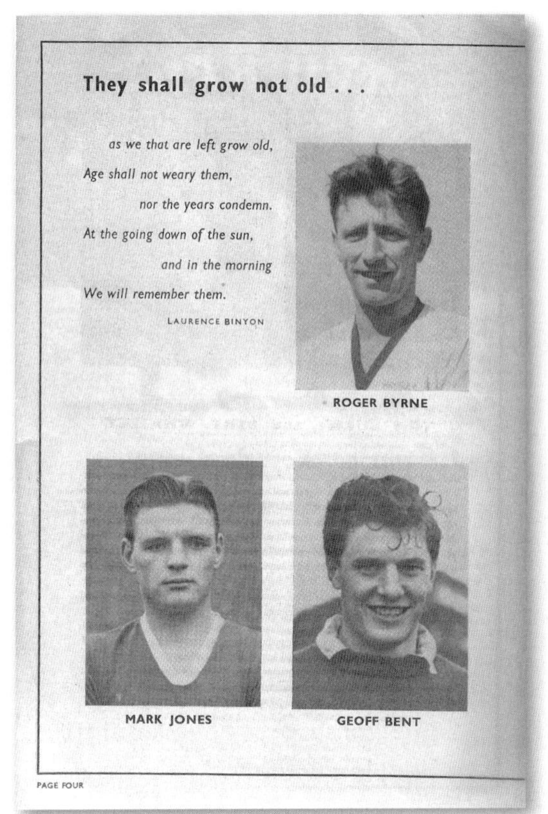
They shall grow not old . . .

as we that are left grow old,
Age shall not weary them,
nor the years condemn.
At the going down of the sun,
and in the morning
We will remember them.
LAURENCE BINYON

ROGER BYRNE

MARK JONES

GEOFF BENT

PAGE FOUR

Above and previous page: **United's first programme after the Munich disaster.**

"I can remember the dressing room was very quiet. I couldn't get Roger out of my mind; I was getting changed where he would have sat. I was wearing his shirt..."

The game was watched by a crowd of 59,848 – the second highest home crowd of the season (63,347 witnessed the derby with City in August), and only United's fifth domestic attendance over 50,000 at this point in the season. This was 6,000 more than the previous cup tie and over 18,000 more than the previous home League game against Bolton. Many non-football followers attended that night, as did the supporters of other clubs. The feeling was that everybody wanted to help the Reds.

The game ended 3-0 to the Reds with goals from Brennan (2) and Dawson, and three days later the first home League game after Munich ended in a 1-1 draw against Nottingham Forest before 66,124 – this would prove to be United's biggest Old Trafford attendance of the 1950s.

Much has been made in the more recent past about the effect of Munich on United and it is clear in pure statistical terms that the disaster did have an initial impact on attendances. The average crowd for the seasons prior to Munich stood at 35,458 (1953-4), 35,960 (1954-55), 39,254 (1955-56) and 45,481 (1956-57). For the 1957-58 season the final average was 46,073, but this rocketed to 53,258 for 1958-59, however by 1962 support had dropped back to a more typical figure of 33,491 (fifth best in the League). This was one of three seasons in the 1960s when support averaged less than 40,000 and it was only when the Reds found major success under Busby in the mid to late Sixties that crowds reached in excess of 50,000 on a regular basis. In general though the Reds spent most of the 15 years post-Munich as one of football's top three best-supported sides and then in the period post 1972 they tended to be the best supported club year after year.

In terms of on the pitch performance and atmosphere around United it is clear the disaster continued to have an effect for many years. In 1958 itself the Reds were swept along on a tide of emotion to the 1958 FA Cup final, but their European campaign ended with a 5-2 aggregate defeat to AC Milan.

The FA Cup final saw them defeated 2-0 by Bolton and Tony Pawson, writing in the **Observer**, gave a realistic assessment of the game:

"In prospect yesterday's Cup Final was more likely to be distinguished by its emotional impact than the quality of the football. So it proved, except that there was little of the expected excitement. Manchester

A post-Munich team photo.

rarely seemed likely to crown their wonderful recovery with this last triumph. Bolton are essentially an effective rather than an attractive team, and they won because they were always marking more closely, tackling harder, and, above all, moving more quickly to meet the ball. Their play was, in fact, ideally suited to upset their opponents.

"Manchester United, who had won through to the Final as much by their enthusiasm and spirit as by their skill, now found themselves outmatched in determination, in strength and in the will to win. Tactically, too, Bolton were their masters, for they kept with relentless persistence to a plan that was simple and effective. Edwards, keeping always at Taylor's side, cut him off from the ball, destroying at once the cohesion of Manchester's attack. Without the inspiration of Taylor's constructive and cunning passes, United's forwards had nothing to offer except the power and thrust of Charlton, who was left to challenge on his own the competent Bolton defence.

"Cope was outstanding in Manchester's defence, playing with a coolness and command that was lacking in the fretful play of their backs and wing-halves."

Manchester United Football Club Ltd.

Football Association Challenge Cup Final

The Directors request the pleasure of the company of

J. Mercer, Esq., and Lady.

at a

Celebration Dinner and Dance
to be held in the Lancaster Room
of the Savoy Hotel, Strand, London
on Saturday, 3rd May, 1958

Reception 7-15 Dinner 7-45 Carriages Midnight
R.S.V.P. (card enclosed) Ordinary Dress

Matt Busby's friend and future City manager Joe Mercer is invited to the 1958 FA Cup final.

Pawson added: *"For Manchester it was a day of dust and ashes as their weaknesses were ruthlessly exposed by opponents who harried them from start to finish. It wasn't that they were overawed by the occasion, simply that they lacked the ability to counter so fierce a challenge.*

"There remained Charlton to save the game for United, and it is a measure of the remarkable advance he has made that he came near to doing it. Bolton's superiority was unquestioned, but twice he nearly snatched the game from them. In the first half he sent Hopkinson diving to save, brilliantly, a shot of tremendous power; in the second, a shot which might have turned the game thundered against the inside of the post and rebounded to the goalkeeper. A year ago Charlton would have manoeuvred the ball awkwardly and automatically to his left, but these shots were hit with equal ease and force with either foot. In midfield his bursts of speed and close control of the ball made him a lonely threat throughout. Surprisingly, however, as the game progressed, he lay deeper and deeper, giving Bolton, who were otherwise untroubled, too much time to guard against his sudden raids.

"From the start it was clear that Bolton were setting too fast a pace for United; and within minutes they were ahead. A long pass from Banks to Birch, a centre to the far post, and Lofthouse came near to rushing the ball in as Gregg hesitated. The corner kept Bolton on the attack, and when Taylor headed clear, Edwards sent the ball back across the goal and Lofthouse, again at the far post, ran in to glide it home. Birch continued to trouble the defence, and once when he varied his long centres by turning inwards himself and shooting left-footed, Gregg for the first time took the ball with his usual confidence. United had their chance at last as Taylor, winning the ball for once, sent a measured pass out to Webster, and Viollet drove the ball over from close in as it was pulled back to him. In the main, however, play was disjointed and destructive, with Bolton neater and more frequent in their attacks."

United trainer Jack Crompton felt United were never going to win that final: *"Coming back and finding what was left of the team. It was a difficult time. We'd lost the final before we even went to Wembley, and once it started we were never in it. It was all Bolton, even though it was a foul on Gregg when Nat Lofthouse scored."*

ATTENDANCE DETAIL SEASON BY SEASON - 1955-1960

Season	City	United	Oldham	Bury	Stockport	Rochdale
1954-55	35217	35960	7760	14174	7339	6202
1955-56	32198	39254	6473	11919	7347	4833
1956-57	30005	45481	8273	11986	9706	6280
1957-58	32765	46073	7469	11775	9994	6352
1958-59	32568	53258	5322	9441	9255	4810
1959-60	35637	47288	4957	10628	6552	4599

LEAGUE POSITIONS SEASON BY SEASON - 1955-1960

Season	City	United	Oldham	Bury	Stockport	Rochdale
1954-55	7	5	54	35	53	56
1955-56	4	1	64	37	51	56
1956-57	18	1	63	43	49	57
1957-58	5	9	59	48	53	54
1958-59	20	2	89	54	65	68
1959-60	15	7	91	51	78	80

CHAPTER EIGHTEEN

MANCUNIAN STYLE

Manchester City, Football League champions of England, were swamped by a seething sea of blue and white bedecked fans at the end of this unforgettable game. Yesterday City, the team that has won more friends than any other in a season of imaginative attacking football, turned on the style. They weaved the patterns, scored the spectacular goals and finally triumphed with a display that defies superlatives. James Mossop, Sunday Express, 1968

MANY people regard the 1960s as the peak for football in the region. Every League side in the region during the Sixties and early Seventies had some success, but there was also some failure. Every side in the region was promoted at least once, but they were also all the victims of at least one relegation.

At an amateur level the FA accepted the affiliation of Sunday teams in 1960, and so the game became more formal at a lower level. In addition, both Saturdays and Sundays were popular times for the various local leagues and there was one place in particular where football's popularity in the region was clear for all to see – Hough End playing fields. Hough End, close to Manchester's Princess Parkway dual carriageway heading south of the city, was a great expanse covered with football pitches. Close to Southern Cemetery, where so many of Manchester's footballing greats including Billy Meredith were buried, the venue was immensely popular. Nationally, people talk of London's Hackney Marshes as being the leading amateur venue, but Hough End was perhaps Hackney's main rival.

Arthur Hopcraft, writing his seminal football classic **The Football Man**, talked of Manchester's venue in 1968. He painted a rather romantic, but fairly accurate picture of a typical Sunday morning:

"At Hough End, a great, low-lying urban plain off one of Manchester's major entry-and-exit roads, the grass bordered on one side by a railway line and on another by a prefabricated housing estate, the goalkeepers line up back to back, only ten yards separating one line of pitches from another.

"Old warriors conserve their wind by playing wily midfield games, suppressing criticism from younger men for their immobility by shouting the loudest and lacing compliments with baritone abuse of referees, often younger than themselves. The pitches are so close, side by side, that the balls whiz muddily from one game into another, striking wingers distractingly as they gather themselves for a subtle centre into

the opposition's goalmouth, startling referees into involuntary blasts on the whistle, whacking spectators in the back of the neck as they scoff knowingly at imitations of the bolt defence and the 4-2-4 formation. Escaped poodles frisk among the players' legs, and lads with Rolling Stones haircuts collide with static veterans like gollywogs flung against a nursery wall. Some of the recrimination tells touchingly of the aching confrontation of Narcissus with his beer-barrel tummy:'What d'yer mean, run? I've bin running. For Christ's sake, roll the ball'."

As part of his research Hopcraft followed a Salford Sunday League team called The Pied Piper through their selection meeting for a game, and his experience was typical of the period:

"We sat around a table drinking pints of mild and ran our minds over the list of players. The left back had played trial games for Birmingham and Stoke City, the left half for Huddersfield and Bury, the centre forward for Manchester City and the outside left for Bolton. Two more of the team were 20 year old twins who had spent their first two years out of school on Portsmouth's ground staff and playing for one of the club's youth teams. The crowd used to call them Pinky and Perky [two popular 'pig' characters from children's television at the time]. I asked the group how many of them had wanted to be professional footballers, and after a silence in which the players looked at each other as if they had been spoken to in French, the centre-forward replied: 'Well, every lad does, doesn't he?'."

Hopcraft captured the essence of football at that time in the region and in his writing he proved how committed many Mancunians were to their game:

"A team manager with a crew-cut and a shortie overcoat told me he knew one old player who had grown so decrepit that no club would give him a regular game; but he turned up week after week with half a dozen jerseys of different colours in his bag, hoping to get a game with any team a man short."

On Hough End during this period the game, more than anything else, was important. Some of the sides competing would be part of a significant organisation – perhaps a major employer's sports and social club – while others would simply be a group of young men keen to play the game. Some of the sides competing would probably have had no more than 12 or 13 members, maybe even a simple eleven, while others may have had the resources to pull together squads of a couple of dozen. The majority of teams both in 1960s Manchester and the Manchester of the 21st Century would have been based around an organisation such as a pub. Often the side would have been created simply because one member of staff, or one of the regular customers, wanted to pull a side together to compete as a matter of pride against a rival pub. Some of the pub sides would last a few years and then collapse, others would continue and develop and become, in effect, the public face of the pub for many years. Football in Manchester had been like this for many years. Think about the formation of the leading clubs in the area. They all came from works teams, pubs, churches and the like.

A quick review of the Manchester FA handbook for 2006-07 shows several pub teams that were created in the Sixties and early Seventies still in existence, these include Fleece FC (from Hyde) and Gardeners FC (from Stockport). Of course it also shows several sides playing home games at Hough End, such as Adlington Academicals FC, and sides created during almost every period of football history. One of the amateur sides listed is Showmans FC, created in 1908 and playing at Turn Moss, Stretford.

Venues like Hough End and sides like South Manchester Maccabi FC (1948) help to bind communities together. Although football by 1960 in the region was a major spectator sport with every one of the region's professional sides proving popular and successful at some point, the true strength of the game was on the amateur playing fields. Saturday and Sunday leagues, together with the various mid-week competitions, gave everyone the chance to be a hero to some degree. Also, by participating in the game at this level, the interest in professional football remained high. Many people would play a game on a Saturday morning then rush off to watch one of the region's main sides in the afternoon. It was all part and parcel of the same thing, and the 1960s and Seventies was a great period for participation. As Hopcraft surmised:

> *"The important point about all this football, varying so much in quality and effort, is simply that it is being played. Hackney Marshes and Hough End display a lot more animation in our bleak urban fastnesses than foreign readers of the* **New Statesman** *might be expected to imagine."*

Of the professional sides in the region, it is worth noting that the first to enjoy success during the Sixties was Bury, the region's first nationally successful side. Bury managed promotion in 1960-61 by winning the Third Division. The club had struggled financially towards the end of the previous decade and massive cutbacks were forced throughout Gigg Lane. The number of teams was reduced from five to three while positions such as Chief Scout and Assistant Trainer were dispensed with. The situation had been grim, however on the pitch in 1960-61 Bury entertained. The promotion challenge, which in the previous season had collapsed, was maintained throughout the season, even when in February captain and influential centre-half John McGrath was transferred to Newcastle for £24,000. The transfer had been vital from a financial viewpoint but brought concern from supporters that the season might peter out. Instead veteran defender Bob Stokoe became the new

BURY F.C. SOCIAL CLUB
THIS WEEK'S ATTRACTIONS
SATURDAY, 16th APRIL
STAR CABARET
VERONICA DEAN
SINGER - ACCORDIANIST
ALSO
DON CARROLL
Whistling Impressionist
Admission:—
Members 2/6 Guests 3/6
SUNDAY, 17th APRIL
STAR CABARET
HARRY CASE
(Case Harry)
COMEDIAN - IMPRESSIONIST
ALSO GUEST ARTISTE
Admission:—
Members 1/- Guests 3/6
Continuous Entertainment . Fully Licensed Bars and Refreshments
WITH YOUR RESIDENT COMPERE, ORGANIST and DRUMMER
BINGO EVERY WEDNESDAY

Mid 60s advert for the Bury Social Club.

PAUL AIMSON, who joined us from York City for whom he was leading marksman, a fortnight ago, has already made his mark for he scored the winning goal against the Wolves. Paul formerly played for Manchester City.

captain and the side remained unbeaten for the rest of the season. That 18 match run had begun before McGrath left, however Stokoe's influence was clear to all fans.

In mid April a point at Bradford City guaranteed promotion and then seven days later a 3-0 victory at Gigg Lane over Hull City brought the Third Division title to Bury for the first time. Several club records were broken as well with Bury's points tally of 68 being their highest under the 2 points for a win system. In addition, the side had netted a record 108 goals in a season; achieved their longest sequence of League wins (9) and longest sequence of unbeaten League matches (18). Off the pitch McGrath's transfer had helped the club to record a profit of £33,168.

Despite the positive nature of the period Bury were stunned when on 4th December 1961 manager Dave Russell resigned. He had agreed to drop down a division and move to Tranmere Rovers. His reasons were an indication of the problems that would affect Bury for the rest of the Twentieth Century:

"The financial offer made to me was so attractive [believed to be between £2,500 and £3,250 salary] that I could not turn it down. There is a huge population on The Wirral and there is tremendous potential at Tranmere Rovers. In any case, everyone knows what Bury's gates are like."

If Bury were unable to compete with sides like Tranmere in the battle to retain a successful manager then what hope would they have when it came to a star player. As time moved on Bury had to rely on a good youth policy, and under their new manager this became particularly strong. 31 year old captain Bob Stokoe was given the role of player-manager, making him the club's youngest manager, earning £30 a week.

Stokoe managed to keep Bury in Division Two during his first season in charge, and then the following season his side reached eighth in the Division – their highest finish since 1937. At one point it had looked as if his side would gain promotion to Division One. But sadly the great freeze of January and February 1963 seriously restricted Bury's chance of glory, and with finances once again moving into the red Stokoe had little money to strengthen the squad. Fortunately Bury's youth policy was starting to pay dividends and exciting teenagers such as Bobby Owen and Alec Lindsay were given apprenticeships. Another to arrive was Colin Bell. Bell was signed from north-east club Horden Colliery Welfare Junior FC for a donation of £25 and was immediately given a professional contract, and a basic wage of £25.

Bell was clearly a skilful player and a host of clubs had shown interest, most notably Huddersfield Town, but Bell chose Bury:

"The move had to be right and I was quite a shy boy in many ways, so I needed to go somewhere where I felt at home. Bury were a homely club and made me feel so welcome. I'd had interest from a few clubs – Newcastle offered me a trial. Arsenal were another. I damaged my back shortly before I went down to London from my home in the north-east and that made me a little uncomfortable. Their manager Billy Wright watched the games we played and selected the ones to stay, and then said to those not selected 'I hope you join other clubs that are not as good as Arsenal!'

SECOND DIVISION

(Up to Thursday, April 7th).

		Home					Away					
	P.	W.	D.	L.	F.	A.	W.	D.	L.	F.	A.	Pt.
Manchester City	33	11	6	0	32	12	6	6	4	28	23	46
Huddersfield Town	35	11	5	1	32	9	6	6	6	22	18	45
Coventry City	34	11	5	2	45	25	5	7	4	16	16	44
Wolverhampton Wanderers	35	13	3	2	47	17	4	5	8	30	34	42
Bristol City	35	7	9	1	21	13	6	6	6	29	30	41
Southampton	33	10	3	4	44	21	7	3	6	28	27	40
Rotherham United	32	11	2	2	40	21	2	7	8	21	39	35
Birmingham City	34	8	4	4	26	18	6	3	9	25	37	35
Derby County	35	10	2	6	42	30	3	6	8	13	26	34
Plymouth Argyle	35	6	8	3	32	19	5	4	9	16	33	34
Crystal Palace	35	9	6	2	23	13	2	6	10	16	33	34
Norwich City	32	7	7	3	28	20	3	6	6	14	18	33
Bolton Wanderers	**34**	**10**	**1**	**6**	**31**	**21**	**3**	**6**	**8**	**15**	**26**	**33**
Portsmouth	36	10	4	4	39	26	2	3	13	21	46	31
Preston North End	33	5	7	3	21	16	4	5	9	23	36	30
Carlisle United	32	13	2	3	38	19	0	1	13	9	30	29
Ipswich Town	34	9	5	3	27	17	2	2	13	14	34	29
Cardiff City	33	8	2	7	30	29	2	6	8	30	39	28
Charlton Athletic	31	7	5	3	26	20	2	5	9	19	35	28
Middlesbrough	34	7	7	4	34	25	0	5	11	13	42	26
Bury	**33**	**8**	**5**	**3**	**35**	**19**	**1**	**2**	**14**	**16**	**45**	**25**
Leyton Orient	34	3	6	7	12	25	2	4	12	17	38	20

OUR GOALSCORERS

FIRST TEAM

Pointer 17, Bell 10, Parry 5, Owen 4, Maltby 4, Bird 3, Griffin 2, Eastham 1, Henderson 1, Kerr (J.) 1, Kerr (G.) 1, Aimson 1, Own goal 1.

SECOND TEAM

Owen 23, Randall 8, Griffin 6, Maltby 4, Claxton 4, Henderson 3, Lindsay 3, Wilson 2, Turner 2, Roberts 2, Alston 1, Hughes 1, D. Cook 1, Clunie 1, Bibby 1, Atherton 1, Campbell 1, Own goals 2.

CENTRAL LEAGUE

(UP TO THURSDAY, APRIL 7th)

	P.	W.	D.	L.	F.	A.	Pt.
Sheffield Utd.	32	22	7	3	83	39	51
Stoke City	35	21	7	7	65	40	49
Everton	36	21	5	10	80	49	47
Wolves	36	18	9	9	67	43	45
West Brom. A.	36	18	9	9	78	52	45
Blackburn R.	34	19	4	11	84	55	42
Liverpool	34	16	8	10	60	44	40
Aston Villa	35	17	4	14	59	55	38
Burnley	32	15	6	11	54	50	36
Newcastle U.	32	14	5	13	66	54	33
Preston N.E.	32	12	9	11	57	52	33
Sheffield Wed.	34	11	11	12	53	60	33
Bolton W.	34	13	6	15	50	61	32
Bury	**35**	**13**	**5**	**17**	**66**	**67**	**31**
Man. United	34	12	7	15	44	47	31
Huddersfield T.	33	11	8	14	38	47	30
Blackpool	32	8	10	14	46	61	26
Man. City	32	8	9	15	37	62	25
Derby County	36	8	8	20	42	71	24
Leeds United	31	5	8	18	36	47	18
Barnsley	33	4	9	20	32	86	17
Chesterfield	32	4	6	22	33	89	14

Above: **The Second Division table as recorded on 12th April 1966 in the Bury-City match programme. Note the Bury statistics showing Colin Bell as second highest scorer. By this time Bell was a City player.**

Opposite: **Bury's Paul Aimson, who passed away in 2008.**

"Both Bury and Huddersfield wanted me to sign, so I was totally open with them and agreed I wouldn't make my mind up until I returned back home and looked at it objectively. The Huddersfield experience went well, but Bury was so much more homely. While I was there I knew I'd sign for Bury, but I wouldn't tell them. They kept pushing me, and I wanted to say yes, but I felt it was more important to stick to the plan. So when I went home I told both clubs of my decision."

Bell immediately felt at home at Bury and the club seemed perfect for his temperament, skill and experience:

"My instincts were right, however I did still feel homesick. It really hit me for about six weeks or so and I know that if my family had suggested I go home I would have done. I'd have packed it all in because I hated that homesick feeling. I'd have got that wherever I went, and I'm glad I chose Bury because in the end I couldn't have had a better start to my career. It was a great period once I'd settled and I felt I was so lucky to be paid for playing. I took each day as it came. That's true of all my career."

Eventually in 1966 Bell became one of the side's most valuable players and ultimately he became another asset the club had to sell. Bell:

"I never thought about moving from Bury. It never crossed my mind, and I certainly didn't think about playing for England. I didn't ask to leave. I loved playing for Bury and never really thought beyond that. I didn't even know City were watching me until the official approach came. In fact it got to transfer deadline day and suddenly I had both City and Blackpool interested in me and I had to make another choice. This time it was stay at Bury, move to Second Division City, or move to First Division Blackpool.

"At the time I didn't know enough about Mercer or Allison to base a decision on, so my decision was based more on league position. City were heading for promotion, while Blackpool were beginning to struggle [they were eventually relegated in 1967], so I thought it would be best to join a club looking forward rather than one heading for struggle. In the end I found that City was a lot like Bury, even though it was a much bigger club, it still had that homely feel. We were all part of the same family. First team players would pop into the laundry room and have a cup of tea with the ladies in there. Sometimes we'd just love being at the ground. I do think football's lost a lot by having training grounds some distance from the home grounds. We felt part of the Maine Road furniture. It was my second home and most mornings we'd get in early to get into the gym for head tennis. If ever you arrived at the ground and found you'd arrived too late to make up a head tennis team you'd skulk around and plan to get in even earlier the next day. That's how I'd felt at Bury as well. The two clubs were always wonderful places to be."

By the time of Bell's move manager Stokoe had also moved on, while Chairman George Horridge had also stood down. At the 1964 AGM he looked back on his 34 years as a director and talked of the hope and ambition of his early years on the Board. As far back as 1930 he had talked of his aim to bring Bury back into Division One and in 1964 he talked of this:

"I regret that I have failed the trust put in me but the club's experiences in Division Two have generally been a series of ups and downs. There is no club with the same small population of less than 100,000 that has a better record than Bury, except maybe Burnley. Perhaps we have not done too well, but I hope the Shareholders will think we have not done too bad a job. I don't suppose that anyone who has not had the job will realise the difficulties and responsibilities. If the club is not doing well you feel there are thousands in the town who look to the Chairman to do something about it. During the time I have been Chairman – I have held the office 19 times – there have been occasions when we have been struggling and then one has realised the burden of the job. I would now like to sit and watch the matches in comparative peace."

A week later Horridge was offered the role of Life President.

In 1967 Bury finished bottom of Division Two, an immediate return followed but the 1968-69 season saw more struggles at Gigg Lane and relegation to Division Three came again. Further struggles followed and in 1971 Bury were relegated to Division Four for the first time. George Horridge had earlier relinquished his position as President to become a director again and he went on to become Chairman again at a time when his respectability and Bury heritage was much needed. Understandably with Bury's relegation almost certain Horridge resigned as Chairman on the morning of the fateful relegation game against Swansea. In a letter to the Secretary, Gordon Hurst, he stated:

"I wish to inform you that I have decided not to continue as Chairman of the Board of Directors when the present playing season is over. I shall regret very much the relegation of the club into Division Four, should this happen. This possibility is not the reason for my wishing to retire and I feel that the position of Chairman should now be occupied by a younger person. I wish you, therefore, to consider this letter as

a request to the Board to relieve me of the position of Chairman and to place it before the Board at the earliest opportunity."

Bury remained a Fourth Division side until promotion under manager Bobby Smith in fourth place in 1974, and the following season they found themselves gaining some national coverage. Tom Tyrell, **Piccadilly's** Sports Editor at the time, believed Bury had a great season:

"They had some young players ready for inspiration and some ex-perienced ones willing to inspire. They fell into the magnetic field that draws the bottom clubs down, but had the ability to blast their way out of the danger zone and finished in a comfortable and respectable position for a first try. They also had their share of glory, some of it short lived. They did well in the FA Cup.... well, they did better than all our other local clubs for Bury reached the fourth round! And in one player they found themselves holding a headline grabber. He was Derek Spence who was 'over the moon' to be picked for Northern Ireland and to play in their first game in Belfast for four years, when they met Yugoslavia in April. Derek's selection was a boost for Bury as well as for the boy himself, and his display in the Yugoslavia game showed everyone that the Irish selectors weren't wrong."

Despite the positives of 1974-75, Bury's experience during the sixties and seventies was typical of the region's smaller clubs and was also a strong indication that smaller clubs could rarely compete with the larger city sides. Throughout Bury's late sixties and early seventies struggles comparisons were being made with Accrington Stanley – a side who were forced to resign from the League in 1962 mid-season due to financial difficulties. Most assumed that a town the size of Bury could hardly support a Fourth Division side, never mind one that its Chairman still hoped he could get back into Division One.

It was a point recognised by Tom Tyrell:

"Life in professional football is a battle all the time these days, and for clubs in an area like ours there has got to be success to survive. The spectators will only turn up week after week if the team carries on winning, and so we get the eternal triangle of success, finance and sur-vival. Few clubs can afford the big wage bills they are faced with week after week; ground maintenance cannot always be afforded, and new players for cash are out of the question. But still Rochdale and Stockport have carried on, thanks to the efforts of fund-raising committees, the ever presents in the small crowds, and the seemingly bottomless pockets of the directors. Football needs its little clubs."

On the face of it the situation was bleak at Rochdale who started the sixties in Division Four and ended the 1974-75 season in nineteenth place in the same division. However, in between those dates Rochdale had achieved promotion from Division Three in 1969 and had also shocked football by becoming League Cup finalists in 1962 – a record for a Fourth Division side and also the first of the region's sides to reach a major final during the decade.

Tony Collins had been Rochdale's manager at the time of the League Cup final, but by the time of promotion in 1969 Len Richley was in charge after a brief period which saw Bob Stokoe take the reins. Alongside Richley was coach Dick Connor. Connor arrived in December 1968 when Rochdale's position was still fairly bleak, as Connor explained in the early 1970s:

"When I first came to Spotland the club was in trouble, in fact, I came in the December and on Boxing Day that year we were due to play at Workington. If we lost that game it meant that we were in the

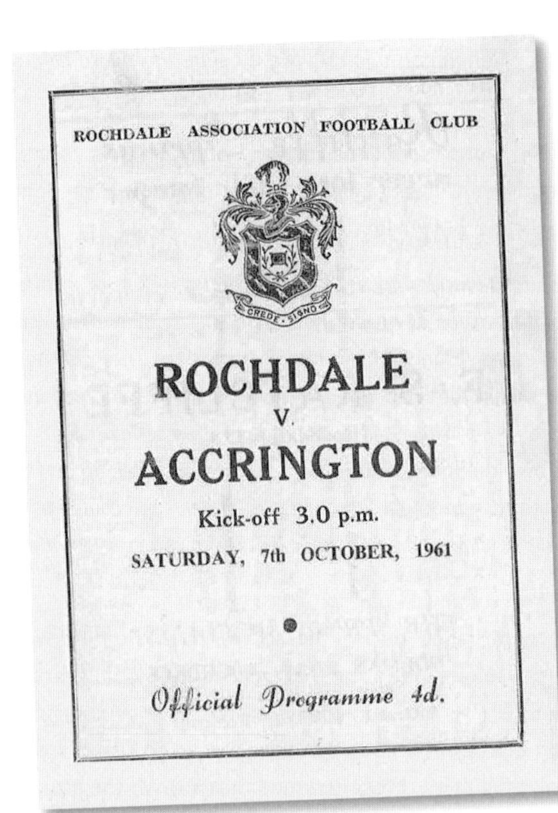
ROCHDALE ASSOCIATION FOOTBALL CLUB

CREDE SIGNO

ROCHDALE
V.
ACCRINGTON

Kick-off 3.0 p.m.

SATURDAY, 7th OCTOBER, 1961

Official Programme 4d.

Left and below: **Two games that no longer count. Rochdale won 1-0 against Accrington Stanley in October 1961and 2-0 at Stanley in February 1962, but Stanley pulled out of the League that season and both games have been expunged from the records.**

Right: **In the fourth round League Cup tie Dale defeated York 2-1 with goals from Hepton and Thompson.**

Bottom right: **12,125 witness a 1-1 draw between Rochdale and Oldham at Spotland on 15th September 1962. However the referee was not entirely happy with the behaviour of fans.**

ROCHDALE ASSOCIATION FOOTBALL CLUB

CREDE SIGNO

ROCHDALE

V.

YORK CITY

Kick-off 7.15 p.m.

WEDNESDAY, FEBRUARY 7th, 1962

Official Programme 4d.

bottom four of the Fourth Division – but we won and really we never looked back. Really I suppose I have been very lucky. They weren't having too good a time here then, and although they had not done too badly when Bob Stokoe was manager, things did not look too promising. But I came here, watched a couple of games, got a few ideas, tried them out and we just went sailing along from there, and in fact we only lost a couple of games between Christmas and the end of the seasons, and of course we won promotion.

"It's a lovely feeling when this happens, and you have a good run, for you can see the players you have brought along putting your ideas into practice. When you see the success coming you feel great."

Connor ultimately became Dale manager:

"Eventually Len resigned and I took over as manager, but I wasn't really worried when I went into the hot seat. I just thought that it would be a good challenge for me. I feel as if I had served a good apprenticeship before I became a manager."

Rochdale's promotion in third place at the end of 1968-69 was the first promotion in their history, although they were a Division Three side immediately after the creation of Division Four, and there was a great deal of hope and optimism around the town. In 1969-70 Dale finished ninth, their highest finish since the days of Division Three North. Connor felt they had managed to surprise most teams:

"We were winning games because people knew nothing about us. They didn't bother watching us and we surprised one or two. Then, when the return matches came around we found that more people knew about us, and had taken the time to find out our little problems and play on them. It wasn't so easy then and we had to change our ideas again to carry on winning – but we did!"

In 1970-71 Dale continued to impress with a famous meeting with Coventry City in the FA Cup third round coming in January. Coventry's manager Noel Cantwell made a rather foolish comment *"Rochdale, where's that?"* at the time and that question came back to haunt him as Dale won 2-1 to reach the fourth round for the first time since 1915. Sadly, the fourth round saw Colchester United defeat Dale 5-0 in a replay after a 3-3 draw preventing Dale from facing one of the giants of the periods Leeds United (Colchester actually became famous for their giant killing act over Leeds that season).

In the League Rochdale finished sixteenth and for the next couple of years Dale seemed stranded in mid-table, and at the end of the 1972-73 season manager Connor's contract was not renewed. There had been some supporter disquiet as Connor's side had become more defensive, but the years that followed were much worse overall. During the early months of his reign Connor had made it abundantly clear that his ambition was to see Rochdale stabilise in Division Three, but he openly admitted that Rochdale had to establish themselves as a selling club:

"The club is not just going to stand where it has been in days gone by. Everyone wants to do something, they are genuinely trying to do something for the public, and that is why I am certain that Rochdale will not go backwards. The revival probably started when Tony Collins was manager here, for Tony began by trying to cut down the age of the team, starting with younger people, and once a thing like this happens, then you are in with a bit of a chance. People now come to our matches to buy our players, and this is something which has never happened in the past.

"There may have been the odd transfer from time to time, when somebody has come along and bought a player to help the club out of trouble, but nowadays clubs are always asking about one or other of our players. The telephone is always ringing with some inquiry about a player, and once the big clubs start contacting you, you know that you are not dead, or out of business.

"Small clubs like Rochdale have to sell survive, I suppose. If we have to sell then it will be sensible selling and not just selling for the sake of getting in some cash."

Connor touched on the issue that would dominate football life for the smaller clubs throughout the decades that followed, and for Rochdale, Stockport, Bury, Oldham, and even Manchester City at various times from the Seventies onwards selling became the only way to survive. Support was not high enough to keep Dale in a challenging position and after Connor's departure the side struggled to build on what had been achieved. In February 1974 only 588 people attended Dale's game with Cambridge – reported at the time as the lowest Football League crowd for 20 years, but is now acknowledged as the lowest since 469 attended Thames V Luton in 1930.

TOPS ... THAT'S THE DEFENDERS

STOCKPORT COUNTY F.C.

FIVE

TOKEN VOUCHER

"THE DEFENDERS" are putting up an impressive case for County. For the Stockport defence is the best in the Fourth Division, having conceded only six goals in nine League games. Next best is eight by Tranmere and second club Southend. Secret is that three of the rearguard, Billy Haydock (pictured right), Peter Jones and Matt Woods have played in every game, while Eddie Stuart and goalkeeper Steve Fleet have missed only one game each.

FIRST TEAM

APPEARANCES

NINE — Haydock, Jones, Woods, Lord, Allen, Price.
EIGHT — Shawcross, Stuart, Fleet.
SEVEN — Quixall.
SIX — Allchurch.
THREE — Goodwin, Henderson.
ONE — Mulhearn, Sykes.

GOALS

Lord	6
Shawcross	4
Allen	2
Henderson	2
Allchurch	1
Own goal	1

GATES

Aug. 26	v. York	7,897
Sept. 5	v. Barnsley	9,068
Sept. 9	v. Chesterf'd	10,265
Sept. 30	v. Southport	13,848

FOOTBALL LEAGUE—DIVISION IV

	P	W	D	L	F	A	Ps
COUNTY	**9**	**7**	**1**	**1**	**16**	**6**	**15**
Southend U.	9	6	2	1	19	8	14
Newport Co.	10	5	2	3	18	12	12
Tranmere R.	9	4	4	1	12	8	12
Aldershot	9	5	2	2	19	13	12
Wrexham	9	3	5	1	17	11	11
Southport	10	5	1	4	18	13	11
Barrow	10	3	5	2	18	16	11
Port Vale	9	3	5	1	11	10	11
Bradford C.	9	4	2	3	17	12	10
Bradford	9	4	2	3	19	14	10
Crewe Alex.	9	4	2	3	16	15	10
Chesterfield	9	3	3	3	12	12	9
Hartlepools U.	10	4	1	5	12	16	9
Luton T.	9	4	0	5	13	13	8
York C.	9	3	2	4	16	17	8
Exeter C.	9	2	4	3	11	12	8
Rochdale	9	3	2	4	9	13	8
Chester	9	2	4	3	10	17	8
Brentford	9	2	3	4	8	15	7
Notts Co.	10	1	4	5	13	23	6
Halifax T.	9	1	3	5	13	21	5
Lincoln C.	9	1	2	6	11	19	4
Barnsley	10	1	1	8	10	22	3

RESERVE TEAM

APPEARANCES

ELEVEN — Reynolds, Parry, Phillipson.
TEN — Holden, Abbott, Cooke.
NINE — Pielow, Mulhearn.
SEVEN — Henstock.
SIX — Goodwin.
FIVE — Alderson, Sykes.
FOUR — Harvey, Henderson.
THREE — Dowthwaite, Brennan.
ONE — Fleet, Allchurch, Bee.

GOALS

Pielow	2
Abbott	1
Phillipson	1
Henstock	1
Goodwin	1

CHESHIRE COUNTY LEAGUE

(Up to and including October 4)

	P	W	D	L	F	A	Ps
Wigan A.	11	9	2	0	25	12	20
Altrincham	11	8	2	1	37	14	18
Frickley C.	11	6	3	2	23	13	15
Ellesmere P.T.	10	5	3	2	20	15	13
Bangor C.	8	5	1	2	19	7	11
Northwich V.	8	4	3	1	22	17	11
Tranmere Res.	11	5	1	5	20	24	11
Hyde U.	8	4	2	2	12	7	10
Witton A.	8	4	2	2	18	14	10
Stafford R.	10	3	4	3	12	11	10
Wrexham Res.	11	5	0	6	18	22	10
New Brighton	8	2	5	1	15	11	9
Runcorn	8	4	1	3	15	14	9
Macclesfield	7	3	2	2	7	8	8
Chester Res.	12	3	2	7	16	20	8
Stalybridge C.	10	3	2	5	12	16	8
Buxton	10	2	3	5	9	19	7
COUNTY Res.	**11**	**1**	**4**	**6**	**6**	**16**	**6**
Oswestry T.	10	2	1	7	15	26	5
Mossley	9	2	1	6	11	22	5
Rhyl	9	1	2	6	9	17	4
Winsford U.	9	0	2	7	4	20	2

County 1966-67 Division Four champions.

STOCKPORT COUNTY A. F. C. LTD.

SEASON TICKETS 1967/8

The prices for Season Tickets have been fixed as follows:—

STANDS B, C, D and E ... £8 0s. 0d.
Ladies/Juniors .... £7 0s. 0d.
STANDS A and F .... £7 0s. 0d.
Ladies/Juniors .... £6 0s. 0d.

RENEWALS

Please note that the latest date for renewal of present season ticket is:—
30th JUNE

NEW APPLICATIONS

We have good seats available, but early booking is advised. Personal or postal applications accepted.

Postal Applications together with the appropriate remittance should be sent to:—

The Secretary,
Stockport County A.F.C. Ltd.,
Edgeley Park,
Stockport.

Division Four champions Stockport announce their ticket prices for the 1967-8 Division Three season.

There were some strong reasons for so few to attend with the most significant being that the game took place on a Tuesday afternoon due to power cuts – these were the days when strikes and industrial unrest meant electricity was restricted. Some clubs, such as City for their League Cup game with Coventry in January, brought in generators to ensure the games could continue, but generating enough electricity to power floodlights at Spotland would have been a significant issue. As well as the electricity issue, the three day week and other strike activity meant people simply could not afford to attend. However, the low crowd does give an indication of how Dale were beginning to struggle again.

Previously, during his spell as manager Connor had hoped he could get the side into Division Two and believed attendances would increase, but a season after his departure Dale were propping up Division Three with only 21 points from 46 games. They had created a few records as well – although no one would have wanted these. Dale had only won two matches (no club had ever recorded so few Division Three wins), and their points tally of 21 was the record lowest total for Division Three at the time.

Stockport's record during the Sixties and early Seventies was similar to Rochdale with promotion in 1967 as Division Four champions being followed in 1970 with relegation. They had started the period as a mid-table Division Four side and ended it in twentieth place in the same division in 1975.

Similarly Oldham started the Sixties in a similar position but of all the sides in the region they were the ones who ended 1974-75 considerably higher than fifteen years earlier. They ended 1974-75 in eighteenth place in Division Two but had faced Manchester United on equal terms that season, and had actually beaten the Reds 1-0 on 28th December. At that time the Latics were in the Second Division relegation zone while United headed the table. ***Piccadilly Radio's*** Tom Tyrell, the United reporter at the time, gave his view on the game in an article at the end of the season:

"The Latics' fans will never forget when United came to Boundary Park and were beaten by a penalty after the referee had missed a goal that was, but didn't count. That goal-that-never-was came when a fierce shot beat Alex Stepney and went into the net, striking a stanchion, then flying out again to be cleared. It looked like a goal from the grandstand, seemed like a goal to the players, and was a goal according to photographers on the line, but the referee didn't see it and it didn't count. A second-half penalty for hand-ball gave Latics their winner and it was a Merry Christmas for the Latics' fanatics."

The transformation in Latics fortunes had come about following the appointment of Jimmy

Frizzell as manager. Former player Frizzell took over as caretaker manager on 30th December 1969 with the side in a desperate position after only winning four of their opening 24 games in Division Four. They appeared to be heading for the nightmare of the re-election process but Frizzell managed to give a positive approach and with a new found confidence the Latics managed to gather enough points to finish in nineteenth place. Inevitably, Frizzell was appointed manager on a full time basis stating at the time:

"I am very pleased with the appointment and the confidence that the board have shown in me. I will do my best to justify it."

Over the course of the following seasons Frizzell more than justified his appointment. Frizzell:

"I was very lucky. I had some great players over the years. There were many, many players who did good jobs. I also bought one or two bad buys, but overall I think it went well."

The following season Oldham reached third place in Division Four, guaranteeing promotion, and they also won the Ford Sporting League – a sponsored competition looking at all League results giving points for goals scored and deducting points for player behaviour. They received a significant cash injection of £70,000 out of the competition, spending it on ground improvements (a requirement of the competition).

A mid-table finish in Division Three followed, before Oldham ended 1972-73 in fourth place, missing promotion by three points. Missing promotion was a bitter disappointment but Chairman John Lowe faced fans and the media to explain that the club's desire was to become a First Division side:

A trademark flying header from Bert Lister gives Oldham a goal at Boundary Park. Lister netted 81goals in 135 appearances between 1960 and 1965. He also had spells at City, Rochdale, Stockport and Altrincham.

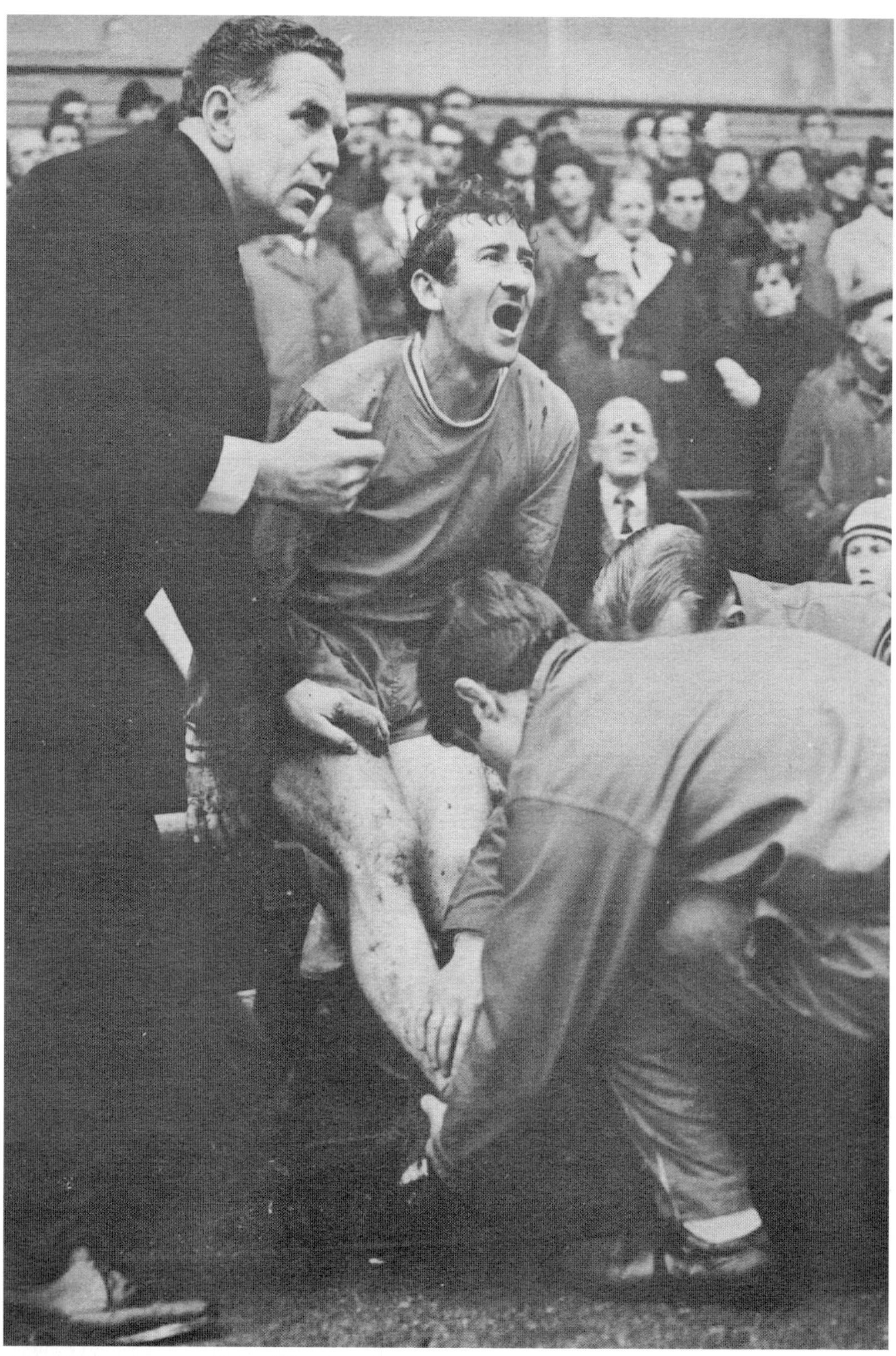

Future Oldham manager Jimmy Frizzell receives treatment while Jack Rowley (manager 1968-9) readjusts his plans.

co-directors, are bitterly disappointed that promotion had not been achieved. We shall continue with the same aim for 1973-74 and, even if we win promotion, we shall carry on afterwards and will not be satisfied until the Latics are a First Division side."

Lowe's Latics progressed under Frizzell and ultimately they won the Division Three title – their first title since Division Three North in 1953 – but sadly Chairman Lowe had passed away in January 1974 and missed the success. At the time of promotion director Arthur Hudson outlined the transformation the club had undergone:

"Four years ago when we were bottom of the Fourth Division we were a joke and commonly referred to as Oldham pathetic. Now we can meet our public with heads held high. We have won back our pride and self-respect and are Oldham Athletic again."

That statement about being 'Oldham Athletic again' is significant as almost every team within the region as at some point been seen by supporters as not being 'theirs'. The creation of FC United during the new century has come about because some Manchester United supporters have felt that United is no longer 'theirs', with the Latics in the early Seventies there was a feeling that the club had been brought back to life. In the mid Sixties Latics suffered financially and this was solved to some extent by the arrival of new Chairman Ken Bates, a man who would later hit the headlines as Chairman of first Chelsea then Leeds United. Bernard Halford was assistant secretary at the time of Bates' arrival:

"Ken Bates bought Oldham in December 1965 and the following February he decided he wanted to change the secretary of the club. He walked in on a matchday morning and had taken some sort of action on the Friday night that I knew nothing about, and he walked in at ten to nine, in his long black coat, and he threw a big bunch of keys right across the office to me. He went 'there you are Bernard. It's all yours now', and that was that. I was secretary."

Bates financed the arrival of a few players within his first year, while also claiming he knew little about football but a lot about business. He felt his business acumen would help Latics become a significant side: *"Europe is our goal, and it can be done."*

The optimism in 1965 encouraged fans, but within three years it became clear that there were issues. He told writer Arthur Hopcraft in 1968:

"When I first went there and started spending money I got letters saying 'God bless you, Mr. Bates, you are our saviour', but when I put the prices up the letters changed. They said 'Go to Hell, Moneybags. What do you know about football?' But what encouraged me was that it was the younger people who were on my side."

Ken Bates, Oldham Chairman.

He added: *"What have we got in football? We've got a handful of people flogging their guts out to raise money to subsidise the game so that other people can buy it at less than production cost. People just don't appreciate how cheaply they've had their football. In South Africa the poor starving African is paying a minimum of seven shillings [35p] to watch a match."*

Standing spectators at some First Division grounds still only paid around four shillings (20p), and Bates' views were not particularly popular in Oldham. In fact, had his spell in charge come in a more modern era, supporters would probably have objected to his involvement from the beginning. Whereas most football chairmen and directors at this point were keen supporters of the club they directed, Bates had made it clear that he had picked Oldham purely for business reasons. In many ways, his selection of Oldham compares with the modern day takeover of Premiership sides by wealthy investors. Bates, who according to reports in the mid-sixties had been a season ticket holder at Burnley during the decade, saw in Oldham a club he could improve and make successful. As a very successful businessman he may have viewed Latics as a good investment. He told Hopcraft in 1968 of his reasons for picking Oldham:

"The only way you can usually get into a football club is in times of difficulties. I wanted to be associated with a poor club which had once been successful. That was important because it meant there was the pull among the public in remembering what the club had been like in the great days. But the first requisite was that there should be a large population. In the north-west I decided there were only two clubs which fitted the bill. One was Stockport, and someone else had already got that, and the other was Oldham. Let's be honest about it. What players want to go and live in Barrow?"

Oldham did benefit under Bates even if he chose them for business reasons rather than a love of the club. Modern day supporters are use to investors without a passion or feeling for their club getting involved, but in the mid-sixties Bates, still only in his late thirties, was an unusual football investor.

Occasionally Bates would take action that would upset supporters, but he always felt he was doing it to help Oldham develop. Halford: *"He did a thing that upset some fans. He brought out the first magazine,* **The Boundary Bulletin**, *and to pay for it he put sixpence on the admission price. Everyone coming in the ground was given one. Well that didn't go down too well with those who just wanted to watch the game."*

Jimmy Frizzell, a player during Bates' time, believes the former chairman made a bigger error: *"He wrote in the 'paper and called the Oldham public the 'lambs of Sheepfoot Lane'. They never forgave him. I think that was the reason the he ultimately decided to get out because he was never really going to win over those people."*

There was also friction within the club and at one point Bates announced he was resigning for business reasons. Then shortly after the 1968-69 season started he announced that he had no intention of leaving. Frequent business trips away were beginning to make it difficult understanding exactly what the Chairman wanted, but then on 17th September 1968 Bates arrived back in England and announced:

"The time has come when I have to concentrate more on my job than on football. After all, football has always been a hobby to me – an expensive hobby at that – and I have devoted more time and energy to it than a lot of people would have done."

Ironically, that same year saw the publication of Arthur Hopcraft's classic football book ***The Football Man***. Bates was featured in Hopcraft's writing as a man with ambition, but also a desire to see Oldham succeed. According to Hopcraft:

"He dearly wants to make good his assertion that 'I think we will be in the First Division by 1970 – just by doing the right things consistently, while other dogs are having their day'. Even if he fails he will at least have gathered the satisfaction that comes to adventurous businessmen of his kind from 'giving yourself an opportunity to exercise your own theories'."

Bates made it clear that he did not want to withdraw his money from the club, but his successor John Lowe felt the financial situation was such that Bates could force the club to close at any point, and so he spent time striking a deal with Bates to ensure financial survival. The on the pitch successes that followed helped ease the financial burden, but also and perhaps more importantly rekindled the interest in the club's fortunes. The eighteenth place finish in Division Two was a remarkable achievement.

As time moved on Bates became known more for his time at Chelsea and then at Leeds but, taking his comments from the 1960s, it is clear that the reasons he chose both Chelsea and Leeds were the same as the reasons he had given for selecting Oldham. He was not known as a supporter of either club, but those clubs both fitted the bill for the type of club he wanted to invest in – *"a poor club which had once been successful"* with the public *"remembering what the club had been like in the great days"*.

For Manchester's two best supported sides the Sixties and early Seventies brought great success, but they also brought failure. City started the Sixties as a struggling Division One side, were relegated in 1963 after an appalling winter which prevented any of the sides from building on any victories they achieved, and then went on an incredibly successful spell under manager Joe Mercer and his assistant Malcolm Allison. By 1975 City had won the title, the FA Cup, the European Cup Winners' Cup, the League Cup and were one of football's most glamorous sides. Incredibly though, during the struggles one of the Blues' directors had actually approached United about the possibility of a merger.

The idea of merging with United shocked supporters and in many ways became the most controversial moment in the two clubs' shared history since the campaign to stop Manchester Central from joining the League. Neither City nor United fans could possibly have been happy with the idea, although Reds supporters would undoubtedly have delighted in winding up their Blue counterparts.

A merger would seriously have damaged football in the region and, no matter how poor City were in the mid-Sixties, there was never any real belief that the club would go out of business. Even in the worst case, the club would have struggled but remained a fallen giant, perhaps becoming the equivalent of a modern day Burnley. Clearly, if Rochdale, Oldham, Stockport, and Bury could survive – and at times thrive – then the better supported City should have a future.

Today the idea may sound ridiculous and, perhaps, a pure flight of fancy, but throughout the 1964-5 season City appeared to be seriously considering the possibility, and amazingly City's Vice-Chairman Frank Johnson had actually come up with the idea.

It appears that Johnson had already angered supporters, and his fellow directors, by proposing the entire Football League should be split into North and South sections, and then he followed this up with the formal approach to United to merge. As with many periods of football history it appears some football directors were totally out of touch with what fans themselves wanted from the game. Furious letters appeared from both sets of fans who were united in their disgust at the idea.

How far the merger would go was unclear, but at the very least, it was suggested, City and United would share one ground – Old Trafford. The whole history of the game in England suggests ground sharing is not something that can work in the Country, certainly not at a senior club level, however cities such as Milan appear to have made it work. In Manchester in 1964 the idea that Maine Road with all its history and heritage could be demolished and City moved into Old Trafford seemed totally ridiculous. It would also have been a tragedy for the region.

The approach by Johnson came towards the end of the 1963-4 season and was confirmed as being genuine by an Old Trafford director, but the discussions – which seemed to occur several times during 1964 – only became public in January 1965. By that time a group of 'rebel' City shareholders led by Peter Donoghue were pushing for changes at Board level. They had already asked for an Extraordinary General Meeting where they were to demand the resignation of the Board. When he heard the news about the merger, Donoghue was dismayed and told Peter Gardner of the *Manchester Evening News*:

"RED DEVILS"

SOUVENIR SHOP

PERSONAL presentation of this panel advert at the Souvenir Shop, (next to ticket office, or hut at Stretford End, and Kiosk in Canti-lever Stand) will (WHILST STOCKS LAST) enable bearer to obtain a special souvenir illustrated metal tray for only 5/-.

DO NOT MISS THIS SUPERB BARGAIN!

"If what we have heard is true this is the last straw. We are determined not to let City die as a club. A merger would only go through over our dead bodies."

Donoghue's group issued a ten point plan to save the Blues. This led to the City board and Donoghue's group announcing they would work together for the good of City.

As for the merger this seemed to be nothing more than a silly idea to reduce City's financial burden by moving the Blues to Old Trafford, but simply making the suggestion caused much worry for supporters in the region. From a wider perspective it also suggested that the financial nature of football meant, even then, that clubs had to carefully balance their ambition with the realities of their financial life.

Some felt that the Blues were a dying club and that they had to find a way forward. Reporter Eric Cooper, the 'Sports Voice of the North', considered City's dismal situation and decided:

"It isn't soccer experts or players Manchester City need right now so much as a psychologist. A man who might analyse the transitions from optimism to pessimism. A man who by his enthusiasm and drive

might fill the gaps between the potential City have shown so often and the failures that have labelled them the most unpredictable team in Soccer. Here is a club that between the wars were Manchester's favourites, reaching the Cup final three times besides winning the League Championship in 1937, while neighbours United were regarded as a music hall joke."

Cooper went on to consider where City's failure began:

"Old timers will tell you that the decline at Maine Road set in when they were relegated a year after winning the League title and a cynical fan lowered the flag to half-mast. Since that time City have twice won promotion from the Second Division and twice more returned. They have also won the Cup, but somehow they have never recaptured the old glory. Supporters – and they could probably command more potential fans for a winning team than their successful United rivals – have been buffeted between hope and frustration until they are tired. The image of Manchester City has changed from the glamorous cavalier football of the 30s to one of abject apathy."

The apathy fortunately did not last but many of the characteristics of the club have continued to this day. Supporters have become the most important aspect of the Blues, while a succession of directors have failed to grasp what the club needs to recapture the dominance it had pre-war. Success has occurred – and the late sixties became one of Manchester's greatest eras with City finding significant success – but City's history from the 1880s through to 1938 provided a legacy which should have been built on, just like the period that followed the positives of the Mercer-Allison era ended with City lacking the vision to build a giant of the European game.

Back in the summer of 1965 when all seemed lost for City, Joe Mercer and Malcolm Allison arrived to re-ignite City's ambition and drive. Glorious successes followed with promotion, the

Neil Young is mobbed by fans after scoring an equaliser at Maine Road in the FA Cup tie with Leicester. The Blues reached the quarter-finals in 1966 despite being in Division Two.

123
124

League Championship, the FA Cup, the League Cup, and the European Cup Winners' Cup all coming in a five year spell. Those achievements brought the most significant transformation in a club's fortunes any of the Manchester region sides had enjoyed. Only Mangnall's transformation of United between 1902 and 1912 came close. What Mercer & Allison achieved for City was remarkable.

For United the early sixties was to be a period when the Munich Air Disaster shaped the club's direction. The 1958 tragedy caused many problems for the Reds and rebuilding the squad and developing a new side was manager Busby's main aim, and inevitably it was a difficult task.

Facing page: **City skipper Tony Book lifts the League Championship trophy at Maine Road in May 1968 prior to a friendly with Bury.**
Right and below: **After winning the FA Cup in 1969, both the League Cup and European Cup-Winners' followed in 1970.**

In 1963 the Reds were almost relegated as they avoided the drop by three points (a controversial derby match gave United the edge and caused City to struggle), but that same season they won the FA Cup by defeating Leicester 3-1 with goals from Denis Law and David Herd (2). United player Pat Crerand remembers: *"I was only here for about 3 months before the cup final when we beat Leicester. The cup final was much bigger then than it is now, and it was a situation where United hadn't done so well in the League finishing third bottom or something and then in the final everybody just clicked at the right time. We abolished Leicester City."*

The win was the first success of Busby's third great side, and it heralded a five year period of success. The Reds were runners-up for the title in 1964, Champions in 1965 and 1967 and European Cup Winners in 1968. Celtic were the first British side to win the trophy, but the Reds were the first to bring the trophy to England. Crerand:

"To win the European Cup was a very sad occasion in many respects because they'd also invited all the families of the players who had died at Munich. You started to think 'would I have been here'. Quite a few of us players wouldn't have been there had these players lived. You also thought about those players and those that were still with us. So it was sadness but also great joy for Matt and everybody else."

Winning the European Cup inevitably caused many to focus on the ten year journey from the disaster at Munich to success at Wembley, but sadly the win seemed to bring a premature end to United's successes. Whether the pressure, strain, and ambition to find that success ultimately

MANCHESTER UNITED F.C. 1968-69 (European Champion Clubs' Cup Winners)

Back Row (left to right) : W. Foulkes, J. Aston, J. Rimmer, A. Stepney, A. Gowling, D. Herd (Now with Stoke City)
Middle Row (left to right) : D. Sadler, A. Dunne, S. Brennan, P. Crerand, G. Best, F. Burns, J. Crompton (Trainer).
Front Row (left to right) : J. Ryan, N. Stiles, D. Law, Sir M. Busby, C.B.E. (Manager), R. Charlton (Captain), B. Kidd, J. Fitzpatrick *Photo : Manchester Evening News*

limited the opportunities that followed is open to debate, however it is clear that despite possessing exceptionally talented players – perhaps individually their side contained the greatest players in the English game at the time – they no longer appeared to have a shared desire for team success. This may appear harsh, however, when City won the title in 1968 it is clear their success was a triumph for the entire team and although nationally supporters would talk about Bell, Lee and Summerbee, in Manchester the part the other players such as Oakes, Pardoe, Doyle, Booth and Young played was clear. The one time City tried to sign a player simply because of his flair and national fame saw the Blues stutter – Rodney Marsh was signed to boost the popularity of the side but his arrival was seen as causing the side to miss out on what had appeared a certain League Championship success (the Blues missed the title by a point).

Of course United possessed arguably the greatest player of all time during their late Sixties triumphs, George Best. Crerand: *"George Best was the first glamorous footballer. He had tremendous talent. An absolutely incredible footballer, but because of his looks he was thrown into the limelight even more. He had this image, but he was actually quite a shy person really."*

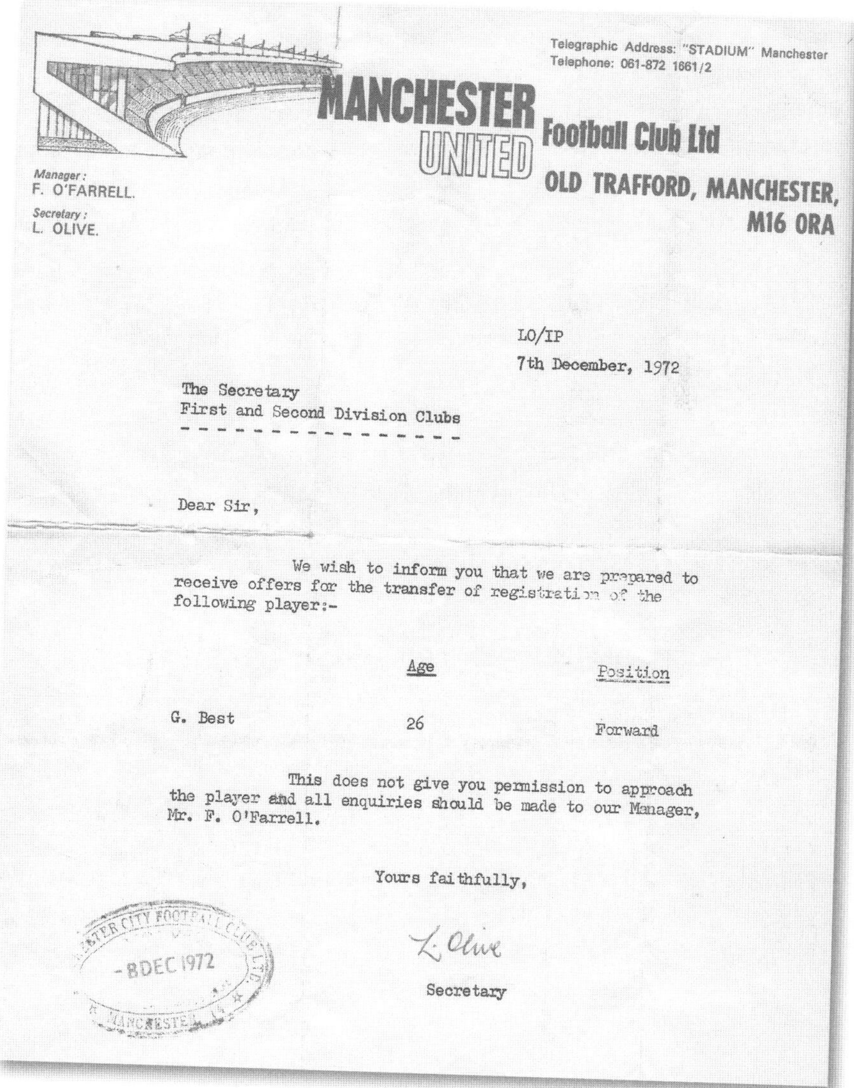

Telegraphic Address: "STADIUM" Manchester
Telephone: 061-872 1661/2

MANCHESTER UNITED Football Club Ltd
OLD TRAFFORD, MANCHESTER, M16 ORA

Manager: F. O'FARRELL.
Secretary: L. OLIVE.

LO/IP
7th December, 1972

The Secretary
First and Second Division Clubs

Dear Sir,

We wish to inform you that we are prepared to receive offers for the transfer of registration of the following player:-

	Age	Position
G. Best	26	Forward

This does not give you permission to approach the player and all enquiries should be made to our Manager, Mr. F. O'Farrell.

Yours faithfully,

L. Olive

Secretary

The shock news that United were prepared to sell George Best. This was City's copy of a letter sent to all senior clubs.

Best played his part in all of United's successes from 1963 to 1974 and found recognition internationally for the quality of his game. His glamour both on and off the pitch helped generate new support for the Reds, but sadly his United career petered out during the early seventies. He walked out of Old Trafford on several occasions, before spending the rest of the Seventies at a variety of clubs in England and the USA, including Stockport County. He managed three games for County in 1975 – his first game saw the crowd rise by around seven thousand to 9,220 – but earlier he had almost joined both Oldham and City.

The Reds had placed Best on the transfer list in 1972 and Malcolm Allison tried to sign him for City – according to Allison, Best wanted to sign but the move was blocked by United. Around that time Oldham secretary Bernard Halford had a meeting with Best. According to Halford, Best verbally agreed to a move to Boundary Park, but that the signing of the contract would have to be done later. They agreed a time and Halford went back to Oldham delighted:

"Imagine the headlines... Oldham sign George Best!"

Halford's delight soon turned to despair when an Oldham director reminded him that Best may not be quite so interested later. The director told Halford the only way of getting Best to commit would be to get his signature on a contract. Halford was told that he should have locked the player in a room until he signed. Deep down Halford knew the moment had gone, but he still went to meet Best at the location and the time the player had chosen. After waiting for what seemed an eternity, the realisation dawned for Halford that the moment Best walked out of the earlier meeting the opportunity was missed. Sure enough Best did not go to Oldham.

ATTENDANCE DETAIL SEASON BY SEASON - 1960-1967

Season	City	United	Oldham	Bury	Stockport	Rochdale
1960-61	29502	37807	12644	10207	6506	3929
1961-62	25711	33358	11324	10518	4824	4024
1962-63	24683	40329	14269	11265	4061	3306
1963-64	18201	44125	12373	8169	4277	3020
1964-65	14753	46521	8184	7784	5739	4686
1965-66	27739	38769	8943	7667	7802	2974
1966-67	31209	53854	9940	8076	9820	2442

LEAGUE POSITIONS SEASON BY SEASON - 1960-1967

Season	City	United	Oldham	Bury	Stockport	Rochdale
1960-61	13	7	80	45	81	85
1961-62	12	15	79	40	84	80
1962-63	21	19	70	30	87	75
1963-64	28	2	53	40	85	88
1964-65	33	1	64	38	92	74
1965-66	23	4	64	41	81	89
1966-67	15	1	54	44	69	89

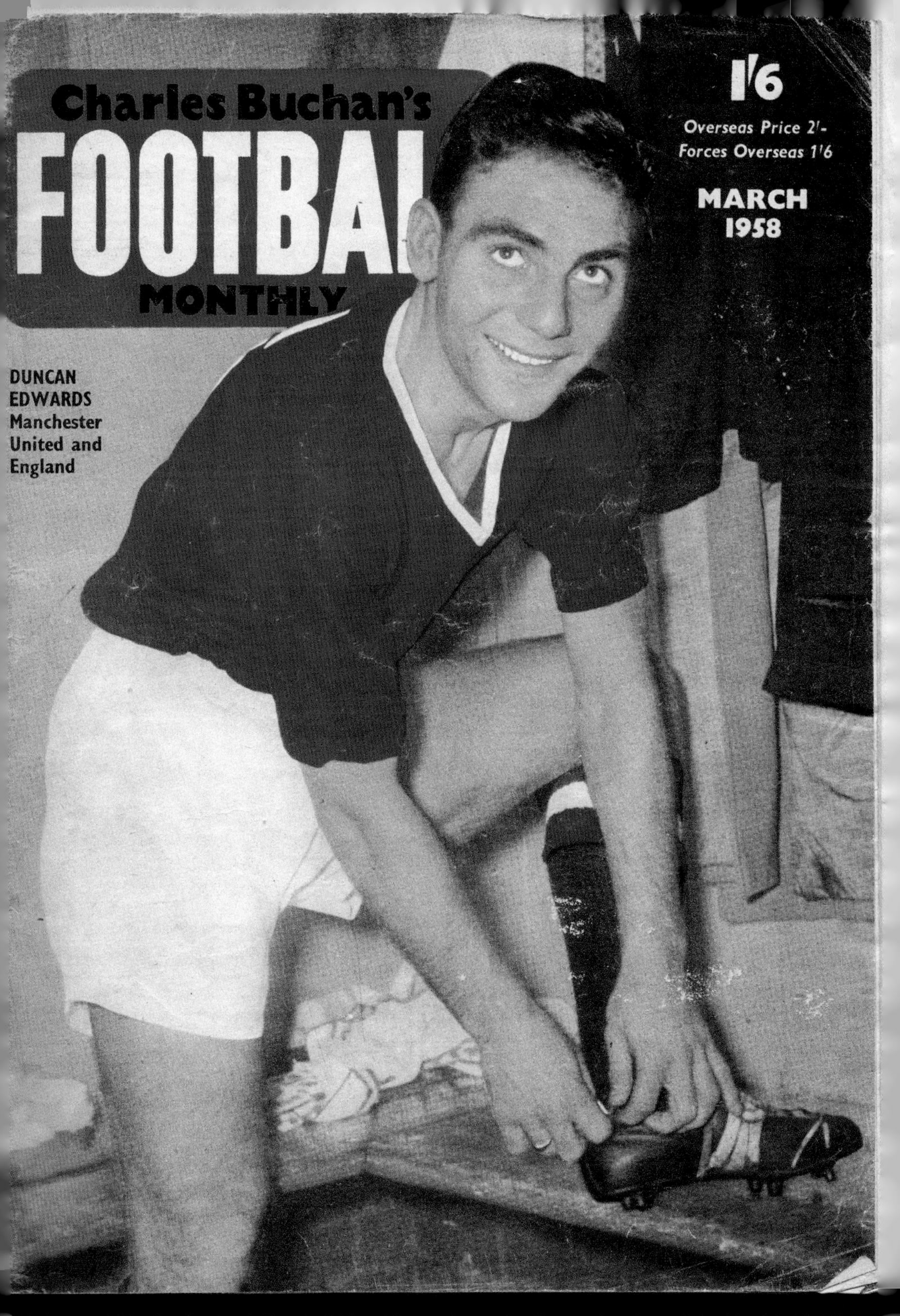

This issue of Charles Buchan's Football Monthly was in production at the time of the Munich Air Disaste

ROCHDALE
v
NORWICH CITY

Nº 72

NORWICH CITY
FOOTBALL CLUB
F.A. CUP SEMI-FINALISTS, SEASON 1958-59

FOOTBALL LEAGUE CUP FINAL (Second Leg)
TUESDAY, 1st MAY, 1962
Norwich City v. Rochdale
PRICE 4d. EACH

THE FOOTBALL ASSOCIATION CHALLENGE CUP COMPETITION
FINAL TIE
BOLTON WANDERERS
v
MANCHESTER UNITED
SATURDAY, MAY 3rd, 1958 KICK-OFF 3 pm

EMPIRE STADIUM
WEMBLEY
OFFICIAL PROGRAMME · ONE SHILLING

MANCHESTER CITY F.C.
MAINE ROAD, MANCHESTER.
LEAGUE DIVISION 1 CHAMPIONSHIP
SATURDAY, 17th AUGUST 1968
Kick-off 3-0 p.m.
OFFICIAL PROGRAMME 1/-

op: **Rochdale were the first of our sides to compete in a League Cup final.** *Bottom left:* **The first FA Cup fina fter the Munich disaster.** *Bottom right:* **League Champions City v European Cup winners United.**

Top left: **Francis Lee celebrates scoring in City's 1968 title decider at Newcastle.**

Top right: **Matt Busby is delighted to bring the European Cup to Manchester in 1968.**

Left: **The Swinging Sixties arrives with two Manchester icons - George Best & Mike Summerbee - sat outside their city centre boutique.**

Top: **On 5th February 1974 a crowd of 588 saw Rochdale in their stylish kit take on Cambridge. This was a record low crowd, but power strikes had caused the game to be staged on a Tuesday afternoon.**
Bottom: **On the 100th anniversary of their 1903 record breaking FA Cup final score Bury finally get to display the trophy at Gigg Lane.**

Two FA Cup final balls (1956 & 1969) and six City FA Cup final shirts - 1955 (Ken Barnes, top left), 1934 (Ernie Toseland, top middle), 1981 (Paul Power, top right), 1956 (Ken Barnes, bottom left), 1926 (Sam Cookson, middle) and 1969 (Colin Bell, bottom right). Sadly, to date shirts from the 1904 & 1933 finals have not been located by City's museum.

Top: **A variety of player-worn shirts in United's museum. The Blue kit on the far right was worn by Brian Kidd in the 1968 European Cup final.**

Left: **City's Robbie Fowler and United's Gary Neville come face to face at Eastlands, 14th January 2006.**

Bottom: **the 2006-07 mini-derby between two teams formed by supporters - Maine Road FC V FC United of Manchester.**

Top: **End of the Road. Maine Road during demolition in 2004.**

Middle: **Old Trafford's North Stand seen shortly after the corner extensions in 2007.**

Bottom: **Michel Platini invites the author of this book to the UEFA Cup handover.**

BURY F.C.

FOOTBALL LEAGUE DIVISION II SEASON 1965-66

№ 177 **BURY v MANCHESTER CITY**

Tuesday, 12th April, 1966 Kick-off 8-0 p.m.

OFFICIAL PROGRAMME 6d.

SEASON 1966-67

GO GO GO COUNTY

FRIENDLY

FIXTURE

COMPLIMENTARY

STOCKPORT COUNTY

v

MANCHESTER CITY

EDGELEY PARK

WEDNESDAY, MAY 17

JOHN CROSSAN

Captain of Manchester City and Irish international inside-forward

Price - Threepence

FC UNITED
OF MANCHESTER

vs Eccleshall FC

INSIDE >>>
THE ROAD TO GIGG AND BEER > PHIL POWER
> LEEK MATCH REPORT > STUART BRENNAN

NOCHEX

OFFICIAL MATCH SPONSOR

CHAPTER NINETEEN

FRIDAY NIGHTS

Some people call some of our ideas gimmicks. I prefer to call them progressive ideas. We were first with the car stickers idea... and not long after the Manchester clubs followed suit. Stockport Chairman Vic Bernard, 1968

BY the late 1960s with both City and United finding major success, there was further pressure on all the less well supported sides of the region. Stockport County, after arriving in the Third Division, tried to accept that the lure of top flight football and the possibility of European success meant that fans would automatically go to City and United first. So rather than compete directly, County took steps to change the public perception of football. Roger Reade, who later became secretary at Doncaster Rovers, remembers County's initiatives:

"They invented Friday night football. Basically, they felt that City, United and I suppose the other First Division teams in the northwest would take their support so they decided to create something different. They came up with a slogan – Go, Go County – and they played matches on Friday nights. It proved very popular and other clubs copied. When I was at Doncaster we switched games to Friday nights for exactly the same reason."

To move fixtures to Fridays meant County had to pay a fee of £100 to the League for each game. It was a large amount but it was well worth it. Chairman Victor Bernard explained to journalist Peter Howard in 1969 that they had little choice:

"What else could we do? How should we have fared for attendances in 1967-68 with City and United doing incredibly well? There's probably only one other club in the country as badly placed geographically as us from the point of view of competition. That's

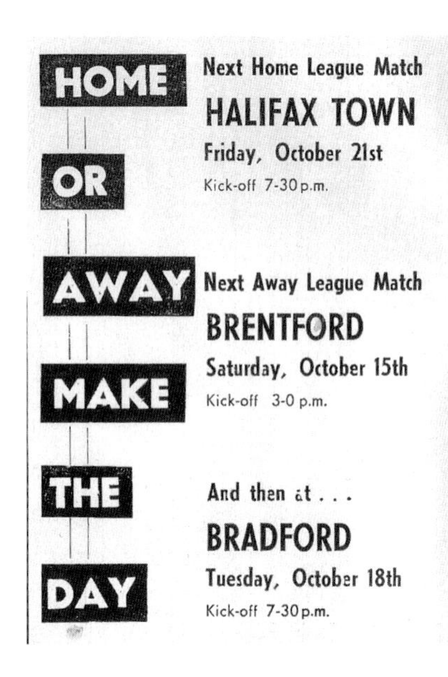

Tranmere, and at least there is the "wide end" of the Mersey between them and Liverpool - and a tunnel you have to pay to go through!

"It can be very hard work, but I've got a great bunch of people to work with, on and off the field. It is a pleasure to work with them, even when we have problems. When this sort of thing happens, it is up to us to get together, sit down and ask - why aren't we getting the crowds we need? Where are we going wrong?"

County goalkeeper Steve Fleet enjoyed the popularity and glamour of his side around this time:

"Everything seemed right at this time… the atmosphere, 'Go, Go, County', famous managers like Bert Trautmann, the television personalities coming to watch games – I think all the cast of Coronation Street were brought down by Victor Bernard. It was a great period when Stockport seemed to be at the centre of the Manchester scene."

In 1968 City won the League, United the European Cup but County's approach managed to ensure they were seen as a modern lively organisation. The Go-Go County slogan was a success, the social club was popular, and the club's bingo brought in £25,000 a year. County were seen as the type of club other lower division sides should emulate. Victor Bernard:

"We don't just copy people. If they have ideas which may be useful to us, fair enough, but we have come up with plenty of our own and shall continue to do so.

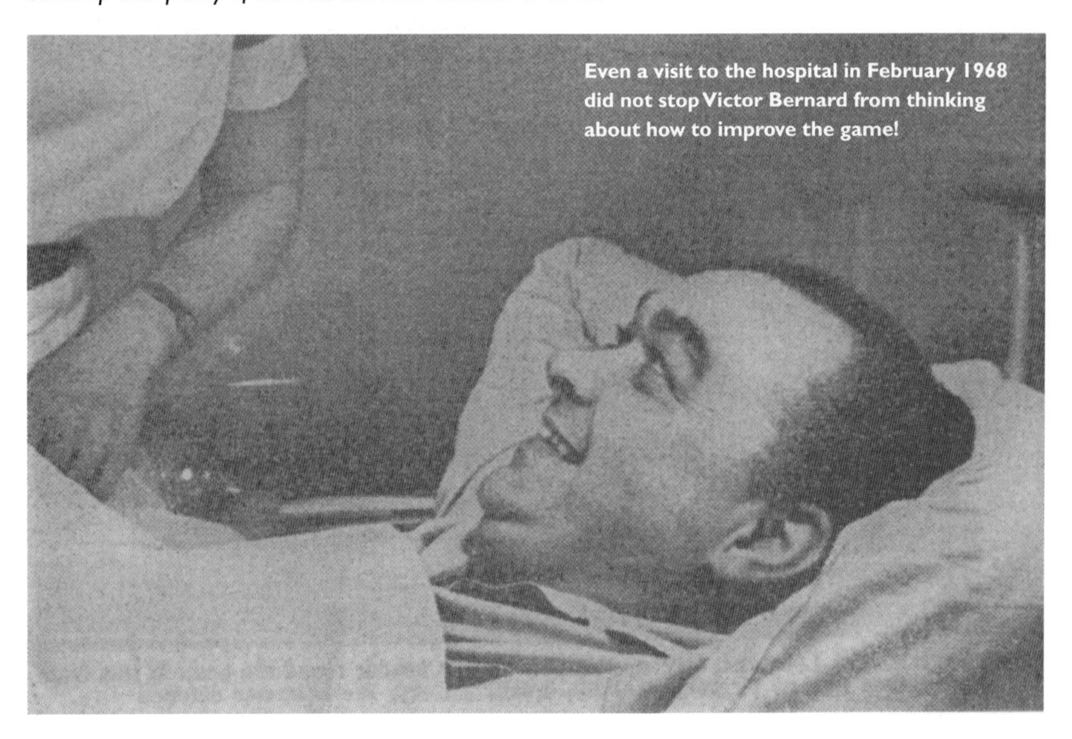

Even a visit to the hospital in February 1968 did not stop Victor Bernard from thinking about how to improve the game!

"The prime object of the social club, for example, is to make money, but we would not worry if it did not make a penny. If it does nothing more than break even the club is providing an extra facility for the fans - and this is the main thing.

"It is our duty to provide the goods for the public of Stockport first. It is our duty to attract them. We want to try and improve the team and facilities at the same time, step by step. The two go hand in hand, I believe. If we can provide all that we feel the people of Stockport deserve and want, and then we don't get the support we deserve, that is the time to worry about the town's reaction. If we want to give the Stockport people the best, then we must aim for the First Division. However, we want to be careful how quickly we get there. I believe it is possible to get to the top too quickly, as some clubs have discovered. If we can reach the top grade, we at County would want to be ready for it in every respect."

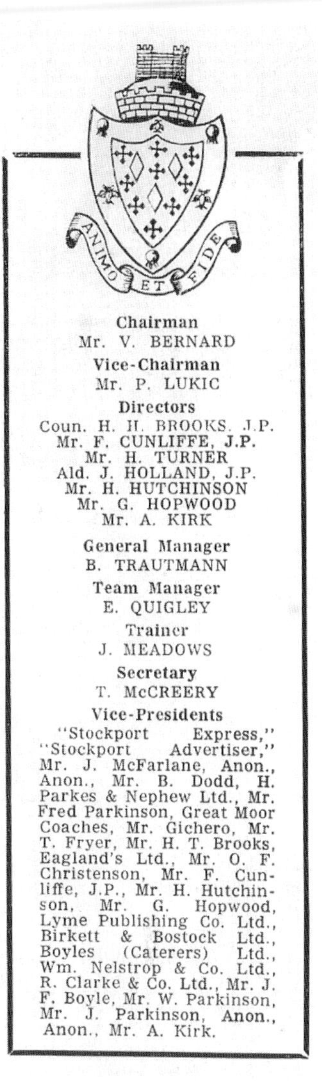
ANIMO ET FIDE

Chairman
Mr. V. BERNARD
Vice-Chairman
Mr. P. LUKIC
Directors
Coun. H. H. BROOKS, J.P.
Mr. F. CUNLIFFE, J.P.
Mr. H. TURNER
Ald. J. HOLLAND, J.P.
Mr. H. HUTCHINSON
Mr. G. HOPWOOD
Mr. A. KIRK
General Manager
B. TRAUTMANN
Team Manager
E. QUIGLEY
Trainer
J. MEADOWS
Secretary
T. McCREERY
Vice-Presidents
"Stockport Express," "Stockport Advertiser," Mr. J. McFarlane, Anon., Anon., Mr. B. Dodd, H. Parkes & Nephew Ltd., Mr. Fred Parkinson, Great Moor Coaches, Mr. Gichero, Mr. T. Fryer, Mr. H. T. Brooks, Eagland's Ltd., Mr. O. F. Christenson, Mr. F. Cunliffe, J.P., Mr. H. Hutchinson, Mr. G. Hopwood, Lyme Publishing Co. Ltd., Birkett & Bostock Ltd., Boyles (Caterers) Ltd., Wm. Nelstrop & Co. Ltd., R. Clarke & Co. Ltd., Mr. J. F. Boyle, Mr. W. Parkinson, Mr. J. Parkinson, Anon., Anon., Mr. A. Kirk.

County's officials as recorded in 1966.

Another side facing the problems of competition from the two First Division sides was Oldham Athletic. As with Stockport Oldham focused on bringing their brand of football into the modern era. Rather than moving games to Friday nights, Oldham concentrated on facilities and the social side. Journalist Peter Douglas had a walk around Boundary Park in 1969 and considered the quality of what he saw:

"Look around the Oldham club and you will be amazed at the facilities they have which rival any club in Division One. Chairman Massey is the first to admit that credit for this is due to former chairman Bates, but the problem as Massey sees it was a growth in facilities that was not accompanied by the support of a team or crowd potential to justify it.

"The ground itself presents an air of being well-kept and yet the cost of upkeep of the pitch and surrounding buildings is enormous. With a stadium that will hold 45,000 people and gates of some 4,000 each week, there is almost the same amount of work involved in maintaining the ground in a good state of repair as if they had capacity crowds every Saturday afternoon. The main stand has been completely re-seated and below it are some of the most modern dressing-rooms that can be found in .the country. Beneath the stand is a very attractive club bar and refreshment room and leading off this are private boxes which can be hired by the season. About half of these are occupied at present, but Oldham is the only club in the country, except Chelsea, that has gone in for this idea. The boxes themselves are very comfortable with private seats, private heating, a Tannoy system that gives the half-time and full-time results and refreshments are provided free of charge during the half-time interval."

Douglas was incorrect in his comment about the private boxes as Manchester United had erected boxes in their new United Road Stand in 1966, however it is true that Latics were ahead of most football clubs. As a comparison Liverpool and City did not install boxes until 1992 and

WHAT SOCCER MEANS TO ME

by the STARS of SHOWBIZ

AS KEN DODD

AS HIMSELF

I'M SOCCER DAFT

says Mike Yarwood

WHEN I PLAYED football as a boy I wanted to be a comedian; now I'm a comedian I'd like to be a footballer. That's why I'm so honoured to be honorary vice-president of Stockport County F.C., my home team.

I've been a fan of the "Lilly-whites" for twenty years and I'm hoping that before long they'll win promotion to the Second Division.

My father used to take me to Edgeley Park in the days of the old Third Division North. I was so small that I couldn't see much of the match and when the brass band came on at half-time I used to cry to go home. I was too small for the school soccer team but when I left school I applied to Stockport for a trial. They turned me down, but I did have a trial for Oldham Athletic. It was no good, I had to come to the sad conclusion that I would never be another Bobby Charlton.

I suppose we all yearn to be like someone we can't. Most people I come across in my career have a soccer idol; in fact, I think we're more conscious of the greatness of soccer stars than most people.

ALL-STARS

Since I've become an entertainer I've played a lot of charity Soccer with the Television All-Stars. I'm a utility forward and have scored quite a few goals in my time. Believe me, when I play opposite some real footballing stars, my day is made.

Earlier this year I had a great time when I did some training with Stockport County.

As an impressionist, I have to spend a lot of time in listening to voices of the famous and then studying their characteristics. I only wish I could study the footwork of Georgie Best and then copy it! But still, I'm not too bad on my impersonation of Danny Blanchflower!

Of course, being in the entertainment business makes Soccer watching difficult, particularly during a long pantomime season. During my last panto season in Coventry I longed to be able to pop along to see the Sky Blues in action, but work comes first. I dread to think of my frustrations if I go to Manchester for pantomime with City and United playing on alternate weeks!

But although I won't be able to watch the August and September games of Stockport County due to my Bournemouth summer season, I'll be there with my fiancée, Sandra, as soon as the final curtain comes down. My new role as honorary vice-president allows me to sit in the directors' box—a far cry from ten years ago when a policeman pushed me back behind the barrier.

RELAX–in the new season

WHERE DO Soccer players go in the summertime? Some go off on summer tours, either with their country or club. Some go off to faraway places such as Ghana or Zambia to coach the local, aspiring teams, or take an extended holiday at home or abroad.

But for Blackpool's tigerish, Scottish wing-half John McPhee there just *isn't* a close season.

On the Soccer field John is perhaps best-known for his tremendous work-rate. Just as the leopard cannot change his spots—John McPhee just can't switch-off his apparently limitless supply of energy when the final whistle blows.

Before he became a full-time professional (with Motherwell) he served a five-year apprenticeship as an engineer. After only two years as a full-timer he was transferred to Blackpool in 1962.

For once, the bright lights and garish palaces of this virtually non-stop home of fun—did not attract. Just married, he and his wife decided to budget for the future.

In a holiday resort such as Blackpool it was perhaps natural that they should take a small boarding house.

Only two years later they moved to a bigger, smarter private hotel on the north promenade and two years later again, they acquired the hotel next door, making the two into one.

Hence—immediately the Soccer season ends, along comes the summer holiday season, and John switches from taking the ball from attacking opponents, to providing the best in holiday fare for up to 120 guests at his Sheraton Hotel.

"It's not all glamour," he says. "In fact it is a lot of hard work, requiring long hours and a lot of tact. So much so that by the time the new season comes along I welcome it *as a relaxation*!"

If he looks after his guests as well as he *looks after* opposing forwards on the Soccer field he could easily become an hotel tycoon.

Twice "player of the year" at Blackpool, he is equally successful as "mine host."

The Sheraton is visible evidence of this.

Try this Middlesbro Goalagram

Using all ten letters of MIDDLESBRO, can you fill in the gaps in the words below. Then rearrange your four completed words into two familiar football phrases.

●EL●RIOU●

T●AI●

CR●W●

WE●●L●Y

Last week: Heading Duel; Home Defenders.

Mike Yarwood - One of Stockport's celebrity fans - featured in the early 1970s.

1993 respectively. Douglas was impressed with what he saw and he believed most of this credit was down to the administration team Chairman Massey had gathered around him, plus of course he was impressed with the Chairman himself:

"If you thought Ken Bates, former chairman of Oldham, was a forthright man, try talking to present man-in-charge Massey. He is an ex–builder, and as blunt a Yorkshireman as you could wish to find. He is now in his ninth year as a director of the club, and with young secretary Bernard Halford, the assistance of a small working committee formed from among members of the breakaway Supporters Club, the aid of a weekly prize bingo, the Golden Goal competition and hard work all round, Massey and his team are struggling to keep Oldham Athletic alive in one of soccer's most depressed areas.

"Almost a third of the cash brought in each week to help Oldham continue comes from sources other than gate receipts. These included a very successful football sweep with prize-money often over £300. A lot of hard work is being done on this by young club secretary Bernard Halford, who, Massey claims, works a seven-day week on behalf of Oldham Athletic. And the chairman himself distributes several hundred ticket books in the course of each week."

This team approach proved to be in contrast with what had gone before. Massey told Douglas:

"We are proud of the fact that we are a group of working directors and I mean work. Before, with Ken Bates as chairman and major shareholder, he took all the decisions. Now we get together and discuss things before any decision is made."

Incidentally, Oldham secretary Bernard Halford, in 2008, was still involved with football as Manchester City's club secretary – a position he has occupied since he arrived at Maine Road from Boundary Park in 1973.

ATTENDANCE DETAIL SEASON BY SEASON - 1967-1969

Season	City	United	Oldham	Bury	Stockport	Rochdale
1967-68	37223	57552	5745	8281	8237	2292
1968-69	33750	51169	3862	7765	7173	5399

LEAGUE POSITIONS SEASON BY SEASON - 1967-1969

Season	City	United	Oldham	Bury	Stockport	Rochdale
1967-68	1	2	60	46	57	87
1968-69	13	11	68	43	53	71

Mid-air meeting (above) between Tommy Taylor (Manchester United) and Alonso, during the first leg of the European Cup semi-final with Real Madrid, in Madrid. Right—dance of a 3–1 victory by Rial and Mateos, both of whom scored. Below, United players rush to acclaim Taylor after he had scored. The Madrid players are also rushing—to argue with the referee. He decided on a goal.

United were defeated 5-3 by Real Madrid on aggregate in the semi-final of the European Cup in 1957 - this was United's first season in the competition.

CHAPTER TWENTY

EUROPEAN COMPETITION

United started the second leg of the European Cup tie two goals down. They had been beaten 5-3 in Bilbao. Under the Maine Road, Manchester, floodlights they gave an exhibition that would have graced a novel. For 43 minutes, United's youngsters battled against tough, experienced opponents who, determined to hold on to their lead, waged a defensive battle. The scenes that followed were almost beyond description. The 65,000 onlookers gave United's players an ovation that has rarely been equalled anywhere 'Charles Buchan's Football Monthly', 1957

DURING the fifty years or so since European football competition was created, Manchester has managed to win four major European trophies. Manchester United were the first of the region's sides to compete in European competition, although initially they played their home games at Maine Road as Old Trafford did not possess floodlights at the time. This means that City's former ground was the first English venue to stage European Cup football.

The Reds became the first English side to enter the European Cup in 1956, although League Champions Chelsea had been invited to join the competition the previous season. The English footballing authorities put pressure on Chelsea not to take part, whereas when United won the title in 1956 they accepted the invitation to compete in the competition. Former United goalkeeper and trainer Jack Crompton recognises that this was not a popular move with the authorities:

"Matt took us into Europe against the wishes of the FA and the League. They did not want any of our teams in Europe and Matt went against their wishes. I think when it got to 1968 and we won the trophy I think part of our happiness was that Matt had been proved right."

The first competitive European match on English soil took place on 26th September 1956 with United at home to Anderlecht in the 2nd leg of the Preliminary round at Maine Road.

In total three United European matches were played at City's stadium. United had defeated RSC Anderlecht 2-0 in Brussels in the first leg of the Preliminary round and a crowd of forty thousand arrived at Maine Road for the return fixture on 26th September 1956. It was a wet and miserable night but a decent sized crowd made up of regular United fans and several neutrals keen to taste European soccer witnessed a goal-feast. Anderlecht, whose coach was Bill Gormlie a former schoolmate of former Blue Frank Swift, could not cope in the Manchester mud and rain and the Reds won 10-0.

In the next round (first round) Borussia Dortmund were defeated 3-2 at Maine Road before 75,598 fans. Again, as well as the regular Reds fans many neutrals attended as most Mancunians during this period were intrigued by the prospect of continental opposition and first class football under lights – the FA and League were still not entirely convinced that football should be played under lights and many clubs, including United, had not bothered to erect lights believing they would prove to be nothing more than a fad.

Busby's United drew with Dortmund in the second leg and the next round – the quarter-final – saw another 70,000 attend Maine Road. The Reds beat Athletico Bilbao 3-0 (6-5 on aggregate) but this was the last United home match to be played at the ground.

The attendances for the last two United European Cup matches at Maine Road remained the two highest home crowds United have experienced in European competition until the redevelopment of Old Trafford in the new millennium. In fact at the time of going to press the Dortmund crowd remains their highest home attendance in European competition (some 400 more than United attracted at Old Trafford for the visit of Lille in March 2007).

The Reds progressed to the semi-final of the European Cup in 1957 and faced Real Madrid. They lost the first leg 3-1 but chose to play the second leg at Old Trafford, hoping the move would build the atmosphere and excitement of the night. Floodlights had now been installed, but United could only manage a 2-2 draw in the second leg and were eliminated from the competition. Interestingly, the move back to Old Trafford backfired as the attendance was some way short of the previous home games at Maine Road. The attendance was 61,676 (according to the *Manchester United Pictorial History & Club Record*), but had the game been staged at Maine Road the stature of United's opponents and the importance of the fixture would undoubtedly have brought a significantly higher attendance – at least 75,000 - and potentially the atmosphere would have helped United to progress to the final.

Bobby Charlton's first European game was the 1957 semi-final second leg with Real Madrid. His last European game came twelve years later in the 1969 semi-final with AC Milan. Interestingly, he scored in both his first European game and his last.

The full record of United's first season in European Competition is:

Attendance	Date	Venue	Result	Round
35,000	12/9/56	Away	United 2-0 RSC Anderlecht	Preliminary
43,635	26/9/56	Maine Road	United 10-0 RSC Anderlecht	Preliminary
75,598	17/10/56	Maine Road	United 3-2 Borussia Dortmund	One
44,570	21/11/56	Away	United 0-0 Borussia Dortmund	One
60,000	16/1/57	Away	United 3-5 Athletic Bilbao	Qtr-final
70,000	6/2/57	Maine Road	United 3-0 Athletic Bilbao	Qtr-final
135,000	11/4/57	Away	United 1-3 Real Madrid	Semi-final
61,676	25/4/57	Old Trafford	United 2-2 Real Madrid	Semi-final

The Reds went on to compete in the European Cup the following season, and of course the tragedy of the Munich Air Disaster occurred during this run. According to many sources UEFA invited the Reds to compete in the competition in 1958-9, however the Football League blocked the move stating that only the League Champions should be allowed to compete in the competition.

On September 25th 1963 United played their first game in the European Cup Winners' Cup – a competition for the winners of Europe's major domestic cup competitions – and they reached the quarter final where they were defeated by SC Lisbon 6-4 on aggregate.

In 1964-5 the Reds competed in the Inter-Cities Fairs Cup – an early form of the UEFA Cup – and they reached the semi-final stage where they were defeated by Ferencvaros. The following season they returned to European Cup action again, reaching the semi-final stage again where they were defeated 2-1 on aggregate by Partizan Belgrade. Inevitably memories of the 1958 tie against Red Star Belgrade and subsequent disaster dominated thoughts.

After missing European competition in 1966-67, the Reds were back in 1967-68 and of course the side went on to become the first English side to win the competition when they defeated Portuguese side Benfica 4-1 at Wembley.

The game was watched by a crowd of 100,000 with a worldwide television audience estimated, by the BBC, at 250 million, and it is worth noting that Munich survivors Bobby Charlton and Bill Foulkes played in the final. United wore an all blue kit.

GORNIK ZABRZE
v
MANCHESTER UNITED
3-DAY
INCLUSIVE ARRANGEMENT
BY AIR FROM MANCHESTER
32 GNS.
For full details contact
GAYTOURS LTD
200
DEANSGATE
MANCHESTER
DEA 7795
WALLACE ARNOLD
TRAVEL LTD
152
ALEXANDRA RD
MANCHESTER
MOS 2402

Details of how fans could travel to United's 1968 quarter-final tie with Polish side Gornik.

The first half saw many negative aspects of play with a series of fouls. Busby later admitted:

"The first half was something of a let down, apart from a heart stopping moment when Eusebio let fly and his shot rattled the bar. A lucky escape. At half time it was still goalless, but eight minutes after the restart it was 1-0 for United with Bobby Charlton – not noted for heading the ball – nodding it home."

The score remained 1-0 until with only ten minutes to go Benfica stunned Wembley by netting an equaliser. Shortly afterwards striker Eusebio managed to break free of Nobby Stiles and blasted the ball goalwards. Busby:

"I was so certain it was going to be a goal that I was saying to myself 'oh no, not again!' I could see the European Cup being snatched from us as Eusebio escaped from Nobby Stiles for virtually the only time in the game. The ball left Eusebio's foot like a bullet from a high-velocity rifle."

Goalkeeper Alex Stepney made a great save and inevitably the game went into extra time. After only two minutes of additional play George Best put United ahead again, slipping round the keeper and gently tapping it over the line. One minute later United scored again with a header coming from Brian Kidd who was celebrating his 19th birthday. Then captain Bobby Charlton scored the third goal in eight minutes and the game ended in an emphatic 4-1 scoreline.

Understandably the media focussed on the feelings of Matt Busby and the memory of Munich. Potentially, his young 1958 side would have won the competition, and many of those players could possibly have been forces at Old Trafford all the way through to 1968. Busby told the media:

"They've done us proud. They came back with all their hearts to show everyone what Manchester United are made of. This is the most wonderful thing that has happened in my life and I am the proudest man in England tonight."

Matt Busby & Bill Foulkes, both Munich survivors, seen immediately after the 1968 success. The emotion is clear.

A decade later as he talked of the famous 1968 victory he admitted:

"Tears rolled down my cheeks as I embraced players, and there was a lump in my throat as I put my arms around Bobby Charlton. It had been a ten year trek from that snow swept airstrip to Wembley, but we had made it all the way and, ultimately, overcome heartbreaks and setbacks to score a decisive triumph. In a way, I felt drained."

Cup winner Pat Crerand enjoyed the game, but post-match he was unable to celebrate:

"Myself and Bobby Charlton had a couple of glasses of champagne, but it had been corked or something. It made us ill, so we couldn't go and celebrate. We missed the dinner! Bobby and I were the first up the next morning though!"

1968 – Manchester became the first British city to have two sides competing in the European Cup - City's Tony Book and United's Bobby Charlton show off their silverware.

City became the second Manchester side to compete in European competition when, as League Champions they entered the European Cup in 1968. This meant that Manchester became the first English city to have two sides competing in the competition – a feat no other city achieved until 1999-2000 when both Arsenal and Chelsea competed in the restructured Champions League.

In 1970 City became the second Manchester side to win a major European trophy when they found success in the European Cup Winners' Cup. The competition saw the Blues face Athletic Bilbao, SK Lierse, Academica Coimbra, Schalke 04, and Gornik Zabrze – Gornik had faced United in the 1968 European Cup quarter final.

The final saw them defeat Polish side Gornik 2-1 at the Prater Stadium in Vienna. However the match was not shown live on British television. This was an exceptionally unusual situation because, even in 1970, any European final would normally be broadcast. However, the FA Cup final between Leeds and Chelsea had gone to a replay – ironically at Old Trafford - and as that was being played on the same night the BBC covered it. ITV, the only other television channel at the time, were unable to broadcast the game live, and so only highlights late in the evening were shown.

In addition to the lack of television coverage there were issues with the venue itself. The Prater Stadium was, at the time, more or less totally open without shelter even for the directors, press and officials. As torrential rain came in bursts throughout the game it was not a pleasant night to either play or watch the game.

Manchester Evening News photographer Eric Graham remembered the weather in 2000:

"I worked for 37 years as a photographer for the MEN - and that was one game I will never forget, there was torrential rain throughout the game, and they only turned on two of the four floodlights for some reason (probably because there were only about 9000 fans in the stadium). The sports writers, in their posh sheepskin coats and expensive mohair suits were falling about laughing in the coach on the way to the stadium in the heavy rain, about how wet us poor 'snappers' were going to get - until they arrived at the ground and discovered that it had no roof! Still, the result was right, for a lifelong Blue - and completely unbiased journalist!"

Fans invade the Maine Road pitch after City's ECWC semi final success over Schalke 04 - the Blues won won 5-1 (5-2 on aggregate) on 15th April 1970.

Joe Mercer also sat in the rain: *"Managers, directors, press and fans alike had to brave the elements together in the open air. I had to sit there with rain running down my neck, my coat was saturated and my shoes were filled with water. But neither Malcolm Allison nor I would budge from that spot as we watched our players drive home their superiority."*

The game itself was very entertaining for those City fans who had made it to Vienna, with the Blues taking control from the start, although pre-match there had been some worries. Supporter John Jennings:

"There were some nerves going to the game, - Buzzer was out injured, Oakes was on pain killers and then Doyle went off injured. By half time we were two up, the first after some unbelievable skills from Franny Lee to set Young up."

As Jennings mentioned City did go two goals in front. Ronald Crowther of the **Daily Mail** reported the moment:

"When Young scored his goal it was only the culmination of 12 minutes of absolute dominance, and his breakthrough was the just reward for intelligent anticipation. Lee, playing with all the fire and fervour that will serve England well in Mexico, shook off three defenders out on the left and hammered in a shot of fearsome power. It struck the foot of the post and then cannoned off the legs of goalkeeper Kostka straight to Young, whose flick into goal was the merest of formalities."

Francis Lee grapples with fans to ensure he keeps hold of the Cup-Winners' Cup after City's success in the 1970 final.

The injury to Mike Doyle occurred only four minutes after the goal. He had badly damaged an ankle tendon in a collision with Florenski and was left in agony on the pitch for two minutes as play went on around him. After what seemed an eternity Austrian referee Schiller allowed City's trainer Dave Ewing on. Doyle was carried off the pitch on Ewing's shoulders as attempts to get a stretcher to him failed. The Blues played on for six minutes with only ten men as they tried in vain to get Doyle back to fitness.

Doyle was replaced by Ian Bowyer and City continued to dominate the tie, then three minutes before the interval Young attempted to dribble through the penalty area and was brought down in a sort of rugby tackle by the Gornik 'keeper. Schiller rightly awarded a penalty and Francis Lee sent a straight, hard shot into the net via Kostka's legs.

Gornik pulled a goal back in the 68th minute when a free kick led to Oslizlo cutting in from the left. He sent a left foot drive past Corrigan, but City remained in overall control against a team that contained seven international players.

At the final whistle the City fans, who numbered some five thousand in a crowd variously reported as anything from 7,968 to around 12,000, invaded the pitch. Supporter Martin Dodd managed to get hold of a special souvenir:

"The game was somewhat of a blur and I sheltered with my mum for most of the game to avoid the driving rain. My brother managed to get on to the pitch at the final whistle and was rewarded with Tommy Booth's shirt which we still have to this day."

In 2008 that shirt was on exhibition in the MCFC museum.

John Jennings was also celebrating of course:

"I happened to bump into Tony Heap, a lad I knew from my St Bedes days, who casually mentioned that he was working in Germany and was translating for City that night! Obviously I had to go for a drink with him after the game! That night turned into a supporters dream. Instead of dancing in the fountains of Vienna I got a taxi to the Schonbrunn Park Hotel, and sat there speechless as the team celebrated their win. At one point I was sitting at a table with Joe Mercer, his wife and top sports writer J L Manning, and into the small hours it felt unreal to listen to Allison, Lee and everyone else as they 'relaxed'.

"I couldn't resist getting a few autographs, - the back of my match ticket was signed by Mercer and

Tony Book brings home the trophy.

Allison, and a post card which I had written to my girlfriend in Leicester became much too valuable to post once it had the signatures of Bell, Lee, Summerbee, Mercer and Allison alongside mine!"

Afterwards the players and management focused on the support they had received from the likes of Jennings. Mercer: *"Our supporters, about 4,000 of them, stood in the pouring rain in Vienna to cheer us on. We are only sorry the rest of them were unable to watch on television."*

Lee: *"We were all thrilled with the fans. But for them there would have been no game at all."*

Vice-chairman Frank Johnson – the man who only 6 years earlier had suggested City merge with United - announced that the Blues were thinking about pulling out of Europe the following season as they were disgusted with the choice of venue:

"This was an absolute scandal. Our fans had to travel a thousand miles to be soaked to the skin. It came close to ruining the whole thing. A European final played before such a handful of people is ridiculous. And we're in the mood to pull out of Europe altogether if we do not get any satisfaction from UEFA. We could have packed 60,000 into Maine Road for this match. But as it is we have lost money on the tie."

He was right about the venue but the idea of pulling out of European competition was not one supporters would have supported. Later, back in Manchester after Malcolm Allison joked that *"Homecomings are becoming monotonous."* Johnson added *"Success is becoming monotonous"* and, even though this was clearly a joke, it was reported seriously in some newspapers.

In Vienna Malcolm Allison enjoyed the celebrations that followed:

"It was a great night. Perfect! Back at the hotel Harry Godwin, our Chief Scout, was playing the piano - all the old songs - while Francis Lee was on top, dancing away, in his underpants. It had to be seen to be believed. But that was the type of thing we did."

Back in England Allison entertained the fans. After hearing the supporters at Manchester's Ringway airport welcoming the team with a chant of *"We won the cup"* he responded with: *"We won another cup!"* Later he told the fans in Albert Square:

"We are the greatest club in Manchester. I am only sorry ladies & gentlemen that we were unable to win more than two cups this year. We decided to let a London club [Chelsea, FA Cup] win something for a change!"

After City's 1970 success, Manchester achieved little in Europe for some time. There were some great individual nights, most notably for City when they defeated AC Milan in 1979 (UEFA Cup) and for United when they came back from a 2-0 defeat at Barcelona to win 3-2 in 1984 (ECWC), but it was not until 1991 when the Reds won the ECWC that real European success was enjoyed. Of course the Heysel disaster of 1985 limited opportunities as English clubs were banned from Europe until 1990 and even then a reduced number of English clubs were admitted for several years.

In 1990-1 Alex Ferguson's United were only at the beginning of their development and entered the ECWC as FA Cup holders. The Reds were the first English side to be allowed back into European competition. A crowd of around 44,000 attended Feyenoord's De Kuip stadium for the final against Barcelona.

Johan Cruyff's Barcelona were regarded as one of the period's strongest sides and with no experience of Europe since 1985 United were expected to lose. Fortunately, the form book was thrown out of the window as United – most notably via Mark Hughes – won the match 2-1. Hughes had briefly been on Barcelona's books during the mid-eighties and the period was not a successful one, but back at Old Trafford Hughes was one of United's most successful and popular players.

Hughes seemed determined to prove from the start that he was at the top of his game and his wonderful attacking style caused Barcelona to play a more defensive game, however the Reds could not capitalise on this control until the 68th minute. Hughes was fouled on the edge of the box with Bryan Robson taking the resulting free kick. Steve Bruce sent a header downwards and Hughes sent the ball over the line.

Seven minutes later Hughes escaped the attention of the Barcelona defence and rounded 'keeper Zubizaretta. Many fans thought he had kept the ball too long and just when it looked like the opportunity was lost he blasted the ball goalwards at a very tight angle from about 20 yards out.

At 2-0 United seemed in total control but then four minutes later – and only eleven minutes from time - Barcelona pulled one back with a Koeman free kick. The final minutes were extremely tense and then as the game entered its final minutes Hughes came close to netting a hat-trick when he was pulled down on the edge of the box. Barcelona's Nando was sent off for the incident but United's chance to increase their lead passed.

In the final minute a poor back-pass from Steve Bruce caused Clayton Blackmore to make a dramatic goal line clearance from Michael Laudrup, but shortly afterwards the whistle went and United had won their second European trophy.

After 1991 United regularly entered European competition as a result of domestic trophy success and also following the changes to the format of European competition when an increasing number of sides were allowed to enter the European Cup, or Champions League, as it was now named. It was as runners up to Arsenal that United entered the 1998-99 European Champions League. This led to the biggest night in United's recent history.

In 1999 at Barcelona the Reds came back against Bayern Munich to win the European Cup and achieve the treble of League, FA Cup and European Cup for the first time. The game became a classic, although for United it certainly did not start that way.

As early as the sixth minute Bayern took the lead with a free kick from Mario Basler. As the game continued, Bayern had plenty of opportunity to increase their lead and only the good form of United 'keeper Peter Schmeichel prevented a second blow for the Reds. Late on an overhead kick from Carsten Jancker, direct from a corner, crashed off the crossbar and for a brief moment it felt as if luck was on United's side.

The Reds had a few chances to equalise but to be frank they seemed some way off seriously testing Bayern's 'keeper Kahn. Then with only around five minutes remaining the Reds began to look invincible.

The transformation came with the arrival of substitutes Teddy Sheringham and Ole Gunnar Solskjær. Several attacks came and then as the game moved into injury time, the fourth official indicated that three minutes would be played. This was when United became dangerous.

The Reds gained a corner causing 'keeper Peter Schmeichel to come forward as he often did in these never-say-die moments. He entered Bayern's penalty area as David Beckham played the corner in. It floated over Schmeichel's head and, after Bayern had failed to clear, it arrived at the feet of Ryan Giggs on the edge of the area. His right-footed shot was weak, but somehow it went straight to Sheringham. Sheringham swiped at the ball with his right foot and the ball ended in the net.

The goal gave United hope of extra-time, afterall there was hardly any time left and surely Bayern could not regain the lead, but then – less than 30 seconds after the restart – the Reds forced another corner. Fearing a Bayern break Schmeichel stayed in his own penalty area and left the outfield players to it.

Beckham again took the corner and this time Sheringham headed the ball downwards. Solskjær fired the ball into the roof of the Bayern goal and gave United a 2-1 lead. The player celebrated by sliding on his knees, mimicking Bayern's earlier celebrations, and was subsequently mobbed by the United players, substitutes and coaching staff. Schmeichel somersaulted!

Alex Ferguson celebrates United's 1999 Champions League success.

The game restarted with Bayern desolate and inevitably United managed to keep their lead until the final whistle. The presentation of the trophy was delayed partly for the erection of a stage on the pitch, partly for television advertising purposes, and partly because the Bayern Munich ribbons had to be removed and replaced with United's. United had come that close to losing the match, and none of the Bayern players could believe what they had experienced.

Reds fans spent the night celebrating along Barcelona's famous Ramblas and then, back in Manchester, the treble-winners' homecoming was recorded as the largest sporting celebration the region had ever known.

Alex Ferguson later said:

"It felt it was meant to be. The fact that it would have been Matt Busby's 90th birthday; the fact that we were playing Munich with everything that means to this club – people who believe in God might see a pattern in that. I mean, I believe, I pray a lot. You have that sense that it all has a meaning."

Most football fans acknowledged it was a major success and that the United side of 1998-99 was one of immense quality. Although a Nottingham Forest fan telephoned the BBC Radio Fivelive 'phone-in 606 to say:

"What've they done? They've just emulated us and won the European Cup twice! We won two European Cups in two years!" Fortunately, he was in the minority.

The following list shows the seasons in which Manchester's sides have competed in European competition:

SEASON	TEAM	COMPETITION
1956-7	United	European Cup
1957-8	United	European Cup
1963-4	United	ECWC
1964-5	United	Fairs Cup
1965-6	United	European Cup
1967-8	United	European Cup
1968-9	City	European Cup
1968-9	United	European Cup
1969-70	City	ECWC
1970-1	City	ECWC
1972-3	City	UEFA Cup
1976-7	City	UEFA Cup
1976-7	United	UEFA Cup
1977-8	United	ECWC
1977-8	City	UEFA Cup
1978-9	City	UEFA Cup
1980-1	United	UEFA Cup
1982-3	United	UEFA Cup
1983-4	United	ECWC
1984-5	United	UEFA Cup

SEASON	TEAM	COMPETITION
1990-1	United	ECWC
1991-2	United	ECWC
1992-3	United	UEFA Cup
1993-4	United	Champions League
1994-5	United	Champions League
1995-6	United	UEFA Cup
1996-7	United	Champions League
1997-8	United	Champions League
1998-9	United	Champions League
1999-2000	United	Champions League
2000-01	United	Champions League
2001-02	United	Champions League
2002-03	United	Champions League
2003-04	United	Champions League
2003-04	City	UEFA Cup
2004-05	United	Champions League
2005-06	United	Champions League
2006-07	United	Champions League
2007-08	United	Champions League

European Trivia

- On 28th May 2003 Old Trafford staged the European Cup final between Juventus and AC Milan. The game ended goalless and after extra time Milan won 3-2 on penalties in front of a crowd of 63,215.
- In 2006 City defeated competition from Turkey, Israel, and Germany to win the race to stage the 2008 UEFA Cup final.
- In 2007 prior to United's European Champions League tie with Lille, the French club hired restaurants at the City Of Manchester Stadium and over 400 fans enjoyed hospitality, a stadium tour, and a visit to City's museum as part of their preparations.
- As a result of their exploits in Europe United have also competed in the 'Super Cup' (winners in 1991) twice and the Intercontinental Cup/World Club Championship twice (winners in 1999, runners up in 1968).
- The highest attendance recorded at a game involving a Manchester side in Europe is 135,000 for Real Madrid V United in April 1957 (European Cup).
- Both City and United have attracted crowds of 100,000 or more for games against Gornik Zabrze in Poland. United attracted 105,000 in March 1968 (European Cup) while City were watched by 100,000 in March 1971 (ECWC).
- Both City and United have played English League sides in significant European competition. In 1971 the Blues were defeated 2-0 on aggregate by Chelsea in the ECWC semi-final. United have faced Tottenham (1st round ECWC 1963-4), Everton (3rd round Fairs Cup 1964-5), and Wrexham (2nd round ECWC 1990-91).

ATTENDANCE DETAIL SEASON BY SEASON - 1969-1974

Season	City	United	Oldham	Bury	Stockport	Rochdale
1969-70	33930	49862	4357	4512	3506	6109
1970-71	31041	43945	9546	3993	3271	4866
1971-72	38573	45999	8016	3502	2477	4387
1972-73	32351	48623	8256	2971	3728	3186
1973-74	30756	42712	10118	4879	2380	1891

LEAGUE POSITIONS SEASON BY SEASON - 1969-1974

Season	City	United	Oldham	Bury	Stockport	Rochdale
1969-70	10	8	87	63	68	53
1970-71	11	8	71	66	79	60
1971-72	4	8	55	77	91	62
1972-73	11	18	48	80	79	57
1973-74	14	21	45	72	92	68

CHAPTER TWENTY-ONE

GLAMOUR & GRIME

"I am delighted to be at Boundary Park, because this is a job which offers an excellent chance for success. From what I saw of Oldham last season I am optimistic. If we can put out a winning team and an attractive team, I am sure we can bring back supporters" Joe Royle, 1982

WHEN United won the European Cup in 1968 they possessed a great team approach, but in the years that followed the Reds gave the impression that the game was more about a group of individuals, particularly after Sir Matt Busby moved away from direct involvement with team matters. As a result United were unable to mount a serious challenge for the title despite having many gifted individuals, and by the end of the 1973-74 season they were relegated from the First Division.

To be relegated so soon after winning the European Cup – inevitably United were the first of the ten British sides who had previously found success in one of the major European competitions to be relegated - was a major shock. Tom Tyrrell, who had followed United for **Piccadilly Radio** during this period and was well known as a popular broadcaster, looked back on United's demise and their subsequent return in the **Piccadilly Radio Soccer Book**:

"Although the blow had already been struck elsewhere, to rub salt into United's wounds Denis Law had scored the goal against his old club which meant defeat at the hands of Manchester City and no chance of survival for the Reds.

"The fans stormed the pitch, the way they have done for years at the end of the season, but in 1974 the game was still in progress. Their action meant the eventual erection of fences at each end of the ground, it brought protests from all quarters, and there were even suggestions that United should be put into the Third Division and not the Second as a punishment!

"All that was forgotten a year later. This time, when the eyes of players and management moistened, they were crying tears of joy, not sorrow. On relegation day Tommy Docherty took me into the physiotherapy room to record an interview for Piccadilly Radio. To me this was a marvellous gesture by a man who was choked with sadness. He had taken Manchester United into the Second Division... his world had collapsed around him... and yet he wanted to speak to the fans on radio. This is what he had to say: 'I'm very upset for the lads and the club, and the spectators. Obviously it's a thing you never imagine can happen and now it has happened, and out of it I feel we've found for the future a very good side. In players like Daly, Greenhoff and McIlroy - and that's in no way being disrespectful to the other players - I feel we've three

players there who are going to be really great players. Players in the true Manchester United tradition, in the future'.

"How true those words turned out to be, as well as Doc's prediction that, 'We'll be back!'. Although United were to set the Second Division alight the following season, at that time a lot of people thought that the United manager was speaking words of bravery and hope, rather than giving a true reflection of his side's ability. The critics were still there last season, but United did plenty to keep them quiet."

United were promoted as champions of Division Two at the end of 1974-75 with Martin Buchan as captain and Tommy Docherty as manager. The following season the Reds momentum continued as they finished third, behind Liverpool and QPR in the First Division, and reached the FA Cup final. At Wembley, United were defeated by Second Division Southampton 1-0.

By the mid 1970s, football was a major industry and United could not afford to be out of the top division for long. With large support following them to every game they bounced back, and under Docherty were poised to challenge for success once more. Likewise City were a highly popular and significant side during a period when glamour seemed to be the major draw. The game had an incredible amount of media focus attached to it. It was no longer simply an activity enjoyed by working men on a Saturday afternoon, it was considerably bigger than that. Many footballers, such as George Best and Rodney Marsh, were treated like glamorous popstars and the game seemed to match the excitement of the period, but the mid-Seventies were also a turning point in supporter behaviour and attitude to the game.

City found success in the 1976 League Cup final, winning the trophy with a memorable overhead kick from Dennis Tueart, after an earlier goal by PFA Young Player of the Year Peter Barnes. The award brought much attention 19 year old Barnes' way:

"I can laugh about this now but at the time it was painful. At the awards I was sat with a couple of the other City players but we also shared a table with a few United men – I couldn't understand that at the time! The guys on our table were telling me I had a good chance of winning and I remember Tueart saying that I had to thank so and so – the list kept growing. When it was announced that I'd won I got up, still with the lads telling me to say this and say that, and as I collected the award from Dickie Davies I was worrying about what to say. I started my speech: 'My Lords, Ladies, and Gentlemen…' I looked around the room and saw there were no ladies. Great start! Then I said: 'I'd like to ah… ah… ah...' I froze!

"Funnily enough the Liverpool players were just in front of me and I remember Kevin Keegan urging me to just say anything. I eventually thanked someone – the players I think – and then I went back to my seat. It was the most frightening experience of my life at the time!

"I got more fan mail that week than at any other time, but it was all from mothers. My own mum thought the volume had gone on her telly! When we played United some time later the Stretford End teased me mercilessly with 'Barnsey, Barnsey, give us a speech… I'd like to ah… ah… !'."

Barnes' memories of that time also show the great rivalry that existed between Blues and Reds and the other teams in the region. The banter from the Stretford End and from the Kippax at Maine Road livened up games and, although sometimes it overstepped the mark, it was always typical of Manchester and Mancunian life at the time. In later years it became harsher and more hurtful, and the Seventies was probably the decade when the transformation most occurred.

In 1996 supporter Harry Hughes, born in August 1902, remembered the rivalry from his childhood:

A very important moment in Manchester football - Denis Law leaves Maine Road on 26th August 1974. This was the date Law retired from football. Many people incorrectly believe that Law retired immediately after the 1974 derby match at Old Trafford. In fact Law's last first team game was actually for City against Oldham on 10th August 1974 in the Texaco Cup. Four days earlier he scored his last first team goal when the Blues faced Sheffield United in the same competition.

"There was a derby game in 1921 at City's old Hyde Road ground and the groundsman arrived very early, about 7am. I don't know why, but it was fortunate he did because all the railings that went around the pitch used to be blue and white, but on this day some United fan had broken in and painted them all red and white – imagine that at City's ground! It seems that he'd got in in the middle of the night. Well, City weren't having that and by the time of kick off the club had painted them all blue and white again! It caused a great deal of merriment in the crowd. The rivalry was friendly then, but we were still rivals! Arguments used to happen of course, occasionally a scuffle, but that was it. You'd certainly never get a player going into the crowd attacking them of course."

By the late Seventies, the abuse flying between the sides was intense and derby day began to take on a different edge. The United relegation, followed by the November 1975 injury to Colin Bell sustained during a tackle by Martin Buchan, both caused the relationship to turn nasty but the situation worsened with the general development of hooliganism and violent activity. Watching football matches became a more tribal event than at any other point in football's history and inevitably the relationship between the supporters of Manchester's sides became more negative. During the early to mid-seventies United fans, in particular, were gaining many negative headlines, and Old Trafford became the first League ground to have perimeter fencing installed to help control fans.

WINNERS EUROPEAN CUP WINNERS' CUP 1970
WINNERS F.A. CHALLENGE CUP
1904, 1934, 1956, 1969
FINALISTS F.A. CHALLENGE CUP
1926, 1933, 1955
LEAGUE (1ST DIVISION) CHAMPIONS
1937, 1968
RUNNERS-UP 1904, 1921
WINNERS FOOTBALL LEAGUE CUP 1970
LEAGUE (2ND DIVISION) CHAMPIONS
1899, 1903, 1910, 1928, 1947, 1966
RUNNERS-UP 1896, 1951

TELEPHONE Nº 061-226 1191/2 TELEGRAPHIC ADDRESS: "FOOTBALL MANCHESTER 14"

MANCHESTER CITY FOOTBALL CLUB LIMITED

REGISTERED IN ENGLAND REGISTERED NUMBER 12272

President: J. F. SMITH *Chairman:* P. J. SWALES
Vice-Chairman: S. H. CUSSONS *Directors:* J. J. H. HUMPHREYS
S. S. ROSE, M.B., F.R.C.S. A. E. ALEXANDER, M.S.I.A. R. HARRIS
I. L. G. NIVEN C. B. MUIR

REGISTERED OFFICE & GROUND
MAINE ROAD
MOSS SIDE
MANCHESTER
M14 7WN

TEAM MANAGER:
A. K. BOOK

SECRETARY:
J. B. HALFORD

12th November 1975

Master Peter Godlin
35 Holcombe Lee
Holcombe Brook
Bury
Lancashire

Dear Peter,

Thank you for your letter, which I have read with interest and fully appreciate.

I agree with your fathers' statement regarding Francis Lee but unfortunately Francis could not understand that there were certain things I felt had to be upheld in the club, and however hard I tried to dissuade him from leaving he would not 'give way'.

Kind regards and all good wishes.

Yours sincerely,

Tony Book

Tony Book (Team Manager)

AKB/JMcC

A fairly frank letter to a young supporter from City manager Tony Book on why Francis Lee left the Blues.

The glamour of Seventies football on the pitch contrasted sharply with the behaviour off it, but for some fans these were the most exciting days to support their club. Not every fan was involved with hooliganism and disruptive behaviour but the atmosphere was intoxicating.

For actor Christopher Eccelston the general mood at United was a major part of the experience. He told the **Observer** in 2002:

"People these days won't appreciate it but for many years after [United's 1974 relegation] United were the underdogs, until we finally won the League in 1993. Us being the underdogs was one of the attractions of supporting United in the Seventies and Eighties. City always turned us over; we were the joke of Manchester. We have enjoyed our success in the Nineties because it took so long to come."

Although Eccelston did not mention fan behaviour, it was a fact that United fans had hit the headlines at the relegation derby of 1974 when supporters invaded the pitch with the aim – or so the media claimed at the time – of getting the derby match abandoned. United were relegated that day, but in truth they would ultimately have faced the drop even if they had achieved a victory over City. The pitch invasion – actually there were two that day – caused the media to focus on the behaviour of supporters and United suffered as a result.

By the time of United's promotion in 1975 the situation was still difficult, despite the fencing in of United fans. A quick review of the headlines documented in the **Rothmans Yearbook** for the opening months of the 1975-76 season show several mentions of the behaviour of United's fans:

19th August – *"United win 2-0 away at Birmingham. Stepney is taken to hospital during the match with a dislocated jaw – reportedly sustained while shouting at a team mate! 26 United supporters are arrested."*
30th August – *"Other trouble spots are Stoke, where there are 60 arrests – the visitors being Manchester U."*
11th September – *"It is announced that there will be a train and bus strike in West London on Saturday as a defensive measure against the invading Manchester U fans on their way to QPR."*

Hooliganism tended to follow the club throughout the mid-70s and whether relegation in 1974 had exacerbated the problem is not known, but the problems continued for several years. In 1976-77 violence occurred regularly. United's trip to Norwich on 2nd April 1977 was typical. The Reds lost the game and the **Rothman's Football Yearbook** for 1977 looked back on the season and recorded:

"Manchester United fans provoke fights at Norwich and Tommy Docherty intervenes personally to calm the situation. Afterwards he says that these hooligans bring shame to the club and the birch should be reintroduced by the Courts to punish them sufficiently."

Four days later **The Daily Mail**, with the opening line of *"Unprecedented measures to beat soccer violence are introduced, with positive action against the notorious hooligans of Manchester United"*, covered the problem in detail and revealed the news that Bristol City were to ban United fans from their ground. Sports Minister Denis Howell said hooligans would be banned – once caught – and United manager Docherty felt Howell's recommendations were not 'tough enough'.

These headlines give an indication of the coverage and, although there is no mention of the region's other clubs, it is true that incidents such as these were starting to appear at most grounds. At City, 1975-6 was the first season in which the large Kippax terracing was segregated by an iron fence from the back of the terracing to the bottom. The fence was placed roughly a third of the way along from the Platt Lane end of the stand. The visitors stood close to Platt Lane, while City fans were housed in the rest of the stand.

During 1975-6 formal segregation at Maine Road was used selectively. The 27th September 1975 derby match was the first fixture in which it was impossible to walk from one end of the stand to the other. The initial barrier barely kept fans apart, and meant home and away supporters could position themselves within a yard of each other. It was still an improvement on previous years when temporary barriers were utilised for derby games at City.

A derby day regular Tony O'Grady talked of the situation at City-United fixtures in 2002:

"When City and United played at Maine Road in the Sixties and early Seventies it was sometimes decided to separate the fans by putting a rope from the back of the Kippax to the front wall. Police manned the rope to separate the fans, but it was hardly the best segregation. I suppose it worked to some extent. But there were a lot of odd scenes. I remember that when United were winning by two goals in a derby a City fan couldn't take it any more and just jumped over the segregation and into the United area. A couple of minutes later he was stretchered out! At another derby the United fans were throwing acid bottles into the Kippax. It was a real battlefield at times."

In 1975-76 City did not want to segregate at all and after the derby segregation was only used for the visit of Leeds on Boxing Day; followed by Aston Villa (7th February 1976), and Everton

(21st February 1976). Interestingly, fixtures which a decade later would be viewed as high risk matches – Newcastle, Burnley, Tottenham, Birmingham, and West Ham – were not deemed enough of a risk to insist on formal segregation. Of course throughout the sixties and seventies supporters at all grounds did initiate their own unofficial form of segregation.

By the start of the 1976-7 season fencing at the front of the Kippax was also a permanent fixture, however fencing behind each goal did not seem a concern at City for some time. The perception was that the rowdier element would only ever watch games from the Kippax terracing, however an incident in the UEFA cup tie with Widzew Lodz on 14th September 1977 shattered that illusion. Basically a fan from the North Stand attacked Widzew's Boniek after the player had scored. The incident had major repercussions for the club.

Firstly UEFA fined the Blues £400 then 19 year old supporter George Beddows was found guilty of using threatening, abusive and insulting behaviour. He was fined £100 and the club banned him from Maine Road, but City were also instructed to erect fencing behind both goals. Initially, the club in consultation with the police and local authority erected the fencing for only high profile fixtures, but as time went by the fences became a permanent barrier between the players and the fans.

When Beddows was found guilty City were keen to publicise the event, hoping it would act as a deterrent. Bernard Halford said at the time:

"We trust that our supporters will take notice of this case, what it has resulted in for the individual and the club, and realise that at all times it has got to be important to uphold the very good name which Manchester City have got.

"Believe me, we are totally aware of the great effort made by the fans to support City and we are delighted with the numbers who turn up on the Kippax and follow the team away from home. But we have to make every effort to reduce trouble, provocation and make the ground a place where any person is proud to come. I have been asked to implore the City fans to cut out the abusive language. It is doing no good for the club and is often at the root of troubles by its very provocative nature. We can do without it and if the fans responsible feel anything for the club they claim so strongly to support, then they will listen to this appeal."

As Old Trafford had terracing on all four sides, fencing was more obvious and many images from the period show young Reds supporters with their red, white and black bar scarves tied to their wrists peering through the fencing. The football on the pitch at most leading grounds in the Country was perceived as being glamorous and of a very good quality, but the experience of watching games for those on the terraces was not a comfortable one. Supporters who first enjoyed the game from the terraces during this era talk affectionately of the experience, and it is clear that for many the tribalism of the game and the camaraderie developed behind the fences added to the experience. The noise, fervour, passion of the Stretford End, the Kippax, the Chaddy End or any of the other more vocal parts of the region's grounds gave supporters their identity and the enforced segregation added to this experience. United supporters still talk affectionately of the power of the Stretford End; City fans boast about the fact that their vocal fans had an entire side, not 'just' an end, and throughout the Seventies and Eighties these spaces became the place to be for the most dedicated of home fans. You were not a true Red unless you experienced the Stretford End.

As time moved on segregation caused other areas of grounds to become passionate spaces – K Stand at Old Trafford was positioned directly behind the away fans terracing, so those wanting to bait fans would sit there. Similarly at City the Platt Lane Stand housed members of the City 'Cool Cats' for a while (a forerunner of the Young Governors). Although the Blues were well established as more of a community club than United, and had already created highly popular organisations such as the Junior Blues and the Social Club, City possessed several hooligan gangs who over time would gain headlines for their activities.

United's hooligan elements were usually simply branded 'The Red Army' by journalists of the period. Inevitably, there were individual groups such as the Cockney Reds and a group known as the Mancs – rivalry existed between the Mancunian Reds and those from outside the region - but as far as the media were concerned any bad behaviour occurring at a United game was carried out by the 'Red Army'.

Hooliganism affected football throughout this period, and grounds did become fortresses. It took the disasters at Bradford (1985) and Hillsborough (1989) to force changes in the treatment of spectators, however the seating of supporters in the top division since 1994 has seriously affected the atmosphere at all grounds. Old Trafford became a shadow of itself, even when over 76,000 were present in 2007-08, with few games generating the atmosphere experienced in the Sixties and Seventies. Peter Barnes, who ultimately would play for both City and United remembers the atmosphere when he made his debut in October 1974. Barnes came on as substitute for City in a League Cup tie at Old Trafford:

"United won 1-0 through a penalty – Jeff Clarke was adjudged to have handled - and Arthur Albiston also made his debut. I came on for Glyn Pardoe and I suppose my main recollection is of the noise generated by the crowd. There were 55,000 there and City fans had the whole of the Old Trafford Scoreboard End. It was a great sight, but coming on for the first time was a little frightening. I remember shouting for the ball and no one hearing me because of the intense atmosphere. I soon realised there was no point shouting."

Crowd safety was a very serious issue for all the region's grounds however there were various times when the safety of spectators took a backseat. Sometimes this was simply because it was not perceived as an issue, for example during the pre-World War Two period when supporters were packed in for big games. Modern day images of football support during that time show groups of happy flat-cap wearing fans. They rarely show photos of disgruntled fans. Even the scenes at Wembley's first cup final in 1923 focus on the role of one white police horse controlling in excess of 120,000 people. The impression is given that fans were easily controlled, but this is not accurate. The Wembley crowd for instance was controlled by many mounted policemen – black and white footage does not easily pick out the darker horses – while fans at all grounds would on occasion break down gates to get in to watch their team. The smaller grounds of the region, and also City's old Hyde Road ground and United's Bank Street venue suffered at the hands of determined fans on several occasions. At Hyde Road gates were smashed open in 1920 for a crucial game with Burnley, while other supporters climbed in to the ground via ropes from terraced houses on Bennett Street – the houses backed on to the Popular Side terracing.

Old Trafford and Maine Road however were much less easy to get in to. In fact during the 20s and 30s the problems of both venues were all about capacity management rather than lock-outs. At United in 1928 Huddersfield faced Sheffield United in the FA Cup semi-final before a crowd of

69,260. This was some way short of the ground's record which, at the time stood at c.73,000 for a cup tie between Bolton and Sheffield United in 1923, but control of fans was a substantial issue. There had been terrible crowd control problems with supporters taking to the pitch on several occasions to avoid crushing. The game itself could not start until the pitch had been cleared by police horses. The journalist Adjutant had been particularly critical of the organisation and as a result Maine Road was to stage the second replay between the same two sides (the first replay went to Goodison and was watched by 53,749). The second replay was supposed to be going to Old Trafford but the scenes caused a re-think. In the end 69,360 attended the Maine Road match.

At City, the provincial record crowd of 1934 became famous in some quarters because fans said they 'got in but couldn't get out', suggesting that the stadium was too overcrowded. Little was said nationally about crowd control then on 9th March 1946 the Burnden Park disaster saw 33 spectators die in a crush. According to the **Manchester Evening News** this was the result of around 200 to 300 people, many of whom were servicemen, charging through a gate to gain admittance. Perhaps as an indication of the general view of the period, it is worth highlighting the newspaper comment:

"Possibly the war has left some people with less respect for law than they used to have."

Naturally, an enquiry followed and clubs were forced to consider safety. Capacities were more sensibly calculated and applied but little else changed until the advent of hooliganism in the Sixties and beyond. The whole dynamic of watching football on the terraces in the region changed as a result of enforced segregation. In many ways separating the fans increased the territorial chanting and view that the terraces were a battleground. Supporters on either side of the segregation fence would throw items over the divide at their opponents – these could be anything but typically items such as stones, darts, socks filled with material, and coins – and supporters on both sides of the divide would be injured. Some would be innocent victims, while others would see it as a battle wound.

While this was going on the police would man the segregation line looking for potential trouble makers and trying to keep the peace. Often the police would move into the ground and remove supporters they felt were guilty in some way. At United the Scoreboard Paddock became the away section, and simply because of its position it was easier for the police to man the two segregated fences at either end. Often a paddock would be left empty to allow a large buffer zone between away fans and United supporters however the biggest issue tended to come from those sat behind the away section. For several games, particularly derby matches, opposition fans would sit directly behind their fellow supporters stood in the paddock, but if away 'seated' support was small (or United reduced the number of seat tickets) those sat behind the paddock would be United fans. This added a different dimension to segregation and caused objects to be thrown from the seats on to those below.

At City pitch invasions after a number of high profile games, most notably Luton in 1983, Charlton in 1985 and Sunderland (Full Members' Cup) also in 1985, had caused the club to increase fencing around the entire stadium. The whole of the original 1923 white perimeter wall was topped with a perimeter fence and viewing was severely restricted. At times in the early eighties fencing had been erected in front of the Platt Lane and North Stands for high profile matches – again City were reluctant to make it permanent – but the Blues were forced to make this permanent over time. Then in December 1985 City took the amazing approach of devoting the entire front page of their match programme for a game with Coventry to the Situation. Under the heading **"A Major Concern"** the club stated:

"Fencing has been re-inforced and been built to a height of 2.4 metres. If this is not effective then we may well have to increase the fencing height to 4.4 metres (around 14 feet). And if there are still 'fans' who consider this a challenge to be scaled then the height will be increased yet again.

"We have also been warned that any breach of the fencing perimeter will result in additional modifications being needed and the top of the fencing will have to be raked back to provide an even greater obstacle to would-be invaders. But who wants to be caged-in to watch a football match."

This unusual step was perhaps an over-reaction by City but with City Chairman Peter Swales being an influential member of the FA at this stage in his life, it was very important for the Blues to be seen as taking a stand.

None of the sides in the Manchester region were the worst in football but they tended to get headlines either because of their own profile, their outspoken directors, or simply because of the large media interest in the region. In 1980 Oldham hit the headlines when Sheffield Wednesday fans invaded the Boundary Park pitch after Wednesday's Terry Curran was sent off. The game was halted for 29 minutes and the media immediately claimed a 'riot' had taken place. A full enquiry followed and the FA commission ultimately blamed Wednesday for not being able to control their fans, as they felt that Boundary Park's safety and security was more than adequate.

By the summer of 1985 the situation across football was grave. The Heysel disaster, rioting at Luton and at Birmingham, and many, many other stories of football violence made the Government determined to act. Even the Bradford fire was often lumped into debates about crowd control with some politicians and other non-footballing people talking of the fire as being the result of hooligan actions – there was talk of flares being fired into the stand but these comments were totally out of context with what actually happened.

Margaret Thatcher's Government insisted on the game taking action and membership schemes and increased fencing became the norm, but still more was demanded. The former Oldham Chairman Ken Bates was by this time Chairman at Chelsea and he seemed to be one of the more vocal footballing figures. He suggested that fans needed to be treated like animals and he went on to install an electric fence. Football fans were horrified, but others were not. Others felt this was an appropriate reaction. Fortunately Bates, who by 2007 was Chairman of Leeds United, did not turn the electric fence on, but it was clear the view across Britain was that the English League clubs had to increase segregation, fencing and security. All fans were labelled trouble-causers.

Supporters started to respond to the negativity by publishing their views and the fanzine industry was created, but on the terraces supporters were continually viewed as unruly animals at all grounds.

As the atmosphere at football grounds worsened, supporters of all types started to come together. The fanzine movement helped enormously while cross-club supporter organisations started to be formed. In addition, the inflatable banana craze started. A City fan called Frank Newton was widely acknowledged as starting the craze when he took an inflatable banana to Boundary Park for the Oldham-City fixture of August 1987. The game was played in torrential rain, the City fans were drenched, morale was low as Oldham equalised, yet the banana was waved throughout. It brought much needed humour to what was otherwise a depressing day.

By Christmas 1988 the banana craze had become a major national story. At Maine Road the number of inflatable bananas and other objects increased game after game with the largest display of inflatables coming at Stoke on Boxing Day 1988 when City fans travelled in fancy dress, and the players entered the field carrying inflatables which they threw into the crowd – City lost the match 3-1!

Other clubs followed the trend with United fans carrying inflatable Devil forks but at Oldham the Latics managed to make a bit of cash following a game with City. City's General Manager, and ex-Latics boss, Jimmy Frizzell objected to Oldham's negative tactics and called them 'yard dogs'. Immediately, the Oldham supporters adopted the name, placing it on flags, and they also carried inflatable dogs to matches. Oldham manager at the time Joe Royle remembers it well:

"We laughed at that. The Commercial manager went out and bought 2,000 inflatable dogs! You then saw the strange sight of grown men walking down the street with inflatable dogs under their arms. The comment didn't bother us at all. I think if you'd have asked Jim half an hour later he wouldn't have said it, but he said it straight after the game. That was his problem. We laughed, though! The Oldham lads took the name to their hearts and it became a nice little earner for the club."

The inflatable craze was a nice diversion, however it did help to get the message across that football fans were not all hooligans. This was something the Government found hard to accept at the time. Then in April 1989 tragedy struck in Sheffield when football faced one of its blackest days – the Hillsborough disaster occurred. The whole question of perimeter fencing and other initiatives such as membership schemes was reviewed. Clearly, the disaster was a major tragedy but it did have the effect of making the authorities talk and ultimately the decision was taken that fencing had to come down. Naturally, this impacted every ground in the region. It took several years for the fences to be totally removed but immediately steps were taken to provide easier access to the pitch in case of disaster.

At Old Trafford – the venue which staged the replayed Liverpool-Nottingham Forest semi-final – perimeter gates were left open, as they were for City's promotion match at Bradford City of the final day of the 1988-89 season. But the biggest change for all major venues was the insistence that standing had to be banned from the top division by the start of the 1994-5 season. The ban would ultimately be phased in for second tier clubs, but as the nineties started it was clear football would change forever for the majority of attending fans.

From a safety point of view, although crowd violence and hooliganism is still present within the game, the actions of the football authorities and the clubs in recent years has been on prevention of trouble rather than reaction to incidents.

Back on the pitch, the Seventies and to some extent the Eighties were a glamorous period. City challenged for the League title on several occasions during the Seventies and in 1976-77 they missed the title by a point – while United managed to finish second in 1980 and 1988. In addition, both sides reached FA Cup finals. The Blues competed in the 100th FA Cup final where they faced Tottenham and were unfortunate to draw 1-1 via an own goal from cult hero Tommy Hutchison. They lost a highly entertaining replay 3-2 and in the years that have followed the story of Tottenham's Ricky Villa has tended to dominate discussions of the final, however City fans rightly point out that the replay contained several great goals, including an amazing volley from Steve

Mackenzie. Villa himself commented at Tottenham's 25th anniversary celebrations that Mackenzie's goal was the type of goal that should have won the final.

The *Daily Telegraph* report of the game tended to focus more on the role of Spurs however:

"Ricardo Villa, who left the pitch in tears on Saturday after being substituted in the 100th FA Cup final, returned to Wembley to score twice and earn Tottenham victory in a hard, exciting replay. After the bearded Argentinian had given Spurs an early lead, Manchester City fought back to equalise, then move in front. But a goal from Crooks and a sensational winner from Villa maintained Spurs' record of never losing a domestic Cup final.

"When Villa was substituted by young Garry Brooke midway through the second half in the first match, with Spurs a goal down, he must have thought his season was over. But Hutchison, who had scored City's goal, deflected a Hoddle chip into his own net to afford Spurs a replay. Manager Keith Burkinshaw showed great courage in keeping faith with Villa for the return, and the Argentinian repaid him by sweeping a loose ball into the net after only seven minutes. Young Steve Mackenzie equalized for City three minutes later with a spectacular volley from 22 yards out, and they went ahead after the interval when Reeves converted a penalty. Spurs were regretting their earlier misses now, but they continued to play good football and press forward, with the other Argentinian, Ardiles, and Hoddle running the midfield. It was a typical piece of Hoddle flair that led to their equaliser after 70 minutes, as he flicked the ball up and over the advancing City defence for Archibald to lay on Crooks's goal. The dramatic winner came seven minutes later. Villa got the ball on the left and began to run powerfully at the City defence. They held off, but he beat one man after another before cutting inside and ham-mering the ball past Corrigan. It was a fitting climax for what had become a classic Cup final."

Across Manchester Tommy Docherty guided United to the FA Cup final in 1976 (losing to Second Division Southampton), and 1977 (defeating Liverpool 2-1), however an affair with the wife of physio Laurie Brown caused the United board to dismiss their manager in July 1977 – just two months after FA Cup glory. Docherty told reporters:

"I've been punished for falling in love. This is the most shattering experience of my football life."

The manager's departure caused the board to bring in a new man – Dave Sexton. Sexton had found success at Chelsea, winning the FA Cup and ECWC (beating holders City in the semi-final), but at Old Trafford the best he could manage was a second placed finish (1979-80) and a cup final appearance in 1979 (losing to Arsenal in a thrilling game). Under their next manager, the flamboyant Ron Atkinson the Reds won the FA Cup twice - 1983 (defeating Brighton in a replay) and 1985 (beating Everton in the game which saw United down to ten men following the sending off of Mark Hughes) – and they also mounted several challenges for the title.

By 1986 the title was the one trophy the Reds were desperate to win. They had seen Liverpool dominant for most of the period since they had last won the Championship and they had also watched enviously as smaller teams such as Derby (twice champions during the 70s), Leeds (champions in 1969 & 1974), Nottingham Forest (1978) and Aston Villa (1981) had all won the title. Forest and Villa had also gone on to win the European Cup, while Arsenal, Everton, and City had all won the Championship in the years that followed Busby's 1967 success.

With the title becoming the only trophy the Reds were desperate to win at this point pressure seemed to mount. As a result Ron Atkinson was dismissed in 1986 and replaced by Alex Ferguson.

ALEX FERGUSON

Manchester City have given youth a chance and worked hard at getting the right kind of youngsters to Maine Road. It's very satisfying to bring your own players through to First Division level and I admire them for the way they have set about it.
But of course when you embark on that kind of policy it takes time and patience. I have no doubt that they would like to be a little further up the table.
It takes exceptional young players to get success quickly and you cannot expect miracles. It will be interesting to see whether they can bridge the gap in the short term. Certainly their policy can be very rewarding and pleasing for supporters in the long run.
The one thing certain as we welcome the Blues to Old Trafford is that there will be little time for theory today.
A derby is a derby. League positions and form guides are of little help, and I know we are in for a tough one. No-one has taken many goals off Manchester City, so defensively they look to have built something solid, which as the away team today will serve them well.
It will be up to us to make the running, something we tried to do last week here only to

end up with a goalless draw which received a great deal of criticism.
I agree it never got off the ground as an entertainment. All I can say is that we did not set out to be negative. I would never be a party to that kind of footbali.
We did in fact try something different in an attempt to spring a surprise on a team which we had to respect as League leaders.
I played Paul McGrath as a sweeper only for Howard Kendall to counter with five in midfield and only one player up front. The result was that the game was congested in the middle of the park and it wasn't until the second half that we were able to reorganise.
It was just one of those unfortunate tactical ploys which Everton succeeded in countering to leave us with a disappointing match.
We certainly didn't play with five at the back, which some have suggested. We played three, with the two full backs pushed into midfield.
Unfortunately Everton played for security. They had been on a wee wobble, and it was important for them not to lose. I know they were worried about coming to Old Trafford.
I might add that the poor state of our pitch didn't help the football. It was very cut up and bumpy indeed, and putting that right this summer will be a priority I assure you.
At least we relished the battle side of it with Bryan Robson and Norman Whiteside in particular showing tremendous appetite.
We will need those qualities this afternoon and with the encouragement of you, our supporters, I am sure we will go all out to chalk up a derby success.
After all, we ARE unbeaten in the League since the turn of the year.

Alex Ferguson

Alex Ferguson gives his views on young players in the March 1987 Manchester derby programme.

It is worth noting that many of United's managerial appointments during the Seventies and Eighties tended to follow a pattern set by City. The flamboyant Docherty was appointed while 'Big Mal' Allison was in charge at Maine Road, then the more sober Dave Sexton took the manager's chair while the Blues were being successful under the thoughtful Tony Book. 'Big Ron' Atkinson was appointed while the flamboyant John Bond ruled at City, and then Aberdeen's successful manager Ferguson arrived at Old Trafford during the City reign of Celtic's great leader Billy McNeill. Officials at United did make it known, particularly during the appointment of Ron Atkinson, that they had looked across at Maine Road and tried to match the Blues ability for grabbing positive headlines when Bond was in charge. Of course all of that was to change during the late 1980s and early 1990s when City embarked on what seemed like a suicide mission, while United chose not to follow City's managerial lead and they stuck with Ferguson through some difficult spells.

It is worth noting that by 1989 the Reds looked as far away from title success as they had been at more or less any point since 1967. When City and United met in the 1989 Maine Road derby the Blues ran out easy 5-1 victors and the chant of "Fergie Out" had been sung with true venom by the away fans, but – and this is perhaps the best example of how the two clubs differed at this point – United did not dismiss their manager in the months that followed, yet City did!

One rumour that did circulate at the time claimed that United would have dismissed Ferguson had the 5-1 defeat been by any other club. Allegedly, there was no way the Reds would give City the satisfaction of claiming the manager's scalp. It is an interesting theory and one which has clearly worked to United's advantage.

Of course United hit the headlines a great deal during the 1980s as a result of takeover – or proposed takeover – stories. In February 1984 the newspaper baron Robert Maxwell made a £10m bid to take over the Reds, then in 1989 Michael Knighton claimed he had taken over the club and was going to take the Reds forward into a bright new era. **Piccadilly Radio** featured an extensive interview with Knighton prior to the Arsenal game on the opening day of the 1989-90 season. James H Reeve, then of **Piccadilly Sport,** remembers:

"The show used to start about 12 then and we had Michael Knighton in for two hours. I asked him his plans for taking over United and after two hours I still hadn't got a straight answer out of him. I was baffled, and then after two hours with me he went off to Old Trafford and did all that juggling on the pitch with the ball. Ultimately, it all failed, but he did get a place on the Board and I've got some headed paper at home from United with his name on as Chairman. So somebody must have been convinced."

In the years that followed, Knighton often claimed that the redevelopment of the Stretford End and the transformation of United into a PLC were instigated by his takeover. It is clear that without the involvement of Knighton it is highly unlikely the Reds would have developed in the way they did during the 1990s, however Knighton himself was only at Old Trafford for a short period before facing a new challenge at Carlisle.

Under Alex Ferguson United went on to win the FA Cup in 1990 (beating Crystal Palace in a replay for the first trophy of Alex Ferguson's reign), and this first FA Cup appearance by Ferguson's side was viewed as a triumph for captain Bryan Robson. The **Daily Telegraph** reported:

"A dramatic late introduction of the partially fit Ian Wright into the game brought Crystal Palace within seven minutes of winning the FA Cup on their first appearance in the final, but Mark "Sparky" Hughes intervened to earn Manchester United a replay.

"Wright has twice broken a leg this season, and his achievement in getting fit enough to claim a seat on the Palace substitutes' bench was no small miracle in itself. Manager Steve Coppell gambled on leaving him there for 69 minutes, but when he unleashed the striker he lit up a hitherto undistinguished match. Bryan Robson had equalised an early O'Reilly goal in the first half, and Hughes had put United ahead after 62 minutes. Wright's two goals were gems in a sea of mediocrity, the first coming with his first significant touch as he destroyed £5 million worth of reputations only three minutes after going on. Both Pallister and Phelan were left floundering as Wright came bursting through from the left and slashed the ball past Leighton in goal. Two minutes into extra time, he scored another superb goal, stealing in at the far post to volley Salako's centre into the roof of the net.

"But Manchester were not to be denied by Wright's spring heeled heroics. In the exhausting last period, class began to tell. Ince, Webb, Phelan, Wallace and Hughes, a large part of the £15 million it has cost to build this United team, all came into their own as men capable of deciding the issue. And no United player was more influential than their remarkable captain, Robson, who carried his team along with the sheer force of his intensely competitive nature. United might have scored three times before Webb and Wallace split Palace down the middle and Hughes beat Martyn to earn them a replay."

That success helped Alex Ferguson keep his job at United – remember many fans had continued to call for his sacking as the season progressed and even after Wembley there were still a significant number of supporters who felt it was time for a change.

Across at City, the Blues began the 1990s as a top flight side, managed by Howard Kendall, however the 1980s had seen the Blues suffer on several occasions. They were relegated in 1983, promoted under manager Billy McNeill in 1985, suffered relegation again in 1987 and then enjoyed promotion in 1989. Chairman Peter Swales was viewed by supporters as holding the club back and on a fairly regular basis since 1983 demonstrations took place against the chairman. For a while "Swales Out" was heard more than any other City chant.

For the other sides in the region, the period was inevitably mixed. Bury spent the mid-Seventies as a Third Division side, but suffered relegation in 1980 – they unluckily finished fourth bottom and missed survival by one point. That same season they did manage to play in a morale boosting FA Cup tie at Anfield. Gordon Sorfleet remembers:

"I was 14 or 15 at the time and Liverpool were the biggest team in football, so going to Anfield was something special. There was over forty thousand there. It was nil-nil at half time but we'd hit the crossbar. Then they brought on supersub, David Fairclough, and that was it 2-0. He scored in the 64th minute and the 81st but we kept going. After the game the Kop applauded Bury off. It's moments like that that stick in your memory. We were a nothing side, but here was the Kop cheering us."

Bury Chairman Bill Allen with Bobby Smith, manager 1973-77. Following Bill's death in 1979, his wife Amelia Allen became the first women director in the Football League.

Above: **Bury's promotion side of 1984-85.**

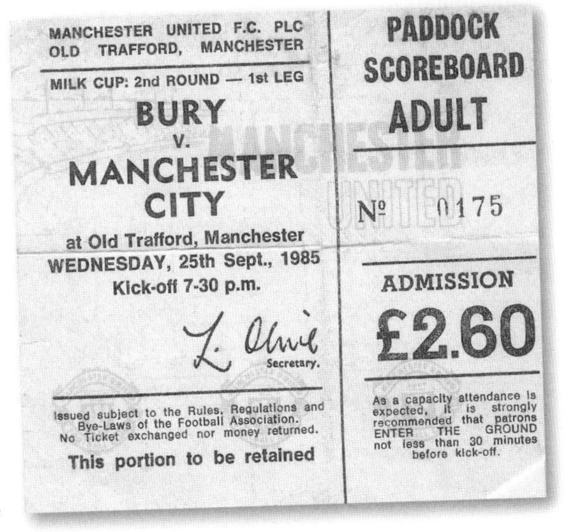

Right: **City defeated Bury 2-1 in the first leg of the second round of the League Cup in 1985 at Bury's home - Old Trafford. At the time it was felt moving the game would bring a larger crowd, however many City fans boycotted the game, and the attendance was only 11,377.**

Despite the occasional high-profile cup tie Bury remained very much a Fourth Division side until 1985 when they achieved promotion to the Third Division.

Stockport spent the entire period in Division Four and at times the club was in serious financial difficulty. In 1978 Mike Summerbee, who had joined the club as a player the previous year, became manager. It did not take him long to realise money was tight and that the 'Go, Go, County' glamour of the previous decade had faded:

"We struggled for money. We struggled for everything! The players' strip was falling to pieces. It couldn't be worn. I was a good friend of Horst Dassler, who owned Adidas and so I called him up and asked for some kit. He'd known me for years because I wore Adidas boots and I said to him 'we've got a problem. We've no money and no kit'. So he asked me what I wanted and I told him we needed everything.

"He asked me what colours we played in. So I told him, and he said that Argentina had just won the World Cup and he had some shirts without the badge on. So he sent us a full set of Argentina shirts – long and short sleeve – and he found us an away kit as well from another team. We were the best dressed team in the division!

"He also sent us a hundred footballs and gave us lots of other bits and pieces."

Stockport eventually dropped this style of shirt following the Falklands' War, but it was not only the kit that needed replacing. Summerbee:

"The dressing rooms were in a terrible state. They were an absolute mess. So I knew someone else

who had done some tiling work for me and he came in and completely refurbished them. He put quite expensive marble down, did all the work, and gave us the best dressing rooms in the Fourth Division! It cost us virtually nothing. Opposition sides would be full of envy when they came to play us."

Despite Summerbee's improvements to the presentation of the club, he did not feel he could give management everything it needed and rather than blindly carry on regardless he moved on. By the end of the 1980s the County manager was Danny Bergara. Phil Brennan, Stockport's press officer, remembers his impact:

"A little Uruguayan bloke turned up in the late 'eighties and more or less overnight the whole atmosphere of the club changed."

The following decade was to be the most successful in the club's history, and so the period pre-1990 should be viewed by County as a rather entertaining if not spectacular prelude to real achievement.

Another Division Four side during the 1970s and 1980s was Rochdale. The period was mostly one of struggle with re-election worries never too far away. This is covered further in the next chapter, but it is worth pausing to consider a brief period when Dale possessed one of the Country's leading entertainers on their board of directors – Tommy Cannon. Cannon, from double-act Cannon & Ball, was known to be a Dale fan and for a while in the mid-80s he invested in the club. Mark Hodkinson, author of **Believe in the Sign**, was a regular on the terraces at the time:

County played their 1986 League Cup tie against Sheffield Wednesday at Maine Road.

"Tommy Cannon was here for a couple of seasons and immediately he was on the front cover of the programme with his arms raised. There were rumours that he was going to land on the pitch in an helicopter. I never actually saw that, so I don't know if it's true or not.

"I don't think he actually put much money in. I think it was just a flirtation really. I think at the same time Bobby Ball was involved with Rochdale Hornets, so it was like 'him and him' sporting clubs at the time. It coincided with a very poor period on the pitch, so he came and went quite quickly."

The Cannon & Ball influence was also felt across at Boundary Park during the eighties when Bobby Ball released an Oldham Athletic version of Cannon & Ball's song **"The Boys in Blue"**. This coincided with success on the pitch for the club.

Rochdale 1975-76.

Jimmy Frizzell and his Oldham team celebrate winning the Division Three championship in 1974.

During the Seventies and early Eighties manager Jimmy Frizzell had established Oldham as a fairly typical Second Division side. They enjoyed a few high points, but seemed unlikely ever to mount a serious challenge for trophy success or promotion. Nevertheless this in itself was a major achievement considering the position the Latics had been in during the Sixties and early Seventies – remember Latics were a Fourth Division side in 1971. It seemed around the region that Oldham were happy with Second Division midtable consistency, but then on 14th June 1982 the shock news was released that Latics had parted company with their popular manager. The club issued a statement saying:

"The board has decided to terminate the manager's employment. The two years remaining on his contract will be honoured along with his testimonial arrangements. There is no particular reason for our decision, but we do feel that the club needs a new challenge, and people coming through the turnstiles. We are hoping for a new impetus throughout the club."

The decision was a bold one and could easily have backfired on the club. Frizzell had been with Latics for 22 years as first player then manager and had achieved a great deal. His replacement was a former City player whose playing career had ended the previous season through a knee injury – Joe Royle.

England international Royle had enjoyed a successful playing career at Everton, City, Bristol City and Norwich City before he took up management. At Everton he was a member of the side that won the League championship in 1970 and appeared in the 1968 FA Cup final side, and at City he was part of the team that won the 1976 League Cup (he also had a goal disallowed).

Royle's arrival at Oldham was seen as a chance by the Board to create a new challenge. They felt it was time for Latics to have new direction and Royle, with no experience of management, was chosen ahead of 29 other applicants.

33 year old Joe Royle arrived at Boundary Park on 14th July 1982 and an incredible period of success for the club was to follow. At the time Royle had no track record of success:

"Although I am a novice as a manager, I am not too proud to ask for advice from the people in the game who I respect, and I am sure that we can make a good job of things at Oldham."

The new manager's first season in charge saw Oldham finish seventh in Division Two – their highest finish since 1930 and four places higher than the previous season - but the following year they dropped to 19th place, five points above relegation.

Much of Royle's managerial career at Boundary Park saw him having to carefully manage the finances. Players came in on free transfers or bargain fees, and Royle tended to bring in players he either knew could deliver, or felt their record proved their ability. Ex United hero Martin Buchan arrived on a free, and Willie Donachie was also to arrive in 1984 but younger players were also developed with players such as Mark Ward proving popular.

Inevitably, Oldham struggled at times but by 1986 Royle's long term planning was starting to take shape. In 1986-87 Oldham came close to promotion to Division One and in previous years their third place finish would have brought promotion but the play-offs had been introduced for the 1986-87 season. This meant Oldham were the first team to miss out on automatic promotion.

Unfortunately, they faced fourth placed Leeds United in the play-offs and they defeated Oldham on the away goals rule. It was a cruel end to the season particularly as the away leg ended 1-0 through a goal in the final minute of the match. At home Oldham were winning 2-0 as the game entered its final minute. Everybody was convinced Royle's men would progress, however another last minute Leeds goal – scored by Keith Edwards who had also netted the last minute goal in the previous match – meant Leeds progressed to the play-off final.

It was a devastating blow, but Oldham's progress had also brought general criticism. Boundary

Boundary Park dilemma for new boss

Why Royle just can't win

By PAUL HINCE

OLDHAM ATHLETIC will soon discover whether their policy of "out with the old, in with the new" will bring the success they have been dreaming about.

For the achievements of the Latics under new manager Joe Royle (pictured left) will inevitably be judged by the standards set by his longserving predecessor Jimmy Frizzell, so controversially sacked shortly after the end of last season.

The Latics board members are convinced that their decision is the right one. But it is Royle, the big ex-England striker, who will be left to provide the ammunition to back up that argument.

In many ways, Oldham's likeable young manager has inherited a Catch 22 situation in his first job on the other side of the soccer fence.

If he can somehow guide his new team to promotion or even improve significantly on last season's placing some will say he merely inherited Frizzell's team.

If, on the other hand, the Latics slip down the Second Division or suffer the humiliation of relegation, it will fuel arguments that Frizzell should never have been sacked in the first place.

The truth probably lies somewhere between the two extremes. Royle, with all his knowledge of the game after a long and successful playing career, is still very much a novice in managerial terms and it would be foolish to expect too much too soon.

And it is difficult to see how Royle can achieve the club's ultimate ambition for First Divison soccer with the players currently at his disposal.

Royle is by no means unhappy at the squad he has inherited, particularly after persuading top-scorer Rodger Wylde to accept a new contract.

And he has a further bonus with promising young striker John Humphreys pushing his claim for a regular first-team place.

Royle believes he knows the players who could perhaps turn the dream of promotion into a reality.

But he knows he must sell before he can buy, and there is every possibility that either Kenny Clements (pictured in action below) or Paul Futcher, the club's two most expensive buys, could soon be pursuing their careers elsewhere.

Paul Hince's incorrect prediction that Joe Royle would find it difficult at Boundary Park. This was made in 1982. By the end of the decade Hince's views had changed significantly.

Park's pitch had been replaced with an artificial surface – at the time the largest in Great Britain. The new 'plastic' pitch had cost £385,000 but allowed Boundary Park to be utilised extensively by the local community. It was a much-needed local asset and one which enabled Oldham to develop both from a financial perspective and a community angle. Inevitably, any team defeated at Oldham tended to point to the pitch and claim the surface worked against them, but in truth Royle's side were performing well away from home as well. Nine of Latics 22 wins came away from home while second placed Portsmouth only won six games away from home, but had managed 17 home wins. In fact Oldham's away record was second only to champions Derby while their total number of home victories was the fourth best in the division.

All of this however was eclipsed in 1989-90 when Royle's Latics enjoyed a tremendous run in both the FA and League Cup competitions. Journalist Tony Bugby reported on Oldham during this period:

"Joe often appropriately describes the 1989-90 season as the 'pinch-me season'. That was due to the fact that Oldham were beating lots of top teams. To have one giant-killing act would have been great, but it was happening round after round in both the League Cup and the FA Cup. It was beyond everyone's expectations."

In the League Cup Leeds, Scarborough, Arsenal, Southampton, and West Ham were beaten as Oldham progressed to the League Cup final, known at the time as the Littlewoods' Cup. Those victories, particularly the 3-1 defeat of Arsenal and the 6-0 thrashing of West Ham, gained national headlines and brought Joe Royle in to contention for a whole host of other managerial jobs. At one point he looked certain to leave Boundary Park for Maine Road but City chairman Peter Swales chose to announce the interest on Friday night football show *Kick Off* and Latics fans attending that night's game at Boundary Park made their feelings known. Royle was touched and stayed.

In the League Cup final Oldham faced Brian Clough's Nottingham Forest. It was the first major final played by the club and many Latics fans were simply delighted to be at Wembley, but sadly the day ended in a 1-0 defeat. Cult hero Andy Ritchie:

"I'd scored in every round, but the one I drew a blank in was the final. But that was a memorable day. Going down Wembley Way and seeing a mass of blue. There were quite a few of us who had lumps in our throats. You just couldn't see any Nottingham Forest fans. It was tremendous."

Oldham were defeated 1-0 by Brian Clough's Nottingham Forest in the 1990 League Cup final at Wembley.

By the time of that Wembley defeat, Oldham had also been knocked out of the FA Cup, but again they had been so close to glory. They progressed to the FA Cup semi-final where they played United at Maine Road. That in itself was another major landmark but the Latics had defeated Birmingham, Brighton, Everton, and Aston Villa in the earlier rounds, and in the semi Oldham drew 3-3 in thrilling game with Earl Barrett scoring the first goal:

Oldham's 1989-90 FA Cup run brought much enjoyment to Latics fans during Joe Royle's 'Pinch Me' seasons. Here Earl Barrett faces United in the FA Cup semi-final.

"I didn't know what to do, to be honest. I thought 'I've just scored the first goal, what should I do now?' because I don't think anybody expected that. It was a great occasion and personally a massive game for me."

Three days later the replay ended 2-1 to the Reds but Latics should have won. Mark Robins scored in extra time to give United the win but Oldham had deserved their chance to play at Wembley.

In the League, Latics finished eighth, four points behind sixth placed Sunderland who achieved promotion via the play-offs, and there was a perception that the cup runs had had a detrimental impact on the league performance. Royle admitted at the end of the season:

"I would have swapped all the Cup games for promotion to the First Division. It would be easy to sit back and say we were this, we were that, everyone loved us and we only missed out because we ran out of steam, played too many games. But the bottom line is we were not good enough. We had a few 'paper tigers' away from home."

James H Reeve, **Piccadilly Radio's** main sports presenter at this time, remembered Oldham's success as Manchester's greatest of the period. With United yet to win the FA Cup and find any success under Ferguson, and City recovering from their 80s relegations struggles, Oldham's progress was significant. Reeve:

"It was the start of a great period for Oldham. They reached the Littlewoods [League] Cup final, they narrowly missed out on the play-offs and promotion – without the other competitions they'd have gone up – and they reached the FA Cup semi-final against United. During that season they'd beaten Arsenal, West Ham – six nil!, Everton, Leeds, Aston Villa, Southampton… all sides regarded as giants in comparison, plus they'd almost beat United in the semi and Forest only beat them 1-0. The League became impossible after all that and they had to play four games over seven days in the final week of the season, and in April they'd played nine games in 26 days including the final and two semi-finals against United!"

The summer of 1990 saw Royle tipped as England's manager, but again he stayed at Oldham, and guided them to promotion as Champions. Some felt Latics would be one of the favourites for relegation and it would be wrong to say Oldham had a great season, however they did end the campaign 17th and Royle guided his team into the first season of the new Premier League. Simply being among football's elite was a major achievement. It is worth noting that many so-called giants, such as Newcastle, are unable to boast that they were founder members of the Premier League.

In 1994 Royle led his side to another FA Cup semi-final and, as with the 1990 meeting, this was against United and again went to a replay with Oldham unfortunate to miss out again. Sadly, relegation brought an end to the Oldham fairytale. It also brought an end to Royle's reign, and the former Evertonian player moved to Goodison as manager, taking Willie Donachie with him as his number two. His achievements at Boundary Park had brought him into contention for a number of high profile jobs. During his spell as manager at Everton he was interviewed by the author of this book about football in Manchester and he talked of the club he played for during the mid-70s:

"City deserve success. It's sad to see the state they are in today, but I'm certain they'll bounce back. And when they do, they will succeed. Manchester is a very wealthy city with a huge population. A population desperate for City to succeed, so when they do they'll find they'll have the fans and the backing of the money men to make the club really strong. If they can turn things around now, they'll have a great future."

As local football entered the 1990s, Oldham and United (under Alex Ferguson), ended the 1989-90 season after appearing in significant Wembley finals. For both sides the new decade would take both clubs to their greatest successes of the modern era. Similarly Stockport were on the verge of a significant leap forward.

ATTENDANCE DETAIL SEASON BY SEASON - 1974-1979

Season	City	United	Oldham	Bury	Stockport	Rochdale
1974-75	32898	48387	12492	5527	2099	1507
1975-76	34281	54750	10456	5936	3238	1594
1976-77	40058	53710	9944	5299	3851	1745
1977-78	41687	51860	9583	4979	4010	1275
1978-79	36203	46430	7045	3782	4142	1767

LEAGUE POSITIONS SEASON BY SEASON - 1974-1979

Season	City	United	Oldham	Bury	Stockport	Rochdale
1974-75	8	23	40	58	88	87
1975-76	8	3	39	57	89	83
1976-77	2	6	35	51	82	86
1977-78	4	10	30	59	86	92
1978-79	15	9	36	63	85	88

CHAPTER TWENTY-TWO

FOOTBALL LEAGUE ELECTIONS

On the day, the voting ended Rochdale 26, Altrincham 25, with two votes not cast, the Grimsby representative being in the wrong part of the meeting room (which prevented him from voting), and the Luton man, who had mixed up the time of the meeting, arriving late; it was believed that the two vote absentees had promised their support for the non-Leaguers. The Dale had survived again, this time by the skin of their teeth.

"Rochdale AFC: The Official History 1907-2001", Steven Phillipps, 2001

FROM the formation of the League through to 1987 entry into the Football League was by means of a ballot. Initially any side – and it really did mean any side – could put itself forward as a possible League side. Existing League clubs would vote on all those applying, plus a number of the League's bottom clubs. When the votes were counted up those with the most votes would be either admitted into the League, or would retain their place.

The system had no direct interest in how clubs were equipped to deal with regular League competition, nor did results on the pitch directly affect the vote. Basically, if a poor performing League side, with little hope of improvement, managed to persuade fellow members of the League that they deserved the place, then they would usually win the vote. By contrast, a forward looking, hugely successful non-League side could apply, but if that side could not secure enough support from the League sides, then they would not be accepted.

From a non-League perspective views varied as to whether this was a good system or poor. For many years, the system did allow non-League sides to basically go from absolute nothing to aspiring League side without having to climb through a pyramid system – imagine if that system had been in place when FC United were created in the 21st Century. Could the new side have created enough support to gain a place?

From a negative perspective, the system tended to favour existing League sides. So much so that for many years during the 1970s and 1980s the same three or four teams appeared at the bottom of the League. This gave the impression that those sides were dead wood and that they had little to offer. Non-League sides felt they blocked all hope and many neutral fans around the Country considered the likes of Halifax Town and, from our region, Rochdale as offering little.

However, supporters of those sides, particularly Dale, could put forward strong, convincing arguments as to why they were worthy members of the League. *Times* Journalist Mark Hodkinson is a passionate Rochdale fan and he has often talked of the strength of feeling between supporters of his club for their side. Often people assume that 'small' clubs are less important, but as football in our region has demonstrated many times, the fans of every club feel as passionately – possibly more so in some cases - for their side as those of United.

Locally, during the 1970s the yearly League elections were often perceived as Rochdale Versus Altrincham. Obviously, this was not quite accurate as Dale were not the only League side fighting to avoid relegation during the period, nor were Alty the only side attempting to join the League, but it gave the media a good story. Dale were perceived as a side that was passed its best while Alty were seen as a non-League giant. Non-League expert Mike Pavasovic:

"Altrincham like to see themselves as a big club – the Manchester United of non-League football. They are a big club but at this time they liked to really present themselves as something significant. They pushed for League football. It was seen as being the next step."

Altrincham were, in the end, probably the unluckiest of all the region's clubs when it came to acceptance into the Football League. They were founded in 1903 and in the early days Altrincham competed mainly in the Manchester League, but in 1908 they became members of the Lancashire Combination and clearly they had ambition.

After World War One the side moved into the Cheshire League and, in the main, they established themselves as a top half of the table side, and they became established at that level for many years.

Sadly the 1950s brought some struggle, but by the end of the sixties they were seen as a progressive 'go-ahead' side. With direction set by Peter Swales and Noel White – two men who would later gain significant positions with the FA but would also become directors of City (Swales) and Liverpool (White) – Altrincham became founder members of the Northern Premier League (it was no coincidence as Swales was one of the League's key instigators) in 1968-69.

In 1969 the *Northern Soccer Annual* focused on the side and the transformation it was undertaking under Swales, White and manager Freddie Pye. Journalist Keith McNee commented on the situation as it was when White & Swales first arrived:

Altrincham 3, Winsford 0

EX-STOCKPORT LEADER Len White cracked Winsford's defensive wall yesterday with a penatly for his new club after 70 minutes of frustration. After that the goals that had been promised came.

White showed that, along with Jack Swindells, the league's leading scorer last year, he is going to be a real threat this season. He scored Altrincham's second after 81 minutes from a Swindells pass.

Taylor got the third a minute from time when he worried goalkeeper Ikin into dropping the ball from a Halliwell free kick.

Bangor C. 5, Mossley 1

Bangor could be in for a good season judging by this goal feast. The star was new inside-right Albert Jackson from Oldham Athletic who collected a hat-trick.

Just before half-time, Bangor blasted in four goals in seven sensational minutes. Jimmy Conde launched the spree when he climbed high to send a dipping headr over goalkeper Tony Tighe. Conde was the architect of the next goal when he cut through on the right and gave Tony Broadhead a chance which he accepted at the second attempt.

Then Jackson took a hand. With 40 minutes gone he won a duel in the air and beat Tighe. The crowd were still applauding when Jackson crossed from 40 yards and Tighe dropped the ball behind the line.

Mossley were shattered. After Len Dickenson got a consolation Jackson got No. 5 with five minutes lemt.

Stalybridge Celtic 1, Runcorn 2

Stalybridge, who included new signing James Burdess, the ex-Oldham Athletic outside right, impressed against a Runcorn team which had six changes from last season. But Stalybridge paid the penalty for poor marksmanship.

Lack of sharpness in front of goal was noticeable in both forward lines, and it was from a scramble in the Celtic goalmouth that Gorrie scored in the 38th minute.

Runcorn held their lead at half-time, but afterwards Celtic were always dangerous with sudden breakaways. After 69 minutes, Boss crossed to the far post for Jones to head the equaliser.

Both teams suffered in the sunshine as they struggled for the winner, which eventually went to Runcorn two minutes from the end. Gorrie hooked a shot just under the bar.

The opening day of the 1968-69 season for ambitious non-League sides Altrincham, Mossley and Stalybridge.

ALTRINCHAM FOOTBALL CLUB

Moss Lane, Altrincham Phone 061-928-1045

Northern Premier League Challenge Cup Winners 1969/70.
North-West Floodlit League Champions 1968/69.
North-West Floodlit League Champions 1970/71.
Cheshire County League Champions, 1965/66, 1966/67; Runners-up 1967/68.
Cheshire Senior Cup Winners 1967.
Cheshire League Challenge Cup Winners 1963/64.

Chairman: Mr. N. WHITE
Vice-Chairman and General Manager Mr. F. PYE
Team Manager: Mr. R. REES
Coach: Mr. A. SAUNDERS
Secretary Mr. D. BALDWIN

Directors
Mr. L. POLLITT
Mr. W. BRIGGS
Mr. M. KLAPISH
Mr. A. POWNALL
Mr. J. PENDLEBURY

FIXTURES, 1971-72

NORTHERN PREMIER LEAGUE

Date	Team	Grd.	F A	1970-71 F A
Aug. 14	ELLESMERE PT. TOWN	H	4-2	—
,, 17	MORECAMBE	A	3-2	1-2
,, 21	STAFFORD RANGERS	A	1-1	1-2
,, 23	BRADFORD PARK AV.	H	2-1	1-0
,, 28	SKELMERSDALE UTD.	H	1-0	—
Sept. 1	SCARBOROUGH	A	1-1	1-1
,, 4	BANGOR CITY	A	0-1	0-2
,, 6	FLEETWOOD	H	2-0	1-0
,, 11	LANCASTER CITY	H	4-1	
	N.P.L. Challenge Cup			
,, 13	GAINSBOROUGH T.	A	1-1	1-4
,, 18	BUXTON	H	1-0	—
	(F.A. Cup 1st Qual. Round)			
,, 20	BRADFORD PARK AV.	A	1-2	1-4
,, 25	NETHERFIELD	H	1-0	5-0
,, 27	MORECAMBE	H	3-0	3-2
Oct. 2	MATLOCK TOWN	A	3-2	1-1
,, 6	FLEETWOOD	A	0-1	3-2
,, 9	EASTWOOD (Hanley)	H	4-1	
	F.A. Cup—2nd Qual Rnd.			
,, 11	GAINSBOROUGH T.	H	0-1	2-0
,, 16	BOSTON UTD.	A	1-2	1-1
,, 23	NANTWICH TOWN	H		
	F.A. Cup—3rd Qual Rnd.		1-1	
,, 27	NANTWICH T. (replay)	A	4-1	
,, 30	WIGAN ATHLETIC	A	0-0	1-1
Nov. 6	OSWESTRY TOWN			
	F.A. 4th Qualifying Round	A	3-0	
,, 13	KIRKBY TOWN	A	3-2	5-4
,, 23	ROSSENDALE UNITED	A		
	F.A. CUP. 1st Round proper		0-1	
,, 27	NORTHWICH VICS.	H	0-0	0-3
,, 29	SCARBOROUGH	H	2-0	
	Watney Challenge Cup			
Dec. 4	WITTON ALBION	A	0-1	
	F.A. Challenge Trophy			
Dec. 18	ELLESMERE PORT T.	A	0-1	—
,, 27	MACCLESFIELD TOWN	H	1-1	0-3
Jan. 1	STAFFORD R.	H	0-0	3-2
,, 8	SKELMERSDALE UTD.	A	0-1	—
,, 15	BANGOR CITY	H	2-0	3-1
,, 17	SOUTH LIVERPOOL	H	2-1	3-2
,, 22	GOOLE TOWN	H	1-3	3-0
,, 29	NEW BRIGHTON	A	4-1	
	Cheshire Senior Cup—1st Rd.			
Feb. 5	MATLOCK TOWN	H	3-0	—
,, 8	GAINSBOROUGH T'nty	A	0-1	
	(Watney Challenge Cup Semi-Final—1st Leg)			
,, 12	GOOLE TOWN	A	1-2	2-1
,, 19	SANDBACH RAMBLERS	A	1-2	
	Cheshire Senior Cup—2nd Rd.			
,, 26	GREAT HARWOOD	A	1-2	1-1
Mar. 4	WIGAN ATHLETIC	H	1-3	1-1
,, 5	RUNCORN	A	4-4	3-1
,, 11	SOUTH LIVERPOOL	A	0-1	0-6
,, 12	GAINSBOROUGH T'nty	H	1-1	
	(Watney Challenge Cup Semi-Final—2nd Leg)			
,, 18	KIRKBY TOWN	H	0-0	5-0
,, 19	BOSTON UNITED	H	1-3	0-0
,, 25	LANCASTER CITY	A	0-2	3-1
,, 27	CHORLEY	H	4-1	4-4
,, 31	SCARBOROUGH	H	4-0	0-1
April 1	NORTHWICH VICS.	A	2-3	0-3
,, 3	MACCLESFIELD TOWN	A	3-0	3-2
,, 7	RUNCORN	H	0-0	3-1
,, 10	GREAT HARWOOD	H	4-5	4-2
,, 15	SOUTH SHIELDS	A	1-0	2-5
,, 18	CHORLEY	A	1-1	1-1
,, 22	LANCASTER CITY	H	5-2	2-2
,, 29	SOUTH SHIELDS	H	4-1	2-3
May 2	NETHERFIELD	A		2-4

NORTH WEST FLOODLIT LEAGUE

Date	Team	Grd.	F A
Oct. 18	WITTON ALBION	H	1-0
Nov. 8	GREAT HARWOOD	H	2-1
,, 17	WITTON ALBION	A	1-4
Dec. 6	GREAT HARWOOD	A	0-1
Dec. 13	ELLESMERE PORT TOWN	H	5-0
,, 20	RUNCORN	A	0-4
Jan. 3	RUNCORN	H	3-2
,, 10	ELLESMERE PORT TOWN	A	3-1

F.A. YOUTH CHALLENGE CUP

Dat	Team	Grd.	F A
Oct. 4th	PRESCOT TOWN (2nd Qual. Rnd)	H	3-4

"As the two young men approached the football club they had no idea of the shock that was in store for them. For when one of them attempted to open the main door - it came off in his hand!

"That was seven years ago. The place:Altrincham Football Club in the heart of Cheshire.The men: Noel White and Peter Swales, two local businessmen who had taken on the job of putting Altrincham back on their feet. They could hardly have been impressed with the ground at Moss Lane - it was poor, to say the least - or its team. They were at the bottom of the Cheshire County League and had to apply for re-election. Yet, within a few years 'The Robins' had taken wing and flown up from the depths of despair to the pinnacle of non-League soccer and the fringe of the Football League.

"White and Swales,who began their business partnership with one small shop selling sheet music and built it into a chain of twenty electrical and television shops - adding a hotel to their empire in the process, brought in another dynamic character to form the 'Big Three' who lifted Altrincham to success manager Freddie Pye. It was a shrewd move, for in the seven seasons since the trio first tackled their problems, the team has won the Cheshire League two years running, missed the hat-trick by three points and also carried off the League Challenge Cup, Cheshire Senior Cup and North-West Floodlit League Cup.The one

trophy to elude them is of course the F .A. Cup, but that has not prevented them from having a mighty fling or two at that one either, and in 1967 they swept through to the Third Round before going out at Wolves.

"Back in their dark days The Robins were glad to pull in attendances of more than 400. Now they command an average of nearly 3,000 - not bad when you consider that each Saturday they must fight the counter-attraction of either Manchester United or Manchester City just a few miles away. But now Altrincham flourish in the Northern Premier League. Peter Swales, previously their chairman, has handed over to his colleague Noel White and become chairman of the new 'Super Set'. Says White: 'We are competing with nineteen other clubs from the North of England now, so the standard of non-League soccer must be better and we could be playing League football within three seasons'."

A 1980 Goal famine? It's Quite Possible!

by MICHAEL BENNETT (Aged 13)
A regular supporter of the Robins

I OFTEN wonder what football will be like in the 1980's. Will all referees be professional by then? Will the size of the pitch have to be increased? Could there even be fifteen players per side? All the evidence suggests that the game may well alter a great deal over the next two decades. Although I cannot foresee many changes in the laws governing the game, there will, I think, be one major change from the spectator's point of view. That change can be summed up in one word: Goals!

Let us look back over the last two decades. In the fifties a game of soccer was truly a spectacle. To see six or seven goals being scored in a match was nothing outstanding. To see your team win 6–1 was nothing to get drunk about. Goals were frequent and plentiful. Goals were EXPECTED by both players and spectators.

Why is it, then, that things have changed so that nowadays so many top matches will end predictably in a goalless draw, or will be won by the single goal? Why? The reason, I think, is fairly straightforward. Tactics. In the days of great players like Matthews and Mortenson, teams used to field five forwards, all of whom were eager to score and all of whom were prepared to "have a go" from 25–30 yards from the goal. Another advantage of the old five-forward was the role of a wingman. In present day soccer, a player wearing the number seven or number eleven shirt is no longer expected to play on the wing. He can often be found helping his full-back, or moving across the field to pass the ball to the other flank. He is rarely seen taking on defenders and creating goals for the "big men" who await high balls in the penalty-area.

Would it not be a good idea to allow wingmen to adopt their orthodox role once again. If they did, the goals might appear again, and the game could once more become the spectacle it was in the fifties and early sixties. For isn't it true that far too many teams today are defence orientated and pay too much attention to keeping the opposition from scoring, instead of going after goals themselves. Surely the old saying "The best form of defence is attack" is just as true today?

Take for example the present England team. Without being critical of the selecting I, along with many others, feel that until Martin Chivers came onto the international scene the English forward line was packed mainly with midfield stars, with very few goal-poachers in the team. On the other hand, a completely different example is that of Brazil. Even after their World Cup win in 1970, there was considerable criticism of their surprisingly lax defence. It puzzled many people that a team with such a superb forward line should be so weak in defence. Brazil's objective was clearly to score as many goals as possible and to concentrate on attack much more than defence. They gambled on being able to overpower the opposition with forceful, attacking play. Their gamble paid off, time and time again.

I cannot help feeling that unless this attractive technique returns to English Soccer very soon, teams will become increasingly defensive in their play, and goals will become so scarce that a 1980 goal famine will not be merely a fanciful prediction.

A Young Altrincham fan looks forward to the year 1980 when he hoped attacking football would result in more goals. These predictions were made in 1972.

The aim of League football within three years was not achieved, and Peter Swales became Chairman of Manchester City in 1973, however by 1977 Altrincham were regularly featuring in the top half of the Northern Premier League. They were not the strongest side, nevertheless when it was agreed that only two non-league sides could be put up for election, with one coming from the Northern Premier and one from the Southern it was sixth placed Altrincham who were put forward from the north.

Sadly, Wimbledon from the Southern League joined the Football League with northern side Workington not re-elected, and Altrincham finishing in last place in the vote. Halifax, Hartlepool and Southport were all re-elected.

Twelve months later Northern Premier champions Wigan Athletic were put forward for election – and were subsequently elected in place of Southport – and Altrincham had to wait until 1979 before their chance came again.

Mossley were the Northern Premier's champions in 1978-79 but Tameside's opportunity of having their first League side since Stalybridge in the 1920s failed at the first hurdle when the Northern Premier felt they were not ready for a challenge. To outsiders the only real contender was second placed Altrincham, and it always felt as if they had been groomed for League status throughout the decade. With Peter Swales now an influential FA figure, it was felt Alty had significant support at several senior clubs.

In 1979 all 4 League clubs up for re-election were successful with Alty finishing fifth, but they were a considerable number of votes (24) behind fourth placed Halifax Town.

By the time of the next vote, non-League football had been restructured and the elite of the two senior non-leagues joined forces to create the Alliance Premier League (later more commonly known as the Vauxhall Conference or Football Conference). This meant that the Alliance would put forward only one side in the hope that a reduced number of clubs would give the aspiring club a larger share of the vote. Altrincham now shone, and they won the first Alliance title by two points. Not only that but their ground was viewed as being considerably better than many of the Fourth Division's best sides, and the club had even spent in excess of £50,000 improving the stadium during the previous season or so.

The time looked right for Alty to be accepted and with strong support from the local media, notably **Granada TV** and **Piccadilly Radio**, and local businesses they seemed ready. A £10,000 campaign helped to convince existing League sides of their potential, while on the pitch a good FA Cup run which had seen them defeat League sides Crewe and Rotherham, before losing 2-1 in a replay to Orient, brought much attention their way. It is also worth noting that in the previous FA Cup campaign Alty had also reached the Third round and held Division One side Tottenham to a 1-1 draw before a replay, at Maine Road, ended 3-0 to the London side.

The groundwork had of course been started in the 1960s and in 1969 journalist Keith McNee had been one of the first to recognise the club's development:

"If League football does come to Moss Lane the club will certainly be ready for it. They have a ground that is almost as good as many League clubs, with a new 1,200-seater main stand, covered accommodation for another 4,000, room for 11,000 fans altogether - and plenty of room for other improvements. Since the arrival of White and Swales the ground has had a £30,000 face-lift and there will be more to come. When it comes down to hard cash Altrincham are one of the glamour sides of non-League. They are backed by a swank £40,000 'Red Robin' club which puts £6,000 a year into the club account. Add to this £600 a week from the club pool - twelve times its original figure - and you have some idea why the Altrincham part-time professionals are among the highest paid in their line of business. The Altrincham outlook is wholly professional. The club employs a full-time ground-staff and even called in a time-and motion expert to run the rule over the social club.

"Messrs White and Swales were the personalities who put Altrincham on a sound financial basis, but the man who has transformed the team into one of the most formidable and respected outfits in non-League is their jaunty boss Freddie Pye. A business tycoon in his own right, he has become a legend in non-League circles, joining Altrincham seven seasons ago as successor to Charlie Mitten, after working his managerial magic on nearby Stalybridge Celtic and Welsh clubs Pwllheli and Nantle Vale. Pye, a tough little character who bears a resemblance to James Cagney has a love of the big-time into which his business success has lifted him. He was born in the back streets of Stockport forty years ago, once drove a £25

shooting-brake, but now drives an £8,000 Rolls Royce Silver Shadow, has a Daimler in his garage for his wife to use, and a string of scrap metal yards and hairdressing salons, plus a weekly column in the Manchester evening newspaper. 'I just couldn't put a figure on their value,' he says of his businesses - yet success has not spoilt him. He remembers the days when he struggled along as an amateur winger with Manchester United ('As a winger, I was a joke,' he admits), before moving to Hyde United in the Cheshire League where as a wing-half he earned the name of 'Tear away Fred'.

"Now, beneath the hard business exterior there lies a sincere personality and he has often been known to go to some lengths to make sure outgoing Altrincham players are fixed up with other clubs. Pye's contract as a manager is lucrative enough for an ordinary man to live well on - but to him soccer is a hobby. 'I love the game and being involved in it,' he explains. 'It gives me a certain amount of prestige and I am better known in Manchester through my football contacts than for my businesses'. Pye numbers among his friends such personalities as Joe Mercer, the Manchester City boss, his assistant, Malcolm Allison, and Sir Matt Busby from Old Trafford. And he demands the same amount of success, in his own sphere, as they demand from their teams. For failure is just not tolerated at Moss Lane - and Altrincham have tasted little of it. From a tiny wage bill at the start of the new era the figure the team boss now has to work with has gone up to around the £200-a-week mark, and among the ex-League stars he has had on the payroll in recent seasons are Albert Quixall (ex-Manchester United and England), Colin McDonald the ex-England World Cup goalkeeper, Bobby Irvine, ex-Stoke and Ireland, Len White (Newcastle and Stockport County) - and many others who made a name for themselves in the League. But undoubtedly his greatest-ever capture is the goal-getting spearhead of the feared Robins' attack, Jackie Swindells, who went via Accrington, Newport and Torquay before joining Altrincham - and setting the Northern non-League scene ablaze with his fan-tastic scoring exploits which he capped in 1965-66 with 86 goals - a club record that looks certain to stand for many years.

"Swindells is so highly thought of that he runs one of Pye's scrap yards. Quixall is a close friend who has a share in another. In fact, no Altrincham player ever goes short of a job and none ever want to leave the club. 'We usually have to give them a push,' says Pye, who since the dark days has risen to the point where he has his own assistant manager.

"Pye thinks highly of his new challenge in the shape of the Northern Premier League: 'It is obviously the best improvement to non-League,' he considers. 'There are no more easy games. It's harder for the players, managers - everybody, so it must be a good thing.' But Pye, the Altrincham directors, and their cocky Robins are equal to the task, restless for advancement. And if the chance of League football comes along it won't be long before they are flying high there too."

Despite all the positiveness of the late sixties and their continued development during the 1970s, Altrincham were not successful in the 1977 election.

Mark Hodkinson: *"I do feel as if it was portrayed that Altrincham were a go-ahead club from south Manchester and that we were on our knees with a ramshackled old ground. That may have been the truth but as a supporter you don't see that. It's too close to your heart. I took it personally. They were after my club and their place in the League. Even though I was quite young I knew we couldn't lose League status."*

"Our main backer was Fred Ratcliffe and he worked hard to influence votes. He really was 'Mr. Rochdale' and he spent a lot on Dale. In fact he's still remembered by a lot of people as the man who saved Rochdale."

BEST CATCH 'DALE MADE

ALMOST forty years ago there was a young football fanatic who watched Rochdale from his own "grandstand"—a branch on a tree in Denehurst Park beside the ground.

And when he was chased off he would wait at the Spotland gates until the last few minutes when the gates were opened. As disgruntled fans left early, the youngster would get on to the ground late, but not too late to enjoy a few minutes before the game ended.

The youngster was Fred Ratcliffe, now chairman of the club and, according to most, the best signing Rochdale ever made.

A self-made businessman, Mr Ratcliffe has been on the Rochdale board for 23 years. He has seen the club through crisis after crisis and is determined to steer the club through its present spot of bother.

He has poured a fortune of his own cash into Rochdale and one is tempted to wonder why anyone should go to such lengths.

UNTHINKABLE

His answer is this: "I suppose I developed an affection for Rochdale in those old days of climbing the trees in the park to watch. For Rochdale to go out of existence is absolutely unthinkable to me. I am not saying how much I have put into the club since I became a director, but I have no regrets.

"Another reason for all my efforts is that I want Rochdale to be a town on the map and there is no better publicity for a town than its football club. Once a town loses its football League status it disappears into obscurity, and I do not want that to happen to Rochdale."

And of the future Mr Ratcliffe has this to say: "We've got to see the club through to the end of the season. Then we're on the mend. We're going in for quality and I reckon that.

Fred Ratcliffe, 'Mr. Rochdale', was a passionate supporter of Dale.

Although Ratcliffe's efforts saw Dale win the re-election vote it had been an exceptionally close race with Rochdale receiving only one vote more than Altrincham. Incredibly, several stories circulated that two sides that had promised support missed the vote!

Hodkinson: *"One story was that the Grimsby and Luton chairmen were travelling to the game together and they had an accident. They missed the vote, and apparently would have voted for Altrincham. I think the story's apocryphal and don't think they ever revealed who they were going to vote for."*

Another version of the story claims that Grimsby's representative arrived at the meeting, but somehow ended up in the wrong part of the building and was therefore unable to vote, while Luton's representative arrived late after getting confused over the time of the meeting. Whatever the truth, it was perceived at the time as a cruel blow for Altrincham. Those two votes would have given Altrincham League status but from a regional point of view they would also have killed Rochdale's long League career.

Neutrals saw this from Altrincham's perspective, but they overlooked the possible impact on Rochdale. At Dale, and inevitably at other struggling sides in our region, supporters care deeply and the prospect of losing their League status would have caused a major downturn in attitudes within the borough. Altrincham were unlucky, but Rochdale could have died as a club.

In 1981 Altrincham were Alliance champions again but this time the vote was not going to be close. Rochdale were recognised as a vulnerable side in 1980 and in many ways were easy pickings, however their League form in 1980-81 meant they were safe while the sides that did feature in the re-election were either exceptionally strong sides going through a bad patch or were clubs who already carried a great deal of support – the sides were Tranmere, Hereford, York and Halifax. Halifax were the weakest but they had finished second from bottom in the Fourth Division (York were bottom) and it would have been cruel to see them evicted. Sadly, Altrincham could only muster 15 votes while the next lowest side was Halifax with 41.

Alty's form dipped considerably after 1981 and the side was unable to mount a serious election challenge. They did win the FA Trophy in 1986 (as they had in 1978) and during the same year reached the fourth round of the FA Cup where they faced York City, after defeating Blackpool and Birmingham City, but by that point they were competing back in the Northern Premier League. In 1999 they were Northern Premier champions, but these days they are more regularly seen as a side whose peak came six years too early. Mike Pavasovic:

"The problem for Altrincham was that they were at a peak when you couldn't gain automatic promotion. After a couple of title wins the failure to win the League election meant that the side broke up. Players wanted new challenges. Had automatic promotion been possible back then, they'd probably be a decent League side today."

In 1987 automatic promotion was introduced and Altrincham's ground would have been good enough to guarantee a League place.

Since automatic promotion to the League was introduced, none of our local Non-League sides have managed to gain promotion. Droylsden won the Conference North in 2007 and stated their aim was League football, but a difficult 2007-08 saw them struggle, along with Altrincham.

As the pyramid system, with automatic promotion, now provides all clubs across the country with the opportunity to progress from park pitch to the Premier League there is the real possibility that sides such as FC United, Droylsden, Altrincham and Hyde United could progress into the Football League. It is worth looking back however, on all the region's clubs who took part in the Election process prior to automatic promotion arriving in 1987.

The following list details all the sides from the region who have applied to join the League. Those in italics were accepted into the League that season, while those applying to rejoin the League due to finishing in the re-election zone are not included. The figures in brackets show the number of votes received.

In total fourteen teams from the region have applied to join the League, with Newton Heath being the first to apply in 1889. It should be noted that most United sources claim the Reds applied to be founder members of the League in 1888 but this is definitely not true.

1889 Newton Heath (1)
1890 Newton Heath (no votes recorded)
1891 Ardwick (4) & Newton Heath (0)
1892 **Ardwick** (automatically entered without a vote into Division 2)
& **Newton Heath** (6 votes, accepted into Division 1)
1894 **Bury** (17)
1895 Fairfield Athletic (no votes recorded)
1896 Fairfield Athletic (3)
1897 Fairfield Athletic (3)
1899 Ashton North End (0)
1900 Stalybridge Rovers (1) & **Stockport County** (28)

1901 Stalybridge Rovers (7)
1905 **Stockport County** (26)
1906 Oldham Athletic (20)
1907 **Oldham Athletic** (17)** & Salford United (0)
1910 Rochdale (1)
1911 Rochdale (1)
1913 Stalybridge Celtic (6)
1919 Rochdale (7)
1921 **Rochdale & Stalybridge Celtic** (25) ***
1929 Manchester Central (2)
1930 Manchester Central (13)
1931 Manchester Central (4)
1946 Hyde United *
1947 Ashton United (no vote performed)
1977 Altrincham (12)
1979 Altrincham (13)
1980 Altrincham (25)
1981 Altrincham (15)

* The first League season after the war saw 14 teams apply to join the League, but as the 1946-47 fixtures were to be those initially planned for 1939-40 no election was necessary. So in a sense the whole application process was a waste of time. Interestingly of the 14 who applied, Hyde United were the only side who did not previously or subsequently apply for election.

** Oldham was elected after Burslem Port Vale resigned, but not as a result of the election ballot.

*** Rochdale automatically elected into new Third Division North while Stalybridge elected as part of voting process.

ELECTION SNIPPETS

Ashton

Ashton North End were a useful local side during the early 1890s. As with most of the other local sides, they mostly competed in friendlies at first, but by 1891-92 they were competing in a league known as the Ashton & District Association Football League. This was a fairly serious competition however at Christmas 1891-2 Ashton faced Hollinwood in a highly controversial match. According to newspaper reports Hollinwood disputed a few decisions and ended up assaulting the referee. The Ashton players also came under attack and supporters – and it was suggested Hollinwood players – threw mud at the Ashton men. There was outrage in the ***Ashton Reporter*** with the Referees Association getting involved. They argued that referees needed greater protection – some things never change – and that teams like Hollinwood needed to learn respect. The debate surrounding the game rumbled on for weeks, but apart from minor punishments little could be done.

Whether it was that experience or not is not clear but Ashton North End decided it needed to move upwards. In 1894 they joined the Football Combination and ended their first season

The Main Stand at Ashton United during the 1980s. Originally Ashton United were Hurst - the first winners of the Manchester Cup.

as champions. It was a remarkable achievement for the side who played off Manchester Road and were nicknamed The Onions, but surprisingly Ashton chose to join the Lancashire League for the following season, despite the Combination being recognised as a significant competition. There were, however, other progressive sides in the Lancashire League including Blackpool and near-neighbours Fairfield Athletic, Stalybridge Rovers, and Stockport County.

1898-99 proved to be Ashton's best season in the Lancashire when they finished third. On 6th May a public meeting was held to decide how the club should develop and a spokesman told the meeting:

"If the public rally round at this juncture, the future of the club would be assured."

He told the audience that he was keen to see the Onions in Division Two and ended with: *"it is now or never."*

In the vote to join the League Ashton (together with another side, Coventry City) received no votes. The Ashton committee were bitterly disappointed and another public meeting was called and held at the Feathers Inn in Old Square. It was not well attended and the decision was taken to fold. By this act the Onions made history by becoming the only side in football's history to fold without playing another game after an unsuccessful bid to join the League.

Incidentally, it is claimed that Arthur Wharton, recognised as the first black footballer in the Football League, played for Ashton during their final season.

Another team from the town applied to join the League in 1947. Hurst formally became Ashton United on 1st February 1947 and the side was full of ambition despite finishing second from bottom of the Cheshire League. This may have looked an ambitious move but there had also been a proposal that the Football League would be restructured with the top 12 clubs of both Division Three North and South forming a new Third Division while the remaining clubs would form regional Fourth Divisions. This would mean that the two new Fourth Divisions would need additional clubs. As that motion was defeated the chance for the 27 teams that applied to be accepted were slim. Ashton United failed in their bid and to date the side has not come as close to joining the Football League.

Manchester North End

In 1925 the Manchester League side Manchester North End considered applying to join the League but for some reason held back. Then on 4th February 1928 the Chairman announced that their League ambitions had been resurrected and that they were seriously considering making a bid. For some unknown reason the application was never made and the club folded in 1939.

Salford United

Little is known of Salford United's roots, but it is clear that the side joined the Manchester League in 1905. Prior to this date no trace has been found of the side competing in other competition, although it is known that a side called Salford AFC existed in 1887. It is assumed Salford United were founded around 1904-05.

They ended their first season 14th out of 16 clubs, but they clearly had potential. Playing at The Willows, which ultimately would become a famous rugby venue in its own right, the soccer side clearly had facilities few contemporary rivals possessed and, with only relatively minor soccer competitors in that area, the club certainly had a large population to support it as it developed.

By the end of the 1906-07 season Salford reached fifth position in the league and were encouraged enough by their development to apply for League status. It was a bold move and on the face of it the side were doomed to failure, especially as fellow north-west sides Oldham Athletic and Wigan Town were also in the election, however the Football League had made it clear in the early years of the Twentieth Century that they were keen to see sides from rugby strongholds apply. Clearly, reading between the lines the League saw rugby, in particular the northern version of the sport, as a threat and wanted to turn rugby strongholds into soccer hotbeds. Salford was a rugby city.

Another plus point in Salford's favour was that it had little competition in the area. The present day boroughs of Trafford, Rochdale, Tameside, Oldham (although that would soon change) and Salford did not possess League sides, while Manchester's sides were both based a little over a mile apart in East Manchester. Salford had the population to support not only a small side, but potentially a successful Division One club.

Despite the encouragement and the benefits of having a club from Salford in the League, the Reds were unsuccessful and received no votes in their favour. Considering both City and United were Division One sides by this point it is unlikely they would have seen Salford as a threat but clearly they did not support the application. Perhaps it was already known at United that the Manchester Reds would be moving to the Trafford area and maybe they eyed the Salford population as their own potential customers.

Salford's failure affected the team's performance in 1907-08 when they could only manage a 13th place finish. The following year they were 8th, and in 1910 they won the Manchester League (after a play-off with Hurst), but United became resident at Old Trafford in February of that season. The lure of the Manchester Reds was too much for Salford United – even the name United would have caused some confusion locally – and so the Salford club disbanded in the summer of 1910. Although Manchester United were only based on the border of Trafford and the city of Salford, they soon became regarded by many Salfordians as their city's team.

In 1940 Salford City was formed, but to date their chance of progression to the Football League has been limited. Unless something dramatically changes, Salford is likely to remain the main competitor with Wakefield for recognition as 'the largest city without a League side'.

Fairfield

Fairfield Athletic were a prominent local side throughout the 1890s with a Lancashire League title to their name in 1895 (Blackpool were second), and an appearance in the FA Cup first round. When they first applied to join the League in 1895 however it is possible many of the voting sides were bitterly opposed to their attempts. The reason being that Fairfield had previously been banned by the Football League from playing friendlies against League sides as, on earlier occasions, Fairfield had allegedly tried: *"tampering with their [opponents] players."* This meant Fairfield had tried to poach the players and, although the ban was lifted by the time of the vote, it was still a relatively sore topic.

The following year they tried again and received one more vote than Tottenham Hotspur, but still they failed. Again in 1897 they applied but after another disappointment they folded during 1897-98. Considering some of the sides who did enter the League during the 1890s and early 1900s Fairfield were unfortunate not to have been elected on at least one of these occasions.

Their ground during this period was at Gransmoor Road and after a Football League inspection in 1895 the local council agreed to carry out improvements to the venue to help the election process. This demonstrates the desire by all in Fairfield to create a League side – a remarkable achievement considering the closeness of Newton Heath and also of Manchester City in east Manchester at the time.

ATTENDANCE DETAIL SEASON BY SEASON - 1979-1989

Season	City	United	Oldham	Bury	Stockport	Rochdale
1979-80	35272	51608	7918	4239	2911	1926
1980-81	33587	45071	6510	2748	2335	2565
1981-82	34063	44571	7023	3533	2540	1837
1982-83	26789	41552	6962	3097	2309	1688
1983-84	25604	42534	6036	2104	2098	1491
1984-85	24220	42881	4713	3591	1895	1434
1985-86	24229	46321	4651	2889	2667	1790
1986-87	21922	40594	6884	2502	2113	2151
1987-88	19471	39152	6907	2565	2272	1939
1988-89	23500	36488	7204	3368	2792	1968

LEAGUE POSITIONS SEASON BY SEASON - 1979-1989

Season	City	United	Oldham	Bury	Stockport	Rochdale
1979-80	17	2	33	65	84	92
1980-81	12	8	37	80	88	83
1981-82	10	3	33	77	86	89
1982-83	20	3	29	73	84	88
1983-84	26	4	41	83	80	90
1984-85	25	4	36	72	90	85
1985-86	15	4	30	64	79	86
1986-87	21	11	25	60	87	89
1987-88	30	2	31	58	88	89
1988-89	22	11	36	57	88	86

CHAPTER TWENTY-THREE

PREMIER POWER

This change is not a matter of greed but of logic and fact. I can see nothing but good coming out of it. Obviously the Premier League will generate more money for the top clubs but that is the only way to compete with the big clubs on the continent like Inter Milan and Marseille.

City Chairman & FA Councillor Peter Swales, 1991

THE 1990s started with Oldham reaching their first major final and United achieving their first trophy success of Alex Ferguson's reign. The future looked bright for at least two of the region's sides, but City also looked to be in a positive position after ending their first season back in the top flight on equal points with the Reds, although it has to be said that both sides had struggled in the League with United finishing one place higher than City in 13th place.

Both City and United were starting to give the impression that they could at long last compete for League honours. For much of the Seventies and Eighties Liverpool had tended to dominate League affairs, but the late eighties and early nineties saw Everton (1987), Arsenal (1989 & 1991) and Leeds (1992) achieve title success. Other sides such as United, Sheffield Wednesday, Crystal Palace, Tottenham, Nottingham Forest and Aston Villa had also challenged, suggesting that the League was truly an open competition.

The Leeds success gave most sides hope and made it clear that a side could still progress from Second Division obscurity – where Leeds had existed for much of the 1980s – to League champions. All this hope though was about to disappear.

The biggest development to hit League football since the creation of the Fourth Division in the 1950s was, by the end of the 1990s, to see the top division become at times a two horse race, occasionally three or four teams would challenge, but the opportunities for the rest of the top division to win the title were, at best, slim.

The biggest story of the early 1990s was the proposed restructure of the League into a Super League of around 16 clubs sitting above the rest of the Football League. On Monday 23rd September 1991 the agreement was made to from the FA Premier League. City chairman Peter Swales was a major supporter of the move and told his club's supporters:

"I believe I have worked as hard as anybody to bring it about. I think it's right for Manchester City and right for football generally. I am sure this club will be far better off in every way. This is the age of the £3m player, top players earning £7,000 a week and of vast sums from TV and sponsorship. It is also an

age when people want to sit down in comfort to watch a football match, to have good toilet facilities and hospitality areas."

Unfortunately the creation of the Premier League was ultimately to have a devastating effect on City with the Blues becoming one of the new league's biggest losers, although by 2008 City were starting to compete at the top again.

Prior to the creation of the Premiership City were one of the game's giants and, although the Blues had not found trophy success since 1976 they had regularly competed, remained a glamorous side, and were still able to attract some of the best players in the Country. Once the new league developed a gap emerged between those teams finding success and those lower down the division. For example after fifteen games of the 1991-2 season at least eleven sides still stood a realistic chance of challenging for the League title, while fifteen years later the situation was such that only two sides were competing for the title. Obviously by 2008 other sides claimed they could compete but only those sides with significant investors seemed likely to challenge United, Arsenal, Chelsea and to some extent Liverpool.

In 1991 after 15 games 11 points separated the top side from 11th place, in 2006 after the same number of games 11 points separated 2nd place from 3rd and this in a league with fewer sides and therefore fewer points available.

City, under Chairman Peter Swales, were one of the most enthusiastic clubs in the creation of the Premier League and so it can be argued that they got all they deserved. Throughout the season club officials and other figures were given space in the club's match programme to air their views. Inevitably, most of them pointed out the financial benefits, but there was one figure who seemed to see the Premier League for what it was. Former City and Bury star Colin Bell seemed to accurately predict the future of the 'Super League' as it was initially dubbed. Perhaps club officials should have listened. Bell, whose views were typical of many supporters and former players, said:

"I cannot see the need for change. We all know it has been coming for years… but why? Football is a great game and the League has survived for a hundred years or so. Why change it? If someone could show me one really good reason for having a Super League I would be prepared to have a re-think, but at the moment I can see more things against it than for it.

"I am sure a lot of the smaller clubs are going to suffer and I'm not so sure the big clubs will benefit either in the long run. When you put the tag 'super' to anything it means super everything. Okay there will be a lot of money coming from television but there will also be super wages and super transfer fees. Everything will snowball and it will be the poor old paying fan who will suffer.

"The enjoyment of the First Division is when the top team plays the bottom and you expect a 6-0 hammering and it doesn't happen. It is the unpredictability of football that makes it such a great game, but a lot of that will be taken away. I'm only guessing but I think if someone conducted an opinion poll on the Super League the majority of the fans would not want it. Having said that, I will be the first to hold my hands up and admit I was wrong, if the Super League works."

Bell's opinions appeared in the City match programme of 18th January 1992 and it is clear his views were more in tune with the majority of football fans across the region than those of club officials at City and United. Ex-Red Steve Coppell who was at this time Crystal Palace's manager was another critic, and it seems the former star players of the region's sides understood exactly what damage the League could do. The PFA were also vocal, although some fans believed the players' views had more to do with their own financial benefits rather than the problems it may cause supporters and the smaller or struggling clubs.

In terms of club officials, both the Blues and the Reds were keen on the new league and it was clear even then that the main reasons were financial. Each side could see the benefits the league would bring in terms of increased revenue, sponsorship, prize money and so on, and while Bell and other former players seemed absolutely spot on, the financial men at each potential Premier League side were excited by the opportunities it presented. City's commercial manager at the time was Phil Critchley, and earlier in the season he gave his views on the opportunities the restructure would bring:

"A challenging time lies ahead for commercial departments but most people agree there are going to be far greater opportunities in the new Premier League. It is absolutely vital Manchester City are in from the start. A lot of money is going to be available. Eventually, this will give the clubs the chance of financial independence."

The financial independence did not come for the majority of clubs for some time, if at all, and it was only when television and sponsorship deals became so great in the new millennium that extremely wealthy overseas investors started to look at English football as a means of investment. However on 18th May 1992 the new Premier League struck the largest television deal in British football history.

The satellite broadcaster **British Sky Broadcasting**, which was struggling to increase the popularity of its own business, worked with the BBC to create a package offering £304m to the Premier League over five years. It was an incredible amount and supporters were genuinely excited with the headline information that the BBC's **Match Of The Day** would show highlights on a Saturday night and that 60 live matches would be shown on Sky per season.

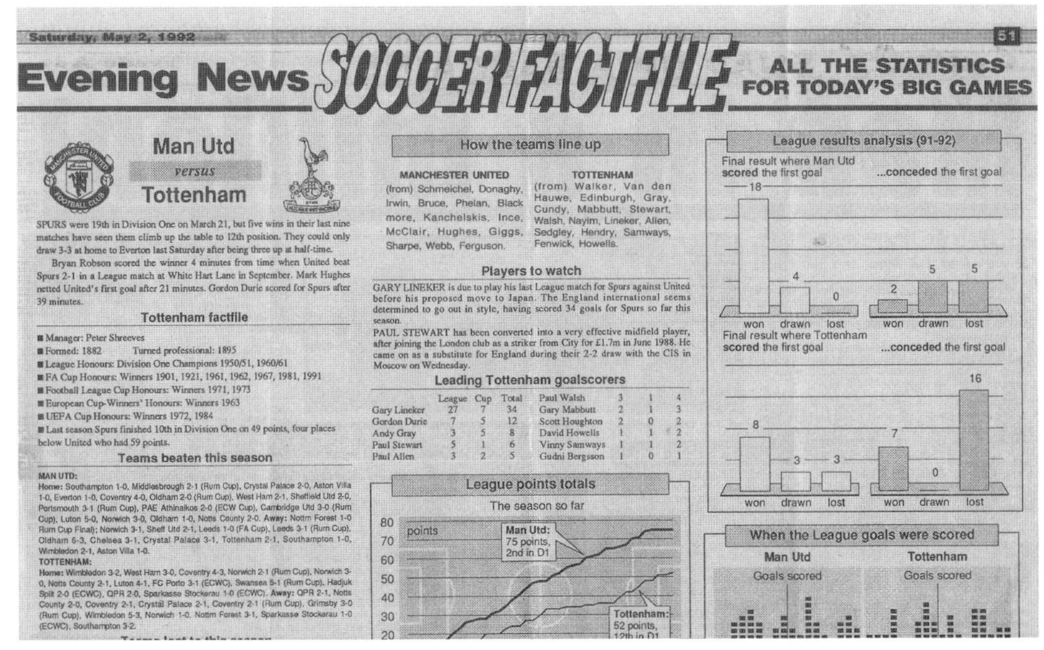

Saturday, May 2, 1992 — 51

Evening News SOCCER FACTFILE — ALL THE STATISTICS FOR TODAY'S BIG GAMES

Man Utd *versus* Tottenham

SPURS were 19th in Division One on March 21, but five wins in their last nine matches have seen them climb up the table to 12th position. They could only draw 3-3 at home to Everton last Saturday after being three up at half-time.

Bryan Robson scored the winner 4 minutes from time when United beat Spurs 2-1 in a League match at White Hart Lane in September. Mark Hughes netted United's first goal after 21 minutes. Gordon Durie scored for Spurs after 39 minutes.

Tottenham factfile

- Manager: Peter Shreeves
- Formed: 1882 Turned professional: 1895
- League Honours: Division One Champions 1950/51, 1960/61
- FA Cup Honours: Winners 1901, 1921, 1961, 1962, 1967, 1981, 1991
- Football League Cup Honours: Winners 1971, 1973
- European Cup-Winners' Honours: Winners 1963
- UEFA Cup Honours: Winners 1972, 1984
- Last season Spurs finished 10th in Division One on 49 points, four places below United who had 59 points.

Teams beaten this season

MAN UTD:
Home: Southampton 1-0, Middlesbrough 2-1 (Rum Cup), Crystal Palace 2-0, Aston Villa 1-0, Everton 1-0, Coventry 4-0, Oldham 2-0 (Rum Cup), West Ham 2-1, Sheffield Utd 2-0, Portsmouth 3-1 (Rum Cup), PAE Athinaikos 2-0 (ECW Cup), Cambridge Utd 3-0 (Rum Cup), Luton 5-0, Norwich 3-0, Oldham 1-0, Notts County 2-0. **Away:** Nottm Forest 1-0 Rum Cup Final); Norwich 3-1, Sheff Utd 2-1, Leeds 1-0 (FA Cup), Leeds 3-1 (Rum Cup), Oldham 6-3, Chelsea 3-1, Crystal Palace 3-1, Tottenham 2-1, Southampton 1-0, Wimbledon 2-1, Aston Villa 1-0.

TOTTENHAM:
Home: Wimbledon 3-2, West Ham 3-0, Coventry 4-3, Norwich 2-1 (Rum Cup), Norwich 3-0, Notts County 2-1, Luton 4-1, FC Porto 3-1 (ECWC), Swansea 5-1 (Rum Cup), Hadjuk Split 2-0 (ECWC), QPR 2-0, Sparkasse Stockerau 1-0 (ECWC). **Away:** QPR 2-1, Notts County 2-0, Coventry 2-1, Crystal Palace 2-1, Coventry 2-1 (Rum Cup), Grimsby 3-0 (Rum Cup), Wimbledon 5-3, Norwich 1-0, Nottm Forest 3-1, Sparkasse Stockerau 1-0 (ECWC), Southampton 3-2.

How the teams line up

MANCHESTER UNITED
(from) Schmeichel, Donaghy, Irwin, Bruce, Phelan, Blackmore, Kanchelskis, Ince, McClair, Hughes, Giggs, Sharpe, Webb, Ferguson.

TOTTENHAM
(from) Walker, Van den Hauwe, Edinburgh, Gray, Cundy, Mabbutt, Stewart, Walsh, Nayim, Lineker, Allen, Sedgley, Hendry, Samways, Fenwick, Howells.

Players to watch

GARY LINEKER is due to play his last League match for Spurs against United before his proposed move to Japan. The England international seems determined to go out in style, having scored 34 goals for Spurs so far this season.

PAUL STEWART has been converted into a very effective midfield player, after joining the London club as a striker from City for £1.7m in June 1988. He came on as a substitute for England during their 2-2 draw with the CIS in Moscow on Wednesday.

Leading Tottenham goalscorers

	League	Cup	Total
Gary Lineker	27	7	34
Gordon Durie	7	5	12
Andy Gray	3	5	8
Paul Stewart	5	1	6
Paul Allen	3	2	5
Paul Walsh	3	1	4
Gary Mabbutt	2	1	3
Scott Houghton	2	0	2
David Howells	1	1	2
Vinny Samways	1	1	2
Gudni Bergsson	1	0	1

United's last Football League game ends with a 3-1 victory over Spurs in May 1992.

Live football had been developing for some time during the 1980s and early nineties with both the *BBC* and *ITV* showing significant live games, however the volume of games to be shown on satellite television was a major development. Live games were to be broadcast on Sundays and Mondays and every club would at some stage in the season be featured – various conditions had been imposed to ensure all sides were represented.

Every club seemed happy with the new arrangements on the face of it but behind the scenes there was a lot of discussion on the subject of Monday night football. Football matches were rarely played on Mondays and any fixture moved would ultimately prove less popular to attending fans than if it was played on a Sunday. Some clubs objected to playing on Mondays, although in truth there was little they could do as they had all agreed to the new television deal. For those who had been outspoken about the benefits of the new League it was a difficult time. They had to publicly support the deal and Peter Swales, as a senior FA Councillor and City Chairman, remained one of the most enthusiastic figures. He was influential in making sure Sky's coverage got off to a positive start and he agreed that City's opening home fixture of the 1992-93 season against QPR would be moved and shown live on the difficult Monday night slot of 17th August. It became the first evening live game on Sky, but the evening proved how out of touch football was with supporters. There was live music on the pitch, dancing girls, and also the arrival of parachutists the Red Devils – once their name became obvious City supporters booed! It all seemed very American and seemed totally out of character with a Monday night in Moss Side. The match ended in a 1-1 draw and as the teams left the field fireworks were set off from the space where the Platt Lane Stand had been demolished (a new stand was in the process of being developed). The majority of fans were cynical of the entire event.

From that point on, no matter what the fans said or did, live television football was to grow, while Colin Bell's views of higher wages and so on proved to be correct. Supporters were inconvenienced enormously as games were moved to ridiculous times to accommodate live television. Morning fixtures, 5.15pm starts and the like caused some to question the point of having season tickets, while match ticket prices rocketed over the following decade or so, so much so that the cheapest adult ticket for the December 2006 Old Trafford derby match cost £35. Fifteen years earlier the same ticket cost £11. By the year 2000 football was no longer the game the majority of fans had grown up enjoying.

As such an enthusiastic supporter of the restructure, Peter Swales should have seen the biggest benefits but the City-obsessed chairman found the development of the Premier League actually forced supporters to question his chairmanship more than ever. Instant success was needed, and the first season of the Premiership ended with City fans frustrated. Their best chance of success, the FA Cup, ended with a highly embarrassing live TV defeat by Tottenham in the quarter-finals. Supporters invaded their pitch, not to fight, but in desperation. They felt let down and betrayed, and within twelve months Peter Swales was no longer chairman as fans campaigned against him. The campaign, which for some had raged since 1983, gained added impetus when ex-player Francis Lee mounted a takeover bid. Lee ultimately became chairman but the Blues entered an appalling period on the pitch.

Lee appointed ex-World Cup winner Alan Ball as manager in June 1995 and the club struggled. Ball, who seemed to lack any idea or feeling of what constituted a good City side, embarked on a clear out which saw the club's biggest stars sold. The team plummeted and were relegated from the Premier League on the last day of the 1995-96 season in farcical fashion. A deflection from City's Lomas gave Liverpool a 6th minute lead in a match the Blues needed to win to stay up. Rush scored Liverpool's second in the 41st minute as City looked dead and buried. Rosler with a 71st minute penalty and Symons both scored to give the Blues hope, but then the Blues decided to time waste in the mistaken belief they were safe. Niall Quinn, on the touchline after being substituted, urged the players to attack, while Liverpool seemed determined to open up play, but the game ended with Ball's side relegated.

Every fan in the stadium knew the situation, but it was clear that the City management had an entirely different view and that Lomas was obeying orders. Alan Ball later claimed that he was the one urging the players to open up play. In his autobiography **Playing Extra Time** he stated:

"We had the ball, so I told Steve Lomas to take it to the corner flag to kill time. He was doing that when I heard that the Southampton goal had been disallowed. I found myself running down the track trying to get another message across and no doubt looking an absolute fool. That is something they bring up in Manchester almost every time my name is mentioned. It was ridiculous. Did people think I would be telling them to play keep-ball in the corner at 2-2 if I knew we still needed to win the match? Of course not."

The memories of fans who were there on the day and BBC television footage of the incident shows Niall Quinn making the run down the touchline urging Lomas to open up play, they do not show Ball. Regardless of the actual events, the fact was that City were relegated in ridiculous circumstances. Niall Quinn appeared on television that night apologising to fans for the relegation but he was not to blame, and his stature in the game increased.

City's struggles continued and at one point it seemed no one wanted to manage the club. Alan Ball lasted into the next season, but by the end of the 1997-98 season Steve Coppell, Frank Clark and Joe Royle had each been appointed manager on a permanent – however long permanent was for City – basis while Asa Hartford and Phil Neal had acted as caretaker managers. The Blues were relegated to the third tier of English football for the first time in 1998. Francis Lee had stepped down prior to the relegation – he had threatened to throw himself off the new Kippax Stand if relegation happened – and many supporters blamed him for the state of the club. Clearly, there had been some poor decisions when it came to matters on the pitch, but off the pitch Lee had instigated a series of major changes for the good.

The Maine Road stadium had improved considerably under Lee with the Kippax Stand proving to be substantially better than the one being planned by former Chairman Peter Swales – from a hospitality point of view the 1,000 seater Millennium Suite was considerably better than anything built at the new City of Manchester Stadium in 2003 – while the developments at the Platt Lane training complex were helping to bring stonger facilities for City's reserve and youth players, and of course the local community. Lee also instigated the discussions for the Blues to move to the stadium being planned for the 2002 Commonwealth Games.

Once Lee resigned as Chairman a new approach was needed. By that time former Blue Joe Royle was manager. He clearly understood the club and the fans and, together with new Chairman David Bernstein, a new fighting spirit developed within the club. Supporters and officials felt they were in it together and with a new found togetherness it seemed as if anything was possible. Players were encouraged to get out and meet fans and the club took a 'back to basics' approach and worked closely with all those elements that City had become famous for over the years – community, supporter relationship, Junior Blues, and representing the heart and sole of Manchester. In fact, under the direction of Chris Bird – initially a PR man for the Club but by 2001 he was the club's Managing Director – the Mancunian identity and relationship with fans became more important than perhaps any other time since the early 1900s.

City's first season in the third tier of English football was not easy and at one point the Blues looked destined for obscurity. Eventually they lifted themselves into the play-offs and although it was far from easy, the Blues achieved promotion at Wembley against Gillingham in 1999. City cult hero Shaun Goater remembers the remarkable events of a day which saw City two goals down with only minutes to spare:

"I saw the celebrations when Carl Asaba scored for Gillingham. The high-fiving on the bench. It was all over and I'm thinking it can't be. Horlock goes and scores and there's only about three minutes to go, and my mind is half and half. You think it's gone, but then there's this roar from the fans and it's building and building. When the injury time boards came up it exploded, and it was as if you'd frozen the game. Told us to get ourselves sorted out and then made us get on with it. That changed it all."

Paul Dickov made it 2-2 in dramatic fashion during injury time and then, after extra-time, City won promotion on penalties. It truly was a highly significant moment in the history of the club and of Manchester. Automatic promotion to the Premier League did follow in 1999-00, but it was the 1999 play-off that really resurrected the Blues.

Journalist Mark Hodkinson followed City for **The Times** that season and he recognised the strength of feeling fans had for their club:

"There was a recognition that City had a heartfelt support and that these supporters had been mistreated to some extent. They had 30,000 who would go every week. Look how bad they are doing. I felt this was totally unfair. How had they been badly mismanaged over the years."

That summer, following promotion, City signed the formal agreement to move to the new Commonwealth Games stadium.

The 1999 play-off final was City's most important game of the modern era, but it has to be stressed that this was also of huge significance to the regeneration of Manchester as a whole. Had the Blues failed to achieve promotion that day it is highly unlikely the City of Manchester Stadium would have been built as a 48,000 seater venue. City would probably have remained at Maine Road, and as a result the financial viability of the new stadium would have been in question.

So many venues have become white elephants over the years that a stadium without a permanent tenant would have cost the region a significant amount and seriously dented Mancunian pride. Without City the structure would probably have been scaled down after the Games, in a similar way to the plans for the 2012 London Olympic stadium. Rather than develop a 35,000 seater stadium for the Games that could be increased to 48,000 it seems likely a smaller permanent structure would have been erected, say with a maximum capacity of 10,000, with an additional 25,000 temporary seats.

The 1990s ended with joy for City and their manager Joe Royle had worked wonders on the pitch. It should be remembered that he helped save the club and managed to bring back a great deal of pride and interest to the club. It is worth highlighting that the decade started with the same

f the City memorabilia up for auction

Story of the Blues goes up for sale

BY ANDREW NOTT

MANCHESTER'S City's season is about to begin with a hammering.

The Blues' history goes under the gavel at a unique auction of memorabilia next week.

Former club director Ian Niven has collected scores of items dating back to the day Maine Road opened in August 1923.

Among the prized documents is legendary winger Mike Summerbee's contract when he moved to City from Swindon in June 1965 for £40-a-week and a £2,000 signing on fee.

Another is the bronze plaque unveiled when the ground first opened and City beat Sheffield United 2-1.

The souvenir programme from that game is also up for sale.

The Manchester Liners vessel, 'Manchester City', was named in honour of the championship win in 1937 — and the ship's bell, later acquired by the club, is up for grabs. Others items include original watercolours of City's famed 70s players and coach Malcolm Allison and team picture from every era.

Mr Niven, from Didsbury, has made a present of the collection fo his son, Ian Stuart, who left the club recently after working in administration at Maine Road for 28 years.

He said: "For some reason they didn't seem to treasure records at the club. But during my time as a director I kept a lookout for thing I could collect.

"Over time it has grown into a significant collection. I believe there will be a large interest in it'

The items — some of which are expected to raise more than £5,000 — go on sale at auctioneers, Capes Dunn, at their offices in Charles Street, Manchester, on Tuesday at 12 noon. Viewing is Monday 10am 4pm and Tuesday from 10am.

1999 City supporters became extremely disappointed when significant items of club memorabilia were sold. Since 2002 the Blues have sought to rediscover items such as these.

man enjoying success across at Oldham. Royle had performed fantastically at Boundary Park to take the side to the League Cup final and the FA Cup semi-finals, but that success was only part of Royle's development of the club. He brought the club a significant amount of excitement, and guided the club through a glorious period in the club's history.

Major trophy success is one obvious way of spotting a great manager, but with Royle his record at both Oldham and City show, that sometimes a manager's greatest achievements are not trophies, but pride, passion and an ability to develop a real spirit of togetherness. The fans of both clubs were part of Royle's family.

In 1990-91 Royle guided Latics through a thrilling season which saw them win promotion as Champions of Division Two. Royle's side had challenged throughout the campaign, and when a 1-1 draw with promotion rivals West Ham on Good Friday was followed with a victory over Plymouth on Easter Monday, it became obvious that this was Oldham's best chance in decades to reach the top division. Oldham and West Ham were neck-and-neck for the title and when Oldham defeated Ipswich 2-1 on 27th April with goals from Ian Marshall promotion was assured.

Royle accurately summed up the feeling when he said:

"The players are elated, but it isn't as if someone scored the winner in the last ten minutes of the last game. Promotion seems to have been with us for a long time."

Achieving promotion was a significant step forward for Oldham but more joy was to follow. The title race was still in progress, although West Ham seemed to have the most chance of success going into the last game. The London club were two points ahead of Royle's men and with the Hammers playing fourth placed Notts County at home and Oldham facing third placed Sheffield Wednesday at Boundary Park it seemed West Ham would be the champions, however Oldham were determined to continue their challenge to the final minute.

Amazingly, West Ham lost 2-1 but as Oldham's game entered the final minute the Latics were drawing 2-2 – after initially going two goals down. This meant that West Ham would still win the title on goal difference, but two minutes later – the 92nd minute of Oldham's final game – the Latics were awarded a penalty. **Piccadilly Radio's** Stuart Pike's commentary of that match and those moments remains one of the most dramatic sporting radio broadcasts in our region. The commentary covered all the key moments, but as the game entered injury time Pike became more and more excited. By the time of the penalty – a good three minutes after the whistle should have blown – he was hysterical and then when Neil Redfearn netted, his emotion was clear.

When the final whistle sounded Pike's voice was barely holding out but he managed to scream:

"Redfearn plays it forward to Moulden... and the referee has blown the whistle. Celebration time. Oldham Athletic have won the Second Division title on the last day of the season in injury time. Absolutely incredible scenes here."

He went on in passionate tone for some time as the Second Division trophy was presented to Earl Barrett: *"It was a sunny day – unheard of in Oldham. It was like a cup final and to come out on top, promoted as champions, was absolutely fantastic."*

Andy Ritchie remembers this as a great day:

"That day was amazing. It was absolutely jam-packed. There were pitch invasions every time a goal went in, which was unsavoury but meant that our game would finish later than West Ham's. If the story's true, West Ham had the cup down at their game and were parading it, not knowing what our result was. They thought we'd drawn, and I think there was a quick removal of the ribbons."

From a media perspective, Stuart Pike's commentary became a classic moment in itself with **Piccadilly Radio's** main sports presenter James H Reeve making the most out of Pike's style:

"It was great for Piccadilly because Pikey encapsulated what most people in Oldham were feeling. I think he almost got freedom of the town! It was great for the station because Oldham's success came at a time when the station was doing well, but we were the first to really celebrate Oldham's development. Pikey

Oldham celebrate promotion in 1991.

was perfect and when a team gets success like that it's not just the fans that celebrate, it's the whole town. Typically people would see the station as a Manchester station, but this proved we weren't just about City and United. Piccadilly became the number one station for Latics and in some ways was the whole town's station. It probably sounds like a drop in the ocean when you talk about the whole of Greater Manchester, but for us it was highly important. We wanted to cover every club and do it well, and thanks to Pikey's... How shall I put this? Individual technique and Oldham's success we managed it."

The penalty scorer was asked what he felt at the time of the spot kick and Redfearn admitted:

"I just closed my mind to everything else going on. All I was concerned with was deciding where to place the shot and making sure of a good strike. I never thought I would miss, but it was a relief and a great feeling when it went in."

The title arrived at Boundary Park, as did the championship trophy but amazingly the trophy had already been engraved with West Ham's name instead of Oldham's. The Latics managed to quickly get it altered, but it did demonstrate how much of an achievement the title actually was.

As a result of Oldham's promotion, the Latics became embroiled in the formation of the Premier League. It was a little unfair as Oldham simply wanted to enjoy their appearance in the top division without the hassles attached to the league restructure, but as a First Division side they had to get involved. Chairman Ian Stott was placed into a position where he had to either support the Premier League or Oldham would find themselves excluded. He said at the time:

"I am not happy at being forced into this position, but I cannot now see anything to prevent the FA from implementing their proposals. We have waited 68 years to regain our place in the top flight, so my personal feelings don't come into it. We simply cannot afford to be left behind, and if nothing happens to alter the situation, we will tell the FA before the August deadline that we wish to be included."

The following season – the last before the restructure - the Latics finished 17th out of 22 sides and had acquitted themselves well, particularly as West Ham ended the season bottom of the First Division. Much had been made in previous years about the impact Oldham's artificial pitch had on the team's performance, although away results prove Oldham were not simply good on plastic, and as a result of increased pressure, and League directives, in the summer of 1991 the artificial surface was replaced by grass. So the record in 1991-2 was even more remarkable as it allowed Oldham to silence any critics.

The highlights of the season had included England international Earl Barrett's goal on 17th August at Liverpool on the opening day of the season; the first victory – a 3-0 win over Chelsea; a 2-1 victory over City at Maine Road; and a 2-0 victory over champions to be Leeds United.

The following season saw Oldham become founder members of the Premier League (They shared the unusual distinction of being founder members of both the Premier League and Division Four with Crystal Palace and Coventry City). That season they narrowly avoided relegation on goal difference on the last day of the season when they beat Southampton 4-3. Royle admitted:

"There have been a lot of shredded nerves and some games have aged me five years. But it's great for us and we've deserved it. We always have a go, we try to score goals. Maybe there's a lesson in that. We play the game with the right attitude; things are never dull with us and surely there's a place in the Premier League for sides like that."

1993-94 brought more positive headlines Latics way as Royle's side reached the FA Cup semi-final for the second time in four years and, as with 1990, their opponents were United. The semi was played at Wembley and saw Neil Pointon put Oldham into the lead in extra-time, but Mark Hughes volleyed an equaliser with only 53 seconds of the 120 minutes remaining. The goal gave United the advantage. Mark Hughes said afterwards:

"Forcing a replay gave us a second chance of reaching the final. We were not going to let that opportunity slip."

Oldham's Andy Ritchie also feels this goal was decisive:

"United came back from the dead with Hughes' volley when we were probably only a minute away from the final, and unfortunately they had a little bit of a quick winger that came back for the replay Andrei Kanchelskis and he managed to knock two in. It was very difficult that one. We'd been close on two occasions and afterwards it knocked a lot out of us. We didn't think we'd ever get that chance again… and we never did!"

The replay ended 4-1 but, as Ritchie implied, the result impacted Latics' overall form. In the League Royle's side only managed three points from their remaining seven games and ended the season in 21st place, 3 points from safety.

Andy Ritchie

Relegation hit hard, but worse was to follow in November 1994 when Joe Royle resigned to become Everton's manager after twelve years at Boundary Park. Royle was genuinely sorry to be leaving the Latics, and most supporters recognised that he had to move on. There had been plenty of stories circulating since the late 1980s that Royle was wanted by one of football's so called giants and, when the club he first made his name as a player called, it was inevitable he had to leave. Royle said at the time:

"Perhaps the time was right for Oldham to make a change as well, and get fresh impetus and ideas. I couldn't turn down the chance to manage a club which has the potential to be one of the biggest, if not the biggest in the country. Everton are capable of winning the European Cup, and that is something we could only dream about at Boundary Park."

As time moves on Everton's chance of winning the European Cup seems to be as far removed as Oldham's was during Royle's time in the town, but in 1994 Royle's views were appropriate. At this stage in football's history the Premier League was still something sides like Everton, City, and Newcastle had a chance of success in. City had finished fifth twice in the early nineties, Leeds had won the League in 1992, and Blackburn – admittedly with strong financial backing at the time – won the Premier League in 1995. It has only really been since 2000 that the Premier League title has become out of reach for the majority of the league's sides.

Royle went on to guide Everton to the FA Cup before returning to the region as City manager in 1998. He arrived too late to seriously affect City's chance of survival, but his record after relegation was predominantly a successful one. For Oldham, the late 1990s were not great. In 1997 they were relegated in 23rd place from the First Division (second tier) and in 1999 they were almost relegated again but a 2-0 victory over Reading ensured they avoided the drop by a point. Incidentally, the side relegated in their place was York City who were defeated 4-0 at Maine Road by Joe Royle's play-off bound City side. It is worth pointing out that Latics were one of only two sides to beat City during the final 24 matches of that season.

Andy Ritchie was Latics manager between 1998 and 2001 and he accepts this was a difficult period for the club: *"You go into management with your eyes open. I think we only spent £65,000 in three years when I was manager, so it shows you that it was tight but that's how it had to be. It gave me a good grounding. I had to wheel and deal and bring in free transfers. I had to work really hard, but I thoroughly enjoyed it there until the time I left."*

While Oldham and City competed in Division Two (the third tier) two sides who had during the eighties usually been seen as minor sides to those had competed in Division One. Stockport and Bury spent part of the 1990s above both City and Oldham. For modern football fans it seemed a bizarre situation, although most Bury supporters would suggest that history shows Bury as a second tier side, while Oldham tended to be a third tier club.

With Bury, the nineties opened with a fifth placed finish in Division Three and secured a play-off place. They faced Tranmere Rovers and after a goalless draw at Gigg Lane they lost 2-0 at Prenton Park. Another play-off appearance followed in 1991 but this time seventh placed Bury faced Bolton Wanderers. A 1-1 draw at Gigg Lane was followed by defeat at Burnden Park. It was another significant disappointment but the feeling of frustration felt was nothing compared to the problems of the following campaign.

1992 started with the Shakers lying twentieth but an excellent unbeaten run followed and Gigg

Lane was full of hope as February dawned. Sadly, injuries to key players, most notably midfielder Phil Parkinson, and suspensions for others caused form to dip. Off the pitch the club were also struggling financially and Lloyds Bank insisted that a player had to be sold if the wages were to be honoured. It was a terrible situation to be in but Bury had no choice but to comply. Colin Greenall was sold to Preston for a particularly low £50,000 price tag. The moment the transfer was made it was clear the Shakers' problems would worsen both on the pitch and off it.

On the final day of the season Bury travelled to Greenall's new club Preston and lost 2-0, causing Bury to be relegated from 'old' Division Three to 'new' Division Three. The side had ended the last season before the restructure of the league in 21st place and thereby dropped into the fourth tier for the first time since promotion in 1985.

The club appeared to be dying and the contrast with United and City at this time was significant. The Reds were to become the Premier League's first champions, and their reserves were to play at Gigg Lane, while City had finished the previous two seasons in fifth place, however the fortunes of two of those teams were about to change briefly. City went on a downward spiral, ultimately competing at a lower level than Bury for a season.

When the 1992-93 season commenced Bury concentrated on recruiting relatively cheap, bargain basement players. It took time for the side to gel as a unit – a robbery in the dressing room at Doncaster on the opening day in which the players lost money and jewellery did not help! – but the final weeks of the year saw the side enjoy an unbeaten run of eleven games. Those results helped lift Bury and they ultimately ended the season in seventh place, where they would compete in the play-offs for the third time in four years. A draw at Gigg Lane put Bury at a disadvantage for the second leg and York City won 1-0 at Bootham Crescent.

The disappointment lingered into 1993-94 and a mid-table finish was the best Bury could manage, but the following season further progress in the League was made, with the side reaching the play-offs once again. This time a fourth place finish saw Bury face Preston, but crucially the first leg would be away from home.

Preston were inevitably favourites for the game. Their tradition and status within the game meant that they were perhaps too confident. In fact coach companies in Preston were advertising their prices for trips to Wembley before the tie had even been played! This confidence actually worked in Bury's favour and David Pugh netted a 41st minute goal to give Bury victory in the first leg.

At Gigg Lane another memorable performance saw Tony Rigby score a screamer two minutes from time. The victory ensured Bury would visit Wembley ten days later for a play-off final with Chesterfield. As with the early century FA Cup finals Bury fans eagerly awaited their trip to the capital and around 10,000 tickets were sold, with 65 coaches – plus numerous private hire minibuses – organised. The excursion was highly exciting for all Shakers, but sadly the game did not go Bury's way. Despite being in control for much of the early play Chesterfield netted a controversial goal. Some said it was offside, some believed there had been a handball, but all Shakers and many neutrals were convinced the goal should not have been allowed. Captain David Pugh summed it up nicely when he later admitted: *"You can't defend against the Harlem Globetrotters."*

A second Chesterfield goal shortly before half time gave Bury an impossible task and the match ended in defeat. It was a cruel end to the season and the visit to Wembley was not in the end a pleasant one.

The following season, 1995-96, saw Bury challenge again, but before they managed that there was a significant change at the top. Manager Mike Walsh, who had been in charge for five years, was to move on. His last game, against Plymouth at the start of September, saw Bury concede five goals. Supporters were furious and the following Monday Chairman Terry Robinson revealed:

"We've had a chat and decided that it's best that Mike relinquishes his duties. There is no animosity and he can hold his head high."

The play-off disappointment had clearly had an impact, and many fans felt it was the right time for a change, but they also felt some sympathy for Walsh. Almost immediately, the fans demanded the appointment of Macclesfield Town's Sammy McIlroy, the ex United man, but Stan Ternent, Walsh's assistant was promoted instead. At the time it was not a popular move and proved, as with so many instances in the lives of the region's clubs that fans views were often ignored. The situation worsened when Ternent appointed Sam Ellis as his assistant. Ellis had in 1990 been Bury manager but had resigned to become Peter Reid's assistant at Maine Road. At that time Bury were in the middle of a crisis, while his arrival at City was not greeted particularly well either.

Gradually, as the season progressed, the mood lifted. Players were bought, progress was made, and Ternent was given the Manager of the Month award in March as Bury seemed destined for automatic promotion. An inconsistent spell followed and Bury appeared to have lost their chance. Supporters knew the play-offs could not be faced again and did all they could to encourage the team forward. However, as the season entered its final day, the situation was such that Bury needed to win at home to Cardiff and hope Darlington suffered at Scunthorpe.

Bury managed their victory but, as so often tends to happen in these situations, Darlington's game had started late. An agonising spell followed but fortunately BBC GMR had decided to provide match commentary of the match so that Shakers fans could hear the news as it happened. Darlington, drawing 3-3, hit the woodwork and nearly caused heart attacks for the 5,658 fans attending at Gigg Lane. Fortunately, when the ten minute or so wait was over the news was clear – Darlington had drawn and Bury were promoted to Division Two (the third tier).

Promotion in third place was a major achievement, but Stan Ternent believed more could be achieved. During the pre-season period he told fans:

"We will be giving it everything we can. The major shareholder and Chairman reckon we have the potential to be in the First Division and it's my ambition to deliver it for them. The word consolidation keeps getting mentioned, but people who settle for second best usually end up with nothing."

Ternent's comments were bold and they were certainly encouraging, particularly as most neutrals predicted they would be relegated, but they proved to be correct. Bury were promoted with a draw at Watford, but nerves were severely tested when a penalty was awarded to Watford with only two minutes left on the clock. Dean Kiely became a hero as he guessed right, saved the shot and kept hold of the ball. A frantic couple of minutes followed before Bury's celebrations could begin. Later that evening the players, directors and other officials celebrated with fans in the Gigg Lane Social Club. It had been a remarkable achievement and then on the final day Bury won 2-0 at home to Millwall to guarantee the title. Stockport finished second as the region celebrated a double promotion. Even more joy was to come when both sides realised they would be facing City on equal terms in 1997-98.

Left: **Bury's Paul Butler in action against City.**
Below: **A fan protests at Maine Road.**

For Bury the games with City were a joy. In September a crowd of 11,216 witnessed a 1-1 draw at Gigg Lane, while millions watched the game live on Sky TV, then on Valentine's Day a 52nd minute goal from Paul Butler caused much upset at City as the Shakers won their first game since 4th November (15 games without a win). Those points helped Bury achieve a 17th place finish but crucially the former poor, so-called 'small' team had finished the season five places higher than the 'giant' City who, along with Stoke and Reading, were relegated to the third tier of English football.

Bury fan Gordon Sorfleet remembers this period fondly:

"After years of being below City this is remembered as one of the best days we've seen. Certainly, in the last decade or so. Paul Butler in the second half at Maine Road... great. The funniest thing about that day was that it was during Franny Lee's time as City chairman, and a City fan came on the pitch, sat down and threw his season ticket away! A couple of days later Frank Clark was sacked as City manager. It was great for Bury to have such an effect. I'd hate to think how the City fans felt at the time - City below little Bury! Great days for us, but pretty poor for them."

Unfortunately for Bury relegation followed in 1998-99, but those two seasons in the second tier allowed many associated with the club to rightly talk of Bury's position within the region and the game. For much of their history Bury have been a second tier club. Many modern day supporters will tend to think of them as a third or fourth tier side but their history proves otherwise. Sadly, the national focus on the Premier League and the European competitions would lead to Bury struggling to attract the right support and finance needed to compete, but at least they have competed and, if nothing else, the 1998-99 season allowed Bury to look down at City for the first time since 1928.

Across at Stockport the 1990s were equally varied. The decade started with County in Division

Four but the 1989-90 season had seen the side finish in a respectable fourth place – missing automatic promotion by one point - and reach the play-offs. Sadly in the play-offs County faced a strong Chesterfield side. Both games ended in defeat with a crushing 4-0 scoreline in the away leg and a 2-0 defeat at home.

Despite the play-off disappointment, Manager Danny Bergara was receiving much praise for converting a side that seemed destined to struggle into a team that appeared capable of beating any team in the division. Stockport press officer Phil Brennan:

"Under Bergara we started to play attacking football in the opposition third. We went up the second year he was here, and we had four Wembley appearances in three years. Typical Stockport we lost all four, but at least we can say we got there."

County's promotion was achieved in 1991 with a second place finish. It was the first time Stockport had been promoted since 1967 and the side's success was even raised in the House Of Commons. Peter Snape, MP for West Bromwich East, had made a speech concerning the rail industry and was then followed by Andrew Bennett, the MP for Denton and Reddish. Bennett told the House:

"I am delighted to follow my honourable Friend, the Member for West Bromwich, East, because he is in extremely good form. I know that he has had a pretty heavy weekend, since his football team has managed to gain promotion from the fourth to the third division. There is a great deal of excitement in Stockport at the prospect. I was pleased to hear that he is in favour of increasing train speeds. He is one of the better-known supporters of Stockport County, and people are dredging up all sorts of stories in the town.

"I am sure my honourable Friend will want to deny one that is circulating… that, when he was working a signal box in Cheadle Heath one Saturday afternoon he slipped all the signals to red and nipped into Stockport County's ground to watch a match for some time, only to discover when shouting with great enthusiasm for his team that one of his supervisors was not far behind him in the crowd. My honourable

Danny Bergara and his Stockport side in 1991.

Friend had to make a hasty return to his signal box. I do not know whether that story is true, but it is circulating at the moment in Stockport."

Peter Snape responded: *"With regard to my honourable Friend's point about celebrations over the weekend, although I support Stockport County and saw them gain promotion on Saturday, my constituency football team, West Bromwich Albion, was relegated from the second division to the third. As a result of that, any joy that I might have expressed publicly had to be muted. The story that my honourable Friend recounted was broadly accurate. However, the signals were not turned to red, they were turned to green. I had switched the signal box out to go and watch the cup match."*

With that matter clarified Bennett then asked: *"I wonder who he will be supporting next season in the third division."*

Snape chose not to respond to that question, presumably for fear of upsetting his constituents.

Further success followed as Bergara's side challenged for promotion from Division Three in 1991-92. This time County reached fifth place and entered the play-offs. They missed automatic promotion by five points, and in the play-offs they faced Stoke. The first match at Edgeley Park ended with a 1-0 victory thanks to a goal from Peter Ward in front of a crowd of 7,537. Three days later the second leg ended 1-1 and County reached the Wembley final. Sadly, Peterborough, who had ended the season in sixth place managed to score first with a 51st minute header. The ball had hit the crossbar and come down on the line. County fans argued that the ball hadn't crossed the line, but it was given.

The final became extremely tense as County searched for an equaliser. Then up popped Kevin Francis to equalise after having an earlier effort discounted. By scoring 'Big' Kevin became the first County player to score at Wembley. He was also already well known as Stockport's biggest star. Known throughout the game, Francis was perhaps the most famous County man of the period,

Danny Bergara and former United star Lou Macari lead out Stockport and Stoke for the Autoglass Trophy final in May 1992. Stoke won the match 1-0.

and he was later voted the accolade of the 'player of the Century' which demonstrates exactly how important he was to the side at this stage in his life and the club's history.

After the equaliser the game looked to be heading for extra time when, in the final minute, Port Vale's Charlery lobbed the ball over Goalkeeper Neil Edwards for the winner. It was a real blow in what was County's second Wembley appearance of all time.

County's Kevin Francis at Wembley in 1992.

Amazingly, only eight days earlier County had made their first visit to Wembley when they faced Stoke in the Autoglass Trophy. The Autoglass Trophy was the sponsored name of the Associate Members' Cup – a competition for teams in the Third and Fourth Divisions of the Football League. Stoke defeated County 1-0, but two Wembley appearances within the space of eight days gave Stockport a great deal of prestige.

Twelve months later County reached both the play-offs and the Autoglass final again. At Wembley in the Autoglass County were trailing 2-0 at half time to Port Vale, but Kevin Francis gave the side hope when he netted a header to give the side hope. The *Daily Telegraph* reported:

"The introduction of the lively Preece immediately offered more space for Francis. First the towering Stockport striker bundled the ball out of Musselwhite's hands, then forced the Vale keeper to save in the air and on the floor. Stockport's pressure deserved reward and it came in the 66th minute. Francis started the move with a pass to Duffield and got up field rapidly enough to meet the cross and divert it unerringly over the advancing Musselwhite's head. Stockport stepped up the pace, Vale wilted and tempers began to fray."

Danny Bergara

The large contingent of Stockport fans in the 35,885 crowd chanted "Danny Bergara's Blue & White Army" and the whole atmosphere swung in favour of County. Significant pressure was applied with County coming close to equalising but sadly, success eluded them and the game ended in defeat.

It was a similar story in the play-offs when Port Vale won 2-1 on aggregate in the semi-finals, and then in 1994 there was heartache again in the play-offs when County reached the final, but were defeated 2-1 by Burnley before 44,806. How much longer could County sustain this record of reaching the play-offs? Sadly, an eleventh placed finish in 1995 and ninth in 1996 meant County missed out entirely, but then 1996-97 became the season fans had hoped for for some time. This time, under manager Dave Jones, County finished the season in second place in Division Two (the third tier), just behind champions Bury.

In addition County reached the semi-final of the League Cup for the first time in their history. They faced Middesbrough but sadly they lost the first leg at Edgeley Park 2-0. Most neutrals would have assumed that was it, and that County would be humiliated in the away leg, but County proved worthy opponents and managed a 1-0 victory at the Riverside Stadium. Sadly, it was not enough to give County their first League Cup final appearance, but it did encourage fans overall, especially as County had come close to equalising on aggregate on several occasions.

The League Cup semi-final appearance and the promotion were two magnificent highpoints in County's season but, unfortunately, Dave Jones soon moved on to Southampton, and was replaced at Edgeley Park by Gary Megson. Often a managerial change so soon after a significant success can have a detrimental effect on the side and could cause the side to stagnate and to struggle, but with County Megson was able to guide the team to an eighth place finish in 1997-98. This was the club's highest position of all time and meant that County were the region's second highest placed side, United being the highest. City were fourteen places below County. There were many high points during the season, including a 2-2 draw with Champions to be Nottingham Forest in April and a 3-1 victory over City at Edgeley Park on 29th November.

After the high of 1998 County remained a Division One side for the rest of the decade, however they finished in 16th and 17th place over the following two seasons. Again they managed great results over City in 1999-2000 – a 2-1 win at Maine Road in December and a 2-2 draw at Edgeley Park in March. Incidentally, with the December victory over City, County's first goal was scored by Alan Bailey who had arrived at Edgeley Park on a free transfer from City. The same player was brought down in the 86th minute which resulted in Tony Dinning scoring a penalty. Dave Espley, writing in the Stockport fanzine the *Tea Party*, later highlighted his feelings of that game:

"It reminded me why I enjoy watching County. County fans get behind their team when things are not going to plan. Maybe that is because as County fans, expectations have already been exceeded simply by playing the likes of City and Blackburn in the league, whereas in Moss Side the opposite is true."

In the other Stockport-City game City took a seventh minute lead via Jamie Pollock, but County took control with Ian Moore netting a 28th minute equaliser and then County cult-hero Mike Flynn netted a second two minutes before the interval. City's equaliser was scored by Richard Jobson in the 78th minute. Phil Brennan believes facing City was one of County's greatest successes of the period:

"A lot of my friends are City fans. My best man's a City fan. Unfortunately, Stockport's got a lot of City fans in it and so for us to be playing on equal terms was great. Then for us to start beating them… it made County fans look forward to going to work or school on a Monday. They were happy days."

County hero Mike Flynn shares those feelings:

"Most of my friends who I have grown up with are season ticket holders at Maine Road. So to go down there and beat them… and to beat them here at Edgeley Park was great. When I scored a goal here against them I ran the full length of the pitch and some of my mates were in the Cheadle End and I went and slid on my knees in front of them. They don't forget that.

"Remember though it wasn't just City. We played against some massive clubs. We had Middlesbrough

here in the semi-final of a major cup competition with the likes of Juninho and Emerson. It was unheard of 'Little' Stockport County. But that period really put us on the map and I played 65 out of 66 games that season, and for such a small club to play so many cup games was astonishing. The fans must have thought they were dreaming."

These were great moments for County but sadly it was not to last. A club record 19 games without a victory followed (28/12/99 to 22/4/2000) and the 1999-2000 season saw County narrowly avoid relegation with a seventeenth place. County were still a Division One side, but considerable effort would need to be made if County were to compete in that division throughout the new century.

Over at Rochdale the decade saw the side continue to compete in the lowest division of the Football League. Dale's best League season during that period came in 1991-92 when they finished eighth under manager Dave Sutton after starting the season with their longest unbeaten run since 1925. Off the pitch however, financial matters were causing serious concern. Increased policing costs – it was announced that police charges would rocket from £893 to £4,259 per match (around £2 per spectator!) – and the creation of the Premier League were perhaps the club's two biggest concerns. Less income from television and the League was anticipated and Dale had no choice but to look at their playing squad and find ways of bringing transfer money in, or of cutting the wage bill. The club had made a trading loss of £181,000 over the year with gate income coming to around £250,000 and wages costing £520,000.

Behind the scenes Dale's commercial department worked hard to improve finances and by 1993-4 the department had raised around £100,000 – a significant amount. Hospitality boxes were now available at £3,000 per season and many other initiatives had been tried during the early 1990s. Of course it helped that the season had seen the side finish ninth, but the following season (1994-5) started with a Lancashire Cup tie against Manchester United. A crowd of 4,290 watched Dale defeat a side that contained David Beckham and Gary Neville 3-2. One of Dale's scorers, Shaun Reid (brother of former City manager Peter Reid), was already viewed by Rochdale fans as being better than some of United's heroes and a range of car stickers had earlier been released reading: ***"Who needs Cantona when we've got Shaunie Reid."*** It is worth noting that Gary Neville made his England debut less than 11 months after his Spotland appearance.

League form was mixed during the 1994-95 season – a 6-2 defeat at Barnet was soon followed by a 4-2 win at Scarborough - but Dale came close to real success in the Auto Windscreens Shield (Associate Members' Cup). They reached the northern final of the trophy after defeating Blackpool, Wigan, Darlington, Stockport, and Bury, but were defeated 5-3 on aggregate. The first leg at Carlisle had been the killer game with Dale losing 4-1 in extremely stormy and difficult circumstances. A gallant fight in the second leg saw Dale go two goals up in 22 minutes, but former Evertonian Derek Mountfield scored for Carlisle and Rochdale's chance of success soon disappeared.

Another northern final came in March 2000. This time they faced Stoke and sadly went three goals behind in the opening half hour. They managed to pull a goal back through the previous season's top scorer Michael Holt, but the 3-1 defeat made it very difficult going to the Britannia Stadium for the second leg. A crowd of 16,896 witnessed another Stoke victory (1-0).

In terms of League position, it is fair to say that Rochdale spent most of the decade in the lower half of the division, but following the birth of the Premier League and the financial problems facing lower division sides, simply to exist and be in a position to compete was a major achievement. Of course, beating Neville, Beckham and Co in 1994 was something many sides were unable to do, but Dale did it!

The story of United during the decade was one of more or less continual success. From the FA Cup win at the start of the period, through to the Premier League title in 1999-2000, the Reds managed to win 13 significant trophies. There were some trophy free years, but in the main the decade belonged to United.

It is worth pausing to consider that both Manchester's two leading clubs were under-achievers during the Seventies and Eighties. Considering both clubs' size, support, and wealth the two decades saw both City and United each win only three major trophies, and neither of them managed to win the title during those decades. At a time when Liverpool (four), Nottingham Forest (twice) and Aston Villa found European Cup success and other sides such as Chelsea, Tottenham, Everton and Ipswich found success in the other European competitions, it was highly surprising that neither City or United could manage sustained success during that twenty year spell. Both sides came close to winning the title (City runners up in 1977; United in 1980 & 1988), but considering the size of their support both clubs can be regarded as under-achievers during that period.

For United, a club claiming by the end of the 1980s to be the biggest in the world (although several continental sides would argue), this was totally unacceptable. United needed to win the title and every time Liverpool found success it hurt, so the 1990s became the Manchester Reds chance to truly shine.

The record of success under Alex Ferguson was greater than any Mancunian would have anticipated at the end of the 1980s. United looked as if they had a few more years of struggle, but success in the FA Cup, then in the European Cup Winners' Cup against Barcelona managed to give the Reds a little more belief in their manager and their side. Incidentally, the ECWC final was played in Rotterdam at Feyenoord's stadium and was an exceptionally tense night as United tried to find success in their first European final outside of England. Mark Hughes proved, as he often did, that he was a man for the big occasion and he netted his first on the 68th minute after a Bryan Robson (named the player of the 1980s by England manager Bobby Robson) free kick had found Steve Bruce who headed goalwards wher Hughes was wiating to pounce.

A second Hughes goal came – from what looked an impossible angle – in the 75th minute. Barcelona's Koeman netted four minutes later, and Clayton Blackmore cleared a shot from Laudrup off the line, but United held on to tehir lead.

Immediately after the final most footballing pundits tipped United for the title in 1991-92. This was to be the last season prior to the Premier League but the difference between top and bottom of the League during this spell was not so great as it was to become later in the decade and Leeds United, who had only been promoted in 1990 after eight years in Division Two, matched United for much of the season. The Reds looked the strongest side in the division from the start despite challenges from Liverpool and City, in addition to Leeds. A point proved when Alex Ferguson picked up the first two manager of the month accolades as the Reds looked determined. By 2nd November Leeds had caught United a little - United were on 31 points from 14 games while Leeds were on 30 from 15 (City were third on 28 points) – but by 26th February United's lead over Leeds had increased to four points and eleven over third placed City.

A month later United were still in pole position but the gap had narrowed to one point although United still had a game in hand, however the Yorkshire side seemed to possess the right approach and Leeds' David Batty admitted in March:

"We feel nearly all the pressure is on Man United. I don't think there is any sign of nerves at Elland Road. We are enjoying our football and whatever happens we'll have had a phenomenal season. We'll just let Man United do the worrying and take each game as it comes."

At the start of April Leeds were thrashed 4-0 by City at Maine Road, and it looked as if the Yorkshire side's title hopes were over. Then United drew 1-1 with City at Old Trafford and by the time of United's next League game (at home to Southampton on 16th) the Elland Road club were heading the table, one point clear of United. In between the City and Southampton game the Reds had defeated Nottingham Forest in the final of the League Cup, sponsored by Rumbelows at the time (ironically a company that a few years earlier had bought out a chain of electrical shops owned by City Chairman Peter Swales).

Although the Reds beat Southampton the pressure seemed to be on United. A draw at relegation favourites Luton and defeat at home by Forest left the Reds one point behind Leeds, but crucially United did still have a game in hand. With three games to go all United needed to do was win their final three games to be guaranteed their first title since 1967. Sadly, they could not manage that and successive defeats at West Ham and Liverpool gave Leeds the title. The Reds ended the season four points behind the Yorkshiremen who, incidentally, had been boosted by the addition to their numbers of a Frenchman called Eric Cantona during the latter half of the season.

Years later Brian McClair commenting on the season in United's illustrated history believed fixture congestion was the difference between Leeds and United:

"We lost it because we had to play so many games towards the end of the season. We lost at home to Forest at Easter when Giggsy and Sharpey decided to go to Blackpool for the night. Then we just couldn't win a game and by the end of it all we had nothing left. We would never take any credit away from Leeds because they stuck ai it doggedly all year. But it was interesting that the change in the back pass law killed them the following season. We were the more exciting team, trying to batter or steamroller the opposition."

The comment about fixture congestion was true to some extent, however in terms of League games United only played one more League game (and one Cup game) than Leeds in April and May, and Leeds had played more League matches in March.

McClair was the man who netted the only goal of the 1992 League Cup final:

"To score in a cup final at Wembley is something that everyone dreams about. People might say now that the League Cup doesn't matter, but at the time the club were more than happy to have some more silverware. It was another trophy and that kept the momentum going."

If the momentum in the League season had stuttered towards the end, McClair was right to say the general momentum of the club continued and the circumstances were right for the side, recognised as English football's wealthiest, to make another serious assault on the title in 1992-3. Ferguson signed a forward by the name of Dion Dublin in August 1992 and the £1m player scored on his full debut against Southampton on 24th August 1992. This was the first victory of the season and followed two defeats and a draw. Dublin's arrival helped establish an attacking frame of mind, and though he is not regarded as one of United's most crucial players of the 1990s, it is true that fate was to play its hand. Dublin's career at United would ultimately help Ferguson make a decision that would set the Reds up for an assault on the League title.

At his home debut Dublin suffered a broken leg and damage to his ankle ligaments. A long fight to regain fitness meant Ferguson had to seriously consider strengthening his side and in November 1992 Eric Cantona was bought for £1.2m. It turned out to be one of the best investments any football side had made in one player, and for the next few years, Cantona thrilled as he helped establish United as real League contenders and European competitors. His full League debut came on 12th December at home to Norwich – 6 days after he had come on as substitute for Ryan Giggs in the Old Trafford derby match. United player Paul Parker believes Cantona's arrival was significant:

"He had something about him. He had a presence. He could have five players around him and still want the ball. You'd give it to him – well you'd have to give it to him. The boss always used to say that he added a new dimension. It's only now when you analyse it that you realise what a difference he made to the team."

From Cantona's debut the Reds were only to lose two League games (one of which was against Joe Royle's Oldham) while they had been defeated in four League games prior to his first appearance.

The first Premier League season had not gone entirely United's way – they were in third place at the start of April and both Norwich and Aston Villa stood a real chance of taking the title, but Ferguson's side managed to defeat Noriwch 3-1 on 5th April, and were in blistering form as they entered the final six games of the season. Victories at home to Sheffield Wednesday (2-1) – according to Paul Parker this was a significant result and set the Reds up – and Chelsea (3-0) and away to Coventry (1-0) and Crystal Palace (2-0) meant the Reds could win the title with two games left to play if Oldham could beat Aston Villa on 2nd May – the following day United would face Blackburn at Old Trafford.

Sure enough Joe Royle's Oldham beat Ron Atkinson's Villa. Peter Schmeichel:

"We trained on the Sunday and while Villa played Oldham, I was having a nap. When I woke up an hour later, I tuned into Teletext to see the result of the Aston Villa game. There were still five minutes to go but Oldham were winning 1-0. Those were five long minutes for me! I switched off the TV, turned on the radio, turned the radio off again, played for a while on the piano, turned on the TV again, went back to the radio, and finally lay down on the floor behind the sofa with my head buried in my arms. And then the final whistle blew. Oldham had won, and we had become champions of England! After 26 years, Manchester United were League champions again, and I was a member of the team that had done it!"

An impromptu party at Steve Bruce's house followed. Paul Parker: *"It was a tough day at the office the next day. In the dressing room players were trying to keep their eyes open and the boss was giving us a semi-serious rollicking before the game for what we'd done the night before, and then at half-time he gave us another for the way we performed in the first half. In the second half we totally blitzed Blackburn. After the game was another party."*

United were by far the most successful of the Manchester region sides during the 1990s.

The long wait was over and success in the very first Premier League season seemed to ignite the Reds in a way no other side managed. Of the other top five sides in the Premier League – Villa, Norwich, Blackburn, and QPR - that season only one would find success (Blackburn Rovers) in the years that followed and even then success could not be sustained. United were the first true beneficiaries of the new style League, but they were also the first to build a strong foundation for the future.

From the moment Alex Ferguson arrived in Manchester he found it hard to accept that City possessed the greater youth set up and that the Blues were developing strong talented individuals such as Paul Simpson, Earl Barrett, Paul Lake, Andy Hinchcliffe, David White, Ian Brightwell and Steve Redmond. He worked hard to ensure the Reds started to succeed and invested heavily in scouting and youth. While players such as Cantona were being bought to bring instant results, by 1993 Ferguson's youth set up was starting to pay dividends. Ryan Giggs, who had previously been part of City's youth set up, was heralded as one of the greatest finds of the Ferguson years, while others such as Lee Sharpe and Lee Martin had also made names for themselves by this point. In addition youngsters David Beckham, Gary Neville, and Nicky Butt had each made substitute appearances at some point during the season. It was this more than anything else, that suggested United would finally find the regular success their size, support, and history demanded.

From 1990 onwards United, under Alex Ferguson, has become a major European power and although they did not find the European success in the 1990s that Liverpool had in the 1970s and 1980s, they did develop their name and reputation in a similar – if not greater – manner.

By the end of the summer of 2000 the Reds had won an amazing six titles, four FA Cups, one League Cup, one ECWC, and one European Cup. They had also found success in the European Super Cup and the Inter-Continental Cup. United were also the richest of our local sides and with success following success it seemed as if none of the others would ever catch them. Bury's Gordon Sorfleet:

"To me the Premier League is ripping the heart and sole out of football and creating an unequal playing field. Take Manchester United... their programme sales for one Champions League game would keep this club running for two years. We can't compete against that! For the bigger clubs it's a business. To us it's still a game.

"The Premier League doesn't really appeal to me. I try not to watch it on the telly. I don't watch Champions League games either, but give me a Second Division or League Two game on and I'll sit there rivetted to it."

The 1990s were undoubtedly a great period for many of the region's clubs across the divisions with United, Oldham, Stockport and Bury finding real success.

ATTENDANCE DETAIL SEASON BY SEASON - 1989-1997

Season	City	United	Oldham	Bury	Stockport	Rochdale
1989-90	27975	39077	9727	3450	3899	2027
1990-91	27874	43218	13247	3572	3562	2238
1991-92	27691	44984	15087	2901	4896	2784
1992-93	24698	35152	12859	2670	5504	2312
1993-94	26709	44244	12563	2597	5090	2657
1994-95	22725	43681	8444	3223	4525	2184
1995-96	27869	41700	6634	3262	5859	2214
1996-97	26753	55081	7045	4502	6424	1829

LEAGUE POSITIONS SEASON BY SEASON - 1989-1997

Season	City	United	Oldham	Bury	Stockport	Rochdale
1989-90	14	13	28	49	72	80
1990-91	5	6	21	51	70	80
1991-92	5	2	17	67	51	78
1992-93	9	1	19	77	52	81
1993-94	16	1	21	83	50	79
1994-95	17	2	36	74	57	85
1995-96	18	1	38	71	53	83
1996-97	34	1	43	45	46	82

CHAPTER TWENTY-FOUR

THE MODERN ERA

I have just read that Stockport County are going to be renamed Man-Stock County and are moving from Edgeley Park to Maine Road in Manchester. I have just double checked the calendar just to make sure that it is not April 1! Dave Espley, "The Tea Party", 2000

WITH United at the height of their powers and City back in the Premier League and planning a move to the stadium being built for the 2002 Commonwealth Games, it looked as if football in the region at the end of the nineties was to be dominated by these two sides. However the biggest development of the new century saw supporters from a range of clubs in the region take a lead in shaping the destiny of their clubs. The commercialisation of football gave many traditional fans an uneasy feel. Then, as the money invested in the game via television, sponsorship and corporate activities increased, non-traditional investors became interested in the English game. Locally, fans felt they were losing their sport.

At Old Trafford, United supporters had successfully fought against takeovers by media moguls Robert Maxwell in the 1980s and Rupert Murdoch in 1999, while City fans had proactively sought to remove their chairman Peter Swales. Despite being a passionate City supporter and Mancunian, fans felt the chairman had let them down in a number of areas. They mounted a "Swales Out" campaign for over a decade before finally getting their way in 1993, but even then it was only the presence of ex-City star Francis Lee that helped galvanise the majority of supporters.

For many supporters in our region the new century was a period when the larger clubs seemed less interested in their views than ever before. Nevertheless – and possibly because of this - direct fan action was soon to have an impact on the structure of football in the region.

The biggest fan related story to seriously alter the direction of one of our League sides was at Stockport. County had enjoyed a successful 1990s with two Autoglass Trophy finals, promotion and an eighth placed finish in Division One (second tier of league football) in 1998. Everything looked positive, then in 2000 rumours circulated that County were interested in moving to Maine Road. It was even suggested the club would change its name. City were scheduled to move to their new stadium in 2003 and Manchester City Council were keen to see another significant sports team move into the stadium. The two obvious candidates were County and Sale Sharks.

County Chairman Brendan Elwood had meetings with Manchester council and seemed particularly keen on the prospect:

"It's an attractive idea because, to be honest, with the crowds and ground we have at Stockport we've been overachieving for the past few years. We feel we would be the best possible leaseholders and could bring more to the Moss Side area than anyone else who might be interested in taking over Maine Road.

"When this possible move was first suggested the majority of the letters we received and comments on the internet were supportive. For those who see Edgeley Park as a sacred ground, I would reply there simply aren't enough pilgrims there."

The move itself was clearly an issue, but for some the worst part was the idea that the club might also change its name. Elwood was more positive:

"Name changes are possible and when we were founded in 1883 we were Heaton Norris Rovers. But I would want to keep some reference to Stockport in the name, Man-Stock County for instance."

The comment was similar to that made in 1902 by Newton Heath secretary James West when he wanted the name Newton Heath incorporated into the new name of his club Manchester United. Although in both cases the logic was right, in practical terms both were non-starters.

Ultimately, Manchester council saw Sale as a better prospect for Maine Road and the Stockport interest waned. Ultimately Sale pulled out, causing a dilemma for the council. Maine Road remained a high quality stadium in parts – remember the 10,000 capacity Kippax Stand was opened in 1995 and also housed the best corporate facilities of any ground in the region (in fact no lounge at the new City of Manchester Stadium could match the size or versatility of the Kippax's Millennium Suite) – but its capacity was too high for most local sports clubs, while its location would always alienate fans from outside of Manchester. This meant that the County interest ended and the council took the decision to demolish Maine Road instead.

With the decision taken to stay in Stockport, County fans should have been happy, however matters on the pitch raised serious concerns. In 2001-02 County were relegated from 'New' Division One - a spell between 24th November 2001 and 13th January saw a record number of consecutive League defeats - finishing the season with just 26 points. In fact relegation came on the 16th March - the earliest post-war relegation. A midtable finish followed, but these were worrying times for fans. County fan Phil Brennan:

"We had four or five years of success, then it dramatically changed. The wheels came off completely. We went down with a record number of goals conceded... least amount of goals scored at home. In 2001 Carlton Palmer became manager and that failed."

Many fans had wanted cult hero Mike Flynn to be the club's manager. Flynn:

"Carlton was getting stick, and I wasn't in the team. A lot of fans were shouting for me to become the manager and I think that helped Carlton make his decision to let me go."

In the summer of 2003 Brendan Elwood sold the club to Brian Kennedy, the owner of Sale Sharks, and the rugby side moved to Edgeley Park. A new company was created, called 'Cheshire Sports', which would have ownership of Stockport County, Sale Sharks & the Edgeley Park stadium. During that same period the demolition of Maine Road commenced causing some to consider what would have happened had either Sale or County moved to Maine Road.

Despite the new opportunities presented by a dual sports club, County struggled further and in 2004-05 they were relegated again. This time they found themselves in Football League Two. The

Football League had been restructured in 2004 with the new League Two being the fourth tier of the national game (equivalent to the early 1990s Football League Division Four). Phil Brennan:

"It got worse. We thought well at least we can have a laugh with teams like Dale, but we used to get battered by every team in that division as well."

That summer a major transformation saw the club's ownership change again. A supporters' trust had been set up to aid the club and on 8th July 2005 ownership was passed from Cheshire Sports to the Supporters Trust. For the first time possibly since formation, one of our region's leading professional sides was now in the hands of its supporters. This is highly significant in the development of the game and meant that County could truly claim to be a club for its fans. So many sides have claimed to listen to supporters and work for their good but once clubs became PLCs with shares listed on the stockmarket – United floated in 1991 – shareholders were the people the companies were accountable to. Inevitably most football shareholders were also fans but, as events at United and City would ultimately prove, anyone with the right financial clout could come in and take over any listed club.

Stockport's Supporters Trust clearly had a lot of problems to resolve, however the very fact that County were now in supporters' hands was a major reason to celebrate. The Trust, acting on behalf of supporters, vowed to only work on objectives voted for by its members and it published its aims. These included:

- To encourage and promote the principle of supporters representation on the board of the club and ultimately to be the vehicle for democratic elections to the board of the club.
- To encourage the club to take proper account of the views and interests of its supporters and of the community which it serves, in its decisions.
- To help raise the profile of the club and encourage new support within the community.
- To obtain from the club a commitment to provide and maintain facilities for the enjoyment of professional football within the area.
- To strengthen the bonds between the club and the community which it serves and to represent the interests of the community in the running of the club.
- To support and encourage the further development of the club's school of excellence and its promotion of and involvement in football in the community.
- To benefit present and future members of the community served by the club by promoting, encouraging and furthering the game of football as a recreational facility, sporting activity and focus for community involvement.
- To be an inclusive democratic organisation that seeks to represent the views of all supporters of the club through open, affordable membership, and consultation and liaison with all supporters and supporters groups, regardless of whether they are members.

The Trust immediately had some serious issues to resolve, mostly from a financial perspective, but on the pitch results were not great and the side came perilously close to relegation out of the Football League. Former player Jim Gannon arrived as caretaker manager before being appointed to the job on a permanent basis on 17th January 2006. Under his leadership, Stockport's fortunes started to turn around, and they managed to pick up 35 points from their final 23 games. They were still on the verge of relegation out of the League on the final day of the season, but County's new spirit was refreshing.

On an extremely tense final day of the season, County held champions Carlisle United to a 0-0 draw in an exceptionally difficult match, while a last minute winner for Leyton Orient at Oxford United sent Oxford down and brought the Hatters to safety. Inevitably, scenes of celebration followed at Edgeley Park.

Survival allowed the Trust to focus on their original aims and plan for the future, and by the end of 2006 the Trust published its achievements since taking over in the summer of 2005. These were:

- Broken even for the first time in a very, very long time, after years of making a trading loss of over £1m per year
- Achieved record season ticket sales
- Brought in a manager who the supporters adore - a manager who guided the club to safety after it was all but relegated into the Conference on Boxing Day and is now building a team that has the potential to fight its way back up the league and into the Championship
- Created and used an open and transparent procedure to appoint a new manager – a procedure that is now being adopted by other clubs
- Put forward a proposal to the local council, seeking to purchase and develop an area of land close to the football ground, which, if accepted, will be beneficial to the local community while putting the club on a sound financial footing with substantial assets.
- Improved the morale of the club's employees, both on and off the field of play
- Started various schemes in partnership with the local council, including a scheme called "Fit To Read," which is aimed at providing help for young people who have reading difficulties

The article ended with further optimism:

"And we're nowhere near finished yet! There is still plenty more to be done in order to take the club back up the divisions where we all want it to be!"

These achievements were remarkable and by the end of 2006-07 County were eighth in League Two. They had missed the play-offs on goal difference, but had ended the season higher than Rochdale and Bury – and near neighbours Macclesfield Town. They were also wearing a kit which had been designed by supporters instead of marketing men and kit manufacturers. That in itself was a refreshing move. Phil Brennan felt positively about the state of the club:

"There's a feel good factor to the club with the football side of things especially. Hopefully we're all back on track now."

By late February 2008 County sat comfortably in a play-off place and it did appear as if the future looked positive once more for Stockport.

During the early years of the decade Supporters/Shareholders Trusts were beginning to develop

at other local clubs, including City, but the supporter movement to gain most coverage during this period saw the development of a side called FC United of Manchester. Although it had been suggested for some time, the creation of FC United was prompted by supporters disgruntled at the takeover of United by American businessman Malcolm Glazer.

Glazer had owned shares in the Reds for at least a couple of years when, in September 2003, it was revealed that he had increased his shareholding to a little over 3% - the figure at which he had to inform the club's management. Speculation quickly followed that he was interested in taking over the club and, by end of October, the Glazer shareholding had increased to almost 9%. A month later it was 15%, and then in February 2004 it stood at 16.31%.

Inevitably it appeared that the American was attempting to gain control of the Reds, and by the following June the Glazer shareholding stood at 19%. Further increases followed until the biggest purchase came in May 2005 when he bought the shares of JP McManus and John Magnier. This took his shareholding to around 57% of the club. Effectively he controlled the club but it soon became clear that he wanted more than just a controlling interest. He wanted the entire club and by 16th May 2005 his shareholding increased to 75%. A month later the size of his shareholding was such that he was able to end the club's PLC status and de-list it from the Stock Exchange. On 28th June Glazer's shareholding came to 98% and this was enough for a compulsory buyout of all remaining shareholders. Glazer appointed his three sons as United board members with Joel Glazer appearing to be the driving force behind the new Reds. In 2006 other family members were added to the board.

In the main, supporters were against the acquisition of their club by the Glazer family, with their main concern being that the family had taken out significant loans and financial agreements to purchase the club. This meant that by 2007 United had a debt of around £660m and interest charges of around £62m a year, however the club still appeared more than financially able to compete.

On the pitch United finished runners up to Chelsea in 2006 and won the title in 2007. They also defeated Wigan in the 2006 League Cup final, and were FA Cup finalists in 2007. These successes were major achievements as Chelsea - with finance no other side could match at the time - and Arsenal were particularly strong during those seasons.

Many supporters cared little who actually owned the club so long as success and tradition continued. As Chris J Taylor wrote in **When Saturday Comes** in April 2006:

"When the takeover was announced, fans tended to fall into one of three categories. Those who called it a day and vowed never to step foot inside a Glazer-owned Old Trafford. Those who would carry on the fight against Glazer from within. And those who didn't really care. And that's fair enough. No one should have to justify their position, just as no one should criticise someone else's."

For many, United had moved a long way from its roots as Newton Heath with Liverpudlian Fredrick Attock as President, or even from its transformation on Thursday 24th April 1902 at the New Islington public hall in Ancoats when Dentonian James Brown suggested that the club's name should be changed to that of Manchester United. So long as quality players were bought or groomed, and trophy success followed it seemed irrelevant who actually 'owned' the club. Others felt differently of course.

In April 2002 Denis Campbell interviewed actor Christopher Eccleston for the **Observer**. In the article Eccleston talked of his love of United but some of his comments about the modern day Reds were typical of many true locally born United fans. These comments were made before the public interest of the Glazer family, but after player Roy Keane had criticised the corporate nature of match day Old Trafford. Eccleston:

"I don't enjoy the Old Trafford experience as much any more because of a lack of atmosphere. Everyone now has to sit and success has attracted a different kind of supporter. It's big business now and corporate entertainment has killed the atmosphere. Roy Keane was bang on with his comments about 'prawn sandwich eaters'. I loved Roy for saying that. However, it's inevitable that United have sought to become more of a global brand than a football club and that has contributed to our success.

"What keeps me wedded to the club is the hard core of homegrown lads like Nicky Butt and Paul Scholes, the Nevilles, David Beckham – Beckham's an honorary Manc because he's been at the club since he was 12 – who have a sense of the club's history. That makes United a little bit special."

Eccleston's views were shared by many fans, and by the time of the Glazer interest the question of who actually owned United was debated at length. Sure shareholders 'owned' the club, but for many the real 'owners' of United were the fans themselves. They had supported the club through good and bad and they had helped make the Reds the brand leader they were. Had those fans turned their back on the club during the 1970s and 1980s when United were one of the game's biggest underachievers (winning only three major trophies during those two decades can hardly be described as success for a side that was regularly either the best supported or second best supported in the League). United fans ensured the club remained a big name.

Those supporters decided it was time to reclaim the club as their own, and the decision was taken to form a breakaway football team. This team was to take the game back to its roots and focus on areas such as community, local pride, identity and, probably above all else, the game itself. Matches would be played in the right spirit. Supporters would be treated as people, and not as cattle (as they had been for much of the 1980s, and more recently at the away European Champions League tie in Lille during February 2007). They would be encouraged to play their part in all aspects of the new club.

Shortly after the Glazer family had gained overall control of United, a meeting by disgruntled

David Beckham was more than just a footballer at United.

supporters was held at the Manchester Methodist Hall on 19th May 2005. At that meeting Andy Walsh, well known for his role with the Independent Manchester United Supporters Association, announced that the formation of a new club would be discussed at another meeting later in the month. Around 2,000 people, including Manchester Central MP Tony Lloyd, attended the meeting. A message of support was read from Eric Cantona and Tony Lloyd also made a statement:

"This football club is something that goes a long way beyond money. I'm devastated about the fact that someone can come along and say this is all mine. We have got to use today as a stepping stone to make sure we build something positive."

There was already a strong example of how a side like this could be created at Wimbledon. The Wimbledon club that had won the FA Cup in 1988 was given permission to move to Milton Keynes in 2002, and two years later was renamed Milton Keynes Dons. However supporters of the original club set up a rival organisation called AFC Wimbledon. This side claimed to be the spirit of the old Wimbledon and has proved relatively successful, while MK Dons dropped down the Football League. Although in 2007 MK Dons reached the League Two play-offs.

To some extent AFC Wimbledon was the inspiration for the United offshoot, and in May 2005 the Dons chairman Kris Stewart attended one of the United fans' breakaway meetings. He encouraged them to make the move, and said that those backing the vision would have the time of their lives. His words were inspiring.

Fans pledged around £100,000 to support a new side. Ultimately FC United of Manchester was created, although the FA had rejected the club's initial name of FC United believing it was too generic. Actually, supporters were asked to suggest names and a vote was taken with FC United of Manchester winning with 44% of the vote. The other choices were all supposed to reflect United's heritage with AFC Manchester 1878, Newton Heath United, and Manchester Central proposed. Of these it is clear that AFC Manchester 1878 refers to the formation of Newton Heath, while Newton Heath United speaks for itself. Manchester Central was claimed to have been one of the suggested names at the club's relaunch in 1902 but, as this book demonstrated earlier, there has never been any actual proof that Manchester Central was a possibility for the Reds. In fact, Manchester Central appears to be a total red herring as no article has been traced mentioning that name back in 1902. The earliest mentions come from comments made by Louis Rocca some years later (who also claimed Manchester Celtic had been suggested), but none of this fits with the documentary evidence from the period. In addition, the name had already been used by a club playing at Alexandra Park at the turn of the century, and was later adopted for Manchester's third club, playing at Belle Vue, in the 1920s. So it is appropriate the name was not selected by the new club in 2005 as it could have provided an embarrassing distraction from the club's main aims.

The formation of FC United demonstrates much that is good about football in the region. Clearly, some United supporters saw those behind the breakaway as traitors, but in truth their actions were a positive step forward. As with any action by supporters, the authorities had to pay attention. They may not have liked what supporters said or did, but they did have to listen. The game cannot exist without fans and even United, with the large support they have enjoyed during the modern era, could not afford to ignore its fans.

Many of the people behind FC United were true fans in every sense of the word. Some of them were highly respected figures within the fanzine movement; football research; and business, while others could be described as typical fans, i.e. those who fifteen years ago would have stood on the Stretford End or sat in the old K Stand creating atmosphere and demonstrating the passion associated with United supporters during that time. One of the founders Andy Walsh believed FC United offered something significant:

"FC United is a way of every single day that we exist of showing that there are fans who want to see a football club owned and run in the interest of its team and its supporters. That's a symbol for the whole of football and not just Manchester United."

Of course, forming the new club was only part of the story and the new Reds had to find players, staff, a ground, and of course a league. In October 2005 Tony Howard, one of the founders of the club, wrote an article for the **Guardian Unlimited** outlining the moves taken:

"Despite press reports linking the club with Brian Kidd and Sammy McIlroy the job of manager was given to Karl 'Margy' Marginson, a fruit and vegetable delivery driver by day, but someone who knew the non-leagues inside out.

"Open trials were then held in a South Manchester suburb and a squad of 30 selected. 'Those who came ranged from lads turning up in Audi convertibles to lads on bikes,' says Margy. 'Some wrote to us from Australia or New Zealand because they wanted to play for United. It was amazing to see the numbers of those who applied'. Of those who attended the club's first training session, 18 came from the open trials. The players, gathered on the field at the back of a Manchester high school, came from a variety of football backgrounds. Jonathon 'Joz' Mitten - whose great uncle Charlie was a member of Sir Matt Busby's first great side, the one that won the 1948 FA Cup - turned down contracts with Conference North sides to be United's No 9. Meanwhile, at the other end of the scale, Matt Weston had played the previous season for Manchester's Sunday League side FC Lokomotiv.

"No one knew what to expect from the first game on a sunny Saturday, July 16 - a friendly at Leigh, near Wigan. But 3,000 turned up and, for the first time in football history, a celebratory pitch invasion greeted a 0-0 draw in a friendly."

Around 900 had applied to take part in the player trials – proving beyond doubt that there was interest – while thousands offered other support. In addition, the Leigh game referred to by Howard gave a very strong indication that the side could succeed. Behind the scenes much had been done by this point to ensure a proper structure for the club was created, and sound foundations were laid. The club had no intention of being a flash in the pan. It was here for good and after being accepted into the Second Division of the North West Counties League – even that was a major achievement – FC United played its first league game at Leek.

Leek County Old School Boy's Club were defeated 5-2 by FC United in a game that had been delayed due to crowd congestion. Inevitably there was a lot of media focus. After the game manager Karl Marginson told journalists why around 2,000 supporters travelled to the game:

"A lot of people have been upset over the past few years with being told they can't sing, they've got to sit down, they can't stand up. Things that they've been used to over the years, going to the Stretford End, sitting and singing with their mates, hopefully we can give something back to them."

It was a good, strong start. Tony Howard explained in the **Guardian Unlimited** why this all-ticket game - the first in the league's history - was significant:

"The all-ticket affair saw 2,500 United fans travel to sleepy Staffordshire, eat all the pies, buy all the programmes and take all three points. It also saw United fans greeted with open arms by pub landlords and locals alike - a new experience for those of us used to keeping our heads down on visits to opposition towns because of the hatred the country feels for MUFC.

"What's more, our eyes have been opened to a whole new ball game - one arrogantly overlooked by so many of us. The game that sees people doing everything for love not money. And it is a joy to speak to the likes of Stan at Leek or Billy at Blackpool Mechanics. Genuine people running a genuine game."

A ground share agreement was set up with Bury, and FC United were able to play in front of four figure crowds on a regular basis in a true Football League venue. For Bury the use of their ground brought much needed income and to some the success of the region's newest club was the salvation of the region's first major trophy winners.

According to Howard one of the key moments during the early days of the club came on 10th September 2005. On that day 67,839 attended Old Trafford for the Manchester derby. Howard:

"A watershed moment came when 2,266 fans snubbed the Manchester derby in favour of FC's clash with Blackpool Mechanics. In that crowd were 600 under 18s, granted free entry in line with the club's policy of encouraging young, local support - a long forgotten demographic at Old Trafford."

Clearly, the crowd at Old Trafford was typical of a derby, however the make-up of those fans was questionable. Prior to the Premier League, United may have had significant followers from other parts of Britain and Europe, especially Malta and Ireland, but one of the great aspects of the derby day crowd was the split between Red and Blue Mancunians. FC United knew how to attract local 'Red' Mancunians, while those at Old Trafford did not appear to grasp the importance of local pride. City themselves made a big point of publicising the difference when the 2006-07 Old Trafford derby saw both sides take to the field with eleven mascots at the request of the Reds. United's mascots came from South Korea as part of promotional activity while City's mascots were all part of their Live4City young supporters organisation. Those City supporters took to the field with Live4City tee-shirts: 'We are Young Mancunians'.

Those connected with the new FC United would have fully understood the importance of derby day. It is the most obvious way to stress Mancunian pride, and not one to focus on overseas activity. FC United's identity focuses on its Mancunian origins.

After the 2006-07 Old Trafford derby City themselves, and a variety of newspapers, most notably the ***Daily Mirror*** covered the mascot story claiming that United may have won the game but City retained the local identity. This was a dangerous move by the Blues especially as City made a similar mistake when good luck messages to the King of Thailand were displayed at their home derby on 19th August 2007 causing a small number of fans to complain. Had City officials not made such an issue out of the Old Trafford mascots then they would have held the moral high ground. Again supporters of both Blue and Red persuasion understood the need to send out the right 'local' message on derby day.

Many City fans recognised the importance of FC United to Mancunian Reds. At the January 2006 derby at the City of Manchester Stadium, a brief chant of *'Only hate FC United'* was heard. It is significant that a City banner appeared at times during the season highlighting rivalry with the new club, while United fans at the derby also had on display a FC United flag. Whether the United officials saw this or not is unknown, but it is clear that those behind FC United do understand Manchester.

A simple look at the FC United badge says a great deal about the new club's Mancunian ambition. FC United's badge is strikingly similar to the Manchester City badge of the 1950s to early 1970s. It is round with a central shield depicting a ship and emblazoned red/yellow lines. That central shield has been taken from the City of Manchester coat of arms with the ship representing Manchester's trading routes, and the lines representing the three rivers of Manchester – the Irwell, Irk, and Medlock (which passes through the Sportcity site and meanders close to United's old Bank Street ground).

City's early badge was very similar with the words Manchester City FC appearing in circles around the shield (in a similar manner to Football Club United of Manchester). Manchester United's own badge originally contained this central shield, however the emblazoned lines were ultimately replaced with the present red devil. The words 'football club' used to appear on the badge but were removed in 1998. Jim White and Andy Mitten writing in the ***Manchester United Top Eleven of Everything Red*** claimed this change as one of the club's biggest own goals:

"According to official sources, the words 'football' and 'club' were removed from the United crest in order to 'simplify the brand image'. Why not just turn it into a £ sign and have done with it?"

Regardless of United's development post the Glazer takeover, FC United were by mid-season 2005-06 a fully formed club with a manifesto firmly stressing its role as a club for its members. The manifesto stated:

"FC United of Manchester is a new football club founded by disaffected and disenfranchised Manchester United supporters. Our aim is to create a sustainable club for the long term which is owned and democratically run by its members, which is accessible to all the communities of Manchester and one in which they can participate fully.

"Although driven by very different circumstances, FC United of Manchester takes as its inspiration a number of supporters' groups who have gone down this route, including AFC Wimbledon, who have offered unstinting support. FC United of Manchester is intended to create a football club which addresses the concerns which many Manchester United fans have had over the last decade or more with how the club and football have developed, culminating in the club's takeover by Malcolm Glazer. We will follow the best traditions of Manchester United's past by developing policies which encourage youth participation in terms of both playing and supporting.

"FC United of Manchester will be formed as a member-owned, democratic, and non-profit making entity on the Industrial and Provident Society company model.The EGM will focus on the election of a board of directors by the members, and the direction of the club over the coming season. We have ambitious and long term plans. Above all we want to be seen as a good example of how a club can be run in the interests of its members and be of benefit to its local communities. However, we are a new club and will require patience in order to reach our goals. With the help of all our members and supporters we are confident we can achieve them."

Supporting those aims the club issued seven core principles:

1. The Board will be democratically elected by its members.
2. Decisions taken by the membership will be decided on a one member, one vote basis.
3. The club will develop strong links with the local community and strive to be accessible to all, discriminating against none.
4. The club will endeavour to make admission prices as affordable as possible, to as wide a constituency as possible.
5. The club will encourage young, local participation - playing and supporting - whenever possible.
6. The Board will strive wherever possible to avoid outright commercialism.
7. The club will remain a non-profit organisation.

Each of these aims made it perfectly clear that FC United were trying to re-establish football in the region as the people's game. Clearly, the League sides would also claim that many of these principles apply to them also, and certainly Bury, Oldham, Rochdale and Stockport work hard on their community links, while City have been recognised for many years as particularly strong in community affairs. It should be noted that five City figures have been awarded MBEs or OBEs as a result of their community or charity work rather than football - Alex Williams MBE (heads City In The Community), Colin Bell MBE (community and charity work), Ian Niven MBE (community work & young people), Shaun Goater MBE (sport & young people), and Bert Trautmann OBE (anglo-German relations).

One of FC United's principles talked of avoiding outright commercialism and one of the most positive aspects of FC United's existence is the fact that they have chosen not to wear a sponsor's name emblazoned across their shirts. The club does have sponsors, but the fact it focuses on its own logo rather than that of a sponsor is an extremely positive step forward. Football fans have become accustomed to shirt sponsorship but many are angry that sponsors' names tend to dominate. Coventry City had a kit during the eighties that had been designed to focus on their sponsors Talbot cars, while a significant number of sides have taken advantage of recent rule changes to have a variety of sponsors on backs of shirts as well as in more traditional positions.

Regardless of the importance of sponsorship, or the positive steps the club were taking to encourage young supporters, it was vital FC United performed well in their first season. If the venture failed on the pitch it would be difficult to develop the club in the way most fans wanted, although simply having a club was a significant achievement in itself. In the end FC United's first season was a tremendous success, with the new Reds winning the North West Counties Division Two. The championship trophy was presented at the home game with Great Harwood Town on 22nd April 2006. A record crowd of 6,023 attended, but Great Harwood managed a 1-0 win. Regardless of success the real strength of the new United was the spirit in which the club possessed. Writing in **When Saturday Comes** midway through that first season Chris J Taylor talked of the joy of the match day experience:

"For the few thousand disillusioned Reds who upped and left Old Trafford in the summer, football has become fun again. Indeed, the game has become of almost a secondary importance. The sense of community that had evaporated at Old Trafford, of going to the match with a group of friends, standing and singing together, and not having to pay through the nose to do so, has returned."

The following season was similarly positive and in 2006-07 they won promotion to the Unibond League as North West Counties Division One champions. During that season they faced Maine Road, a club set up by Manchester City supporters at the City Social Club in 1955. To many the season's games between FCUM and Maine Road were viewed as mini-derbies and Maine Road even moved their home game to Stalybridge Celtic's ground so they could accommodate a larger crowd. They had hoped to stage the game at City's 5,000 capacity reserve venue the Regional Athletics Stadium (known as the Mini-COM to fans) at Sportcity, but the move failed.

So what of the future for FCUM? The club issued a series of aims for the following years in November 2006. These aims included:

- reach Conference North by 2009.
- attract an average of 5,000 supporters per home game by 2009.
- building a 7,000 - 10,000 capacity stadium, as central to Greater Manchester as possible, by 2012.
- develop training facilities by 2009.
- start a women's team for the 2007-08 season.

How realistic these aims are remains to be seen as, for example, FCUM would need to win promotion in every one of the club's first four seasons, however it is true that each of these aims are achievable. Aside from FC United's rise through the divisions, the most interesting development would be the development of a 7,000 capacity stadium. Board member Adam Brown, and also the researcher behind a number of football reports, claimed that discussions with local authorities in Greater Manchester were under way. He also said that the FA and Football Trust were being consulted. In November 2006 he admitted:

"There are no fixed plans for a stadium as yet. There are no deals that have been done that we are keeping quiet about, and no sites sorted out. All the speculation is wrong.

"But we can't realise the potential of this football club without our own ground. It's incredibly ambitious what we are trying to achieve at FC United, and we have to be patient and realistic about how things develop. If we get this right, it will help to change football by providing a good, visible example of how English football could be run."

Finding a site is likely to be an issue, however the football ground expert Simon Inglis has a view that **The Willows**, the home of Salford City Reds RLFC, would be suitable for many reasons, including its close proximity to what Inglis suggests is United's heartland support. The ground has a capacity of 11,363 and has a significant amount of terracing. It also retains a traditional sports ground feel. Salford are planning to move to a new home in Barton, near the aerodrome, but that move has hit a number of problems. If they do manage the move then clearly their old home would be available.

Inglis's suggestion does look feasible, however the Willows is probably not an ideal venue for FCUM in the long term for two reasons. Firstly, the ground is on a problematic site and has restricted access alongside the two main sides (preventing extension as well). Secondly, the venue is in Salford. Inglis does not recognise that as an issue, but Mancunian Reds and Blues would fully understand the statement a base in Salford would make.

The fact the venue is restricted would prevent FCUM from developing the site if and when the club grows. If the new Reds manage to develop at their current rate it is highly possible the side would be competing at either the lowest level of the Football League or the highest level of non-league by 2012. Once that occurs the potential of the new side could outgrow a stadium of that size, plus of course each level of the pyramid structure of the League has strict guidelines for ground requirements.

In terms of location, the aims of FC United suggest the club want to regain United's Mancunian heritage. To do this it would make sense to establish a venue within the City of Manchester with, ideally, a site in Newton Heath or Clayton becoming home. This would certainly establish the side as a true Mancunian outfit and would also allow the club to focus on United's pre-Old Trafford heritage.

Of course, sites in East Manchester are at a premium, however the prospect of moving there would make an interesting comparison with the development of Manchester Central in the 1920s and 30s. Central, as detailed earlier in this book, were set up by a former City director who was dissatisfied with the move of the Blues from East Manchester to the border of Rusholme and Moss Side. Despite its main aim of giving City fans an alternative 'local' side, the development of the club began to impact United. Initially, this was insignificant, but when Central were accepted into the Football League Third Division North it soon became apparent that the side would challenge the struggling United. City and United combined to stop the new side, but with FC United it is highly possible the new club could seriously damage City's attempts at capturing the 'local' identity.

City believe they are the community club of Manchester and certainly their recent history points to a lot of local success, however a move by FC United into East Manchester would challenge that view. Even if FC United were never to make it into the Football League, their community approach would inevitably impact on City. In addition, lower prices and the traditional aspects of attending football would make FCUM an attractive alternative for local youngsters. Already the club has had a television series on satellite broadcaster Channel M – as did City for a season – however no other non-league side has managed to gain so much media interest. In fact none of Manchester's lower division League sides has had such coverage in recent years.

Whatever happens the FCUM story is a very interesting development for the game in the region. As time moves on it will inevitably have an impact on the existing League sides. Whether it ultimately changes anything at United is debateable, but already it has had an impact on Bury (mostly positive), and has also helped to increase interest in the lower leagues. Bury's Gordon Sorfleet is an interested observer on the development of the new Reds:

"It's not really about the Americans coming in and taking over a football club. It's about affordable football. I think they call it 'punk football'. It's about enjoying yourself. I've been to a few FC United games and the atmosphere is unbelievable."

At least one Bury fan finds one aspect of the FC United experience a bit annoying. Chris Bainbridge, writing in **When Saturday Comes** in September 2006, commented on his support for the project but added:

"Most of the FCUM fans I know have developed a unique and novel way of starting every single conversation. 'Oh, hi Steve,' I'll say, 'how are you doing?' 'Four thousand three hundred and twenty-four!' (or whatever) they will invariably reply. 'How many did you get last time?' I am a firm supporter of the FCUM project, I agree with their grass roots, fan-based approach, their total commitment to democracy and inclusiveness, and I believe other clubs, including Bury, should learn from FCUM's example. It occurs to me, however, that a percentage of their fans are only there because they can't resist backing the winning team (even if that is only in North West Counties League Division Two) and they can't resist being the biggest show in town (even if that town is only Bury). Jumping on the bandwagon? Now, where have we seen that before?"

Criticism of FC United did increase during 2006-7 with United supporter Ashley Shaw, a regular contributor to **When Saturday Comes** on Mancunian matters and author of a book on the Francis Lee era at City, highlighting differences between supporters in March 2007. He talks of FC United's community aspirations and plans and adds:

"Yet this season these same good intentions appear to have caused friction with certain elements within MUFC's support. As a consequence the fans of the two clubs appear to have drifted further apart, the schism made all the worse by United's improved form, which has glossed over the long term implications of the Floridian takeover. A sticker campaign that took the slogan 'Love United, Hate Glazer' as a catchphrase of solidarity with FC has since been hijacked by new stickers featuring the slogan 'Love United, Hate FC', while a tempestuous derby against Salford City in November provided an opportunity for United 'loyalists' to parade a banner calling FC supporters 'Judas Scum'. While this does sound a bit Life Of Brian, there are serious issues to be addressed."

Shaw commented on the threat of hooliganism and then added:

"With attendances down by 20 per cent (or an average of 500 per match) from last season and the well of sympathy so evident in the first season drying up as media interest has switched elsewhere, together with the potential hooligan problems mentioned above, it's clear FCUM are finding life tougher one and a half seasons on.

"Sir Alex Ferguson's criticism hasn't helped in this respect, either; in fact it might have had rather more impact than at first imagined. Fan groups criticised Ferguson when he said of the anti-Glazer protesters: 'They carried on to the degree where they actually thought they should have a say in the running of the football club'. Ferguson's statement was blatantly contrary to his earlier support of the anti-Glazer coalition. Yet perhaps the manager understands the rank and file supporters better than some assume. By initially opposing the Glazers and later accepting them, Ferguson has acted like the vast majority of Manchester United supporters and his words seem to have persuaded many in the Old Trafford stands. With United riding high and attendance records being broken on a fortnightly basis, life for FC is likely to get harder before it gets easier."

The future of any of the teams in our region is unclear, however it is obvious that success does have a direct influence on the attitude of fans. During 2007 it soon became clear that many

Programme Sponsor

MR. MIKE READ

Our thanks to Mike for his sponsorship of this special edition programme. Mike is currently starring in the West End with his show 'Cliff the Musical', but he always finds time to follow the progress of the Shakers.

Some celebrity fans do not give anything back, but DJ Mike Read does provide support to Bury.

City supporters would willingly accept an investor – any investor - without really questioning his background if that investor could guarantee a return to significant trophy winning ways. Likewise, the feeling that the Glazer-induced debt would prevent United from competing with Chelsea appears false and therefore many Reds appear to have accepted the American owners – or at least are no longer openly critical of them. The fans of FCUM and MUFC need to establish themselves as separate entities without directly worrying whether one group are 'traitors' or 'scabs' as some have suggested. It is possible to support both sides, just as many fans of United or City have followed the fortunes of Rochdale, Stockport, Bury and so on, but supporting one should not immediately put the fan at odds with rival supporters.

Whatever develops, the FC United development is one that most genuine football fans and Mancunians should watch with interest. Whatever the future of the club, simply creating the organisation has done enough to make those at established clubs within the region take note.

Supporter control of football clubs is spreading throughout the region. Before FCUM was formed two Oldham fans, Alex Metcalfe and John Connolly, formed a supporters' trust with the aim of helping the Latics. It was initially set up to provide financial help to the club after the departure of Chairman Chris Moore. Moore had bought Oldham in 2001 but the trouble began some time before that date. The years following Joe Royle's departure had not been great and supporters had campaigned against Brewers JW Lees, who originally had owned the ground but by the mid-1990s had the controlling interest in the club. Lees, unable to provide the financial backing a club hoping for Premiership football needed, sold the club to other members of the board.

In 2001 Moore took over and hoped to re-establish the side as a top flight club, but the surprise departure of popular manager Andy Ritchie mid-season – despite taking the Latics to top spot in Division Two (old Division Three, modern day League One) – and the appointment of Mick Wadsworth in his place caused fans a great deal of concern.

Oldham finished ninth in the division that season (2001-02) and Wadsworth was replaced by his assistant Iain Dowie. The side narrowly missed out on promotion, losing in the play-offs to QPR, but worse was to follow when Chris Moore announced he was ending his interest in the club. He stated that he could no longer afford to pay the £50,000 a week to keep the club afloat. He offered to give away his 95% controlling interest and write off the £4m he had loaned.

In June 2003 on BBC GMR the news was revealed that Oldham were close to closure and that £150,000 was needed urgently to keep the club afloat. Around the same time the supporters trust was formed and efforts across Oldham were made to raise the money to save the Latics. Jack Scott, writing on the website www.jklatics.com, outlined how grim the situation was:

"[Latics] now have no assets whatsoever to convince a judge to grant an administration order. It's so grave that if the players' wages are not paid by Friday 27 June, they can give notice and walk away. The club shop has had to close it's doors, the bank account is frozen and there remain to be paid Inland Revenue monthly bills from 19th June which could result in the Revenue serving a winding up order at any minute.

"At that time, Oldham Athletic Football Club will cease to exist. There looks like being no last minute reprieve such as has happened at other clubs. Talks with potential new investors broke down."

A charity football match with some of Latics' biggest names from seasons past helped, as did the sterling work of many supporters, but the situation remained precarious for some considerable time. The 2003-04 season began without a clear way forward. In the end Oldham entered into administration during October and the financial crisis deepened. Then Marketing Manager Sean Jarvis and club accountant Neil Joy agreed to purchase the club for £1. Chris Moore also agreed to write off £4.5m owed to him by the club at that point.

Investors were still being sought and in February 2004 it was announced that the FA had approved a takeover bid by three New York based English businessmen - Danny Gazal, Simon Blitz and Simon Corney. Blitz announced:

"We are pleased today to start a new era at Boundary Park. We now expect to complete the purchase. I would like to pay tribute to those involved in the negotiations, including the FA, the Football League and of course the administrators, PKF. I would also like to mention Latics supporters and the Supporters' Trust, who have been very patient with us during negotiations and have demonstrated fantastic support."

The new investors sold 3% (for £200,000) of the club to the supporters trust as both a thank you for their guidance, and as a means of ensuring fans played a significant part in the direction of the club. The trust would also receive a seat on the board of directors.

Since that time the trust has helped the finances of the club improve. A mini-bus has been provided; money has been given to aid player purchases; and ground developments have been considered. There have even been discussions on significant ground developments. But more than these achievements the very fact that Oldham, like Stockport, exists at all owes a great deal to its supporters.

Across at City, the club's recent history has seen many changes. The most significant of which was the move to the new City of Manchester Stadium. This was first suggested back in the late 1980s, but by the early weeks of the 1999-2000 season City had formally agreed to leave Maine Road. The move came in 2003 – a year after Kevin Keegan had guided the Blues to promotion.

Inevitably, the last season at Maine Road became an emotional one as supporters and officials focused on the move. The last game of the season was Maine Road's final game and, in typical City style, ended in a 1-0 defeat by Southampton.

Emotional scenes surrounded that game but more sadness came during the first few weeks of the close season. The stadium's final days were marked with tributes to Marc-Vivien Foe – the scorer or City's final goal at the old ground - who passed away during an international match for Cameroon. His death was a major shock and for some his loss added to the emotion of moving. It is a little known fact that the Blues had actually handed over the keys to Maine Road to the council at the time of Foe's death, and the council gave special dispensation to the Blues to man the reception area for a few additional days as fans signed books of condolence and left tributes around the Main Entrance.

Foe's death was not the first to occur on the pitch, or as a result of something happening on the pitch, for any of the sides in our region. There have been several stories over the years with the shock death of City player Di Jones coming in 1902. Jones cut his leg in a public practice match and died shortly afterwards. Another player, Bury's Sam Wynne died on 30th April 1927 at Bramall Lane. Wynne, a former Oldham star, collapsed after 38 minutes of the Bury game with Sheffield United while trying to place the ball for a free kick. He was stretchered off but by the time he had reached the dressing room he had passed away with a cerebral haemorrhage. The game was abandoned at half time and the entire gate receipts for the replayed game were given to the player's widow. In addition Bury set up a trust fund raising £1,400.

Clearly the sadness of Foe's early death affected the Blues for some time, as did the departure from Maine Road, but moving to the new stadium did provide lots of optimism. The Blues opened the new venue with a high-profile friendly with Barcelona, and then followed this with a UEFA Cup tie – the first competitive game in the new stadium. However, the first season at the stadium was not a success - City finished sixteenth, two places above the relegation zone (eight points clear of the drop). As with so many moments in the club's modern era it was City's support that impressed. Kevin Keegan:

"They are the greatest thing about this club and the level of support we have enjoyed throughout a very poor season has been amazing. Thirty thousand of them bought season tickets for next year without even knowing what division we would be in. What we've done to deserve this is beyond me."

This was – and still is – the most positive aspect of City. Support throughout the 1990s and new century for the side has been high and, although attendances are small in comparison with United's modern day crowds and did drop off at an alarming level in 2006-07, the Blues remain amongst the best supported sides in the country. But has the club deserved that support in recent years?

The Blues have been under-achievers since the early 1970s. Throughout the club's history the team have been able to find success on a fairly regular basis. By 1970 the club had enjoyed four distinct periods of true success - some would argue there had been more - spread over six decades, and by the early 70s support for the club was high. However, since 1971 when Joe Mercer was pushed 'upstairs' the Blues have won only one major trophy – the 1976 League Cup. They have earned promotion of course, and in 2002 winning the Football League Championship allowed them to proudly display the old Championship trophy, however for a club that claims to be 'massive' - as United fans put it - the Blues have underachieved for too long. The fans deserve more.

Few teams, including the likes of Newcastle and Chelsea, could retain such a large support without finding significant success. In fact Newcastle's average crowd was c.16,000 as recently as 1991, while Chelsea averaged 18,000 for several seasons in the 90s and 12,672 in 1983!

In recent years City fans have felt let down. Some blame those involved with the club since the move to the new stadium; some blame Alan Ball; while others point to Peter Swales. In truth the fact City have failed to be amongst the Country's trophy-elite for so long is a combination of many factors. However, as the decade moved on each of the club's past failings meant that any new 'failing' hit fans harder than before. In many ways the City of the period 2003-07 was no longer judged on the activities of that season, but on years of missed opportunities.

When the Blues lost a FA Cup quarter-final tie to West Ham in 2006 the blow set a downbeat tone for the rest of the season and, ultimately, impacted on supporters throughout 2006-07. When that season saw defeat in the quarter-final of the FA Cup at Blackburn the feeling amongst the large City contingent at Ewood Park was worrying. Fans severely criticised the side, with many fans absolutely disgusted with the club's failure.

For the majority of City fans floating around the Premier League without any chance of trophy success was not acceptable, and City supporters did deserve more. Those in control of the club recognised this and throughout the period following the move to the new stadium it was clear they were actively looking for investors. That did not appease the fans however, and City supporter Steve Kay, who runs the **www.mcfcstats.co.uk** website, performed a survey of fans in February 2007. His findings painted a depressing picture of life as a Blue at that time.

Kay wanted to identify how fans felt and, although his sample was very small, he discovered that 45% of those responding admitted they would be giving up their season ticket for 2007-08 while another 15% were seriously considering giving up. Only 21.7% of existing season ticket holders were to buy a ticket for the following year.

Clearly Kay's sample was too small (almost 70 people responded) to accept the findings as conclusive, however it did raise a lot of debate amongst supporters on various websites and blogs. Kay published some of the comments he had received. These included:

"I gave up my season ticket at the end of last season (so did my partner). I no longer felt part of the club, Stuart Pearce asking me to get behind the team, stewards threatening me with loss of season ticket when I did. High prices for the effort of the team, multiple changes of kick of times/day, now doing as the team does.... turn up when I feel like making the effort. Kick of times/days changed at whim of Sky, price of tickets, my hard earned money going in to the pockets of players who don't try and laugh in the face of the fan, money going out of the game (which could keep down the price of tickets) and in to agents pockets, lack of atmosphere, and lastly we are no longer fans, but customers and are expected to buy the corporate image, clap politely and go home. This is my club, not the Board's, the players' or the manager's but I now feel that they no longer want me as I may wake some of the 'customers' up by singing. I could go on and on and on!"

"Fed up with the prices, the fixture changes and the lack of direction of MCFC and their board, no loyalty to us the fans who have been going for years. The regular match-going fans are being priced out of the game, clubs are more interested in big money and corporate/TV deals than loyalty to their own supporters. It's pure greed. More enjoyment watching non league games!"

"Club appears to have no ambition, why are smaller clubs such as Bolton, Reading, Portsmouth etc out-performing us? It's a sad thing to say, but I enjoyed it more when we were in the old 3rd division, the club was in dire straits but everyone pulled together from the Chairman to the Tea Lady i.e. we all felt part of the family that is 'MCFC'. No truthful information from the Board on the state of the club, which direction it's going. Why should I give my hard earned money to this? I could go on and on."

Many of these concerns were also raised by those United fans who had created FC United. The Glazer takeover pushed many United fans over the edge, while at City it was actually a takeover that started to encourage fans that the future could be bright. The arrival of Dr Thaksin Shinawatra, the former Prime Minister of Thailand, did raise some supporter dissatisfaction, however this was nowhere near the level witnessed at other clubs taken over. Even at Liverpool, ironically a team Shinawatra had shown interest in, demonstrations against their American owners occurred during 2008.

During summer 2007 the media focused on Shinawatra's political record in Thailand, while City supporters tended to focus solely on which manager and players the new owner may bring in. The new manager was former England coach Sven Goran Eriksson. Again the majority of fans took to Eriksson immediately while the national media, again, focused on the negatives of his time with England. A pattern was emerging during 2007-08 whereby the national media tended to misunderstand the views and activities of City fans. This all came to a head with the February 2008 Manchester derby, but more of that later.

Following Eriksson's appointment City appeared a side transformed, and the new manager established a new top flight record for the Blues of nine consecutive home League victories from the start of the season. He also created a side that many felt could qualify for European football in his first season. Whether this positive air continues over the following years is open to debate, but certainly Shinawatra has made it clear he wants City to match United in every department.

Off the pitch Shinawatra made few changes with the general management of the club. Apart from a restructured board, which saw former player Dennis Tueart leave the board, little changed. Chairman John Wardle took on the role of Deputy Chairman, while Alistair Mackintosh remained as Chief Executive. Supporters had anticipated – even expected – more widespread changes.

Presumably, Shinawatra and his advisors will make further changes as they get more involved with the club, but as the season neared its end it was abundantly clear that the vast majority of City fans enjoyed the transformation on the pitch that Shinawatra had made possible. At the end of the Old Trafford derby in February 2008 City fans locked in after the game sang songs in praise of the former Thai Prime Minister, and they seemed genuinely delighted with the Thai takeover. Likewise the new directors were keen to show their colours. These directors included a rather delighted looking Sasin Monvoisin – one of two ladies on the City board.

City fans did come in for a significant amount of criticism however in the build up to that game. The match was played four days after the fiftieth anniversary of the Munich Air Disaster and many newspapers and footballing figures seemed keen to stress the negative aspects of football support. They claimed City supporters would be disrespectful and would disturb the minute's silence being held pre-match to remember the 23 victims of the crash.

The level of criticism was extremely high and yet – and this is very significant – few national newspapers, television companies and radio stations understood what the disaster actually meant to the majority of Mancunians. Had they realised this then it is possible they may have actually started to believe in the fans.

Television and radio debates raged on whether the Blues would be silent. National newspapers severely criticised them before the event had even taken place. ***The Times*** was perhaps one of the more level-headed newspapers but even they tended to focus on the negatives. Every City fan was seen as being guilty before the event even occurred. ***The Times*** even included an interview with United star Paul Scholes - who they regarded as a man who should know how City fans would react, after all, they stated, he had grown up with the rivalry. Scholes was reported as saying:

"I think the only thing you have to worry about is the minority of City fans who might want to cause trouble. They lost someone in the accident as well, so I hope their fans are not disrespectful. There is always that few who might cause problems. They've referred to the accident a few times in the past and I just hope they can come to their senses on the day. It would reflect badly on their club, but that's not stopped them in the past, has it?"

Putting a footballer in the position of talking about this was wrong, and the approach taken by all the national media seemed wrong. The *Daily Mirror*, whose football section 'Mania' is produced in association with AIG (United's sponsors), devoted significant space to the view that City fans would delight in singing songs about the disaster.

Unfortunately for the Blues, a minute's silence held prior to an England friendly at Wembley on the anniversary of the disaster was brought to an end after only 27 seconds as a number of England fans were "effing and blinding" according to *The Times'* Simon Barnes. This, so the majority of the media believed, was nothing compared to how City supporters would behave.

By this time much was being made of the fact that former City and England captain Frank Swift died in the crash – although the FA had neglected to mention his name at the England match and only focused on the United players who died. *The Times* suggested fans should keep quiet for "Frank's sake" and, although this was an improvement on some of the national coverage, it was still the wrong approach.

Many City fans have for several years been talking of the Munich disaster as a tragedy for Manchester. The disaster killed 23 people. Inevitably, it was significant that eight of these were United players but it was not simply about those players. Likewise it was not simply about Frank Swift. To limit the focus actually did more damage, and increased resentment amongst fans.

Back in 1958 all Mancunians understood what the disaster meant, but in the years that followed some supporters – both blue and red – felt the disaster was not being recognised for its effect on the whole of Manchester. City fans became angry that the other victims, including Swift, were not included in United's memorial at Old Trafford and never appeared to be remembered when the disaster was discussed, while Mancunian United fans occasionally felt the disaster was being used at times as some form of marketing activity. This point was demonstrated when fans expressed their disgust that a new Munich tribute on the East Stand façade included the AIG sponsors logo. In the build up to the anniversary this was attacked with paint.

Over the years some City fans have sung about the disaster. Likewise some United fans have sung about Hillsborough to antagonise Liverpool fans. But this does not mean that all City or United fans feel like that.

On the day itself City fans behaved impeccably – a point re-iterated by Old Trafford's safety announcer after the game which itself led to a chant of "*We are impeccable!*" Clearly, there should have been no question about this, but as so many people had criticised, abused, and insulted those fans in the build up to the game, City supporters had every right to stress the point. Sadly, as they left the ground post match many of those fans, including women and children, were abused by people claiming to be United fans on Sir Matt Busby Way and its environs. The spirit of togetherness did not continue outside the ground.

Elsewhere the new century has seen Bury reach seventh place in Division Three (old Division Four) in 2003, but struggle in the years that followed. They ended 2006-07 as the lowest placed of the region's League sides with a 21st place finish in League Division Two (fourth tier). This was their lowest finish of all time and gives a false impression of the stature of the Shakers. For most of their history they have competed in one of the top two divisions, but their 2007 position provided a good indication that the game had changed into one where funding is paramount. It would be a major tragedy if Bury were to be relegated out of the League.

Across at Rochdale the side went from a fifth place Division Three (fourth tier) finish in 2002 to narrowly avoiding relegation out of the League in 2004. Dale did reach the FA Cup fifth round in 2003 – equalling their run in 1990 – but the future looks destined to match the club's more recent past. Perhaps the highest point of recent seasons was the 7-2 thrashing of Stockport County by Dale on 24th March 2007. That result came shortly after County had established a Football League record of nine consecutive wins without conceding a goal, and helped Dale achieve a ninth place finish – only five points below a play-off place.

At the time of going to press Dale are on the verge of a play-off place again, however competition is extremely tight in League Two. Nevertheless, it is refreshing to see that Dale still have potential and it would be a major boost for the region if they could re-establish themselves at the level they held in the early 1970s.

■ HOLDING FIRM ... Droylsden's Dave Cameron holds off Bishop's Steven West

DROYLSDEN 3 BISHOP AUCK 2

BY TONY GLENNON

DEADLY Danny Byrne headed Droylsden's 100th goal of the season to send them through to the Unibond League Cup Final for the first time in their history.

Byrne's second goal of this bruising contest saw the Bloods reach their ton. But, more importantly, it was the one which finally saw off a spirited if at times excessively robust Bishop Auckland side.

Dave Cameron had fired Droylsden in front on the stroke of half-time, but Bishops drew level early in the second period and were threatening an upset until Byrne scored twice in seven minutes to sink them.

Even then, the visitors managed to pull a goal back from the penalty spot, but Droylsden held on to earn a final against Hucknall.

Despite having started the tie as strong favourites, Premier high-fliers Droylsden found it hard early on against their mid-table First Division opponents.

And Bishops had a chance to snatch a shock lead in the 25th minute when Stuart Irvine, close to the left-hand corner flag, pulled a cross back to Shaun Hope, who wasted the opening by flashing a fierce, angled shot a yard over.

It appeared to shake the Bloods out of their lethargy and they quickly came close to striking the first blow, as Byrne raced threateningly on to Leroy Chambers' headed flick, only to shoot fractionally wide under pressure from Brian Ross.

Byrne then forced a fine save from Marc Riches, the keeper getting down quickly to parry his angled drive, and there was finally a sense that Droylsden were starting to warm to their task.

Home skipper Garry Burke was led from the field in the 35th minute with blood gushing from a big gash on his forehead – an injury he sustained after a high challenge from Irvine.

Burke soon reappeared with his head bandaged and was quickly celebrating, along with the rest of his teammates, as the Bloods grabbed the lead two minutes into first-half stoppage time.

Bishops got themselves in a tangle trying to deal with Neil Hall's dangerous cross from the right, and the ball somehow found its way to Cameron, who then had the easy job of lashing it into an empty net from point-blank range.

Bishops had earned themselves few friends with their muscular approach in the opening period, and referee McGee finally reached for his notebook a minute after the restart, to book Nick Scaife for launching recklessly into Cameron.

But it was Droylsden who should have been cautioned for some dreadful defending which allowed the visitors to draw level in the 52nd minute.

Neil Maddison profited from a series of half-hearted tackles to X escape to the by-line, before crossing for Irvine to blast home from 10 yards.

The equaliser gave Bishops fresh heart and then Droylsden were incredibly fortunate not to fall behind on the hour.

Home 'keeper Paul Phillips inexplicably allowed a shot which had taken a seemingly harmless deflection off Burke to slip through his hands, and was so relieved to turn and watch the ball trickle inches wide.

Bloods' boss Dave Pace's response to his team's display was to make a double substitution in the 62nd minute, sending on Gareth Morris and Ciaran Kilheeney for Chris O'Brien and Chambers.

Morris blasted a shot against a post after being teed up by Byrne as Droylsden finally seemed to sense that the tie was in danger of slipping away.

And they dramatically regained the lead in the 71st minute.

Murphy slid a pass through to Byrne, who, having at last slipped the leash, waltzed round Riches and squeezed a shot just inside a post for his 22nd goal of the season.

Byrne struck again seven minutes later as Droylsden finally took a firm grip on the game. This time, he stooped to head home a Kilheeney cross – the Bloods' 100th goal of a memorable campaign.

But Droylsden almost gifted Bishops a way back into the game when Burke was adjudged to have handled just inside his own penalty area, and Irvine stepped up to send Phillips the wrong way.

Bishops' sub Andrew Shingleton then contrived to shoot over as Droylsden grimly held on.

After defeating Bishop Auckland, Droylsden beat Hucknall Town in the final of the Unibond League Cup in 2003-4.

Of course, of all the sides in the region, United remain the most successful of the modern era. Since the summer of 2001 the Reds have won the Premier League (2002-03 & 2006-07), the FA Cup (2004), and the League Cup (2006), and by mid-March 2008 the Reds were still competing for the Premier League title and in Europe.

From a financial viewpoint, United's turnover has reached astounding levels and the fears of many fans that the Glazer takeover would ultimately restrict United's ability to compete seem unfounded. Similarly, the occasional defeat does not seem to impact on United's long term pulling power – the day after the defeat to City in the February 2008 Manchester derby United's museum and shop were packed with visitors, tourists, and supporters from all corners of the world.

Looking to the future football in the region remains strong, however there are several issues which are impacting on supporters' enjoyment of the sport. The domination of the Premier League and the extensive television coverage make life difficult for clubs outside of the top division, and even means sides recognised as traditional trophy winners have little to compete for. At the same time admission costs have priced many fans out of the game, while initiatives such as the idea of a '39th' game per season for each Premier League side played overseas seem more interested in increasing revenue than satisfying traditional supporters. Whether the '39th' game idea develops further seems unlikely as FIFA and many others, have expressed serious concerns. However it is clear the Premier League will continue to look at ways of developing its product around the world.

Despite the negatives football remains the most popular sport in the region, and the region remains one of the Country's most significant zones. People often talk of Liverpool, the north-east, Bristol and other areas as soccer hotspots, but none of these regions have the history, heritage, volume of clubs, and supporter base that the Manchester region has. Every borough of Manchester, excluding Salford, has had a Football League side within its boundaries at some point, while the region also contains some of the most famous non-League sides the game has known.

If the changing face of football at the highest level drives some traditional fans away, then non-League sides such as Droylsden, Altrincham, Stalybridge, Maine Road, Hyde and of course FC United are likely to benefit. These sides offer excitement and entertainment, and possibly some of our sides on the fringes of the Football League may produce the region's next League side. Journalist Mike Pavasovic believes Tameside could produce something new:

"There has always been the argument that one quality side from Tameside could survive in the League. In fact some have suggested a couple of the higher profile sides merge to create a 'Tameside United' with the aim of making it into the League. With automatic promotion teams like Droylsden have proved that they can get into the Conference, or Blue Square Premiership as it is now, and with strong backing from the entire borough promotion to the League could be possible. On the other hand, there remains a lot of rivalry between the sides. Personally, I cannot see Hyde United and Stalybridge Celtic getting together to support the same team.

"The Ashton clubs may work together – there's been a lot of talk of that over the years. If it did happen there's a brand new ground on Ashton Moss which could accommodate League games. Curzon Ashton have moved there, so maybe a Tameside club could work there. The identity of the borough has grown in the last decade. People do talk of Tameside as one location, whereas in the past no one ever claimed they came from the borough. We were all from Hyde, Stalybridge, Dukinfield and so on."

Potentially a Tameside League club would help the borough identity become recognised further.

The quality of football in Tameside, and at our other non-League sides may not be as great as that played in the Champions League, but at least the supporter experience is a traditional one. It is the game that matters, not the finance.

Football has a tendency to take supporters on a journey through every range of emotion possible and certainly the region as a whole has experienced a great deal. From Bury's Second Division Championship win in 1895 through to United's Premier League win in 2007, the region has known great success, failure, tragedy, and so on. No one knows what the future holds, but it is clear that the Manchester region will continue to ensure it plays a part in every aspect of footballing life.

ATTENDANCE DETAIL SEASON BY SEASON - 1997-2007

Season	City	United	Oldham	Bury	Stockport	Rochdale
1997-98	28196	55168	5586	6177	8322	1847
1998-99	28261	55188	5585	5475	7898	2113
1999-00	32088	58017	5394	4025	7411	2774
2000-01	34058	67544	4970	3444	7032	3240
2001-02	33059	67586	5812	3914	6245	3431
2002-03	34564	67630	6699	3226	5489	2740
2003-04	46830	67641	6566	2892	5315	3277
2004-05	45192	67871	6462	3032	5000	2690
2005-06	42856	68765	5797	2594	4772	2808
2006-07	39997	75826	6334	2588	5514	2898

LEAGUE POSITIONS SEASON BY SEASON - 1997-2007

Season	City	United	Oldham	Bury	Stockport	Rochdale
1997-98	42	2	57	37	28	86
1998-99	47	1	64	42	36	87
1999-00	22	1	58	59	37	78
2000-01	18	1	59	60	39	76
2001-02	21	3	53	66	44	73
2002-03	9	1	49	75	58	87
2003-04	16	3	59	80	63	89
2004-05	8	3	63	85	68	77
2005-06	15	2	54	87	90	82
2006-07	14	1	50	89	76	77

A reproduction of the oldest known shirt connected with Manchester City - this was the black shirts worn by Gorton in the mid-1880s.

CHAPTER TWENTY-FIVE

THE COLOURS OF MANCHESTER

Wherever a big city has two major soccer clubs, there has to be a major colour contrast for territorial reasons. The followers of the two clubs wish to be able to distinguish themselves from one another and it is particularly important that, at an annual 'local derby', when the rival local sides meet, each should be wearing their home colours. So it is that Manchester United are red and Manchester City are blue "The Soccer Tribe", Desmond Morris, 1981

FOR most modern day fans the home colours of each of our local sides are set, never to be changed, however it is appropriate to highlight that none of our sides have continued to wear the same coloured home shirts since the beginning of their life. Of all the League teams in the area however Bury can be proved to have worn their recognised kit the earliest.

Bury adopted white shirts and blue shorts in 1888 with the first game in this kit being a 2-1 home defeat to Halliwell on 8th September, although it has to be stressed that Bury did drop these colours for two seasons immediately after the First World War – they wore red and white hoops for a while. According to Bury's official records the colours were adopted by accident. In April 1888 the Bury minute book recorded:

"Mr J Openshawe had kindly offered to give a sufficient quantity of blue serge to the club, of which to provide 18 pairs of pants for next season."

Once the shorts or 'pants' were made committeeman Tom Hargreaves proposed on 21st August 1888 that the club obtain white flannel for shirts to be made. It is recorded that the flannel cost 1/6d per yard and that each shirt would cost one shilling to make, and Bury historians believe the blue shorts had guided the club towards picking a kit that was already worn by the already-famous Lancastrian clubs Preston North End and Bolton Wanderers.

The other Manchester area side that has worn its recognised colours since the 1800s is City. The Blues were definitely wearing Cambridge blue shirts with white shorts in 1894 when Ardwick became Manchester City, and research for this book suggests they wore those colours several years earlier, possibly from the 1880s. Some publications have claimed that City/Ardwick wore white shirts however this does not seem to be true and a more likely reason for white being mentioned is that City's pale blue shirts had simply faded – the Blues were known to wear their kits until they almost fell apart.

Interestingly, research for this book has discovered that key information on Ardwick's shirts actually resides in documentation stored at United's museum. These records show that Ardwick's shirts were royal blue and white when they entered the 1887 Manchester Cup competition. This is the first documentary evidence showing that City or its predecessors wore a form of blue, but clearly the shade and style (it is understood the shirts were striped but they may have been quartered) was not typical of City's later kits. It does clearly show however that the club were the first of our local clubs to adopt a colour, if not shade, and stick with it. 1887 was a significant year, as that was the season the club took on a more professional outlook. The club developed its first truly enclosed venue at Hyde Road and changed its name to Ardwick AFC.

The shade of blue City is recognised as wearing was initially referred to as Cambridge Blue and then Sky Blue, but at times the shade has been slightly darker. Actually the shade of blue worn by City since the move to the City of Manchester Stadium is quite light when compared to City's traditional kit. The shade of blue worn during the sixties was darker and is much more in keeping with the club's traditional shade of sky blue. Today's blue appears too pale.

The 1926 FA Cup final shirt, dubbed 'cornflower blue' at the time, is slightly darker than traditionalists would expect. However, it is a fact that City is the only side to have worn light blue consistently throughout their League history. It is worth noting that Coventry City's use of sky blue came as a direct result of a Coventry director watching the 1955 FA Cup final and admiring City's battling spirit when they went down to ten men. He wanted his side to show the same commitment and eventually Coventry adopted City's colours.

Why blue and white? There is strong information to suggest light blue was selected because of links with the Masonic community. Many former directors of Manchester City talk of the Club as having strong links with Freemasonry and the colour is regarded as a key Masonic colour. It is used to symbolise friendship and is a very important colour in terms of community spirit. Even if the Masonic links are false, it is clear that the people responsible for selecting a very light shade of blue, together with virtuous white, deliberately chose the colour because of its meaning.

Interestingly, the club's first known colours were black with a white 'Maltese style' cross. These shirts were presented to the side by one of the club's original founders William Beastow. As with the use of Cambridge blue some have suggested that this version of the Maltese Cross did have significance within the Masonic community of east Manchester. The majority of historians have suggested the white cross proves the link with St. Mark's was still evident, although this type of cross did not have any direct link with the local church.

French citizen and Manchester football historian Jean-François Maillé has his own view of what the cross meant:

"I believe the cross is not specifically a Maltese Cross. It's more a Patée Cross, which was the pattern for the Victoria Cross introduced in 1856. Local employer Richard Peacock was elected Liberal MP in 1885 – a year after he donated £5 to Gorton AFC and Beastow presented the black shirts to the team. We know that Beastow and Peacock were leading figures in the Gorton area - Beastow was an influential member of the Conservative Party. Peacock was interested in the football team, possibly to help his political aspirations, and he'd also donated money to St. Mark's church over the years.

"To me, the cross on the shirt is a political statement - It is a support to the Monarch and to the courage of the soldiers who fought for the Empire. Also, it could be a badge of honour for the players, a way to encourage their fighting spirit, to be as courageous as a soldier. It is something that a Conservative politician could do. In the book Manchester The Greatest City *it is said that during Gorton AFC's first annual dinner 'Hearts of Oak' and 'The Old Brigade' were sung. These are military songs.*

"The fact that Ardwick have been highlighted as wearing royal blue and white in 1887 adds weight to the idea that the club was in 'support of the monarch'."

More than anything else the Masonic influence does seem far too strong to suggest the shirt's colour and branding is co-incidence. Councillor William Beastow was known to have very strong links with freemasonry and was a senior figure within Ashbury Masonic Lodge No.1459. Maillé's views actually fit with this idea as freemasonry and loyalty to the monarch do go hand in hand.

Recently another theory on City's roots and the white cross has proved popular with United fans who see this story as humorous. According to David Winner, the author of **Those Feet**, an organisation called the White Cross League, founded by Ellice Hopkins, was particularly strong in Manchester in the 1880s and that its aims were to encourage purity, self control and chastity. Winner suggests this may have had a bearing on the use of the white cross on Gorton's shirts, however this is a total red herring as the White Cross League wasn't actually formed until 1886 – two years after the club first wore the cross. Despite being inaccurate, it has provided United fans with an opportunity to ridicule the Blues.

Interestingly one of Gorton's rivals, Earlestown AFC, played in white shirts with a black Maltese Cross during this same period.

Across at United the club has become famous for its use of red, however according to most sources the side only truly adopted red shirts in 1902, when they became Manchester United. ***The Manchester United Official Illustrated History*** records:

"The new era brought a change of strip to red shirts and white shorts and these have remained Manchester United's colours to the present day."

This is of course incorrect as the club have had two significant spells since 1902 where the use of red was limited. During a significant spell in the 1920s (1922-26) their predominant colour was white, and in the 1930s they wore cherry and white hoops for a couple of seasons.

During 1997, shortly before his death, City supporter Harry Hughes (born in 1902) remembered the state of 1930s United and how this affected their kit:

"I worked in Trafford Park then, and all the locals were United fans. I was working nights and when Saturday morning arrived a couple of them asked 'are you going to see the Rags today?' I didn't know what they meant, and then they explained that United fans had started to call the team the 'Rags' because they were so poor that their kit looked like rags. So after that I knew who they meant, but when I mentioned the Rags, they'd go, 'who the Hell are you talking about?' They didn't like the opposition saying it."

It should be noted that the website **www.prideofmanchester.com** claims United wore red & white stripes during the Edwardian period - presumably at some point between 1901 and 1910 - and their site shows a shirt similar in style to the famous Sunderland shirt of the period as evidence. An image of United appears in ***The Pride Of Manchester*** book showing the 1913-14 side wearing stripes, but this may have been their away colours. In addition, the *Manchester Evening News* announced on 8th August 1903 that United was to adopt a new playing kit of *"new jerseys of bright red cashmere with red collar and white knickers and black stockings with blue tops."*

Some organisations, most notably the Association of Football Statisticians, carry information on United wearing red earlier than 1902. In fact it is believed the club may have worn red and white quarters in 1892-93 when they first joined the League. There is no photographic evidence to support this and all images discovered of Newton Heath during 1892-93 continue to show their kit as being of a similar design to the green and gold halves shirt.

It seems unlikely the Heathens wore red and white quarters during 1892-93 but research for this book has located images purporting to show City against Newton Heath from c.1898 which saw City's opponents as wearing quartered shirts of dark and light colouring. Could this be red and white quarters? Another image from 1898 appears in the *Manchester United Pictorial History and Club Record* of the Heathens' Lancashire Cup winning side wearing striped shirts.

The exact reason United selected red is not known. Their use of green and gold during their Newton Heath days is fairly obvious – the Lancashire & Yorkshire Railway used these colours – but red simply appears to have been part of the new start enjoyed by the club in 1902. If it is true that red and white quarters were used in the 1890s then this simply seems to be a natural progression.

The use of white with a red V in the 1920s was linked with United's success in the 1909 FA Cup final. That day the club wore white shirts, reportedly selected by comedian George Robey - who had also helped City's planning for their 1904 final - and bought from the shop co-owned by Billy Meredith, which had a red V and a red rose representing Lancashire.

The academic Desmond Morris performed a significant amount of research into the colours used by clubs for his book *The Soccer Tribe*. He identified that red was often selected by teams wanting to appear more aggressive in battle:

"It is the most conspicuous of all colours, especially at a distance, and it has a powerful symbolic impact as the colour of blood, energy, life, force, power and intensity."

His comments on blue provide an interesting comparison:

"In many ways it is the opposite of red, being the colour of peace, calm, harmony and loyalty. Perhaps its secret lies in the direction of the message. Perhaps its greatest attraction is the comforting signals it sends out from one team mate to another, rather than the message of violence transmitted by bright red costumes towards the enemy. If this is so, it would make up for its lack of fierceness in attack by having a calming, confidence building effect within the ranks of the team wearing it."

From a regional perspective, white is another popular colour, but Morris found this more difficult to understand. In the end he felt:

"The only explanation for its popularity is that it does have one other symbolic 'label', namely that of the hero."

One aspect of football shirts that should be commented on is the inclusion of a club badge or emblem. All sides wear a badge on their shirts. For every side the badge has been adapted over the years based on reasons of pride – making sure the emblem represents the best aspects of the club – and for commercial needs. For the two Mancunian League clubs the City of Manchester coat of arms has played a part in the development of their badges.

From 1894 City utilised the coat of arms as their own, and when United moved to Old Trafford the Reds painted the same emblem on their main stand roof. However, neither side wore the emblem in their first cup finals – City (1904) simply wore Cambridge Blue shirts with no emblem, while United (1909) wore an emblem of a red rose, representing Lancashire.

The first side to wear the coat of arms on their shirt was City for the 1926 FA Cup final, and the Blues have worn it for every major final since (including the 1986 Full Members Cup, but curiously not the 1970 ECWC). United adopted the emblem for their 1948, 1957 and 1963 FA Cup finals but have tended not to use it since (they did wear it for the 1968 European Cup final though).

In 1958 United did wear another emblem which over the years has confused many supporters. The emblem was a bird and many publications since have claimed the Reds wore a phoenix on their shirts to highlight the spirit of the club rising out of the ashes of Munich, but this is untrue. Even on the 50th anniversary of the disaster the BBC made the mistake of saying United wore a phoenix to emphasise the re-birth during their half-time coverage of the England-Switzerland friendly on 6th February 2008. In fact the bird is exactly the same bird that forms part of Manchester City's current badge, and is actually an eagle. In 1958 supporters were suggesting the badge was a tribute to Munich, but in truth the emblem had been created by the city council in 1957 as the official badge of the City of Manchester. The council wanted organisations to use this instead of the formal coat of arms.

In 1958 the **Manchester Evening News** carried the story:

"Just to forestall any speculation, Manchester United's new Wembley badge is not a tribute to Germany or to Munich. The eagle forms part of badge which has recently been granted to the City of Manchester. It is not strictly part of the coat of arms, though it is complimentary to it. Permission for its use has been accorded to Manchester United for the Cup final. A town hall official explained that the eagle was not Germanic in origin or design, but was symbolic of Manchester's connection with ancient Rome. The 'M' is the fesse dancettee recording the association with an ancient family which were Lords of the Manor. Though it looks like an M it is not in fact. The ring around it is symbolic of Ringway. The mural crown is the symbol of municipal corporation. It is in silver to symbolise clean air - in the provision of which Manchester has played a pioneer role."

As mentioned earlier, the eagle now forms part of the City badge adopted during the summer of 1997, although the club also utilised the logo on handbooks and other material produced during the late fifties and early sixties. The 1997 badge was designed to incorporate significant elements of Manchester life and also to try and present a new image. A Latin motto 'Superbia in proelio', meaning 'Pride in battle', was added – the English version of this motto now appears above the City of Manchester Stadium tunnel.

The badge also incorporates the ship over the three emblazoned lines from the Manchester coat of arms. A version of this formed part of both City's and United's first post war badge. Over the years many have incorrectly assumed the ship in all versions of Manchester's emblems represents the Manchester Ship Canal, however Manchester's coat of arms predate the Ship Canal. The ship actually represents Manchester's trading links, focusing on the canals developed during the

18th and early 19th centuries, such as the Bridgewater. The three diagonal stripes on the coat of arms signify the three rivers of Manchester – The Medlock, Irwell, and The Irk – and on City's 1997 badge these lines have changed to blue and white to match City's traditional colours, although the first post war City badge correctly had these as red and gold.

The City badge also includes three gold stars. The stars are simply for styling purposes. Interestingly stars are often utilised in some countries to signify League triumphs, or by Champions League contenders to signify European Cup wins. United were the first English side to adopt stars after winning the Champions League in 1999, and for their European games in 1999-2000 the stars appeared on their shirts. In 2001-02 Liverpool wore four stars on their shirts and then added a fifth in 2005-06, while United have chosen not to wear stars since. Despite the popular view that winning the European Cup or similar allows clubs to wear stars as a right, clubs can chose when to adopt stars at will. The only formal recognition awarded by UEFA following European success was the UEFA badge of honour introduced for teams that have won the trophy five times, or three times in a row. Only five sides, including Liverpool, are allowed to wear this at the time of going to press.

Apart from United's red rose in 1909 and badges worn by City as Gorton (1884) and on club material as Ardwick (1887), the first recognised logos of the two main Manchester clubs were in existence from the 1950s through to the early 1970s when commercialisation first meant the sides had to gain control of their merchandising operations. Those original badges both contained the central shield of the City of Manchester coat of arms, although it had been adapted slightly by each club.

City surrounded the central shield by two circles, between which was a sky blue background and the club's name in gold lettering, while United surrounded it with a similar design to their modern day version (incorporating the red devil for the first time), although the name Manchester United appeared in the top section in gold on a red background, and Football Club appeared in gold on a white background in the bottom section. Two roses separated those two sections, where today footballs appear.

Both City and United's badges appeared in colour in the 1959 book ***The Encyclopedia of Sport,*** as did logos for Bury (the coat of arms/today's club badge), Rochdale (the coat of arms of Rochdale), and Stockport County (an adapted version of the Stockport coat of arms). Oldham was not included, but at that time the book would probably have shown the Oldham coat of arms. Latics have used this on occasion, however during the early 1950s – starting with 1951-52 season – Oldham wore a badge on their shirts that was basically a shield with the letters OAFC sloping across the centre separating sections that included a rose (top section) and an owl (bottom). George Hardwick, Latics manager, has been credited with designing, or at least helping with the design of this badge. The owl of course has always been a feature of both Oldham Athletic, and the Oldham coat of arms. This emblem appears to have lasted about five seasons on the club's shirts.

Stockport wore their version of the Stockport emblem during the late fifties and early sixties, while Rochdale wore their coat of arms during the early sixties. In fact Stockport is believed to have worn an emblem on their shirts for League games throughout the 1924-25 season.

The first of the two 'Manchester' sides to wear a badge on a regular basis in the League was City who announced on 29th August 1970 that their badge of the period would be worn during the

1970-71 season. United first wore a badge on a regular basis during 1972-73 but by that time the original design had been altered to a version of the present badge. The only significant difference between today's badge and that version was that it included the wording of Manchester United Football Club instead of just Manchester United, although it should be recognised that the use of two footballs in the logo itself does still make this a football badge.

So clearly City and United were many years behind the others in wearing badges for League games, although as far as can be told the use of the white cross in 1884 (Gorton, City's predecessor) is the first emblem of any kind adopted by our region's present day League sides. Interestingly, Bury are believed to have worn a badge on their shirts from 1888-90 but, like Gorton these were in the days prior to joining the Football League. They did also wear an emblem during the early 1950s and in the 1960s they wore the Bury coat of arms for a while.

It should be stressed that the emblems of each of our region's clubs have varied over the years, and that some clubs, such as City and Stockport, have altered their badges as part of an attempt to wrestle control for merchandise income back to the club.

The following details provide snapshot information on the kits worn by our local sides throughout the decades. Inevitably, each club may have changed its kit in between these dates, however the information aims to provide a general feeling for how the sides have adapted their predominant colours over the years. For details of specific kits worn by each of the region's clubs the website ***www.historicalkits.co.uk*** carries a colour impression for each side, season by season.

TEAM COLOURS OF LOCAL SIDES AS RECORDED c.1885

TEAM	COLOURS
Gorton AFC, (City)	Black shirts with a white Maltese Cross, white shorts
Bury	Chocolate & blue halved shirts, white shorts
Newton Heath (United)	Green & gold halves, blue shorts

TEAM COLOURS OF LOCAL SIDES AS RECORDED IN 1887-8

TEAM	COLOURS
Ardwick (City)	Royal blue & white striped shirts, white shorts
Bury	Chocolate & blue striped shirts, black shorts
Newton Heath	Green & gold halves, blue shorts

TEAM COLOURS OF LEAGUE SIDES AS RECORDED IN 1894

TEAM	COLOURS
Bury	White shirts and navy blue shorts
City	Cambridge blue shirts, white shorts
Newton Heath	Green shirts with gold edging, white shorts
Stockport, 1895	Blue & white striped shirts, dark blue shorts

TEAM COLOURS AS RECORDED IN 1904

TEAM	COLOURS
Bury	White shirts and navy blue shorts
City	Cambridge blue shirts, white shorts

United	Red cashmere shirts, white shorts, black socks with blue tops
Rochdale, 1907	Blue shirts, white shorts
Stockport	Red & white striped shirts, blue shorts

TEAM COLOURS OF LEAGUE SIDES AS RECORDED IN 1921

TEAM	COLOURS
Bury	Red & white hooped shirts, dark blue shorts
City	Cambridge blue shirts, white shorts, dark blue socks with light blue tops
United	Red shirts, white shorts, black socks
Rochdale	Black & white stripes, black shorts, black socks
Stockport	Broad white stripe, with smaller blue stripes at side, blue & white sleeves, white shorts, black socks with blue & white tops

TEAM COLOURS OF LEAGUE SIDES AS RECORDED IN 1923

TEAM	COLOURS
Bury	White shirts, dark blue shorts
City	Cambridge blue shirts, white shorts, dark blue socks with light blue tops
United	White shirts with a large red V, white shorts, black socks
Rochdale	Black & white stripes, black shorts, black socks
Stalybridge Celtic	Dark Blue with white sleeves, white shorts, blue socks
Stockport	Broad white stripe, with smaller blue stripes at side, blue & white sleeves, white shorts, black socks with blue & white tops

TEAM COLOURS AS RECORDED IN 1934

TEAM	COLOURS
Bury	White shirts and navy collars, dark blue shorts
City	Sky blue shirts, white shorts
United	Cherry and white hooped shirts, white shorts
Oldham	Blue and white halves, white shorts
Rochdale	Black and white stripes, white shorts
Stockport	White shirts, blue shorts

TEAM COLOURS AS RECORDED IN 1960

TEAM	COLOURS
Bury	White shirts, navy blue shorts with white stripe, navy blue socks with one white ring
City	Sky blue shirts with white V neck and trimmings, white shorts, sky blue and white hoped socks
United	Red shirts with white V neck and trimmings, white shorts, black socks with red and white tops
Oldham	Blue & white shirts with white V neck and trimmings, white shorts, blue socks with white tops
Rochdale	White shirts, black shorts, red socks
Stockport	White shirts, black shorts with white seam, red, white and black hooped socks

Bobby Charlton in the United strip of 1973.

TEAM COLOURS AS RECORDED IN 1966

TEAM	COLOURS
Bury	White shirts, royal blue shorts
City	Sky blue shirts, white shorts, maroon & blue socks
United	Red shirts, white shorts, red socks
Oldham	Orange shirts, royal blue shorts
Rochdale	White shirts, black shorts, white socks
Stockport	Royal blue shirts, royal blue shorts with white trim

TEAM COLOURS AS RECORDED IN 1974

TEAM	COLOURS
Bury	White shirts, royal blue shorts
City	Sky blue shirts, white shorts, blue socks with claret and white tops
United	Red shirts with white trimmings, white shorts, black socks with red top and white band
Oldham	Blue shirts, royal blue shorts, white socks
Rochdale, 1973-4	White shirts with a blue & while diagonal stripe, blue shorts, blue socks
Rochdale, 1974-5	Royal blue shirts with white collar and cuffs, white shorts, blue socks
Stockport	White shirts with blue collars and cuffs, white shorts, white socks with blue top

TEAM COLOURS AS RECORDED IN 1984

TEAM	COLOURS	AWAY COLOURS
Bury	White shirts with thin blue stripes, royal blue shorts, white socks	All yellow
City	Sky blue shirts with white collar and cuffs & white stripe down sleeve, Sky blue shorts with white trim, sky blue socks with white rings rings on top	Red and black striped shirts, black shorts, black socks
United	Red shirts with red, white & black trim, white shorts, black socks with with red top and 3 white bands	White shirts with black & red trim, black white trim shorts, white socks with 3 black bands
Oldham	Royal blue shirts with red and white trim, white shorts with blue stripe down the side, white socks	All white
Rochdale	White shirts, blue shorts, white socks	White shirts, green shorts, green socks
Stockport	Blue and white striped shirts, blue shorts, blue socks	Yellow shirts, green shorts, green socks with yellow bands at turnover

TEAM COLOURS AS RECORDED IN 2006

TEAM	COLOURS	AWAY COLOURS
Bury	White shirts with blue sleeves and patterning, royal blue shorts with white sides, royal blue socks	Sky blue
City	Sky blue shirts with white sleeves, Sky blue shorts, sky blue socks	Navy blue, navy blue shorts, navy blue socks
United	Red shirts, white shorts, black socks	Blue shirts, blue shorts, blue socks
Oldham	Royal blue shirts with white trim, royal blue shorts with white trim, white socks	Navy shirts, navy shorts, navy socks
Rochdale	All blue	All white
Stockport	Blue shirts with white chestband, blue shorts, white socks	Black and yellow shirts, yellow shorts, yellow socks

NICKNAMES

In the main supporters rarely use the nicknames the media tend to suggest for their clubs, It is unlikely you will ever hear fans talk of City as "The Citizens" or County as "The Lillywhites" for example. Naturally, it is possible but extremely unlikely during the modern era.

There are of course nicknames given to each of the clubs by rival fans, and in some cases names that originally started as names by one set of fans and then altered by the others. There are also names used for periods under particular managers such as Busby Babes.

The following section gives simple details on some of the nicknames that have been used, or are alleged to be used, by fans of our clubs. This is not a comprehensive list and excludes names such as "Yard Dogs" – a name used by City manager Jimmy Frizzell as criticism for the Oldham style of play in a game during the 1980s and then briefly adapted by Latics fans as a symbol of triumph over the Blues.

Bury

The Shakers

City

The Blues/Sky Blues
City
The Citizens
The Maine Men
Manchester
Gortonians (1880s)
Ardwickites (late 1880s/ early 1890s)
Hyde Roaders (1910s)
The Brewery Men (1890s to 1923)
The Cits (1900-1904)

United

The Reds
The Red Devils
United
Manchester
Newton
The Heathens (to 1902)
The Coachbuilders (1880s)

Oldham

The Latics

Rochdale

The Dale

Stalybridge Celtic

The Celts
Celtic

Stockport

County
The Hatters
The Lillywhites

CHAPTER TWENTY-SIX

THE GROUNDS

Of the making of football grounds there is no end. And such has been the growth of interest in the popular winter game that the modest grounds of the 80s, when professionalism was in its infancy, would prove quite unequal to present day requirements. "The Umpire", 1910

THE history of our clubs and their grounds are inevitably inter-woven, however the stories of our venues are somewhat different to the clubs themselves. The following sections provide information on each of our region's League grounds and of significant other venues in the region.

BURY STADIA

Since formation Bury have only had one permanent home – Gigg Lane – but this home is a perfect example of how traditional football grounds in the region have developed.

GIGG LANE (SINCE 1885)

Gigg Lane was originally part of the Earl of Derby's estate and shortly after formation, the Bury committee started negotiations for a field at the south-west corner of the farm with Thomas Barlow, an agent for the Earl. Barlow lived at Bankfield Farm (present day Bankfield Nursing Home) and the land was known locally as "Mr. Barlow's field, Gigg Lane." Agreement was reached for Bury to pay an annual rent of £25.

Bury Wesleyans played on a field further down Gigg Lane at the time and, according to Bury historians, it is highly possible that a team called Gigg Rovers occupied the site of Bury's new ground.

As with the rest of the region's early venues there were no facilities at the time the ground first opened. A rope separated spectators from the pitch and a fence ran along the length of Gigg Lane. Fans had to access the ground via a narrow admission gate on Gigg Lane almost opposite Brierley Street.

The first recorded game took place on 6th June 1885 between two specially invited clubs - Accrington (winners of the East Lancashire Charity Cup) who beat their local rivals Church 4-2 before around 500 fans. Afterwards the Accrington President, Mr J.P. Hartley, commented that he believed that the new Bury club would be successful.

It is recorded that the first stand was erected at Gigg Lane in 1887-8 on the south side. Initially a Mr. H. Brierley said he could build a 300 capacity stand for £44 but as the project developed costs increased and the eventual bill reached £50 11s. 8d. Although the additional £6 or so sounds relatively small it did cause significant issues for the club and Bury had to set up a stand fund. Fans who subscribed 10/6d or more were given a free stand ticket for the remainder of the season. The stand was officially opened on 5th November 1887 when a crowd of 2,000 watched a Lancashire Junior Cup victory over Heywood. It was a very important moment for the club and on the frontage of the new stand roof the letters BAFC were proudly displayed. It also meant that the players could now change at the ground instead of at the Pack Horse Hotel.

One significant moment in which Gigg Lane beat the majority of the region's other venues came on 5th November 1889 when 7,000 attended the ground's first floodlit match. "Wells Patent Lights" were placed around the pitch in the hope they would illuminate the turf well enough for a game, and Bury defeated Heywood 5-4. Those same lights had been utilised on 26th February that year when Newton Heath played Ardwick at Belle Vue, but as far as can be ascertained Gigg Lane was the first of the region's eventual League venues to stage a floodlit game (there are comments in newspapers of a floodlit game at the Hyde Road ground between Ardwick and Preston in the 1880s but no actual date has yet been identified).

During these early years, Gigg Lane was constantly being improved. In 1890 fencing was erected along the Gigg Lane side and Manchester Road end, and then in October a contract was issued to construct uncovered stands around the ground. Then in 1891 it was announced a 1,000 seat main stand was to be built on the northern side and that this would house dressing rooms and offices and would cost around £335. It was opened on 7th November 1891 and the **Bury Guardian** reported that it was *"Equalled by few, excelled by none."*

Later that month supporters were able to buy hot and cold refreshments at the ground for the very first time. Clearly Bury were moving forward at a fast rate and in 1894 improvements were made to enclose the venue with a 6ft fence built on Gigg Lane and six turnstiles erected opposite Brierley Street. All of this work prepared the side for its move into League football and in 1895, after winning promotion to Division One at the first attempt, the original stand on the south side was demolished and replaced with a £330 large open stand bringing the capacity to around 20,000. Other improvements included enlarged dressing rooms, a referee's room, and the installation of sinks.

Bury won the FA Cup in 1900 and 1903 and as a result the Cemetery End had a roof installed and then a new South Stand roof was built in 1906, but the most welcome change, certainly for female attendees, came in January 1913 when the club decided to erect the ground's first ladies toilet at a cost of £4 12s 6d.

The ground remained much the same until the 1920s when several significant ground developments occurred. First the two end terraces were rebuilt and then on 29th May 1924 the biggest development commenced with the Main Stand being rebuilt. It had its cast iron supports and roof removed and then a large steel framework was erected behind the existing wooden structure and extended backwards. This was to allow the seating capacity to increase from 1,920 to 5,600. The paddock along the front of the stand was made steeper, cutting below pitch level, while the banking on the other three sides of the ground was improved (although actual terracing was not laid at this point).

Further work took place at the South Stand. This was converted from a standing area to a 2,000 seated stand for the first time, while in the south-east corner a Boys terrace was built and a few years later this was roofed. Facilities outside the ground were improved with the present day car park developed on what was previously a field, while the original turnstiles were moved into a new wall of 24 turnstiles. Once fans entered Gigg Lane they then had to pay an additional fee if they wanted to transfer to a particular part of the ground – a system that was also adopted at other venues (During the 1930s and 40s Maine Road ground admission brought entry to the terracing and then fans would pay an additional amount to move under the Platt Lane roof). The difference with Bury was that this system remained in operation until 1981.

Gigg Lane in the 1930s.

All of these ground developments came to a total outlay of £12,000 but there were problems throughout the development. A national building strike in July caused all work to stop but negotiations between the club and the union allowed union workers to be recruited directly (not via an established building contractor) but this meant the club had to take a much more hands on approach.

The redeveloped ground opened on 30th August 1924 with a Division One game against City, although there were still many areas of the ground not quite finished. League President John McKenna opened the reconstructed ground and a then record crowd of 33,523 watched City win 2-0.

In 1938 the Manchester Road stand was built for £3,440 after a public appeal, meaning Gigg Lane had cover on all four sides – something neither Maine Road nor old Trafford could manage until the 1970s – but inevitably the outbreak of war prevented further developments occurring. Then in 1949 the South Stand paddock area and the Main Stand paddock were improved with concrete terracing and crush barriers replacing earth banking and similar forms of terracing. This development may have been brought about as a result of the Burnden Park disaster of 1946.

Other than general maintenance nothing of note occurred from a ground development point of view until a storm caused the Cemetery End roof to blow off in 1952. The roof was around fifty years old but the club did not have any funds available to replace it immediately, and so after dismantling the remaining structure the terrace remained open for the following decade. In fact it was not until the Supporters Club started their 'Stand Fund' during 1955 that moves were made to sort out the problem. Fans initially wanted to have an identical stand to the Manchester Road End built but the end was improved piecemeal. In 1956 the fans paid for concrete terracing costing £850.

While the Cemetery End remained roofless other developments did occur, the most significant being the switching on of the Gigg Lane floodlights on 6th October 1953 – this made Bury the first team in the northwest to switch on their lights as they beat Maine Road to this landmark by 8 days. In 1957 an additional £3,000 was spent on improving the quality of the lights.

Apart from crush barrier improvements in the late 1950s, it was not until 1962 that significant change was to occur with the Cemetery End at last getting its roof. The new 3-bay covered stand cost around £10,000 with the Supporters Club contributing a significant proportion of the money. It was announced that the 3 bays would eventually be added to to make this a larger 5 bay stand, but with finances tight the second phase never did occur. Nevertheless, Gigg Lane was recognised as a nice, neat, traditional style football venue. Bury press office Gordon Sorfleet remembers how he felt when he first started attending the ground:

"All the lads at school were United, City, Liverpool, even Bolton, but for me once I came here there was nowhere else better. I was hooked from the start."

It stayed like this for most of the following two decades and then the Bradford Fire caused the football authorities to take a serious look at the facilities on offer at all grounds. As Gigg Lane contained a significant amount of wood and traditional style stands the ground suffered considerably. The old Boys Stand was demolished immediately, although it had been used on the night of a celebratory friendly between promoted (to Division One) City and promoted (to Division Three) Bury a few days after the fire.

Other changes affected the Main Stand and its capacity was slashed by around 71% with only the use of around 1,500 seats (out of around 5,000) being designated as safe. The rear section of the Manchester Road End was fenced off and the entire capacity of the ground had dropped to around 8,300 from around 35,000 thirty years earlier. The situation looked exceptionally bleak.

Flooding at Gigg Lane in 1966.

Financial problems affected the club and, in truth, the prospect of improving the venue had to take a back seat as salvation more than anything else was the main concern. Then in 1992, at a time when the structure of league football was being changed (which saw Bury relegated from Division Three to the renamed Division Three), decisions were taken to tackle the ground issues.

On the 17th June 1992 the first steps were taken to strip out the old Main Stand, remove the South Stand roof and reprofile the Manchester Road terracing in order to convert the stand into a seated area. The Main Stand was completely stripped and then refurbished with new concrete steps, cladding, seating and so on. Basically it became a new stand and now seats around 3,300. This is still a relatively low number for such a large stand, and maybe the club would have been better ripping down the old stand in its entirety and building totally afresh, however this stand has ensured the ground has retained character.

Building work was relatively quick, however it still meant that several games had to be played in a two-ended ground before the new Main Stand opened on 17th October 1992. Two years later the replacement South Stand was officially opened, but this all-seater stand was smaller than the club had wanted due to opposition from local residents. It still held around 3,300, plus facilities for the disabled, but it should have been taller.

Further developments occurred over the next few years with the Cemetery End redeveloped with a new stand built in mid-1995 at a cost of around £400,000. In 1996 the Manchester Road roof was extended down to the pitch with seating installed in the new section.

Gigg Lane is now a modern looking venue that somehow manages to retain its traditional feel. It has also been a well used ground since the 1990s with a variety of additional activities and clubs using the venue. Swinton RLFC used Gigg Lane for a while, as did United for reserve fixtures, but today FC United have established the venue as their temporary home. How long this continues depends on how FC United develop, but it is clear that Bury need the income and so long as FC United fans accept that without Bury their club's initial couple of years would have been difficult, then this form of groundshare does look as if it could work for some time. Long term however FC United want their own stadium, but Gigg Lane to many remains a perfect venue.

Gigg Lane is the region's oldest League ground. It is also a well loved venue that has managed to combine tradition with the modern needs of the game. The ground deserves to host a high level of football, and hopefully in 100 years when the history of football in Manchester is analysed further, the ground will still be an important venue.

MANCHESTER FC STADIA

Manchester FC are a Rugby Union side and have never been a Football League side, but they were Manchester's first entrants in the FA Cup and they are in effect Manchester's oldest association football club. Their venues, pre 1890, are significant as they staged FA Cup semi-finals and Manchester's first significant soccer games.

Home Grounds

Alexandra Park, Moss Side (1860-62)

Whalley Range (1862-1901)

Mabfield Road, Fallowfield (part of present day Platt Fields, 1901-08)

Littleton Road, Salford (1908-1914)

Moor Lane, Kersal (1919-1968)

Cheadle Hulme CC (1968-1970)

Grove Park, Cheadle Hulme (Since 1970)

WHALLEY RANGE 1862-1901

Richard Sykes worked with other members of Manchester FC to set up the ground at Whalley Range. Initially the land was rented from the de Trafford family, and according to the Manchester FC 125th anniversary brochure it was positioned close to Brooks Bar on the right side of Upper Chorlton Road. Interestingly the players would usually meet and change at the Queen's Hotel on

Portland Street (some sources suggest they would occasionally meet at The Grand Hotel but this seems less likely) in the city centre and then travel to the ground by coach and horses.

In 1874 the club bought the ground and over the rest of its history it staged many significant rugby fixtures, including the Calcutta Cup of 1885, and two FA Cup semi-finals. It also staged the 28th February 1885 Home International soccer game between England and Ireland. A crowd of around 6,000 saw a 4-0 English win.

MANCHESTER CITY STADIA

Since playing their first competitive game as St. Mark's Church (West Gorton) in 1880, the club is known to have played at eight different home venues.

CLOWES STREET/THOMAS STREET 1880-81

It says much about how the early history of football has been viewed in Manchester that the only plaque commemorating the history of City is actually incorrectly positioned. The blue plaque detailing City's formation is positioned on the boarded up Aces public house (named after the Belle Vue Aces speedway team) off Clowes Street, West Gorton. A more accurate and appropriate place for this would be on the Working Men's Club on Gorton Villa Walk. That building is the closest to the actual site of St. Mark's Church. It is particularly galling that football's role in Mancunian life gives City only one blue plaque in the city and that this has been incorrectly placed, with few specific details. In addition it is a little ironic that the walk that follows the original line of Clowes Street (where City were formed) is called Gorton Villa Walk - Gorton Villa FC was one of the club's biggest rivals throughout the 1880s when the City side still retained strong links with the area.

Traditionally football histories have claimed the club's first ground was on Clowes Street (Gorton Villa Walk) itself, but during the last decade research by the author of this book has identified that it is highly improbable that Clowes Street could have been the site of the first pitch as most of the area was already highly developed with residential and industrial buildings. In addition, the oldest surviving match report talks of the first game taking place in Longsight. This seems to be an error on the part of the writer (probably one of the church committee) as the St. Mark's vicarage was south of Hyde Road in an area known variously as Newton Detached or Longsight and so he may have submitted the report from the vicarage itself.

Recent research has concentrated on the location of the first pitch. There are many conflicting views, however the author of this book believes the first game was actually played next to Brooks & Doxey's Union Iron Works on Thomas Street, a road running parallel to Clowes Street. Maps from the late 1880s suggest there was some wasteland next to the original factory and this land was more or less directly north of St. Mark's Church. In addition, a ***Reporter*** newspaper article from April 1879 proves this Thomas Street spot was used for recreational activity. Under the heading ***"One lad stabbed by another at cricket"***, the unfortunate story was told of violence between West Gorton youngsters. A 14 year old was stabbed by a 15 year old on this site:

"The lads were playing at cricket along with some others in a field behind Thomas Street."

It is highly likely the players would have changed in the Church, or its school/church rooms, and walked along William Street – the road St. Mark's actually faced on to – to the land. Walking around this area today easily establishes the close proximity of all these locations.

Sadly, after over two decades of specific research there is no conclusive proof that this was the first pitch, and in 2006 descendants of an early club official suggested the first pitch was actually on land bordered by Armitage Street, Hyde Road and Clowes Street, although maps of the period suggest little space was available for a pitch in 1880.

As with Newton Heath's first venue, it has to be remembered that whichever location was utilised in 1880 this space was nothing more than rough land. The first reported home game was on 13th November 1880, with the first opponents being the Baptist church from Macclesfield. Both teams fielded 12 players, and the pitch markings would have been questionable – reports from later in the decade suggest local residents knew about rugby but not association football – and St. Mark's are known to have played a further two home games that season (Arcadians from Harpurhey on 27th November 1880 and Hurst on 26th February 1881). The Hurst report gives an indication to the quality of the ground:

"The ground was in a very sloppy state, and consequently the falls were very numerous."

It is highly probable St. Mark's played a few more matches at home that season, however the records simply do not exist.

Today the site believed to be the first pitch is currently the car park for an office block, which for most of its existence has been the home of computer firm ICL (Fujitsu) on Wenlock Way (renamed Thomas Street).

Interestingly, all of this area – in particular the houses on Gorton Villa Walk (former route of Clowes Street) and the shopping parade occupying the St. Mark's site – has been used for the Channel Four television series ***Shameless*** which features a Manchester City supporting family, and on matchday today many City fans park their cars in this area while attending games at the City of Manchester Stadium.

KIRKMANSHULME CRICKET GROUND 1881-82

The first true pitch was the Kirkmanshulme Cricket Club ground positioned on the southern side of Hyde Road on Redgate Lane, midway between St. Mark's Church and the rectory on North Road. This five acre site provided the young club with terrific opportunities although, apart from a pavilion in one corner of the ground, there were few facilities.

It is believed Edward Kitchen, an influential committeeman and player, suggested the move to this ground, it was positioned close to Tank Row where he was living at the time.

The club are known to have played five games out of twelve matches at the ground that season. Again they may have played more but the club's own records were destroyed in a fire in 1920 and reports tended only to appear in the ***Gorton Reporter*** and even then not every game was reported on.

The club's first home meeting with Newton Heath (present day United) on 4th March 1882 attracted an attendance of around 5,000 – some 2,000 more than the North Road fixture the previous November - with spectators stood along the touchline (the outer edges of the cricket pitch). The match ended 2-1 to St. Mark's.

According to early club histories, at the end of the season the Kirkmanshulme C.C. asked the footballers to find another ground as their playing surface had been badly damaged. Maybe this had been caused by the Newton Heath attendance, West Gorton's last game at the Cricket ground, or maybe it was simply because of the general wear and tear on the pitch, who knows. It seems more likely that cricket officials were concerned that the football club was becoming more popular than the long established cricket club.

Eventually the cricket club disappeared as the area became more industrial and the popularity of the neighbouring Belle Vue Pleasure Gardens increased. The site was used as car parking for Belle Vue for a time, but by the mid 1980s the site had become derelict. The ring road, which ultimately leads to the City of Manchester Stadium, cuts through the site as it makes its way from Longsight, across Redgate Lane, and on to Hyde Road. This road has brought new life to the area and modern industrial units and other buildings have been erected here.

QUEEN'S ROAD 1882-84

For the start of the 1882-83 season St. Mark's moved to land off Queen's Road, approximately three-quarters of a mile east of Clowes Street. The land is believed to be the present day Gorton Park and, if this is true, this is the only actual former home of either City or United still staging football today.

In the 1930s a City historian referred to the venue as Clemington Park and also Clemington Downs but neither name has ever been used as far as can be ascertained by Gortonians, nor is it one that appears on official records. It is believed this was some form of joke between club officials who perhaps tried to make it sound grander than it actually was - supporters at the turn of the century are alleged to have called it 'Donkey Common' as donkeys and other animals connected with travelling fairs and Belle Vue were supposedly kept there on occasion. During the 1940s a booklet called Famous Football Clubs – Manchester City referred to this ground:

"In later years this ground developed into a park, but it looked more 'parky' than anything else in those days."

As with the name of the venue, the history of St. Mark's during this period is equally confused. Match reports suggest only three home games were played there in 1882-83 and five the following season, and that there was a merger with another local team. While material written during the 1930s and early 1940s – a time when some of the original founders were still around – suggest around twenty games (ten at home) were played each season.

Although little proof exists today, it is clear that this venue was the first to last more than one season, and that it was the first venue which allowed the side to seriously play football.

In 1884 the club split with the original St. Mark's men renaming their club Gorton Association Football Club, while the others created West Gorton Athletic. That side survived for a few years, first at Queen's Road, then near the Gorton Brook Hotel at the top end of Clowes Street, but eventually the side folded.

Over the years that followed the club's move the park was developed into a more formal affair, partly due to the finance of the brewer Stephen Chester Thompson – who was also City's main benefactor for several years. Nowadays Gorton Park remains a small but popular space for football. New housing was being erected around it in 2007 and so, potentially, the value of this footballing space will remain for many years.

PINK BANK LANE 1884-85

Once the club split, the newly named Gorton AFC, chose a site on Pink Bank Lane in desperation in October 1884 as most of the other recognised local sporting venues were already occupied. Player Lawrence Furniss – probably City's most influential figure of all time due to a variety of significant activities during his life - was the man who identified the potential of the site and club secretary Edward Kitchen negotiated a rent of £6 a year.

Although the site was not equipped for football it was relatively close to the old Kirkmanshulme Cricket ground and the St. Mark's rectory. It was referred to as "The Pink Bank Lane Ground" in a report of the Gorton-Gorton Villa derby match of 14th March 1885 when Gorton won 3-0. Interestingly, the oldest known surviving photograph of the club was taken in October 1884, around the time of the move to Pink Bank Lane, and it is believed this was taken at the new ground on the club's first day there.

Gorton moved on at the end of the season and since Gorton's departure, Pink Bank Lane has been re-developed a couple of times. One side of the Lane houses the Belle Vue Athletics Centre, which was utilised during the 2002 Commonwealth Games.

BULL'S HEAD HOTEL, REDDISH LANE 1885-87

Apart from Maine Road, this venue was by far the furthest distance away from the St. Mark's birthplace the side has ever been based at. Right on the border of Gorton, Reddish and Denton, the Bull's Head Hotel is roughly two miles from Clowes Street. The venue was used for a variety of sports in the years prior to Gorton's residence and the committee would have known of its potential. In one month alone, July 1882, the **Gorton Reporter** covered activities such as Rabbit coursing, pigeon shooting and quoits all at the Bull's Head, or Reddish Lane ground as it was often called.

The Bull's Head ground was a large site and, of course, the public house's facilities were also extremely useful (particularly after a difficult game!). Gorton were charged £6 per year rent to use the ground and to change in the public house, and the landlord also gained from improved beer sales. The first Gorton football game to be staged there was a 1-1 draw with Earlestown on 3rd October 1885, and the last known game there was against Pendleton Olympic on 30th April 1887. According to early club histories the landlord asked for a rent increase and so the side moved on.

Today it is difficult to identify specifically where the pitch was. In 1906 the original Bull's Head was replaced with the present day public house, while early twentieth century/late nineteenth century terraced housing covers the neighbouring area. It is believed the housing directly behind the Bull's Head occupies the site of the pitch, however there is one significant open space a short distance behind the public house. This is a playing field for a local school. Potentially, this could have been the site of the old pitch.

HYDE ROAD, ARDWICK 1887-1923

The most important move in the club's history came in 1887. The selection of the new ground caused the club to take on a much more professional outlook. It also allowed the side to return to its roots, as the new venue lay closer to the club's spiritual home, St. Mark's Church, than any of the previous venues other than perhaps the one utilised during the first season.

Club captain Kenneth McKenzie recognised the potential of wasteland located close to his workplace. This land was a decent size, but it was basically a dead space in between railways, a factory, and a terraced street. It was owned by the Manchester, Sheffield, and Lincolnshire Railway Company and after serious negotiation, they rented it to Gorton for £10 for a period of seven months.

As the venue was outside the Gorton borough the club decided to relaunch as Ardwick AFC. A circular was issued on 23rd August 1887 and the inaugural meeting was held at the new headquarters of the club, the Hyde Road Hotel, on 30th August. This public house was also used as dressing rooms for several years, and in 1887 it is believed the side adopted royal blue and white striped shirts for the first game at the venue. This is understood to be the club's first use of blue.

Within a decade the Hyde Road ground developed into a major venue. In 1905 Hyde Road staged an inter-League game between Ireland and England (footage from this match is the oldest surviving footage of a Mancunian game) and the FA Cup semi-final between Newcastle and Sheffield Wednesday. By that time the ground possessed one significant grand stand, a large Popular Side terracing, a mixture of uncovered seats and terracing behind one goal, terracing behind the opposite end, and a small 'Boys' Stand' in one corner.

The stadium was often packed with crowds of 40,000 or more, although it is impossible now to identify the actual attendances of games at this time. Journalists would state that the crowd was around 40,000, while it is known that the Blues regularly downplayed the number that were actually present for financial and safety reasons. A few games, most notably a Cup tie with Sunderland in 1913 and a League game with Burnley in 1921, caused local journalists to question the Blues management about safety, organisation, and attendance of games at Hyde Road. The majority of significant games seemed to be played with a packed crowd inside the stadium and scenes of chaos outside.

ROUND THE COUNTRY.

A.N.—Nov: 8-1920

Manchester City's Grand Stand Burned Down.

MIDNIGHT BLAZE.

(From Our Own Correspondents.)

MANCHESTER CITY have suffered a great blow by a disastrous fire which broke out at their ground late on Saturday night, and which completely demolished the grand stand, players' dressing-rooms, and the offices of the club.

Shortly after eleven o'clock flames were seen issuing from beneath the structure which runs the whole length of the ground, and apparently the fire had originated at what is known as the Galloway end. An alarm was raised, but the outbreak spread with such great rapidity that though the Manchester Fire Brigade answered the call very promptly, the building, which is wholly of wood, was doomed before their arrival.

WATCHING THE FLAMES.

In just over an hour the whole erection, which was valued at several thousands of pounds, was burnt to the ground. The flames could be seen for miles around, and thousands of people were attracted to the ground. A strong body of police was drafted to the scene; but a great number of people by that time had assembled beneath the shelters on the far side of the enclosure, and when the supports of the roof collapsed the leaping flames revealed them standing together as on the occasion of an important match.

The stand was capable of seating about 5,000 people, and, in view of the club's difficulties with regard to accommodation, the loss is a very serious one.

Mr. J. E. Mangnall, the secretary of the club, who was summoned to the ground, informed an *Athletic News* representative that, although the damage was covered by insurance, it was impossible to estimate the loss the club would sustain, especially having regard to the fact that the accommodation on the ground had been inadequate for a long time past.

Mr. Mangnall added that he was not prepared to make a statement with respect to any renewed offer which might be made for the use of another ground in the city. It would be a matter for consideration by the board of directors.

How the fire originated has not been ascertained.

A few weeks ago the City Club entered into an arrangement for transferring their headquarters to Belle Vue; but the new ground cannot be ready for at least two years.

The Hyde Road fire of 1920 seriously damaged the ground, but City's spirits remained high.

FOOTBALL HUMOUR.
S.CHRON. NOV.28.1920
"I Wouldn't Leave My Little Wooden Hut for You."

There is no love lost between the two big Manchester football clubs, and the feeling has not been improved since the United first offered and then refused the City the free use of the Old Trafford ground for League matches.

Evidently a wag had been at work in the musical department prior to the match at Hyde-road yesterday, for just before the United team entered the field the band played with great pathos "I Wouldn't Leave My Little Wooden Hut For You," and followed by "Home, Sweet Home."

Despite the capacity of the ground, newspaper stories regularly suggested the ground's future was limited. In 1904 the club almost moved to Belle Vue and almost every year from then on stories would circulate saying the Blues were about to announce a significant move, but nothing concrete ever occurred. Then, just as United were planning their move to Old Trafford the Blues announced they would improve Hyde Road.

In September 1910 the Blues opened their newly refurbished ground. Clearly, Old Trafford was a fantastic new venue but here, in the middle of Ardwick, City had dramatically improved facilities on three sides of their popular ground. In many ways this transformation in 1910 was similar to the events of 2003-6 when City moved to their new stadium. While the Blues talked of the quality of their new venue in 2003, United were busy improving Old Trafford to show their fans and neutrals that their venue still had a great deal to offer.

During the 21st Century United's capacity was increased significantly, as were the club's corporate facilities, while in 1910 City's redevelopment did little to change Hyde Road's capacity, but it did improve facilities for a vast number of fans. The Blues erected multi-span roofs on the three remaining open sides, improved seating behind one of the goals, improved catering facilities, and refurbished the offices and player related areas.

The Hyde Road ground was able to boast that, in 1910, it provided shelter for a total of 35,000 spectators and importantly all four sides had cover – neither Old Trafford nor Maine Road could match this until 1971 (Maine Road). So, while Old Trafford led the way in terms of complete concrete stadium, Hyde Road led the way in terms of facilities for all fans.

Despite the rebuild, the real issues of the venue could never be overcome. These all related to its location, size and entrances. Hyde Road simply could not be enlarged due to the close proximity of the railway and Galloway's Boilerworks, nor could its entrances be improved. The committeemen searched for a new venue, but it was not until the period after World War One that any real progress could be made.

In March 1920 Hyde Road became the first provincial ground to be visited by a reigning monarch when King George V attended City's victory over Liverpool (some sources claim King Edward VII also attended the ground at the turn of the 20th Century however this is totally untrue, and the photographic evidence produced to justify the claim actually show City officials at the visit of future Prime Minister – and City patron - Arthur Balfour in 1900). Eight months after the King's visit disaster struck when fire destroyed the 21 year old Main Stand. The rest of the stadium survived (during 2000-2002 City's official website claimed the ground was totally wrecked but that was a wild exaggeration), but without the main dressing rooms and best seated stand there were real issues for the club.

The Blues should have moved immediately and they did have discussions with United about moving to Old Trafford, however the local media were highly critical of United, accusing them of opportunism. According to the *Athletic News* the terms were:

HIS MAJESTY KING GEORGE V. AT HYDE ROAD, MANCHESTER.
MANCHESTER CITY v. LIVERPOOL, PLAYED ON MARCH 27th, 1920.

"City should take the equivalent of last season's gate in the corresponding match and that the remainder should belong to the United. As gates have increased by 30 per cent at the very least in the First Division matches the Manchester City directors declined to entertain the proposal, and no wonder Manchester United did not in our opinion manifest the much-vaunted League spirit.

"They missed a great opportunity to make the club popular by a fine sporting act. The followers of Manchester City have greater affection for the old club than ever. And they have formed a just opinion of their neighbours."

For City manager Ernest Mangnall, the former United manager and the man viewed by many as the one responsible for the development of Old Trafford, this was a serious blow. According to City sources he felt let down and, as a result, City made the decision not to pay this excessive rental to Mangnall's former club. Hyde Road was patched up while longer term plans were made. Interestingly, this brought national attention with reporters from all over the United Kingdom checking on City's progress. The **Glasgow Evening Times** was particularly impressed:

"Manchester City must have some good friends. They are of course the popular club in Manchester. It was surprising to find a fine new stand, estimated to hold 6,000 spectators, rising to the height of 25 tiers on the site of the old structure. In addition, extensive new terracing had been carried out, and new dressing rooms for both teams and offices had been erected. Talk about the building of an American city!"

Seven days after the stand was completely destroyed the ground staged a League match watched by 35,000. Journalists, directors and the like were seated behind the goal at the Stone

Yard End (the stand sat around 2,000 behind a paddock), while the players changed at Galloway's boilerworks. On 27th November 1920 (3 weeks after the fire) the Blues faced the Reds. In 1996 City fan Harry Hughes remembered the period with pride and how, after United's offer had been rejected, the Blues transformed the ground:

"City politely refused saying 'Don't worry we'll have a grandstand!' and y'know we did! We had one built by the time we played United. It was made of tongue and groove and varnished. In fact you could still smell the varnish all over the ground. It was pretty rough, but it served its purpose, and as it was all new wood it must have been ten times stronger than the old stand.

"As usual the band came out, formed a circle on the pitch and played all the popular songs of the day. Then they started playing 'I wouldn't leave my little wooden hut for you' and the crowd wasn't slow to notice that, and we all started laughing. Then the referee came on, blew his whistle at the band and told them to get off! So as they marched off they played 'Home Sweet Home' - very apt, very witty!"

Discussions with Belle Vue Pleasure Gardens were taking place behind the scenes on the construction of a new stadium, while life at Hyde Road was proving difficult. The Blues were challenging Burnley for the League, and in March 1921 the two sides met at Hyde Road. Harry Hughes remembered that the crowd for this match was probably the largest Hyde Road crowd ever:

"I managed to get near the front. They had little wooden railings around the pitch to keep the crowd off the turf, but there was never any real danger in those days. Soon the ground became packed beyond ordinary comfort - and we didn't ask for a lot in comfort in those days! Some 'strong arms' lifted me up and put me over the railings onto the turf itself - the holy of holies! Anyway, behind me, right at the back there was a huge wooden door with a padlock on - it would have been one of the large exit gates. While I was safely on the pitch, I heard a tremendous noise and turned to see the gate broken down, all splintered, and the crowd surging in. As I was on the pitch I just missed being involved, just missed being crushed. I was lucky, others were injured."

Max Woosnam in action at Hyde Road in 1922. This is the only known image of the roofed Galloway End.

City's Sammy Sharp training at Hyde Road during the early 1920s.

The *Daily Dispatch* reported the amazing scenes in full - including the details of a stand fire that was quickly dealt with and the fact that many supporters took up positions on the roof itself. Secretary Ernest Mangnall was criticised heavily by the media, but all those connected with the club knew that the size of the ground was now too much of a limiting factor.

Hyde Road survived until 1923 with the last game being a public practice match in August 1923. The ground was dismantled over a period of a couple of years, but elements of the ground have survived into the 21st Century. In the late 1990s metalwork from one of the multi-span roofs was rediscovered as the roof of a factory in Sale. The building has since been demolished, but another section of roof still survives today as a football stand at Halifax Town's Shay Stadium. City sold the stand and a few turnstiles to Halifax for £1,000, and this stand remains a key feature of the Shay, however since the mid-1990s redevelopment plans for the Shay have frequently predicted the demise of the stand but financial problems have ensured the stand remains.

Over the years many writers – both from a City perspective and a neutral stance - have claimed Hyde Road was dilapidated and a poorly constructed ground, but in truth at the time of the King's visit in 1920 the oldest stand was only 21 years old, while the three other stands possessed roofs almost ten years old. Those roofs gave the venue a uniformed presence – something only Old Trafford since the late 1980s and the City of Manchester Stadium have matched – and the fact that one of these stands (slightly remodelled) is still being utilised at a football venue today, almost ninety years after the Hyde Road ground closed, suggests the ground was far from dilapidated. Hyde Road's problems were the fact it could not be enlarged, and its limited number of entrances. It is worth noting that some sources claim the site was needed for tramway developments however this is a myth. It is true that the site did later form part of the Hyde Road tram (later bus) depot, but that did not occur for several years. The outline of the old pitch survived and is visible on an aerial photo from around 1926. The site's use as part of the tram/bus depot only came because the land was vacant.

At the time of going to press exciting plans for the redevelopment of the Hyde Road site are being made. For many years, the site was used as a storage yard for containers and lorries, after several years use as a skid pan for the Hyde Road bus depot.

As with all the other local venues charity matches, local finals, and other events were staged there. One of the most interesting fixtures however had to be the 'Pancake Tragedy Charity Match'. Although the specifics of exactly what occurred are too detailed to include here, it is known that at least one person (Mr. RP Bolger) died when a Pancake Day event ended in disaster at Smithfield Market. Teams representing the fish and fruit markets competed against each other at Hyde Road on Monday 28th February 1910 at 3.30pm to raise money for Bolger's widow and family. Four thousand stand tickets had gone on sale, with over half sold four days before the game was scheduled. Considering the day and time of the game this was a remarkable achievement, but the tragedy had grabbed public consciousness for a while. United scout Louis Rocca played for the fruit team in the match.

Also, in 1956 when City staged their homecoming parade the Blues held a function in conjunction with the ***Manchester Evening Chronicle*** at the Belle Vue Pleasure Gardens. This function extended the homecoming so that after the usual reception at Manchester Town Hall the bus then made its journey back out of the city centre, down Hyde Road and on to Belle Vue. According to the ***Evening Chronicle*** Hyde Road was decked out in blue and white buntings with houses, shops and pubs around the Bennett Street & Clowes Street area covered in messages and banners congratulating the Blues. In addition, the largest crowd outside of the city centre gathered in this area which, the ***Chronicle*** pointed out, proved the strength of support the Blues still possessed close to their old ground.

MAINE ROAD, MOSS SIDE (1923-2003)

The Twenties saw City seriously consider how best to capitalise on their popularity. With a capacity of around 40,000, the Hyde Road ground was too restrictive. For some time City actively considered moving to Belle Vue but they eventually rejected the two sites they were offered (present day greyhound stadium, and the venue that became the Speedway Stadium from the 1920s until 1987) as they were too small. In addition they wanted to build the best club ground in England and needed a site that gave them free reign. As part of the Belle Vue complex the independence and identity of the club and its venue would have been challenged. Nevertheless when, on 9th May 1922, the news was revealed that City were to move away from east Manchester to the border of Rusholme and Moss Side it was still a major shock for east Mancunians.

City's new £5,500 site offered significantly more than any other location could, and the media seemed genuinely impressed with the Blues' ambitious plans. The new sixteen and a quarter acre site was to see a stadium built with an eventual covered capacity of 120,000 developed in two phases – or so the Blues claimed. The first phase, to be opened in time for the 1923-4 season, would see the Blues build a grandstand seating somewhere in the region of 15,000 and terracing for 55,000. Once that phase is completed, said the report, City would extend the terracing and erect a roof around the three sides to form a sort of 'C' around the grandstand, thereby reaching the incredible capacity of 120,000.

The original scheme had claimed the new venue would be 'The English Hampden', however in the years that have followed many City and neutral writers have incorrectly claimed Maine Road was developed as 'The Wembley of the North', and that the architect, Charles Swain, had tried to match the London venue. This is a total myth as both venues were being built by Sir Robert McAlpine in 1922-33. In fact there was actually a great deal of rivalry between the northern

Maine Road during construction in 1923.

builders and their southern counterparts. Wembley did actually open a few months before Maine Road, but crowd control issues at the first FA Cup final meant that Wembley did not have a good reputation in 1923.

According to some reports City adjusted their plans as a result of chaos at Wembley:

"The lessons of Wembley have been taken to heart, and a feature of the ground will be six tunnels communicating with the terraces, giving easy access to all parts."

Any comparison with Wembley would have shown the success of the Mancunian architect, planners, and builders in creating a stadium on time, to budget, and with proper crowd control and safety features.

Outside the stadium, a 500 space car park was developed and, in front of the grand stand, a forecourt capable of holding at least twenty thousand (very useful during the 1980s & 1990s for demonstrations!). Unlike Hyde Road it allowed ingress and egress on all four sides and City's architect Charles Swain designed the venue so that 120,000 people could evacuate within a 'very few minutes'.

There were two significant figures behind the development of the new stadium – manager Ernest Mangnall and Chairman Lawrence Furniss. At the time of opening it was suggested that the stadium should be named after Furniss, but the Chairman clearly felt that no venue should bear the name of a living member of the club. Instead the first time the name Maine Road appeared in print as the ground's name came on the morning of the game:

"The main entrances will be in Maine Road, by which name the ground will be known, for the time being at all events."

Maine Road itself was a relatively insignificant street in 1923, but in the previous century the road had the name 'Dog Kennel Lane' and it had been a fairly significant but meandering route south of the city, with its final southern section ultimately becoming modern day Princess Parkway. The street was renamed in stages when the area was developed during the late 1800s and the name 'Maine Road' was selected. It appears this was done for a very important reason, but over time the specifics have been lost, although a newspaper report from the early twentieth century talks of an event which had taken place around 40 years earlier. The journalist claimed that in the 1860s a prominent member of the land-owning Lloyd family paid for a group of local men to fight in the American Civil War.

If this is true then possibly a link with the state of Maine was established – Maine forces fought in many significant battles and these groups did contain non-American volunteers.

Another version of the story appeared in the **Manchester Guardian** during 1904, but in this version the journalist claimed the Lloyd family had recruited 150 local volunteers to fight in the American War of Independence. Significant battles occurred in Maine and many Manchester men did fight in the war, but the specifics of the Moss Side/Rusholme men are not clear. In 1812 further battles took place with the British aiming to recapture Maine in a battle described by the Americans as the second War of Independence. Whether any of these stories had a bearing on the renaming of the street is unclear, but it is obvious that the street was renamed for a specific reason.

By the time the stadium opened the plans had been amended and instead of one 'grandstand' seating around 15,000, the Main Stand would hold 10,000 under the largest roof span of any stand at any football ground in the country. In addition, the terracing looping around the pitch would hold somewhere in the region of 75,000 spectators - some 20,000 more than the original plan. The sensible capacity of Maine Road at this time was probably around 80,000, though City's management felt it could hold 90,000, and *The Topical Times Sporting Annual* for 1934-5 stated a figure of 86,000. This was a phenomenal figure for a team used to playing in a cramped 40,000 capacity venue.

City Manager Ernest Mangnall was one of the significant figures behind the move and was involved with the planning. It should be stressed that he had also been instrumental in United's move to Old Trafford and it seems he wanted to ensure the new venue offered more than even Old Trafford did – it should be remembered that Mangnall left the Reds only two years after United's move and it is understood he felt disappointment when the Old Trafford plans were scaled down. At City Mangnall helped the Blues develop a stadium that was not simply the best in the region, it was the biggest and best club ground in England, although Mangnall was not entirely happy again that City's plans had also been scaled down. A year after the move he was replaced as manager – perhaps Mangnall's vision for Mancunian football was greater than either club.

The possibility of extending Maine Road to cater for the desired capacity of 120,000 did exist – at the time car parking was not viewed as essential and the large space behind the Kippax and the area between the terracing and the perimeter wall could have been utilised - however, the effort and cost to extend each section of terracing for a capacity that would rarely be tested seemed pointless. Nevertheless, what Swain, Mangnall, Furniss and City had achieved was still remarkable. On the eve of the stadium's first game the *Manchester Evening News* seemed particularly proud:

"That this vast stadium should have been practically completed between April 24 and August 24 of this year is the subject for wonder and admiration. It unquestionably creates a record in building construction, and it is a splendid testimonial to the organising powers of the contractors, Sir Robert McAlpine and Sons.

"Most people were freely sceptical as to whether the enclosure would be ready for tomorrow. A month ago it did not seem possible that it could be, but by the employment of hundreds of skilled workmen all but the internal work on the huge stand has been completed, and even the remaining task will not occupy more than a fortnight. As already stated the enclosure will accommodate well over 80,000 spectators."

The *Manchester Guardian* commented on the overall impression of the ground and the Main Stand:

"This ground is the last word in the provision of comfort and security for (and against) the explosive force of the great crowds that follow the League teams. There is something almost barbaric in the impression which, when it is full, it makes on the observer. As one comes on it suddenly from Claremont Road, a great rounded embankment towers up in front, and over it at one side looms the highly arched roof of a stand whose dim recesses cannot be discerned at all except from the ground level. Only the fresh green paint on the front of it, picked out with gold, detracts from the broad impression of size and power, giving a rather incongruous air of neatness and modernity. The Grand Stand by itself is an elaborate mechanism only to be afforded by the rich town club. For long after the match was over curious crowds explored its many staircases by which the holders of all sorts of tickets are conducted without fail or confusion to their various seats. The topmost section sits aloof and remote at an incredible distance from the field. Like a squall falling suddenly from the hills, its clapping came at times in sudden gusts from far away."

In the main, newspaper reports of the opening match - a 2-1 victory over Sheffield United on 25th August 1923 - focussed on the stadium rather than the game with the *Manchester Guardian* particularly impressed. The newspaper provided a whole range of statistics on the venue, making note of the size of the tunnels and of the terracing, especially the Popular Side (latter day Kippax) of the ground where there were 110 tiers of steps at its highest point. It seemed the most fantastic venue:

"Come in and take your ease but here, inside these barriers, you stay and by these great pits and tunnels, quietly and quickly you depart. This scheme in its simplicity and great scale suggests power and force in the way that a pyramid does, or a Babylonian tower, and there could scarcely be a better scheme to represent the passionate concentration of fifty or eighty thousand men and women on the fortunes of the field below."

During its first season the stadium demonstrated its worth as on 8th March 1924 a crowd of 76,166 – at the time the highest crowd ever assembled at a football venue in Manchester - watched the Blues face Cardiff in the F.A. Cup, and a decade later the gates were closed before the game for the first time in the stadium's history. The official attendance figure was 84,569 - it remains the largest provincial attendance.

Eleven months later 79,491 watched City's League game with Arsenal. At the time, this was the highest attendance for any League match, and by 2008 only one other League ground has held a higher attendance (Stamford Bridge 82,905 Chelsea V Arsenal October 1935). It is worth noting that the current record League crowd is held by Maine Road. This was set in 1948 when Manchester United attracted 83,260 for their League game with future champions Arsenal.

Much has been made over the years of City's planning (or lack of) abilities, however pre-World War Two the Blues did make significant progress in their Maine Road development plan. Architect Swain's original plan was always to perform the initial build, and then when finances allowed he wanted to extend the venue on a regular basis. Relegation in 1926 affected Swain's plan, but by the end of the 1920s the Blues were able to consider the plans again.

It seems Swain had wanted to develop the stadium at regular four-yearly intervals, and he planned to increase the size of the stadium by extending the three uncovered stands and roofing them in stages. The first stage was the Platt Lane corner, completed in 1931. The second stage was the extension of Platt Lane (completed in 1935); the third was the Main Stand/Scoreboard End corner (scheduled for 1939/40); fourth phase was to cover the rest of the Scoreboard End (scheduled for 1943/4); and the final phase was to be the enormous extension to the Popular Side (latter day Kippax, due for development by 1950).

Had war not intervened then the Maine Road of 1950 would have been covered on four sides with a capacity in excess of 100,000 (based on 1920s legislation).

The 1931 build saw the Platt Lane/Main Stand corner terracing reprofiled to match the rake of the Main Stand. Additional seating and a roof was also erected. Four years later the Platt Lane terracing increased and the roof extended over the rest of the Platt Lane Stand. These developments increased the capacity to around 88,000 possibly more (this assumes the record crowd of 84,569 had been the absolute maximum in 1934 -although a capacity of 86,000 was recorded in 1934).

In 1937 League Champions City had toured Germany and became the first English side to play in the ultra-modern Berlin Olympic Stadium and inevitably saw the facilities on offer. The Blues were an exceptionally wealthy club at this point and the capacity of Maine Road had been tested on several occasions. It is possible the plan to redevelop the Main Stand/Scoreboard corner may have been delayed a little while the Blues considered redeveloping the whole of the Scoreboard End and corner. However war brought a halt to City's plans for good.

After the war circumstances changed for the club and the first significant post war development was the installation of floodlights in 1953. Four years later the Popular Side was extended slightly, roofed, and renamed the Kippax Street Stand. The extension was not as great as the one planned when the stadium first opened, but at least the roof meant the stadium provided covered accommodation for over 50,000 fans. Few League grounds could compare.

The newly roofed Kippax soon became the home of City's more vocal fans, and supporters used to love to boast that whereas most other grounds found their more passionate support positioned behind a goal, City's occupied a full side.

In 1963 the Platt Lane Stand was seated with row after row of wooden benches. These were placed directly onto the original terracing – the 1931 conversion of terracing to seating in the Platt Lane corner had seen the terracing reprofiled to match the Main Stand. This was not a particularly forward-looking development, but it did mean that Maine Road housed more seats than any other British club - around 18,500 - something that continued throughout the 70s and early 80s with the development of the 8,120 capacity North Stand. In 1964 the floodlights were replaced with much higher – and more powerful – floodlight towers, and this was followed in 1967 by improvements to the Main Stand roof. The middle section of the roof was replaced by a rather odd looking construction which allowed an unhindered view for the directors and those in the most expensive seats, but it did nothing to improve the look of the stadium.

In 1971 the original Scoreboard End was demolished and replaced by a new cantilever stand. Initially the stand was terracing, but after a year the management decided to turn this stand into a seated stand, and the North Stand was born. At the same time amazing plans to demolish the Kippax Stand and replace it with an incredible structure that would also allow vehicles to drive onto the roof of the new stand, where drivers would be able to watch the game from their own cars, were made. Former Chairman Eric Alexander later revealed:

"The plans were aimed at creating a sort of private viewing area, while also improving facilities for Kippax regulars. The two big issues in the early seventies were the increasing shortage of good car parking spaces, and the lack of good quality facilities at the Kippax side of the ground. The plan would have improved both situations considerably."

The plan was abandoned when Peter Swales became Chairman in 1973. From then on Maine Road's development was piecemeal. Apart from security features such as the installation of perimeter fencing, little of note changed until in 1981 Swales announced a £6m redevelopment of the stadium. The first phase saw the Main Stand roof replaced again, this time with a distinctive cream coloured barrel affair. Later phases were supposed to see the Platt Lane replaced by a similar stand to the North Stand, and a new roof (matching the Main Stand) erected over the Kippax. Executive boxes were to be positioned in the roof of the Main Stand.

The Main Stand roof, held up by two enormous stanchions, was erected at a cost of £1 million. Relegation in 1983 caused the other redevelopment plans to be halted.

Maine Road at the start of the 1980s.

Over the years it has been claimed that City were never very good at making plans for stadium development and had they actually thought long term the venue would have always been the leading club stadium, however this is not entirely true. City were the first of our clubs to make a serious attempt at planning the development of their ground and from 1923 through to World War Two, three stages of the club's six stage plan to develop a 100,000 plus all covered stadium had been completed. War in 1939 ended the first detailed plan.

Post war it was not planning that was City's problem, it was the carrying out of the plan (that is perhaps a more worrying aspect for fans and something which also affected City on the pitch during the post-Mercer club's existence). During the late 1960s the Alexander family made significant plans to redevelop the Scoreboard End and Kippax, but the arrival of Peter Swales as Chairman halted these. Swales own plans for redeveloping the Kippax and Platt Lane end ended with relegation in 1983.

Apart from the replacement of seats in the Main Stand and North Stand, the construction of a new scoreboard in the Platt Lane/Kippax corner, and the increase in perimeter fencing, little obvious development occurred until 1992. The Platt Lane Stand was demolished and the rather smaller Umbro Stand (renamed Platt Lane in 1997) was erected in its place at a reported cost of £6 million. This cost was viewed as being excessive, however it did include 48 executive boxes on two tiers. This stand, quite simply, ended all possibility of Maine Road ever being a major venue again. It was opened in March 1993 – by a group including Peter Swales and Peter Kenyon (United's future Chief Executive).

In 1994 the Kippax Stand was demolished following the creation of all-seater legislation and

By JOHN CROSS

GOLD medallists Jonathan Edwards and Paula Radcliffe last night made a last ditch plea for the City of Manchester Stadium to become the new home of British athletics.

The £110million arena has been a huge success in hosting the Commonwealth Games but will be handed over to Manchester City and become a football stadium when the competition finishes on Sunday.

The Premiership club will inherit the stadium for nothing and will only have to cover running costs and give the council half their gate receipts for crowds of over 32,000.

Despite Edwards and Radcliffe giving British athletics a huge boost with their gold medals in the triple jump and 5,000 metres on Sunday, the sport will again be left without a national home.

UK athletics saw the 2005 World Championships snatched away last year when the government abandoned plans for a new stadium at Pickett's Lock in north London. There are no other proposals.

Edwards, 36, whose Commonwealth Games victory gave him a grand slam of Olympic, European and World titles, savaged the decision to give the stadium to the football club, managed by Kevin Keegan.

He said: "Basically it seems they are handing it to Manchester City on a silver platter for nothing. It's a disgrace. It's public money we are talking about but it's going to just a few people who support Manchester City.

"It's probably too late to do anything about it because it's been signed, sealed and delivered and yet it's a real shame. It's a super stadium for athletics with a super atmosphere.

"I didn't ever think I would enjoy such a great atmosphere or experience anything like it in this country."

Radcliffe, who will tonight try to add the 10,000 metres gold medal to her 5,000 metres success, added: "The biggest shame is we are losing this stadium and our memories are not going to be here.

"It's terrible athletics does not have a stadium capable of hosting a major championship. Hopefully something can still be done about it.

"I'm sure Manchester City have enough money to build another stadium. Why are they getting this one as a present?"

City will leave Maine Road for their new home – which had £77m of public money provided by Sport England – for the start of next season.

But City chairman David Bernstein yesterday defended the deal.

He said: "This stadium could never have been built without the support and help from Manchester City.

"It would never have got off the ground without a long-term tenant.

"It would have become a white elephant without us because athletics does not attract the same number of spectators as football."

BERNSTEIN: Hit back at claims

Following the success of the 2002 Commonwealth Games, athletes ignore the fact that City's new stadium would not have been built without the Blues involvement.

a new stand was completed in stages over the course of the following eighteen months. For a time City's capacity was as low as 19,000. The new 10,000 seater stand was officially opened by Bert Trautmann. Francis Lee was Chairman by this time and he had significantly improved the design of the Kippax making it a three tier stand, housing the best facilities at any football ground in the north-west, however due to the appallingly small Platt Lane Stand the capacity of Maine Road was the lowest for a City venue since 1899. As with Hyde Road in 1920 the ground's capacity seriously limited City's development and income.

While the Kippax was being developed Francis Lee made dramatic and impressive plans to redevelop the rest of Maine Road. His idea was to extend the other three sides of the ground to allow for a construction similar to the new Kippax, and a capacity of 50,000. These plans were warmly viewed by supporters. However, at the same time Lee was in negotiation with Manchester City Council and other bodies for City to become tenants of the new stadium being proposed as part of Manchester's bid to stage the Olympic Games. Three successive Olympic bids failed, but the city was awarded the 2002 Commonwealth Games. It was decided City would move there, but in the meantime Maine Road's capacity had to increase. Temporary stands – one nicknamed the Gene Kelly stand as fans became accustomed to 'singing in the rain' - were erected in the Kippax corners and a variety of other locations from 1997 onwards.

In May 2003 Maine Road staged its last game, and so a mere eight years after the official opening of the new Kippax, and ten after the Platt Lane Stand was built, Maine Road was redundant. As with Hyde Road, City did not move because Maine Road was dilapidated or derelict, it was because a better opportunity presented itself.

This fact is proved further by the events of 2002-03 when both Stockport County and Sale Sharks looked at moving to the stadium. Ultimately neither side moved in, but for a while it seemed Sale in particular would make the venue their home.

During 2003-04 the stadium was demolished. By the start of 2007 the land had been completely cleared and plans were being finalised for the development of houses and businesses. One of the companies involved was called Lowry Homes – interestingly the artist LS Lowry was well known for being a City supporter.

Various objects from Maine Road were salvaged by City's museum, including two of the mosaic signs originally positioned over exit gates. One of these has been reconstructed and now forms part of City's memorial garden at the City of Manchester Stadium.

Since the move some City fans have regretted leaving Maine Road. They feel the passion and atmosphere of the old venue cannot be matched, and some have even suggested that Francis Lee's plans of 1994 to extend the North and Platt Lane Stands and redevelop the Main Stand would have brought a higher capacity (50,000), been a cheaper alternative to the new stadium, and crucially would have helped City retain their identity. City secretary Bernard Halford recognises that from a business sense it was important to move, but it did not stop his heart being torn apart when the move occurred:

"We had to move from Maine Road. Times change and the all-seater meant our capacity was far too small. We'd gone from being the largest ground in the country to one of around 30,000. We had to move. Things have to change, but inevitably it was a real wrench leaving Maine Road. I still tell people I'm going to Maine Road. My car still heads in that direction."

It is fair to say there are still many fans who continue to look back on what the club lost when it moved from Maine Road for some time. The old ground is always likely to be viewed as the spiritual home of City.

THE CITY OF MANCHESTER STADIUM (FROM 2003)

It took approximately fifteen years from the first mention of the plan to move to a new stadium to the move itself. Today, most tend to think of the stadium development as being discussed from the mid to late 1990s, but in truth the discussions started many years earlier.

During the mid-to-late 1980s Bob Scott – a key figure behind the resurgence of the Palace and Opera House Theatres – developed an audacious plan for Manchester to stage the 1992 Olympics. The eventual news leaked out during 1986-7 and Peter Swales, City's Chairman, was consulted on whether the Blues would consider moving to a new venue. For many it seemed like a ridiculous idea. The chance of London staging the Games seemed decades away and Manchester, struggling with identity issues during the Thatcher years, seemed even less likely than the capital to stage a significant multi-sport event. Nevertheless the **Manchester Evening News** focussed on the story and eventually a front page headline – ***"£100m site for Blues?"*** – made the plan feel real. Within the article Peter Swales stated:

"If it all happens and the stadium is built, it is something we have got to be interested in. It is at a very early stage. We have spent a lot of money at Maine Road and the new stadium would have to be something pretty special to make us move. The Olympic Bid committee have explained what they are trying to do and I think it is a very bold, adventurous plan to bring the Games to Manchester."

As time moved on and Manchester's Olympic dreams grew the idea developed. In addition, it is known that Peter Swales had discussed a variety of ideas with a number of organisations including turning the Kippax car park at Maine Road into a supermarket (the Kippax Stand would have been redeveloped with a significant reduction in capacity!). So from Swales' point of view a move to a new stadium did seem possible.

As Manchester never was awarded the Games – it should be remembered though that Manchester's attempts did pave the way for London's successful 2012 bid – a new 60,000 capacity venue was not constructed, however the city did stage the 2002 Commonwealth Games. Manchester City's role in that bid guaranteed that a permanent quality venue was erected (without the Blues a much smaller venue with temporary stands would have been utilised). Swales had gone by this point, and new Chairman Francis Lee pushed to ensure City played their part in all matters relating to the stadium. He wanted a 50,000 capacity stadium (similar in size to Maine Road during the 70s and early 80s), but he had resigned as Chairman over a year before the actual contract was signed. New Chairman David Bernstein pushed forward with the plans and following promotion in 1999 he signed the contract guaranteeing City's move.

Alongside a serious need to strengthen on-the-pitch activity Chief Operating Officer Chris Bird and director Alistair Mackintosh focussed on the specifics of the stadium development and the move. Bernstein, Bird & Co. knew that City fans had remained loyal throughout the struggles, and they recognised that Maine Road's permanent capacity of around 32,000 was woefully low. In fact from the moment Lee became Chairman in 1993-4 the capacity of the Maine Road had been far too low.

In December 1999 Prime Minister Tony Blair laid the first stone of what was to become the City of Manchester Stadium, and work progressed to develop a 35,000 capacity athletics venue. The idea was that the stadium would be built in two phases with initially the top two tiers of the West and East Stands constructed, and the South Stand upper tier developed. A large temporary seated stand was built at the northern end, and the bowl contained the athletics track.

After the Games the plan was to lower the pitch by almost 10m in parts, build the entire lowest tier, construct a new North Stand, and fit out the stadium to create a near 48,000 capacity.

By summer 2002 the popularity of the Games meant that an additional 3,000 temporary seats were installed to raise the athletics capacity to 38,000. Immediately after the Games work commenced on reconfiguring the stadium. The temporary stands were dismantled within days of the end of the Games, and work commenced on lowering the pitch. This was lowered by over 6m with tons of earth removed (this then raised the land at the top end of the stadium to create a large car park). The lower tier was then constructed and the North Stand was erected.

The new capacity was approximately 48,000. In fact at the time of construction there were only three League venues bigger – Old Trafford, St. James' Park, and the Stadium of Light, which claimed to house 48,353. From a pride point of view supporters had hoped for between fifty to sixty thousand as Lee's plans first suggested. This would have made the ground a contender to stage the European Cup final and similar events, plus it would have helped the Blues gain a better average attendance and been more in keeping with the club's history. Nevertheless, as the Blues had only spent two of the previous seven seasons in the Premier League (City's worst ever spell on the pitch) the move still showed a remarkable faith in the loyalty of fans.

David Bernstein and Chris Bird had committed the Blues to the move and to the expense necessary to make this the most modern footballing venue in the country. Sadly, neither man was at the club by the time the move occurred. Both men had resigned during 2002-03 with deputy Chairman John Wardle replacing Bernstein and Alistair Mackintosh ultimately becoming the Club's Chief Executive.

The club spent over £30m in developing the stadium and, when the valuation of Maine Road is considered (this was handed over to Manchester Council), it is clear the move cost the Blues in excess of £60m. The council also receive a share of gate receipts and other stadium income. Naturally, the club did gain, on a 250 year lease, the most modern stadium in the Country and one that raised the bar as far as football stadium development is concerned.

The stadium opened as a footballing venue on Sunday 10th August 2003 when the Blues defeated Barcelona 2-1 and four days later the first competitive match saw City defeat Welsh side Total Network Solutions 5-0 in the UEFA Cup Qualifying Round.

Since opening, the stadium has continued to evolve. Seating changes have been made in many areas – the directors' box was reduced in size and additional seating was added at the back of the second tier corners – and a television commentary box has been erected in the south-east corner of the second tier. A second television gantry was created at the front of the third tier of the West Stand as the main gantry, housed at the back of the third tier, was too high for football action whereas it had been perfect for athletics. The West Stand has also been renamed the Colin Bell Stand after an internet vote.

Other developments include the creation of a Memorial Garden – the first of its type at a major footballing venue. The Garden contains stonework from the Hyde Road Hotel, a mosaic from Maine Road, and a tribute to Marc-Vivien Foe.

At the north end of the stadium City have built a two storey building housing the City Superstore, the City Social and the club's award-winning museum and tour. There are also two impressive mosaics of Joe Mercer, appropriately positioned on Joe Mercer Way, created by renowned mosaic artist Mark Kennedy.

Inevitably, the stadium has won various architectural awards and remains the most awe-inspiring new building in Greater Manchester. It has also been used a model for stadium development with various organisations, including Arsenal, the Chinese Olympic authority, the London Olympic committee, and South African sporting groups spending significant time understanding the strengths and quality of the new stadium.

In 2006-7, after significant bidding from the club, Manchester council, Marketing Manchester and other bodies, the stadium was selected to stage the 2008 UEFA Cup final. The venue was not large enough to stage the European Cup, but it stood head and shoulders above the other UEFA Cup contenders.

MANCHESTER UNITED STADIA

Since formation as Newton Heath (L&Y) in 1878, the club has played at four different home League venues (plus home FA Cup fixtures at Goodison Park and Leeds Road in 1948).

NORTH ROAD (1878-1893)

North Road (now renamed Northampton Road) was the club's first recognised home. Initially, as with so many venues in the region, it was nothing more than an open field. The ground was positioned close to the works of the L&Y Railway and therefore was an obvious choice for the workers to use for their new sports organisation in 1878.

Initially games between different sections of the works would have taken place there but by the 1890s the development of Newton Heath into a football club meant the venue had to accommodate crowds of four figures or more. When Newton Heath joined the Football League in 1892 the ground held significant crowds such as c.16,000 for the visit of Nottingham Forest on New Year's Day 1893, but the venue was not really equipped to deal with such a large volume of support.

Facilities had been poor – in the early years the Three Crowns public house half a mile away on Oldham Road was used as dressing rooms, and then the club moved to the more imposing Shears Hotel for a while before finding offices at 33 Oldham Road. The pitch itself was described in the **History of The Lancashire Football Association** published in 1928:

"In places it was as hard as flint, with ashes underneath that had become like iron, and in others thick with mud."

Whether this was simply a later historian looking back and making assumptions on the quality of the site is not clear but the nearest report of the ground's state comes in the **1901 Newton Heath Bazaar Programme** which states:

"The ground was little better than a clay pit, its surroundings a quagmire. After you had entered the bottom gate, it was quite a work of art to steer clear of pools of water, but when once you got there you were all right, if it didn't rain. If it did rain, you just – well, if you've never experienced it you cannot possibly be enlightened."

As far as can be surmised from plans and maps of the period the ground's entrance would have been positioned on North Road itself, and there may possibly have been refreshment facilities of some description on the East Side of the ground. Sadly, no photographs have to date been found providing evidence of how the ground looked, but it is fair to say it would have been very basic for most of the club's time. Some construction work is believed to have been performed in 1887 – the same year the forerunner to City had established a new home at Hyde Road – though how extensive that was is not known. It is known that two stands were erected in 1891 capable of holding around 2,000 people.

The venue itself was owned by the Deans and Canons of Manchester, in effect Manchester Cathedral, and legend has it that they were dissatisfied that the Heathens were charging admission prices. The church leaders rented the land to the L&Y Railway and they sub-let to Newton Heath. Both the railway company and the church gained income from the arrangements, but clearly with football still in its infancy, and church values being strong, the Heathens had little chance to change the church's mind.

For most of its existence since that time, the site formed playing fields and then from the fifties Moston Brook High School. A red plaque was erected on the site commemorating United's birth. Today, the area including most of the railway sidings connected with the original Newton Heath days, has been cleared for new developments. A business park is being erected and today the offices for Fujitsu cover part of the original pitch. It is an interesting coincidence that both City and United's very first grounds have during the last decade been home to offices for the electrical firm Fujitsu.

BANK STREET/LANE (1893-1910)

The club's next ground was two miles from the centre of Newton Heath and was actually in the Clayton area of Manchester. This would later cause the club many issues, but in 1893 the new ground was the only real option.

The area around the new ground was developing rapidly with industry growing across Clayton and surrounding districts, and so the ground was surrounded by industry, chemical works, a railway, and terraced housing. It was not a glamorous spot, although the beautiful Phillips Park was close by.

According to the *Manchester Evening News*, during June 1893, the land was to be rented from the Bradford & Clayton Athletic Company (although material in the same newspaper in 1902 suggests a different owner) and considerable work was ongoing to transform the venue into a significant home for League football:

"The ground ought to be a commodious one, and no doubt when the first of September comes it will be fully equipped. The only doubt that remains is as to whether the ground will be convenient from a Newton point of view."

Whether it was the location, or the poor performance of the side is not absolutely clear, but the Heathens did not develop in the way most sides would have anticipated following the move. Finances were poor and by 1901 the ground was not viewed well be supporters, opponents or the media. On 16th January 1901 the *Athletic News* commented:

"When funds allow, I hope the directors will make an effort to improve the ground. Its fittings are altogether inadequate and obsolete."

Despite the negativity on the pitch and on the terraces, the Heathens did make some very interesting moves during their final couple of seasons as Newton Heath. Perhaps the most significant was actually the agreement made with the *Manchester Evening News* for the newspaper to set up an office at the ground. This was an unusual move at the time, however with rivals City getting significant coverage in the Edward Hulton owned sporting press, the Heathens felt a tie up with the *MEN* would provide huge benefits. From the newspapers point of view it gave them the chance to establish a more populist style – the paper was not known for its football coverage at the time. From that point on the *MEN* was the Heathens/United 'paper while the *Evening Chronicle* was the City 'paper.

In 1902 the club collapsed and was re-launched as Manchester United. This immediately led on to significant ground developments. These included the creation of a large embankment at the Bradford end of the ground, and another opposite the main stand on what was known as

A rare photograph of United's Bank Street ground from the early years of the Twentieth Century and (below) a modern day view taken from a similar position but pointing straight across the pitch.
Bottom: **A view towards Eastlands from the original site of Bank Street's centre-spot.**

the Popular Side (running the full length of the pitch more or less in a line from Ravensbury Street). A refreshment bar was erected in the centre of the Popular Side, and it was claimed in one **Manchester Evening News** report from July 1902 that the Popular Side had covered accommodation for 10,000.

On 10th July 1902 the **Manchester Evening News** provided a more extensive article on the redeveloped ground and reported that the improvements had lifted the capacity to around 50,000, although a year later the same newspaper claimed the capacity was 40,000. The 'paper tempered this however with a comment that *'the venue is still somewhat inadequate'*. The newspaper claimed that the club should have and would have moved from Bank Street but they simply could not find a new venue. It also reported:

"The field of play is enclosed by a stout hoarding, some four feet in height, and a cinder track has been provided along the Bradford side for the use of players."

The report added that the Bank Street side was to be covered and that the 'old' covered stand was to be improved for high priced ticket holders. In addition player facilities were in the process of being improved with the dressing rooms being converted into a large gymnasium with vapour and other baths erected. A new set of dressing rooms would also be built.

Despite the rebirth of the club, football was still not understood by all Mancunians. On 2nd September 1903 the **Manchester Evening Chronicle** journalist 'The Odd Man' reported that a few days earlier he had decided he needed to get out and write a feature on Manchester United. Presumably he was keen to understand how the side and the venue had developed, but the specific purpose of his article was not clear. In the end he wrote a slightly humorous story of his journey and of his experience. As he had never been to the ground and did not know the Clayton area he asked passers by to point him in the right direction. One told him that he could not miss the ground as it had a bright red flag flying from it. 'Odd Man' headed up Bank Street and spotted a bright flag:

"When I traced the letters on the banner, and saw distinctly 'MUFC' which to my unsophisticated eyes appeared to be a new way of spelling 'MUFFS', I thought this could not possibly be the place, but it was!"

Despite 'Odd Man's' comments most Mancunians began to understand the importance of football and over the following years both United, and Bank Street began to improve and prove popular. In 1904 £500 was spent on stand improvements, and then two years later a partial redevelopment of the ground saw a 1,200 capacity open stand built in the Stuart Street corner of the ground. This joined on to the Reserved Stand (for season ticket holders only), while reports claim that at this time the largest stand was "The Embankment" behind the goal at the Electric Works End. In 1906 a much-improved Embankment held 12,000, although plans of the site make this an unlikely claim if we assume the Popular Side (Chemical Works side, opposite the main stand) held around 10,000. According to reports from 1906 a roof on the Popular Side was to be extended, and that this was by that time known as the "Sixpenny Stand" alongside the Chemical Works.

These developments appear to be the last substantial changes at the ground, and with United developing a successful team on the pitch the Reds decided to move on. The pollution from the nearby works may have been a factor in the decision as, according to the **Manchester Guardian** match report for the Portsmouth FA Cup replay of 16th January 1907:

"All the time the struggle was waging the 30 Clayton chimneys smoked and gave forth their pungent odours, and the boilers behind goal poured mists of steam over the ground."

By March 1909 the ground was sold to Manchester Corporation and leased back to United until the new stadium at Old Trafford was ready.

Many United publications talk of a Bank Street stand roof collapsing approximately a month after United moved out of the old ground, however the timing was actually much more dramatic than that. On Christmas Day 1909 a crowd of around 25,000 (the second highest of the season at that point) witnessed a 3-0 defeat by Sheffield Wednesday in what was expected to be the last match at Bank Street. However building problems at Old Trafford caused delays and on 22nd January the old ground was forced to stage another League game. This time a miserly crowd of around 8,000 (the second lowest of the season) saw an entertaining 5-0 defeat of Spurs but the match should have been played at Old Trafford.

Significant delays in the new ground's construction brought an air of uncertainty across the club but Old Trafford did manage to stage its first game on 19th February. However, according to the authoritive **Umpire** newspaper, produced the following day, the move to Old Trafford had proved absolutely vital:

"On Thursday last the grand stand on the old ground suffered severely, being almost swept away by the hurricane. The roof was blown across the street, alighting on the houses opposite, the hoarding at the back of the stand was blown out, and there is a mere wreck of a stand left. What a tragic ending, and how singular that it should happen at the present time."

So the destruction of the Bank Street End stand occurred before Old Trafford staged its first game. With Old Trafford not quite complete at the time of the storm the question of whether United would have sought to stage another match at Clayton has to be considered. Clearly, the Reds were keen to move to the new ground as soon as possible, but they had already delayed the opening on a couple of occasions – the 1909-10 season was anticipated to start at Old Trafford. The destruction of the stand guaranteed the Liverpool match would be played at the new ground, but had the storm not occurred it is possible – though probably not likely – that the Liverpool match would also have been switched to Bank Street with Sheffield United opening the ground in March.

Research for this book has included reviewing every piece of Manchester press from this period and it does seem likely that the game would have been staged at Old Trafford no matter what – the club could not afford any more delays – however the storm made sure the Reds had no viable alternative.

It is worth noting that many say the collapsed Bank Street stand proves the poor condition the ground was in at this point, however that cannot be entirely accurate. The stand was not the newest in the game, but in real terms it was not that old having been roofed as part of the improvements of 1902. In addition the storms were described by the **Evening Chronicle** of 17th February as a hurricane that lasted three hours and that they had brought loss of life and the destruction of several buildings in the region, including a tall chimney on John Dalton Street and many walls in the city centre. A 16 year old died in Stockport when a building collapsed on him.

As with City's Hyde Road ground, and indeed Maine Road, at the time of the move Bank Street was not dilapidated and many areas were less than a decade old. However, in comparison with Old Trafford the ground was not equipped for modern football.

The Umpire took the destruction of the Bank Street stand as an opportunity to pay tribute to the old venue:

> *"Still, the stand has done its work, and the ground answered a long and useful purpose. If it had the power to tell its life story, what a history of trials and triumphs! Clayton can boast a proud record. Manchester United is dead. Long live Manchester United! Clayton has at best been a temporary shelter, and now we welcome a new United and usher in a new era. It is a cordial good bye."*

According to records at United's museum despite the damage to the stand, the ground was still used for Reserve fixtures until December 1911, although the 25th February 1910 *Manchester Courier* gave a report on United's first reserve game to be played at Old Trafford in the Combination. The remaining timber at Bank Street was apparently sold to Keyley Bros for £275.

For years the site stored coal and such like for the nearby power station but today it is relatively clear. It now forms part of the car park for the Velodrome, close to Manchester City's present stadium, and a red plaque appears on a house on Bank Street opposite the site of the ground. Some City fans park here on match days.

A simple visit to the site in this state easily allows visitors to picture the size, scale, and position of the old ground.

In recent years discussions on some fan-based websites have suggested this could be redeveloped into a new home for FC United. That would certainly provide an interesting twist to the development of the game in the region.

One final point concerning the old ground worth making is that for many years after the Reds left Bank Street the United Hotel public house on the corner of Mill Street and Ashton New Road survived. The pub had been one of John Davies' brewery's houses and was known originally as

The United Public House - named after the Reds. This was sited close to the Bank Street ground, however had the building survived until the modern day, it would now be positioned at the traffic lights next to 'B of the Bang', only yards from City's stadium.

the Queen's Hotel. Due to its proximity to the Bank Street ground the pub was renamed and continued to recognise United's history through to its demolition in the 1970s as part of the slum clearance programme.

The site is now on the ASDA side of the traffic lights, opposite the B of the Bang sculpture, off Alan Turing Way (the remodelled and renamed Mill Street). It is interesting to consider whether the pub would have been renamed had it survived until the present day and City's occupation of the area.

OLD TRAFFORD (FROM 1910)

At formation as United in 1902 the Reds had considered moving from Bank Street however time and opportunity was limited, and so investment had to be made in the old ground. However, with the financial support of wealthy brewer John Davies, United had for the first time in a decade direction. It was Davies' Manchester Brewery Company which bought the site at Old Trafford and it was his decision for the Reds to move there. In fact while researching for this book officials at United have expressed the view that Davies may actually have been planning to build a new brewery or bottling plant at the site – its close proximity to the ship canal and the huge Trafford Park industrial estate made this a good location – and that only problems with the authorities prevented that.

Whether that view is true or not, it is clear that the selection of Old Trafford was somewhat of an odd one. Some writers, most notably Simon Inglis, justifiably talk of the area as having a rich sporting heritage – *"part of the old Trafford Park estate where sport and leisure had been concentrated since the 1860s"* – but football itself had never actually taken hold of the area despite several significant clubs being based there in the 1880s. In addition, east Manchester, where both United and City had been born, had also enjoyed a rich sport and leisure industry but also had the advantage of a densely populated working class, eager to support the working man's game.

Old Trafford was, as the **Salford Chronicle** remarked, *"a more salubrious"* area than Clayton, but the game of football was still very much the working class obsession. As JAH Catton wrote in the **Athletic News** on 8th March 1909:

"Clayton is situated in the very heart of a working class community, and dominated on every hand by about forty huge stacks of chimneys, belching forth Cimmerian smoke and malodorous fumes. No doubt there are those who feel thankful for a football ground in the vicinity, as it does tend to remind the immediate residents that there is some space left where the toiling people can be amused in a healthy and vigorous manner that pleases them."

The Old Trafford site was also a considerable distance across Manchester – over five miles from the club's Newton Heath heartland – and not particularly easy to get to. Of course there were trams and trains traveling to that part of the region, but a United supporter working at say the Bradford pit close to Bank Street - the pit was situated where the City of Manchester Stadium is today - on a Saturday morning would have to travel into Manchester city centre first, then out to Old Trafford in time for a 3pm or 3.30 kick off. If his shift finished at 2pm he would have virtually no chance of getting to the match, whereas had that same supporter been attending Bank Street then he would have had time to finish his shift at 2pm, get washed and changed, have a quick lunch then soak up the atmosphere in Davies' United Hotel before a short walk to the ground.

The move to Old Trafford was the furthest any club had ever moved. The previous 'furthest' was Sheffield Wednesday who moved around three miles when they left Sheffield for Owlerton (Hillsborough) in 1899 and, like Wednesday, United were moving outside of the city's boundaries. It was a major gamble. It was also one which financially crippled the club for more than two decades.

Despite the negatives ambitious plans were announced in March 1909. These were ultimately scaled down – the original plan was for a capacity of 100,000 with 12,000 seated, and covered terracing for 24,000 – but what was delivered was still significantly better than any earlier venue. It should be noted that despite Old Trafford's modern day appearance, there are still some elements of the original design that can be identified today, almost 100 years later. These include the original players' tunnel that was described as planned by JAH Catton, under the pen name Tityrus, in 1909:

"The directors, players, and officials will obtain access to the field from a tunnel which will debouche from the centre of the stand. The offices for the secretary and clerks will be constructed in a portion of the ferro-concrete terracing, almost facing the bridge over the Cheshire Lines. Between the grand stand and the railway there will be an enclosed street 45 feet broad – entirely reserved for private motors – not public vehicles."

The article also focused on the pitch and the general shape of the ground:

"The ground will be rectangular in shape, with the corners rounded, and it is designed so that everybody will be able to see. The pitch will be excavated to a depth of nine feet from ground level, so that the boundary or containing wall which is to surround the whole place will only be 30 feet high. There

A rare photograph of Old Trafford during construction. This image was found at Maine Road during the 1980s and in the 1990s appeared in a book on City with the suggestion that the ground is Hyde Road. However, this is clearly Old Trafford. It is believed the original image formed part of Ernest Mangnall's collection. Mangnall was a key figure behind the development of both Old Trafford and Maine Road.

are numerous entrances and spacious exits and it is estimated that a full ground can be emptied in five minutes. Altogether the entire area of the new home of Manchester United will be 16 acres. The outward circumference of the ground will be about 2,000 feet. The ground will be 630 feet long and 510 feet broad, the width of all the terracing being 120 feet."

Although the dimensions do not make it clear, the site did have one major flaw – and perhaps demonstrates clearly that this location had not been picked initially by Davies for his football club – and that was that it had to be constructed on an east-west axis rather than north-south. Typically, football grounds were designed with the main stand on the west side of the pitch and the goals being at the northern and southern ends. The reasons were simple – first neither goalie had to directly face the sun and second the directors and wealthier customers would not have their vision impaired by a glaring sun (assuming kick offs would be at regular footballing times!).

Old Trafford's site did not allow enough space for such a significant venue to be constructed on a north-south axis. An impressive ground could have been constructed but something would have had to give. Having said that it may actually have meant that the main entrance could have been constructed on Warwick Road and, therefore, brought a much more impressive entrance to the stadium.

Regardless of these issues the stadium was developed and the **Manchester Evening Chronicle** of Tuesday 15th February 1910 under the heading: ***"A Fine Ground"*** included an article detailing the strengths of the new venue's size:

"Given fair weather, it is quite possible that all football records for Manchester will be exceeded by the crowd which will assemble to watch the game. At least 45,000 people can be accommodated on the Sixpenny side alone."

The report went on to explain that the Sixpenny side was actually more than a side and that it covered both ends as well. It also highlighted that the Main Stand possessed a variety of seats, including some modern tip up seats. Continuing with the attendance theme it gave an assessment of the total capacity:

"It is estimated that the ground will give a good and comfortable view of the game to about 65,000 people. A small army of men are at work on the approach, and the top of Warwick Road is being widened. There will be a broad cinder path right round the walls of the ground."

In terms of admission charges the **Chronicle** claimed these would be reasonably priced at: 6d, 1 shilling, 1s 6d, and 2s (modern day coinage would be 2.5p, 5p, 7.5p, and 10p). One disappointing aspect for fans was the news that the ground would not serve alcohol for its opening game. On 17th February the **Manchester Evening Chronicle** reported on the story of J.H. Hargreaves, the landlord of the Dog & Partridge on Chester Road who had applied to the authorities to sell liquor within the Old Trafford ground. The licensing committee rejected the request, although they did agree to meet on 25th February where they could assess the organisation of the ground and United's operation.

Nevertheless the opening was eagerly anticipated and it was announced that the Old Trafford Cricket Ground train station would be opened especially for the first game. The **Salford Chronicle** of 19th February 1910 reported:

"There should be a great crowd this afternoon to see the Liverpool open the new ground. Of course the ground is not completed properly yet, but for all that everything is nearing completion. It is to be hoped that the new ground will prove a good speculation and now that the United ground is in a more salubrious neighbourhood the people of Manchester will support them well. The club deserves support."

Under the headline ***"The new ground but a bad start"*** the **Salford Chronicle** of 26th February 1910 focussed on the opening day crowd:

"There was a good crowd at United's new ground, which was described in these columns a week ago, on Saturday, when Liverpool opened the same. Yet the crowd was not as big as one expected for the occasion, and unfortunately the game ended in favour of the visitors, who recovered an apparently lost position in exactly the same manner as that United won at Newcastle the previous week.

"The result was a bitter disappointment to the home team and to their supporters present. It would have been nice to have inaugurated a new era in their history by a win, but it was not to be."

United had been leading 2-0 at half time, with Sandy Turnbull netting the historic first goal. Despite this great start, somehow United lost their way and were defeated 4-3. The **Manchester Courier** claimed the attendance for the Old Trafford opener was 50,000 with a *"fair number who got in without paying."* Around 5,000 of the 50,000 were said to have gained free entry.

It seems some of the boundary walls were not as complete as they ought to have been while some windows were also not fully finished causing some to sneak in, while other reports talk of gatemen unable to cope with queues letting people in for free, but this seems unlikely as the mechanics involved with turnstile operation at the time would have meant that the only time saving that could have been made would have been the actual handling of the cash. The operator would still have had to click the turnstile forward for each individual customer, regardless of whether they paid or not.

Whether the move impacted the organisation of the club is not clear but seven days after the Liverpool game the Reds were defeated 7-1 at Aston Villa – a result the **Salford Chronicle** claimed was a *"record defeat"*. The newspaper was particularly sympathetic towards the Reds at this point and was keen to see the side develop. As part of its match report for the Villa defeat it talked of the negative atmosphere surrounding the Reds and said:

"Every sportsman will extend sympathy with the United club at present."

Louis Rocca was a key figure behind the development of United and his band of supporters are seen here at the opening of Old Trafford in 1910.

The following week the *Salford Chronicle* continued its support of United with coverage of the first victory at Old Trafford. The Reds defeated Sheffield United 1-0 and the 'paper focused on the crowd:

"There can be no question that United's new quarters have resurrected a new interest in the club. There was another splendid attendance to witness this game and every bit of clever play was cheered to the echo."

By that time Wanderer of the *Manchester Evening Chronicle* was also a fan of United's new location:

"Only those who have frequently visited Clayton can appreciate the pleasure it was to attend a match in this delightful part of the city."

The venue staged the 1911 FA Cup final replay and the 1915 final, dubbed the Khaki final because of the large volume of soldiers attending. These were watched by crowds of 58,000 and 49,557 respectively, while United's biggest home crowd of the period was 60,000 for the Manchester derby in September 1910.

So everything looked positive, however financial problems caused by the move and later (1927) the death of Davies affected the club for many years. In addition crowds fell off and the ground was left for some time in its original state.

In the 1930s progress started to be made again however. By that time City had moved to Maine Road and Old Trafford had competition for staging significant neutral games. The first problem for United came in 1928 when the 69,260 crowd for the Huddersfield V Sheffield United semi-final replay was poorly controlled. The game went to two further replays – one at Goodison and significantly one at Maine Road. A slightly larger (69,360) crowd at City's ground brought many positive comments the Blues way. Nevertheless, Old Trafford continued to stage semi-finals and then in 1933 the Popular Side (United Road/North Stand) terracing was covered.

One of the peculiarities of Manchester football is that both City and United possessed significant covered terracing at their Bank Street and Hyde Road grounds, but both Old Trafford and Maine Road were short of terracing cover until the 1930s.

From that point on United continued to take ground developments seriously. In 1935 a train station was constructed at the ground – a very important move – and in 1936 work was carried out on improving the terraces.

In 1938 the two corners of the Main Stand were covered in a similar manner to the 1931 Platt Lane corner at City. These corners had been built at a larger scale than the rest of the terracing originally, and the back of these corners matched the original size and scale of the entire stadium. This meant that some of Archibald Leitch's original plans could be progressed to some extent, however the outbreak of war ended the possibility of further developments.

On Tuesday 11th March 1941 Old Trafford was hit by bombs dropped by the German Luftwaffe. The highly industrialised Trafford Park had been the target and by daybreak the news of damage to Old Trafford was circulating around Manchester, although the *Manchester Guardian* did not mention the ground by name. Due to the wartime situation the newspaper did not want to give away too much information and reported:

"Slight damage was done to dwelling-houses in one or two working class districts and slight outbreaks of fire were reported from a football ground and a training institute."

The 'slight damage' saw a bomb hit United's Main Stand. The stand was almost completely wrecked, while the pitch was scorched by the blast. City contacted United and offered the use of Maine Road immediately, and the first home United match to be staged at City's ground was the 5th April meeting with Blackpool in the North Regional League. The Seasiders' won 3-2 before a crowd of around 2,000.

Further wartime matches followed over the course of the next four years with United paying the Blues an annual rent of £5,000 plus a share of the gate receipts. Initially City was to use United's training ground, The Cliff, for reserve fixtures, but both sides also used Old Trafford at times.

After the war United were granted £4,800 to help cover the costs of tidying up the venue, and then a further £17,478 was given to help rebuild the Main Stand and damaged terracing. This allowed the redevelopment of Old Trafford to commence and between 1945 and 1949 the Main Stand was rebuilt, as was the terracing at the Popular Side (United Road).

The Reds returned to competitive action at the rebuilt ground on 24th August 1949 with a crowd of 41,748 witnessing a 3-0 victory over near neighbours Bolton. Between 1949 and 1954 the offices and administrative areas of the stadium were rebuilt and improved, and then in 1957, following United's first appearance in the European Cup, the Reds decided to erect floodlights.

Two years later the Stretford End was covered. During the modern era, an article in **Red News** called ***"The Birth of the Stretford End"*** focused on this momentous development:

"At the beginning of 1959, at a Board meeting, it was decided to improve the facilities in the stadium. The dilemma was which part of the ground would they improve? It was decided to increase the capacity

Fans making their way to Old Trafford during the late 1950s.

at the Stretford End by taking the terracing a little higher and also putting in 1500 seats and building a covered stand. At the Scoreboard End, they decided to rebuild the old Scoreboard by demolishing the old wooden/corrugated structure and erecting a purpose built brick structure.

"Work began immediately the '58/'59 season ended and continued throughout that summer. When the '59/'60 season began, the work had been completed and the ground had a completely new look to it. United opened that season away to West Brom at the Hawthorns, on Saturday August 22nd, losing 3-2 in a terrific game which I recall attending, mainly for Bill Foulkes scoring a wonderful goal with a diving header which flew like a rocket into the back of the net. Unfortunately for United fans, Harry Gregg never saw it and it happening in the last few minutes of the game, proved to be the winner for Albion!

"The following Wednesday evening, August 22nd, the first home game of the season was played against Chelsea and 57,674 fans poured into the ground to watch United lose 1-0. The team that night was; Gregg; Greaves, Carolan; Goodwin, Foulkes, McGuinness; Bradley, Quixall, Charlton, Viollet and Scanlon. The Streford End in those early days was no more vocal than the Scoreboard End, and most of the noise during matches used to come from the Popular Side or Glover's Side as it was then known, and which is now where the North Stand is situated. It was like that until the 1962 World Cup Final competition which had taken place in Chile, was over. During that World Cup, apart from Brazil retaining the trophy which they had won in Stockholm in 1958, and the rough play the competition had witnessed, the thing which is remembered most is the chanting which came from the Brazilian fans. They would clap their hands in rapid succession and finish by chanting 'Braaaaa- zillllllll'. Chanting was unheard of on British grounds up until then but at the start of the '62/'63 season, British fans started to copy the Brazilian chant.

"At the start of that season, the Stretford End started to come into its own, and it was the area where most of the young fans began to congregate. It was also no coincidence that the emergence of the Streford End began with the arrival of a certain lithe, athletic, blonde, inside forward from Torino by the name of Denis Law! He'd been signed by Sir Matt during that close season and on August 18th, 1962 in the first game of the season, against West Bromwich Albion, he played his first game for Manchester United. 51,685 fans turned up and the United team that sunny afternoon was; Gaskell; Brennan, Dunne; Stiles, Foulkes, Setters; Giles, Quixall, Herd, Law and Moir.

"United attacked the Stretford End in the first half, and in the eighth minute of the game, Giles had the ball out wide on the right. He was hemmed in by Graham Williams (the same full back George Best was to face a little over a year later on making his debut for United) the Albion full back. As Williams jockeyed Giles, the United man feinted to go outside but then suddenly checked back and made half a yard of space for himself. He hit a hopeful cross into the area designed to land around the penalty spot. It seemed a 'nothing' ball until that is, there was a blur of red and white, sprinting into the penalty area at full pace. A prodigious leap, and the body seemed to hang in the air for an eternity. The timing had been perfect, and there was a quick turn of the blonde head as the ball was met full on with the forehead. The ball absolutely rocketed into the back of the Albion net to give United the early lead. It was a classic goal, and it mattered not one iota to those United fans who were stood on the Stretford End that afternoon, that just over eighteen months previously, the scorer had been turning out in the sky blue of Manchester City!

"The scorer had fallen as he landed and picking himself up he wheeled away in front of the Stretford End, his right arm raised in the air, his finger pointing to the heavens, and his face aglow with that wonderful smile. The roars of approval rolled down that Stretford End terracing and the fans came tumbling down in waves to greet their new hero. We were beginning the dawn of a new era – we had our first 'king' – and the Stretford End had been born. The sight of Denis Law wheeling away in that classic pose after scoring

was to become a familiar sight in the years that followed. For those of us stood there that day, little did we know the pleasures in store for us all during those coming years. The Stretford End grew in stature from that moment on and the chants became more discernable and vociferous. It was the start of an era that we became to know as 'Best, Busby and Bachus' – but it was also the beginning of the 'Stretty End' and the start of some wonderful, memorable experiences to come!"

In 1962 Old Trafford was given a grant of £40,000 to spend on reconstructing the Popular Side in preparation for the 1966 World Cup finals. The cantilevered United Road stand was constructed at a cost of around £350,000 and included, for the first time at a leading football stadium, private boxes. It was not the first cantilever stand in English football, but it was perhaps the most impressive of the period and allowed supporters to stand in the front paddock or sit in the raised second tier, or sit in a private box. For the first time three types of supporter could be accommodated. Interestingly the 1967 film ***Charlie Bubbles*** features one of the private boxes to symbolise the disappointment of a boy taken to watch United V Chelsea from the glass-fronted box. The boy is separated from his heroes and does not have the typical football experience both he – and most football fans of the period – wanted.

The new stand was designed by architects Mather and Nutter who have remained involved with the reconstruction of Old Trafford through to the modern day.

From that point on Old Trafford, unlike almost every other League ground, has been developed based on a specific plan. Whereas most sides tended to develop a stand at a time without really thinking about how that stand blended into the others, United focused on giving the venue a strong visual unifying identity. It took thirty years to achieve the complete stadium with the following significant developments along the way:

1963-65	United Road (North) Stand built
1973	Scoreboard End redeveloped (providing cover on all four sides)
1975	Executive Suite and restaurant overlooking pitch installed at Main Stand
1984	Executive Suite extended and Main Stand Cantilever roof installed
1985	Main Stand/Scoreboard End corner cantilever roof installed
1987	Floodlights installed on roof and pylons removed
1990	United Road terracing converted to seating
1992-93	Stretford End redeveloped

The ground became all seater in 1994 with the remaining paddock area at the Scoreboard End having seats installed on to re-profiled terracing.

In essence the Old Trafford plan of the early 1960s was now complete with each side of the stadium covered by a sleek cantilever roof but, as it was now an all seater stadium and the Reds were enjoying a highly successful period on the pitch, it was agreed that the completed stadium was no longer big enough for Ferguson's successful side. The desire to see the Reds was increasing daily and the stadium capacity was woefully inadequate. Every other city in England would have been delighted with a venue of that size (c.45,000), but with City contemplating a move to a new stadium and United's pulling power growing it was clear that Manchester needed more.

In March 1995 it was announced that United were to extend and redevelop the United Road Stand. The 20 acre industrial estate on the opposite side of United Road had been bought for

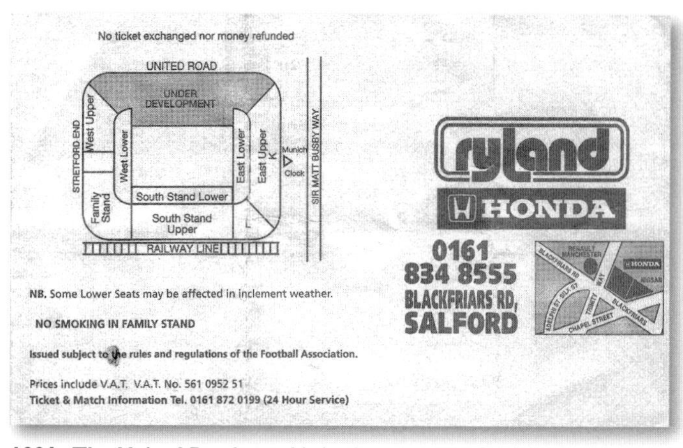

1996 - The United Road stand is in the process of being rebuilt as this ticket ground plan shows.

£9.2m, and a new near 26,000 capacity North Stand (United Road) on three tiers was built between 1995 and 1996. But still this was not enough.

The Main Stand was refitted in 1998 and since then both ends have been extended and now match the North Stand. In addition, during 2006 the club redeveloped and extended the two corners adjacent to the North Stand, and these quadrants have provided significantly improved corporate facilities and raised the capacity to over 76,000, making it the largest Manchester venue since the mid-fifties. Some fans have been critical of the development of corporate facilities over the years, however they do provide a significant income to United and to City. In fact City's move to their new stadium in 2003 caused the Blues to gain many headlines and awards for the quality of their corporate facilities and, as with United's move to Old Trafford in 1910 and its impact on Hyde Road, this is believed to have played its part in United's planning.

The increase in capacity has allowed United to dominate the average attendance charts in a way no other club has ever managed, and with regular commentary appearing suggesting the stadium will be developed further, it appears Old Trafford's position as England's largest League

Old Trafford in 2004.

ground will continue for many more years. The stadium has hosted many Internationals, semi-finals, five games during the 1996 European Championships, plus one European Cup final, however now that Wembley Stadium is open once more it seems Old Trafford is unlikely to stage international matches on a regular basis again. That is a major shame as Manchester has demonstrated time and again that its venues can provide an atmosphere the capital finds hard to match.

Today Old Trafford attracts fans from all over the world and on non-match days its museum and tour proves very popular, however within the ground on matchdays it is clear local fans still feel part of the fabric of the club. Banners positioned at the Stretford End mostly talk of United's place in Manchester. So, although United have succeeded in becoming a global brand, there does still appear to be a Mancunian heart.

MAINE ROAD (1941-1949 & 1956-7)

The use of Maine Road by Manchester United came in two distinct phases. The first was following the bombing of Old Trafford during the war and immediately after. The second came when United needed to play European Cup matches under floodlights.

In 1946 the first United 'home' crowd of over sixty thousand to watch United at Maine Road was 65,112 for the game with Middlesbrough on 14th September 1946.

The Football League's record crowd of 83,260 is held by Maine Road for United's 1-1 draw with eventual League champions Arsenal on 17th January 1948. Joe Mercer captained Arsenal that day and United ended the season as runners-up. The crowd for the United-Arsenal game remains the record crowd for a League fixture and, until the recent enlargement of Old Trafford, United's top four League attendances had all occurred at Maine Road during this period.

On 7th April 1948 the first Manchester derby with City away at Maine Road took place and was watched by a crowd of 71,690 – around 6,000 less than the City home fixture. City player George Smith claims that despite City being the away side, the Blues always insisted on using the home dressing room for these matches, while City supporters did not have the same opportunity to retain home advantage. Those with seats would have to choose other seats if United had sold those tickets to their own supporters.

In 1949 82,771 watched United draw 1-1 with Bradford while 81,565 witnessed their 8-0 victory over Yeovil. Both matches took place in the FA Cup with the Yeovil match gaining national coverage. Yeovil had developed a fantastic reputation as giant killers after knocking out Second Division Bury and First Division Sunderland, and everybody wanted to see them play. Over seven thousand travelled from Yeovil, while many neutrals also joined the queues for the tie. Main Stand seats, which had a face value of 5 shillings and 7 shillings and six pence, were exchanging hands for figures between three and six pounds.

Twenty minutes before kick off the ground committee chose to close the gates. According to reports there were still hundreds locked outside. The attendance was not a record – even United's game with Bradford had attracted more – but because of the involvement of Yeovil the match has always been significant. Mancunian Harry Bramble attended the game:

"People have often asked me whether I supported United that day or not and the truth is that I came to Maine Road to see them get licked! I knew they wouldn't but I hoped they would. I think most of us felt the same. Yeovil offered a great Cup fairytale story."

United's Best Home Attendances at Maine Road (1941 to 1949)

Attendance	Date	Opponents	Type of Fixture
83,260	17/1/48	Arsenal	FL (Arsenal Champions)
82,771	29/1/49	Bradford	FA Cup 4th round
81,565	12/2/49	Yeovil Town	FA Cup 5th round
74,213	28/2/48	Preston NE	FA Cup 6th round
71,690	7/4/48	Manchester City	FL
71,623	26/3/48	Bolton W	FL
70,787	4/12/48	Newcastle United	FL
70,434	7/2/49	Bradford Park Avenue	FA Cup 4th round replay
66,967	7/4/47	Wolves	FL
66,485	22/1/49	Manchester City	FL

United's Average League Attendances at Maine Road (1946 to 1949)

Season	Average Attendance	Lowest Attendance	Highest Attendance
1946-7	43,945 (4th highest)	8,456 (Stoke)	66,967 (Wolves)
1947-8	54,890 (3rd highest)	35,509 (Everton)	83,260 (Arsenal)
1948-9	48,808 (3rd highest)	20,158 (Middlesbrough)	70,787 (Newcastle)

NOTE: United's average attendance for the first season back at Old Trafford was 43,282, and reduced to 39,008 in 1950-1. By 1954 it was down to 35,458, and didn't surpass the 1946-7 figure (United's lowest at Maine Road) until 1956-7 (45,481 – the best in the League). The 1947-8 figure was not surpassed until 1967-8 season.

One interesting statistic from United's time at Maine Road concerns their lowest League crowd at City's home. On 5th February 1947 8,456 witnessed United's 1-1 draw with Stoke. This is incredibly almost exactly a tenth of Maine Road's record crowd (84,569) for City's cup match in 1934 also with Stoke.

The second period when United used Maine Road for home games came in 1956-7 when the Reds became the first English side to enter the European Cup. The details of this are covered earlier in this book.

OLDHAM ATHLETIC STADIA

Since formation as Pine Villa in 1895 the club has played at four different home venues.

HUDSON FOLD (1895 & 1900-06)

Hudson Fold, Westhulme, was the home of Oldham County, who had leased the venue from John Robinson. Robinson owned 22 acres in between the Union Workhouse and the Pine Mill and County spent some time creating a pitch by levelling the land, installing drains and placing top soil and turf. Their first game was on 7th September 1895 and two months later another team, Pine Villa (present day Oldham Athletic), was set up and they agreed with County to share Hudson Fold with games taking place on alternate Saturdays.

Sadly Pine Villa were forced to look for another venue later in the season when County created a reserve side. The club moved on before returning to Hudson Fold again in 1900.

At Hudson Fold Athletic (the name had changed in 1899) made steady progress and started to establish themselves, ultimately joining the Manchester League. As a result the venue was improved and Latics tended to look after the ground well, although it did cost them a great deal to ensure the venue was up to standard. The playing area was extended by six yards and widened by ten yards. In addition the spectator facilities were improved with banking erected on all sides and a new pavilion built.

In 1903 new drains were erected following problems with the pitch, but the season that followed was a controversial one with some of the 4,000 crowd causing trouble at the end of a 3-0 defeat against Tonge FC, resulting in the ground being closed for six weeks by the FA.

At the end of the season discussions with the new owner of the ground – a Miss Clegg of Lytham St. Annes – proved difficult and Latics looked at moving back to the site that became Boundary Park. However, changes in the structure of Latics resulted in the new committeemen vowing to improve Hudson Fold instead. They erected a new main stand, improved the dressing rooms, and erected a fence around the pitch.

Despite this expense, the club moved back to Boundary Park in 1906. Oldham had become more professional and ambitious in their outlook and decided to make a serious bid to join the League. They failed in the 1906 election and its possible that the Hudson Fold ground was recognised as a weakness, although Latics were already committed to a move to Boundary Park by the time of the vote.

In 1924 part of Hudson Fold became Westwood Park and today Westhulme Avenue is the closest landmark to the pitch.

BERRY'S FIELD (1895-98)

The move to Berry's Field, behind Garforth Methodist Church on Garforth Street (Chadderton, close to Middleton Road), was one of necessity as Pine Villa were still in their initial season and were neither wealthy enough to rent a quality venue, nor experienced enough to know exactly what they needed.

As far as can be ascertained the ground was nothing more than an unenclosed pitch – actually there were two – and there were no facilities for changing. According to some sources a Smithy close to the Featherstall & Junction Hotel was used as dressing rooms.

As the side developed a move became essential and in 1898 the club moved again. Today the site of the pitch is developed with housing and some industry.

SHILOH (1898-99)

The Shiloh ground became the club's home for one season only and even that started late – the first home game coming on 12th November (the sixth fixture of the season). It was the last season before the transformation into Oldham Athletic and so was clearly a transitional period for the club. The Black Cow Inn was used as the club's headquarters and after one season the side moved on.

In 1925 Elk Mill was erected on the ground and this was the last traditional cotton-spinning mill built in Lancashire (the last to spin cotton on mules). When it ceased operation at the end of 1998 it was also one of the last cotton spinning mills still operating in the North West. The mill was demolished in 1999 and the site now forms part of a retail park.

SHEEPFOOT LANE/BOUNDARY PARK (1899-1900, SINCE 1906)

This ground was originally used by the club in 1899 when they reformed as Oldham Athletic. In fact, at that time, the venue was known as the Athletic Grounds and so the move also had a bearing on the club's new name – Oldham are the oldest of all the Athletics playing in the Football League or Premier League.

Originally the ground had been the home of Oldham County and they played their first game there in September 1896. County had been offered the ground on a 21 year lease and they developed a running and cycle track, a tennis court and a bowling green, as well as football facilities and a stand. Sadly, the expense was too great for the club and in 1897 a winding up order was served and the club ceased to be. Despite the relative quality of the ground it did not stage competitive football on a regular basis until Pine Villa reformed as Latics and moved there, but it did stage rugby (Werneth RLFC played there 1901-03 and Oldham RLFC played A team fixtures there for a while).

The ground was owned by JW Lees Brewery and after a dispute with the owners Latics chose to return to Hudson Fold in 1900, however the ground always offered more potential than any other local venue and in 1906 Latics returned after negotiating a seven year lease with the brewery.

A stand was built with dressing rooms, baths, a recreation room and all the facilities deemed essential for a professional soccer club (including a snooker table). There were two stands at this point. The Main Stand was a rather traditional looking affair with a paddock in front and built into the gabled roof was a viewing platform. Typically at grounds these areas would be used by journalists or important attendees.

Opposite the Main Stand stood the Broadway Stand, also nicknamed the Flat Stand (the roof was flat). This stand was built in 1907 and also housed a viewing gallery on its roof (which survived until shortly after World War Two). Often supporters would stand on this roof for a better view, while manager David Ashworth is reported to have run up and down the roof following action on the pitch.

In 1908 with assistance from Archibald Leitch – a famous architect who would later design Old Trafford – the pitch was re-drained and re-turfed, and then five years later the club invested in a new Main Stand. This stand was actually developed in stages over several years and contained a large seated section (with 1,092 tip up seats for officials and wealthier fans) behind a concreted paddock. In addition terracing in other areas of the ground was improved while the roof of the old main stand was remodelled and installed at the Chadderton Road end of the ground to provide cover for 1,200 fans. In total the capacity was viewed as being around 45,000 with 18,000 being able to stand at the Rochdale Road end.

These ground improvements came at a time when Latics were enjoying a good period on the pitch, however the outbreak of war ended any chance of the side finding major success and as a result ground developments also took a back seat. In fact it was not until 1927 that the next major development took place. This was the erection of a large roof on the Chadderton Road End.

The roof was anticipated to provide cover for around 12,000 but disaster struck as the development entered its final stages. A hurricane caused the roof to come crashing to the ground and work had to start again. The roof was expected to cost £3,000 but clearly the storm damage caused Latics some financial worries – if nothing else the roof would be delayed. Eventually it was finished but throughout its life there were concerns whenever there was a particularly strong wind or bad storm – even in October 1987 a game had to be postponed because sheeting had blown off the roof and the local authorities refused to let the game take place.

Despite those worries Boundary Park was by 1930 a significant venue and in January of that year it attracted a record crowd of 46,471 (receipts £3,116) for the visit of Sheffield Wednesday in the FA Cup. It was an amazing tie – heralded as one of the best games ever staged in Oldham – and ended 4-3 to Wednesday. Four years later the same sides met again with another huge crowd of 46,011 witnessing a 1-1 Boundary Park draw. Interestingly the replay was watched by a lower figure of 41,311 at Hillsborough.

Despite these highs Oldham had dropped to Division Three North by the outbreak of World War Two and ground developments took a back seat. The venue was routinely painted and terracing touched up and so on, but little of note occurred until 1950 when Sheepfoot Lane itself was improved – for years the road was nothing more than a dirt track – and then the Sheepfoot Lane terracing was concreted with the help of a donation from the Supporters' Club.

A few years of struggle again limited developments but in 1961 floodlights were erected at Boundary Park. The cost was around £18,000 (paid for with support from a public appeal) and League Champions Burnley were the visitors for the inaugural game under lights. According to grounds expert Simon Inglis Oldham were the last Lancastrian League side to install lights, but Oldham were still only four years behind United who had to install lights for European football.

Five years later, with Ken Bates in charge of the club, Boundary Park was given a face-lift. Private boxes were installed during the summer of 1966 at the back of the terracing in front of the Main Stand. These boxes, though relatively basic, allowed the club to generate greater income and with a relatively large amount of terracing available around the ground Latics felt the move was an

The approach to Boundary Park in 1937.

easy one to make. Other improvements followed throughout the mid to late sixties, despite the departure of Bates as Chairman.

Journalist Peter Douglas highlighted the changes in the **Northern Soccer Annual of 1969**:

"Look around the Oldham club and you will be amazed at the facilities they have which rival any club in Division One. Chairman Massey is the first to admit that credit for this is due to former chairman Bates, but the problem as Massey sees it was a growth in facilities that was not accompanied by the support of a team or crowd potential to justify it. The ground itself presents an air of being well-kept and yet the cost of upkeep of the pitch and surrounding buildings is enormous. With a stadium that will hold 45,000 people and gates of some 4,000 each week, there is almost the same amount of work involved in maintaining the ground in a good state of repair as if they had capacity crowds every Saturday afternoon. The main stand has been completely re-seated and below it are some of the most modern dressing-rooms that can be found in the country. Beneath the stand is a very attractive club bar and refreshment room and leading off this are private boxes which can be hired by the season. About half of these are occupied at present. The boxes themselves are very comfortable with private seats, private heating, a Tannoy system that gives the half-time and full-time results and refreshments are provided free of charge during the half-time interval.

"The players themselves have first-class facilities with modern dressing-rooms for both home and away teams. The whole of the premises under the stands is fully air-conditioned and centrally heated by a gigantic oil-fired boiler. There is a modem laundry with all the latest equipment and a drying room with another one in course of construction. Where the Supporters Club and other premises under the stand have had to be sealed off, special air-conditioning has been installed and giant ducts pass under the stand to provide fresh air without having to open the windows. There is a special tea-room for the Press and visitors, and the boardroom has an acre of rich green carpet that would not disgrace a West End hotel."

He went on to provide details about the technology housed within the Main Stand:

"The boardroom, indeed, would rival that of any First Division club. It is large and light and airy, tastefully furnished in modern style, and Massey points to the modern telephone system: 'We have three telephone lines, two of them ex-directory and a fantastic inter-corn system. From here I can ring the offices, the club, the Tannoy control centre, the treatment room, the dressing-room, everywhere'.

"The treatment room is perhaps the piece de resistance. Here they have not one, but three treatment couches, each with radiant-heat lamps and the latest electronic equipment for dealing with sprains and injuries. The whole treatment centre is under the direction of a university graduate physiotherapist and such is the fame of his skill and the club's facilities with private cubicles and all the latest gadgets, that many private patients are treated there. Naturally, with the small staff they maintain at Oldham, it's essential to have players in the peak of fitness. And, thanks to the skill of the physiotherapist and the most up-to-date equipment, it is possible to have them back and fit by the following Saturday, following almost any kind of injury."

Two years after those comments Boundary Park saw the development of a new stand – the Ford Stand – on the site of the oldest part of the ground the Broadway Stand. The old stand had been existence from the club's earliest days at the ground and the opportunity to replace came when Latics won a competition sponsored by Ford which provided £70,000 to be spent on ground improvements. The new stand was taller than the old and, like the main stand opposite, it had a seated upper tier behind a terraced paddock.

Some have suggested the new stand was merely a modern version of the old stand and to some extent there is some truth in that – the roof was basically flat with a series of stanchions holding it up – however it did allow the number of seats in the stadium to increase and provided some of the best views in the ground. It also provided space under the stand for additional facilities.

The saddest part of the stand's development however is that Latics were struggling financially at this point and so the £70,000 could have been put to better use elsewhere had Oldham been allowed to. Similarly, had Latics had some spare cash they could have built a much more impressive stand, afterall the new one only provided seating for around 1,400. Around the same time City built their 8,200 seater cantilevered North Stand for £325,000. Building costs cannot easily be proportioned however if Oldham had been able to top up the Ford money with an additional £50,000 it is possible they may have been able to build a small, modern cantilevered stand housing say 2,000.

As with the other clubs in the region the following decade saw the introduction of fences and segregation, and on 27th December 1980 the ground's new undersoil heating system was used for the first time. It had been installed the previous close season and Latics were only the second Division Two side to install such a system – they also beat many Division One sides including United. Interestingly, it was the same 'Meltaway' Swedish system utilised at Maine Road, although at £60,000 it was around £15,000 more than City paid a year earlier.

From then on many of Boundary Park's developments came as a result of legislation or success on the field. For example, in 1983 the Rochdale Road End terracing was reduced to ensure the club could make sure it was of the right quality. However there was one highly controversial development which was to bring Latics a great deal of opportunity and significant criticism – the installation of a 'plastic pitch'.

The artificial surface was installed at a cost of around £385,000 (with around £305,000 subsidised from Oldham council) in June 1986 and consisted of 8,415 square metres of fibrillated polypropylene. The first League game on the new surface was a 1-0 victory over Barnsley in stormy conditions. From that point on any side defeated at Boundary Park could point to the surface as being 'their' problem but the new pitch helped Latics survive. It was estimated that an extra £50,000 a year was being raised through hiring out the venue.

In the summer of 1991 the artificial surface was removed following legislation that League football was not to be played on that type of surface and the Latics lost a substantial income generator. On the new surface though Oldham were proving successful – some claimed it had been because of the plastic but the club's rise continued into the post-plastic period. That Joe Royle inspired Oldham success also saw supporter facilities developed with 3,634 seats installed in the Chaddy End and an improved roof.

In 1992 the Rochdale Road terracing was demolished and replaced by a £1.95m cantilevered stand. This holds around 4,700 seats and is the neatest area of the ground.

Since that time the ground has been improved in stages with the Main Stand undergoing a £450,000 refurbishment in 1994, and of course seating has been installed on the paddocks in front of the Main Stand and on the Broadway side. There are also executive viewing spaces on stilts in the two Chaddy End corners.

Of course the ground has also been used from time to time for rugby league, especially since the demise of the Watersheddings ground in 1997 and Oldham Roughyeds currently play most

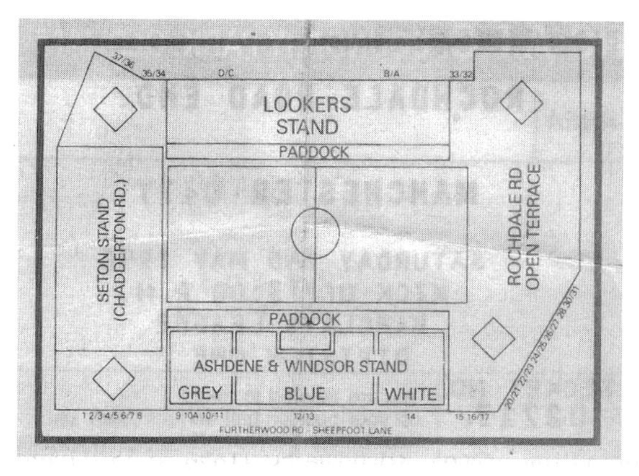

A plan of Boundary Park as seen on the back of match tickets in 1992 (above) and 1993 (below).

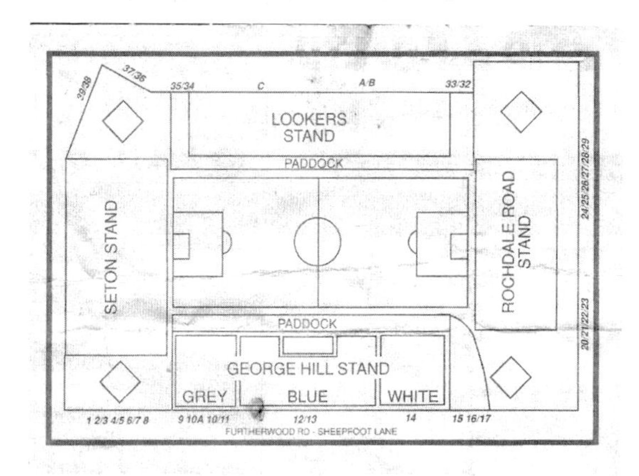

of their home games at Boundary Park, although only the Main Stand tends to be open for their fixtures.

Looking at Boundary Park today it is clear there is room for improvement and there has been considerable debate on the redevelopment of the ground and its surrounding areas. The Broadway side of the ground appears to be the weakest, however the venue still retains a strong identity and any transformation needs to consider what makes Boundary Park so special to Latics fans. Clearly, as a Premier League venue it struggled at times, but at least it improved without a drastic overall and subsequent loss of identity. How it develops from now on is still being discussed but on 15th February 2006, plans were unveiled which would see every stand other than the Rochdale Road end redeveloped in some way to create a 16,000 seater stadium. The plans also suggested the ground would have a four-star hotel, conference and banqueting facilities, significant office space, apartments and a leisure & fitness club with swimming pool.

There was also a campaign by the Latics Supporters Club Canada to build a permanent memorial or tribute to Bobby Johnstone, the great footballer who many fans remember as the greatest to appear at Boundary Park. The campaign aims to either name a stand in his honour or develop some other significant tribute. On the LSC Canada website former secretary Bernard Halford is quoted as a real fan of Johnstone's time at Oldham:

"He transformed the club, no doubt about that. He had the crowds flocking down Sheepfoot Lane, even though Athletic were in the Fourth Division. I think it was the only period in my life when I regularly told lies. On match days the phone never stopped ringing. 'Is Johnstone playing?' Bobby might have been sitting in my office with his ankle in plaster, but I had to say he was playing, otherwise the fans wouldn't have turned up. It really was as cut and dried as that.

"I can't think of any player having an impact on any club like he had. The gates were three thousand and the first game he played the gate was eighteen thousand. So he multiplied the gate by six, and while he was there it never really went down to its old level."

Only time will tell whether Boundary Park alters substantially – during 2007-08 there were further proposals to redevelop the site - or Bobby Johnstone is given a memorial, but at least Boundary Park remains the focal point of football in Oldham, as it has done for well over a century.

ROCHDALE STADIA

Since formation Rochdale have only had one permanent home - Spotland.

SPOTLAND (SINCE 1907)

Spotland was in existence as a significant local venue before the formation of Rochdale AFC, although its name in the early days was St. Clements playing fields. A rugby club – St. Clements – was based there in the 1890s and when the big split came in rugby St. Clements chose to remain a Union side, while Rochdale Hornets became a Northern Union (Rugby League) side. St. Clements clearly made the wrong choice and in 1897 they folded.

Harvey Rigg, the leaseholder and a significant local businessman, had been the rugby side's secretary and he managed to find new tenants in the original Rochdale FC (1896 to 1901) and then Rochdale Town (1901 to 1903). After Town's failure Rigg invested his time in looking at the alternatives and in 1907 the present day Rochdale AFC was created to occupy the ground.

The new club's first game on the ground was a public practice match, attracting an attendance of 350, then a friendly with Oldham on 3rd September was watched by 2,000. The first Manchester League match occurred on 7th September with another 2,000 witnessing a 2-2 draw with Tonge.

Various minor ground improvements occurred over the first few years, then in 1912 significant developments saw the capacity raised to 15,000, although it is fair to say the ground was still not much more than a basic football enclosure.

In February 1914 Rochdale bought the ground outright for a fee reported as £1,700. Permanent developments followed with the building of a 700 seat Main Stand. This stand was for many years the smallest main stand in the League, and survived until it was replaced in 1992.

Understandably the terracing was improved over the years and shortly before joining the League the Pearl Street End saw its banking improved with railway sleepers providing a footing on the otherwise cinder banking.

Disaster hit the club shortly after joining the League when the Main Stand roof blew off, causing £500 worth of damage. Despite a poor first season joining the League allowed Dale to think more long term and in 1925 the central section of Pearl Street was roofed. Two years later the Willbutts Lane side was also roofed.

In 1929 Bradford City – the division's leaders – helped attract a then record crowd of 20,945 to the ground, and although it is perhaps a little hard to visualise today, the ground regularly held five figure crowds.

The Supporters Club performed further improvements to terracing during 1937 but post war the biggest Rochdale issue from a national perspective was the notorious slope of the pitch. The surface dropped by five feet with the Pearl Street goalmouth being higher than that at Sandy Lane. So in 1948, prior to a FA Cup tie against Barrow, the turf at the Pearl Street end was removed, the additional five feet dug out, and then the turf re-laid. Sadly Barrow complained and the game was moved to Boundary Park instead.

The extra earth was then used to create the hill/Spion Kop at the end of the Pearl Street terracing. Crush barriers were installed here in time for the cup tie with Notts County on 10th December 1949 and the new – and current – record attendance was set at 24,321. During the fifties the official capacity was recorded as 32,000 but this was never tested, despite visits from Chelsea (17,817) and Leeds (21,526) which were expected to fill the venue.

In August 1954 the main stand caught fire, needing another extensive rebuild costing £350, but earlier that year saw the significant development of floodlights at Dale. The lights were switched on for a friendly with St. Mirren in February 1954 – three years before Old Trafford installed them and only four months after Maine Road.

Considerable ground improvements had been going on in the background throughout the post war period as Rochdale's Supporters Club worked hard to pay for improvements and also performed improvements themselves. A programme of concreting the terracing had been going on for several years, and then in 1961 the supporters paid £6,000 for a roof to go over the Sandy Lane End.

In 1966 the main stand was hit again by another disaster – the roof collapsed following a particularly heavy snowfall. Five years later Sir Matt Busby switched on Spotland's new floodlights – by that time he had realised just how valuable they were to football – after Coventry City had refused to play under the old lights the previous year.

The following couple of decades were not particularly kind to Spotland as in 1980 the ground was secretly sold to a company owned by the then Chairman for £175,000 – considering the excellent development work performed by supporters over the years this was a major insult. Fortunately, for fans the Chairman's other businesses struggled and Dale were able to buy the ground back at a cut price £83,000 from the Official Receiver in 1982.

Other problems to face the ground came following the Bradford Fire in 1985 and Hillsborough disaster in 1989. The Pearl Street End was closed temporarily following the Bradford fire in 1985 and the ground was in a desperate state.

Spotland photographed in 1976.

Mark Hodkinson, author of *Believe in the Sign*, recognised the poor state of the ground at this point:

"This ground was an absolute mess. It was falling down around us. You couldn't explain how bad it was."

From the mid-80s until 2001 significant change did occur at the venue on a regular basis. In addition Rochdale Hornets moved into Spotland in 1988-89 and in 1990 a partnership was created with the rugby club, the football club and the local council. This has allowed the venue to become a remarkable home although not every action taken has been welcome – the ground name was changed to the Denehurst Stadium but Spotland remains the real name as far as most are concerned.

The sale of Hornets' old ground and various grants allowed Spotland's main stand to be replaced in 1992 by a new £1.1m 2,000 seater stand. A couple of years later 12 executive boxes were built into the stand that was officially opened on Boxing Day 1992 at the match against Scunthorpe.

Earlier in 1992 the Sandy Lane End had suffered from storm damage. There were also some safety concerns and so the stand was refurbished and is now the only standing area of the ground. It holds 1,898 fans.

The Pearl Street End was the next area to be updated and in 1996 it was given its biggest ever makeover. The old stand and terracing was demolished to make way for a £900,000 all seater stand. This was formally opened by Nat Lofthouse before a friendly against Bolton in October 1997. This remains the most popular area of the ground for fans and it also houses the family stand.

Spotland undergoes a 90s transformation.

The transformation of Spotland did not end there however and after the old stand was demolished in January 2000, a new 3,644 seater stand was developed at the Wilbutts Lane side during 2000-01. This houses away supporters but has been designed in such a way as to allow home fans to use the stand when the need arises. It also houses the television gantry – something needed much more frequently in the modern era than at any previous time in the ground's history. The development of this stand brought the capacity of the ground to 10,208 but more importantly meant that Spotland was a great modern venue for watching football and rugby.

Mark Hodkinson feels the redevelopment of Spotland has shown that there are a lot of people who care about the club:

"I remember the transformation started and when one of the stands opened I remember looking at it and thinking, 'look what somebody's bothered to do'. People really do care."

According to Rochdale's official website the Wilbutts Lane Stand brought the club's redevelopment plans to completion and when Dale's home is compared to other traditional lower League venues, it is clear Spotland is now an exceptionally modern venue. It may not have the character of the old stands, but it is certainly more than equipped for modern day sport at a lower League level. Comparisons with venues such as the Shay (Halifax) and Millmoor (Rotherham) show that those managing Spotland know how to develop a good community venue.

STALYBRIDGE CELTIC STADIA

Home Grounds

Joe Walsh's Meadow, Spring Hollows (1906)

Bower Fold (Since 1909)

BOWER FOLD (Since 1909)

The early years of Stalybridge Celtic are not particularly clear and, despite a few mentions of friendly games, it was not until 1909 that the club truly developed. Bower Fold at this time was nothing more than a field, although it had been used by Stalybridge United and Stalybridge Christ Church in local competition.

Herbert Rhodes, the captain of Stalybridge CC and a key figure behind Celtic, spent £100 on levelling the pitch and erecting barriers around the playing surface. It was a fairly rough and ready venue, and then according to various sources shortly after the First World War a 500 seater main stand was constructed. This became a familiar part of Bower Fold for the following seventy years, although a photograph appearing on the Celtic website dated 1913 shows both the main stand and a covered enclosure opposite already in situ. It is fair to say the stand does look new in the image, and it appears as if the roof opposite is in the process of construction.

The largest recorded attendance came on 8th February 1921 when an official crowd of 10,400 watched Dick Kerr's Ladies play a Rest Of Lancashire side. The unofficial crowd for this is believed to have been around 12,000, while 9,753 is the record Celtic attendance and was established on 17th January 1923 when West Bromwich Albion were the visitors in the FA Cup.

By the time Celtic joined the League in 1921 the ground's terracing had been reinforced with railway sleepers and there was also additional covered accommodation with a roof running behind one goal as well as opposite the main stand.

Bower Fold 1913 (above) and the 1980s (below).

Various improvements have occurred over the years, and in 2004 the capacity of Bower Fold was recorded as 6,108 with 1,200 seats. Today the ground possesses two impressive stands. One of these, opposite the Main Stand, has been named The Lord Tom Pendry Stand after the former local Labour MP and shadow Minister for Sport.

STOCKPORT COUNTY STADIA

Since formation in 1883, the club is known to have played at seven different home venues, excluding FA Cup ties played at grounds such as Maine Road.

HEATON NORRIS RECREATION GROUND (1883)

As with most of the other sides of the region Stockport's early homes were not particularly significant venues. The first of these was the Heaton Norris Recreation Ground, off Wellington Road North. Sadly, all the club's records were destroyed in a fire at Edgeley Park in 1935 and unfortunately there are no official comments on the state of this ground, or the other early venues. Suffice to say that this venue could have been nothing more than a basic field and presumably the players would have changed in a nearby public house or other relatively public building.

It is not known how many games were staged here.

HEATON NORRIS WANDERERS CRICKET GROUND (1884-5)

It is known that the club moved to this cricket ground at some point in 1884 with some sources believing the move occurred during the first season (1883-84). The first game identified by Stockport historians Phil Brennan and Richard Harnwell was against Stalybridge on 11th October 1884 (a 3-0 defeat).

Again little is known about this venue, and today the site is located adjacent to Ring Avenue, close to the modern day Pyramid building.

CHORLTON'S FARM (1885-6)

This venue was another of the club's short stay homes and according to Brennan and Harnwell the exact location has never been accurately identified, however Dave Twydell, writing in *Grounds For a Change*, believes the venue was located off Didsbury Road and he states that it was in a very rural setting at the time.

HEATON NORRIS CRICKET GROUND/ASH HOTEL (1886-7)

This home, off Manchester Road, would have been another fairly basic venue however the Ash Hotel itself was already known as a sporting venue. Naturally, the ground was known for cricket but maps from the 1840s also show a bowling green. No doubt the players would have used the facilities of the pub.

Today the Ash Hotel still exists and a short distance behind the pub, off Whitehill Street, there is a large recreation ground which houses playing fields. Lancashire and Cheshire Amateur Football League side Norris Villa SM play there.

WILKES FIELD, BELMONT STREET (1887-89)

The club's next ground was located off Wellington Road North close to a site now occupied by All Saints Primary School and it was here that the side was able to charge an admission fee for the first time. In addition attendances of around 2,000 were recorded here.

Today the site is heavily developed, but in the 1880s much of this area was still relatively rural.

NURSERY INN, GREEN LANE (1889-1902)

Initially this venue was nothing more than a basic field however it was here that the club developed into a significant side and as a result the ground also progressed. Within nine months of moving in the ground became enclosed and a wooden stand – erected by the players and committee members – was built on the main (west) touchline opposite the Nursery Inn side of the pitch.

A large embankment was erected at the northern end and another at the southern end. Dressing rooms were provided in a barn at the side of the Nursery Inn and all spectators had to enter the ground via an opening between the pub and the barn. They also had to walk around a

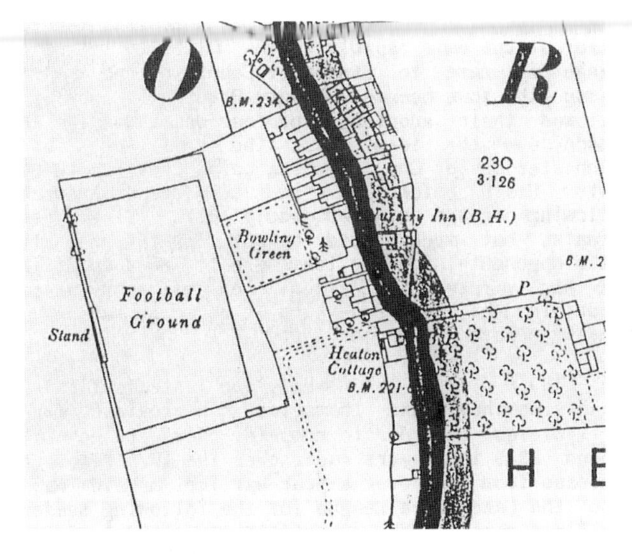

Stockport's Nursery Inn ground in 1895.

bowling green – presumably this caused an issue for larger crowds leaving the venue in a hurry.

Today the Nursery Inn is not the original public house (it was built c.1930s) but it does give an indication of the location of the original ground. This was positioned behind the site of the modern day pub. It is worth noting that a popular bowling green still appears behind the modern day pub.

EDGELEY PARK (SINCE 1902)

It is a little ironic that Edgeley Park started life in 1891 as a rugby league venue and at the time County moved there in 1902 Stockport Rugby club were based there. The rugby side, despite being founders of the Northern Union (Rugby League) was in decline while the association game was rapidly becoming popular in the area.

Clearly the facilities and potential of the new venue was significantly better than the earlier grounds, and County did all they could to improve the stadium and stamp their identity on it. The first major development following County's arrival was the installation of a roof on the back section of the Popular Side of the ground. This is believed to have provided cover for around 1,400 fans at the time.

In 1913 the next significant development was the erection of a main stand on the Hardcastle Road side of the ground. This replaced the earlier changing facilities and gave the club offices and various players' rooms, and allowed County to present themselves as a forward looking club despite struggles on the pitch (they ended 1912-13 in 19th place in Division Two but the League only consisted of 2 divisions at the time). This stand included 500 seats.

Ten years later a roof was erected over the Cheadle End of the ground – in the 60s and 70s this became a lively, noisy, passionate and popular spot to watch County – and it housed around 3,000 standing spectators. The stand was relatively small and compact, but it was the type of traditional footballing end that fans felt was their space to represent their club.

Over the years that followed improvements were made to terracing, including the creation of a new larger barrel roof on the Popular Side in 1927 and an extension to this in 1934. Then, in 1935 the future of Edgeley Park was seriously threatened when the Main Stand was destroyed by fire. It seems the fire started at noon on 23rd July and quickly enveloped the entire stand and houses on the opposite side of Hardcastle Road. According to the ***Cheshire Daily Echo*** the entire stand was completely destroyed within 45 minutes while the houses suffered 'fallen in' roofs and badly damaged frontages. Fifty people were made homeless while club captain Billy Bocking was highlighted as being a bit of a hero as he had worked with the fire brigade and other members of staff to save as much club property as possible (including his own boots).

BENNETTS' OPTICIANS, STOCKPORT, CHESTER

CHESHIRE DAILY

NO. 14,175. 51st Year. TUESDAY, JULY 23, 1935.

DISASTROUS FIRE HAVOC

COUNTY'S GRAND STAND GUTTED

11 HOUSES AND A WORKS DAMAGED

HOUSEHOLDERS' ALARM

FURNITURE REMOVED INTO STREET

THE GRAND STAND AT EDGELEY PARK FOOTBALL GROUND, STOCKPORT COUNTY'S HEADQUARTERS, WAS GUTTED BY FIRE THIS AFTERNOON, AND ELEVEN HOUSES AND A PRINTING WORKS ADJOINING WERE ALSO SERIOUSLY DAMAGED.

Fortunately, though the ground is situated in a thickly populated district, there were no serious casualties. Several

ALLEGATIONS AGAINST COLONEL

ARTILLERYMAN'S STORY OF PHOTOGRAPHS

DEFENCE'S SUBMISSION

"CASE BROUGHT FOR BLACKMAIL & REVENGE"

To-day's Racing.

GOOD DEAL'S EASY IN LEICESTERSHIRE

DEFEATS CHARM THREE LENGTHS

Gordon Richards ac... the Hat Tr...

July 1935 and Stockport's main stand burns down

Inevitably, the fire forced the club to act and a new Main Stand (the present one) was built at a cost of around £7,000. This initially sat 2,000 but more importantly included good quality dressing rooms and offices. Significantly, the stand was officially opened by the Football League's President Charles Sutcliffe. This is highly important as Sutcliffe was always in demand for occasions like this and although a modern day audience may not care so much for a League or FA official carrying out such a task, in 1930s England the League's President was regarded as a very significant figure. In addition, he had actually turned down an offer by Arsenal to open their new £100,000 East Stand on the same day. That season saw County take off on the pitch as well and they ended the campaign as champions of Division Three North.

In the mid fifties the Popular Side roof was extended with a sloping section joining on to the 1920s barrel roof and the stand was renamed the Barlow Stand after long serving Chairman Ernest Barlow who died in 1954. Shortly afterwards County beat United by installing floodlights around six months earlier than the Reds. These were used for the first time in October 1956.

The Barlow Stand was reduced in size in 1978 with the old barrel roof dismantled and the section fenced off. A five-a-side pitch was installed in this area, but the loss of terracing was significant, as around 16,000 had stood on this side during the 1950 record crowd of 27,833 for the FA Cup tie with Liverpool.

Edgeley Park received the Johnstones Paint treatment during the Sixties.

During the mid 1980s significant changes saw the Railway End reduced by a third and the terracing concreted over – this had mainly been railway sleepers, cinder and gravel for the first 100 years of the ground's history. The Main Stand paddock terracing also disappeared at this point and with it went one of the ground's most entertaining features – the drawbridge. For years the drawbridge had been lowered across the paddock from the players' tunnel to allow the teams to walk straight on to the pitch without having to go down the stepped terracing and then back up at pitch side. Either side of the players' tunnel a re-profiled paddock had seats installed on to it.

Perhaps the worst aspect of the mid-80s developments was the demolition of the Cheadle End. The Bradford fire immediately brought serious concerns at almost every ground in the country and County suffered a great deal. The Cheadle End was ordered to be demolished by safety inspectors and for the next decade this end was open with nothing more than a walkway behind the goal.

In 1993 the Barlow Stand terracing was reprofiled and 2,411 seats were installed under the 1950s roof, and two years later a new Cheadle End stand was erected (four times the depth of the original). To do this the club had to buy a timber yard and social club that had been behind the original stand, but they also ran into problems with local residents who complained when the plans were unveiled. In the end a smaller stand than originally planned was constructed but this still is a significant structure. It houses around 5,000 seats and hospitality facilities, and cost £1.5m when built. Interestingly, its architects were the same company, Howard & Seddon, who were responsible for the new Kippax Stand at Maine Road opened the same year. This is by far the most modern part of the ground.

The Railway End was the next to be altered and in 2001 around 1,600 seats were installed on the terracing.

Today the capacity of Edgeley Park is around 10,600 and the 1990s were a great period to enjoy games here, however the most dramatic changes to the venue came as a result of ownership issues detailed elsewhere in this book. These changes ultimately led to Sale Sharks moving in and County almost leaving their home. Now County is owned by a supporters' trust but the ground is owned by Cheshire Sports. As this book goes to press there are stories that supporters would like to see the trust buy back the ground, however whether this is possible remains to be seen. One area where the trust has been able to make a difference however, is in the recognition by the local council of the importance of the venue. Edgeley Park has been awarded one of ten prestigious Blue Plaques given by the local council to commemorate famous local places and people.

All football clubs and also former venues in the region should receive similar recognition from their council.

GROUNDS AND CAPACITIES

The following tables show the varying capacities, record attendances, and receipt details at significant points in local football history.

CAPACITIES & ATTENDANCES 1933

TEAM	CAPACITY	RECORD ATTENDANCE
Bury	40,000	33,872, V Bolton, 3/1/25
City	86,000	76,166 V Cardiff City, 8/3/24
United	80,000	73,000, Bolton V Sheff Utd, 24/3/23
Oldham	52,000	47,671, V Sheff Wed, 25/1/30*
Rochdale	25,000	20,945, V Bradford City, 30/4/29
Stockport	27,000	24,804, V Bradford City, 2/2/29

* Note: This attendance is often recorded as 46,471 but in record books from 1934 (and into the 1970s) it is recorded as 47,671.

RECORD ATTENDANCES & RECEIPTS 1966

TEAM	RECORD ATTENDANCE	RECORD RECEIPTS
Bury	35,000, V Bolton, 9/1/60	£4,775, V Bolton, 9/1/60
City	84,569, V Stoke, 3/3/34	£20,212, Blackburn V Bolton, 22/3/58
United	76,962, Wolves V Grimsby, 25/3/39	£41,263 10s 6d, V Partizan, 20/4/66
Oldham	47,671, V Sheff Wed, 25/1/30	£7,664, V Liverpool, 27/1/62
Rochdale	24,371, V Notts County, 10/12/49	£2,285, V Notts County, 10/12/49
Stockport	27,833, V Liverpool, 11/2/50	£4,600, V Liverpool, 3/2/65

All attendance records still stand in 2008.

CAPACITIES & RECORD RECEIPTS 1974

TEAM	CAPACITY	RECORD RECEIPTS
Bury	35,000	£7,039, V City, 3/10/72
City	52,500	£30,888, V United, 3/12/69
United	60,500	£104,000, Leicester V Liverpool, 30/3/74
Oldham	30,000	£9,269, V Burnley, 26/1/74
Rochdale	28,000	£2,836, V Doncaster, 7/4/69
Stockport	24,904	£6,771, V Norwich, 1/11/72

CAPACITIES & RECORD RECEIPTS 1985

TEAM	CAPACITY	RECORD RECEIPTS
Bury	22,500	£22,200, V Nottm Forest, 17/1/78
City	52,600	£239,476, Everton V Liverpool, 28/3/84
United	56,925	£192,956, V Juventus, 11/4/84
Oldham	26,324	£44,998.30, V City, 20/4/84
Rochdale	15,000	£8,834 V Telford, 7/1/84
Stockport	16,000	£23,515 V Liverpool, 24/9/84

CAPACITIES & RECORD RECEIPTS 1993

TEAM	CAPACITY	RECORD RECEIPTS
Bury	12,000	£37,000, V Bolton, 19/5/91
City	39,800	£469,419, United V Oldham, 8/4/90
United	45,000	£432,345.80, V Legia Warsaw, 24/4/91
Oldham	17,004	£129,365, V United, 9/3/93
Rochdale	5,600	£46,000, V Burnley, 5/5/92
Stockport	9,720	£50,152, V Stoke, 3/3/93

CAPACITIES & RECORD RECEIPTS 2003

TEAM	CAPACITY	RECORD RECEIPTS
Bury	11,669	£86,000, V City, 12/9/97
City	35,150	£512,235, United V Oldham, 13/4/94
United	68,210	£1,124,195.24, V Olympiakos, 23/10/01
Oldham	13,559	£138,680, V United, 29/12/93
Rochdale	10,208	£46,000, V Burnley, 5/5/92
Stockport	10,817	£181,449, V Middlesbrough, 26/2/97

CAPACITIES 2006

TEAM	CAPACITY
Bury	11,669
City	47,726
United	76,212
Oldham	13,624
Rochdale	10,208
Stockport	10,641

EIGHTH YEAR OF PUBLICATION.

MANCHESTER EVENING CHRONICLE

Football Guide for 1911-12

Illustrated with Photos and Sketches

Price ONE PENNY.

CHAPTER TWENTY-SEVEN

THE MEDIA

Granada had a great stroke of luck in being able to make quick arrangements to show hundreds of thousands in the North-West the triumphant return of Manchester City. The seething crowds, the scenes on the Town Hall steps and the speeches of the players made a brilliant piece of intimate camera work. Manchester Evening Chronicle, 1956

ACROSS the region, the media has always played a significant part in the development of the game. Local newspapers such as the **Gorton Reporter**, **Bury Times**, and **Oldham Evening Chronicle** have promoted and supported our teams. In addition, many national sporting media organisations have either been born in the region, or have had bases within the Manchester conurbation.

The following sections provide background to the significant forms of the media affecting football in the region.

NEWSPAPERS

According to JAH Catton, the **Athletic News**' Tityrus, the first regular footballing newspaper pre-dated most of the Manchester clubs. In 1926 he wrote his memoirs and gave his views on the earliest sporting publications:

"In November 1878 there appeared the first issue of a weekly periodical called **The Goal – The Chronicle of Football.** *I never heard of this publication until I looked over a miscellaneous lot of books bought for me by a very kind friend at Usk.* **The Goal** *was surely the first of football papers, and it seemed to have been issued by a Mr. E.M. Fraser, of The Crescent, 169 Camden Road, London, NW. Less than two years afterwards* **The Athletic News** *was produced and in 1886 my first contribution to its columns was signed 'Ubique'. But these weekly prints did not speed the football editions of the evening newspapers. Some editors seized on this idea owing to the birth of several sheets called* **Saturday Night**. *They were entirely devoted to sport – and chiefly reports of football matches.*

"The **Saturday Night** *newspapers and the application of the telephone to press work hastened the football editions, which were at one time the bane of my existence. In the middle of the 'eighties I thought it was a great feat when the National Telephone Company 'tapped' a wire by affixing an instrument to one of their posts for me to send a report of a big match. If I recollect rightly this was an exciting replayed Cup tie on neutral territory.*

"Nowadays [1926] there is a separate entrance for members of the Press to a private gallery or reporting box, and there the journalist can 'talk' his report through an instrument on the desk in front of him to the offices of his newspaper. This is part of the advent of luxury – belonging to the era of the tip-up seat and the Cup and Saucer Act as half-time, unless a more powerful dope than tea is preferred. The modern football reporter has much more creature comforts than his predecessor of forty years ago. Nor were the players of that distant period so pampered as many of them in these days. They seldom resented Press criticism, for they accepted praise and blame just as they would fat and lean meats. 'Twas all part of the game and all in a lifetime."

By the start of World War One the newspapers were already influencing the direction of some of our local clubs and the selection of players. At City probably the most important media link of football's pre-1990s *Sky TV* involvement was established at the start of the Twentieth Century. Edward Hulton junior was a significant newspaper magnate who had been given responsibility for much of his father's business interests. Edward Hulton senior had initially worked on the *Manchester Guardian* and then went on to found a number of leading newspapers in Manchester including in 1871 *The Tissue* (in 1873 this became the *Sporting Chronicle*), in 1875 the *Athletic News*, in 1885 the Sunday Chronicle, in 1897 the *Manchester Evening Chronicle* and in 1900 the *Daily Dispatch*, and he helped to establish Manchester as a major newspaper centre. Hulton senior passed away in March 1904 – a month before City's first FA Cup final appearance – and he was later buried at Brooklands Cemetery, near Sale.

Edward Hulton junior, who had helped with the formation of the *Evening Chronicle* in 1897, was a very keen sportsman and owned horses that won the Derby and the Oaks, and he was captain of Royal Lytham & St Anne's Golf Club, but it was his interest in football which became significant from a Manchester perspective.

During the early years of the twentieth century City's leaders were determined to establish the Blues as a major power and one local businessman, John Allison, took the lead role in finding other investors. Inevitably, his contacts included the wealthy newspaper baron Edward Hulton junior and Hulton was easily persuaded to help the club. Hulton became a director in 1900 and between 1902 and the summer of 1904 he was Chairman of the Blues.

From that point on Hulton's sporting 'papers regularly reported on behind the scenes events at City and was often first to cover the club's leading stories. For example, shortly after Hulton came on board his *Athletic News* began attacking City secretary-manager Sam Ormerod, and it was not long before the manager was replaced by a man Allison and Hulton had a high regard for – former Celtic founder Tom Maley. 37 year old Maley went on to become the first City manager to find success.

Sir Edward Hulton Junior.

Hulton must have had a significant part to play in Maley's arrival, after all Hulton did become Chairman around the same time. It is also known that the Hulton family were strong Catholics and this may have had a bearing. Interestingly, much has been made over the years of the role of religion in Manchester's two prominent clubs. Significant figures at both United and City have said at various times in each club's history that religion played a part in the development of those sides with City being a protestant club and United a catholic side. It is true that City's roots lay in the Church of England and that prominent figures in United's development have had significant catholic interests, however the involvement of Hulton, Maley and so on prove that City were not a club where religion dominated activity. From its earliest beginnings as a church side the Blues never really focused on the religious aspects and they always tried to establish City as a club for all Mancunians regardless of religion, class, and birth-nationality. At United, modern day personnel claim there is no evidence to suggest that religion ever played a part in the development or direction of the side, although Frank Worrall's *Celtic United* book talks of Louis Rocca encouraging Catholic priests to act as unofficial scouts for the Reds, and the book also describes how United were known as the 'Catholic club' of England.

With Hulton's involvement City became one of football's most featured – and successful – sides of the period. All Hulton's newspapers carried City material and the *Athletic News* tended to include photographs of City's home games at the expense of other sides. Hulton's coverage certainly helped promote the side and encourage Mancunians to support the club, while his financial support helped create a quality side. The two combined made the Blues a major power and inevitably City's success helped increase newspaper sales. It is no wonder that Hulton's *Athletic News* was highly critical of the F.A. when City's illegal payments scandal brought a premature end to the Blues first golden era.

In 1907 Hulton was diagnosed as having Bright's Disease and his consultant believed he had only six months to live. In the years that followed Hulton gradually transferred his main business interests to London (his wife was not a fan of northern England) and he bought the *London Evening Standard* in 1916. He eventually sold his entire newspaper empire for £6m to his neighbour Lord Beaverbrook in 1923 and two years later Hulton passed away. His death made front page news in the *Sunday Express*. Beaverbrook said at the time:

"His body failed him just as his mental powers were reaching maturity... He died too young to hold the place to which his greatness entitled him."

Hulton's son, Edward Hulton the third, launched the *Picture Post* magazine in 1937 and the name lived on for many years as one of the world's leading photo agencies, the Hulton Archive (although this is now known as Getty Images). Sadly though, despite the focus on Mancunian football during the period pre-World War One, few of the hundreds of action photos covering games at Hyde Road and Bank Street during that time exist as part of this collection.

Hulton's influence remained through to the latter half of the Twentieth Century. The modern day entertainment venue The Printworks was the main location for Hulton's newspaper businesses, while the *Manchester Evening Chronicle* – a newspaper Hulton created in 1897 – continued to exist through to 1963. This newspaper forms a very important part of our story of Manchester football.

Once Hulton established the *Evening Chronicle* he ensured it held a more popular style of

ALWAYS A WINNER

★

THE BEST INFORMED, UP-TO-THE-MINUTE, FOOTBALL EDITION

FRANK SWIFT ON SOCCER

Best Reports - Most Results

FOOTBALL EDITION

reporting than the existing *Manchester Evening News* (founded in 1868). It also reported on association football while the *Evening News* still had not got to grips with the importance of the game to the city. Inevitably, because of Hulton's City connections the *Evening Chronicle* became known as a City 'paper. This view persisted until the end.

Potentially because Hulton's *Evening Chronicle* started to prove the value of covering football, or maybe because of its links with City, the *Manchester Evening News* started to show interest in the game and in 1901 they negotiated with Newton Heath to create office space at the club's Bank Street ground. From the moment the Heathens allowed the *Evening News* to set up their own office, the two evening newspapers seemed to establish a blue identity for the '*Chron*' and a red identity for the '*News*'.

Both 'papers did provide substantial coverage of both teams, and of the others in the region, however they did tend to show more of a bias to 'their' side. The *Chronicle* established a Saturday night sporting edition called *The Manchester Evening Chronicle Football Pink*, and the *Evening News* established the *Football Green*. *The Pink* was by far the more popular of the two but both newspapers would be in competition to be the first to hit the streets with match results, reports and league tables.

Queues would form as, in the days before portable radios, the quickest means of finding out results was always via the Saturday sporting newspapers.

By the beginning of the 1960s the *Chron* was still a very popular 'paper with a circulation recorded as 250,000 but the *Evening News* had always managed to retain a larger share of the classified advertising market. Without this, the *Chron* was not as financially viable as its rival and when the Thomson Organisation gained control of the group that owned the *Chron* in the late 1950s it was determined to focus on the northern edition of the national newspapers published in Manchester.

In 1961 the *Guardian* and *Manchester Evening News* group gained control of the *Evening Chronicle* and the organisation published both evening newspapers as separate identities before eventually in 1963 the group pulled the plug on the *Chronicle*. Whether City's own fortunes – the Blues were relegated in 1963 after a few seasons of struggle – had affected circulation is not clear, but it is known that the *Guardian* group needed to maximise income from its Manchester evening newspapers to fund *The Guardian* newspaper's transfer to London (remember that today's *Guardian* was for most of its life the *Manchester Guardian* produced in the city as a national).

The *Evening Chronicle* ceased to exist despite its popularity and the nightly Manchester paper became known as *The Manchester Evening News and Chronicle* for several years before the words 'and Chronicle' disappeared altogether. For many Mancunians the belief that the *Chron* was blue and the MEN red has persisted and even today there are a significant number of City supporters who refuse to buy the MEN because of their view that it remains a red-obsessed newspaper. It is true that at the time this book went to press in 2008 United tended to receive more positive coverage in the MEN than City, but this does not appear to be as a result of bias from the 'paper. Far from it. In fact many of the newspapers leading journalists are known to be blue. It appears that the extensive coverage of United is because United's media department are simply more accessible and determined to get their stories out than City's.

Whereas City's local newspaper coverage tends to focus on on-the-field activities, which are not necessarily always positive, United's local coverage tends to feature more off-field activities. Both sides perform extensive work in the community with City winning more awards and recognition within the community, but United's tends to get the most coverage.

Once the newspapers merged, it was inevitable that the decision to kill off one of the sporting 'papers would follow. In the end it was decided to terminate the Saturday night *Football Green* (the Evening News' publication) and retain the Chronicle's *Football Pink* (although its title was modified in a similar manner to the evening 'paper).

The *MEN Pink* as it ultimately became known continued to exist until 2006 when the *MEN* pulled the plug claiming a lack of sales. Various reasons were given from the widespread development of the internet, satellite TV and so on to the fact that few significant games were being played at 3pm on a Saturday. *The Pink* was produced on a Sunday for a while, but the MEN claimed it was not a success.

Since the *Pink*'s demise local sporting coverage has plummeted, and minor-leagues and sports which had previously been guaranteed space in the 'paper have to fight for space in the regular *MEN*. It is a major shame and disappointment that a city as large as Manchester is no longer able to sustain a weekly, Saturday night sporting 'paper. This is particularly disappointing when it is remembered that Manchester has for much of the last 150 years produced a substantial number of leading newspapers, including many significant sporting titles.

Former City player and leading *MEN* sports journalist for many years Paul Hince talked of the *Pink* in 2006:

"Back in the early 1970s when I joined the MEN *Sports Desk, Manchester was second only to London's Fleet Street as a major printing centre in this country's newspaper industry. All the north-west, north-east and Yorkshire editions of the national newspapers were printed right here in this city. These were the 'hot-metal' days when newspapers were not published at the push of a button. When the* Evening News *presses began rolling from midday onwards, the whole building came to life. You could feel the vibration under your feet and the sensation never failed to excite me. It was almost as though you were working inside something that was alive and breathing.*

"Saturdays, for me, were the highlight of the working week. The Football Pink *was in its pomp and the match reports we sent in were hair-raising adrenalin rushes. Everything we did was off-the-cuff because there was no time to take notes. A match would finish at round a quarter-to-five, and 15 minutes later the '*Pink*' - with full match reports and final scores - would be available on every street corner in the city centre. To this day, I still don't know how we managed to achieve that. Of course, because of that tight time schedule in producing the Saturday evening football edition, occasional bloopers could be found in the* Pink *if you looked carefully enough.*

"Dictating a Stockport County match report down the phone to a copy-taker back on Deansgate, I observed that the home striker had limped off after pulling a muscle in his thigh. **The Pink** *that night reported that the home striker had limped off 'after pulling a muscle in his thing'. He wouldn't have limped off if he had done that - he would have been sent off. Almost as comical was the copy-taker's error when transforming my word 'ricochet' into the name Rick O'Shea!"*

In the early days of the game the journalists had great power and could impact the game in a variety of ways. Inevitably, comments on a player's performance would be read and analysed by the competing clubs and also by representatives of the other clubs keen to identify how other games had been played. In the days before television it was impossible for clubs to see matches they were not involved with unless they sent scouts or spies to other grounds, and so the words of the journalists were studied in detail. JAH Catton occasionally claimed credit for helping players' careers develop via the text of his articles:

"On January 29 1912 I attended a match at the Den, the ground of Millwall, when the amateurs of the North met the amateurs of the South. There were some excellent players in both elevens, and I was able to use my voice in favour of one man on each side. The South won by three clear goals, but the North would have been absolutely overwhelmed had it not been for the goalkeeping of Edward Taylor, who was described on the card as a player of Liverpool Balmoral.

"Taylor protected his charge in magnificent fashion. Not for years had I seen a goalkeeper with such judgement and handicraft. Although his side was beaten I, of course, awarded to Taylor the tribute that his prowess had earned. Nor were my words measured, for the ink was enthusiasm and the pen [my slave] who slaved away to express what I felt."

The glowing tribute was read throughout the Manchester region, with at least one of the region's clubs showing interest. Catton:

"A few days later the manager of Oldham Athletic rang me up on the telephone and coolly asked me if Taylor was as good as I had said! I told him that I was not in the habit of writing what I did not believe. He replied that he would try and sign Taylor for his club, and he did."

Taylor joined Oldham then later was signed by Huddersfield Town for a fee of around £2,000. As well as Taylor, Catton also claimed that he recommended another player from the game at Millwall to another Manchester club:

"Edward Hanney, then the amateur centre-half back of Reading, played such a fine game that I went out of my way to advise Manchester City to get the assistance of this player. They hesitated, and went down to Elm Park to watch him before they did so, but eventually they brought him to the old ground at Hyde Road, and never regretted it."

FILM & TELEVISION

Some of the region's earliest significant games were filmed by media companies for display in local halls and public houses, however little of this early coverage exists. We know that Bury and City's FA Cup finals of 1903 and 1904 respectively were filmed and shown in venues around the region in the days that followed but to date no surviving footage has been located.

It is also known that footage does survive of United in 1902 and of City's Hyde Road ground in

City's FA Cup training at Buxton is filmed for cinema audiences in the mid-1920s

1905. This Hyde Road footage is believed to be the oldest surviving film of a Manchester League ground, although the author of this book is convinced several games involving Manchester's sides were filmed prior to that date.

By the 1920s coverage of local games became more commonplace and organisations such as *British Pathe* and *British Movietone* retain strong footage from the decade. In 1937 the *BBC* televised the FA Cup final and all the postwar finals involving our clubs have been shown live on television. Initially, only the *BBC* broadcast the final live but during the mid-1950s the independent television companies began broadcasting. Locally *Granada* began broadcasting on 3rd May 1956, however their franchise only covered weekdays and *Associated British Corporation* (*ABC* – also a well known cinema chain) held the franchise for weekends. *ABC* began broadcasting from the converted ABC cinema in Didsbury on 5th May 1956 – the same day City played Birmingham City in the FA Cup final. Recognising the pulling power of football the new television company, which had already been broadcasting in the Midlands since February, launched its northern operation with the FA Cup final. This was followed by local celebrities joining journalist Ludovic Kennedy for a news programme, and then The Adventures of Robin Hood.

This coverage meant that the 1956 final would enter history as the first shown live on both the *BBC* and *ITV*. This caused the local newspapers to cover the television story extensively with the *Manchester Evening Chronicle* focusing on the differences between the two sides. The *Chronicle* observed that the *BBC* would take full responsibility for the filming the game and that they would have four cameras positioned in the stadium – this was an amazing number according to the coverage! Two cameras would be placed behind the royal box, in front of the restaurant, with another at the royal box itself and another directly above the scoreboard on the west side of the ground (opposite the players tunnel). The *BBC* commentator Kenneth Wolstenholme would be sat with the two main cameras.

ITV's footage of the game would come directly from the *BBC*, however the independent

Billy Meredith seen during filming for *The Ball Of Fortune* - a feature film he appeared in during 1926.

station decided to concentrate more on its commentators who were set up in a separate position some distance from the BBC. The ITV commentators had a much more popular feel to them with their main man Peter Lloyd being joined by Wolves star Billy Wright and City's former hero Frank Swift. Incidentally, the radio commentators included Manchester journalist Henry Rose, which means two of the main commentators would later become victims of the Munich Air Disaster.

It seems the 1956 final was the first to receive extensive coverage and also a gimmicky aspect to encourage viewers to stick with one channel. Clearly ITV won the war from a Manchester perspective by having the hugely popular Frank Swift in their commentary team, however the BBC staged an entertainment show on a Mersey pleasure boat straight after the final with leading stars Jimmy James and Anne Shelton watching the final via a large screen on the boat and then talking about it throughout their own show. At 7.15 there was also a show on BBC called "Today's Sport" which guaranteed members of the winning team would appear. They also announced a special one hour highlights show would appear on Sunday for anyone who wanted the see the game again.

It really was the first occasion football had so much focus throughout an entire weekend's schedules, but for Mancunians the coverage got even better when Granada TV, who had missed out on the game because it only held the weekday ITV franchise, announced they would show City's homecoming live on the Monday night. The *Manchester Evening News* reported on 7th May, the day of the homecoming:

"City's triumphal arrival will be covered by Granada TV cameras. From 6.45 to 7.30 the 'Travelling Eye' will be in Albert Square to show the team's arrival at the Town Hall and their reception by the Lord Mayor. Said Granada administrative chief Mr. Jim Phoenix: 'This is an experiment. We don't know of any outside broadcast being arranged at such short notice'."

The broadcast did not go exactly to plan as City were delayed, and so experienced radio broadcaster Gerry Loftus was left to fill in time in his first TV broadcast by describing the scene outside the Town Hall for nearly 30 minutes before the team bus appeared. According to David Lowe – an American TV advisor helping the station in its first few weeks – the broadcast was: *"the most exciting outside broadcast I have ever seen here or in the States."*

The following day's **Evening Chronicle** commented:

*"**Granada** had a great stroke of luck in being able to make quick arrangements to show hundreds of thousands in the north west the triumphant return of Manchester City. The seething crowds, the scenes on the Town Hall steps and the speeches of the players made a brilliant piece of intimate camera work."*

As time progressed Manchester football became a key part of television coverage, with the **BBC** introducing ***Match Of The Day*** in 1964 (United featured on the third show, 5th September 1964), and then in 1969 Granada commenced regular football programming. In 1972 the Friday night preview show ***Kick Off*** was launched and from that point on every side in the northwest was featured, although inevitably ***Granada*** tended to focus on the larger sides of the region.

Sundays saw regional highlights in a programme known as the ***Kick Off Match***. For supporters of City and United this tended to mean that their side would feature almost every other week – sometimes more often! When this was combined with the coverage on BBC's ***Match Of The Day*** it meant the larger sides were always on television, or at least always on the shows available. League football was still restricted to highlights on ***Match Of The Day*** (Saturday nights), ***Kick Off*** (Sunday afternoons) and occasional midweek shows, however live football was restricted to internationals and the FA Cup final.

This meant that supporters would still attend the game, not knowing what would be shown, and then at the ground they would spot the cameras. The sight of **BBC** or ***ITV*** vehicles would itself bring some excitement with supporters post match re-arranging their plans to ensure they watched the relevant show. There was no perception of missing a game because you would be able to catch it later on television, instead the sight of the cameras would bring more interest and excitement, and fans would hope for an even better performance than normal as this would help prove their club was worthy of the coverage.

As so few matches were actually shown the **BBC** and ***ITV*** agreed a process for selecting their preferred games on a monthly basis. Before the season started, they would toss a coin to decide who should have the first monthly pick of matches, after which they would alternate each month. One negotiator was selected by the ***ITV*** companies to represent their views, and assuming he won the toss for initial selection, he would pick his first choice game, and then the **BBC** man would pick their number one from the remaining games. As the **BBC** had the prime time slot for football (Saturday nights) and the independent companies featured more games ***ITV*** would then make the next three selections. The **BBC** would then pick the next match.

If **BBC** were choosing first they would get their preferred game, followed by ***ITV*** selecting games two, three and four, and then the BBC would take the fifth match. If more games were to be shown then the selection would go back and forth between the BBC and ITV.

The League did however create strict selection criteria to ensure as wide a selection of clubs as possible. During the mid-Seventies, out of sixty games per season, the BBC had to cover ten Second Division matches and four from the lower divisions. They also had to visit every First Division ground at least once each season. From a Granada perspective, as one of the larger regions the company had to show at least five Second Division matches and two from the lower divisions.

The Seventies were a great period for Granada and Kick Off and Manchester region fans loved their off beat approach. As the decade progressed Kick Off tended to be used by the clubs as one of their greatest promotional outlets. City, in particular, seemed to see the potential the programme had for publicising games and Chairman Peter Swales made sure he was a regular on the show. For a while he even became a horse-racing tipster – years later he admitted he knew little about horse racing and that he only did it to ensure City gained more of a focus. The return of Malcolm Allison to City in 1979 was announced first on Kick Off.

Mike Whalley, a Bolton Evening News journalist, has written his views on the history of the programme:

"Kick Off became renowned during the Seventies for some of its more eccentric feature ideas, which once included getting Francis Lee to dress up as a psychic medium (complete with crystal ball) to forecast the results of the weekend's FA Cup ties. Sinstadt also turned up on the set of Coronation Street to ask the cast members for predictions ahead of the 1977 FA Cup final. There was even a Kick Off Christmas choir, made up of North West players singing festive hymns.

"In January 1978, Kick Off introduced an up-and-coming young reporter signed from Liverpool's Radio City. His name? Elton Welsby. Welsby began to share presenting duties with Sinstadt towards the end of the 1970s, even taking on commentary duties for a couple of games during the 1978/79 season. By the early 1980s, Granada decided it was time to freshen up its coverage. The Kick Off Match became Match Night in 1980, while Sinstadt left Granada the following year (although he stayed with ITV for another two years, transferring to TVS in Southampton, before going freelance and then joining the BBC in 1985). Welsby took over the main presenting duties, helped by Denis Law and new commentator Martin Tyler, brought in from Yorkshire TV."

As the 1980s progressed football coverage became more of a national concern and evolved into The Match, followed by a 'live' version of the show. Elton Welsby and Martin Tyler became key figures, but ITV's favoured commentator Brian Moore – known in Manchester as ITV's FA Cup final and international presenter – was inevitably the lead man.

Since that time Granada has created a variety of highlights packages, depending on the various television agreements, and in 1989 Kick Off was revived for a while. Again City's Chairman Peter Swales tried to ensure the programme was used as one of the club's promotional outlets and on 1st December 1989 he went on the show to publicly state that City wanted to appoint Oldham's Joe Royle as their new manager. As Oldham were due to play Blackburn that evening the power of Granada's coverage was proved when over 10,000 fans at Boundary Park made their feelings known and urged Royle to stay. Royle did stay, and City fans were appalled at Swales' approach, but from a television perspective it was a great scoop.

By 1992 the BBC were showing goal clips of a large number of games and so the majority of teams would appear, however Stockport County were one of only seven League clubs who had not featured as a main match. The others were Aldershot, Darlington, Doncaster, Hartlepool, Maidstone and Reading. Inevitably, the wide scale coverage of football since 1992 and the advent of Sky TV meant that almost every match staged would appear on a channel somewhere, but that has not stopped supporters of Stockport feeling frustrated at the lack of focus given to them by the BBC.

The BBC have tended to focus on Premier League and FA Cup football in recent years, however as recently as November 2006 Stockport had still not been given appropriate coverage, as far as supporters were concerned on the channel. County fan Russell Griffin left the following message on the BBC Sport internet site on 9th November 2006:

"Given the formula for choosing games, my own team (Stockport County) can't have been far away from a live match as we are away to Exeter. Hope you can bear us in mind for future rounds if we get through - we are apparently the only league club never to have been featured in the lead game on Match of the Day! The closest we came was when we beat QPR in the third round in the early 90s but it still wasn't the lead game. There is an obvious news angle in featuring us as we are one of the very few clubs run by a supporters trust and are starting to hit form again after several years of decline."

The BBC responded that they were aware of Stockport's position and commented that they would like to feature them later in the competition, however they had featured Exeter against United a few years earlier and felt unable to feature the same club so soon. Perhaps neutrals would have preferred them to feature Manchester United and the other Premier League sides less.

Nowadays, all Premiership games tend to feature on Sky TV and the BBC, with Granada/ITV focusing on the Football League. Games tend to be selected more for their national appeal, although Granada does try to ensure all local League sides are covered. Inevitably, the larger sides tend to dominate, and when City were out of the Premiership during the late 1990s it brought a major boost to Granada, although it has to be remembered that ITV did have Premiership coverage for some of this period as well.

Inevitably, of all the clubs within the region United tend to be featured more on a national perspective. As well as domestic football the Reds tend to be ITV's preferred side for European coverage. The Reds have also created their own satellite television channel – MUTV.

In 2000 a new broadcaster entered the local television scene, Channel M. By 2006 Channel M were making inroads into sports coverage and the channel, broadcasting from the Urbis building in the city centre, created a City specific programme, Inside MCFC, and also introduced a show on FC United. It is believed this was the only show anywhere in the world on a non-league side and, although it inevitably focused on the new Reds, it did allow some of Manchester's other non-league sides to be featured. This was a significant boost for local football and an extremely positive step by the station.

By the start of the 2007-08 season Channel M were producing football debate shows, history shows, and a weekly programme focusing on all aspects of the game in the style of Granada's old Kick Off show.

As the new century progresses it seems clear that Channel M may take on the role of the region's leading football broadcaster from Granada. Channel M retains an identity and direction in keeping with the region's number one sport, while *Granada* has sadly taken on more of a national/international appeal, although clearly *Granada* still has more viewers, football rights and so on.

It is worth noting that there have been plenty of mentions of our sides in drama, documentary, comedy and other forms of television and film. These range from the use of Edgeley Park and Bower Fold in *Coronation Street* to films such as *Bend It Like Beckham* and *There's Only One Jimmy Grimble*.

FIRST APPEARANCES ON MATCH OF THE DAY

TEAM	DATE	RESULT	COMPETITION
United	5/9/1964	Fulham 2 United 1	Division One
City	5/2/1966	Bristol C 1 City 1	Division Two
Oldham	21/5/1966	Oldham 3 Oxford 0	Division Three
Bury	16/3/1968	Torquay 3 Bury 0	Division Three
Rochdale	16/11/1991	Gretna 0 Rochdale 0	FA Cup 1st round
Stockport		No main match appearances between 1964 and 1992	

MANCHESTER FILMS

It is widely held that prior to *Match of The Day* little footage of games involving local clubs had been seen, however throughout the research for this book significant footage of games involving most of our sides from several decades before the *BBC*'s main coverage began has been identified. These games were either filmed for cinema audiences as part of a news reel such as *British Movietone* or *Pathe News*, or for audiences in public houses and halls. The following list provides an indication of the earliest known footage featuring our local sides. If anyone knows of earlier, or more significant footage please contact the author care of the publishers.

EARLIEST SURVIVING MANCHESTER GAME FILMED:

Burnley V United, 6th December 1902

This Match was filmed by Sagar Mitchell and James Kenyon and was to be shown at the Burnley Mechanics Institute, however United won 2-0 and the footage was not shown until the *BBC* featured it as part of their series on Mitchell and Kenyon in 2005. The *BBC* proclaimed this as 'the oldest United footage' but the researchers at the National Fairground Archive are aware that many other games exist from the northwest and that some of the unidentified footage may show United/Newton Heath, or indeed any of the other local sides.

EARLIEST SURVIVING GAME FILMED IN MANCHESTER:

The Football League V The Irish League at Hyde Road, 14th October 1905

This Match was filmed by Sagar Mitchell and James Kenyon and was shown in Ardwick. The footage focused on the players taking to the field, and the crowd, as well as some match action. This has never been broadcast on television, but is an exceptionally brilliant study of football in the early years of the last century and provides a wonderful view of the old Hyde Road ground.

EARLIEST KNOWN CUP FINAL FEATURING A MANCHESTER REGION SIDE FILMED:
1903 F.A. Cup Final, Bury V Derby, 18/04/03

Although periods in this game were filmed, research has failed to find any surviving footage from the match. Similarly the 1904 FA Cup final between City and Bolton was filmed and shown in Manchester in the days that followed, but no trace survives. The author would be delighted to hear from anyone who possesses any actual footage of either game. Copies may possibly have resided in Bury & Derby or Manchester & Bolton in the years that followed.

EARLIEST CUP FINAL FEATURING A MANCHESTER SIDE BROADCAST LIVE ON TELEVISION: The 1948 FA Cup final, United V Blackpool, 24/04/48

The first final televised live on the BBC was in 1937, and United were the first of our local sides to appear in the final after this date.

FIRST FA CUP FINAL BROADCAST ON BOTH *BBC* & *ITV*:
The 1956 FA Cup final, City V Birmingham City, 5/5/56

Both *ABC* (*ITV* weekend franchise holder) & *BBC* broadcast the game live.

EARLIEST LEAGUE CUP FINAL FEATURING A MANCHESTER SIDE BROADCAST ON TELEVISION: The 1962 League Cup final (2nd leg), Norwich V Rochdale, 1/5/62

It does not appear as if the first leg of this final was filmed, but the second leg was televised by *Anglia TV* in East Anglia. Interestingly, *Angli*a's record of the coverage says:

> *"Norwich win the League Cup on 4 goal aggregate. Rochdale doing most of the attacking. Hill shoots - saved by Milburn. Good view of crowd. Hill scores for Norwich. Hill shoots - Milburn again clears. Presentation of trophy to skipper Ron Ashman from Mr Len Shipman, of the Football League Management Committee. Team posing with their trophy."*

This appears to be the oldest surviving footage of a Rochdale game, although it is likely there was an earlier Rochdale game filmed.

EARLIEST SURVIVING VIEWABLE MAINE ROAD GAME:
Billy Meredith's Benefit Match, Meredith's XI V Rangers & Celtic XI, 29/04/25

An extremely poor quality film survives of a match featuring Meredith at Maine Road. The game is definitely not a City match, although it does feature Frank Roberts and Charlie Pringle, and is attended by a significant crowd. The footage concentrates on Meredith pre-match, and also shows the Kippax and the Platt Lane end. For much of the action, the camera is placed close to the Platt Lane goal.

Although the footage is officially recorded as "Meredith 1926", it is definitely not from 1926.

EARLIEST SURVIVING VIEWABLE GIGG LANE GAME:
Bury V West Ham United, Division Two, 2/04/23

West Ham and Bury were challenging for promotion (West Ham succeeded, Bury had to wait until 1924) and this game was filmed by *Gaumont*. West Ham won 5-2, but the following year interest in Bury must have been high as on 21st August 1924 Gaumont also released footage of Bury in training, and on 30th August 1924 they filmed Bury V City – the Shakers first game back in Division One.

EARLIEST SURVIVING VIEWABLE STOCKPORT GAME: Stockport V South Manchester, 3/05/24
Little footage of Stockport exists but this game has survived.

EARLIEST SURVIVING VIEWABLE OLD TRAFFORD GAME:
Bradford City V Newcastle United, FA Cup final replay 1911
This excellent footage shows a relatively new Old Trafford and includes the presentation of the Cup. It is believed footage from United V Newcastle 15/10/10 exists, though at the time of going to press this has not been verified.

EARLIEST SURVIVING VIEWABLE BOUNDARY PARK GAME:
Oldham V Tottenham Hotspur, FA Cup 3rd round, 14/01/33
This footage shows good quality images of the 6-0 defeat watched by 16,662.

EARLIEST SURVIVING VIEWABLE OLDHAM ATHLETIC GAME:
Brighton & HA V Oldham, FA Cup 1st round, 8/01/21
This *Gaumont* footage shows Oldham defeated 4-1 at Brighton.

FIRST MANCHESTER GAME TELEVISED: United V Blackpool, 1948 FA Cup Final

FIRST CITY GAME TELEVISED: City V Newcastle, F.A. Cup Final, 7/5/55
City lost 3-1 but this was the first City game broadcast live on television.

FIRST MAINE ROAD GAME TELEVISED: City V Wolves, Division One, 15/12/56
This was Trautmann's first game back following his cup final injury and was screened on *BBC TV*'s *Sports Special* programme. It does appear however that at least one of United's European Cup games played at Maine Road in 1956-7 may have been televised.

FIRST OLD TRAFFORD GAME TELEVISED: United V Real Madrid, European Cup, 25/4/57
This was the European Cup semi final and was shown on *ITV*.

GRANADA TV'S FIRST OUTSIDE BROADCAST:
The 1956 victorious homecoming by City, 7/5/56
Granada TV started broadcasting on 3rd May 1956 and took the opportunity, the following Monday to test out their new outside broadcast equipment. They filmed part of City's FA Cup homecoming.

ABC (North) TV'S FIRST BROADCAST: The 1956 FA Cup final, 5/5/56
ABCTV started broadcasting from Didsbury a few minutes before the FA Cup final and this was their very first television broadcast in the north of England.

FIRST MANCHESTER DERBY FILMED: United 0 City 1, Division One, 7/9/1912
The French company *Pathe Journal* have 19 seconds worth of footage of a Manchester game from 1912. From viewing the section available it appears, though it is not conclusive, that this is the September 1912 derby match. The game is clearly at Old Trafford, and shows what appears to be a City corner. A man looking like Bill Eadie (City) is filmed close to the touchline.

FIRST MANCHESTER DERBY ON MATCH OF THE DAY: City 0 United 0, Division One, 17/8/68
The League Champions against the European Cup holders.
FIRST LIVE MANCHESTER DERBY: City 1 United 1, Division One, 26/10/86
The first derby of Jimmy Frizzell's reign and the last of Ron Atkinson's period at United. The match ended in a 1-1 draw. *ITV* televised the match.

FIRST LIVE LEAGUE GAME ON *SKY TV*: City V QPR, Premier League, 17/8/92
This was the first Monday night League match broadcast live on *Sky TV*. City Chairman Peter Swales was delighted with the contract agreed with the satellite company and was keen to see City play a prominent role in televised soccer. Dancing girls, live music, 'Red Devils' parachutists and fireworks greeted this momentous occasion. City drew 1-1 on a cold, dark night in Manchester.

RADIO

When talking of radio's coverage of Manchester football most people tend to think of the local stations *Radio Manchester* and *Magic 1152*, and both of those stations can trace their coverage of football back to the early 1970s. However, Manchester's role in football broadcasting stretches back to almost the beginning of radio in the Country.

The very first FA Cup final to be broadcast live on radio was City's 1926 final against Bolton. This was broadcast on the *BBC* but was not a national broadcast with the game being relayed to public halls in Bolton and Manchester as a test. The following year's cup final became the first true radio broadcast, and by the time a Manchester side next appeared in the final (City V Everton, 1933) cup final broadcasting was a regular occurrence.

Locally, the *BBC* first broadcast in 1922 as Manchester station *2ZY*, and this was transmitted from the Metropolitan Vickers Electricity works in Old Trafford, and during the 1930s football coverage developed via the *BBC*, however a local football focus did not come until the arrival of *Radio Manchester* and *Piccadilly Radio* in the 1970s.

Radio Manchester first broadcast on 10th September 1970 and used football to help identify its role in Mancunian society, and then on 2nd April 1974 *Piccadilly* first broadcast. From the start *Piccadilly* was keen to be a livelier and more modern station. It focused on music and sport with Tom Tyrrell taking on the role of Sports Editor. At the beginning of the 1975-76 football season the radio station published a *Soccer Annual*. In that annual Tom Tyrell, who was also the United reporter, gave his view on the first year of *Piccadilly* sport:

"When I was first appointed Sports Editor, I decided that while the most important clubs for us were the two Manchester clubs, we had also to cater for our listeners in Bolton and Oldham, in Bury and Rochdale, over in Stockport, even in Altrincham, Macclesfield and in Wigan, where soccer isn't big league, but is certainly big time.

"I lined up a team of reporters, and tried to maintain a regular man at each ground for many different reasons, but mainly so that the fans could identify with your own reporter. Brian Clarke is responsible for coverage of Manchester City;Tony Pullein looks after the Southern end of the fixture list whenever our clubs are playing down that way;Jim Hancock goes off to Gigg Lane to follow the Shakers; Henry Matthews looks after Oldham Athletic, and Peter Keeling sees that Bolton Wanderers fans have something to smile about on a Saturday. Matt Proctor has also turned his hand to soccer, with games ranging from Rochdale and Stockport to City and United's away games. We've been to Wigan and Altrincham for Cup games, but rely on local journalists to keep us informed of the weekly action in the Northern Premier League."

On Saturdays Piccadilly Sport, lasting over four hours, was hosted by Andy Peebles and Tom Tyrell on alternate weeks. In addition, Tyrell also hosted Soccer Special from Old Trafford – a programme aimed at entertaining fans in the stadium as well as those listening to the station. When City was at home Vince Miller would host the show from Maine Road.

Piccadilly brought a much more entertaining and lively approach to the game and by the late 1980s their Saturday coverage was by far the best in the region. By that time the studio host of Piccadilly Sport was James H Reeve. Reeve remembers this time as a very enjoyable one:

"When Radio Manchester came along in 1970 suddenly the local sides started to get proper radio commentary. Radio Two, I think, had provided match commentary of City and United for some time, but not every week and not from a local perspective, so Manchester gave us all something local. Then when Piccadilly came along its whole image was a bit more irreverent and the station became popular and it knocked Manchester back a bit. Manchester was always a sort of serious 'establishment' view and it didn't quite establish a style that suited most Mancunians.

"The very nature of independent radio encouraged a more popular style and football was key. By the time I was working there I'd been doing the late night phone-in and they asked me if I'd have a go at sport.

Phone in - and speak to the Doc!

I'm a City fan so I was keen and said I'd have a go. Anyway, I managed to get away with waffling on about football for a few weeks and then they said that I was going to double-head it with someone else. It turned out to be Tommy Docherty. The Doc had already been given his chance not long after his dismissal at United by **Piccadilly**. *That was a bold move because the Docherty story [Docherty had an affair with the physio's wife at United, but later married her] at the time was highly controversial and* **Piccadilly** *took a gamble. It shows you how the world has changed – Ron Atkinson was on dictionary corner [***Countdown***] the other week and no one even mentioned his fall from grace.*

"Anyway, I used to joke on the show that I didn't want to work with a Red, but it was a great time. I'd met him once a few years before we started working together when I gave him the V sign when he pulled up next to me at the traffic lights in Sale! I hoped he didn't remember me. Anyway, with Tom and me the banter just worked. We didn't plan it or anything we just got on with it. I used to call him Docherty in a public school way and we had a great rapport.

"As time went on we developed the show into a sort of performing troupe. It was a bit like **It Ain't Half Hot Mum**. *Every reporter had a part and an image. We gave the impression Brian Clarke was 'round the bend'. John Gwynne had a ringmaster's sort of voice so we played a long with that. Tom Tyrell was always Mr. Smooth so we'd try and undermine him and so on. I was surprised people took to it in the way they did and we used to get complimentary remarks and also friendly banter. We were fortunate that at that time United hadn't embarked on their great run of success, so both City and United were fairly even and that allowed us to focus on the positives and the negatives.*

"Actually, from a negative perspective my time at **Piccadilly Sport** *came around the time Margaret Thatcher or Colin Moynihan called football a 'social evil' and we'd had the problems at Heysel, and then the Hillsborough disaster. The issue from the Government was hooliganism, not safety, and when I was presenting the show I had this feeling that we were entering the final fro of football as a major sport. It really was a dark time for the game so we tried to lighten it, but we also tended to develop alongside the fanzine movement. We tried to cover the same issues that fanzines were highlighting and, more than any other station at that time, we were allowing fans to raise any issue and were trying to get the clubs to discuss them.*

"One of the peculiar aspects of the broadcasting agreements at the time was that at first we could do three score inserts per half of the match but during those inserts you could only summarise. You could not commentate. That was a definite no-no! Then when commentary was allowed that was also strictly controlled. It was agreed we could do second half commentary but we could not announce which game we would cover until after the start of the game in case it damaged the attendance.

"I used to bend the rules as much as possible. I'd try and announce it about twenty seconds before the start of the game, just as we were going up to the news. If the League found out they'd go mad and you would be in real danger of losing the licence. I tried to play it a little bit and at one point Tommy Docherty would do his bit in the studio with me and then we'd send him to a game for the commentary. So I used to make the odd comment like 'Docherty's heading off south more than that I cannot say' or 'we've just heard he's getting off the Mancunian Way going west'. Anyone listening would be able to guess that south meant City and west United and so on. It was still a major risk and the clubs themselves were expected to help police this. We had lots of discussions with people like Bernard Halford at City and he was adamant we could not say anything. Every time we took liberties he'd get worked up.

"We used to get calls and letters from people asking for a lift off Tom. He'd leave here relatively normal and by the time he'd driven twenty minutes to the ground he'd be a raving lunatic!

"From the ground the reporters had to use telephone lines and it was all fairly basic and the quality was poor. So our guys used to unscrew the mouthpiece of the old telephones and wire up our commentary kit with crocodile clips, but you couldn't let anybody see you do this because it was illegal and you would be made an example of. At the end of the game you'd have to screw it all back together again in case the telephone engineers spotted that you'd been tampering. Then ISDN lines came in and you had to pre-book them but these were limited at most clubs and regularly failed, so you'd have engineers crawling around as you started to broadcast.

"By the 1990s costs escalated and the show was always the most expensive to produce so new management tried to kill it off. It was a big mistake in some way because **Piccadilly Sport** *attracted people to the station and it was believed – but we couldn't prove it – that the show encouraged people to listen to* **Piccadilly** *at other times. The sport helped to develop an identity for the station.*

"John Pickford used to have to control everything and he did it exceptionally well because for almost every Saturday show something would go wrong at one of the grounds. Brian Clarke once arrived at Bournemouth and had left his broadcasting gear back in Manchester... others would be locked out. Tom Tyrell had a real problem once and we all made the most out of this because it was a great story, and I guess it showed the versatility of the station. He arrived at Stamford Bridge and there'd been some sort of mix up and there wasn't a ticket for him. He couldn't get in and there was nothing he could do. Anyway, he saw Alex Ferguson and he had a spare ticket, so Tom used that. But the ticket wasn't for a commentary position it was just for the stand, so one of Fergie's mates had a mobile 'phone – one of the early ones. It was like a brick. So Tom used it to do the score flashes.

*"Tom called us to do the flashes and because he was sat in a regular seat, every time he 'phoned you could hear some bloke giving him abuse, 'You northern ******'. For us in the studio it was getting funny, but for Tom it was a bit awkward to say the least. He must have said something to the bloke to try and get him to stay quiet, but it went the other way and when we went to Tom he started his summary and then*

Part of the GMR commentary team for the last Maine Road City-United derby in 2002-3. Arthur Albistion, Jimmy Wagg, Peter Barnes and Ian Cheeseman.

the other bloke started to get really nasty. There was a lot of noise and we could hear the crackle of the 'phone but didn't quite know what was going on. Next time we went for a score flash it turned out Tom had been chucked out for fighting! He was completely innocent, but the stewards just chucked a few of them out, including Tom. So then he stood by one of the gates, peeping through and was able to describe half the pitch.

"United had been losing but they equalised, so we went over to the Stamford Bridge car park to catch up with him and he said 'I was looking through the gate but when United started to attack a steward came and stood on the other side of the gate and has blocked my view!' It was great radio."

As football entered the 1990s **Piccadilly**'s sporting importance declined. Changes to local radio and various takeovers, restructures and so on caused the role of sports broadcasting to be questioned, however there were still some great moments. Reeve:

"When Oldham were fighting against relegation from the Premier League in 1993 there was a crucial game between Latics and Southampton, and in London Crystal Palace were playing Arsenal. So John Pickford arranged for us to take commentary from a London station – LBC I think – and we'd give them Oldham's commentary. It meant we could both switch and catch up on the other game. Oldham needed to win. Anyway I was back in the studio listening to both games – there was noise everywhere because we wanted to make sure we heard everything – anyway at one point Oldham were 'down' and Stuart Pike was commentating on Oldham and trying to sound positive. He was saying things like 'there's only one goal in it' and so on, but in truth everyone felt low. Then Arsenal scored against Palace! I signalled to John Pickford and he told Pikey 'two-nil Arsenal'. Pikey gave up on his sentence and screamed 'and Arsenal have scored' and at that moment Boundary Park erupted. We heard it through the speakers and it was a great, great feeling because we knew they'd all heard Pikey's commentary. It couldn't have been more than 2 seconds after we'd heard, and we felt fantastic because we felt we'd brought the news. You suddenly realise that you're part of something special."

This high was soon followed by a **Piccadilly** low as restructures affected the sporting heritage of the station:

*"We had a new chairman who came round to do a 'young Mr. Grace' and have a look around. He brought his daughter and chose to come on a Saturday afternoon. It was not the best time to come because you simply cannot predict what's going to happen. Anyway, they go into the control room and John Pickford's doing his best to act as tour guide and keep everything respectable. He's telling them of the number of reporters we've got; the variety of games we're covering and so on. All very impressive, then he starts giving examples of what we do... 'We have Stuart Pike and Tommy Docherty at Boundary Park and we can speak to them here... I'll demonstrate... Master Control to Boundary Park... Master Control to Boundary Park' and Pikey replies 'is that you John?' 'Yes, Master Control here' and Pikey immediately says 'John, you won't f***ing believe what's happened here'. John interrupts and tries to get Pikey to tone it down without giving away what's happening but Pikey's carrying on 'Tommy Doc's just farted in the press box! They've had to clear the place. It's F***ing disgusting!' John's trying to talk over him, but the damage was done."*

Piccadilly's influence waned and by 2007 the station had undergone a number of changes but was now branded as ***Magic 1152*** and football once again played a key part in its broadcasting schedule, while the local **BBC** station had also established itself as a major provider of football coverage. Hosted by Jimmy Wagg, *Radio Manchester*'s matchday football show provides many of the elements that made *Piccadilly*'s sporting name. A regular phone-in with a variety of players and coverage of the region's major sides, plus lower division teams, ensures a strong sporting identity.

FANZINES

During the 1980s when football was at a low, supporters were perceived by the media as being 'a problem'. The view often expressed in the media was that fans were all hooligans and that they had to be controlled and in some cases eradicated all together. Threats appeared in official publications warning supporters that they would be punished and so on. Old Trafford was the first ground to introduce perimeter fencing during the mid 1970s, while the Manchester City match programme for a game against Coventry in 1985 talked of perimeter fencing being increased to a ridiculously high level if fans did not behave – the truth was that fans had invaded the pitch to celebrate at the end of a couple of games and City did not want to pay the fines being threatened. These were not acts of hooliganism, but that is the way fans were being viewed.

The disasters at Bradford (fire) and Heysel (violence) in 1985 caused supporters to react against the views being expressed by the Government and footballing authorities and a new culture started to appear. Those attending games knew the truth about fan behaviour and knew there were problems, but they also knew that there was a significant gap between what the authorities felt and what the fans experienced. Television and official publications tended to focus on either the glamour of the game, or the grime, but never portrayed the sport as fans experienced it.

During the mid to late eighties all that changed and a fanzine culture developed. Fanzines are unofficial publications and during the eighties they were perceived as a major threat to established publications and the leading footballing figures. Dave & Sue Wallace were the founders of City's *King of the Kippax* fanzine which began during City's Second Division days of the 80s but continues to this day. Sue:

"When we began the Club did all it could to stop us. I think Peter Swales viewed us as a serious issue and I think he associated us with all that was bad about fans – he didn't seem to understand that we were trying to give supporters their voice. Through fanzines supporters could say what they really felt. Officially we were not welcome, but inevitably a lot of City's own staff bought the fanzine and agreed with what was written. One official at the club used to send someone out to buy it every issue until we started sending him a freebie!"

The same situation existed at most clubs and ultimately fanzines themselves became a regular feature of the matchday experience for fans. The first publication recognised as a football fanzine was *Foul*, which ran from 1972 - 1976. Locally, almost all of our teams were featured at some point with Peter Swales, City's Chairman from 1973 to 1993, even taking part in an interview. However *Foul* was not to last and was only a stepping stone on the way to the real fanzine explosion of the eighties.

In March 1986 *When Saturday Comes*, a national fanzine, was produced after a few club based publications, most notably the *City Gent* (Bradford City), had already appeared. This encouraged fans throughout Britain to focus on getting their views heard and by 1989 the following local fanzines existed:

City

Blue Print
Electric Blue
King of the Kippax

United

Red Issue
Red News

By the mid 1990s this list grew to include:

Bury

Where were you at the Shay?

City

Blue Print
The City Set
Citizen
Electric Blue (later renamed Bert Trautmann's Helmet)
King of the Kippax
Main Stand View
Out of the Blues
Purple Reign
Singing The Blues
This Charming Fan
True Blue

United

By the Swords United
Celtic United News (combined with Celtic fans)
Cula Review (combined with Celtic fans)
Echoes From Old Trafford
Hell Fire Club
In League With the Devils
Independent View
The K Stand
Man U Magic
Northern Exposure
Our Day Will Come (combined with Celtic fans)
Red Attitude
The Red Devil
Red Issue
Red News
The Shankhill Skinhead
There's Only One United
Tiocfaidh ar la (combined with Celtic fans)
United We Stand
Walking Down The Warwick Road

Oldham

Beyond The Boundary
Boundary Bulletin
The Exploding Latics Inevitable

Rochdale

The 92nd Club
The Dark Blues
Exceedingly Good Pies

Stockport

1-0 County
County Calling
No More Pie In The Sky (also covers Notts County)
The Tea Party

Mossley

Stuffed Like A....

It is also worth mentioning that some other clubs' fanzines referred to our teams in their titles. These include the Preston fanzine ***Hyde! Hyde! What's The Score?*** and the Peterborough United fanzine ***Blue Moon*** which was originally known as ***Blue Moon is a Man City song for F**k sake***.

Many other fanzines have emerged over the years in the region, and by the late 1990s the influence of the fanzines was clear, as they had helped to successfully fight the imposition of ID cards and encouraged some clubs to open up a little. At United the fanzines had formed part of the campaign against Rupert Murdoch's potential takeover of the club, while at City they had positively supported the campaign to remove Peter Swales as Chairman. That also led to City appointing a 'fan on the board' and this was ***King of the Kippax***'s Dave Wallace, although it proved a difficult task representing all fans. In addition, Wallace was only able to attend certain sections of Board meetings and was not consulted on issues, which fans would have felt strongly about (for example the appointment of Alan Ball – five seconds with Wallace would have made the Board realise this would be a difficult one to sell to fans).

At United the formation of FC United of Manchester has come about mainly through figures associated with Reds' fanzines, proving the value of using the movement to create a voice and action.

Sadly, the new century was to see the demise of many fanzines as the internet, blogging, and a general fan-friendly approach from some areas of the media led to many fanzines calling it a day. In addition, many of the people who had been involved with the fanzine movement when it first began had also become part of the established media – whether this was a positive move proving the media's approach had changed or a negative move showing that the writers themselves had succumbed to the established style of writing is open to debate.

One fanzine which found itself unable to continue was Stockport County's popular 'zine **The Tea Party**. In 2001 editor Dave Espley decided the 100th issue would be the last. The fanzine, named via a loose link with "Alice In Wonderland" (the Mad 'Hatter'), began in 1991. At the time of the fanzine's demise Espley told the **Stockport Express**:

"It has been a thoroughly enjoyable ten years both as a County fan and as editor of **The Tea Party**. *Apart from winning promotion and reaching the semi-finals of the Coca-Cola Cup, the highlight was probably the FA Cup victory over Queens Park Rangers in 1994. It put us on the footballing map and gave us some great national media coverage.*

"On the down side, the club actually tried to get us banned for breaking street trading regulations in 1993. After doing some research, we found out that magazines and newspapers were exempt from that piece of legislation.

"The magazine has been looking a bit stale for a while, partly due to the falling number of regular contributors. While still representing far better value and being a far better read than any other County publication, it has become a bit repetitive. It seems as though the magazine is drawing to a natural halt. The fact is that sales are down to a level which means they occasionally do not cover the costs. I have always said that when that happened I would stop. I am extremely grateful to the loyalty from readers over the years. They are clearly intelligent people who realise that supporting a football club is about more than blind devotion to every aspect of the club's administration."

In 2008 many local fanzines still exist including the well established **Red Issue**, **United We Stand** and **King of The Kippax,** however internet forums have tended to dominate fan culture in recent years. Dave Wallace:

"At **King of the Kippax** *we continue to offer an outlet to all fans and we try to ensure we represent as many supporters as possible. Amazingly though, after around twenty years, we're still getting people asking us 'is that the programme?' Sometimes you wonder how fanzines have been missed by some fans."*

The fanzine culture forced clubs to change and allowed supporters to gain a voice. From a Mancunian perspective that was a very important achievement.

CHAPTER TWENTY-EIGHT

THE MANAGERS

Every manager should have a hobby. Mine is Soccer!

Sir Matt Busby, 1968

THE following is a list of the region's significant trophy winning managers. It excludes the Charity Shield, European Super Cup and similar, but does include all divisions of the Football League and the Premier League, the FA Cup, League Cup, European Cup, UEFA Cup, and ECWC. Had any of our sides won the Associate Members' Cup or Full Members' Cup then they would also have been included. Similarly the list does not include runners-up in cup or league competitions, nor promotions other than division winning promotions.

Inevitably, some of these managers have achieved considerably more than the following table suggests. Joe Royle, for example, won only one championship (Oldham in 1991) but he also took Oldham to the 1990 League Cup final, and guided City to back to back promotions in 1999 and 2000. Likewise Stockport's Danny Bergara achieved a considerable amount during his six years at County, including promotion from Division Four and two Wembley appearances, but he fails to appear in the table because his side did not finish first in their division, nor did they win a trophy. From a County perspective his achievements should always rank highly.

Where two or more managers have won the same number of trophies these have been listed according to stature of competition (Europe, Premier/Div One League, FAC, League Cup, then each division in turn). If the success achieved was equivalent then the managers have been listed in date order (for example Tom Maley and Tommy Docherty). This table is correct at the time of going to press and does not include 2007-8 season.

Please note: The 'Trophies per playing season' figure has been calculated by dividing the number of trophies by the number of seasons. If the manager has only won trophies at one club then the calculation has been performed only on the service at that club (for example Ernest Mangnall's record only considers the years he was at United).

Manager	Team(s)	No of Significant Trophies	Trophies	Trophies per playing season
Alex Ferguson	United (1986 -)	18	European Cup, ECWC, 9 Premier League, 5 FAC & 2 League Cup	0.86
Matt Busby	United (1945-69)	8	European Cup, 5 League Championships & 2 FACs	0.33
Joe Mercer	City (1965-71)	5	ECWC, FAC, League Cup, League Championship & Div 2 Championship	0.83
Ernest Mangnall	United (1903-12) & City (1912-24)	3	2 League championships & 1 FAC	0.33
Wilf Wild	City (1932-46)	2	FAC & League Championship	0.26
Harry Hamer*	Bury (1887-1907)	2	2 FAC	0.1
Ron Atkinson	United (1981-86)	2	2 FACs	0.4
Tom Maley	City (1902-06)	2	FAC & Div 2 Championship	0.5
Tommy Docherty	United (1972-77)	2	FAC & Div 2 Championship	0.4
Les McDowall	City (1950-63) & Oldham (1963-65)	1	FAC	0.08
Tony Book	City (1974-79)	1	League Cup	0.2
Albert Duckworth*	Bury (1892-95)	1	Div 2 Championship	0.33
Sam Ormerod	City (1895-1902) & Stockport (1903-05)	1	Div 2 Championship	0.14
Harry Newbould	City (1906-12)	1	Div 2 Championship	0.17
Peter Hodge	City (1926-32)	1	Div 2 Championship	0.17
'Archie' Scot Duncan	United (1932-37)	1	Div 2 Championship	0.2
Sam Cowan	City (1946-47)	1	Div 2 Championship	1
Joe Royle	Oldham (1982-94) & City (1998-2001)	1	Div 2 Championship	0.08
Kevin Keegan	City (2001-05)	1	Div 1 (old Div 2) Championship	0.25
Albert Williams	Stockport (1919-24)	1	Div 3 (N) Championship	0.2
Bob Kelly	Stockport (1936-38)	1	Div 3 (N) Championship	0.5
George Hardwick	Oldham (1950-56)	1	Div 3 (N) Championship	0.17
Dave Russell	Bury (1953-61)	1	Div 3 Championship	0.13
Jimmy Frizzell	Oldham (1970-82) & City (1986-87)	1	Div 3 Championship	0.08
Stan Ternent	Bury (1995-98)	1	Div 2 (old Div 3) Championship	0.33
Jimmy Meadows	Stockport (1966-69) & (1974-75)	1	Div 4 Championship	0.33

* The early careers of Bury's secretary-managers are not entirely clear. Some sources quote secretary Harry Hamer as the guiding figure throughout the period 1887-1907 while others say that Albert Duckworth had sole responsibility for team matters during the promotion season of 1894-95. Others say that team matters were decided by a three man committee which saw

MR. H. S. HAMER.
Mr. H. S. Hamer is probably one of the best known club secretaries in the North of England. He took a leading part in the agitation which culminated in fixing the wages limit for professionals. At home he is universally esteemed as a man thoroughly conversant with his business, and with the best interests of the club at heart.

Duckworth take a lead role. For the purposes of this table Duckworth has been recorded as the main 'manager' for the promotion season, while Hamer takes the title for the FA Cup successes.

Hamer was appointed Bury Secretary in November 1887 and it was a position that, apart from one season, he held for the following 26 years. Recognised by Bury historians as a 'shrewd and knowledgeable man' Hamer was one of the club's most influential figures,. He helped the side develop and grow, and of course become the region's first truly successful side. Sadly, after 27 years continuous service to the club, he died on 21st December 1913. Almost two years alter his son, Frank Hamer, took over the role (he had previously been assistant secretary). Later he became the club's financial secretary and, like his father, dedicated much of his life to the Bury cause.

Looking at the other managers recorded above, it is worth noting that the only manager to date with a one trophy per season record is Sam Cowan. Cowan was City's manager for less than a season (2nd December 1946 to 30 June 1947) and arrived at the Blues when they were fourth in Division Two and some have suggested the Blues would have won promotion that season regardless of Cowan's involvement, but the manager himself disputed that:

"When I came on 2nd December to the club they were fourth in the table and an indifferent side. They won 22 games on the run and made promotion to the First Division virtually safe. No matter what anybody connected with the club might say, I have not been a failure."

Cowan was dismissed as, due to family commitments, he remained living at Hove, near Brighton, and travelled to Manchester during the week to carry out his duties. The directors felt more was needed from their manager and they tried to insist he moved to Manchester, but he refused.

Sadly, Cowan's departure was not a good one for City. The former captain's appointment had been made as an attempt to counter the attraction of Matt Busby's United. Busby, a former Blue FA Cup winner, was

Future managers Matt Busby and Sam Cowan are joined by Eric Brook on a training session at Maine Road during their time as City players in the 1930s.

a popular player and many City fans had begun following United (remember they were also playing at Maine Road) as they wanted to see Busby successful. Cowan was by far a more popular City player, and his appointment seemed perfect – crowds had grown under Cowan with the increase bringing an average a little short of 40,000 (some 4,000 more than the Championship winning season of 1937).

The following sections provide biographical detail on each of the managers who have guided their sides to the English championship (Football League pre 1992 & Premier League since 1992) from our region. We start with the only man to manage both City and United, Ernest Mangnall.

MANAGER PROFILE

JAMES ERNEST MANGNALL

Born: Belmont, Bolton, 1866 **Died:** 13th January 1932

Ernest Mangnall was the first man to bring United trophy success – with a side containing the key members of the Blues 1904 FA Cup triumph – and was also credited with being instrumental in United's move from Bank Street, Clayton (roughly where the Velodrome is close to the City Of Manchester Stadium) to Old Trafford.

Prior to joining the Reds he had been a director at Bolton Wanderers, and then after two years at Bolton, he moved on to Burnley Football Club where he took the role of secretary (27th December 1899 - 1903). Earlier he had been a noted amateur footballer, rugby player, boxer, swimmer, athlete and cyclist. According to the 1928 *History of the Lancashire Football Association*, he was still a record holder at various cycling events in the Bolton area, and he had cycled from Bolton to John O'Groats, then from John O'Groats to Land's End. He became the Honorary Secretary for Bolton Harriers and was well known as a cross country athlete.

Mangnall had been educated at Bolton Grammar School and, according to some sources, he played inside right for the school football team and then for their Old Boys' side. There is also evidence he played competitively at county level and it is believed he played in goal for a Lancashire FA trial game at Accrington against North Wales in July 1879. Lancashire won the match 2-1, and Mangnall is reported as appearing several times over the following years.

At United (September 1903 - August 1912), he managed to obtain the services of Billy Meredith and many of the other banned City stars for relatively small sums of money, and with the City men he brought United 2 League Championships – the first ever won by a Manchester region side - and the F.A. Cup. Without Mangnall's recruitment of these men it is highly unlikely United would have achieved any form of success during this period. United fans should remember Mangnall as their first greatest manager, especially as he had transformed the club following their collapse in 1902.

In 1906 the *Manchester Evening News* wrote a profile of him and included:

"For a team to be successful a good secretary is almost as necessary as a good centre-forward, and

Manchester United are fortunate to possess a gentleman of the ability of Mr. J.E Mangnall. Only those who are acquainted with the inner workings of the club can have any conception of the important duties he has been called upon to fulfil, and the fact that since Mr. Mangnall took office the period has been one of steady and continuous progress is sufficient testimony of his ability. Careful to a degree, Mr. Mangnall is yet one of the most keen and enthusiastic sportsmen connected with the game, and by his tact and unfailing courtesy he has done much for the club. His extensive knowledge of the game and its players has been placed unsparingly before his employers, and as a judge of players he has few superiors. Upon Mr. Mangnall fall the duties of secretary and manager, and during his three years' connection with the club he has proved himself a model official. The esteem in which he is held by the players was shown last Saturday when he received a most flattering reception on rising to receive one of the promotion medals."

In addition to this fantastic record on the pitch Mangnall is recognised as one of the key figures behind the development of Old Trafford. In those days the secretary-manager was responsible for many of the off field activities as well as playing matters and Mangnall would have found the period 1909-1910 difficult as the Reds move to their new ground was delayed and, due to financial restrictions, even scaled down.

Mangnall ultimately fell out with the directors at Old Trafford within the first two years at the new ground. Whether this was over finance, ambition, or interference is not clear but as the Reds were still struggling to pay off the debts created by the move to Old Trafford it seems he simply saw more opportunity at City. Billy Meredith, still a United man at this time, wrote openly of his admiration for his former boss:

"The Manchester United team will, of course, greatly miss Ernest Mangnall, who has left to manage Manchester City. Even though he and the Directors of Manchester United have not agreed on a number of matters, there is no doubt that Ernest Mangnall was a very fine manager. No man in the Country, except perhaps Will Cuff of Everton, could have run such a club with so much success on so low a cost. I should say that Mr. Mangnall and Mr. Cuff stand alone in the managerial world. Mr. Mangnall is about the best judge of a player serving a club in England. Apart from that, the new Manchester City manager knows how to buy and sell at the best profit to his own club. He should do well at Hyde Road. If he succeeds he will probably make enemies, because it is well known that he is to have a free hand. I know him, and I feel confident that he will not be content until the club is run at a big profit."

Mangnall arrived at Hyde Road in 1912 but the most incredible aspect of his arrival was the way it was carried out. Mangnall had been United's leader since 1903 and had achieved so much while there that no one could ever have expected him to move. However, City were still regarded as the region's more popular club, and so there was a perception that Mangnall could achieve even more with the Blues.

Never before had a manager left a major club for its biggest rivals after so much success, but what made the story more of a sensation was the fact Mangnall had agreed to become City manager while still in office at Old Trafford, and that he had watched City's opening game at Notts County when he was supposed to be with United at Arsenal. As City did not formally have a secretary-manager on that day it is believed he actually helped the directors select the side and carry out other duties. The Blues won the game 1-0 while 'his' United side drew 0-0 at Arsenal, and then five days later he was still in charge of United for the Manchester derby of 7th September 1912 at Old Trafford.

Some historians dispute that Mangnall was officially United's manager on the day of the derby, but leading newspapers of the period, most notably the **Umpire** and the **Daily Dispatch**, are perfectly clear that he was officially in charge. City won the Old Trafford match 1-0 despite being down to ten men for most of the game. Mangnall, according to one report, was delighted with the City win despite, officially at least, still being a red. *"United speeded their manager rejoicing with two points to his new club"* read one article.

The following Monday Mangnall moved into his office at Hyde Road, and within a few weeks his new side were looking like Championship contenders:

"Manchester City stand out boldly as the only first class team in the two divisions of the League, the Southern and the Scottish Leagues, with the highest possible points to their credit. The Citizens of Manchester have earned every point in September. Other clubs have remained undefeated, but they have not annexed the maximum marks. Nine years have passed since Manchester City commenced a campaign in this stimulating style."

The title did not arrive, however Mangnall did develop a decent-looking side by the time of the First World War. In fact the Blues were proving a highly popular side to watch, so much so that the ground could hardly cope. A notorious cup match with Sunderland in February 1913 had to be abandoned due to overcrowding. Incredibly – and this is difficult to appreciate today – the team manager was also responsible for the management of the ground at this time and so Mangnall was held responsible for all matters concerning safety and crowd control as well as picking the team and buying the players. One reporter 'Veteran' accused Mangnall of spending too much time with the team and said:

"I am rather surprised at Mr. Mangnall being caught napping, but it may be that he has been away with the team and had had little to do with the home management."

The Blues finished fifth in Division One at the end of the 1914-5 season. During the hostilities he kept the club alive and brought some trophy success in the wartime tournaments that replaced the League.

After the war, Mangnall's side became very popular and he had to focus on ground issues as well as team matters. As secretary-manager Mangnall was held totally responsible for all activities at Hyde Road and, with the Blues filling the 40,000 capacity on a regular basis, Mangnall regular had to face the press, the FA, the Football League, the council, and the police to explain why chaotic scenes were being experienced game after game in the streets around the ground.

In 1920 fire destroyed the Main Stand and exacerbated the problems Mangnall faced. He approached his former club United about using Old Trafford but they met his request with terms that were ridiculed in the press. Perhaps they still felt a little aggrieved about his departure almost a decade earlier. Mangnall's view was that City had to move from Hyde Road. Its forty thousand capacity was far too small, and the manager worked with club officials, most notably another former City manager Lawrence Furniss, to plan the development of a new ground. For many years the Blues had looked at moving to Belle Vue, and it is believed Mangnall was the man who changed the club's thinking. A move to Belle Vue would have been the safe option but it would not have offered the club the same potential as a move to Maine Road could. At the same time as these debates, Mangnall guided the Blues to second place in the League and their popularity increased further.

By the start of 1921-22 far too many people were missing out on watching City, and the ground move was still occupying much of his time. Then in 1922 he announced that City would be creating an "English Hampden" on the Moss Side/Rusholme border.

In 1923 City moved to Maine Road, and in Mangnall's final season (1923-4) he almost managed to guide City to the FA Cup Final. With the 49 year old Billy Meredith back in Mangnall's side, City were defeated by Newcastle. That run was important as it perhaps demonstrated the reason why Mangnall had been determined to join the Blues back in 1912 for his City side attracted a few magnificent attendances including over 76,000 for a cup tie with Cardiff. At the time this was the largest crowd for any footballing fixture played in Manchester including three FA Cup finals. Mangnall knew City's strengths and after 13 years in charge he must have felt a great deal of satisfaction at seeing such a large crowd in the stadium he had pushed for.

The following May the directors surprisingly decided not to renew his contract. Although It seems likely he may well have chosen to step down, feeling that there was little more he could achieve at Maine Road. After leaving the Blues he became a director of his home town team, Bolton, and was a significant figure within the PFA. He died of a cerebral embolism in 1932 at St. Annes.

In addition to his roles at Burnley – his first club as secretary – United, City, and Bolton, he was also the man responsible for founding the Central League (1911, while secretary at United) and the Football Managers' Association. He also became an official of the Lancashire FA in 1918. Today, he remains one of the most influential football administrators of all time, and although most associate him with United he actually managed City for a longer spell. Items connected with his career, including his family scrapbook of Manchester City cuttings, are stored in the Manchester United museum archive at Old Trafford.

Modern day football rarely remembers men like Mangnall, however his place in the history of Manchester must always remain a significant one. He was United's first truly great manager, and he also restored pride and passion to the Blues. In addition, he was the key figure in the development of Old Trafford and of Maine Road, and instrumental in many other aspects of Mancunian footballing life.

MANAGER PROFILE
WILF WILD

Born: 1893 **Died:** 12th December 1950

Wilf Wild was one of Manchester's greatest managers and was only the second man to bring the League Championship to the region. He was City's longest serving manager and in terms of success remains Manchester's fifth most successful manager of all time, behind Ferguson, Busby, Mercer, and Mangnall. He was the first Manchester manager to win the FA Cup at Wembley.

He joined the Blues in 1920 as assistant secretary to United's first successful manager Ernest Mangnall, and it is clear he must have gained a great deal from him. At that time though, Wild assisted Mangnall mostly on the administrative side.

Although Wild was delighted with his role, he felt the responsibility which Mangnall had was too great and the assistant did more than most to ensure the responsibility for team matters and other administrative duties were split. Wild felt he could see a more productive way for the club to

Wilf Wild with the League Championship trophy in 1937.

develop and as time moved on he urged the club's directors to split the role of manager and secretary.

The big change coming in 1924 when Mangnall's contract was surprisingly not renewed. Wild worked with the directors to encourage a new approach, and former Oldham manager David Ashworth was appointed to look after team affairs while Wild focused purely on secretarial duties. At the time this was a novel – some would say revolutionary – approach.

From then on Wild helped to shape the two distinct roles, but Ashworth did not last long, and when his replacement Peter Hodge resigned in 1932 Wild was viewed by the directors as being more than capable of managing the two roles as one. It seems likely Wild would not have sought this approach, but he did agree to 'giving it a go'.

As anticipated Wild performed exceptionally well in the combined role, and in his first couple of seasons he guided City to consecutive FA Cup finals (winning in 1934). Interestingly, footage from the period leading up to the cup final shows all the players of the period training at Maine Road, and then flashes a few seconds of Wild who is stood close to the tunnel waving several pound notes at the camera. The scene was created to get the message across that Wild was a very busy man sorting out the game by game arrangements and did not have much time to train his side. Perhaps the idea to depict him in this way had come from Wild himself who still seemed keen on having the secretary-manager role split.

With Wild splitting his time between the two roles the club could hardly have complained if the side entered a period of mediocrity but instead his team became one of the leading forces in the game, and Wild seemed to possess a Midas touch. It should be noted that during 1934 Wild had responsibility for crowd control, safety issues, control of accounts and payment of wages, and Maine Road was undergoing a significant development programme which saw the erection of the Platt Lane Stand in 1935.

In 1936-7 he managed City to their first League Championship after selecting exceptionally talented players of the calibre of Alec Herd, Sam Barkas, Matt Busby, Peter Doherty, and Frank Swift. Despite the success Wild was also a victim of City's peculiar unpredictable streak when, the following year, the Blues were relegated. They remained a Division Two side until after the war, by which time Wild was determined to relinquish control of team affairs.

Former Captain Sam Cowan was recruited in December 1946 – it seems this was entirely Wild's idea - and Wild finally succeeded in his desire to see the roles of manager and secretary split for good. Sadly, Wild passed away in December 1950 while still the club's secretary. His wife Betty also worked at the club and she remained a popular presence through to her retirement in the 1960s. She later moved to Lytham St. Annes.

MANAGER PROFILE
SIR MATT BUSBY

Born: Orbiston, 26 May 1909 **Died:** Cheadle, 20 January 1994

Signed from Denny Hibernian on 11th February 1928 Matt Busby took some time settling at City. In fact, it's not the type of story City fans like to mention, but the Blues were responsible for Matt Busby making Manchester his home. The Busby family were planning on emigrating to Canada and only the efforts of the City management – and left back Phil McCloy who looked after him during a period of homesickness - caused those plans to be cancelled. Had Busby emigrated then clearly his managerial career would not have occurred.

Before that great managerial career commenced Busby was a noted player and did feature in two FA Cup finals with City. He was also very popular with supporters.

His City debut came in 1929, against Middlesbrough, and was the first of eleven appearances that season. Initially signed as an inside forward, over the course of the next couple of years City would convert him to a stylish half-back. Around the time of his debut Busby had actually been seen as a possible signing for the Reds. City manager Peter Hodge is alleged to have told them *"Give me £150 and he's yours."* The reply came back that United did not 'have 150 pennies, never mind pounds', and so Busby continued to make a name for himself at Maine Road.

In 1933 he appeared in the FA Cup final for the Blues and earned a Scottish cap against Wales. The following season he was a member of City's FA Cup winning side and at the start of the following season the *Topical Times Sporting Annual* announced its six sportsmen of the year with the leading footballer being Busby. The annual believed that he was the best right half back in Britain and claimed that his 'ball control is wonderful'. The article went on to stress his strengths and reminded its readers that Busby was at long last winning the kind of international recognition he deserved. Two years later the *Manchester Guardian* claimed:

"In Matt Busby, City have at best a player who has no superior as an attacking half-back."

Busby joined Liverpool for £8,000 from in March 1936 and was immediately made captain. He led the team with distinction but as with many players at the time found much of his career taken from him through the outbreak of war. Once the war ended he was offered a coaching role at Anfield but he had already agreed to take on the manager's role at United. Talking of Busby's time at Liverpool, Bob Paisley (Liverpool player and highly successful 70s and 80s manager) later said:

"He was a man you could look up to and respect. He'd played the game and people like him weren't solely tied down with tactics, which was a valuable lesson for me".

At United Busby found a side with a badly damaged ground, financial worries, and many other problems, but in his first season in charge he guided the Reds to second place in the League. It has often been said that Busby had no experience of management at this point and clearly that is true, however, he had taken on the lead role for many wartime matches he took part in. The likes of Joe Mercer, Frank Swift, Stan Cullis, and others collectively managed the Army, RAF, and representative sides during this period, and it is no coincidence that Mercer, Cullis, and of course Busby would become established as modern day managers/coaches by the end of the 1950s.

The following season he guided the Reds to their first major trophy since 1911, when they won the FA Cup by beating Blackpool. It was the first time United had played at Wembley Stadium and to many at the time it was the biggest success they had ever known. That summer he managed the British Olympic soccer side at the London Olympics, but more success was to follow for United as the years that followed saw the Reds challenge time and time again for the League title. The Championship eventually arrived in 1952.

After Busby guided the Reds to their second title under him in 1956 the club was invited to compete in the European Cup and, despite the desire of the English authorities, Busby guided his side into the competition. That season the Reds reached the semi-final stage, and also won the League Championship again.

Sadly the 1957-58 European campaign saw tragedy as the Munich Air Disaster decimated Busby's side, and almost cost the manager his own life. Much has been written about this period, but it has to be stressed how close Busby was to passing away. Inevitably, much of the period that followed saw Busby trying to rebuild United into a force.

In 1963 the Reds came close to relegation but managed to win the FA Cup and that triumph, against Leicester, seemed to convince many associated with the side that League success could follow again. The following season Busby's United were second to Liverpool, and then in 1965 they won the title on goal average from Don Revie's Leeds United.

An emotional return to the European Cup followed, with the Reds reaching the semi-final stage for their third successive appearance in the competition, and then Busby guided his side to another League success in 1966-67. This was followed by the winning of the European Cup at Wembley in 1968. After the success Busby told reporters:

"They've done us proud. They came back with all their hearts to show everyone what Manchester United are made of. This is the most wonderful thing that has happened in my life and I am the proudest man in England tonight."

It was a highly emotional night and much of the focus was on Busby himself. Less than a year later 59 year old Busby announced his retirement:

"It's time to make way for a younger man... a track-suited manager".

He claimed the pressures of managing a leading side were becoming too great for a man of his age, and he added that he would now take on the role of general manager. He told reporters:

"United is no longer just a football club. It is an institution. I feel the demands are beyond one human being."

Potentially, winning the European Cup had brought Busby his last remaining ambition, and maybe

Busby and Mercer caught in 1970 chatting over the garden gate.

he felt drained by the club's exploits over the previous decade. Sadly, the years that followed were not great for United, and as time progressed the achievements of Busby began to look even more special than perhaps they had felt at the time. Certainly, until the arrival of Alex Ferguson, United were unable to find the kind of continual success that Busby had created.

Another spell in charge of team affairs did follow at the end of 1970, but Busby ensured his direct involvement was brief. He recognised that it was time for someone else to lead the side. Later he became a director of the club, before passing away in 1994. United had become Champions for the first time since 1967 the season before his death.

Today there are several tributes to Busby around Manchester. There is Sir Matt Busby Way, the renamed Warwick Road on which Old Trafford is built, and a statue of him at the stadium itself, however the biggest memorial to the great United man is Manchester United itself. Without Busby it is highly debateable whether United would ever have become a powerful club, and the best attended in England. No man is bigger than United, however Busby's legacy is that United became a giant of a club.

■ MANCHESTER United will soon be unveiling a huge bronze statue in memory of Sir Matt Busby, which will have pride of place outside Old Trafford.

This will be the official tribute to the man regarded as the founding father of the club as we know it today, on the lines of the bust of Joe Mercer, which Manchester City have on show at Maine Road.

Both Joe and Sir Matt, wartime pals when they served together as physical training instructors and played in the same army team, were men of the people with a warmth which won them many friends.

MANAGER PROFILE
JOE MERCER, OBE

Born: Ellesmere Port, 9th August 1914 **Died:** Hoylake, 9th August 1990

City's most successful manager and the only manager to win five trophies in his first five seasons with a club from the Manchester region, Joe Mercer was already a major footballing figure prior to joining the Blues.

As a player Mercer won the Championship with Everton and Arsenal (twice), and also captained the Gunners to FA Cup success. He made his first England appearance shortly before the war and went on to captain his country. He was a model professional, and only stopped playing at the age of 39 when a collision resulted in a broken leg.

Both Evertonians and Arsenal fans still remember his playing days with affection and it is fair to say that at Arsenal Mercer was regarded as one of the greatest Gunners of all time. It is only really as a result of the side's recent successes that his name has slipped down the Arsenal list a little – in the late 1980s he was introduced on to the Highbury pitch as the best Gunner of all time. Once his playing days came to an end Arsenal fans urged the directors to appoint him as manager on several occasions. Ultimately he did move into management but not with the London club, although it is known he almost applied for the job but held back at the last minute.

His first managerial role was at Sheffield United where he inherited a struggling side. Inevitably, the Blades were relegated but Mercer struggled to take them back to Division One. They did reach sixth place in 1958 and were challenging in 1958-59 but Mercer had taken them just about as far as he could. In December he was offered the Aston Villa job and the prospect of working at one of the game's elite clubs (as Villa were perceived at the time) excited him.

Despite their history and heritage Villa were a struggling side and relegation followed in May 1959, however Mercer had anticipated this when he took the job, and the Board gave him time to push forward with his ambitious plans. As with his friend Busby at United, Mercer focused on youth, and within two seasons of the relegation his young side had found success winning the Division Two championship and the League Cup. City journalists and officials have often claimed he was a failed manager prior to arriving at City, but in terms of trophy success he had achieved more than most had prior to joining the Blues – the League Cup (plus another League Cup final), Second Division Championship, and two F.A. Cup semi-finals.

During his early managerial career he often hit the headlines for the bold, stylish, exciting football his sides played and many other teams showed interest in him. In the early sixties a media campaign demanded Mercer be made England team manager (after ex-Red Walter Winterbottom).

Mercer decided he was not ready for the post and chose not to apply. He did take on the role of under-21 boss though, when Alf Ramsey became England manager.

In the Sixties "Mercer's Minors" as Villa became known (the fifties had seen Cullis's Cubs at Wolves and of course the Busby Babes) demonstrated a very entertaining style of play and enjoyed several good cup runs. Unfortunately, pressure increased at Villa and by 1963 fans were desperate for Villa to win their first Championship since 1910. Mercer's relatively young side were still not ready for that and, as a result of the pressure, Mercer became ill. Eventually he suffered a stroke.

At Villa he had taken on too much – in addition to the playing side he was also a major player in the development of a new stand – and while he lay at home ill the Villa board decided to terminate his contract. Villa's loss was Manchester's gain.

After a year out of the game he joined the Blues in July 1965. His doctor had tried to dissuade him but admitted to Mercer's wife, Norah:

"He may as well die doing the job he loves, than sit at home and die of a broken heart."

Mercer decided to bring in a youthful coach and sought out Malcolm Allison, a young former West Ham player he had been impressed with at FA Coaching sessions. Mercer said around this time:

"The chance was irresistible. I knew that people had written me off. There were doubts about my health, but I had no lack of confidence about my ability. Allison was magnificent. I knew we had a chance with Manchester City. Although they were in the Second Division they were a club with a tradition and a ready-made public."

Promotion in 1966 – and a good FA Cup run - was followed in 1968 by the League Championship. The FA Cup followed, and then in 1970 he became the first person to guide an English side to a major European and domestic cup double.

With a fierce take-over battle (which eventually led to Peter Swales becoming chairman) forcing Mercer and Allison on to opposite sides in 1970, the following seasons were difficult. On 7th October 1971, two days after a League Cup defeat at Bolton, a three hour board meeting ended with City announcing that Allison was to be Team Manager with Mercer taking on a role as General Manager. It was clearly a compromise and one that never really succeeded. To many it was clear the former Everton player's time in Manchester was nearing its end

In June 1972, after the new board of directors had removed his car parking space and taken away his office, Mercer felt it was time to move on. It was a shabby way to treat the club's greatest manager and even today this period is one that embarrasses fans and shows the Blues in an exceptionally bad light. Mercer was treated appallingly by the new regime who believed Allison had brought all the success on his own. It is worth noting that City were only to win one major trophy (the 1976 League Cup) in the thirty years that followed.

Regardless of what the new Directors felt, the fans recognised Mercer's enormous contribution. Shortly after his departure the City Supporters' Club invited him to their annual ceremony and presented him with a silver tea service. It was a touching moment for Mercer, but for supporters too it was a key moment as it brought to an end the most glorious period in the club's history.

It is also worth noting that Mercer and Allison, as a partnership, were being lined up as successors to England manager Sir Alf Ramsey around the time of Mercer's departure from Maine

Road. Mercer was aware of the approach but Allison was not, and ultimately the end of the Mercer years at City not only ended City's period of glory, it also ended the prospect of Mercer & Allison managing England together.

After City Mercer joined Coventry with Gordon Milne, and won a manager of the month award, then in 1974 he took control of the England side on a caretaker basis. His brief period in charge helped bring new life and excitement into the national side. Entertainers such as Frank Worthington and quality players such as Kevin Keegan were given great opportunity to entertain and excite. It was a great summer, and Mercer was asked to continue on a permanent basis, but because of a painful back condition he declined feeling that he would not give England he felt they needed. It was a major shame that the Mercer-Allison partnership had ended prematurely in 1972 - surely the two men would have offered more to England than Don Revie managed.

After Mercer had put the fun back into English football, he became a Coventry City director until 1981 when he returned to Merseyside to retire. He kept involved with various footballing panels - young player awards, judging Spot the Ball etc. - and made a large number of journeys to Wembley and to Tranmere Rovers (his father's old club). Throughout the late 80s City supporters asked the club to appoint Mercer to a role worthy of his contribution. It was suggested he become club President by some fans and, for a while, Peter Swales said the club would approach their most successful manager. Mercer passed away peacefully in his favourite armchair in August 1990 on his 76th birthday after suffering with Alzheimer's in later life. Sadly, no official approach ever came from Peter Swales or City to welcome their old manager back.

Since the end of Peter Swales reign as City Chairman the Blues have welcomed Mercer's widow, Norah, to the club, and during 2007-08 she was a popular presence on matchday at the stadium. The last decade or so has seen a Joe Mercer Suite opened at Maine Road; a street was named after him at the City of Manchester Stadium, and in 2005 two outstanding mosaics of Mercer were unveiled on Joe Mercer Way at Eastlands.

MANAGER PROFILE
SIR ALEX FERGUSON

Born: Govan, 31 December 1941

Alex Ferguson became United manager in November 1986 after finding success as manager in Scotland. He had spells at East Stirling and St. Mirren before establishing his name with Aberdeen. At Aberdeen he managed to break the Rangers-Celtic domination by taking the club to the Scottish Premier Division title in 1980. Further success followed with the Scottish title coming again in 1984 and 1985, and the Scottish Cup in 1982, 1983, 1984 (double winners) and 1986. Of course his greatest achievement at Pittodrie was winning the European Cup Winners' Cup in 1983 with a 2-1 extra time victory over Real Madrid in Gothenburg.

A spell as Scotland manager came after Jock Stein's death, and Ferguson managed Scotland from 1985 to after the 1986 World Cup finals. Inevitably, this helped bring him to the attention of other clubs and interest from Tottenham, Wolves and Scottish side Rangers came, but it was United who appointed the former Rangers player in 1986.

By the start of the 1989-90 season with no actual trophy success Ferguson's job looked vulnerable and the media regularly reported that his time would soon be up, and when the Reds

were defeated 5-1 by City in September supporters made clear their views. Chants of "Fergie Out" came from the United faithful while the following day's newspapers claimed his reign was almost over, yet it now seems clear that the City victory helped to keep him in his job. It is highly unlikely the Reds would have given City fans the satisfaction of seeing their leader dismissed immediately after the derby. In addition the Michael Knighton takeover was still rumbling on, so it is possible the United Board were unable to make such a significant change at this point.

Soon afterwards Howard Kendall arrived back in the northwest after a spell in Spain and his arrival immediately made him the bookmakers' favourite to take over at Old Trafford, but an amazing sequence of events saw City dismiss their manager Mel Machin; attempt to appoint Oldham's Joe Royle; and then persuade Kendall to take over at Maine Road. This immediately ended the prospect of Kendall's appointment, but by Christmas Ferguson still looked vulnerable. Then it all changed.

A great FA Cup run saw the Reds reach the 1990 Cup final where they defeated Crystal Palace in a replay. Ferguson still had his critics but with trophy success his immediate future seemed assured. Then in 1991 the Reds reached the League Cup final and won the European Cup Winners' Cup. This was United's second European trophy and immediately lifted his status to a similar level to Manchester's two other European trophy winning managers Matt Busby and Joe Mercer. The one significant difference however was that both men had also found League success. This was something the modern day Reds wanted more than anything else at this point.

In 1993 Ferguson managed to achieve something only four previous Manchester managers had achieved and he guided his side to the title, except by this point the highest domestic league competition was the Premier League and Ferguson's Reds became the inaugural title winners.

Since 1993 Ferguson has pushed United on to new levels of success with the 1998-99 season proving to be a major landmark for the Reds. That season United won the European Cup, FA Cup and Premier League – the three most significant trophies any English side has ever competed for – and Ferguson became recognised as one of the game's greatest ever managers. It is also worth noting that Ferguson has overtaken Matt Busby's record of achievement.

Busby won the European Cup, five domestic titles, and two FA Cups while by the start of 2006-07 Ferguson had guided United to the European Cup, European Cup Winners' Cup, eight domestic titles, five FA Cups, and two League Cups. Ferguson's success has been achieved over a shorter period than Busby's, although it must be recorded that Busby's success came in two stages and that the Munich Disaster brought a premature end to the success of that side.

Over the years many of the coaches around Ferguson have changed, as have the players, and whenever a player or coach has moved on the media has been quick to forecast the end of Ferguson's triumphs. Each time the media has been wrong and in many ways the manager has taken United on to a new level.

During recent seasons the sudden rise in status of Chelsea has also caused many to suggest that United's strength under Ferguson would be challenged. Inevitably, that has occurred to some extent, however in 2006-07 Ferguson's side proved they were still determined to challenge. They won the Premier League title by six points.

Whatever the future holds for United, it is clear that while Alex Ferguson is involved the Reds will always be seen as title challengers and European hopefuls. It is also obvious that his record of achievement is unlikely to be matched by any manager for a considerably long time, if ever.

Former Oldham manager Jimmy Frizzell recognises that Ferguson has been a great manager for the region:

"When you look at the way it was when he first came down. He had that wee spell where he almost lost his job, but since then he has been the best manager in Britain. Probably in the world. I don't think anyone can ever match him."

Former United star Paul Parker feels United's success owes everything to the manager:

"He has been there the duration. There has been no one more important. You can talk about players, but they've come and gone. He's been there through it all. He was written off and he's come out even stronger. He took a lot of pounding when Chelsea started to find success. People who used to back him were quick to dig him from behind. He was written off. Then he's come back and won his ninth Premiership and proved them all wrong."

United captain Gary Neville summed up Ferguson's contribution to United well when, at the time of the manager's twentieth anniversary at United, Neville told journalists:

"Matt Busby was always seen as the godfather of this club and you would never have thought there could be another Matt Busby but we have one, and he is the manager now. Alex Ferguson has surpassed Sir Matt's achievements and in 20, 30 and 40 years' time people will look back and see United as being formed by two great figures rather than one. He is Manchester United"

CHAPTER TWENTY-NINE

THE FA CUP

> *For the first occasion in the history of the English Association Cup the final tie was played out of London, and the Manchester Athletic Ground was the scene of the encounter on Saturday afternoon. The sun shone brilliantly, and the sight was one such as had never previously been seen at a football match in any part of the world.* The Sporting Chronicle, 1893

THE FA Cup was the first national competition any of the sides from the region competed in. It was also the first competition to attract a crowd of over 60,000 to the city and today four out of the top five attendances in the region were for FA Cup games. In addition, two FA Cup finals and two FA Cup final replays have been played in Manchester. The first of these occurred in 1893 and was in fact the first FA Cup Final, excluding replays, to be played outside of London.

The 1893 final was played between two significant clubs of the period - Wolverhampton Wanderers and Everton. At that time both Newton Heath and Ardwick were League sides of course, but rather than pick either of their homes, the FA chose to stage the game at the Manchester Athletic ground in Fallowfield. This venue was opened in May 1892, but Manchester Athletic club had originally been based in the Old Trafford area, with its only stand backing on to Talbot Road to the east of the present day Lancashire CC ground.

The Manchester Athletic Club was set up in 1887 by Tom Sutton, editor of the **Athletic News** – a leading sporting newspaper of the day – and moved to Fallowfield in May 1892. So at the time of the 1893 final it was one of the Country's newest venues. Access to the stadium was off Whitworth Lane, and it is fair to say it was not the best placed venue in Manchester's history, as it appeared to be tucked behind houses and in between fields and other sports facilities (the present day Firs Athletic Ground/Armitage Centre, Manchester University sports facilities lie to the south of the site).

Why the stadium was chosen is not entirely clear, although the **Athletic News** connections may have played a part. Inevitably the final could not be played at Goodison Park, at the time recognised as the most impressive football stadium, and Manchester was probably seen as an appropriate city to stage the final in. Whatever the actual reasons, it is clear that the organisers were unaware of exactly how popular football was becoming in the north. A crowd reported as 45,000 with gate receipts of £2,559 should have guaranteed future finals at the arena, but in truth the day had been a difficult one, with crowd control a major issue.

A FOOTBALL MATCH AT MANCHESTER.

The view here given represents a match between the Wolverhampton Wanderers and the Everton Club, at Fallowfield Ground, Manchester. The vast crowd therein shown is a good proof of the absorbing interest which a first-class football match now arouses in almost any of our great centres of population, but especially in the northern and midland counties. Year by year this interest has grown, until now a match is often witnessed by tens of thousands. Even cricket does not in the north draw such crowds of spectators, or excite for weeks previously such animated discussion as an important match at football, and such a scene as here depicted well illustrates the innate love of the British people for manly sports.

R. Banks, Manchester.]

THE FALLOWFIELD FIASCO DURING THE MATCH BETWEEN WOLVERHAMPTON WANDERERS AND EVERTON IN 1893.

This photograph was taken soon after the kick-off, and shows the touch-line clear. Later on the crowd swarmed on to the field and interfered with the game. The match was, however, finished.

(From a photograph kindly lent by the Football Association.)

Scenes from the 1893 FA Cup final at Fallowfield

In total it was estimated that a figure potentially as high as 60,000 may have attended the game, but even the 45,000 known to have been there was several thousand more than the ground should have coped with. According to the newspapers of the day there were significant problems controlling the crowd. The *Sporting Chronicle* highlighted some of the issues:

"The sun shone brilliantly, and the sight was one such as had never previously been seen at a football match in any part of the world. The only regret that can be expressed is that there was not a larger force of police to maintain order. As it was, there were several small encounters between individual policemen and the crowd, and some of the latter went home with cracked heads. The palisades were mounted and every point of vantage occupied, with the result that the little army of pressmen who were present were only able to give poor accounts of the game. In fact, a large portion of it could not be seen from the pavilion, where most of the reporters took refuge."

The Chronicle highlighted a few key moments from the match, which ended 1-0 to Wolves, and then concluded its report with a final comment about the control of the fans:

"A large number of people were admitted without payment, and the police – 192 in number – were singularly inactive in the performance of what might be supposed were their duties."

The *Athletic News* hinted at the problems of the crowd when they wrote:

"The Wolverhampton Wanderers, after nearly stunning a policeman with one shot, won the Cup by a goal from the foot of Harry Allen, a fine figure of a man, who was renowned as a centre half-back."

THE ENGLISH CUP FINAL.

EVERTON v. WOLVERHAMPTON WANDERERS.

A TREMENDOUS CROWD.

WOLVERHAMPTON VICTORIOUS.

For the first occasion in the history of the English Association Cup—if we except the drawn game between Blackburn Rovers and West Bromwich Albion, which was replayed on the Derby County ground, in the season of 1885-6—the final tie of the English Association Cup was played out of London, and the Manchester Athletic Ground was the scene of the encounter on Saturday afternoon. The sun shone brilliantly, and the sight was one such as had never previously been seen at a football match in any part of the world. The only regret that can be expressed is that there was not a larger force of police to maintain order. As it was, there were several small encounters between individual policemen and the crowd, and some of the latter went home with cracked heads. The palisades were mounted and every point of vantage occupied, with the result that the little army of pressmen who were present were only able to give very poor accounts of the game. In fact, a large portion of it could not be seen from the Pavilion, where most of the reporters took refuge.

It was a very hard match, but not a particularly scientific one. The crowd behaved in admirable fashion, and kept clear of the lines all through. The spectators had every opportunity of breaking through, but they had evidently come to see the match, and behaved themselves accordingly. The first half was very much in favour of Everton, and they had hard lines on many occasions, but the "Wolves" reversed the order of things in the second half, and had just as much of the play and experienced similar luck. The game was won by sheer pluck and determination, and although the shot which scored was somewhat lucky itself, it was a grand effort on Allen's part. This occurred about half an hour from the finish, but it was palpably the deciding point, for Everton did not play up with anything like determination, and taken altogether it was a very quiet and not excited cup-tie. In the first half it seemed any odds on Everton winning, for during that period they played a very telling game; but immediately a re-start was made the "Wolves" went at it in a most vigorous fashion and fairly overplayed their opponents. Their defence was very prominent, and Baugh has hardly ever been seen to more advantage, whilst Swift was very useful. Rose had not a great deal to do, but he often showed great nerve, especially in the first half. The half-backs were very strong, and Allen was perhaps the best, but both Kinsey and Malpass did well. The forwards were not at all brilliant. Topham occasionally contributed some capital runs, but the biggest surprise was Wykes, who worked unceasingly, and was always about when required. As a whole, the forwards were more useful than brilliant, and this is a feature not to be despised in any team. Everton played a disappointing game in the second half. In the initial period they were all right, and in the play ought to have won before the interval, but they afterwards fell off a lot, and allowed Wolverhampton opportunities which they ought not to have had. Their forwards were good in the first half,

Since 1893 much has been made of the problems of the day and in some publications the game has been dubbed "The Fallowfield Fiasco". To some extent this is true as there were problems with fans encroaching on to the pitch and at one point the referee discussed with the FA the possibility of abandoning the game, but in other ways it was not so much the venue that was at fault it was the failure to understand the lure of the game in the north.

With both Everton and Wolves reaching the final it was clear both sides would bring a significant number of fans to the final, add to that the growing interest in the game in Manchester and it was inevitable a large crowd would attend.

Writers since 1893 have tended to overlook the fact that the 45,000 crowd was around 13,000 more than the next highest FA Cup final attendance, and that the game was initially moved from the Oval because it was agreed the London venue could not cope with the size of crowds football was starting to attract. Comments on the quality of the venue do seem misplaced because, other than a recognised 'modern' football ground such as Goodison Park, it is unlikely any venue could have coped with that size of crowd at the time. True football venues needed to be developed.

The journalist JAH Catton from the **Athletic News** wrote in 1926 that he believed it was the popularity of the game that was more significant than the inadequacy of the venue:

"It was said that the arrangements were indefinite and casual but no forethought could have rendered an enclosure, good enough for an ordinary athletic festival, the rendezvous for an event which was attracting thousands more people as each spring returned."

The founder of the League, William MacGregor, writing in the 1905 publication **The Book of Football** also believed the popularity of the game had not been fully appreciated:

"We were then at the beginning of the really big modern gates, and it is an admitted fact that the Association and the officials who were in immediate charge of the game woefully underestimated the interest that the match was destined to arouse. I do not know that any blame attaches to them; it is so easy to be wise after the event."

The site of the 1893 final as it looked during the 1950s.

Wanderers Avenue was so named to commemorate Wolves' first F.A. Cup win in 1893. They beat Everton, who were hot favourites, by one goal to nil, at Fallowfield, Manchester. A replica of the Cup (right) was put on one of the walls

According to MacGregor it was poor sightlines that had caused the problems:

"The people were perfectly orderly for a time, but they could not see what was going on, and consequently those at the back grew restive. They saw a nice open space between the people close to the ropes and the players, and they naturally tried to get there. They pushed and fought, and then they threw clinkers and turf at the people in front. Finally, the strain became too great for the barriers, which were frail, wooden palisadings; they crashed in at many points, greatly to the danger of the reporters on one side of the ground, and soon there was wild confusion. However, the people wanted to see the play; there can be no doubt on that point; and, although there were interruptions to the game – the crowd were often encroaching over the touchlines – the match was finished.

"A great many people were injured – few seriously, I believe – and more than one football journalist carried home with him traces of the excessive enthusiasm which the crowd manifested."

The Fallowfield ground did not stage any further FA Cup finals, but the following season it was deemed worthy of staging an FA Cup semi final when Bolton defeated Sheffield Wednesday 2-1. The crowd that day was a more manageable 22,000, but the fact the ground was chosen does prove that the FA did not at the time view the 1893 game as the big catastrophe later generations would.

Five years later another semi-final was staged there but this time crowd control became a much bigger issue. Liverpool were leading Sheffield United 1-0 at half time when the match was abandoned, officially because of crushing and darkness. The game had commenced about thirty minutes late – around 4pm – and frequently fans encroached on to the pitch. Each time the game had to be halted with one stoppage reported by Sheffield officials as lasting fifty minutes. At 5.45pm the first half came to an end, and the FA had already decided that the game should be abandoned, however fearful of what might happen the FA insisted the players return to the field while they managed to get the match takings out of the ground and in to a safe location. Once the money was away, the game was abandoned. The replay took place at Derby County, and Fallowfield never again staged a major footballing fixture. The next semi-final in the city was played at City's Hyde Road ground in 1905.

For the Fallowfield venue many other significant events were held there. In rugby, Fallowfield staged the England-Scotland international of 1897 and the Northern Union Challenge Cup (Rugby

League) finals of 1899 and 1900. Athletics were staged there, including the Amateur Athletics Association championships of 1897 and 1907, while the venue mostly became known for the rest of its history as a cycling arena. In 1934 it staged the cycle races in the London Commonwealth Games (most other events were staged at White City, London), and in 1955 the famous cyclist Reg Harris helped purchase the venue from the Manchester Athletic Club with the aim of developing it further. It was later renamed the Reg Harris stadium but struggled financially. In the early 1960s it was sold to the University, but unlike the neighbouring Firs/Armitage centre it was allowed to deteriorate.

The 1915 FA Cup final between Sheffield United and Chelsea became known as the Khaki final due to the large volume of servicemen at the game.

In 1994 the venue was demolished and today student accommodation covers the site and, like so many other significant footballing landmarks in the region (including Belle Vue, Hyde Road, and the Imperial Hotel) there is no permanent memorial to the venue in Manchester. Unlike those other sites though there is a memorial commemorating the 1893 final elsewhere. In Wolverhampton a street called Wanderers Avenue was built to commemorate their FA Cup success, and on one of the walls a stone replica of the Cup and the simple inscription "Fallowfield 1893" was erected. That section of the street, often referred to at the time as Fallowfield Terrace, was built close to the Wolves' ground of the period in the Blakenhall area.

Scenes from the 1911 FA Cup final replay at Old Trafford. Bradford City beat Newcastle United 1-0 in front of 58,000.

FA CUP FINALS PLAYED IN MANCHESTER

1893 Wolverhampton Wanderers 1 Everton 0, 45,000, Fallowfield
1911 Newcastle United 0 Bradford City 1, 58,000, Old Trafford (replay)
1915 Sheffield United 3 Chelsea 0, 49,557, Old Trafford
1970 Chelsea 2 Leeds United 1, 62,000, Old Trafford (replay)

FA CUP SEMI FINALS PLAYED IN MANCHESTER

Whalley Range

1882 Blackburn Rovers 5 The Wednesday 1 (replay)
1883 Blackburn Olympic 4 Old Carthusians 0

Fallowfield

1894 Bolton Wanderers 2 The Wednesday 1
1899 Sheffield United 0 Liverpool 1 (second replay)
(abandoned at half-time due to crowd trouble and darkness)

Hyde Road

1905 Newcastle United 1 Sheffield Wednesday 0

Old Trafford

1910 Barnsley 3 Everton 0 (replay)
1914 Burnley 0 Sheffield United 0,
1921 Wolverhampton Wanderers 3 Cardiff City 1 (replay)
1923 Bolton Wanderers 1 Sheffield United 0
1928 Huddersfield Town 2 Sheffield United 2
1930 Huddersfield Town 2 Sheffield Wednesday 1
1931 West Bromwich Albion 1 Everton 0
1939 Wolverhampton Wanderers 5 Grimsby Town 0
1968 Everton 1 Leeds United 0
1971 Liverpool 2 Everton 1
1974 Liverpool 0 Leicester City 0
1989 Liverpool 3 Nottingham Forest 1
1996 Liverpool 3 Aston Villa 0
1997 Middlesbrough 3 Chesterfield 3
1998 Newcastle United 1 Sheffield United 0
1999 Newcastle United 2 Tottenham Hotspur O
2001 Arsenal 2 Tottenham Hotspur 1
2002 Arsenal 1 Middlesbrough 0
2003 Arsenal 1 Sheffield United 0
2004 Sunderland 0 Millwall 1
2006 Chelsea 1 Liverpool 2
2007 Blackburn Rovers 1 Chelsea 2

Maine Road

1928 Huddersfield Town 1 Sheffield United 0 (second replay)
1946 Derby County 4 Birmingham City 0 (replay)

1947	Burnley 1 Liverpool 0 (replay)
1950	Liverpool 2 Everton 0
1951	Blackpool 0 Birmingham City 0
1953	Bolton Wanderers 4 Everton 3
1954	Preston North End 2 Sheffield Wednesday 0
1958	Bolton Wanderers 2 Blackburn Rovers 1
1960	Blackburn Rovers 2 Sheffield Wednesday 1
1973	Leeds United 1 Wolverhampton Wanderers 0
1975	Fulham 1 Birmingham City 0 (replay)
1977	Liverpool 2 Everton 2
1977	Liverpool 3 Everton 0 (replay)
1979	Manchester United 2 Liverpool 2
1985	Manchester United 2 Liverpool 1 (replay)
1990	Manchester United 3 Oldham Athletic 3
1990	Manchester United 2 Oldham Athletic 1 (replay)
1994	Manchester United 4 Oldham Athletic 1 (replay)

MANCHESTER'S FA CUP RECORD

Ever since Bury's FA Cup victory of 1900 the region has been one of the strongest in the country for cup glory. The FA Cup was the first significant national trophy won by the region's sides, although both Bury and City had also won the Second Division title during the 1890s. Since the dawn of the Twentieth Century three of the region's sides have won the competition, while another side, Oldham, have reached the semi-final stage.

The full breakdown of Manchester's FA Cup finals is:

YEAR	MANCHESTER SIDE	OPPONENTS	SCORE	ATTENDANCE
1900	Bury	Southampton	4-0	68,945
1903	Bury	Derby County	6-0	63,102
1904	City	Bolton	1-0	61,374
1909	United	Bristol City	1-0	71,401
1926	City	Bolton	0-1	91,447
1933	City	Everton	0-3	92,950
1934	City	Portsmouth	2-1	93,258
1948	United	Blackpool	4-2	99,000
1955	City	Newcastle	1-3	100,000
1956	City	Birmingham City	3-1	100,000
1957	United	Aston Villa	1-2	100,000
1958	United	Bolton	0-2	100,000
1963	United	Leicester City	3-1	100,000
1969	City	Leicester City	1-0	100,000
1976	United	Southampton	0-1	100,000
1977	United	Liverpool	2-1	100,000
1979	United	Arsenal	2-3	100,000

1981	City	Tottenham	1-1 (aet)	100,000
1981 (Replay)	City	Tottenham	2-3	92,500
1983	United	Brighton & HA	2-2 (aet)	100,000
1983 (Replay)	United	Brighton & HA	4-0	100,000
1985	United	Everton	1-0 (aet)	100,000
1990	United	Crystal Palace	3-3 (aet)	80,000
1990 (Replay)	United	Crystal Palace	1-0	80,000
1994	United	Chelsea	4-0	79,634
1995	United	Everton	0-1	79,592
1996	United	Liverpool	1-0	79,007
1999	United	Newcastle United	2-0	79,101
2004	United	Millwall	3-0	72,350
2005	United	Arsenal	0-0 (aet) *	71,896
2007	United	Chelsea	0-1 (aet)	89,826

* In 2005 Arsenal won 5-4 on penalties

NOTE: Finals detailed above pre-1923 were all played at the Crystal Palace Grounds. Those between 1923 and 2001 were played at Wembley, and United's finals in 2004 & 2005 were held at the Millennium Stadium, Cardiff. The 2007 final was the first at the new Wembley Stadium.
The total of FA Cup successes by the region's sides stands at: United 11, City 4, and Bury 2.

HOW THE GAME WAS WON AND LOST.

DAVID JACK'S CUP FINAL DISTINCTION.

WONDERFUL GOALKEEPING BY DICK PYM.

"OLYMPIAN'S" COMMENTARY.

Bolton Wanderers set the seal on their fame as Cup fighters by winning the Football Association Challenge Cup for the second time in three years at Wembley Stadium on Saturday, David Jack, scoring the all-important goal when the game had only 13 minutes to run.

There was not a great deal between the teams in one of the hardest games and incidentally one of the best Finals I have ever witnessed, the quality of the football being a credit and worthy of two of the outstanding teams from the County which has a strong claim to be regarded as the hub of Soccer football.

His Majesty the King gave expression to the popular sentiment when, in handing the Cup to Joe Smith at the close of a thrilling struggle, he said he thought the Wanderers just deserved their success. Thus was avenged the defeat inflicted upon the Bolton team by the City in the Final tie of 1904, and that by a goal the legitimacy of which could not be questioned.

Butler takes his nerve powder

A great save by Pym, on his knees to deal with a shot from the Manchester City attack

Bolton's mystery powder sees the Trotters defeat City 1-0 in the 1926 final.

FA CUP TRIVIA

- ***The first FA Cup tie played in Scotland saw Manchester FC defeated by Queen's Park 15-0 in December 1883.***
- In November 1991 Rochdale emulated Manchester FC by playing a FA Cup tie in Scotland. Dale faced Gretna in 1991-92. Gretna were the first Scottish side to play in the competition proper for 105 years.
- ***The biggest victory in any round of the FA Cup saw Preston North End defeat local side Hyde FC 26-0 on 15th October 1887.***
- The biggest win in a FA Cup final saw Bury defeat Derby 6-0 on 18th April 1903.
- ***City director Albert Alexander senior provided the horses and carriages for both City and United's first FA Cup homecoming parade. United asked Alexander to lead their 1909 homecoming because of his experience with the first historic homecoming in the city five years earlier.***

Replay not all ticket

By Bryan Brett

ROCHDALE have warned fans that their FA Cup replay against Scottish club Gretna at Spotland on Wednesday is not all-ticket.

There was some confusion following false information given out immediately after the draw at Gretna but Dale stress that fans can pay at the turnstiles on match night.

Dale had 900 supporters with them at Gretna and will be hoping to attract additional support from outside their area because for the historic visit of a Scottish club.

The incentive for both clubs is there, with a home tie against Huddersfield the reward for the winners.

Big boys

Gretna are setting their stall out early. "Small clubs bringing big boys like Huddersfield to grounds like ours is what the FA Cup is all about," says secretary Keith Rhodes.

"Staging the game on our ground will give us a chance of getting through and meeting a First Division club. Before we can start thinking about that we must dispose of Rochdale."

That is precisely the Rochdale view, although they accept they must play a lot better than they did at Raydale Park. The return of Steve Doyle should bring better balance to midfield while manager David Sutton will also be looking for more penetration in attack.

- The highest team score in a FA Cup semi-final stands at 6, and was first achieved when City defeated Aston Villa 6-1 on 17th March 1934 (Fred Tilson netted 4 goals – also a record).
- ***The highest individual total of goals scored by one player in any round of the FA Cup stands at 10. On 31st August 2002 Paul Jackson netted ten goals for Stocksbridge Park Steels V Oldham Town (Stocksbridge won 17-1). This equalled Chris Marron's 10 goals for South Shields against Radcliffe Welfare United on 26th September 1947.***
- Norman Whiteside became the Youngest FA Cup final goalscorer when he netted against Brighton in the 1983 FA Cup final. He was 21 years and 212 days old.
- ***It is known that Billy Meredith either played in, or attended every FA Cup final appearance by City or United from the creation of the competition up to and including 1956. In total he attended Eight Manchester finals (six for City & two for United).***
- The oldest player in any round of the FA Cup is Billy Meredith who played in City's semi-final against Newcastle on 29th March 1924. He was 49 years and 8 months old.
- ***United have won the FA Cup more than any other side. Their 11 wins is one more than Arsenal at the time of going to press.***
- Bury's 100% record from two FA Cup finals is only bettered by the first FA Cup winners Wanderers who have competed in five finals without defeat.
- ***In 1926 City became the first FA Cup finalists to be relegated in the same season. Interestingly, the second side to achieve this dubious distinction was Leicester who were defeated by City in the 1969 final. United's 1983 opponents Brighton were the next side to equal City's bizarre record.***
- In 1956 Bobby Johnstone (City) became the first man to score in consecutive FA Cup finals at Wembley.

- ***The 1933 final was the first to see players wear numbered shirts. Everton were 1 to 11 with City 12 to 22 (goalkeeper Len Langford wore 22).***
- The biggest crowd for an FA Cup match, apart from the final itself, stands at 84,569 for City V Stoke on 3rd March 1934 at Maine Road. This remains the highest crowd in the Manchester region, and is still the record for any game outside of London or Glasgow.
- ***Between 1927 and 1945 Rochdale went 13 FA Cup matches without a win. This was a record, but has since been eclipsed by Leeds United (Leeds went 16 matches between 1952 and 1963 without a win). Rochdale's run ended with a 2-1 victory over Stockport County on 17th November 1945.***
- In 1963 it took United just 82 days from playing their first FA Cup match to winning the final. This is the quickest amount of time taken to become winners. That season appalling weather caused the FA Cup third round to be delayed until 4th March, with the finals staged on 25th May 1963.

- ***United shocked the football world in 1999-2000 when they refused to compete in the FA Cup. As reigning European champions they competed in the FIFA Club World Championship in Brazil – a tournament scheduled to last two weeks in January – and felt they could not take part in the FA Cup. That year however the Third Round was staged in the middle week of December with the Fourth Round occurring in the second weekend of January. Most neutrals and many United fans were horrified at the club's decision. Gillingham were re-instated into the competition after winning a 'lucky loser's' ballot and they faced Aston Villa in the Third Round. Had United agreed to compete in the FA Cup as well as the World Club Championship they would have had time to face Villa, and had they been successful (which would not have been guaranteed) it is possible their fourth round tie could have been delayed or that a reserve side could have competed instead. After the decision to withdraw from the competition there were many different possibilities suggested, but United decided to be the first League team since 1951 to withdraw.***
- In 1957 Stan Crowther played for Aston Villa against United in the FA Cup final, and the following season he made history by becoming the first person to play for two clubs in the competition during the same season. He was transferred to United in the wake of the Munich Air Disaster and was given permission by the FA to play for the Reds despite making an earlier appearance for Villa in that season's competition.
- ***Alec Herd played for City in the 1933 and 1934 FA Cup finals and his son David played for United in the 1963 final.***
- Billy Meredith faced Bolton in the 1904 FA Cup final and his son in law Charlie Pringle faced the same side in the 1926 final. Meredith won the FA Cup as a player with City (1904) and United (1909).

- ***Gary & Phil Neville both appeared in the 1996 FA Cup final. Phil made a full appearance, while Gary came on in the 89th minute. Both players made full appearances in the 1999 final against Newcastle.***
- Mancunian Dave Bennett played for City against Tottenham in the 1981 final (and for Coventry against Spurs in 1987) while his brother Gary, another former Blue, appeared for Sunderland in 1992.
- ***Jackie Blanchflower was a member of United's 1957 FA Cup final team, and ended up playing in goal after Ray Wood was injured, while his brother Danny played for Tottenham against Leicester in the 1961 final.***
- Bobby Charlton played for United in the 1957, 1958 and 1963 finals, while his brother Jack was a member of Leeds' 1965, 1970, and 1972 Cup final teams.
- ***Brian and Jimmy Greenhoff became the third set of brothers to play together in a 20th Century FA Cup winning team. The brothers faced Liverpool in 1977 with Jimmy scoring the winning goal.***
- In 1969-70 the FA introduced a third place play-off match for the defeated FA Cup semi-finalists. It was not a success but United were the first to compete when they faced Watford at neutral Highbury on 10th April 1970. The game ended in a 2-0 Red victory with goals from Brian Kidd in front of 15,000. The idea was subsequently abandoned after only 4,000 watched the 1974 game between Leicester and Burnley at Filbert Street.
- ***Lancashire cricketer Jack Dyson became a FA Cup winner in 1956 for City, while in 1958 Fred Goodwin became the second Lancashire cricketer to appear in an FA Cup final for one of Manchester's clubs when he played for United.***
- Overseas players – the first Dane to play in the FA Cup final was United's Jesper Olsen (1985).

Drama at the 1956 final - City 'keeper Bert Trautmann receives treatment. Later it was announced he had broken his neck.

The first German was City's Bert Trautmann (1955). The first Channel Islander was Billy Spurdle (1955). The first Frenchman was Eric Cantona (1994). United's Arnold Muhren (1983) was the first Dutchman, Andrei Kanchelskis (1994) was the first from the Ukraine, and Dwight Yorke (1999) the first from Tobago.

- ***Matt Busby was the fourth and Joe Mercer was the eighth to both play in and manage a FA Cup winning side. Busby played for City in their 1934 success and managed United to their 1948 and 1963 victories. Mercer captained Arsenal to their success in 1950 and managed City at the time of their 1969 victory.***
- Alex Ferguson has managed more FA Cup winning teams than any other man – the record in March 2008 stands at 5 wins.

POSTCRIPT TO ALTRINCHAM'S BIG DAY AT SPURS

AGONY . . . linesman Monk waves away angry players after his 'foul throw' decision had ruled out a goal

DUEL . . . Stuart Terry with Darren Anderton

King salutes Robins' fans

■ ALTRINCHAM boss John King paid tribute to his club's fans for their superb support during the 3-0 FA Cup defeat at Spurs, writes RICHARD FROST.

■ "I'd like to thank the fans who were right behind us all the way. We lost but we had a great backing and I would like them to know that the club appreciates their support," said the Robins' boss.

■ King agreed that winger and top scorer Stuart Terry had enjoyed a fine game and added: "He is good player who could move on in the game. But we've got a lot of good players.

■ "Our biggest disappointment was having a goal by Shaun Constable ruled out. If it had been 2-1 with 18 minutes left, anything could have happened."

After defeating former League side Southport and Division Three's Wigan, Altrincham were beaten 3-0 by Premier League Tottenham in the 1994-95 FA Cup.

- ***The first player to play in three FA Cup finals for one of the region's clubs was Sam Cowan (City – 1926, 1933, & 1934). The first for United was: Bobby Charlton & Bill Foulkes (1957, 1958 & 1963).***
- The record attendance for a FA Cup semi final stands at 80,470 for the replay between Derby and Birmingham City played at Maine Road on 28th March 1946. This was also the record for a midweek FA Cup game in England until the 1981 FA Cup final replay between Spurs and City (92,500). This was also eclipsed in 1983 when 100,000 witnessed the Brighton-United replay.
- ***The lowest FA Cup semi-final crowd stands at 17,987 for United V Crystal Palace at Villa Park on 12th April 1995. The police had asked fans to boycott the match following the death of a Palace fan at the original game.***
- In 1992 the fourth actual FA Cup trophy was introduced. Of the Manchester region sides, only United have won this version of the trophy. Interestingly, none of the Manchester region sides won the first FA trophy, however all three of the region's victors did find their first successes with the second trophy. This was based on the original design and was won by Bury (1900 & 1903), City (1904) and United (1909), however United's success was perhaps also the trophy's downfall. In 1910 the FA discovered the trophy had been copied for a minor competition in the Manchester area. It is believed that someone copied the trophy after seeing it at United. The FA ordered a new one to be made and the third trophy – which followed the more familiar present day design – was first awarded in 1911. Both City and United won this trophy with the Blues winning it in 1934, 1956 and 1969 and the Reds in 1948, 1963, 1977, 1983, 1985 & 1990.
- ***Eric Cantona became in 1994 the first player to score two penalties in a FA Cup final.***
- The 1981 FA Cup final replay between City and Tottenham was the first to be played at Wembley.
- ***Kevin Moran was the first player to be sent off in a FA Cup final (1985)***
- The first FA Cup tie to be played on a Sunday was Cambridge United V Oldham, which ended in a 2-2 draw in January 1974.

CHAPTER THIRTY

THE LEAGUE CUP & OTHER COMPETITIONS

With costs rising, and attendances falling, attempts were naturally made to bring more money into the game. One such way was the creation of more competitions. These proliferated in the 1960s, parallel with the growth of European football. Alan Hardaker's own baby, the League Cup, was the most prominent. "The Story of Football", Phil Soar & Martin Tyler, 1986

THE League Cup was the brainchild of Alan Hardaker, who was secretary of the Football League from 1957 to 1979. Hardaker felt a competition based on a more European format of home and away legs rather than the traditional English style of one off knock out games, would be more financially viable and more attractive to the game's smaller sides. Clearly income from FA Cup games is shared between competing clubs, however the very nature of the FA Cup is that games are played based on which club's drawn first. The League Cup's two-legged format guaranteed a game at the larger, more popular club as well as a home tie.

The first of the region's sides to appear in the League Cup final was Rochdale who appeared in the second League Cup final (1962) while Joe Mercer's Aston Villa side had won the inaugural competition. Sadly, this major moment in Rochdale's history has largely been ignored and even at the time few newspapers covered the story in detail. Even locally the story that Denis Law was expected to sign for United from Torino occupied most of the local press sports sections – it is interesting to note that the ***Manchester Evening Chronicle*** contained an extremely large number of letters urging the Reds not to sign Law and create a 'one man team'! From Rochdale's viewpoint the main coverage following the first leg of the game in the main Manchester press focused on the potential income from the competition. Future head of ***Granada*** sport Paul Doherty, son of City's former hero Peter Doherty, wrote in the ***Evening Chronicle*** of Friday 27th April 1962 (the day after the tie):

"The 85th minute shot from balding Bill Punton probably did more than just goal damage to Rochdale's League Cup final hopes at Spotland – it seems strong enough to knock the bottom out of this two-legged tie.

"For the Punton goal was Norwich's third of the night, and with a three goal lead and home ground

advantage to come for Norwich officials fear next week's gate figures will be trimmed. But Rochdale will be banking a fair sized sum for their efforts at home. They pulled in £1,1640 from the 11,123 crowd, and after share outs and expenses it should boost the funds so far to more than £3,000 in the League Cup.

"One thing Rochdale do face: a £500 pay out to their players even if they lose. The winners get £750."

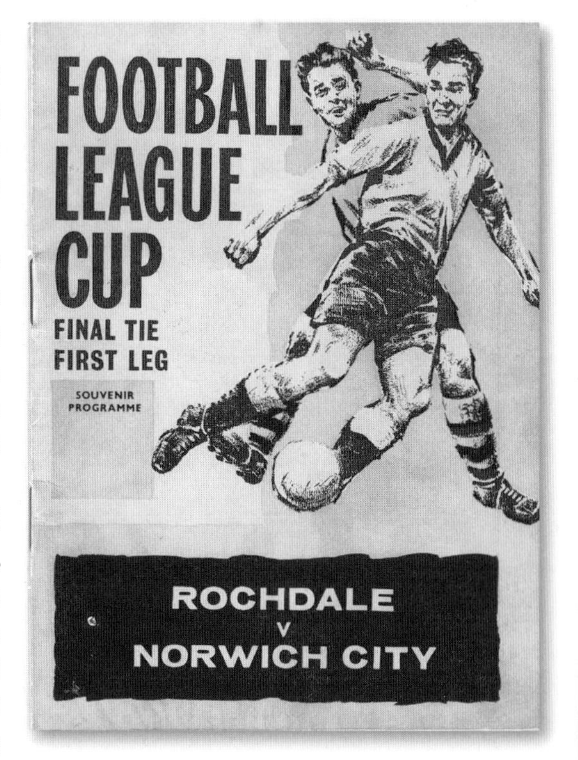

Surprisingly the **Chronicle** did not even cover the second leg of the final, although **Anglia TV** did film the game and broadcast this in their region. Their own notes of the highlights claim Rochdale had most of the play.

Initially many of football's biggest clubs boycotted the competition, particular those competing in Europe. It was not until the final was moved to Wembley and then when a European place was granted to the winners that the competition became of interest to all League sides.

All the local sides, including City and United, entered during the first season, however the Reds boycotted the competition between 1961 and 1966 and again in 1967 to 1969. In fact 1969-70 was the first season all 92 League sides entered the competition and this was also the first time any of the region's sides won the trophy. City were the winners and their run saw them defeat Southport 3-0, before a thrilling 3-2 Maine Road victory over Bill Shankly's great Liverpool side in the third round. Goals from Colin Bell & Francis Lee ensured a 2-0 defeat of Everton in the next round, and then QPR were despatched 3-0 in the quarter-final, leaving City to face Matt Busby's United in the two-legged semi-final. This was only the second significant semi-final between the two sides (the first had been the 1926 FAC semi at Bramall Lane which the Blues won).

In the 13th minute of the first leg, Colin Bell sent a half volley past Alex Stepney. Stepney performed exceptionally well under intense pressure from Bell, Lee and Oakes in the first half, and managed to keep the Reds in the match. In the 66th minute Bobby Charlton equalised, causing City to rue their missed chances. However, the gloom was lifted in the 88th minute when Ian Ure felled Francis Lee in the penalty area. Penalty expert Lee sent the ball low to Stepney's right to bring a 2-1 victory.

As the players left the field George Best exchanged words with referee Jack Taylor and appeared to knock the ball out of his hands. The Irishman was fined £100 and suspended for a month as a result.

In the second leg, City youngster Ian Bowyer netted first, but the Reds fought back. Goals from Paul Edwards and former Blue Denis Law made the scores level on aggregate, but all that was to change with only eight minutes remaining. City were awarded an indirect free kick. Francis

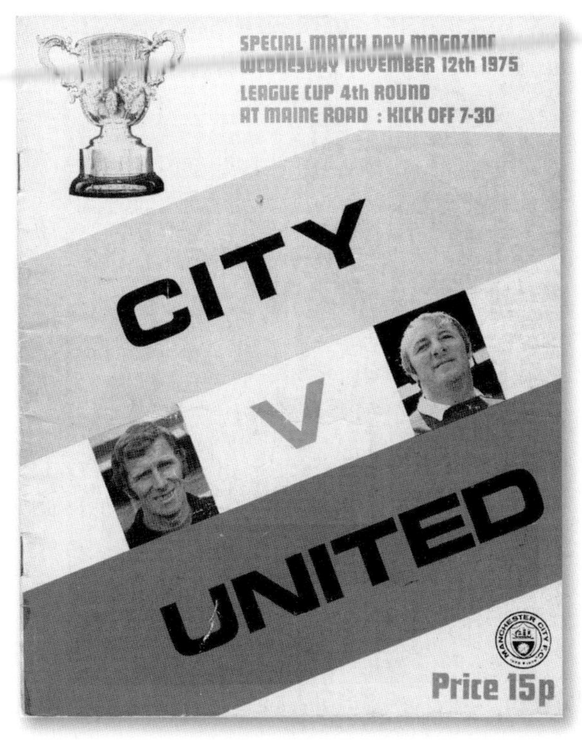

Lee seemed to ignore the signal and fired the ball goalwards. Stepney went to catch it, but fumbled and the ball went loose. Mike Summerbee proceeded to bury it in the net. Had Stepney allowed Lee's shot to enter the net no goal would have been given. City reached their first League Cup final by means of a 4-3 aggregate victory over their biggest rivals.

The final, against West Bromwich Albion, was played only 36 hours after City had returned to England from a ECWC tie in Portugal. Freezing conditions had brought transport chaos and caused many to wonder if City would be in the right frame of mind for the final. A fifth minute goal from Jeff Astle seemed to suggest that Albion would have the upper hand, however City fans need not have worried as City took control. Francis Lee played the best game of his career, while Mike Doyle slid home the equaliser in the 60th minute. Unfortunately, Summerbee was forced to leave the field shortly afterwards with a hairline fracture of the leg.

In extra-time Glyn Pardoe scored his first goal of the season to give City a deserved 2-1 victory and their first League Cup trophy. It also brought qualification for the European Fairs Cup, the predecessor of the UEFA Cup. Interestingly, that competition only allowed one entrant from each city, causing Mike Doyle to joke that qualification had helped him achieve an aim:

"That's not bad for my new campaign and car stickers – 'Keep United out of Europe'."

Mercer joked: *"If we can win the ECWC and so qualify to defend it next season, maybe the authorities will let us flog our Fairs Cup place to the highest bidders!"*

In the end City did not need their Fairs Cup place as they did win the ECWC, but six years later the region's second victory in the final saw the Blues defeat Newcastle 2-1 and qualify for the UEFA Cup.

In 1983 United were defeated by Liverpool in the Reds first League Cup final, and then in 1990 Oldham became the fourth of the region's sides to play in the League Cup final. Piccadilly Radio chose to broadcast live from Wembley. Presenter James H Reeve remembers the excitement if the weekend:

"That weekend it was the Rugby final on the Saturday with Warrington and Wigan there and then it was Oldham and Forest on the Sunday, so London was like Greater Manchester that weekend. It was great and we were desperate for Oldham to win. Everyone liked Oldham and Wembley was full of Oldham fans, of course, but City and United supporters went as well to cheer them on. It was a great atmosphere but sadly it wasn't to be."

The full breakdown of Manchester's League Cup finals (including 2007-08) is:

YEAR	MANCHESTER SIDE	OPPONENTS	SCORE	VENUE	ATTENDANCE
1962 (1st leg)	Rochdale	Norwich	0-3	Spotland	11,123
1962 (2nd leg)	Rochdale	Norwich	0-1	Carrow Road	19,708
1970	City	WBA	2-1 (aet)	Wembley	97,963
1974	City	Wolves	1-2	Wembley	97,886
1976	City	Newcastle Utd	2-1	Wembley	100,000
1983	United	Liverpool	1-2 (aet)	Wembley	100,000
1990	Oldham	Nottm Forest	0-1	Wembley	74,343
1991	United	Sheff Wed	0-1	Wembley	80,000
1992	United	Nottm Forest	1-0	Wembley	76,810
1994	United	Aston Villa	1-3	Wembley	77,231
2003	United	Liverpool	0-2	Millennium	74,500
2006	United	Wigan	4-0	Millennium	66,866

LEAGUE CUP FINALS PLAYED IN MANCHESTER

1962 Rochdale 0 Norwich City 3, 11,123, Spotland
(first leg, second leg at Norwich ended 1-0 to home side)

1977 Aston Villa 3 Everton 2, 54,749, Old Trafford (second replay)

1978 Nottingham Forest 1 Liverpool 0, 54,375, Old Trafford (replay)

1984 Liverpool 1 Everton 0, 52,089, Maine Road (replay)

LEAGUE CUP TRIVIA

- ***City's Tony Book was the first man to win the League Cup as a player (1970) and as a manager (1976).***
- Three of the Manchester region venues have staged League Cup finals. These are: Spotland (venue for 1962 final), Old Trafford (venue for 1977 & 1978 replays), and Maine Road (venue for 1984 replay).
- ***Rochdale became the first Fourth Division side to reach the final (1962) and their meeting with Norwich was the first not to feature a side from the top division.***

1976 League Cup final Tony Book and capt Mike Doyle.

- The first ever winners of the League Cup were Aston Villa, managed by future City & England manager Joe Mercer.

MANCHESTER'S FA TROPHY RECORD

The Football Association Challenge Trophy was created by the FA in 1969 for semi-professional sides from leagues such as the Football Conference, Southern League, Isthmian League, and Northern Premier League. Clubs at lower levels of the National League System play in the FA Vase.

The idea was for this to complement the FA Amateur Cup, however this competition was abolished in 1974, and so the leading amateur clubs entered the Trophy. The final was traditionally held at Wembley Stadium, but due to the redevelopment of the old stadium the final has since been staged at League grounds such as Upton Park and Villa Park.

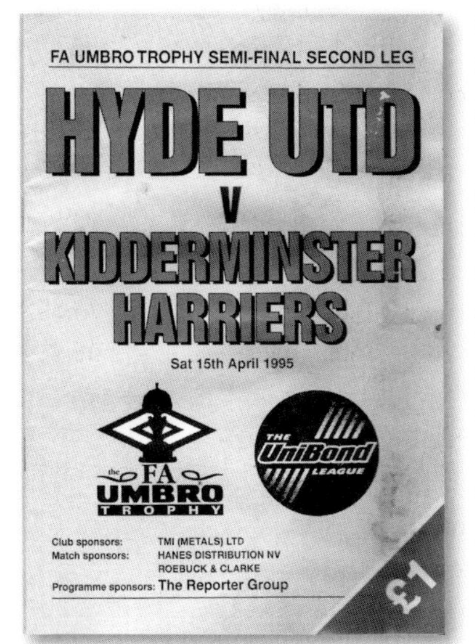

The trophy itself has a good history as it was initially presented to the FA in 1905 by a barrister, Ernest Cochrane, who wanted it to be used in an international competition between England, the USA and Canada to promote football in North America. That competition was never instigated and the trophy only really proved worthwhile when the new competition was created.

The following table details those sides within the region who have reached the final. It should be noted that many other sides from the edges of the region, such as Witton Albion, Northwich Victoria and Macclesfield Town, have reached the final as well.

YEAR	MANCHESTER SIDE	OPPONENTS	SCORE
1978	Altrincham	Leatherhead	3-1
1980	Mossley	Dagenham	1-2
1982	Altrincham	Enfield	0-1 (aet)
1986	Altrincham	Runcorn	1-0

MANCHESTER'S FOOTBALL LEAGUE TROPHY RECORD

The history of the Football League Trophy can be traced back to the Texaco Cup from the early 1970s. This was a competition for English, Scottish and Northern Irish sides and City and Oldham both competed in the competition at times.

In 1975-76 the Irish element was dropped and the competition became the Anglo-Scottish Cup. In 1981 the Scottish clubs pulled out, by which time the senior English clubs had chosen not to take part. The competition evolved into a knock-out style trophy for sides from the bottom two divisions and was renamed the Associate Members' Cup (sides in the top 2 divisions were Full Members of the Football League, hence the title of the 1985-86 competition City reached the final of). Since 1984-85 the tournament has been sponsored under various titles. It was the Autoglass Trophy when Stockport reached their finals, and the Auto-Windscreens Shield when City competed in the competition for their one and only time in 1998.

The following table details those sides within the region who have reached the final.

YEAR	MANCHESTER SIDE	OPPONENTS	SCORE	VENUE
1979 (1st leg)	Oldham	Burnley	1-4	Boundary Park
1979 (2nd leg)	Oldham	Burnley	1-0	Turf Moor
1992	Stockport	Stoke City	0-1	Wembley
1993	Stockport	Port Vale	1-2	Wembley

MANCHESTER'S FULL MEMBERS' CUP RECORD

The Full Members' Cup was a competition created in 1985 following the ban on English clubs from competing in European competition. There were two competitions created that season with those sides that should have been in European competition – including United – taking part in the Screen Sport Super Cup, and the majority of other First Division and Second Division sides playing in the Full Members' Cup.

The competition lasted for seven seasons and City were the only Manchester side to reach the final. This occurred in the competition's first season (1985-86) when the Blues faced Chelsea in a thrilling final the day after City had drawn 2-2 at Old Trafford in the Manchester derby. The final ended 5-4 to the London club and was watched by an attendance of 68,000 at Wembley Stadium.

MANCHESTER'S CHARITY SHIELD RECORD

The Charity Shield was first competed for in 1908-1909, replacing the Sheriff of London Charity Shield (no Manchester side competed in that competition) that had been introduced in 1898-99. It continued the concept of the professionals playing against the amateurs of the earlier competition.

The first match was between the League Champions (and professionals) Manchester United and Queens Park Rangers (amateurs). This match went to a replay, although that concept was later abandoned. Both games were played at Stamford Bridge and according to reports of the period the competition was not highly regarded and the games were relatively informal, end-of-season affairs.

The professionals versus amateurs concept was eventually dropped, and the competition evolved into one which would typically see the League Champions face the FA Cup winners. It was moved to the start of the season in 1959 and moved to Wembley in 1974.

The competition was renamed the Community Shield in 2002.

The following table details those sides within the region who have played in the match.

YEAR	MANCHESTER SIDE	OPPONENTS	SCORE	VENUE
1908	United	QPR	1-1	Stamford Bridge
1908 (replay)	United	QPR	4-0	Stamford Bridge
1911	United	Swindon Town	8-4	Stamford Bridge
1934	City	Arsenal	0-4	Highbury

United V QPR - the first Charity Shield appearance by any of our sides.

1937	City	Sunderland	2-0	Maine Road
1948	United	Arsenal	3-4	Highbury
1952	United	Newcastle	4-2	Old Trafford
1956	United (winners) & City		1-0	Maine Road
1957	United	Aston Villa	4-0	Old Trafford
1963	United	Everton	0-4	Goodison Park
1965	United	Liverpool	2-2 (held jointly)	Anfield
1967	United	Tottenham	3-3 (held jointly)	Old Trafford
1968	City	WBA	6-1	Maine Road
1969	City	Leeds	1-2	Elland Road
1972	City	Aston Villa	1-0	Villa Park
1973	City	Burnley	0-1	Turf Moor
1977	United	Liverpool	0-0 (held jointly)	Wembley
1983	United	Liverpool	2-0	Wembley
1985	United	Everton	0-2	Wembley
1990	United	Liverpool	1-1 (held jointly)	Wembley
1993	United	Arsenal	1-1 (Utd won 5-4 on pens)	Wembley
1994	United	Blackburn R	2-0	Wembley
1996	United	Newcastle Utd	4-0	Wembley
1997	United	Chelsea	1-1 (Utd on 4-2 on pens)	Wembley
1998	United	Arsenal	0-3	Wembley
1999	United	Arsenal	1-2	Wembley
2000	United	Chelsea	0-2	Wembley
2001	United	Liverpool	1-2	Millennium
2003	United	Arsenal	1-1 (Utd won 4-3 on pens)	Millennium

2004	United	Arsenal	1-3	Millennium
2007	United	Chelsea	1-1 (Utd won 3-1 on pens)	Wembley

CHARITY SHIELD TRIVIA

- ***The most successful team in the competition is United (12 outright wins and 4 shared).***
- The highest scoring game was United's 8-4 win against Swindon Town in 1911.
- ***Tottenham goalkeeper Pat Jennings scored against Manchester United in the 1967 Charity Shield.***
- The 1956 final should have been staged at Old Trafford (as it was usually played at the home of the League Champions) but it was moved to Maine Road to enable the game to be played midweek under floodlights. It was watched by a crowd of 30,495.

MANCHESTER'S FA YOUTH CUP RECORD

The following tables details Manchester's finalists in the FA Youth Cup. The competition was first competed for in 1952-3.

YEAR	MANCHESTER SIDE	OPPONENTS	AGGREGATE SCORE
1953	United	Wolves	9-3
1954	United	Wolves	5-4
1955	United	WBA	7-1
1956	United	Chesterfield	4-3
1957	United	West Ham	8-2
1964	United	Swindon	5-2
1979	City	Millwall	0-2
1980	City	Aston Villa	2-3
1982	United	Watford	6-7
1986	City (winners) & United		3-1
1989	City	Watford	1-2
1992	United	Crystal Palace	6-3
1993	United	Leeds	1-4
1995	United	Spurs	2-2 (Utd won 4-3 on pens)
2003	United	Middlesbrough	3-1
2006	City	Liverpool	2-3
2007	United	Liverpool	2-2 (Liverpool won 4-3 on pens)
2008	City reached the final as this book went to print		

The only FA Youth Cup final featuring two Manchester sides was in 1986. This was watched by crowds of: 7,602 (at Old Trafford) and 18,162 (at Maine Road).

WOMEN'S FOOTBALL

The Women's FA Cup was introduced in 1971 and at the time of going to press no side from Manchester has reached the final. Likewise, no side from the region has won the National Division of the Women's leagues.

In 2006-07 City and Stockport County had a ladies side competing in the Northern Division (2nd tier of Women's football), together with Curzon Ashton LFC, while Manchester United had scrapped their ladies team a couple of years earlier.

Women have played a significant part in football in the region. Obviously, there have been many female fans of all our clubs over the years but women have also held significant positions within the men's game, for example the founder of St. Mark's Church team (present day City) is widely acknowledged as Anna Connell, the daughter of the rector of St. Mark's.

As far as the women's game itself is concerned, the game does have a long history in the region. The famous side Dick Kerr's Ladies played in the region on occasion – in 1921 they recorded a crowd of over 10,000 at Stalybridge.

There have been many women's teams created and based in the region over the years with the mid-80s seeing the professional clubs taking more of an interest, often via their community programmes but also via dedicated supporters, to create women's sides. City, United, Oldham and Stockport all developed decent women's sides during this period and the City ladies team even featured on the Saturday morning show ***The Wide Awake Club*** with a feature filmed at City's Platt Lane complex.

Over the years the professional League sides became more interested in the women's game and, whereas the initial formation of the female sides was officially supported but in truth was simply accepted, the 1990s saw most of the region's clubs become seriously involved with the female version of the game. In addition more recent times have seen some of the women's sides not affiliated to professional men's sides occasionally supported via community activities of the leading sides, or encouraged to merge with women's teams affiliated to male League sides.

In Stockport, County have had a women's team since 1989 and were one of the first of the smaller clubs to embrace the idea of the female game and the side soon proved to be a success. In 1997 a major recruitment drive took place and several senior players were encouraged to take up coaching roles within the set up, and in the years that followed considerable effort was made by County and another highly important side, Stockport Ladies, to establish a stronger women's game in the area. Discussions took place for the teams to merge, and in 2000 the Junior sides were brought together, then the following year the two clubs joined together as Stockport County Ladies. Since that point County have become one of the region's leading sides.

From a national perspective, the Manchester region has yet to find true, major success, however the battling spirit and determination of many of the region's sides suggests this will ultimately follow. Manchester does however hold a great place in the history of the game as for many years the Women's FA was based at the Corn Exchange building in Manchester city centre. The organisation moved out in the early 1990s, but it says much about the region that it was Manchester that provided a home during a period when the game developed rapidly.

More recently, in 2005 the City of Manchester Stadium staged the first game in the Women's European Championship. In that game England defeated Finland 3-2 before a crowd of 29,092.

As the new century moves forward it seems the trio of Curzon Ashton, Manchester City, and Stockport County are the most likely of our sides to find national success. In 2007 both City and County reached the fourth round of the Women's FA Cup, while Curzon had been knocked out by County in the third round.

When Headachy take Genasprin The SAFE Brand

Sunday Dispatch

MARCH 4, 1934

THE ONLY WAY—CUP-TIE VERSION

ARTHUR THOMPSON, the "Sunday Dispatch" photographer, shows in this page of pictures the remarkable adaptability of the Cup-tie fan. These striking photographs were secured during his wanderings among—or behind—yesterday's record crowd of 84,569 at Maine-road, Manchester.

"FROM A TUNNEL I saw minute headless players and spectators in many weird attitudes."

"HIS WHITE SCARF made an excellent foot support."

"A PRECARIOUS PERCH reminiscent of a pole-squatting record bid."

"NICELY BALANCED on a steel girder at the top of a 30ft. bank."

"HERE IS INGENUITY—It was only an old perambulator chassis, but it served."

"TWO MEN ON A BRICK, and a girl's tight-rope act."

"THIS FLEETING GLIMPSE of the ding-dong struggle I obtained by climbing on to a friend's shoulders."

Printed and Published by the ASSOCIATED NEWSPAPERS, LTD., at Northcliffe House and Carmelite House, Carmelite-street, E.C.4, and Northcliffe House, Deansgate, Manchester 3. March 4, 1934.

The record crowd for any game in Manchester (indeed for any English game other than a final in London) stands at 84,569 and was set in 1934 at Maine Road when City beat Stoke in an FA Cup tie.

CHAPTER THIRTY-ONE

SUPPORT

Without the atmosphere they create, without their fierce loyalties and their intense longings, the whole sport would collapse, not merely for financial reasons, but because it would lose its spirit – its tribal agony and its tribal joy. "The Soccer Tribe", Desmond Morris, 1981

OVER the years much has been made about the loyalty of fans, the volume of support received and so on. During the last fifty years Manchester United have, without doubt, been the best supported side in terms of average attendance, however this has not always been the case. In fact the level of support United now attract week in week out is over double their all-time average League attendance.

The following table and bar chart provide an overview of the level of support enjoyed by the region's League sides during their seasons in the Football League and Premier League up to 2007. Stalybridge have been included on the bar chart and their average support for two seasons is a few hundred greater than Rochdale's. However, it is clear that Rochdale has had a significantly longer League history than Stalybridge.

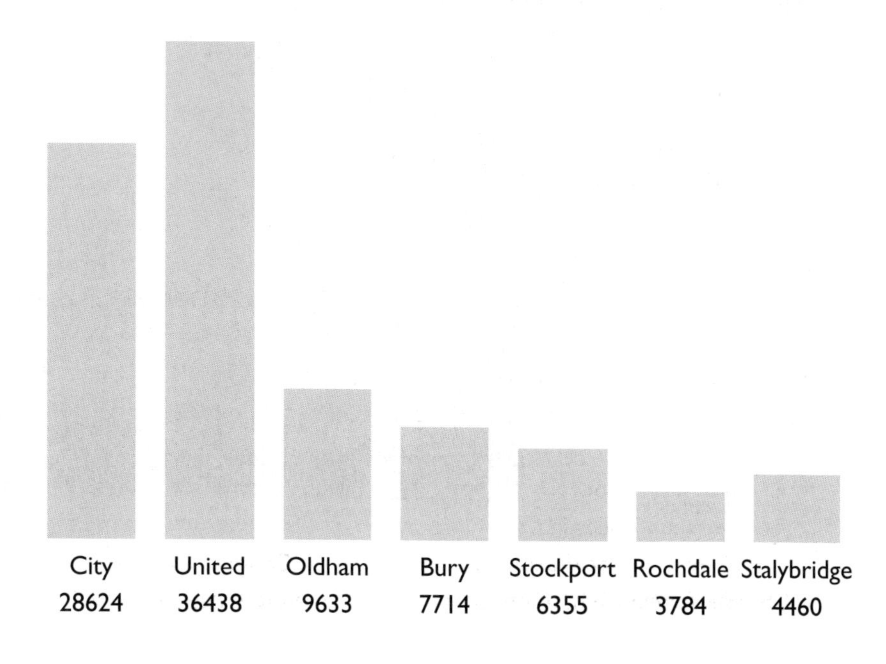

United fans at the Maine Road Scoreboard End in February 1948.

Please note that the average attendance for all games has been calculated by taking the aggregate crowd for every game and then dividing this by the exact number of games.

This figure cannot be totally accurate as the majority of attendances pre World War One, and many in between the wars, were not accurately recorded. However, as this situation existed for each of our clubs it is fair to assume that the same margin of error existed for each club, and therefore the net effect would be negligible.

The redevelopment of football grounds during the 1990s affected attendances somewhat and it is worth noting that attendances were seriously reduced for some of our clubs for several seasons. This is most obvious at the highest level with City whose ground was three sided for most of the 1992-93 season and for most of the 1994-95 season (the capacity of Maine Road at the start of 1994-95 was just under 20,000 at a time when interest was at a significant high following the takeover by Francis Lee).

At Old Trafford the dramatic rise in capacity and attendance since 1996 has increased United's all-time average by over 3,000 from a 1996 all time figure of 33,318, while City's move to their new stadium in 2003 has increased the club's all-time average by a mere 500.

The following table takes a look at the average attendance of all the significant League and non-League sides within the Manchester region during 2005-06. In the main it ignores sides outside of the boroughs of Bury, Manchester, Oldham, Rochdale, Stockport, Tameside, and Trafford. However, a couple of teams slightly outside of those areas have been included, such as Flixton.

The average attendances in this table have been taken from the figures available for the 2005-06 season. This means that those sides in North West Counties Division Two during the season, such as Cheadle Town, will have benefited from a large crowd against FC United of Manchester.

For 2006-07 it is known that the average attendances of NWC Division One sides, such as Salford City and Maine Road, were much higher for the same reason. For up to date information on average attendances at all levels of football check out www.tonykempster.co.uk.

It is worth noting that although FC United appear as the fifth best supported side in the region, both Rochdale and Bury's all time average support remains higher than FC United's average.

Club	Attendance 2005-06
Manchester United	68765
Manchester City	42856
Oldham Athletic	5797
Stockport County	4772
FC United of Manchester	3059
Rochdale	2808
Bury	2594
Altrincham	1048
Stalybridge Celtic	540
Hyde United	463
Droylsden	424
Leigh RMI	233
Cheadle Town	229
Mossley	229
Radcliffe Borough	207
Ashton United	202
Chadderton	192
Flixton	159
Oldham Town	149
Curzon Ashton	131
Woodley Sports	124
Trafford	98
Salford City	97
Abbey Hey	52
Maine Road	52

Their fan club girls are fanatics

By KENNETH MOOR

MANCHESTER City have a supporters' club which proudly boasts it is one of the few recognised by the directors of a football club.

Manchester United have a fan club—'the only one recognised by the board.'

As secretaries, both have ladies who are football fanatics. Both deplore Soccer hooliganism. Both have around 2,000 members.

There the similarities end.

Manchester City Supporters' Club was founded in 1928. There are 14 branches up and down the country. Subscriptions are 3s. a year.

Dances

On match days, members are admitted to Manchester City's Social Club—claimed by manager Roy Clarke, much-capped former Welsh international, to be 'the biggest and finest of its type in Europe'—on production of their card.

The supporters' club organises dances and concerts to raise funds. They sell club ties at 13s. 6d. and half-crown lapel badges.

Secretary Mrs Edith Whelan says: 'Over the past three years we have made very favourable progress.'

She has been secretary for six years, says her husband is a football widower, and first saw Manchester City as a shawl-swathed babe-in-arms, carried to the Hyde Road ground by her father.

Mrs Whelan, a company cashier, says: 'We are proud and jealous of the name of our supporters' club. We are pledged to expel members who are involved in trouble. This hasn't happened yet.'

Objects: to support Manchester City and organise trips to away matches. To stamp out hooliganism.

Manchester United's Fan Club was founded in 1963. It has no branches. Subscriptions are 10s. a year.

There are no club functions but members receive a free 16-20 page magazine in January, April, and December. At present the club's badge, featuring a red devil on a silver background, is also free. From September, members will have to pay an extra 2s. 6d. for it.

Secretary Miss Dorothy Woolley, who puts in 30 unpaid hours a week, says: 'In the first year we had a £70 loss. Now we make a modest profit which is put aside for emergencies.'

She has been secretary for four years, is respectfully called 'Miss' by the younger members of the committee, and watched United for the first time five years ago.

Cheering

The club committee meets weekly in a hired room.

Objects: To keep supporters in 32 countries up to date with club affairs and to sell pictures of star players. More than 100 letters weekly are written giving news of United.

Some are to explain that the fan club can't arrange match tickets.

Last night, from their stand seats, Mrs Whelan was cheering the Blues, Miss Woolley the Reds.

ATTENDANCE STATISTICS

The following table highlights Manchester's biggest crowds, including cup finals, World Cup matches, European Championship games, internationals and all neutral fixtures. This should show the top ten crowds, however with Old Trafford's capacity now larger than the tenth highest, United's own record crowd for Old Trafford has been included.

It is worth noting that City's former home Maine Road has staged more attendances over 80,000 than any other League ground. With the increase in Old Trafford's capacity during recent years, United's home has now held more 70,000 plus crowds than any other League ground. Maine Road had held this record until the latter stages of 2006-07 – up to that point 32 games had attracted crowds of 70,000 or more to City's home.

Manchester's Highest Attendances

ATTENDANCE	DATE	VENUE	GAME	COMPETITION
84,569*	3/3/34	Maine Road	City V Stoke City	FA Cup
83,260**	17/1/48	Maine Road	United V Arsenal	FL (Arsenal Champions)
82,771	29/1/49	Maine Road	United V Bradford PA	FA Cup
81,565	12/2/49	Maine Road	United V Yeovil Town	FA Cup
80,480	27/3/46	Maine Road	Birmingham City V Derby County	FAC semi final
79,491***	23/2/35	Maine Road	City V Arsenal	FL (Arsenal Champions)
78,000	20/9/47	Maine Road	City V United	FL
76,962	25/3/39	Old Trafford	Wolves V Grimsby	FAC semi-final
76,166****	8/3/24	Maine Road	City V Cardiff	FA Cup
76,129	3/3/56	Maine Road	City V Everton	FA Cup
76,098*****	31/03/07	Old Trafford	United V Blackburn Rovers	Premier League

* = This remains a record for a provincial match.

** = This remains the League's record attendance but appears in United's records as 81,962.

*** = this was the League's record attendance at the time.

**** = The attendance against Cardiff in 1924 was a record for any football match in Manchester at the time (including three FA Cup finals)

***** = with the capacity of Old Trafford reaching 76,212 in 2006-07 it is likely that any attendance detailed lower than this figure may be surpassed at some point soon. At the time of going to press the Old Trafford crowd highlighted was the highest United home crowd for a competitive fixture at Old Trafford.

Buses ready to take fans from Old Trafford in the 1950s.

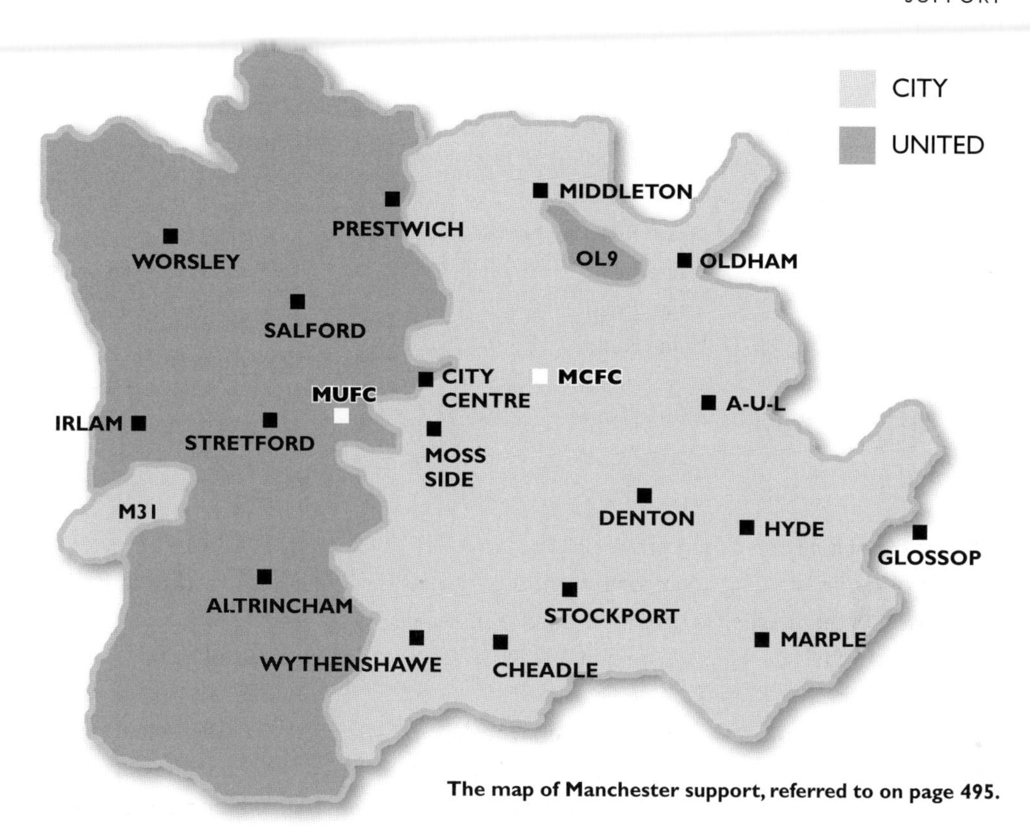

The map of Manchester support, referred to on page 495.

SPREAD OF SUPPORT FOR CITY AND UNITED

In 2002 Dr. Adam Brown from the Manchester Institute for Popular Culture at Manchester Metropolitan University published an analysis of the location of United and City season ticket holders under the title *Do You Come From Manchester?* His analysis took season ticket information supplied to him by the two clubs for 2001.

His analysis was based on 16,481 City season ticket holders and 27,667 United season ticket holders. Interestingly, both sets of figures were significantly lower than the clubs themselves claimed to have at this point – City have since admitted their season ticket figure was c.25,000 at this point, while United's was estimated to be in excess of 40,000. This suggests the two sides withheld certain information, though it is unclear why.

As this is the official information provided by both sides, however, it is important those figures are taken as accurate, and certainly Brown accepted their statistics as being the only true ones available at the time.

Brown's research concluded that around 40% (6,678) of City's season ticket holders resided in a 'M' postcode district, while 29% (7,808) of United's resided in 'M' postcodes.

For this publication efforts have been made to obtain accurate, up to date, information from all of the region's clubs on the current level of season ticket holders. Sadly, Bury, United, Oldham, Rochdale, and Stockport have for various reasons been unable to provide the material. Only City has provided more up to date information (season ticket holders for 2005). As a result it has been decided not to update City's statistics with the larger 2005 sample as this would have been unfair on the other clubs.

For this reason, the same statistical information available to Brown has been utilised to attempt to paint a picture of support for both Manchester sides within the region.

The material available provided the following number of season ticket holders based on Manchester 'M' post codes and a few of the neighbouring SK, OL, WA and BL postcodes:

Post Code	City	United	Total Season Ticket Holders	Post Code	City	United	Total Season Ticket Holders
M1	20	27	47	M32	196	394	590
M2	4	53	57	M33	419	820	1239
M3	13	52	65	M34	528	367	895
M4	19	16	35	M35	265	184	449
M5	46	108	154	M38	11	39	50
M6	102	228	330	M40	311	242	553
M7	60	115	175	M41	320	560	880
M8	74	109	183	M43	305	181	486
M9	234	172	406	M44	77	149	226
M11	104	89	193	M45	180	280	460
M12	48	36	84	M46	30	80	110
M13	44	24	68	OL1	37	31	68
M14	261	88	349	OL6	162	126	288
M15	26	21	47	OL7	88	77	165
M16	102	212	314	OL8	72	64	136
M17	0	18	18	OL9	164	202	366
M18	146	97	243	SK1	67	43	110
M19	245	150	395	SK2	233	161	394
M20	411	254	665	SK3	186	116	302
M21	238	210	448	SK4	367	312	679
M22	277	163	440	SK5	249	156	405
M23	250	165	415	SK6	379	310	689
M24	395	348	743	SK8	664	637	1301
M25	195	329	524	SK14	359	225	584
M26	122	192	314	SK16	176	124	300
M27	175	336	511	WA14	186	356	542
M28	162	470	632	WA15	315	534	849
M29	80	184	264	BL4	36	87	123
M30	140	261	401	TOTAL	10418	11417	21835
M31	43	33	76				

Clearly, the M postcode represents the main Manchester districts, however it does not directly relate to the City of Manchester, for example Denton is officially in Tameside yet its postcode is M34.

Throughout City and United's modern history much has been made of whether one side or the other represents the majority of Mancunians. As the above postcode statistics show there is not actually a great deal separating the number of season ticket holders for each side, however there are some districts which are significantly more blue than red and vice versa.

To provide a simple analysis of the preferences of each postcode district the total number of each side's season ticket holders within a district has been compared to identify whether the district is red or blue. This has then been plotted on to a map of Manchester (see page 493).

No assessment has been made on the percentage of fans living in that area, or the total population of the district, and so it is clear this map can be challenged and should only be used as a guide.

Some districts are very similar in their support, for example the M1 postcode has 20 City season ticket holders and 27 United. On the map this therefore appears as a Red district, however in terms of percentage support Brown calculated that 0.12% of City season ticket holders lived there and 0.10% of United's. Those percentages have been ignored as the population of each district has not been utilised and therefore it is impossible to say what percentage of the district's population is blue or red. Instead the analysis focuses on absolute numbers of ticket holders.

Similarly, as data had not been available for the other clubs, it is probable that certain districts would have a larger number of season ticket holders for other clubs. For example, OL1 is recorded as City yet, in total, City and United combined only have 68 season ticket holders there while Oldham Athletic would surely have a larger figure.

It is worth noting that the area of Cheadle (SK8) has United's second highest total of season ticket holders but is regarded as Blue because City have more, while Sale (M33) is City's third highest concentration of fans but is also United's number one post code district.

Naturally, only the data available has been used and this ultimately limits the coverage across the region. Most of Tameside is covered by the map, though not all, and strong areas of footballing support in the east and south such as Cheadle Hulme, Bramhall, and Mossley are excluded. City is particularly well supported in the SK postcodes, while a Mossley Reds flag has been a familiar presence at United games for many years. Despite these limiting factors, the map and data should still be used as an indicator of support.

Looking at the map, even if we accept there are inaccuracies in the data, it seems fairly obvious that support is divided with United leading the way in west Manchester and City in the east. There are many reasons for this but the main one is simply that the Blues were formed in the east, established themselves as a major side while based there, and when they moved to Maine Road, the east could still easily access public transport to reach Moss Side.

United were also born in the east, however they moved to west Manchester at a time when public and personal transport options were limited. Many of those supporters left behind found it difficult to travel across town due to work commitments, money and transport, and so ultimately support declined. However the move did allow the Reds to dominate football affiliations in the west (although this map takes no account of the lure of teams such as Wigan, Bolton and the Merseyside clubs).

In terms of United's birthplace, the Reds were originally born in Newton Heath (represented today by postcode M40) and then found success playing at Clayton (M11), close to City's current stadium. Even in 2001, prior to City's arrival in this area, these two districts had more City season ticket holders than United, but the Reds' figures were not too far behind.

Brown's analysis looked at support around each club's ground location and he produced the following statistics based on Old Trafford and Maine Road. Please note figures for the City of Manchester Stadium (M11) as recorded in 2001's season ticket figures have also been included for comparison purposes.

	CITY	UNITED
Number of Season Ticket holders in M14	261	88
% of Season Ticket holders in M14	1.58	0.32
Number of Season Ticket holders in M16	102	212
% of Season Ticket holders in M16	0.62	0.77
Number of Season Ticket holders in M11	104	89
% of Season Ticket holders in M11	0.63	0.32

These figures surprisingly show that even before City had moved to their new home, the number of City season ticket holders living in an area close to United's old Bank Street ground was greater than United's support in that area. This strengthens the view that United's move across Manchester to Old Trafford did have a significant effect on those left behind as explored earlier in this book.

It is worth noting that United's season ticket support was consistent in the two 'City' areas, and that the Blues had more season ticket holders on United's home patch than United did on City's. Was this some form of statement by City residents living close to Old Trafford – in 2001 City had a thriving supporters club based in the area – although it should be recorded that Old Trafford is on the very edge of the M16 postcode and many of the residents of M17 are closer to the ground than those in M16. In M17 City had no season ticket holders according to the statistics in 2001, while United had 18 (0.07% of their season ticket database).

City fans stand in the seated North Stand at Maine Road during 2002.

United chasing a record

By RONALD CROWTHER

MANCHESTER UNITED are now within easy reach of the all-time season attendance record for any club in the Football League. Even before last night's derby their average had reached 56,619.

This is running ahead of the record of 56,473 set up by Newcastle United in season 1947-48.

With a sell-out assured for the visit of Liverpool to Old Trafford and the championship struggle almost certain to keep enthusiasm on the boil, there can be little doubt that a new record will be set up.

In the history of the Football League there have been only five instances of clubs topping 50,000 average for a season. United, who with 53,984 last season went nearest to Newcastle's record, have done so twice.

In season 1958-59—the one after Munich—they had an average of 53,033. The other clubs to exceed 50,000 were Tottenham in 1960-61, the season of their League and FA Cup double, with 53,315, and Everton, in their championship season of 1962-63, with 51,460.

Newcastle's record still stands out as a football phenomenon, because it was established in Division Two. Admittedly it was a promotion season, but that early post-war side, with great personalities such as Jackie Milburn, Joe Harvey, Frank Brennan, Jackie Fairbrother, George Stobart, and Tommy Pearson, did not finish up as champions. In the final table they were three points behind Birmingham City.

Growth

Manchester's pulling power this season when as League champions, they are also fighting for the European Cup, is not surprising. But last season, when they topped 50,000, they were in no European competitions.

When I asked manager Matt Busby if he could explain this growth of interest he told me: 'I believe it to be a combination of things. The World Cup gave English football a big boost. And, as I see it, it is becoming more and more a family entertainment.'

Secretary Les Olive added: 'We have noticed that many more women are coming to games, particularly teenagers. I believe our facilities have added to the attractiveness of football at Old Trafford, where we have seats for 18,500 people.'

In their bid for the record United lead a trend that is bringing greater prosperity to the game generally. For the overall picture is one of Football League gates running at a figure of more than a million and a quarter up on last season.

By the end of the season they may be two million up on 1966-67, and in that season they rose by 1,695,616 on the previous one. That was the biggest seasonal gain for 19 years.

The news on 28th March 1968 that United were aiming to beat the all time highest average attendance, set by Newcastle in 1947-48. They succeeded and ended the season with an average of 57,552.

The story of football in this region suggests that were we able to turn the clock back say 100 years to a time when both sides found their first successes, and also were based close to their birthplaces, the map would look somewhat different. Potentially the area west of the city centre would hardly have registered as a footballing region at all, while each of the individual towns of the region would have supported their local club. The area of support for City would still have been predominantly the east of the region but would probably have ended at M34 (Denton), and would possibly have stretched down to some of the SK postcodes but only those close to Reddish (City were based on the border of Gorton and Reddish for a while) and easy travelling distance of the Hyde Road area.

United's support would probably have come from the north and the north-east with the strongest support in M11, M35 and M40, and maybe stretched into OL9 (hence the present day support in that district). Most of Tameside would have supported the local sides such as Hyde and Stalybridge Celtic, while support in Oldham, Rochdale, Stockport, and Bury would have focused on each area's local club.

One of the biggest issues affecting support, though it is hardly been considered over the years, has been the impact of the slum clearance programmes of the 1950s to 1970s. Much of City and United's traditional heartland was demolished during this period with supporters pushed to the very edges of the conurbation. Many Gorton, Clayton, Ardwick, Bradford, and Beswick residents were moved to new housing estates miles from the city centre such as Hattersley (SK14), Haughton Green (M34), and Gamesley (SK13). The initial inhabitants of these estates still regard themselves as Mancunians, even though none of those estates fall within the City of Manchester boundaries, and it is true that these areas remain strong in their support for both sides.

Those inhabitants have helped to colonise their neighbouring towns to some extent and, thanks to the influence of Gamesley and the ease of rail travel (a direct route takes City supporters from Glossop, Gamesley and Hattersley to Ashbury's near Sportcity, while a simple change in Manchester city centre takes Reds on to Old Trafford), Glossop is strong in its support for both Manchester sides.

Looking to the future, it is clear the map of support will change. In fact with both City and United's increase in season ticket holders since 2001, and City's relocation, it is possible it is already somewhat different. As time passes will the influence of City in M14 and surrounding districts reduce? It is already known that United's community programme has started to work with some of the schools previously regarded as City's in this area.

Will City's support in East Manchester grow stronger? And what about the impact of FC United of Manchester? Dr Adam Brown, whose research in 2002 raised the question *"Do You Come From Manchester?"*, was one of the founders of FC United and, at the time of going to press, is a board member of the new club. One of FC United's aims is to find a permanent stadium. If the side moves to Newton Heath or Clayton, as some hope, will this reduce the number of season ticket holders for both the Blues and the Reds in these areas?

Only time will tell. What must be remembered however, is that the number of season ticket holders is only one indicator of support and over time that in itself may not be a significant enough sample to work with. Supporters of both clubs have realised that with the increase in capacities at both clubs during the last few years, it is no longer absolutely vital to buy a season ticket and many games – including the 2005-6 derby at City and 2006-7 derby at United – had tickets on open sale the day before the game.

In terms of non-season ticket holders, the arrival of FC United caused many United fans to return their season tickets and transfer match day allegiance to the new club. In the main those fans still remained United supporters – some would say they are amongst the most passionate – but they no longer attended United's home games. Any survey performed in the future must look at three types of support – season ticket holders; other 'attending' fans; and those that claim allegiance but do not go. It should also include detail of every side in the region. Only then will we have a true picture of Manchester's support.

CHAPTER THIRTY-TWO

THE RECORDS

THE following sections provide information on a variety of local and national competitions, and focus on the success of our teams within these competitions.

THE MANCHESTER CUP

The Manchester Cup was first competed for in 1884-85 and was the first major competition the region's sides could take part in. The original trophy was replaced in 1887-88 by the present day trophy, which cost 60 guineas to produce. The original trophy became the Manchester Junior Cup and was first won by Hurst Nook Rovers in 1888 (co-incidentally that same trophy was first won by another side from Hurst when it was inaugurated in 1885 as the Manchester Cup).

From 1888 the competition became known as the Manchester Senior Cup and was the first significant trophy won by Newton Heath (United), Ardwick (City), Bury, Rochdale and Stockport. Occasionally drawn finals would see the trophy shared between the two competing clubs, and this happened in 1903 with Bury and City and then in 1912 when Rochdale (shared with United) won the cup for the first time.

A close up view of the Manchester Cup.

Despite its original importance the competition was not viewed particularly positively by Manchester's leading clubs in the 1960s and the final of 1964 which saw United defeat City 5-3 marked the end of City's involvement in the competition. United also pulled out and the competition waned.

Between 1980 and 1998 the competition was suspended, and then a decision was taken to resurrect the tournament with the reserve sides of the leading clubs taking part. Since that time City, United, and Oldham have once again found success with memorable finals. In 2005 the trophy was proudly displayed at City's museum after the Blues had defeated United in the final, and then in 2006 United's museum had the honour of displaying the trophy after victory over Oldham Athletic.

The following provides a full list of the competition's winners.

1885	Hurst
1886	Newton Heath LYR
1887	West Manchester
1888	Newton Heath LYR
1889	Newton Heath LYR
1890	Newton Heath LYR
1891	Ardwick
1892	Ardwick
1893	Newton Heath
1894	Bury
1895	Bolton Wanderers
1896	Bury
1897	Bury
1898	Stockport County
1899	Stockport County
1900	Bury
1901	Manchester City
1902	Newton Heath
1903	Bury & Manchester City
1904	Bury
1905	Bury
1906	Bolton Wanderers
1907	Manchester City
1908	Manchester United
1909	Bolton Wanderers
1910	Manchester United
1911	Manchester City
1912	Manchester United & Rochdale
1913	Manchester United
1914	Oldham Athletic
1915	Stockport County
1916-1919	No Competition
1920	Manchester United
1921	Bolton Wanderers
1922	Bolton Wanderers
1923	Stockport County
1924	Manchester United
1925	Bury
1926	Manchester United
1927	Crewe Alexandra
1928	Manchester City
1929	Manchester City
1930	Wigan Borough
1931	Manchester United
1932	Manchester City
1933	Manchester City
1934	Manchester United
1935	Bury
1936	Manchester United
1937	Manchester United
1938	Bolton Wanderers
1939	Manchester United
1940-1946	No Competition
1947	Competition Abandoned
1948	Manchester United
1949	Manchester City
1950	Oldham Athletic
1951	Bury
1952	Bury
1953	Oldham Athletic
1954	Bolton Wanderers
1955	Manchester United
1956	Competition Abandoned
1957	Manchester United
1958	Oldham Athletic
1959	Manchester United
1960	Bury
1961	Bolton Wanderers
1962	Bury
1963	Bolton Wanderers
1964	Manchester United
1965	Oldham Athletic
1966	No Competition
1967	No Competition

1968	Bury	1979	Droylsden
1969	Oldham Athletic	1980-1998	No Competition
1970	Oldham Athletic	1999	Manchester United
1971	Dukinfield Town	2000	Manchester United
1972	Mossley	2001	Manchester City
1973	Droylsden	2002	Oldham Athletic
1974	Oldham Athletic	2003	Oldham Athletic
1975	Hyde United	2004	Manchester United
1976	Droylsden	2005	Manchester City
1977	Mossley	2006	Manchester United
1978	Ashton United	2007	Manchester City

MAJOR TROPHY SUCCESSES OF MANCHESTER'S SIDES

The following list details, by season the major successes of Manchester's teams. Included within the table are the Champions (Premier/Football League), FA Cup winners & finalists, League Cup winners & finalists, European winners & finalists, Autoglass winners & finalists, Associate Members' Cup, winners & finalists, Full Members' Cup winners & finalists, and the champions of the other divisions. Runners-up in the various divisions or promotion places are not documented.

Season	Success
1894-95	Bury Div Two Champions
1898-99	City Div Two Champions
1899-1900	Bury FAC winners
1902-3	Bury FAC winners, City Div Two Champions
1903-4	City FAC winners
1907-8	United Champions
1908-9	United FAC winners
1909-10	City Div Two Champions
1910-11	United Champions
1921-22	Stockport Div Three (N) Champions
1925-26	City fac finalists
1927-28	City Div Two Champions
1932-33	City fac finalists
1933-34	City FAC winners
1935-36	United Div Two Champions
1936-37	City Champions, Stockport Div Three (N) Champions
1946-47	City Div Two Champions
1947-48	United FAC winners
1951-52	United Champions
1952-53	Oldham Div Three (N) Champions
1954-55	City fac finalists
1955-56	United Champions, City FAC winners
1956-57	United Champions, United FAC finalists

1957-58	United FAC finalists
1960-61	Bury Div Three Champions
1961-62	Rochdale League Cup finalists
1962-63	United FAC winners
1964-65	United Champions
1965-66	City Div Two Champions
1966-67	United Champions, Stockport Div Four Champions
1967-68	United European Cup winners, City Champions
1968-69	City FAC winners
1969-70	City ECWC winners & League Cup winners
1973-74	Oldham Div Three Champions, City League Cup finalists
1974-75	United Div Two Champions
1975-76	City League Cup winners, United FAC finalists
1976-77	United FAC winners
1978-79	United FAC finalists, Oldham – Anglo-Scottish Cup finalists
1980-81	City FAC Finalists
1982-83	United FAC winners & League Cup finalists
1984-85	United FAC winners
1985-86	City FMC finalists
1989-90	United FAC winners, Oldham League Cup finalists
1990-91	United ECWC winners & League Cup finalists, Oldham Div Two Champions
1991-92	United Super Cup winners & League Cup winners, Stockport Autoglass Trophy finalists

THE BURY GUARDIAN, SATURDAY, APRIL 25, 1903.

PRESS COMMENTS.

A few cuttings from the Press will serve to show the general opinion of the final tie:—

Never in the history of the final tie has the result been so one-sided as it was on Saturday at the Crystal Palace. Had both teams been at their best, there is no reason to doubt that the game would have proved a close one, but the Derby players, on their form of Saturday, had no chance whatever.—"Daily Telegraph."

Something like a debacle—tha was the Cup final. As a Southampton director remarked after the game, "Our display was bad enough, but at least the four goals against us were good ones. This was more like opera bouffe."—Morning Leader."

Briefly and candidly the Cup final was a fiasco. Nothing like it had ever been seen before. Bury defeated Derby County by six goals to none, and it might have been twenty. That it was not is testimony to the mercy exercised by the winners rather than to the defence of the losers, who have something to regret in the protraction of the season till players are stale and not sufficiently sound to do themselves full justice.—"Daily Chronicle."

Make every excuse you can possibly find, and you are bound to regard the final of 1903 as about the worst. All you can say is that Bury were decidedly the superior team, express your regret for unfortunate Derby, and wish them better luck another time.—Mr. J. J. Bentley.

Backers of Derby County knew after five minutes play that they were on the wrong horse. The best play for the losers was undoubtedly that of their captain, A. Goodall, who played a sound game for his side.—K. S. Ranjitsinhji.

Derby County never showed the slightest ability to either win the Cup or to hold their antagonists in check, although the Midlanders were sorely handicapped by being badly served in goal, for Fryer ought never to have played, owing to an accident on Easter Monday, from which he had not recovered.—"Athletic News."

I never saw Derby County play a poorer game than in this match, for they were weak all round

(From the "Daily Dispatch.")

1992-93	United Champions, Stockport Autoglass Trophy finalists
1993-94	United Champions & FAC winners & League Cup finalists
1994-95	United FAC finalists
1995-96	United Champions & FAC winners
1996-97	United Champions, Bury 'New' Div Two Champions
1998-99	United European Cup winners, United Champions, United FAC winners
1999-0	United inter-continental Cup winners & Champions
2000-1	United Champions
2001-2	City 'New' Div One Champions
2002-3	United Champions & League Cup finalists
2004-5	United FAC finalists
2005-6	United League Cup winners
2006-7	United Champions & FAC finalists

MANCHESTER'S FIRST SUCCESSES

The following successes were the first in each respective division/competition and ignore the various League restructures or name changes. For example, United's Premier League success of 1993 is equivalent to League Champions (1908, United), while City's 2002 Division One Championship success is equivalent to Second Division Champions (1895, Bury). Likewise United's Rumbelows' Cup success of 1992 is the same as City's in 1970.

In addition to Manchester's first actual trophy wins, the table also details first final appearance and, for the Fairs Cup and UEFA Cup, the furthest round reached as no side from our region has appeared in finals for these competitions.

Competition	Year	Team
Manchester Cup Winners	1885	Hurst
Lancashire Cup Winners	1892	Bury
Second Division Champions	1895	Bury
FA Cup Winners	1900	Bury
League Runners Up	1904	City
English School's Trophy Finalists	1906	Manchester Schools
League Champions	1908	United
Charity Shield	1908	United
Third Division Runners Up	1924	Rochdale
English School's Trophy Winners (joint)	1932	Manchester Schools
English School's Trophy Winners	1934	Manchester Schools
Third Division Champions	1937	Stockport
FA Youth Cup Winners	1953	United
League Cup Finalists	1962	Rochdale
Fourth Division Runners up	1963	Oldham
Inter-city Fairs Cup Semi-finalists	1965	United
Fourth Division Champions	1967	Stockport
European Cup Winners	1968	United

Intercontinental Cup Finalists	1968	United
League Cup Winners	1970	City
ECWC Winners	1970	City
FA Trophy Winners	1978	Altrincham
Anglo-Scottish Cup Finalists	1979	Oldham
UEFA Cup Quarter-finalists	1979	City
FMC Finalists	1986	City
(Euro) Super Cup Winners	1991	United
AMC Finalists	1992	Stockport
Intercontinental Cup Winners	1999	United

ALL TIME LEAGUE POSITION

The following table shows the all-time final League position for each of our League sides. For each side a final place per season has been allocated to each side based on the total number of teams in the League at that time. This has been calculated by taking the total number of sides in each division and calculating a final place. For example, in 2006 Rochdale were 82nd in the League based on 20 sides in the Premier, 24 in the Championship, 24 in League One, and Dale finishing 14th in League Two.

For seasons when Division Three North & South existed, the final position of sides in Division Three North has been calculated as if the southern division did not exist.

The 'final' League position for each club for each season has then been averaged based on each club's number of League seasons to create a final position. Surprisingly this calculation shows that none of our sides would make an all-time top ten, however a similar calculation for post-war seasons would show United's average position as being slightly below fifth place.

United	City	Bury	Oldham	Stalybridge	Stockport	Rochdale
11	15	42	43	53	58	72

CHAPTER THIRTY-THREE

BIBLIOGRAPHY

THE following books are significant works in the development of Manchester football. For some of the clubs in the region there have been plenty of books written detailing almost every major moment in the club's history. Some of these have been significant works but occasionally, most notably with United and City, publications have been released simply to cash in on a particular aspect of the club.

The list that follows is not meant to be a comprehensive review of all Manchester region publications, but it is intended as a guide to further reading. In addition, the majority of works featured here have been written by supporters of the respective clubs. All of these books have been consulted during the production of this book.

General

The Football Man, Arthur Hopcraft, 1968
A History Of British Football, Percy M Young, 1968
British Sports Past & Present – Soccer, Denzil Batchelor, 1954
The Book of Football, various, 1905
Association Football & The Men Who Made It, various, 1905
League Football & The Men Who Made It, Simon Inglis, 1988
Denied FC, Dave Twydell, 2001
Football Through The Turnstiles Again, Brian Tabner, 2002
The Rothmans/Sky Sports Yearbooks, 1970-2008
The Complete Record of The FA Cup, Mike Collett, 2003

Club Specific

Bury FC 1885-1985, Peter Cullen & Paul Greenlees, 1985
Bury FC, Peter Cullen, 1999
An Undividable Glow: The First Ever Book on the Formation and First Season of FC United of Manchester, Robert Brady, 2006
Mottram Road to Maine Road – A History of Football In Hyde, Mike Pavasovic, 1985
Manchester FC – 125 Year History, Len Balaam, 1985.
Manchester City Football Club: Souvenir History, Fred Johnson, 1930
Manchester City, David Williams, 1947

Manchester City: Meredith to Mercer and the F.A. Cup, Eric Thornton, 1969
The Manchester City Football Books, Peter Gardner, 1969-1979
Manchester City Football Club: Official Record Handbook Commencing 1892, Bill Miles, 1976
The Manchester City Story, Andrew Ward, 1984
Manchester City The Complete Record, Ray Goble & Andrew Ward, 1987 & 1993
From Maine Men to Banana Citizens, Gary James and Keith Mellor, 1989
The Battle For Manchester City, Alec Johnson, 1994
Blue Heaven, Ian Penney, 1996
Manchester The Greatest City, Gary James, 1997 & 2002
Manchester City The Complete Record, Gary James, 2006
Manchester City – 125 Years Of Football, Gary James, 2006
Century City, David Wallace, 2007
Manchester United, Alf Clarke, 1948
Manchester United Football Club, Alf Clarke, 1951
Manchester United, Percy M Young, 1960
The Manchester United Story, Arthur Barker, 1977 & 1979
There's Only One United, Geoffrey Green, 1978
The Manchester United Football Books, David Meek, 1966-1980
Winners & Champions: The Story Of Manchester United's 1948 Cup Final and 1952 League Championship Winning Teams, Alec Shorrocks, 1985
Manchester United A Complete Record, Ian Morrison & Alan Shury, 1986, 1990 & 1992
Manchester United A Pictorial History & Club Record, Charles Zahra, Joseph Muscat, Iain McCartney, & Keith Mellor, 1986
Heathens & Red Devils, Keith Mellor, 1987
Illustrated History of Manchester United, Tom Tyrell & David Meek, 1988 & 1994
Red Devils In Europe, David Meek, 1988
Manchester United Player By Player, Ivan Ponting, 1989
Manchester United The Betrayal of a Legend, Michael Crick & David Smith, 1989
Back Page United, Stephen F Kelly, 1990
The Gibson Guarantee, Peter Harrington, 1994
The United Alphabet, Garth Dykes, 1994
United – The Story Of Manchester United in the FA Cup, Steve Cawley, 1994
United We Stood, Richard Kurt, 1994
Are You Watching, Liverpool?, Jim White, 1995
The Official Manchester United Official History, Justyn Barnes, Adam Bostock, Cliff Butler, Aubrey Ganguly, Graham McColl & Mark Wylie, 2001 onwards.
Manchester United The Top 11 of Everything Red, Jim White & Andy Mitten, 2005
United: A History of Manchester United (The United Opus), Justyn Barnes, 2006
History of Oldham Athletic FC, 1933
The Team From A Town of Chimneys, Stewart W Beckett, 1982 & 1990
Oldham Athletic The Complete Record, Garth Dykes, 1988
Keeping The Dream Alive, Stewart W Beckett, 1991

Pine Villa & Oldham Athletic – A 100 Year Journey, Stewart W Beckett, 1995
Forward With Dale – A History of Rochdale AFC, Brian Clough, 1981
The Survivors – The story of Rochdale AFC, Steven Phillips, 1990
Rochdale AFC, Steven Phillips, 2001
The History Of Stockport County AFC, Simon Myers, 1966
Stockport County Centenary, 1883-1983, Tom Turton & Howard Jones
Stockport County A Complete Record, Peter Freeman & Richard Harnwell, 1994
A Pictorial History of Stockport County 1883-2006, Phil Brennan & Richard Harnwell, 2006

The Munich Air Disaster

The Day A Team Died, Frank Taylor, 1960
The Team That Wouldn't Die, John Roberts, 1975
Duncan Edwards, Iain McCartney & Roy Cavanagh, 1988
Tommy Taylor of Manchester United & Barnsley, John Kennedy, 1994
Roger Byrne, Iain McCartney, 2000
Harry's Game, Harry Gregg & Roger Anderson, 2002
Bill Foulkes – Manchester United & Beyond, Bill Foulkes & Ivan Ponting, 2003
The Lost Babes, Jeff Connor, 2006

General Manchester Footballing Works

My Story, Matt Busby with David R Jack, 1957
Don Davies: An Old International, Jon Roberts Cox, 1962
Living For Kicks, Denis Law with Kenneth Wheeler, 1963
Piccadilly Radio Soccer Book, Tom Tyrell, 1975 & 1976
A-Z of Manchester Football: 100 Years of Rivalry, Derek Brandon, 1978
Denis Law: An Autobiography, Denis Law with Ron Gubba, 1979
Kicked Into Touch, Fred Eyre, 1981 & 2006
Another Breath Of Fred Eyre, Fred Eyre, 1982
Football Wizard: The Story Of Billy Meredith, John Harding, 1985
A Strange Kind Of Glory: Sir Matt Busby & Manchester United, Eamon Dunphy, 1991
Football With A Smile: The Authorised Biography Of Joe Mercer OBE, Gary James, 1993
What A Game, Fred Eyre & Roy Cavanagh, 1983
Taking The Mike, Fred Eyre, 1991
The Pride Of Manchester, Steve Cawley and Gary James, 1991
Free The Manchester United One, Graham Sharpe, 2003

Venue Specific

Old Trafford Theatre Of Dreams, Iain MCartney, 1996
Farewell To Maine Road, Gary James, 2003
Played In Manchester, Simon Inglis, 2004
Engineering Archie (Archibald Leitch – football ground designer), Simon Inglis

SUBSCRIBERS

The author & publishers would like to thank all the patrons and subscribers to this volume. Your support of this project is appreciated.

Number	Subscriber Name	Favourite Manchester Region Team	Favourite Manchester Region Player
1	The British Library		
2	Gary James		
3	Trevor Hartley		
4	Keith Barraclough		
5	Brian Gurney	Manchester City	Eric Brook
6	Dr. John O'Connor	Manchester City	Colin Bell
7	David J Price	Manchester United	Eric Cantona
8	David Williams	Manchester City	Bert Trautmann
9	John Barlow	Stalybridge Celtic	Matthew Barlow
10	Robert Dickson	Manchester City	Colin Bell
11	Gary Dickson	Manchester City	Peter Barnes
12	Alan Whiston	Droylsden	Dave Cameron
13	Phil Brennan	Stockport County	Terry Park
14	Malcolm Plaiter	Manchester City	Colin Bell
15	Dave Wallace	Manchester City	Bert Trautmann
16	Peter Wilson	Manchester City	Bert Trautmann
17	Anna Lee	Manchester City	Micah Richards
18	Sean & Jane Riley	Manchester City	Dennis Tueart/Andy Morrison
19	Geoff Clegg	Manchester City	Dennis Tueart
20	Laurence P Ward	Manchester City	Bert Trautmann
21	Stephen Rigby	Manchester City	Trevor Francis
22	Michael Joseph	Manchester City	Micah Richards
23	Bill Perkins	Manchester City	Colin Bell
24	Andrew Zuill	Manchester City	Colin Bell
25	David John Smith	Manchester City	Colin Bell
26	Don Hinchcliffe	Manchester City	Gio Kinkladze
27	Judith Hughes	Manchester City	Gio Kinkladze
28	David Glynn Hall	Manchester City	Colin Bell
29	Graham Anthony Hall	Manchester City	Dennis Tueart
30	Alison J Smith	Manchester City	Francis Lee
31	Paul Newton	Manchester City	Colin Bell
32	Steve Armstrong	Manchester City	Johnny Crossan
33	Alex Barlow	Manchester City	Shaun Goater

34	Michaal Wilson	Manchester City	Colin Bell
35	Nick Shaw	Stalybridge Celtic	Don Cooke
36	Roger Haigh	Manchester City	Mike Doyle
37	Barry Taylor	Manchester City	Neil Young
38	Baz Riley	Manchester City	Bert Trautmann
39	Christopher Roland Jones	Manchester City	Paul Dickov
40	Kevin J McGovern	Manchester City	Colin Bell
41	John & Alex Leigh	Manchester City	Bobby Johnstone
42	Keith Edgeley	Oldham Athletic	Roger Palmer
43	John Doran	Manchester City	Paul Dickov
44	Alex Culshaw	Manchester United	Bryan Robson
45	Jonathan Culshaw	Manchester United	Denis Irwin
46	Derek Barnes	Manchester United	Denis Law
47	Dave Miller	Manchester City	Colin Bell
48	Jonathan Poole	Manchester City	Colin Bell
49	Michael Crick	Manchester United	
50	Peter Moulds		
51	Garry Griffin	Manchester City	Colin Bell
52	Steve Worthington	Manchester City	Dennis Tueart
53	Mark Hodkinson	Rochdale	Bob Mountford
54	L Kershaw	Manchester City	Colin Bell
55	Michael Grayson		
56	Edward Garvey		

Publisher of limited edition football books.

For information on future Manchester related publications see our website.

PO Box 822, Halifax, West Yorkshire, HX1 9FX

Website: **www.manchesterfootball.org**

Email: info@manchesterfootball.org